Also by Kumkum Sangari

Women and Culture
Recasting Women: Essays in Colonial History
From Myths to Markets: Essays on Gender

Politics
of the Possible

Politics
of the Possible

Essays on

Gender, History, Narratives,

Colonial English

Kumkum Sangari

Anthem Press
London

Anthem Press is an imprint of
Wimbledon Publishing Company
PO Box 9779
London
SW19 7QA

This edition first published by Wimbledon Publishing Company 2002

British Library Cataloguing in Publication Data
Data available

1 84331 051 1 (hbk)
1 84331 037 6 (pbk)

1 3 5 7 9 10 8 6 4 2

For

MY MOTHER AND FATHER

SHAMU AND RAUMI

Contents

Preface

I am deeply grateful to Ravinder Kumar for institutional support as director of Nehru Memorial Museum and Library, for his unfailing encouragement, intellectual exchange, personal warmth, for putting himself out in innumerable ways; to Anuradha Kapur and Amit Gupta for their generous help, unflagging encouragement, and their care in selecting the essays for this collection; to Indu Chandrasekhar and Rajen Prasad without whom this collection would neither have been conceived nor completed; to friends who shared my anxieties and enthusiasms; to those friends who took the trouble to read and comment and who I have acknowledged individually at the end of each essay; to my family for sympathy, support, questions, and all they did over these years; to snegnu and binio and gnuiya who know why.

The bulk of this volume was enabled by a UGC fellowship, the cooperation of Indraprastha College, the facilities offered by NMML and the unfailing assistance of the NMML library staff. Chapters 5, 6, and 7 were facilitated by a British Council and Charles Wallace grant for using the India Office Library in London, and the revision of chapters 6 and 7 by the unstinting generosity of James Nye at the library of the University of Chicago.

'Women against women' is unpublished, 'The amenities of domestic life' doubled in the revision though I have retained the original title. The other essays were too locked into the urgency of their own moment of writing, too tightly structured to alter or renew in a substantive way. They have, however, been extended a little with additions in text and endnotes, and cross-referenced. Details of publication are given at the end of each essay.

Between the lines

Introduction

It seems artificial to fix a set of essays written over several years into a single schema except to say that they are 'literary', contentious, gendered, and if history is seen as an act of denaturalization, they may even be historical. The contentions are deeply embedded, usually neither immediately visible nor fully articulated. This under-explanation stems in part from the other concerns—oral devotional compositions and hagiographies, nationalist and contemporary reformulations of gender, religion, law, and culture—that circulate beneath them but slip in only as questions or assumptions. And, in part from my need to step aside from polemic to work out alternative ways of connecting hitherto discrete histories for which there was neither a readymade method nor a short cut. Nothing but the slow labour of tentatively mapping specific intersections between narratives, 'literature', patriarchies, religious and cultural categories, and, in Walter Benjamin's famous formulation, trying to grasp the constellation that one's own era has formed with definite earlier ones.

Instead of offering a summary I will enumerate the different ways in which this book can be read, take apart what it in fact brings together, surface some connections between the essays, and chase some of the contentions within them.

In and out of 'literature'

With some exceptions, the Eng Lit that I grew up in was configured as a fully-formed (self)conserving field fenced in by a paradigmatic New Criticism. It compelled an extraordinary sensitivity to individual texts but usually illuminated them against dim historical backdrops, foregrounded the eternal antinomies of individual and society, flux and permanence, the chaos of life and the formal unity of canonized texts, and resolved these in subtle renditions of paradox and equipoise, empathetic disclosures of ambivalence and irony. Having receded from earlier comparativist models as well as the reformist ambitions of its colonial and nationalist forebears into a resolutely 'apolitical' metaphysic of the text, it frowned on range as superficial dilettantism, as that fatal incapacity to know the text well enough. In sum, this was an Eng Lit that inhibited consistent engagement with theoretical questions which involved stepping outside the shelter of specialism and canon, suppressed not merely the historical relations of colonization and the British and Indian energies through which the field had come into existence and was institutionalized, but also the class and gender distinctions through which it was (re)produced. All this combined with those pressures that were palpably present 'outside' the classroom to shape the nature of my reaction and preoccupations. This collection thus marks both a personal trajectory from Eng Lit to the template of 'English' in India and a complication of earlier Marxist and feminist agendas with questions about the interanimation of narrative forms, patriarchies, religious ascriptions, and cultural categories.

My break with the naturalization of textual immanence takes the classic route of seeing the properties and usages of narrative forms (marvellous realism, domestic and historical novels, romance, qissa, epic, prescription, textbooks), devices (kingly boon, female conversation, disguise, jealousy and political exhortation), organizing tropes (female incitement, the so-called Muslim interregnum) and epistemic modes (realist, modernist, postmodernist) in relation to their historical and ideological locales. In the process a number of 'texts' are reworked. Some are from the well-known canons of Eng Lit (Henry James's *Portrait of a Lady*, Jane Austen's *Mansfield Park*, John Ruskin's *Sesame and Lilies* and *The Two Paths*), Urdu literature (Nazir Ahmad's *Mir'at ul-Arus*, Altaf Husain 'Hali's *Majalis un-Nissa*), ancient epic and prescription (the Valmiki *Ramayana*, the *Manusmriti*), or have become 'postmodern' icons (James's *Wings of the Dove*, Gabriel Garcia Marquez's *Hundred Years of Solitude*, Salman Rushdie's *Midnight's Children*). Others are lesser known (J.A. Dubois's *Hindu Manners, Customs and Ceremonies*, Sara Ellis's *Women of England*, Gauri Datta's *Devrani Jethani ki Kahani*,

Romesh Chandra Dutt's *The Last of the Rajputs*, Madame Blavatsky's *From the Caves and Jungles of Hindustan*, Arun Joshi's *The Strange Case of Billy Biswas*), while some of the nineteenth-century works discussed are now virtually unknown (Ramprasad Tiwari's *Riti-ratnakar*, Ahmad Husain's *Istri Updesh*, the multiauthored *Chhabili Bhatiyari*). A sizeable number fall into the amorphous area of the 'non-literary', the 'ephemeral', and the archival such as prescriptive manuals, school textbooks, the proceedings or tracts of learned societies, reformist caste associations and religious organizations, polemical pamphlets or articles, nationalist songs, colonial taxonomies, British Orientalist essays, missionary treatises, administrative and institutional documents. The constitutive ideological field on which canons and concepts of 'literature' depend was in fact cross-generic and part of a much wider matrix of social evaluation.

New forms of circulation and consumption made the fluctuating boundary between the literary and the non-literary more volatile even as colonial cartographies struggled to settle them. The essays work on the way the literary and the non-literary, writing and orality pass through and configure each other, reposition questions of genre, authorship, address, and reception (chs 1,6,7,8). The censorious separation of high from low and the interfaces between the two are gendered, as in the incorporation and deflection of popular fiction in high textuality (ch. 2), or in the assimilation of colonial and nationalist ethnography into a contemporary, marketable 'ethnicity' (ch. 4). Chapter 6 disentangles the affirmation and transgression of emergent ideologies in school textbooks and caste reform tracts by a 'popular' romantic qissa. Most of the Hindustani writing taken up here and in chapter 7 belongs neither to a residual orality nor to high literacy but to an intermediate orality that evades the closures of print and encapsulates the uneven emergence of a small-town intelligentsia. This intermediate orality that moves in and out of print is also a mark of the continuous restaging of first-generation literacy—that persists even today in India—so that the break between the written and the oral has never quite congealed into a finalist rupture. In fact the peculiar synthesis of narrative illustration, school textbook, educational treatise, polemical tract, ancient prescription, medieval devices of collation and their passage through orality in the late nineteenth century speak, similarly, of an uneven crystallization of new genres and discourses.

Most of the essays develop a relational ground for theorizing forms, genres, and literary criticism that cuts across provincial or nationalist oeuvres. Taken together, chapters 2 to 7 suggest that colonial urgencies governed not only the renovation of British conservatism, paternalism, and organicism from the early nineteenth to the early twentieth century but also generated the tension between a quasi-religious and an instrumental role for literature that characterizes the Ruskinian and Jamesian aesthetic, F.R. Leavis and New Criticism. High modernist styles were formed in the crosshatches of romantic organicism, early nationalism, the aestheticization and scientization of non-European peoples and belief systems (ch. 4). The singular conservatism of Anglo–American modernism, often played out in the adoption of englishness by 'loyalist' emigrés, had a more obvious alignment to imperial power especially in the genealogy of its ambivalence about modernization (chs. 2,3,4). Chapter 4 traces the route through which the aesthetic of this modernism became one of the modalities by which Eng Lit could be absorbed into a so-called indigenous aesthetic and produce synthesizing, quasi-transcendental, self-commemorative readings of the very same conservative modernists in India. Thus T.S. Eliot's monumentalist notion of European tradition, at once timeless and temporal, could be retimbered to house an apologetic nationalism and an antimodern hubris covalidated by 'Hindu' philosophy. An object of acquisition more than inheritance, of discriminating yet depersonalized surrender, it permitted a retrieval of our own 'spiritual' past as well as (in defiance of Kipling) allowed the glory of east and west to meet in the wholeness of 'art': in sum, made us citizens of India and of the world, the bearers of a nativist cosmopolitanism.

Some of the ideological locales of the transition from realism to literary modernisms too were cross-national (chs 1,2,3) while two of the lineages of realism in British and Indian writing can be traced to disparate processes of embourgeoisement and a colonial pedagogy encased in reformist narratives of patriarchal improvement (chs 1,5,6). The differential authority of mimetic narrative in terms of its discrepant locations and the size and literacy of the middle class it sought to represent is evident in the uneven texture of causality, individuation, and 'unmasking'. Thus Mahesh Chunder Deb's hesitant individualization of himself in "A Sketch of the Condition of Hindoo Women", and none at all of the women he seeks to uplift stand in stark contrast to the cultural mobility of the acquisitive emigré and the settled monadism that James seeks to mask and renounce through his heroine in *Portrait*. Whereas Deb's self-flagellating language of lack was confined to affective exposure and predicated on a yearning for women compatible with 'literature', James's language combined the expansive energy radiated by the rapid industrialization of America with the cultural capital amassed by Europe—which together allowed him to partake of, even annex, metropolitan power and distance the sordid reality of colonial extraction from which it emanated (chs 2,5). The ephemeral, 'non-literary', and now archival writing explored in the essays was more openly and assertively purposeful; though written from differing positions it was central to the production of organizing concepts of aesthetic value, tradition, culture, in effect, the cognitive grids of the colonial period. As political and as mediated as the canonical, it not only provided the ground for the formation and reception of 'high' literature but manufactured at once the 'national' heritage of England and the 'civilizational' heritage of India.

The imbrication of British literature in colonialism was as much a matter of the characterization and institutionalization of English, the deep structure of narrative and prescriptive genres, as of their alignment with other disciplinary fields and the hierarchical distribution of literary status (chs 5,6,7). Thus anthropology and sociology, along with travelogues and primitivization, assembled an instrumental data-base for governance, fabricated normative categories and reductive comparative schemas of racial/national virtues and vices, which were in turn recuperated by conservative modernism within the binding aesthetics of depth and surface, fragment and collage (chs 1, 4); some of these have now crept under the overlaps between colonial indigenism, modernisms, and postmodernism (ch. 1). The first five chapters together suggest a link between the earlier and later phases of colonial typification and canonization and subsequent modernist and poststructuralist appropriative and classificatory procedures, especially in the shift in metropolitan authorization from the documentary and mimetic to anti and nonmimetic or even 'irrational' modes.

If these essays function at one level as a critique of Eng Lit, Lit Crit, the category 'literature' in India or in metropolitan academies, they also seek to subject this field to other pressures, refuse 'literature' as either a given or an autonomous entity. Thus the emergence of novelization in school textbooks of the United Provinces (UP) —*Mir'at ul-Arus*, *Ritiratnakar* and *Devrani Jethani ki Kahani*—is situated on the mixed terrain of social practice and female labour, the anxiety of patriarchal prescription, and the imaginaires of romance which together standardized a dyadic emplotment of reform and misogyny (chs 6,7). The stubborn regularity of altruism and misogyny in the accounts of administrators, missionaries, historians, British Orientalists, the small-town and urban intelligentsia is meshed with political imperatives, class formation, caste discrimination, and patriarchal rearrangement (chs 5,6). The generic transmutation of a narrative unit, female incitement, is connected to the layered shifts from pre-state formations to monarchy and primogeniture compacted in the Valmiki *Ramayana*, and to the street rhetoric of contemporary Hindu communalism (ch. 8). In chapters 4, 5 and 6 'English' is refigured as a tutelary social ensemble on the gendered precinct of class and religion, and as one which, assimilated or replicated in regional linguistic formations, belies the indigenist projection of the Indian 'vernaculars' as necessarily opposed to the 'western', as unblemished by anglicization and colonial ideologies. In UP for instance, narration and prescription in Hindi, Hindustani, Urdu composed a field in which the authority of three transregional ensembles— Sanskrit, Persian, English—was played out and relocated. Colonial English itself doubled as a guarantor of a universal secular modernity and a purveyor of indigenist and antimodern ideologies.

My broad attempt, then, has been to resist the isolation of 'literature' as a discrete object of enquiry and 'return' it to its generative matrix: the interaction of formal elements, ideological ensembles, and social processes. As the essays try to show, literature, taken in the widest sense (a sense that can account for the contingency of the category itself), may acquire an apparent autonomy through the indirect and complex relation it bears to this productive matrix, but in practice it enters social relations, enacts or filters social tensions, and acts as a material force in the formation of class and gender distinctions. Indeed in the colonial period literature was institutionalized precisely on the twin assumptions of pedagogic social agency and autonomy, of instrumentality and transcendent value. And it was this duality that led not only to its own exorbitation but to the canonization of particular genres such as British domestic realism which, even as they laid out the scenarios of moral worth and female subjectivity, in fact mediated imperialism (chs 2,3,5). English literature could legitimate colonial rule precisely because its disavowal of material power and appeal to higher values created an aura of autonomy that not only glossed over its own contradictions and helped English nationalism to universalize itself as a bourgeois 'humanism', but covertly synchronized moral value with monetary value.

The essays can also be read as a form of suspicion of the hidden pedagogies of doubt claims, of the idea that postmodernism is "the discourse *of* the periphery" because it is a discourse of fragmentation and heterogeneity.[1] Antifoundational epistemologies, precisely like the idealisms and normative universalisms they reject, have finite political locales and determinate social bases. If the power axes of knowledge systems must be questioned then poststructuralist doubt claims—that push imperialized formations into posing as the 'other' of the Enlightenment, turn (ex)colonial subjects into the privileged site of epistemic doubt—too cannot be exempt from scrutiny (ch. 1). To me, as a student of Eng Lit, it was only too evident that textuality, ambiguity, and semantic indeterminacy had done ideological 'work' for a sanctioned, imperious discourse of literary criticism and aesthetic value even before the poststructuralist 'turn' was institutionalized on the level ground of narrative and counternarrative, and that demonstrable pluralities of meaning were not inherently radical or transformative.

The narrativization of enigma, secrecy, semantic difficulty, uncertainty, have had precise though diverse ideological locations. Thus the simultaneous production of opacity and value in *Mansfield Park* tied willed (female) ignorance to colonial instrumentality (ch. 5). The conflation of secrecy with the sacred in Blavatsky's *Caves and Jungles* inflated and internationalized Hinduism, recast it as scientific–spiritual enigma, an uncharted mystical frontier (ch. 4). Secrecy was linked in *Portrait* to antifeminism, the growth of mass culture, the gendering of privacy; uncertainty in *Wings* locked the authority of realism into the elision of a 'dissident' modernism to compose an aesthetic of hermeneutic freedom that obscured the degree of James's consent to his own metropolitan class authority (chs 2,3). Garcia Marquez, however, inscribes an enigma into *Chronicle of a Death Foretold* to manifest the political and patriarchal opacities of neocolonialism (ch. 1).

Colonization in particular engendered structural occlusions and scissions, undesignated absences and subsumptions, systemic obliquities and instabilities that in-formed genres and epistemic modes. Spatial disjunctions radically altered the constitution of selfhood: middle-class women were fashioned across the colonial divide through a discursive 'realism' crafted from an unseen India and an un-visited Britain—profoundly ideological 'clarities' emerged from what was in fact unknown or invisibilized while a range of opacities emanated from quite specific occlusions (chs 5,6). These spatial and other disjunctions helped to transform the zones of surplus extraction into sites for the production of 'symbolic' value(s) impervious to 'rational' enquiry which could be consumed in both metropolis and colony (ch. 4). The 'classic' epistemic difficulty that defined high Anglo–American modernism (*and* made it canonical) partly arose from the ways in which it internalized or extrapolated from such material regimens of obscurity, compressed and formalized its own engrossment in metropolitan relations. In this modernism, the desired wholeness of bourgeois identity as much as its mourned/celebrated fractures, its compulsive distancing of the materialities that ground its self-universalization and its nomadic assimilation as much as its heuristic revolts, anomie, alienation, or self-irony, inaugurated new styles of negotiating and displacing 'old' colonial accumulations (chs 1,2,3,4). These 'limits' of representation, governed by regional and global networks of class, patriarchal and imperial power, produced difficulties of cognitive mapping that are only too easy to reify into epistemic doubt per se. The politics of social and disciplinary location and the connections between local, metropolitan and colonial geographies as they bear on realist, modernist and postmodernist epistemologies, then, are central to the whole question of meaning.

Polysemy, the excess of meaning, too is indissociable from determinate contexts. The generic frameworks and numerous other ways through which narratives transcend the literal or univocal, the plural reading positions they carry, are as contextual as univocity (chs 3,6). Thus the multiaccentuality of signs in *Chhabili* is predicated on the traffic between print and performance, the fluidity of belief systems, unevenness of class and literacy, instability of gender and caste definitions. In other words, the prismatic transitiveness of a text is not seen as a function of the inherent ambiguity of language but as the interplay of its aggregated densities, latencies, and formal imperatives, with new interpretative ensembles aligned to the axes of social division and contest that in turn increase the layers or refractions. The historical sediment, variation, and social indeterminacy that multiply points of view can be further occulted into epistemic doubt or, as for Garcia Marquez who proffers the enigma in a radical way, they can be the point of entry for a transformative politics.

My effort to loosen or rework text/context divisions, then, stems not from the now mandatory rejection of the grand narrative of history but from the need to disengage from an externalist view in which literature and history stand 'outside' each other, or at best 'behind' each other as distillation and corroboration. As such it is an attempt to work literary analysis (except in matters of emphasis, detail, particularity of a form or a text) of the "labour of representation" (Pierre Bourdieu's phrase) and the study of social stratification/transformation into each other, and also to make 'literature' visible as itself an object of these same historical processes, especially in the modes of its institutionalization, consumption, and reutilization.

Finally, the collection suggests different possibilities for theorizing subcontinental literatures in terms of lineage, periodization, conjuncture, and national provenance, a theorizing that is reducible neither to an ethnography of local context nor to an 'alternate' canon with its own (hagiographic) genealogy. This would rest on the specificity of forms and of conditions of production, the new structures of determination that emerged in the colonial conjuncture, and the particular political and institutional formations that overdetermine 'intertextual' recurrence within logics of segmentary social change. An intertextuality read neither as a mechanism internal to texts or discourse nor as the anthropological synchronicity of a 'cultural system', but, as I suggest in the case of misogyny, altruism, incitement, as a formal mark and particular style of affiliation between texts that takes shape in the dynamic of the social relations they refract and institute. Taken together the essays hope to open a space, albeit gesturally, for charting the ways in which the dispersals, recursivities, involutions and enclosures of precapitalist literary production were replotted through·their interaction with new local and transnational forms of fusion, recursivity, parochialization and categorization. And in the process redoubled the density, the accretions, the nodes of condensation in even the most prosaic and 'lowly' of tracts.

'Literature' in the colonial period, given this multiplicity of shaping pressures and the co-production of 'exclusive' national heritages is, I suggest, at some levels definitionally not a 'national' but a mixed field, contextually instantiated. Its historical curvature could perhaps be transcribed through a method that can describe the loops between transnational and transregional constellations, the oral and the written, reading clusters and individual intentionalities, and can apprehend their contradictions by isolating, provisionally, ideological configurations. A method that can regroup texts, trace their antecedents, mobility, ideological pliancy, conjunctural teleologies, shifting address, and social effectivities. The essays in this book do in fact try to map transnational ideological configurations—British and American, British and Indian, Latin American and metropolitan— that have pressed a patriarchal bourgeois consciousness into high modernism, 'Indian spirituality' into a gendered and primitive unconscious, and 'third-world' narratives into a postmodernist rubric. The need to develop such a method, to which I will return, may become apparent as I indicate some of the contentions which underwrite the essays.

Which anticolonialism?

If the well-tailored jacket of colonial English did not quite fit, then some of the anticolonialisms on offer have also been uncomfortable. This was, and remains, a question of context and location. The incremental growth of economic imperialism, Hindu communalism with its marauding tactics and investment in a majoritarian polity corresponding to a primordial religion, the defensive (self)articulation of difference in identitarian politics, have been accompanied by new patriarchal rationales for each. The splitting of compacts of civil decency in patriarchal–communal–casteist violence based on primordial differentialism as well as of the left–feminist–secular unities arrayed against it, alongside a visible shrinking of space for public protest in the 1990s have been the daily conditions for the reception of cultural theories. In this volatile political conjuncture, given the common lineage and overlap between some politically antagonist positions, the many connections of the colonial period with the present have become even more fraught. And at the same time, those anticolonialisms which have been marshalled in defence of these developments, or provided no way to oppose them, or functioned in ways that allow different types of cultural differentialism to converge, have become more disturbing.

In the wide spectrum of opposition to colonialism three currents have an especial bearing on gender and culture. The first is the continued circulation—as historiography, as commonsense—of an early twentieth-century anticolonialism whose vocabulary was compromised by a patriarchal and colonial patrimony, and mortgaged to a dyadic grid that laid out a national space affected by the western. This, shorn of its secular aspirations, can still be seized by the Hindu right to mobilize national–cultural particularities (ch. 8). The second is a communalism which pushes culture as a 'Hindu' nation premised on patriarchal antimodern antiwesternism, deploys hard religio–cultural identities to unify it, exalts a Hindu–Aryan past. The third is a strand in contemporary academic theory structured around a critique of (post)Enlightenment rationality and colonial modernity as embodied in the nation or elite nationalism. It opposes communalism but largely on the ground of its modernity, tends to be soft on or untroubled by premodern essentialisms, or pits a postcolonial identitarianism against a (post)Enlightenment universalism; and, paradoxically, by not breaking with the nation-state as a naturalized site of *cultural* particularity for struggles between 'cultures', jeopardizes its own project of reconceptualizing the nation.

The difficulty lies not in the occasional entanglement of these discrete currents but in that each is shackled to the same theoretical precondition (cultural differentialism) and its paraphernalia (cultural authenticity/autonomy) on a political terrain where assumptions of cultural difference have considerable social force, ideological ramification, and can be manipulated to debunk the left and disband whatever remains of the secular–nationalist consensus. For instance, Hindu communalism posits a double rupture—first Muslim invasion then modernity; some anti-Enlightenment theory indexes a single rupture—the epistemic violence wrought by (post)Enlightenment modernity through colonization. The one inscribes medieval and colonial history as a logic of (Hindu) subjection and reaction; the other lingers on the religious and private domain as a unique sphere of cultural difference defined in response/reaction to colonial subjection/modernity. The one fulminates against 'imported' ideas and 'imitation' and directs its energy into rescripting an 'alternative' modernity that is 'modern-but-not-western' (a formulation directed especially at women) either by bodily transposing the modern onto the ancient (a paradoxical denial of novelty to the modern) or by casting the religious premodern as a rival of the secular modern; the other condemns the political derivation of national elites, sets out to write difference into 'our' modernity, and often stages premodern 'survivals' as an answer to the modern, without pausing to reflect on the implications. Any anticolonialism premised on rupture caused by invasion seems especially problematic when a powerful system for othering Muslims and Christians on the *same* premise is already violently in place. And how would the model of schism, itself so taken up with the rupture of an undifferentiated premodern, help to dismantle the tripartite Hindu communal model of golden age-decline-rejuvenation which invokes a pure and recuperable womanhood in a pre-Muslim past? How will the impossible lure of indigenist cultural difference or aesthetic autonomy displace the Hindu communal myth of origins? How will an allegation of modernity embedded in a polarization of us against the (usually monolithic) 'west' challenge its denial to 'nonwestern' women of any horizon of self-definition other than their 'own' culture?

   It would be reductive to compress this complex field, at once diffuse and familiar, into single-authored positions in the span of an introduction, and doing so may deflect the issues, namely, that anticolonialisms with otherwise differing political and theoretical premises can still recluster or revamp the same set of dyads: colonial imposition–'native' response, authenticity–'inauthentic' derivation, tradition–modernity, western universalism–nonwestern particularism. And that these dyads rely on some form of cultural exceptionalism as subject of loss, nostalgia, retrieval, invention, as irreducible difference, or as a precondition for resistance.

And of course all these terms are gendered in their formulation, referents, or effects: women in one way or another have paid the highest price for cultural exceptionalism. An egalitarian feminism, however, forces a critique not only of colonialism and capitalism but also of precapitalist essentialism, culture, and patriarchies; it cannot but recognize that patriarchy was neither a gift of Muslim invaders, as Hindu communalism likes to claim, nor as anti-Enlightenment arguments can imply, largely an effect of colonial rule and imposed modernity. Given the precapitalist history, the persistence, and the repeated reconstitution of patriarchies, the issue is far more complicated than a nationalism derived or divided off from Enlightenment rationality. Can the nation as a condensation of (post)Enlightenment modernity be the privileged object of feminist critique if patriarchies did not originate in colonialism or nationalism and are unlikely to terminate with the demise of nationalism(s)? If the nation-state has been the object of left–feminist critique—as stabilizer of patriarchies, as broker of imperialism—it has at the same time been the determinate horizon of struggle for livelihood and rights, work and wages. In other words, even at the risk of abandoning some types of anticolonialism altogether, feminism must point to both the regularity and the reformulation of patriarchies, and as a corollary, sift and distinguish between various anticolonialisms to uncover their assumptions.

In retrospect, much of this collection can be read as interrogating, in different ways and with varying intensity, these anticolonial dyads whose conceptual weakness became especially vivid when faced with such vexed questions about patriarchies. I believe that if the question of inequality in practice and in theory is to be confronted, and if the formation of culture under capitalism is to be understood as an eminently transnational, structured and ideological process located in the materialities of class, patriarchies and politics, then claims to cultural exceptionalism have to be replaced by the claim to specificity.

Yet the stake in specificity too has to be demarcated from both the neo-orientalist claim to ontological difference[2] and the kind of contextualism that retreats from 'grand' theory into a local theorized as the preferred 'oppositional' site of difference–resistance. Even when specificity refuses to function as an alibi for irreducible particularism, it still needs to be reconstructed if it is to enter concrete

contexts and theory into a dialectical relation, to negotiate the materiality of the formation of class and culture without recourse to a
paradigmatic European model, to define with precision the types of
unevenness engendered by colonization and capitalism. In sum, this
would be a specificity that emerges from an older Marxist tradition
of the situated critique of social formations—in both their determining and transformative capacities—and sets out to articulate culture
and patriarchies with class *and* non-class features, with the asymmetry, blockage and contradiction in local, national *and* transnational imperatives.

The perspective on colonization which took shape gradually
and underwrote my essays (not all at once, all together, or in the same
way) rests on specificity understood as unevenness, relationality,
cross-national historical intersection, and political affinity. And, it
can be pinned down in a series of related propositions that revolve
around a single one: British colonization of the subcontinent was a
collision of two well-developed patriarchal class societies. It was a
juncture, grossly unequal, in which two class processes intersected:
the consolidation of the middle classes in Britain and the emergence
of new classes in India.

The subcontinent had prior histories of state formation,
centralized political systems, class division and notions of empire,
tribal as well as 'feudal' formations with corollary institutions and
intermediate classes, elaborate taxonomies of social stratification,
sophisticated modes for rationalizing the cognate structures of gender and caste inequality, material and ideological means for guaranteeing these divisions of labour, and different degrees of extension of
state authority into the familial complex.

Further, a number of cultural processes that have currently
come to be associated solely with colonization in postmodern/post-
colonial theory had been taking place over the centuries: linguistic
choices in layered multilingual formations; sporadic interaction between the local, regional, and cosmopolitan, that is, 'vernacularization'
at different social levels and the braiding of high sanskritic culture
into vernacular formations; disjunction and interplay between oral
and literate cultures; the segmentation of knowledge (as sacred, as
monopoly over the written) and its arrogation as social power by
elites and upper castes; minutely detailed forms of legal codification,

social surveillance, literary and aesthetic taxonomy that were stapled to class, caste, and patriarchal distinctions. Diverse epistemologies, notions of selfhood, and forms of writing accompanied cultural 'intrusion' (from within and without) with varying effects. The play of essentialism, instrumentality, and legitimation on ruling group models often invoked the authority of the past and shaped a corresponding vocabulary of 'derivation' that could be adapted by incoming groups.[3] Claims to cultural continuity thus were at times a ruse within local processes of mobility or allied to political and ideological collaboration between ruling and invading groups. What is more, there were settled modalities for proselytization (not only Islamic but also Buddhist, Jain, Vaishnav) and the hierarchical assimilation of tribes into the brahminical caste order.

In effect, either the Indian subcontinent was always already colonial, postcolonial, postmodern, and can be recoded along with other plural social formations into a continuous prefiguration of postmodernist fragmentation. Or, this history of extraordinary adaptation, importation, in-migration, settlement, these ancient techniques of exclusion, othering, discrimination, surveillance, and structuring diversity indicate the naiveté of reading colonization as the *unique* invention of regimes of difference, as the *originary* moment of 'alien' imposition and epistemic rupture, as the *sole* engine of cultural violation, as the *founding* moment for 'native' derivation. Given the prior presence of discontinuities, what was both unprecedented and a decisive break was not these cultural processes per se but the impositions made by capitalism. Culture, then, may more appropriately be seen as a series of reconfigurations in which capital overdetermined by colonization both used and transformed earlier cultural processes. Within this there were subtle shifts and remodulations beneath seemingly continuous processes; practices that persisted were either spatially, temporally, and ideologically repositioned or integrated; certain types of change were recoded as (patriarchal) 'conservation'; and the practices and discursivities that emerged on old or familiar terrains were often neither vestigial remainders nor fitted the classic model of transition but were part of new constellations. A paradigm of culture that reads the advent of colonialism in terms of cataclysm and genesis implies some preceding unbroken and uncontested culture, conflates culture and economy, and cannot register the range of nuances between resilience and atrophy within a logic of uneven change. It tends instead to fall into a before-and-after tradition–modernity dyad of enchanted and disenchanted worlds, languages, knowledge systems.

Since the transition to capitalism in Britain was not uniform either,[4] an entangled, mutually constitutive yet jagged history emerges. In nineteenth-century Britain too the reconstellation of older forms of aggression with discrepant modes of governance and control sharpened ideologies that could negotiate the tension between ascribed status and acquired wealth or endorse the value of 'continuity'. The question of specificity, then, can be posed not as one of uneven versus even development but, more accurately, of different types of unevenness. First, as necessary and inherent to the logic of capital that expands through uneven differentiation of sectors, geographies, and labour forces, and creates several "economies" before it dissolves precapitalist relations or "destructures and restructures" precapitalist institutions.[5] Second, as engendered by the precapitalist histories of metropolis and colony, the character of colonial rule and emerging classes, and how these came to be articulated. Thus the regional disparities and cultural etiquettes on the Indian subcontinent (in all the respects listed earlier) along with the state and class formation underway in the eighteenth century not only determined the nature of the social relations spawned by capitalism but decisively shaped the weight and distribution of the four major modalities of colonial rule: violent disruption, coercive imposition, structural interlock, and ideological collaboration.

The logics of unevenness unfolded simultaneously as disjuncture and concurrence at various levels. Class formation was itself temporally uneven and regionally segmented in India. The new patriarchal and cultural pressures among the landowning and middle classes were pegged to both their social dominance and political subordination (chs 5,6,7). Ideological ensembles crisscrossed or fluctuated in terms of heterogeneous origin, gender disjunctions, class fractions, intra-class conflicts, qualitatively different levels, trajectories, valences of embourgeoisement, particular caste and religious constellations (chs 1,5,6,7). Prolonged piecemeal annexation, direct rule punctuated by paternalist phases of selective 'non-interference' in 'native' customs and religions in the presidencies alongside indirect rule in the princely states created another set of time-lags. Within the logic of capitalist exploitation of enclaves of precapitalist organization, the princely states functioned materially as backward pockets, ideologically as 'traditional' sectors distinct from the presidency showcases of 'enlightened' reform. Combined with the discrepancies between the relatively amorphous or new and the settled middle classes, both within and between regions, this process produced a systemic concurrence of disjunct formations that was crucial to the definition and circulation of cultural categories as well as to the local refashioning of increasingly generalized or transnational ideologies. For instance, not only was it conducive to the valorization of rajputs (as anti-Muslim patriots with self-immolating wives) in Bengal, but the time-lag between the Bengal middle class and its post-1857 counterpart in UP turned these compensatory narratives and Bengali reformist ideologies of embourgeoisement into a significant patriarchal force in the north where, however, they took a regionally distinct shape (chs 4,6). The creation of different types of elites—a 'new' aristocracy was schooled at the same time as the middle class in separately designed institutions—alongside exclusionary systems of 'constituency' education (Hindu, Muslim, Eurasian, Christian converts) in the presidencies (chs 5,6) also belongs to this paradigm of colonial governance.

Specificity thus entails some reperiodization. Different levels of change within India—economic, political, cultural—were not only spatially segmented and class differentiated but had different rates of disjuncture. Nor did literary forms, ideologies, divisions of labour, the organization of households, and patterns of daily life change in tandem. There could be extensive overlaps, small yet significant transitions, untidy layers, anachronistic juxtapositions or incongruities. In some areas such as domestic labour old and new factors joined to ensure persistence (ch. 7), in others the colonial political economy induced drastic changes.

Finally, concurrence and disjuncture were an effect of substantive material and ideological variations in colonization as a whole—informal trade empire, slave regimens, enforced labour migration and diasporic plantation settlements, direct and indirect rule, decimation of native populations followed by resettlement— and in the modes of production (tribal, agrarian, feudal, tributary) on which it was overlaid or imposed. The intersections and time-lags produced by these disjunct contemporaneities were central to the formation of culture both within and across national boundaries. The traffic from colony to colony in techniques of governance, labour both enslaved and indentured, and in ideologies of race, caste, and gender too was inscribed in this dynamic of concurrent modes of colonization. As indeed was the circulation and internationalization of forms of antiimperialism.

The presence of these differential temporalities[6] within the 'modern' is for me not a question of pluralization—as the proliferation of diverse imperial and imperialized subjects/identities, as a multiplicity of modernities lived out in 'many worlds' across the globe with disparate possibilities and constraints. Rather it is primarily one of historicizing concurrence, disjuncture, and the systemic production and patterning of difference by atomizing/homogenizing cultural processes inside, and often beyond the nation-state in order to extend a socialist theory of asymmetrical "historical trajectories".[7]

Thus the contrary characterization of India, its precolonial polities and religions, and the colonial mission by the British hinged on preservation as much as intervention, emulation as much as reform.[8] These were not discursive antinomies. Nor were they merely expedient narratives of conquest and consolidation. Rather they marked the contradictions which arose from the structural interlocks and ideological confluences of colonial rule with existing and emerging stratification, divisions of labour, and patriarchal arrangements in the dual context of class formation and selective 'non-interference', and need some elaboration. I believe it was the ponderous presence of all the features and structures of inequality enumerated earlier, which the colonial state and comprador groups could often jointly utilize, that gives a special importance to structural interlocks and complicit discursivities at particular class levels. However, the material accommodation of a small section played out in patronage, clientilism, political alliance, or displays of loyalism are less significant than the ideological consolidations that occurred through them. The more so because indigenist rhetorics have obscured the extent to which their own religious and patriarchal categories, description of (national) culture, and framework for opposing colonial intervention were smelted in this crucible. A culturally 'authentic' formation was gained by foregrounding the blatant onslaught and repression of the colonial state, and blurring what was in fact a complex field of institutional and class interaction bearing contradictory and collusive ideological tendencies.

The complicit schemas, the blends of disparagement and approval which circulated from the end of the eighteenth century (and not in British Orientalism alone) were crucial in the configuration of female knowledge, domestic labour and other patriarchal arrangements, the casting of Hindu men as politically docile but patriarchally 'autonomous', the production of a modern-but-not-western woman who later became a sign of cultural singularity and 'nationalist' intransigence, the demarcation of a transcendant domain of custom and belief, the restitution of colonial versions of 'native' traditions and institutions, the compilation of an organic and usually 'Hindu' past, the institution of anti-Muslim rhetorics, and the tailoring of a spiritual east and a materialist west (chs 4,5,6,7,8).

As this 'transnational' colonial grammar passed through an equally occulting romanticism and 'scientism', the salvation schemas of German Indology and conservative modernism, and as non-European religio-mysticisms were appropriated from metropolitan locations, a regenerative India came to be crafted. Certain etiquettes for the negation of western superiority/modernity were devised along the way which could lock into the Spenglerian spectre of the decay of western civilization as well as the relegation of modernity in the name of anticolonial indigenism. Religion became at once the special lack created by modernization and the panacea for a modernity that was quite compatible with it: the discoveries of modern science coincided with the essential truth of the east (ch. 4). An indigenist scientism fastened the discourse of health onto domestic labour, knotted the discourse of hygiene with purity–pollution, and biology with caste (ch. 7). This is recycled even today especially by the Hindu right.

The pragmatic assimilation, stereotyping strategies, and parade of patriarchal features as marks of distinction from other religions/cultures by the Hindu right were also pieced together in this constellation of non-interference, loyalism, and collaboration (chs 5, 6,8). For instance, the ideological trope of the so-called Muslim interregnum—that is, the constitution of Muslim rule as a dark moment between a pristine Hindu India and the restoration of Hindu cultural prestige under British rule—became a recurrent, organizing discursivity sustained and refuelled by different situations. It appears in British historiography and the administrative discourse of first noninterference, then divide-and-rule, as responsible for Hindu victimage and as guarantor of Hindu loyalty (chs 5,6). It comes attached to loyalism as proof of British benevolence and Hindu male capacity to take the onus of reform (ch. 5); as part of a 'Hindu civilizational' claim to cultural exceptionalism and an (retrievable) original essence (ch. 4); as an abnegation of Hindu male agency that posited change as a product of external interference (ch. 6). It hooks pragmatically into intra-class conflict over jobs, scripts, and community claims (ch. 6). It is mustered to exonerate Hindu men, to conceal the fact that patriarchies had solidified within the caste order long before Muslim rule; and put to work to purify Hinduism, withdraw women from syncretic practices, concoct a rationale for reforming and educating them (chs 5,6). It persists even now but, in a peculiar transmutation of loyalism into transgression, as a preamble to violence in which Hindu women incite effeminate Hindu men against Muslims (ch. 8).

The very areas encoded as signs of cultural autonomy—classical and vernacular languages, religious ascription, womanhood, patriarchies, were shaped collaboratively, as indeed was their opposite, the sign of 'native' derivation–colonial imposition—English. In fact the categories of English and Sanskrit, Hindu women and English women developed relatedly—through educational institutions, the apparatus of textbooks, treatises and domestic ideologies, debates in journals, voluntary societies and caste associations on the woman question, marriage expenses and the introduction of English —as ensembles that clubbed class mobility, religious and caste ascription with patriarchal arrangements, and produced a notion of culture as a form of conscious cultivation (chs 5,6). The simultaneous constitution of ideologies about women and 'literature' in conservative British nationalism also crystallized into allied notions of female knowledge and agency. The pre-scripted them-and-us rendition of colonization worked to hold apart what were interpenetrative categories though it was, paradoxically, itself crossbred within a local and transnational field of determinations that structured culture in both India and England; and it served in the metropolis, as in the colony, to mask the similarity and intersection of class processes and patriarchies. Thus 'co-authorship' did not necessarily disperse colonial authority or resolve it in the comfort of dialogy but often *reconfigured* it.

A recognition of complicity, then, calls the assumptions and procedures of anticolonial cultural differentialisms into question. Indian middle-class and landowning groups did not only subscribe to the so-called modernizing venture and (post)Enlightenment universalism, as some anticolonialisms claim, but also to the very preservation, formation, and recasting of cultural differentialism. Premodern temporalities and so-called primordial categories centred on religion, caste, and gender were instituted as principles of differentiation; a 'colonial' indigenism was improvised in which precolonial typologies could cooperate, coalesce with, or be rechanelled by colonial taxonomies.[9] The resulting coincidence of the "mark of the plural"[10] with the mark of the primordial created a genetically unbridgeable (gendered) gap between us-and-them, coded as a non-individualized group/community identity incommensurate with 'western' individualism. This had several consequences: a concerted opposition of individuation for women, a presentation of change as the persistence or erosion of discrete sacred–cosmological–symbolic complexes, a related suppression of both the specific accommodations and material arrangements through which these complexes were filtered, and their dilution or recombination on the amorphous, overlapping terrains 'below' (ch. 6). And, it generated a covert compatibility or alignment between this 'primordial–premodern' and a conservative 'modern' deeply attracted to cohesive religious systems (chs 4,6).

In sum, the notion of cultural autonomy, the *terms* of the difference it sought to mark, the very demarcation of the 'private' domain it was to be marked in, were eminently colonial in their ideological bearing. Far from being a disjuncture with modernity, they were among its structured coordinates. The so-called non-bourgeois, non-secular, non-universalistic, mytho-religious, affective markers of the middle-class universe were not, as is believed, resistant to assimilation into the categories of the European imperial modern (and as such unavailable to secular interpretation), but fairly well assimilated into the colonial political imaginary of pragmatic non-interference, patriarchal governance, and indissoluble cultural difference.

That is, there is some continuity between the older languages—traditionalist, romantic organicist, antiwestern, antimodern, conservative modern—for fixing and essentializing difference, and contemporary theories about 'alternative' traditions and modernities in so far as they rely on intense and rigid particularisms, single out non-class at the expense of class features, turn women, peasants and religion into the special sites of danger, loss and, need I say it, of recovery. In effect, among other things, colonialism patterned a culturalist language of mourning that was also the language of self-congratulation. A language that blurs, or, at worst, provides an alibi for patriarchal privileges.

Ironically, it is the gender question that unravels this collaborative primordial–premodern subject. As my essays suggest, the issue of patriarchies was as material as it was ideological, the gendered division of labour assisted class differentiation, and unpaid domestic labour was central to class formation (chs 5,6,7,8). The colonial state's own implication in the preservation and reform of patriarchies was locked into the creation and reproduction of classes, the maintenance of class boundaries and labour pools (chs 5,6,7). (The state was as distressed by the market economy as the middle class when the prostitution it patronized was at stake (ch. 7)!) What emerged were jagged patterns of persistence and change, differentiated transitions, patriarchal rearrangements that articulated existing with emerging forms but actively *blocked* ruptures. And, as chapter 6 shows, patriarchal practices themselves not only made it impossible to evade the articulation of class with non-class factors but also raised another crucial issue: the contradictions between class formation and community claims. 'Communities' were premised on a within and a without while women were construed across religions as the innermost sanctum of religious communities as well as the porous borders through which 'other' religions trickled in. However, there were no such 'withins' in existing patriarchies which cut across primordial features of social organization and stuck neither to religious boundaries nor conformed to identitarian claims (chs 6,7).

If I seem to overemphasize collaboration, it is not in order to underplay resistance to colonialism, the critique of its economic and political programmes, the justifiable reactions to its hegemonic drives. These shaped both colonial governance and its demise. Nor do I want to erase the violence and ruthless extraction of colonial rule or to suggest that the presence of complicitous Indian agencies can diffuse or whitewash the implications of imperialism. Rather, I want to draw attention, first, to the confluences or transverse interlocks that laid out the cognitive grid of anticolonial dis-courses of singularity and still undergird definitions of the 'pre-modern', the 'modern', and cultural 'autonomy'. Second, to those anticolonialisms which solidi-fied around alibis of collaboration well before the beginning of orga-nized nationalism and installed a compensatory relation between 'cultural' refractoriness and economic pliancy (repeated even today in Hindutva politics). And finally to address the one-sidedness of theories which homogenize colonial procedures and so return to the protean contest between tradition and modernity.

The tradition–modernity dyad, both in its early sociological forms (as pragmatic debit–credit sheet of gains, losses, compromises) and its present anti-Enlightenment variant (as inventory and infla-tion of non/pre/antimodern enclaves, deflation of the modern) pre-sumes that some autonomous entity entered India either as an agent of violation, an emblem of European cultural otherness, or as object of imitation and derivation. It replicates the procedures of euro-centric diffusionism, a "nineteenth-century elite myth-formation" that set out to unify a special European identity[11] in which cultural processes flowed out from Europe to non-European sectors from the fifteenth century while Europe's own cultural dynamic, like its eco-nomy, was a self-generated miracle unaffected by the wealth and innovation seized from the colonies. And this internalist model of dichotomized historical development has shaped imitation–deriva-tion whether as nationalist lament, indigenist condemnation, or postmodern/postcolonial anti-Enlightenment diatribe. It is heavily mortgaged to conceiving of colonization as a confrontation of two coherent preconstituted entities, pre-formed in separate geographical locales, each immaculate—and never as themselves products of tran-sactional, transnational processes, intensified, altered, or made itine-rant by capitalism, and at many levels jointly formed in the pressure of precapitalist essentialisms, producing new entities at the site of interaction which proliferated in the colony and returned to remake the metropolis.

Further, the centuries of European colonial extraction and

accumulation that preceded British rule in India had already suffused
and racialized European discursivities. What came to be described
and legitimated as European knowledges were neither unitary nor
autonomous but hybrid formations that enfolded and systematized
'other' knowledges, other hierarchies. 'Local' knowledge was transformed into European knowledge and thence travelled back into
indigenist claims, performed different ideological functions in its
European and Indian locales. The making of metropolitan identity
was implicated politically in 'native' resistance and dissent. Even
nationalism was not a 'finished' entity made in the metropolis and
exported to the 'periphery' but an interactive field.[12] By the nineteenth century Britain's entanglement in class, caste, and gender divisions in India shows up in its own social history and classificatory
schemas: in the management of class struggle, the willed self-
containment of its pastoralism, ideologies of prostitution, labour and
domesticity, the often cognate codification of caste and race, the fit
between racism abroad and evolutionary doctrine, eugenics and the
regulation of female sexuality at home (chs 4,5,6,7). If Indian upper-
caste ideology had attributed widowhood to female literacy then
evolutionists insisted child-bearing women be "intellectually handicapped" as a "penalty to be paid for race predominance", that English women pay the sacrificial "tax" demanded by nature for the
ascent of civilization, and that mental development would render
them partially or completely infertile![13] The qualities ascribed to
Victorian women on the basis of 'science' too were similar to those
ascribed to Hindu women and men on the basis of religion: greater
respect for authority, a weaker notion of individual freedom, conservative attachment to custom yet too dangerous to be given political
power. An emphasis on cultural imposition and 'native' derivation,
then, can suppress the fact that colonialism extrapolated from and
mediated the extant as much as it invented the new. Indeed the
questions can be rephrased. What accounted for the span and the conjoining of these patriarchal operations that immured women as the
self-limiting, self-correcting subjects of modernity?[14] What was the
precise relation between the modern-but-not-western woman in India
and the western-but-not-fully-modern woman in Britain?

    If on one side (post)Enlightenment thought was overdeter-
mined by colonial expansion, then on the other side its 'inbreeding'

was marked by exploitation, repression, exclusion of women, blacks and the poor, its professed universalism undercut by elitism, racism, and 'western' superiority.[15] It was not universalized in Europe and even less so in the colonies. Caught in a dialectical history of proliferation and blockage—as an abstract set of egalitarian values with emancipatory potentials and as an ideology of capital threatened by the political concretization of these potentials for the underprivileged, as questioning old hierarchies but renewing masculinist essentialisms and devising normative hierarchies to justify colonial domination, as recuperated in libertarian or antiimperialist agendas even as its own unitary premises were fissured by the imperial arenas in which it was played out (ch. 5)—it was not quite the inexorable engine it is made out to be. The fact that much of colonial rule and education, ideologically and strategically, was itself carried out under the signature of either the irrelevance, sectorization, dilution and withholding of the Enlightenment project, or of outright opposition to it (chs 5,6,7), makes me doubt if colonization can be attacked solely as a purveyor of the Enlightenment, or if a critique needs to be mounted in these terms. Thus the crosshatch of existing exclusionary divisions in India with the hidden exclusions within 'liberal' ideology and its difficulty in granting full individuation or citizenship to women and 'others' *renewed* the force of ascription along lines of class, race, and gender. The claim to equality, then, is not an 'internalist' demand for completion of the Enlightenment project but based on a double evaluation—of precapitalist essentialism *and* the essentialization of the premodern, of the assumption that Enlightenment ideals must not be imitated or applied in India *and* the uneasy association of liberal universalism with colonial indigenism—that radically repositions it. What is now at issue is precisely to maintain the tension between a critique of its ideological pretensions as unfurled in the chauvinist rhetoric of the colonial 'mission', a historical appraisal of the controlled or curtailed implementation of its egalitarian values as intensifying European and Indian cultural differentialism, as nurturing both eurocentrism and a reverse indocentrism,[16] *and* the (still) continuous reclamation, generalization, and renovation of its emancipatory potential from 'below'. The notion of a ubiquitous Enlightenment merely obscures the transformation of imperial nations and their cultural trajectories, and impedes alternative analyses that

neither defend nor demonize colonial modernity, that do not save
the dubious legacy of colonial particularism in order to reject its spurious universalism.

Cultural mixing: in a secular frame

This argument for the mutually shaped, shared yet discrepant histories of imperial and imperialized countries was first laid out
in the early 1980s in "The Politics of the Possible", and no longer
needs reiteration. However, the way I then defined hybridization—
as a relational and political process resistant to right-wing or ethnocentric notions of authenticity but vulnerable to postmodernist reclassification—needs to be refined. Hybridity now occupies many
sites and other pressing questions have emerged. What notion of
culture is this relationality and mixing to be located in? Which theoretical framework is the destabilization of fixed national–cultural
boundaries to be mobilized for? In other words, what is at issue is not
merely the dyadic and originary models of colonialism but the
viability of the pluralizing schemas (centred on hybridity) that are
replacing them. Both the jumbling of cultures within the palimpses-
tic aesthetics of the modern and an itinerant or evenly circulating
modernist cosmopolitanism deflect the structured contexts or flatten
the torsions of modernity (ch. 1). Floating modernities that take local
root in unexpected recompositions, regroup, distort or transform
'imported' models, place mixed inventive identities within a flux of
constantly permuting ensembles, rest on a notion of many or alternative modernities that can sink into banal relativism and dissolve
the material questions of inequality and circulation of cultural categories in a comforting equivalence between the original and the copy.
On the other hand, the generalized marginality that some post-
colonialisms propose and the hybridity they offer, whether as 'third-
world' prerogative—its very own mark of (non)identity with the
'west'—or as resistance to cultural imperialism via bricolage and
indigenization, seems at once too metaphoric and too strategic. It
normalizes a (universally suppressed) regimen of difference but
claims for this a superlative political efficacy. The hybrid staged as
the ambivalence, doubling, splitting of colonizing and colonized subjects, as a discursive position for native circumvention and undermining of colonial authority from 'within', as troubling binaries of

ruler and ruled, seems to be content with transgression and does not perceive boundaries in a dialectical way. The insertion of culture and its diversity into a processual, 'world-systems' schema to celebrate an unbelonging in which the hybrid evacuates nation-centred grand narratives, disturbs or fractures the (so-called) 'homogenous', 'integrated' culture and 'western' unitary rationalism of the postcolonial nation-state, and is positioned as the migratory, unhoused, restless border-crossing object of an equally nomadic nonlinear historiography, is also problematic. After all the very fluidity and crosscutting of modes of legitimation is itself an issue, as in the case of patriarchal arrangements and ideologies which not only denaturalize the global mobility of capital but expose the limits of even premodern diversity and syncretism. Hybridity, then, has become a conflictual sign. Itself interstitial, interrogatory and inescapable, decentering and foundational, it nevertheless sets out to dispense with all binaries, essentialized identities, and national divisions. It at once removes the stigma of colonial assimilation carried by national bourgeoisies *and* outmodes their nationalism.

If the hybrid is now a talisman that does many kinds of work, the weight of the sharing too has shifted from agonist versions of the 'intimate enemy' to the transnational arenas of hybridization or creolization of diasporas. The energy of this emblematic hybridization, the variation of inflections and critiques, require detailed discussion.[17] My abbreviated and provisional claim here is that even diasporic hybridization is mired in nation-states of origin *and* residence as sites of self-definition and struggle, migration alters both the place of departure and the point of arrival, and mobility is as complicated by differing political and power relations as immobility, as open to substantive disaggregation. Hybridization is an aspect of shared histories but does not subsume them. What is more, neither hybridization nor shared histories *necessarily* require demographic dislocation, imply pluralization or pose a challenge to colonialism, nationalism, or imperialism. They are simply integral to colonial and class processes within capitalism.

As most of my essays show, in one way or another, colonization and capitalism accelerated the process of cultural mixing. And they did this *across* the political spectrum from left to right. Colonialism itself produced a set of conditions conducive to a range of articulations of precapitalist with romantic, liberal and conservative essentialisms, abstractions and universalisms. It is possible that the prolonged process of segmentary change and partial embourgeoisement on the subcontinent also necessitated these combinatoires —in which case, howsoever unprecedented and co-authored the resulting ensembles may be, they can be understood only in relation to the transnational ideologies of a capitalism that developed simultaneously in national and global frameworks.

To rename these asymmetries as our 'own' modernities, as pockets of resistance, and bask in the glow of cultural ownership can not only circuitously reconstruct an 'inimitable' indigeneity that rested till now on authenticity-in-difference, but also reify unevenness and provide a culturalist justification for the disparities enforced by capitalism in imperialized countries. Though it has the advantage of evading pure alterity, absolutist racism or ethnic (en)closure, this too can become another form of exoticization—unique blends of them and us, a hybrid indigenism or indigenist hybrid that by mixing the 'west' with the rest can be consumed as novelty (as endless recombination, as rapid relegation), 'deregulate' or denationalize culture for the postmodern marketplace. In effect, hybridity can recoup some of the cultural nationalism it wishes to jettison or be retethered to the same alterity it sets out to escape.

The uncritical celebration of mixed identities, then, is premature precisely because they are not definitionally disruptive or subversive. Syncretic social practices could emerge or be sustained by convergent interests among lower castes and classes, as in UP, without yielding either a heretical principle or a coherent politics of choice. Religious syncretism could suspend or negate some patriarchal rationales, forge social solidarities that undermined harsh differentialism, but did not resolve other aspects of segmentation or patriarchal oppression (ch. 6). More unambiguously, cultural mixing can be reactionary, conservative, sectarian, transparently clientilist, and redouble access to power. Patriarchies have been reformulated by splicing older, extant and emergent practices and ideologies (chs 5,6,7). The reterritorializing procedures of the Hindu right are syncretic even though it ideologically rejects intermixture: it captures religious and cultural signs from earlier and/or fixed spatial or temporal locations and releases them into new ones, and carries a strong politics of assimilation—a hybridization geared to erase its own signs through authenticity claims (ch. 8). Multinational products and ope-rations can self-effacingly adopt the customs of the con-quered—no meat in MacDonald's burgers on Tuesdays in New Delhi: a mutually constitutive indigenization and globalization meet effortlessly in 'taste' and, ironically, select and ratify a sectional practice, turn it into an undifferentiated 'Hindu' norm, and that too in a context where the Hindu right has been pushing vegetarianism as part of its anti-Muslim/Christian agenda. Local difference can be accommodated in the new universalism of the market by a neo-modernism that no longer finds it profitable to make oversharp distinctions between 'west' and 'nonwest', and invests happily in particularist 'traditions' as long as they are not accompanied by uncouth, that is, protective nationalisms.[18]

Hybridization then is a problematic category because it carries no single fixed moral, political, or cultural valence. It blurs and redraws lines of cultural difference but these may not always be lines of political dissent, nor even egalitarian. If colonial indigenisms or patriarchies were grafts or alloys they did not for that reason become less oppressive, only differently so. Emphasizing cultural mixing can only serve as a preliminary move that, by disputing pri-mordialist claims, clears a critical space for the historically ground-ed explanation of the uneven features of intracultural mixing, but hybridity cannot in and of itself produce a definitive theory or any-thing more than a gestural politics. The crucial question, then, is not that hybridization constantly breaks down the lines between them and us but how it subsequently reassembles on political lines, its political affiliations (latent or explicit), and its sphere of effectivity (national or cross-national).

As may be evident, I want to retrieve cultural mixing, sel-ectively, both from the flabby axiom that all cultures and identities borrow and invent, and from many of its present usages, and refor-mulate it for a now unfashionable secular project. If culture is a con-tested field of continuous appropriation and reclamation, and the work of analysis the equally steady one of disentangling the entan-gled, cleaning up concepts muddied through everyday use, then the domain of 'radical' commonsense is not an exception. In order to re-animate the historical force of mingled histories as a ground and a resource for the secular, it may be useful to first revert to the older meanings of hybridization: new recombinations of elements from previously separate territories whether as conscious break with the notion of tradition as continuity, as unintentional mixture, or as a fusion of disparate elements.[19] And, at the same time, recover the materiality, the historical forms and logics of all the allied processes of synthesis, syncretism, eclecticism, permeation, translation into other frames of reference, alongside the varied valuation and tolerance of cultural mixing and not-belonging in the past, in order to understand how these processes have both mediated and themselves been redesigned by the increasing availability of hitherto discrete options/practices as simultaneities.

A retheorization of the irreducibly heterocultural history of the subcontinent has to be complicated by the multivocal registers of precapitalist cultural mixing, 'relativization', and cross-fertilization that occurred within the logics of mercantilism, conquest, migration of peoples and knowledges (as in medieval traditions of travel and comparativism[20]) and that were corralled into structures of conflict and reciprocity. If there was often a surprisingly high valuation of migrancy, of real and invented claims of having-come-from-elsewhere, this also indicated distributions of power. If the intermittent conceptions of a multireligious society emanated from courtly accommodations above, they could also spring from anti-brahminism, syncretic popular faiths, devotional movements and other protests below, and carry some egalitarian potentials. However, even though 'mixing' was always accompanied by contrary processes of essentialization, compartmentalization and redivision, the formalization and individuation of compounds, as well as intrusive supersession by dominant modes through de/re-culturation, cultural purity was never on offer.

Surfacing the complex social and ideological process—that led to innumerable mutual translations and re-formations with Arabs, Turks, Persians, intertwined the histories of resident and incoming groups—can to some extent challenge the primordialist attack on composite identities, the routine moves of Muslim demonization, the myth of separate 'Hindu' and 'Muslim' cultures. It can invalidate the notion of hard religious identities or the desyncretizing manoeuvres of islamicization and hinduization since the nineteenth century in relation to the cohesive regional contexts of separate and syncretic faiths (ch. 6). However, by the same logic, foregrounding intermixture also undoes some of the classic moves of anticolonialism. If we were composite, syncretic, invaded, even before the onset of British rule, then on what do we base our opposition to the cultural change that occurred with it? Shouldn't the British too be let off on the ground of prior and continuous contamination, of being as hybrid as Indians? Some remodulations and shifts are bound to occur.

First, it would blunt the edge of the dubious anticolonialisms implicated in patriarchal assertion, anti-Muslim/Christian agendas, Hindu-communal or other exclusivist ideologies, and metropolitan relations of dominance. The critique of the systemic features of colonialism would be recast in ways that did not replicate its own procedures. The terms of present opposition would alter to include the way colonial interaction structured these same dubious anticolonialisms, and the new pressures that have congealed them into orthodoxies. To show that colonial hindu/englishnesses were transnational combinatoires, false unities papered over a host of inequalities, would release the debate from both static and hyper-mobile paradigms, and privilege the question of transformation over that of origins.

The second and logical consequence of the dispersal of all claims to cultural authenticity through the interlaced formation of culture would be more nuanced and gendered forms of historicization. A full recognition of the specificities of cultural mixing as a continuous process on the subcontinent—that expanded and intensified with capitalism and was mediated and qualitatively transformed by being placed within new forms of exploitation and expropriation in the colonial period, pressed into the contrary logics of embourgeoisement and secularization on one side, and casteist, communal, and patriarchal ones on the other—would break down the colonial/postcolonial problematic in its present form. The stake itself would shift to the actual transactions and teleologies of mixing in relation to the axes of social division and political power; to the unequal potency and lack of equivalence between various kinds of intermixture; to the conjunctural valences and 'reframing' of hybrids within new systems of meaning or control. In effect, instead of relativizing culture or making an inert hierarchy of hybrids, richer models for the contextual and contingent determination of new ensembles and receptivities may emerge.

Finally, it would also involve a direct confrontation of contemporary political choices and locations, a shift from the narrow project of decolonization to the wider one of genuine democratization, which has the advantage of being able to address areas that historically and analytically either fall outside the ambit of (anti)colonialism, or in which it has become recessive, or where invoking it is positively misleading. The weight of opposition then would perforce fall not on culture alone but also on its predicates—the social relations of class, the inegalitarian and systemic logics of capitalism and imperialism. We do after all inhabit a milieu where there are crippling cultural and economic transnationalisms and politically enabling internationalisms, where the formation of culture can be cross-national, and where the nation-state as the determinate site of political critique and struggle (in the context of a resurgent economic imperialism) cannot be vaporized (or diasporized), even though all that was solid is indeed melting into air!

From altruism to misogyny

As is evident, this book is also about the reformulation of patriarchies. It rereads colonial male reformism and some of the verities of contemporary historiography through the key issues of labour and structures of remuneration and allocation within the family, the forging of a patriarchal consensus (chs 6,7,8), the regulation of literacy and consumption, the tension between women's paid/unpaid work and new notions of status and conjugality (chs 6,7), the ideological and disciplinary divisions of public and private, the locations of women's consent and agency, the persistent blocking of languages of self-interest for women and the equally persistent structuring of desire (chs 6,8), the transnational play of domestic ideologies in creating 'other' women on lines of religious, caste, class and racial difference (chs 5,6,7), the overlap between supposedly different patriarchal systems (British, Hindu, Muslim), and indeed their joint construction (chs 6,7).

With the formation of the colonial state the numerous and often abrasive interactions and articulations between existing, emerging, overlapping, and conflicting patriarchal systems created confluences and triggered contests; these were within and between mobile castes and classes and/or in the name of anticolonialism. The preoccupation with describing and regulating gender difference was not only coupled to the wider question of negotiating change but itself set out to mediate, monitor, adapt to and even effect transitions, often in the guise of continuity. In this respect the unrelenting, often answering descriptions of femaleness and womanhood in the colonial period were a part of the construction and reproduction of higher 'value(s)' that both represented and disguised class, patriarchal and imperialist relations, condensed many anxieties, and built a hegemonic yet flexible repository of, at least notionally, premodern values that could be recycled at will (chs 2,3,5,6). Women, then, were beneficiaries not so much of reformism as of its inconsistencies and contradictions.

Altruism was not only the governing ideological framework of colonization but central to gender formation in nineteenth-century India and Britain. Domestic ideologies that sought to put women's self-interest into abeyance also worked to connect the two. They brought precapitalist systems of domination into new relations with the materialities of class formation producing, as it were, an overlap of euphemisms and of interests. The pastoralization of the home, the emergence of structures of surrogate power for women along each axis of social difference, and changes in notions of philanthropy were all part of a broader colonial process that inscribed gender inequalities in different registers for middle-class Indian *and* English women (chs 5,6,7). And of course for labouring women below: low class/caste and tribal women (supposedly sexually unrepressed, free from patriarchal regimens) were objects of control or later, in a reverse move, absorbed into a quasi-anthropological version of authenticity as 'others' of schooled middle-class women (chs 4,6).

In the male reformist lexicon women were passive embodiments of an enduring domesticity, the domestic domain was the last 'uncolonized' bastion of a vanishing freedom. In fact the domestic domain was altering and prescription *was* an aggressive discourse of change. Even the alibi of cultural fixity—at once subject to decline and capable of rejuvenation—was geared to deal with mobility. Domestic ideologies stitched worldliness and manipulation into normative roles. They sifted the 'customary', reconstituted the textual (scriptural texts increasingly became primers for a partial embourgeoisement), negotiated emergent bourgeois ideologies, brought domestic labour in line with female literacy, male jobs and markets, settled compacts for class, caste and religious differentiation, at once redefined, expanded and circumscribed female volition and agency, made avenues from domestic management to institutional power: imperial and racist for English women, communal and casteist for Hindu women. Indeed the moral power bestowed on middle-class women rested on othering. In sum, the public and private were neither mutually exclusive nor had static impermeable boundaries: the middle-class home was as colonial and as political a site as any other.

The related thematic of women's consent to patriarchal arrangements and to dominant ideologies is plotted along the graphs of class, caste, and colonial power. Consent stretches beyond compensation and compulsion into orchestrating antifeminisms, dividing women, uniting some women—the traditionalist memsahib with the 'new' loyalist higher-caste and ashraf women—against others, and into the changing semantic of the good wife or *pativrata* (chs 2,4,5, 6,7,8). The partial shift to bourgeois notions of female volition itself carved a politics of male conferral. The essays situate some of the locales of proffered, deflected, disguised and indirect female agency, unpack the multiple relations between patriarchal delegation, narrative and prescriptive forms, women's labour and literacy.

Literacy too is a recurring theme, and intended to unsettle rather than confirm the formulaic nineteenth-century reformist narrative of women's 'uplift' or emancipation through education. The biases of colonial reformism—gender-determined differences in the content of syllabi, reiteration of religious instruction and familial ideologies in school textbooks, the fixing of domestic labour and its (punitive) social relations into the curriculum—were compounded by even deeper structural imperatives to curtail female knowledge and lock the whole question of literacy into class, caste, communal, and imperial social compacts (chs 2,5,6,7). In both respects, this was a collaborative enterprise of administrators, missionaries et al. and mobile sections among the upper and middle castes and classes. The tenuous generic divisions between official textbooks and tendentious treatises made for a peculiar interchangeability in which the textbook for girls emerges as a form immersed in its own origin and rationale, primarily 'about' itself (even in its content), and encapsulates the full discourse and limits of colonial male reformism (chs 6, 7). And, in tandem with administrative policies, reveals that even as it opened some new agential possibilities, colonial education worked to restrict if not close circuits of knowledge for women.

The insistent question then is—literacy in what? Was this any more than a literacy in patriarchal norms hardened through the new authority of print, or anything other than an active blocking of a secular notion of womanhood by the state and middle classes? The relation of first-generation literacy for many women in the late nineteenth century to the new politics of religious identity is inescapable (chs 6,7). Ironically, even as 'Hindu' women were set up as emblems of an anticolonial indigenism, they played a mediating role in the cultural and ideological transmission of 'English'. The shifting interpellation and variations in prescription, the friction between orality and print, and the gaps between the design and use of education may have been more productive than literacy per se.

As class and communal subjects, nineteenth-century middle-class women were produced by male discourses before they began to reproduce them. As almost all the essays show, male tutelage was a colonial fixation while the male projection of consenting female voices in a variety of contexts (that included transposition from the Smritis and Puranas) was also remarkable, and seems to have been as necessary to the reproduction of patriarchies in Britain as in India. However, beyond a point, my designation of nineteenth-century Indian prescription as a 'male' discourse has to be bracketed because of its imbrication in orality, performance, social practice, in the fact that women were the chief practitioners and thus teachers of domestic labour, in free borrowing and plagiarism, in translation and inter-regional itineraries, in the as yet subdued notion of individual authorship, in the reliance of authorship on other social modes of authorization—such as the state or colonial moral authority in which English women too were implicated.

The selective definition and attempted homogenization of Hinduism were linked not only to class and colonialism but to the reformulation of patriarchies and a 'private' sphere—through gendered divisions of labour, prescription, symbolic attribution, othering—by both state and civil society. Domestic ideologies acquired a contradictory location; they consolidated both patriarchal unities and particularities, and as such played a part in the communalization of identities. Chapters 6 and 7 look at the cleavages they made between women as well as at shared proprietorial and class codes, the consensual patriarchal arrangements that spread across religious—Hindu, Muslim, Christian—and to some extent caste lines. Patriarchal practices and discursive formations not only structured daily life but coalesced into public–political identities enacted (and contested) by women (chs 5,6,7,8). The range of these discursivities and the high levels of consent displayed in textbooks by the 1870s attest to the making of a pernicious cultural indigenism before organized communalism emerged, provoke a rethinking of the standard periodization of both communalism and the state's involvement in carving a political Hinduism prior to the inception of divide-and-rule policies.

The 'thickness' of detail of patriarchal ideologies from different times and spaces is not a product of ethnographic ambition or the literary habit of careful reading. Rather, it both reproduces my own shock of familiarity and is a subterranean articulation of the complex itinerary of prescriptive texts across regions and historical periods, the transnational (re)formation, the long duration and resilience of patriarchies as a consequence of their conjugation with other systemic forms of oppression (chs 4,5,6,7,8). In fact misogyny may even have crystallized in the contradiction between patriarchies and other social structures. In the Valmiki *Ramayana* bad women (Kaikeyi, Manthara) are necessary to establish the good woman's duty and a patriarchal order, while masculinity is tied to changing modes of male authority and royal legitimation (ch. 8).

The colonial terrain of masculinity was jointly constituted with femininity and, like it, a shifting one: it appears as an aggressive and martial Englishness (ch. 5); as a cosmopolitan male gentility/passivity that recoups its 'renounced' masculinity either as profit or tutelary spectatorial omniscience (chs 2,3); as conventional upper-caste/class sexual promiscuity or the restraint of the reformed middle-class male (ch. 6) that later dovetailed with Gandhian nationalism and was vested in sole wage earning (ch. 7); as rejuvenated by encounters with the 'primitive' and as the recovery of a gendered 'unconscious' (ch. 4); as rajput male virility founded on protecting women endangered by Muslims (ch. 4). Now a generalized 'Hindu' masculinity has been extrapolated from such 'protection' that needs, in Sadhvi Rithambara's speeches, to be prodded and activated by women (ch. 8).

Misogyny too recurs in the essays—largely by virtue of its own astonishing ubiquity than by my design—and seems to have been a wedge for dividing women (chs 5,6,7,8). Misogyny was elaborated as a series of proscriptions on women's curiosity, conversation, leisure, sociability, mobility, consumption et al. It is textual, theological, rhetorical, ventriloquist (in the male use of women's voices), operates in every domain from the sexual to the educational, domestic, and religious. It could be attached to women's illiteracy, domestic mismanagement, unwaged work, widowhood, sexual license, or to their religious eclecticism. It settled most heavily on low-caste working women and prostitutes partly because of the contradictions between the relocation of their labour in a market economy that threatened to level distinctions between women and between sellers and commodities, the reformist emphasis on monogamy and standardized marriage, the widening of the ideological split between marriage and prostitution, and the new semantic adjacency between wives and prostitutes (chs 6,7).

Misogyny was at once the glue that bound genres (prescription and romance, textbooks and fiction) and men (British and Indian, Hindu and Muslim, missionaries and administrators, pandits and maulavis) in common structures of hate and a fissile mechanism that worked at the interface of social divisions and produced absolute differences. The two together generate complex grids of social consensus and conflict that cut through existing patterns of political affiliation and antagonism and reassemble on gendered lines. If in England idealizing desires and punitive misogyny about overconsumption went hand in hand as a rationale for racial superiority, as the price levied by imperial expansion or a mask for male acquisitiveness (chs 4,5,7), in India they worked through a patriarchal anti-colonialism and othering that took advantage of new possibilities for diffusion opened by print. In late nineteenth-century UP, excess consumption by higher-caste men (in dress, money, women) was said to breed an indolence and moral corruption associated with Muslims and the British, and endanger a proper masculinity, but excess consumption for *all* women unilaterally intensified an already extant misogyny (chs 6,7).

The simultaneous, interdependent constitution of race, caste, class, religious difference, and misogyny does turn the multiple location of women into an object of critique. It suggests that the gender question, and consequently a feminist politics, demand an analysis of the dialectical relation between different systemic structures of class, cross-class and non-class oppression, and must stem from an understanding of the junctions, intersections, contradictions and continuities between them, rather than settle into a primordialist identity politics that uses one category to dislocate another. Class, race, religion, community, caste, gender. Each can be used to drive a wedge into the other. And much of this can remain a display of disaligned positionality that never reconnects with the unities in oppressions.

Configurations: mapping the possible?

These essays can be read as casting about for a method that could convey a sense of the number of things I wanted to do, and settling, always hesitantly though differently, on a configural one. A method that could acknowledge the weight of relationality and make theoretical space for more than it demonstrated. Mapping configurations at particular historical intersections could situate discursivities within the materiality of patriarchies and class formation and address the specific unevennesses, transitions, and variations in each. A configural method could also indicate the ideological confluences or repertoires generated by colonialism, the recursive cultural traffic between metropolitan and imperialized formations mediated by local circuits of production, circulation and consumption of texts and concepts, histories of refashioning and dissent, punctuated at each stage by changes in form and meaning that were governed by asymmetries of power, resources and social locations. Finally, it could chart the webbed histories of literatures, religions, patriarchies, mark the way their meanings were isolated and recomposed in the same domains.

These essays both separately and in combination try to map ideological configurations. For instance, the configuration centred on altruism moved in and out of the so-called public and private domains, shaped these divisions, and produced languages for both upward mobility and othering. It not only moved between colonial sites and Britain but branched out via Ruskin, as a redemptive principle for British mercantilism and imperial power, to connect with the Jamesian project which drew the patriarchal capital of Europe honed in theatres of colonization into a Euro-American configuration—the colonial tutelage of Ruskin seeped into the *Portrait* (chs 2,5). On the other side, this configuration travelled as an indigenist reformism from Bengal to UP (chs 6,7). Ironically, the Deobandi and liberal Aligarhi reformism crafted in UP—Ahmad's *Mir'at* and 'Hali's *Majalis*—was to return in subsequent decades to Bengal as an influential model of 'Muslim' reformism. Another trajectory can be traced in the reconstellation of altruism and othering (that valorized non-contractual social relations legitimating gender and caste-based divisions of labour) with the symbolic reconstitution of the upper-caste widow in British and north-Indian reformism to a crossroads where Ruskin meets Gandhi (ch. 7). And yet another line can be drawn from gendered agential modes, implicated in civilizing and monitoring colonial subjects, to the current redeployment of the rhetoric of altruism by women on the Hindu right (ch.8).

The possible can be read in this book through other registers too. Neutrally, as the coordinates of the conjunctural relational possibilities between genres (oral and written), as the historical conditions of their re-semanticization, as the tension between the determinate and the possible. Negatively, as the histories of latency and suppression, as curbed potential, as the ideological opening of possibilities for women that were predicated on other forms of repression, as the closures secreted in ideologies of plurality. Positively, as a more sensitive feminist historiography, a reinflection of culture that can keep radical alternatives open for an integrative political praxis in a time of left 'recession', as social possibilities for the secular in a situation that seems to deny it, as historical possibilities created by contradictions that did not have inevitable outcomes, and as resistant elements produced through the contradictions *between* multiple structures of oppression.

Some of the contentions in this essay have been expressed in the 'oral' domain of lectures (University of Cornell, La Trobe University) and seminars (Nehru Memorial Museum and Library, Jawaharlal Nehru University, Delhi University, Hamdard University, Indian Social Institute, Centre for Transcultural Studies (Chicago), Dyal Singh Evening College) between 1994 and 1998, while the argument on colonialism and hybridization in this form was made at the Centre for Asian Studies, University of Toronto, the Forum for Contemporary Studies, M.S. University, Baroda, and the Institute of Panjab Studies, Chandigarh, in 1997 and 1998. I am grateful to Anuradha Kapur, Svati Joshi, and Indu Chandrasekhar for their comments.

The politics of the possible

or the perils of reclassification

The nonmimetic narrative modes of Gabriel Garcia Marquez and Salman Rushdie inhabit a social and conceptual space in which the problems of ascertaining meaning assume a political dimension qualitatively *different* from the current postmodern scepticism about meaning in Europe and America. Yet such nonmimetic modes, emerging from countries that have been subject to colonial regimes, also seem to lay themselves open to the academized procedures of a peculiarly Euro–American, historically singular, postmodern epistemology that universalizes the self-conscious dissolution of the bourgeois subject, with its now characteristic stance of self-irony, across both space and time. The expansive forms of the modern and the postmodern novel appear to stand in ever-polite readiness to recycle and accommodate other cultural content, whether Latin American or Indian. The ease with which a reader may be persuaded to traverse the path between such nonmimetic modes and postmodernism— broadly defined here as the specific preoccupations and 'sensibility' of both contemporary fiction and of poststructuralist critical discourse—may well lead us to believe they were indeed made for each other. There is not much to be gained by surveying the literature on the subject or in quibbling with individual readings, since the question here is obviously much larger than the 'misreading' of any single writer. The question concerns the way writings from the 'third world' (a term that both signifies and blurs the functioning of an economic, political, and imaginary geography able to unite vast and vastly differentiated areas of the world into a single 'underdeveloped' terrain) are consumed in the 'west' (a term produced to opposite effect by the same procedures). My intention here is to examine the politics of this conjuncture by locating those aspects of their narratives that provide, or at least seem to provide, a *mode of access* for the at once diverse and homogeneous discourse of poststructuralism, and which enable their habilitation as texts of a near-canonical Euro–American postmodernism.

I

Garcia Marquez's marvellous realism is a mode of perception grounded in the political and historical formation not merely of Columbia but of Latin America. Not only is the inscription of the marvellous in the real produced by the colonial history and cultural heterogeneity of Latin America—but the disjunctures in the *understanding* of the real are also equally mediated by and refracted through the apparatus of various kinds of domination, colonial and neocolonial, underwritten by feudal survivals and reactive nationalisms.

The cultural heterogeneity of Latin America is at once different from and determined by the 'linear' history of Euro–America, which both nests inside and shapes Latin American history, often by erasure. The simultaneity of the heterogeneous is a matter of historical sedimentation that results from the physical coexistence over time of different ethnic groups (native American–Indian, Arab, African, Indochinese, Asian, Spanish), each laden with its respective cultural freight of language, myth, oral narrative, magic, superstition, Roman Catholicism, Cartesian education, and modern rationalism. Simultaneity is the restless product of a long history of miscegenation, assimilation, and syncretization *as well as* of conflict, contradiction, and cultural violence. It is also the unique history of colonization by the Spanish colonizer who, now as cultural hybrid, faces across a time-lag the changed configuration of those social forces that once produced the conquistadores. Although a hybrid social formation has an unusual and resistant retentiveness, it would be a mistake to read this as simply the inert absence of change, succession, and continuity. The piecemeal assimilation of European (and American) culture is difficult either to reject or to homogenize: first, because in a contradictory way it is both something that is *owned* as well as something to be *resisted*, and second, because of an 'uneven' material development that, contrary to the unidirectional laws of 'progress', enforces the coexistence of primitive agriculture with advanced technology and export economies.

In a complex way Latin American history *secretes* the history of Europe and in turn renders it ironic. Garcia Marquez's intent is obvious when he points out in his Nobel Lecture that "the statue of General Francisco Morazan [1792–1842, the last president of the Central American Federation] erected in the main square of Tegucigalpa is actually one of Marshall Ney [1769–1815, one of Napoleon's commanders], purchased at a Paris warehouse of second-hand sculptures."[1] It is thus a history that forbids (or ought to) either a simple relation to or a linear interpretation of the past and that insistently raises the question of *how* it is to be known. If the Latin American coastline saw the simultaneous influx of black African slaves and Swedish, Dutch, and English pirates, then surely it is more than merely symbolic for the patriarch to see from his window the ships of Christopher Columbus and the ships of the US marines anchored simultaneously in his harbour. Within this context it is not surprising that Garcia Marquez does not set up the real and the marvellous as antithetical realms.[2] He neither construes himself as the 'other' nor indulges in a simpleminded rejection of rationalism: he refuses to consent unthinkingly to parallel and essentialist categories such as primitive and modern, tribal and rational. For Garcia Marquez, "even the most seemingly arbitrary creation has its rules. You can throw away the fig leaf of rationalism only if you don't descend into chaos and irrationality."[3] So in *The Autumn of the Patriarch* the 'sainthood' of the dictator's mother is rationally exposed as fraud, shown to be a lucrative part of several illusions imposed on him even as other 'miracles' are instated as 'real', for instance, the dictator's secret knowledge of a salt that can cure lepers and make cripples walk. The *margin* for arbitrariness, the casting up of the strange, the incongruous, the peripheral, is the *product* of a historical situation. At this level marvellous realism embodies a *specific* social relation. The apparent 'novelty' of marvellous realism results from its immersion in a social matrix wherein improvisation is not merely a formal literary reflex but a function of living in the world.

Finally, the cultural simultaneity of Latin America must be distinguished from the cultural synchronicity available in the so-called 'first world'. In Latin America it is a matter of historical conjuncture in which different modes of production, different social formations, and different ways of seeing overlap as the ground of conflict, contradiction, change, and intervention, both local and foreign. Not only is Big Mama an emblematic figure in this respect—her power is described in "Big Mama's Funeral" as being at once seignorial, manorial, papal, electoral, *and* mercantile (she runs a financial empire)—but the 'feudal' forms and practices implanted by Spanish colonialism are shown to be reappropriated by emerging power structures. Thus the cruellest killer in *The Autumn of the Patriarch* is Jose Ignacio Saenz de la Barra, the last scion of aristocracy and a sort of medieval prince of darkness.[4]

In contrast, the synchronic time of the modern and of the postmodern in Euro–America is an *end* product of the now discredited linear time of modernity and progress. The synchronic vision of culture in Euro–America takes shape through the conglomerative modality of collage as "different times and different spaces are combined in a here and now that is everywhere at once."[5] Synchronicity, as it inhabits dominant institutions and discourses, is the joint apogee of a cultural modernism and a consumer culture, the instant availability effect of the spatialization of the museum and of the push-button archive, as well as a matter of the recurring renovation of style through new juxtapositions. It must, of course, be said that the cultural heterogeneity produced in Europe and America through internal class stratification, ethnic difference, and immigration also has both an oppositional and vulnerable relation to the influential apparatus and dominant discourses of 'high' culture.

The double disjunction of a hybrid simultaneity and of the economic and ideological deformations of neocolonialism is the condition within which the real is perceived and also the condition within which both authors and texts are produced. Consequently, the problems of meaning and representation that beset the countries that were colonized are very different from the slippage of meaning and of the 'real' which currently confronts the *academic* discourses of Europe and America. To say this is not to claim the possibility of arriving at some essential indigenous truth by a more tortuous route, but to insist that the epistemological problem is *itself* a historical one. Both meaning and the need for locating meaning are conjunctural; and it is useful to maintain a distinction between the realized difficulty of knowing and the preasserted or *a priori* difficulty of knowing. And if we agree, then surely the problem of meaning for imperialized formations is also at bottom entangled in the problems of social and political aspiration and radical reconstitution, whereas the tenuousness of meaning in much of Euro–American cultural production, equally a product of this historical conjuncture, is one in which the felt absence of the will or the ability to change things as they are can become the voice of epistemological despair. For many of us, the difficulty of arriving at 'fact' through the historical and political distortions that so powerfully shape and mediate it leads not to dismember finally either the status or the existence of fact. Rather, it tends to assert another *level* of factuality, to cast and resolve issues of meaning on another, more dialectical plane—a plane on which a notion of knowledge as provisional and of truth as historically circumscribed is not only *necessary* for understanding, but can in turn be made to *work* from positions of engagement within the local and the contemporary. For me, this is the precise function of Garcia Marquez's marvellous realism as a cognitive mode.

II

Garcia Marquez's marvellous realism not only emerges from the contingent, simultaneous, polyphonic contours of his material world, it is also a transformative mode that has the capacity both to register and to engage critically with the present and to generate a new way of seeing. Though he digs beneath the rational encrustations of colonialism to uncover ways of storytelling that existed before or that have subcutaneously survived, he avoids that familiar ideological bind, the swing from disillusionment with an inadequate rationalism to an easily available mysticism—in some sense, mutually constitutive categories brought into play by colonialism. Marvellous realism answers an emergent society's need for renewed self-description and radical assessment, displaces the established categories through which a succession of Europeans and Americans construed other cultures either in their own image or as alterity, questions the capitalist myth of modernization and progress, and asserts without nostalgia a localized preindustrial realm of possibility. In *One Hundred Years of Solitude* the "almost" two-hundred-year-old Francisco the Man sings the news in songs he has composed, "accompanying himself with the same archaic accordion that Sir Walter Raleigh had given him in the Guianas". In these songs he "told in great detail the things that had happened in the towns along his route . . . so that if anyone had a message to send or an event to make public, he would pay him two cents to include it in his repertory".[6] In fact, it becomes impossible to idealize a folk culture which on examination proves not only to be crafted from the contingent but to be hybrid as well!

As a mode, marvellous realism is attached to a real *and* to a possible. The seamless quality of this mode, the difficulty of distinguishing between fact and invention, brings an enormous pressure to bear upon the perception of reality. For example, do the incipient rebels in *The Autumn of the Patriarch* actually slice up and dine on the cooked corpse of their comrade? Are two thousand children really kidnapped and massacred because they have discovered how the general rigs the lottery so that he can win every time? The unanswerability of the questions throws them on to another plane.[7] If the real is historically structured to make invisible the foreign locus of power, if the real may thus be other than what is generally visible, if official versions are just as visible and visibly 'real' as unofficial versions, and if even the *potentially* real is a *compound* of the desired and the undesirable, then marvellous realism tackles the problem of truth at a level that reinvents a more acute and comprehensive mode of referentiality. The brutality of the *real* is equally the brutality and terror of that which is *immanent*, conceivable, potentially possible.[8] Besides, if the farthest reaches of imaginary construction alone can equal the heinous deformations of the real, then marvellous realism must exceed mimetic reflection in order to become an interrogative mode that can press upon the real at the point of maximum contradiction. The difficulty of fixing meaning itself is located as a part of social transactions and of ideologies. In this sense the difficulty of distinguishing between fact and fiction becomes a *political* difficulty that bears upon the ethical difficulty of functioning as 'real' human beings.

Marvellous realism discovers a figurative discourse that produces a knowledge inseparable from its performance in language, image, and metaphor, and that can be understood in its total configuration but not necessarily explained. Through it Garcia Marquez legitimizes the status of the possible as valid knowledge. He realigns a notion of history as a set of discoverable facts with a notion of history as a field of diverse human and cultural possibility. His narratives figure a dynamic relation of past to future in which the present is seen in terms of its potential and in which the varied creative abilities of his culture are embodied in the very capaciousness of the narrative itself. The act of perception is relative yet historically determined; indeed, reality is alterable *only because* it is both relative and determined. The recognition of such relativity is precisely the recognition that the world is open to change: it is necessary to prevent a foreclosure by a single meaning so that different meanings may become possible.

There is nothing purely formal in Garcia Marquez's choice of mode. In one sense the performative aspect of the style lies outside the text in already existing ways of seeing,[9] and relies not on the shock of novelty but on shared structures of knowledge and belief. Even in its most 'excessive' moments the intent of the style is neither to surprise nor to draw attention to its own uniqueness (as in most Euro–American modernist fiction), but to convey the *shared* social bases of an extraordinary or singular effect.[10] Thus, metaphor is treated literally: torrential tropical rain is a downpour that lasts for several years, old age and physical decay are manifest as green slime on the teeth, Colonel Buendia's distance from reality is a white chalk circle demarcating ten feet of space around him, Amaranta Ursula leads her devoted husband into Macondo "by a silk rope tied around his neck". Metaphor is turned into *event* precisely so that it will *not* be read *as* event, but folded back into metaphor as disturbing, resonant image. This is a technique that can make palpable a whole range of natural and social phenomena, and can mime the operative modalities or political effectiveness of an ideology without recourse to the mimetic mechanics of 'exposure'. A good example of the 'naturalization' of an 'unnatural' relation as well as of the necessary *re*-presentation of the already known is the collection of the sea by the Americans (not in repayment but as "surety for the interest" on unpayable debt), which is then neatly parcelled and transported to Arizona. The perverse fertility of the dictator who allows this to happen—manifested in the algae and lichen, sea-flowers and sea-animals that grow on his body—ostends the barrenness of the sea-bed. And yet I must add that the literalization of metaphor is neither an arbitrary trick nor a homogenizing device but is capable of fine discriminations. The obliterated banana company workers who vanish with no trace and are declared never to have existed are the exact opposite of the nude saint, Remedios the Beauty, who ascends to heaven along with the sheets hung out to dry—just as the protean Mr Brown of the banana company is the opposite of Melquiades with his many lives. Different kinds of gullibility and 'magic' are at work here: the first kind signifies the official (and in this case alien) extinction of human value; the second represents some of the local exigencies of survival.

III

Garcia Marquez's narratives direct attention to the *social, collective, performative,* and *manifold processes* by which *meaning* is *generated,* to *parole* instead of *langue.* Unlike Euro–American postmodern fiction, which directs attention to the abstract processes whereby meaning is either generated but never found, or is lost in the finding (for example, Italo Calvino's *Invisible Cities*), the selfconscious textuality in Garcia Marquez's narratives is grounded in an overplus of meaning, a barely controlled semantic richness. The conscious technical complexity of the texts does not ask to be read as an effect either of the autonomy of language, or text, or even as a gesture toward the autoreferentiality of art. Rather, the narratives gesture toward the *autonomy* of the *story* in its *semantic* aspect: stories exist above and beyond the storytellers who relate them, the language in which they are told, and the narrative structures in which they are held; stories are as protean as the people who tell and retell them, remember and forget them, repeat or improvise them. Stories are as malleable as human history. Garcia Marquez's fiction is not encumbered by the myth of the originality either of the author or of the narrative. Stories exist inside a continuous social space within which they can be remodelled and recombined. Little stories drop from long narratives to become full-fledged tales, or full-fledged tales are compressed into cameos and reinserted into long narratives.

Garcia Marquez's marvellous realism, then, is an interactive mode based on a notion of collectivity (a social relation *and* a political desire) which the narratives *figure* forth in several ways. The storyteller *and* the stories have a shared existence in a social matrix that is always prior to their telling. Though the narrative voices change, neither these voices nor the voice of the narrator is highly individuated in the bourgeois sense of being authored/authorized by a singular subjectivity or a single perspective. *The Autumn of the Patriarch* enacts the polyglot dialogue of different social voices in a hybrid, power-riven culture. There is a polyphony of voices—the dictator, his mother, soldiers, commanders, soothsayers, many nameless women and men—which are to be deciphered at the dialogic and representative level, not at the level of individual motivation or internal psychological consistency. The long sentence in *Autumn* contains "multiple monologues"[11] that shift between first, second, and third person, singular and plural speech, that both address and answer. A single sentence (like Spanish as a language) may incorporate, though never proportionately, the socially disparate voices of both oppressor and oppressed. In the episode of the general and the beauty from the dogfight district, the two voices are meshed, they *make* each other's separate reality. The interactive narration replicates the way in which people construct and are mutually constructed by their social relations. It also allows for a comparative standpoint which gives free "permission to narrate" from a number of places within the narrative rather than privilege any one place. No place in the narrative is exempt from scrutiny.[12] The narrative is 'open' in the sense that it creates a figurative space for "interventions on the part of those represented".[13] However, this method also *controls* the generation of meaning without preempting it; by providing multiple voices within the narrative, it *fixes* the social locus of the production of meaning. This heterogeneity constitutes the particular mode of the text's orientation toward the listener/reader— a heterogeneity that telescopes but does not set out to efface the contradictions between contending social voices.

The function of the long sentence in *Autumn* is not to achieve a higher degree of individualization and formal sophistication but to pile up stories, all part of the same story told by different voices. Each sentence is a story or even a series of stories: the sentence cannot stop because all the stories are *connected*. In Henry James's fiction, syntactical elaboration is an endorsement of uncertainty and a site for the formation of an aristocratic bourgeois consciousness. In Joseph Conrad's fiction, syntactical complexity gestures toward an ineffable universe wherein mystery begins to underwrite and overdetermine imperial history. In William Faulkner's fiction, the long sentence becomes a sign of the incestuous involution of the American south and simulates the relentless claustrophobia of oppression that leaves no space to breathe or time to punctuate and is impossible to stem or stop. The style of *Autumn* is closest to Faulkner; however, the ideological locus of the long sentence is finally different from all these writers. The long sentence is an index of the *fecundity* of the repressed, of the barely begun and unfinished—*not uncertain*—stories simmering beneath the strident sounds and tight enclosures of dictatorship, and so gestures toward unopened possibilities. From within the loops and whorls of narrative bursts the recognition that the stories people tell will never finish, that they will strain and break through the controlling constraints of grammar. The speech of many unnamed storytellers gels, coheres, contradicts, overlaps, and is retold. The long sentence shows that heteroglossia—the genuine plurality of unmerged and independent voices—is not an achievement, but a continuing struggle between contending social forces that, like the sentence, has no 'natural' culmination. The sentences accumulate into a narrative that displays the collective, digressive quality of an oral narrative, which invokes the submerged life of a ravaged people and marks their glimpsed resilience. Within a hybrid culture like Latin America (unlike sealed tribal formations) the traffic between oral forms and written forms is not necessarily one-way. Though subject to the mediation of colonial and class relations, the written too finds its *way back* into orality;[14] since the written and the oral are both interdependent and improvisatory, neither is simply at one with itself. Together they *begin* to describe a field within which "values are not reified but volatile"[15] and have to be returned to the whole business of living.

Further, collectivity is infused at the level of the *subject* itself, in the 'I', just as it is infused in the single sentence. Individuality is a truly connective definition—that which connects the subject to a social matrix—so that it is the richness of contextualization that *sets off* the notation of personal particularity and differentiates the individual, rather than the social collectivity itself as being subject to the unique perception of a bourgeois individual. The solitary ageless dictator is a "composite character",[16] the sum of several Latin

American dictators, as well as an infinitely divisible character, held together by his function. The complexity of the dictator is the complexity of his contradictory social construction (as agent and pawn, protector and destroyer) and revealed interaction rather than of an 'internalized' individuality wherein the full connection between private and public then needs to be wrested from the 'unconscious' or from other 'concealed' realms. This composite and divisible mode of characterization is able to show the individual shapes of tyranny and to represent dictatorship itself as a complicit social institution, diffused throughout the social fabric, both supported from within the country and propped up from without.

The ideological space Garcia Marquez's texts occupy is composed of a series of openings and closings. Causality is complex; the narratives are composed simultaneously at many levels and literally held together by repetition and retelling. The narratives return to fixed points again and again from different directions. Repetition is the mnemonic glue that binds the stories as well as that which allows the stories a point from which to depart in a *different* direction. It both preempts surprise and encodes a desire to totalize, to resist fragmentation and to structure the new through the familiar,[17] and it builds upon the notion of improvisation wherein each performance is at once exceptional and obedient to a given structure; each performance can be repeated, yet no two performances are identical, for each is always open to the transformations of a particular context. Thus repetition is the ground of both the *new* and the *same*. The stillness of repetition, even in an early piece like "Leaf Storm", is not just a sign of fatalism and despair.[18] At one level, the style pulls out on to the surface and lays bare—in conjuncture rather than in essence—the fatalistic way in which events are perceived and enacted in the consciousness of the townfolk. At another level, the same memory that enables the closures of repetition also proves to be the agent of historical sense and of political understanding, that is, it provides the openings. In *One Hundred Years* Jose Arcadio Secundo's persistent memory is the only record that remains of the banana company massacre; the plague of insomnia which leads to collective loss of memory is equivalent to the loss of a usable past, of a historiography, indeed of historical agency.[19] So Pilar Ternera reads the past in the cards. Memory functions as flexible, collective, material practice open to improvisation and personal reminiscence (but not dependent on it), and is different from the kind of memory which is central to the modernism of T.S. Eliot and of Marcel Proust. For them memory becomes the often conservative, always individuated, organizing principle of poems and narratives designed to cope with cultural fragmentation, to authorize singular visions (which ironically intensify the experience of fragmentation), to preserve a 'monumental civilization' as 'heritage' through quotation, and to relive it through nostalgia.

Collectivity in-forms the thematic and structural preoccupation with the enigma or the unsolved puzzle in Garcia Marquez's narratives. What is problematized is not meaning 'itself', but the recovery of meaning in specific contexts. The emphasis is on why, in a particular situation, an unequivocal answer cannot be found. The lampoons of *In Evil Hour* reveal what everybody knows, the familiar becomes unfamiliar and takes on the character of a revelation, but the authorship of the lampoons remains a mystery. The priest says that the lampoons are a "terrorism of the moral order"; Cassandra the soothsayer finds out that they are written by everybody and nobody; Judge Arcadio, the self-styled detective, knows that the clues are so varied that it cannot be individuals or even a conspiracy; the mayor simply uses the opportunity to reimpose a fascist rule on the town. The lampoons (like the subversive leaflets) are an efflorescence of the submerged life of the town—what is known has to be continually brought to the surface and reunderstood.

The Chronicle of a Death Foretold is also structured as an unsolved enigma: the whole town is shown trying to understand *why* Santiago Nasar is murdered *after* the virtual complicity of the entire town in not preventing the murder has been previously established. People gather in strange surrender to witness a murder that has been announced; though the murderers wish to be prevented even the priest does not stop them. Guilt is collective. The town wants to understand its own role and responsibility in the matter: "None of us could go on living without an exact knowledge of the place and mission assigned to us by fate."[20] And even as people claim to understand the motive for the murder—honour in a male chauvinist society which requires brides to be virgins—the murder obviously remains senseless. The narration, with its attentive, 'factual' rendering of many voices by a single narrator, and its scrupulous reconstruction of the movements of both the victims and the killers, consciously attempts to compensate for its own inadequacy. The inability of the narrator or of the town *finally* to understand becomes in this case equivalent to the townspeople's inability to change. The unsolved enigma at this level is not an index of an indeterminable reality but the failure, in historical terms, of the will of a people.

At another level, the text exploits, for local ends, the colonial notion of the enigmatic 'native' (for instance, the mysterious Arab or the inscrutable Chinese). The enigmatic native is a familiar orientalizing trope that encodes, first, the incapacity of most colonizers to apprehend the 'native' save as alterity, and second, the reserve, resistance, interested information, or secrecy that colonizers repeatedly encountered and that probably indicated both a recalcitrance and a conscious strategy on the part of 'natives'. The stereotype of the enigma—in its origin, if not in its use—is at bottom dialogic. Again, the colonizers' notations of the enigmatic 'other' were systematically accompanied by vigorous attempts (by missionaries, anthropologists, ethnographers, and administrators[21]) to penetrate into the substratum of truth and of material resources. So the political, institutional, and discursive links between the female (the powerless and the colonized), chastity (the hitherto unconquered and unknown), enigma (the impenetrable object of scrutiny), and colonization are deep historical ones. The very form of *Chronicle of a Death* is *gendered*: structured as female, the form becomes a critique of the content (the subjection of women to the violating codes of a chauvinist society), and functions to protect the already violated woman from further violation or further surveillance. The question of whether Santiago Nasar is guilty and, if not, then who deflowered Angela Vicario ("raised to suffer"), remains unanswered. The unanswered question is not an invitation to further guesswork, but addresses itself to whether the question itself is worth asking or is necessary to answer, whether the question itself is not the first in a series of violations of which the murder is a culmination.

At a third level, to maintain the text as enigma is also to maintain a resistance to being construed as an object of scrutiny. The enigma produces strain and anxiety in those who seek to inspect and understand it; it rejects the voyeurism, extractiveness, and instrumentality of 'sight' as it is shaped by the double determination of capitalism and colonization;[22] it exercises power by sustaining insecurity and by openly refusing to surrender its 'meaning'. Enigma, as structure, endures by virtue of what it withholds, retains the attention it has caught, and acquires a political stamina. The structure of the unsolved enigma in *Chronicle of a Death* is more than a mode of collectivity: it is crafted both as a *resistant* mode and as an *interrogative* mode, both as an *outer* imposition (the way whole continents may remain subject to dominant ways of seeing and not seeing) and as an *inner* imposition (to maintain oneself as an enigma *for* oneself is to fail in political understanding and social will). Such a structure can convey simultaneously a sense of latent energy and of lethargy: it can bring the pressure of *not knowing* to bear with a certain intensity on the problems of *not doing*. To not see is to abnegate responsibility; not to be seen is to be isolated or to be left to perish, a fate that may not be merely individual but collective. The investigating magistrate, tracing the sequence of events leading to the death of Santiago Nasar (a man whom all were watching but never quite seeing), writes: "*Fatality makes us invisible*" (p. 113).

IV

The preoccupation with circular time and the rejection of linear time in Garcia Marquez's narratives are often read as evidence either of his fatalism or of his primitivism. However, the absence of a single linear time need not be read as the absence of a historical consciousness, but rather as the contextual operation of a different kind of historical consciousness. The play of linear time with circular time achieves its cognitive force through marvellous realism's capacity to generate and manage various kinds of alignments, tensions, and discontinuities between sequential and nonsequential time.

Garcia Marquez's critique of the linear time of rationality and progress in *One Hundred Years* is levelled from inside the suspicion, well-founded in the Latin American context, that the development of science and technology within the structures of neocolonialism may guarantee continuous dependence. There is a 'marvellous' passage where bananas become the fruit of empiricism and thence the fruit of empire. After eating a bunch of bananas, Mr Herbert assesses Macondo's potential:

> When he finished the first bunch he asked them to bring him
> another. Then he took a small case with optical instruments out of
> the toolbox that he always carried with him. With the suspicious
> attention of a diamond merchant he examined the banana meticu-
> lously, dissecting it with a special scalpel, weighing the pieces on a
> pharmacist's scale, and calculating its breadth with a gunsmith's
> calipers. Then he took a series of instruments out of the chest with
> which he measured the temperature, the level of humidity in the
> atmosphere, and the intensity of the light . . . but he did not say
> anything that allowed anyone to guess his intentions. (p. 211)

The talismanic notion of technology as a type of 'magic' art,
or as the required miracle that will bring with it the wonders of
prosperity, is played off against the equally problematic possibility
of an indigenous alternative science which of course does not
materialize. Local attempts to construct such a science—the attempts
to use magnets to discover gold or to use the daguerreotype to
establish the existence of god—are shown to be romantic failed
attempts that can, at best, offer only a utopian faith in the possibility
of rediscovering, or rather, of remaking, one's own reality.

However, the wonders of technology that "dazzle" the
inhabitants of Macondo—the "frightful" train that is "like a kitchen
dragging a village behind it", the bulbs, the phonographs, and the
telephones—are not presented merely as an instance of primitive
naiveté, but as a historical irony. Technology does not cross the seas
as a mere emblem of 'progress', but as a broker of profit that easily
represents itself as magical and opportunely insinuates its own
calculable properties as miraculous. Christopher Columbus has no
qualms about representing his scientific knowledge of the stars as
shamanistic power:

> With a solemnity worthy of the adventures in boys' books, he takes
> advantage of his knowledge of the date of an imminent lunar
> eclipse. Stranded on the Jamaican coast for eight months, he can
> no longer persuade the Indians to bring him provisions without
> his having to pay for them; he then threatens to steal the moon from
> them, and on the evening of February 29, 1504, he begins to carry
> out his threat, before the terrified eyes of the caciques. . . . His success
> is instantaneous.[23]

Cortes's conquest of Mexico is no doubt made easier by his claim that his information comes not from human informers, but from the supernatural realm that communicates with him through a ship's chart and a compass.[24] Mr Herbert and his captive balloons (a business "which takes him halfway around the world with excellent profits") belong to this hoary tradition of magical invention and intervention; he gets his comeuppance when the inhabitants of Macondo, working on a different cultural logic of exposure to magic, come to consider his "invention *backward*" after having seen and tried the gypsies' "flying carpets" (p. 211; my emphasis).

Through the expansion of time beyond linearity, Garcia Marquez moves beyond the simplifying oppositions of rational and irrational, and attempts to introduce the notion of time as a structure of values, as in his treatment of death. There are two kinds of death in *One Hundred Years*: first, the horrible brevity of the massacres of the civil war, colonial rule, and the imperial fruit company, and second, an older, integrated, more acceptable way of dying. The first Jose Buendia dies slowly, publicly, under a chestnut tree. Deaths are expected, accompanied by premonition and warning. Prudencio Aguilar is killed in a duel; and when, after dying, he seeks his assassin for company, the living understand and accommodate him:

> When he finally identified him [Aguilar], startled that the dead also aged, Jose Arcadio Buendia felt himself shaken by nostalgia. "Prudencio" he exclaimed. "You've come from a long way off." After many years of death the yearning for the living was so intense, the need for company so pressing, so terrifying the nearness of that other death which exists within death, that Prudencio Aguilar had ended up loving his worst enemy. (p. 76)

This older form of death bears remarkable similarities to prebourgeois, medieval forms of dying in Europe described so brilliantly by Philip Aries in his book *In the Hour of Our Death*. The natural and daily presence of the dying and the dead among the living, the popular belief in an intermediate space between death and the definite conclusion of life—in sum, a death that is neither a complete separation nor a total annihilation—is, with the emergence of a secular individual in Europe, replaced by a notion of dying as anxious and privatized, and of death as an end, as decomposition, and as stigma. In *One Hundred Years* this prebourgeois (or 'marvellous') death functions along an axis of value that it also betokens; not only does it literalize that zone of intensified memory in which the living can still experience the recently dead as almost alive, nearly sensuous beings, but it also comes to signify a collective management of the time of mortality and cannot be taken literally as a gullible inability to distinguish the real from the not-real. The same people who write letters and send verbal messages through Amaranta to their dead, refuse to accept the "resurrection" of a dead actor in a new role in a different film; and when it is explained that cinema is an illusion, they refuse to waste time "to weep over the acted out misfortunes of imaginary beings" (p. 209).

Further, Garcia Marquez attempts to develop a mode that can take cognizance of time as it is experienced. Prophecy, the structural obverse of memory, is not merely a means of self-enclosure within a relentless circularity, but part of a complex notion of causality that takes into account both the perceived concurrence of mythic time within a cultural simultaneity and the felt experience of enclosure within a seemingly deterministic logic. Prophecy, as notation, may be taken to signify the popular perception of events to be one in a series of extra-economic determinations that make up what we call history.

The narratives are obsessed with the quality of time and derive a special intensity from prolonging stagnation, oppression, decay. On a political level, the stagnant time in *One Hundred Years* is imposed by a determining history of colonial and neocolonial exploitation that puts Latin America out-of-date, keeps it in thrall, fixes it in another time. Stagnant time is thus both indigenous *and* alien, in the sense that it is *re*-imposed by the logics of Euro–American domination. Further, since linear time is also embedded in Macondo as the long history of Euro–American intrusions in some form, and so as its *own* history, there is no such thing as pure or uncontaminated indigenous time. It is significant that the concurrent or circular time of Macondo is not only invaded or interrupted by the gypsies who bring alchemy, but also exists in dialectical relation with the several entries of linear time. Thus, the banana company builds a separate enclave within Macondo, fences off circular time in order to exploit it. Linear time is as 'impure' and as oppressive as circular time.

Finally, if circular time is a metaphor for historical inevitability, then it is important to notice that it does come to an *end*. Pilar Ternara perceives incest as a cyclic retardation of linear time: "the history of the family was a machine with unavoidable repetitions, a turning wheel that would have gone on spilling into eternity, were it not for the progressive and irremediable *wearing* of the axle" (p. 365; my emphasis). If circularity wears out, becomes bankrupt like other historical fates, so does linearity. The conclusion of *One Hundred Years* at once images and ironizes a decadent European apocalypticism, described by Vyacheslav Ivanov as a "feeling, at once oppressive and exalting, of being the last in a series".[25] The conclusion is poised in a liminal space and in an in-between time, which, having broken out of the binary opposition between circular and linear, gives a third space and a different time the chance to emerge. Similarly, the end of the dictator's life in *The Autumn of the Patriarch* is described as "the good news that the uncountable time of eternity has come to an end" (p. 206). The end of eternity is the end of *known*, even conceivable, time; it comes out on the other side of both the cyclic and the linear. The irrevocability of this end as end insists on a new beginning, but the modalities of the new or clues as to how it will come about are absent.

The power of Garcia Marquez's narratives lies in the insistent pressure of *freedom* as the *absent horizon*—which is neither predictable nor inevitable. The way marvellous realism figures collectivity and takes metaphor to excess indicates a reality that exceeds the space allotted to it by its own history. The excess of meaning bursting out of its present time into an imaginable (or probable) time exerts immense pressure on his narratives. This may be an absent freedom, but it is not an abstract freedom: it is precisely that which is made present and possible by its absence—the lives that people have never lived *because of* the lives they are forced to live or have chosen to live. That which is desired and that which exists, the sense of abundance and the sense of waste, are dialectically related.

V

Salman Rushdie's narratives may employ a comparable nonmimetic mode, but they can neither be bracketed with Garcia Marquez's, nor seen as continuous with postmodernism, and need to be 'contextualized' separately. Here I can undertake no more than to sketch in his problematic historical location. If Garcia Marquez creates a subsuming and transformative mode that, drawing on substantive indigenous narrative modes, can also rework and relegate the epistemologies of both realism and modernism, Rushdie's narratives play provocatively with disparate ways of seeing, yet are riven by the strain of double coding for different audiences. Further, drawing on culturally distinct modes, they are caught between different ideological systems, pressured by different demands. In the attempt to negotiate two terrains Rushdie's narratives confirm and unsettle much on either side.

The diverse, diffuse, and class-divided relationship with English culture and the English language, in part the product of a mode of colonization unaccompanied by any large-scale influx of British settlers in India, makes Rushdie's insider/outsider position both representative and precarious. For instance, sections of the middle class residing in India can be as 'anglicized', 'alienated', isolated, or equivocal about their cultural alignments, as can emigrés. In some sense, while Rushdie sets out to represent a post-independence, middle-class ethos, his narrative too is shaped by the contradictions inscribed in the formation of this class. The introduction of first realist, then modernist modes under the aegis of colonialism in nineteenth-century India occurred in contradictory combination with insistent, ideologically fraught reconstructions of a precolonial past. These latter were determined as much by the cultural formation of this class and the way it was assembled from heterogeneous groups as by the political economy of imperialism, which has since prolonged the moment of 'uneven' development long after the end of direct political rule. The notable religious and linguistic diversity of India was and remains subject both to fabricated divisions and to imposed homogeneities in the interests of political control. Rushdie also undertakes an archaeological (and necessarily distanced) excavation of an emigré's past, working from within a contingent modernism that is produced, even imposed, by cultural displacement and compelled to accept its own hybrid character. In his use and remaking of English as an Indian vernacular, as well as in his conscious arrogation of an 'international' literary ancestry, he attempts to break from both unconscious influence (the site of more devious cultural insinuation) and a parochial or indigenist nationalism (often tied in binary relation to its chosen adversary 'western' modes). His 'internationalism' thus can potentially be an incisive restructuring of the possibilities already latent in India's political and social history of complicities, inter-penetrations, and direct appropriations.

The social formation of the Indian subcontinent, then, is in many ways amenable to Rushdie's fabulous realism. Rushdie draws on extant narrative modes, especially the epic and the folktale. The informality of the epic structure—the scope for interpolation, digression, accretion, in addition to its self-ascribed status as history or *itihaas* (for example, the *Mahabharata*)—has allowed it in the past to represent ideological collectivities as well as to permit the expression of contesting world views. The serial character—that is, stories nesting inside and/or leading to each other—of folktales (for example, the *Panchatantra* or the *Katha Sarit Sagar*) and their ingenuous, improvisatory, yet generic, underindividuated 'oral' narrators are a significant resource for Rushdie. Further, his fabulation finds a fertile ground not just in classical and oral traditions but also in a still extant social perception of art. This perception does not always constitute the real and the not-real as a binary opposition, but as coexistent; and in it, sacred and secular art forms can be read as miracle or *chamatkar*, signifying not the presence of the miraculous per se but an elasticity and a capacity for wonder on the part of the listener/viewer/reader, that can give the quality of a revelation. As an aesthetic of creativity and response this is quite different from the consciously engineered 'surprise' of the unexpected juxtaposition that is central to much Euro–American modernism. Modernism in fact derives its energy from a steady opposition to realism: realism is the implied or habitual mode of perception that has to be countered or subverted.

In *Midnight's Children* Rushdie attempts to play with these two ways of seeing and so, perforce, with two different conceptions of the subject. The form of the narrative has an epic intention; unfinished stories give a sense of unending possibility; the narrator's choice of story is presented as merely one of several. The totalizing yet open epic structure exists cheek-by-jowl with an epistemological mode (based, like Euro–American modernism, on an acknowledged yet decentred realism) that privileges faulty sight, peripheral or incomplete vision, limited perception, deliberate fallibility, and the splinter effect—in short, with a covertly totalizing quasi-modernist aesthetic of the fragment. To some extent, the narrative finds its dynamic in the modernist challenge to premodern forms and vice versa.

The narrator, Saleem Sinai, is also split through the centre. On the one hand, he is a scribe and storyteller, and his favourite god is Ganesh—not surprising considering Saleem's nose and occupation. His narrative method combines the compendious knowledge of a pandit with a preauthorized orality: he reads out what is written to the nonliterate Padma, as well as writes what he hears, and so attempts to forge a conscious relation between the oral and the written. The narrator and the narration toy with the idea of the writer as expressing a transindividual consciousness. The narrator humbly makes repeated attempts to establish the story as larger than himself. But the narrator and the narration also make different kinds of moves and are imbricated in a different kind of 'self'-consciousness. The narrative incorporates the criteria by which the text might be judged, speculates on the narrator's motivation, biographical formation and 'role', and ponders the status of fiction vis-à-vis the 'real'—displays the characteristic modernist preoccupation with the composition, fictiveness, and self-reflexiveness of narrative.

The conflation of an 'oral' narrator with a modernist narrator leads to an interesting parodic result—they send up each other. If Ganesh breeds with Tristram Shandy to hatch Saleem Sinai, then who is the butt of the joke? The ineffectual, Shandyesque Saleem, who despite asserted humility makes repeated attempts to establish himself as more important than the story, to present himself as an agent of history, parodies both the historical aggrandizement of the (impotent) individual—the paradigmatic protagonist of nineteenth-century realist fiction—and the vaunted epicality of his own narrative. The often indulgent autoreferentiality of the postmodern idiom is opened up for inspection and irony, especially as the narrative's own substantive alignment is with the specificity of colonial and contemporary experience on the Indian subcontinent. Finally, by wearing its technique on the sleeve, as it were, the narrative is able to display to Indian middle classes the doubleness of their own parentage, the making of their urban habitat, of their popular culture, and of their 'despair'—an image of their own peculiar hybrid formation wherein too many things have "leaked" into each other. However, somewhere in this region where two ways of seeing intersect lies the curious desire of the narrative to confirm both ways of seeing. While the parodic mode works at the expense of both epistemologies, the allegorical mode (albeit problematized and contested), which sets up the narrator as both child and fate of independent India, attempts to conjoin the two. Saleem Sinai is to be at once the voice of the individual and of a collectivity, to be spectator and participant, to be unique and representative.

Such a position is precarious precisely because neither parodic rejection nor large-hearted assimilation is a sufficient confrontation of the formation of Indian middle-class subjects; the axes of their hybridization, both through a history of precolonial syncretism and through colonial transactions, are not identical with the paradigmatic 'literary' formation of either a coherent bourgeois self grounded in a realist ontology, or a self-fracturing 'high' bourgeois subject suffused with alienation. In sum, degrees and forms of embourgeoisement are at issue. For instance, here 'alienations' too have a different social genesis and literary–cultural valencies, and different political locations. The repetitive, obsessive quality of a fragmented individual consciousness, though grafted on, does not always stick, as in the amnesiac Sunderbans episode where Saleem, in Buddha-like apathy, regresses into an inner landscape. The strain of negotiating the treacherous terrain between two worlds surfaces in the way the Sunderbans episode tropes the journey through the jungle/ hell as an outer projection of inner torment, and almost falls into the psychologizing metaphors, which go at least as far back as Conrad, where the darkness within the imperial bourgeois consciousness became identical with the fetid darkness of the jungle. Again, the narrative embraces all mythologies in an effort to activate an essentially plural or secular conception of Indianness; it even appears at times to grasp Indianness as if it were an overly abundant torrent of religious, class, and regional diversity, rather than a complex and contradictory articulation, in different historical conjunctures, of caste, class, and cultural difference and conflict, 'othering' and syncretism, prejudice and political use, that can scarcely be idealized. Through the diversity of its narrative techniques and the diversity it seeks to record, *Midnight's Children* effects something that verges on an indigenized 'tropicalization' of the subcontinent.

Rushdie's is a fertile project. It relies on the received or preexisting transformative capacity of Indian narratives and listeners/readers; but can it be said to be itself transformative, to effect a different mode of understanding, to offer to remake the reader? Running aground on the shoals of parody and allegory, he scarcely uses his freedom as a professed fabulist. The totalizing and meandering potential of his chosen form cohabits uneasily with a modernist epistemology of the fragment, the specific perspectivism of a bourgeois subject. Further, unlike Garcia Marquez, for whom the 'arbitrary' is a notation of the loose, recalcitrant residue of a complex, sedimented social formation, for Rushdie, the 'arbitrary' is perilously close to becoming a notation of that avid cultural nomadism which invites assimilation into a postmodern marketplace. However, in the ability and attempt to play both with different conceptions of the subject and with different ways of seeing, a play licensed by this historical moment as well as by the (politically and ethically fraught) intersection between the so-called 'nonwestern' and the postmodern, his narrative opens the way toward more incisive descriptions of related cultural formation.

VI

What are the modes of access into such nonmimetic fiction for contemporary Euro–American, academic, poststructuralist discourse? In what sense are the openings provided by the fiction itself, and in what sense are they constructed by the critical discourse?

As my argument maintains, the hybrid writer is already open to two worlds and is constructed within the national and international, political and cultural systems of colonialism and neocolonialism. To be hybrid is to understand and question as well as to represent the pressure of such historical placement. The hybrid, lived-in simultaneity of Latin America, at once historical, hierarchical, and contradictory, is also the ground for political analysis and change. And yet for these same reasons, hybridity as a position is particularly vulnerable to reclassification. The 'modern' moments of such nonmimetic fiction emerge in fact from different social formations and express or figure different sets of social relations. Though forged within the insistent specificity of a localized relation, the very differences of such fiction are read as techniques of 'novelty' and 'surprise' in much of Euro–American academic discourse. Novelty guarantees assimilation into the line of postmodern writers not only because the principle of innovation is also the principle of the market in general,[26] but also because the postmodern obsession with antimimetic forms is always on the look-out for new modes of 'self'-fracture, for new versions of the self-locating, self-disrupting text. From this decontextualizing vantage point various formal affinities can easily be abstracted from a different mode of cognition; the nonmimetic can be read as antimimetic, difference can easily be made the excuse for sameness. The transformative spaces in a text—that is, those which do not readily give up their meaning—are the crucial node of its depoliticization. The enigma in Garcia Marquez's narratives can be read as a radical contextual figure or can be recuperated as yet another self-reflexive instance of the postmodern meaning/representation problematic. The synchronic time–space of postmodernism becomes a modality for collapsing other kinds of time—most notably, the politically charged time of transition. And further, since postmodernism both privileges the present and valorizes indeterminacy as a cognitive mode, it also deflates social contradiction into forms of ambiguity or deferral, instates arbitrary juxtaposition or collage as historical 'method', preempts change by fragmenting the ground of praxis.[27]

However, it is difficult to understand postmodernism without at the same time understanding the appropriative history of Euro–American 'high' modernism. Raymond Williams points out that modernism is governed by the "unevenness . . . of a class society", and this—along with its mobility and dislocations, which find a home within the "imperial metropolis"—leads to the characteristic experience of "estrangement and exposure".[28] Nonetheless, modernism, or more specifically, the dominant and definitionally privileged tendencies within it, also enter into and are governed by another set of relationships. Modernism is a major act of cultural self-definition, made at a time when colonial territories were being reparcelled and emergent nationalisms were beginning to present the early outlines of decolonization. As a cultural ensemble, modernism is assembled, in part, through the internalization of jeopardized geographical territory—which is now incorporated either as 'primitive' image/metaphor or as mobile nonlinear structure. Though often intended as a critique, such incorporation often becomes a means for the renovation of bourgeois ideologies, especially with the institutionalization of modernism. Ironically, the 'liberating' possibilities of an international, oppositional, and 'revolutionary' modernism for many early twentieth-century writers and artists from the colonies came into being at a time when Euro–American modernism was itself recuperating the cultural products of imperialized countries largely within an aesthetic of the fragment. The modernism they 'borrowed' was already deeply implicated in their own history, being based partly on a random appropriation and remodelling of the 'liberating' and energizing possibilities of their own local or regional 'traditions'.[29] Not only have the critical practices which have developed around modernism been central to the development of an assimilative bourgeois consciousness, a powerful absorptive medium for transforming colliding realities into a cosmopolitan, nomadic, and pervasive 'sensibility', but the freewheeling appropriations of modernism also coincide with and are dependent on the rigorous documentation, inventory, and reclassification of 'third-world' cultural products by the museum/library archive.[30] Modernism as it exists is inconceivable without the archive, and the archive as it exists is inconceivable without the political and economic relations of colonization and capitalism.

Modernist problems of knowing and representation continue to inform postmodernism. Though the organizing role of individual perception—which could legitimate perspective—and the cohesive role and concept of 'art' have lost their ability to bind the aesthetic of the fragment into a 'whole' and are indeed challenged and 'unmade' by postmodernism, there are distinct ideological and historical continuities between the two. Not only has the destabilizing of the image that modernism effected now been extended into the prose of postmodern critical theory and refined anew, but a postmodern aesthetic continues to raid the 'inarticulate' cultural forms of the 'third world', 'textualizing' a geographically lost terrain (for example, Roland Barthes's *Empire of Signs*).

Postmodern scepticism is the complex product of a historical conjuncture and is constructed as both symptom and critique of the contemporary economic and social formation of Europe and America. But postmodernism does have a tendency to universalize its epistemological preoccupations—a tendency that appears even in the work of critics of radical political persuasion and that results, notably, in analytic procedures that reconstitute an overly consolidated, unidirectional 'west'. On the one hand, the world contracts into the 'west'; a eurocentric perspective (for example, the post-Stalinist, antiteleological, anti-master narrative dismay of Euro–American Marxism) is brought to bear upon 'third-world' cultural products; a 'specialized' scepticism is carried everywhere as cultural paraphernalia and epistemological apparatus, as a way of seeing; and the postmodern problematic becomes *the* frame through which cultural products of the rest of the world are seen. On the other hand, the 'west' expands into the world; late capitalism muffles the globe and homogenizes (or threatens to) all cultural production[31]—this, for some reason, is one 'master narrative' that is seldom dismantled as it needs to be if the political agency and differential economic, class, and cultural formations of imperialized countries within a global economy are to be taken into account. The writing that emerges from this position, however critical it may be of colonial discourses, gloomily disempowers the 'nation' as an enabling idea and relocates the impulses for change as everywhere and nowhere. Because it sees the 'west' as an engulfing 'centre', it perpetuates the notion of the 'third world' as a residue and as a 'periphery' that must eternally palpitate the centre. This binary centre–periphery perspective is based on a homology between economic and cultural domination (or even on two related conflations—of capitalism with the 'west' and of capitalism with cultural production), and like the discursive structure of self and other, cannot but relegate the 'third world' to the false position of a permanent yet desired challenge to (or subversion of) a suffocating 'western' sovereignty.[32] From there it continues to nourish the self-defining critiques of the 'west' conducted in the interest of ongoing disruptions and reformu-lations of a self-ironizing bourgeois subject. The 'third world' so con-strued is at once infinitely malleable and essentially impermeable.

Such scepticism does not take into account either the fact that the postmodern preoccupation with the crisis of meaning is not everyone's crisis (even in Europe and America) or that there are different modes of de-essentialization which are socially and politically grounded and mediated by separate perspectives, goals, and strategies for change in other countries. Postmodern scepticism dismantles the

'unifying' intellectual traditions of Europe—whether liberal humanism or Marxism—but in the process denies to all the truth of or the
desire for totalizing narratives. There is no necessary or obvious
connection, as is often assumed, between an 'international' radicalism and the decentering of unitary discourses (or of the projects of the
Enlightenment and modernity). To believe that a critique of the
centred subject and of representation is either equivalent to or sufficient as a critique of colonialism and its accoutrements is in fact to
disregard the different historical formation of subjects and ways of
seeing that have actually obtained from the conjoint operation of
colonization and capitalism; and this belief often leads to a naive
identification of all nonlinear forms with those of the decentred postmodern subject. Further, the crisis of legitimation (of meaning and
knowledge systems) becomes a strangely vigorous 'master narrative'
in its own right, since it sets out to rework or 'process' the knowledge
systems of the world in its own image; the postmodern 'crisis'
becomes authoritative because it is inscribed within continuing power
relations and because, as an energetic mode of "acquisitive cognition",[33] it is deeply implicated in the structure of institutions. Indeed,
it threatens to become just as imperious as bourgeois humanism,
which was an ideological manoeuvre based on a series of affirmations,
whereas postmodernism appears to be a manoeuvre based on a series
of negations and self-negations through which a 'west' reconstrues its
identity as "a play of projections, doublings, idealizations, and rejec-
tions of a complex, shifting otherness".[34] Significantly, the disavowal
of the objective and instrumental modalities of the social sciences
occurs in the academies at a time when *usable* knowledge is gathered
with growing certainty and control by Euro–America through advanced technologies of information retrieval from the rest of the world.[35]
In a somewhat pontifical diagnosis of the crisis of legitimation and the
loss of credibility in the "grand narratives" of emancipation, beginning with the French Revolution and culminating in Marxism,
Lyotard concludes that "our role as thinkers is to deepen our understanding of what goes on in language, to critique the vapid idea of
information, to reveal an irremediable opacity at the very core of
language".[36] To take such postmodern scepticism seriously may well
entail stepping outside it in order to examine how, on the one hand,
the operations of neocolonialism and globalization (based on such

vapid information) continue to be confidently carried out abroad and, on the other hand, 'return' as the crisis of meaning/representation/legitimation at home. Postmodernism, like modernism, may well turn out to be, in some respects, another internalization of the inter-national role of Europe and America. If the appropriation and internalization of the unknowability (or undecidability) produced in the contested and contradictory social space of gender, class,[37] and imperial relations in nineteenth-century Euro–America provided both models of the self and grounds for the epistemological and ontological preoccupation of modernism, then perhaps the question of the *present locales* of undecidability is an urgent one.

The history of the so-called 'west' and the history of the 'non-west', or, more accurately, the histories of imperialist and imperialized countries, are by now irrevocably different and irrevocably shared. Both have shaped and been shaped by each other in specific and specifiable ways. Linear time or the project of modernity did not simply mummify or overlay the so-called indigenous times of colonized countries, but was itself open to alteration and was reformulated and reentered into discrete political and cultural combinations. Thus the history of Latin America is also the history of Euro–America and informs its psychic and economic itinerary. The cultural projects of *both* the 'west' and the 'nonwest' are implicated in a larger history. If the crisis of meaning in Euro–American academies is seen as the product of a historical conjuncture, then perhaps the refusal either to export it or to import it may be a meaningful gesture, at least until we can replace the stifling monologues of self and other (which, however disordered or decentred, remain the orderly discourses of a bourgeois subject) with a genuinely dialogic and dialectical history that can account for the formation of different selves and the construction of different epistemologies.

This essay was first presented at a conference on Marquez and Latin America held in Hyderabad in September 1984, and subsequently published in the *Journal of Arts & Ideas*, 10–11 (Jan.–June 1985). A longer version was published in *Cultural Critique*, no. 7 (Fall 1987), and presented at the University of California at Berkeley and at Santa Cruz, and at the Janwadi Lekhak Sangh in 1987. The essay would not have been possible without the help of Ranjan Batra, Anuradha Kapur, Badri Raina, and Sudesh Vaid.

Of ladies, gentlemen, and the "short-cut"

or choosing unfreedom

Who was she, what was she, that she should hold herself superior?
Henry James, *The Portrait of A Lady*

The Portrait of A Lady (1881) is part of a wider discursive structure simultaneously implicated in shifting class alignments, in the 'power' relation of two countries, in the redistribution of gender attributes, and in a redefinition of culture interested in the formation of a higher bourgeois consciousness which is encoded in its formal textual characteristics. The specific paradigm of individuality created in the novel identifies 'femaleness' as a mode of higher bourgeois consciousness, deploys femaleness as a thematic for desired cultural change, and in the process draws on the individualism latent in nineteenth-century feminism even as it marginalizes the more disruptive aspects of this feminism. This paradigm, partly a product of literary modernism and influential in post-Jamesian critical theories, is of special relevance in unpacking the essentialist notions of femaleness that are often implicit in contemporary feminist criticism.

Modes of consciousness and self-consciousness, identity and experience, personality and subjectivity, are constructed in response and reaction to the pressures of a given historical moment and are neither self-sustaining nor perennially 'male' or 'female'. Femaleness is neither the 'natural' property of women, nor an eternally subversive other, nor even, beyond a point, the product of a special experience. It is not an essential, homogeneous quality at the *core* of all women waiting to be discovered once social oppression and repression are removed. Like maleness, femaleness is not a fixed inalienable quantity: it is, rather, a mode of *social* being and so a historically specific value which can be redistributed and reformulated. Structurally related to maleness, femaleness is integrated or isolated in various ways in different cultural formations and is often vital to their maintenance. It is very far from being, even theoretically, an uncontaminated area which can be inhabited by women alone or analysed by itself—and so as a category of redemption, celebration, transgression, blasphemy, or authority, femaleness has only limited assertive value. A feminist criticism which demarcates female experience, tradition, or culture as privileged enclaves loses the ability to articulate the complexity of historical process, to rupture and prise apart the wholeness of given social constructs at one of the most vulnerable points of contradiction—the inequality of women.

James, an expatriate shaped by and shaper of two cultures, constructs a mutually sustaining opposition between the emptiness of America and the fullness of Europe, invents women who represent neither themselves nor patriarchal attitudes alone but carry the weight of assorted cultural meaning. Elizabeth Allen traces a conflict between woman as "sign" and woman as "self" or "consciousness" in James's fiction.[1] I doubt if there is any 'self' outside its representation in *The Portrait*; it seems to me that the selfhood or consciousness of Isabel Archer is itself a social sign, a representation, which cannot be isolated from its social and historical construction. Indeed the urgency and seductive power of the novel emanate from its historical location at the intersection between the discrepant ideological and cultural currents of England, America, and imperial expansion in the late nineteenth century.

My reading of the novel is retrospective, taking into account the historical time which intervened between the original text and its revision, the decades in which its themes unfurled and in which the 'intentions' of its author intensified. I have interleaved the revised New York edition of *The Portrait* (1908) with the texts which cluster around James's visit to America in 1905—*The American Scene* (1907) and the essays on "The Speech" and "The Manners of American Women" (1906–07).

The title of the novel lays bare the assumptions of class, culture, gender, and aesthetic theory, and indicates their interrelationship. *The* portrait seems definitive, final, whereas *a* lady seems to be one of several, one of her kind, generic. *Who* is the lady? Within the terms of the nineteenth-century English novel she is yet another young heroine facing the inevitable choice of husband and choosing wrongly—"a young woman affronting her destiny", portrayed with a familiar mixture of indulgence and irony. Given its genre, it seems odd that the questions students often ask—why doesn't Isabel Archer get a divorce or go away with Caspar Goodwood—should still be regarded as irreverent and 'irrelevant', as unjust to the novel and to James's intentions. In fact, both the irrelevance of the questions and the inhibiting terms of the answers are embedded in a whole social and cultural edifice. If the novel is to be even adequately relocated in its historical matrix then the questions have to be altered: not simply *how* women are represented but *what* they represent, not merely *how* James deals with his women characters but *why*.

I

The word 'lady' comes to define Isabel's social relationship, and to gather for her the still significant dignity of its lineage even as she is allowed the advantage of its newer usages. In England the broadening usage of the word 'lady' is full of historical reverberation. From a word denoting fixed rank (the female analogue of 'lord'), it comes to be a word which expresses the cultural aspirations of, as well as connotes the means for, the upward social mobility of the bourgeoisie and the petit bourgeoisie (the female analogue of 'gentleman'). The medieval lady was both a representative and a symbol of her class. A member of feudal aristocracy, she cultivated a life of leisured elegance, finer feeling, intellectual subtlety, and polished manners; she was the object of chivalrous devotion, and if propertied, her person was subordinated to her possessions.[2] In the eighteenth century the word widened to denote "a woman of superior position in society", and in the nineteenth century a 'lady' could be "a woman whose manners, habits, and sentiments have the refinement *characteristic* of the higher ranks of society".[3] By the 1880s the word thickens with other historical meanings. The Victorian middle class defined itself by the leisure of its women, in implicit opposition both to the working classes and to the entry of women into professional market-oriented jobs.[4] The "perfect lady" as "leisured", "helpless", and "ornamental", as the desired ideal of the middle class,[5] was once again assuming a symbolic and representative role. In American nineteenth-century usage the word 'lady' denoted "a woman of high social standing" as well as "a woman of distinction";[6] here ladyhood could be an attribute of personal achievement. In her social meaning the American 'lady', like her English counterpart, was a vehicle for upward mobility. As Ann Douglas points out, the mid-nineteenth-century middle-class American woman in the northeast, disestablished from her role as domestic producer into a domestic consumer, was at the same time becoming a "lady". Her leisure, "whether hypothetical or actual", was increasingly "treated as the most interesting and significant thing about her", so that the significance of her new role comes to reside in "her connotations rather than her actions".[7] Isabel Archer then is a lady by virtue of the fact that she is neither a working nor a working-class woman: the selective realism of the novel is ideologically a matter of exclusion and repression. As the 'self-made' product of a New England elite and of American democracy rather than of the more rigidly class-stratified England, Isabel's claim to be distinct, to be exclusive, is intended to outstrip that of the solid, insulated Victorian middle class: though it is a claim to aristocracy which, even more than theirs, will be made on affluent, uncontestable bourgeois ground.

Both the word 'lady' and its history are mobilized in the process of defining a new aristocracy, the word 'lady' is in fact the *site* of an ideological struggle for a new definition of the 'exclusive' carried out in response to changing social formations on *both* sides of the Atlantic. Entangled in the blurring of social divisions in England and in America, James responds full-bloodedly to the need for a new aristocracy to define itself in terms other than wealth or blood, to find just inheritors for what was to him an unquestionably valuable cultural heritage. In England, from the 1880s onward, there is a visible "confusion" and "convergence" between the aristocracy and the commercial bourgeoisie as the nobility "contaminates" its patrician spirit by "venturing unreservedly into the world of business", and the parvenu bourgeoisie enter the nobility in increasing numbers through intermarriage and the distribution of peerages. American heiresses were actually in vogue in England at this time.[8] Were the matter to rest here, Isabel could simply marry Lord Warburton and claim ladyhood through the effective union of wealth and birth. But the aristocracy itself does not qualify, for if not already decadent its scions are handicapped by the fact of being born into it, and so of being confined in preordained roles like the "radical" Warburton and his compliant sisters. The patrician upper middle class lacks vision, for by the late nineteenth century it has settled into "aristocratic pretensions and authority".[9] In England, perhaps the most suitable candidate for James is the influential, professional, and intellectual middle class—a group to which he himself, though born a millionaire's grandchild, came to belong. However, the *true* inheritor is the *select* representative of the American bourgeoisie endowed with an unlimited vision of human capacity. The newly rich American, marked by the vulgar and levelling excesses of democracy, corrupted by the brash acquisitiveness and conspicuous waste of the Gilded Age, is not eligible. Nor does the American businessman qualify in person, for that "obscure, but not less often an epic, hero" is "seamed all over with the wounds of the market and the dangers of the field and launched into" a time-consuming and "boundless ferocity of battle".[10] Clearly, for James American men continued to supply "all the canvas, and the women all the embroidery".[11] So it is the businessman's daughters—his "immitigable womankind . . . who float, who splash on the surface and ride the waves, his terrific link with civilization, his social substitutes and representatives, while, like a diver for shipwrecked treasure, he gasps in the depths and breathes through an airtube"[12]—at once guardians of culture and consumers in the making, who come to symbolize the noble spirit of youth and the leisured best of American democracy. If the values of the English/European aristocracy are to be *preserved* then they have to be gently plundered by the sensitive scions of American democracy, whose economic mobility is an apparently unimpeded, already accomplished fact, and whose potential for cultural mobility is infinite. The notion of potential here is not potential for change, but rather a potential for spongelike absorbency and intelligent assimilation, for further enrichment of the already rich, for becoming the epitome of an already existing culture.

   Cultural mobility becomes operative through the joint modes of acquisition and inheritance, is ratified by the relation of America to Europe, and is both cause and symptom of James's expatriation. James's enthusiastic letter to T.S. Perry in 1867 is worth rereading in this context:

> I think that to be an American is an excellent preparation for
> culture. We have exquisite qualities as a race, and it seems to me that
> we are ahead of the European races in the fact that more than either
> of them we can deal freely with forms of civilization not our own,
> can pick and choose and assimilate and in short (aesthetically etc.)
> claim our property wherever we find it. To have no national stamp
> has hitherto been a defect and a drawback, but I think it not
> unlikely that American writers may yet indicate that a vast intellec-
> tual fusion and synthesis of the various national tendencies of the
> world is the condition of more important achievements than any
> we have seen. We must of course, have something of our own —
> something distinctive and homogenous —and I take it that we shall
> find it in our moral consciousness, our unprecedented spiritual
> lightness and vigour. In this sense at least we shall have a national
> *cachet*.[13]

The key terms in this process are exclusiveness, free choice, mobility,
and an almost imperial expansiveness; indeed it is a process in which
an American can profit from the imperial expansion of Europe more
effectively, and more selectively, than Europeans themselves.

The heritage of the aristocracy must be maintained as an
elite enclave if it is to remain a privilege worth sharing. James clearly
partakes, like English aestheticism and French Symbolism, in the
"ideology of rarity which endeavours to value the art object by
placing it beyond the reach of the multitude".[14] For James, exclusiveness functioned as a defence against the growth of mass culture,
against the ethic of personal fulfilment through the appreciation of
high culture (which was becoming the property of the common person
and attendant on the increased availability of art and literature), and
against the cultural heterogeneity of immigrant 'melting-pot' America.
In "The Manners of American Women" he reminds us

> that the art of meeting life finely is . . . *the art of preparations*. There
> is always a thrill for us at home in the observed operation of our
> law that anyone may become among us, at two minutes' notice,
> anything possible or impossible, even a gentlemen, even a lady; but
> the deeper impression attaches, none the less, to the *exhibited
> effects of being tutored*, which correct usefully our too habitual,
> too national belief in the sweet sanctity of free impulse.[15]

Even Isabel considers that the "essence of the aristocratic situation" is "'to be in a better position for appreciating people than they are for appreciating you'".[16]

James's novel enacts yet another democratic opening up of exclusive privilege to those not born to it, and simultaneously curtails it through the use of the inheritance device. Not only is the money cleansed for Isabel because it is both inherited and deserved, but there is a significant conflation of inherited wealth with inherited tradition. As Jules Zanger writes of the nineteenth-century American novel:

> in an age of growth, centralization and industrialization of the community, the inheritance theme affirmed the uniqueness of the singular self. It identified the recipient with a successful (that is cumulating) past in a period brassily dominated by new money . . . offered a special validation of the individual . . . repudiated the crushing social environment and affirmed individual possibility and special fate in a world otherwise determined.

Or, as James put it in *The American Scene*: "Money in fact *is* the short-cut".[17]

Adopting a cultural heritage is above all an act of free choice. Indeed *because* it is an act of free choice it signifies a higher form of bourgeois humanism than the landed aristocracy is capable of—they belong merely by birth. James wrote passionately of himself in 1881: "My choice is the old world";[18] and Isabel believes that for her the aristocratic life consists of "the union of great knowledge with great liberty" (2: p. 198). James's expatriation creates the space for a notion of a freefloating bourgeois aristocracy which can *afford* to be a set of attitudes, a privilege to be earned and appropriated which—in its vaunted internationalism—can inhabit London or New York or Paris with equal ease.

Ironically, it is James's expatriate status and his critical distance from America which allows him to culturally legitimate American expansionism without subscribing either to a crass materialism or to crude nationalism. The superior position of the American vis-à-vis European culture, as James describes it in his letter to Perry, coincides with America's expanding, expansive role. Between 1870 and 1900 America was investing a growing amount of capital in Europe and was increasingly perceived as a major challenge to

Britain's industrial supremacy.[19] Mr Touchett represents an American "banking-house" in England (1: p. 49), his fortune is presumably a product of this transaction, and he expects his son to "carry on the grey old bank in the white American light". At this time, then, America had both the old and continuing rationale as well as a new reason to represent itself to England/Europe, and to create the terms through which it was viewed. The characteristic Jamesian theme of American wealth—"spiritual lightness and vigour" versus the density of English/European culture—finds its shape in the inverting power relations between the two countries/continents, and so finds its characteristic difficulty in reconciling the power of wealth with the power of moral purity.

James's notorious despair over America's alleged emptiness in *The American Scene*, his dread that those empty spaces which could be filled through specialized exchange with Europe may now be endemic, often blurs the fact that this same sense of emptiness empowers his fiction, both dictates and lends its blankness to his experiments in the acquisition and inscription of culture. This then is the actual promise America holds for him:

> The very *donnee* of the piece could be given, the subject formulated: the great adventure of a society reaching out into the apparent void for the amenities, the consummations, after having earnestly gathered in so many of the preparations and necessities. . . . *Never would be such a chance to see how the short-cut works*, and if there be really any substitute for roundabout experience, for troublesome history, for the long, the immitigable process of time.[20]

Though the promise fails collectively since America has no "time for history", and is now an "apotheosis of the raw", a monstrous appetite with an unappeasable "*will to grow*",[21] the same failure perversely justifies individual versions of "the short-cut"; the questionable success of James's fine discriminations makes them seem even more necessary to him.

It is not sheer perversity which leads James to play out the fate of Isabel, the expansive Emersonian individual with transcendental notions of freedom and of American 'promise' in restrictive Europe, and so doom her to unhappiness. Isabel is the *ground* on which new modes of cultural selection and evaluation are to be tested and evolved, modes which reinflect gender to assist shifting class alignments. She is the womanly and so contradictory carrier of an appropriative notion of culture through whom both lesser and grosser forms of appropriation, as well as dilettantism and decadence, are to be excised—partly by a ritually repeated rejection of her suitors and by the exposure of her husband. Her fate, at once exceptional and representative, is also the fate of an idea—the idea of a *willed* adoption of 'culture' developed within the matrix of Anglo–American liberal belief in individual independence and free choice, and the American transcendental ethic of self-reliance and self-development, both of which enter into contradictory, even self-negating, relation with their material underpinning in laissez-faire and the individual's struggle for success within capitalist competition. Isabel, the lady, is framed in more senses than one.

II

Isabel's ladyhood rests not only on how she is placed in relation to nineteenth-century feminism, to other women in the novel, but also on James's conception of femaleness as the pliable medium of subjectivity through which to constitute a bourgeois consciousness, which is at once a matter of class and of literary form. Isabel's identity depends largely on what she is not; the significance of her marriage comes to lie in what she does not do.

The very conception of Isabel as lady involves a response to and reformulation of the disturbance caused by feminism on both sides of the Atlantic. James does not separate the question of women from what was for him the overarching question—the state of culture and civilization in America. The growth of the suffragette movement, the access to new educational and employment opportunities, and so perforce to options other than marriage in the 1870s was followed in the 1880s (especially in England) by the opening up of issues such as dress, marriage, sexuality, incompatibility, divorce, and adultery, as subject matter for public debate and fiction. The term 'New Woman' was often an abbreviation for this cumulative activity. For James the confrontational assertiveness of the New Woman was virtually an extension of the untutored state of American women as a whole. Together they constitute an unsurpassable 'vulgarity' best treated in the comic or ironic mode. In quasi-Ruskinian tones James describes

American women as "the unfortunate 'queens'" to whom there was seemingly no one to suggest the possible privilege and profit, even for competent queenship, that may proceed from a recognition of the *related* state". These American queens have had

> no wholesome social rigour of any sort to reckon with. Social rigour exists and becomes wholesome from the moment social relations of a more composite order . . . are attested, established, embodied things, involving attention and deference, involving the sacrifice of easy presumptions, and the mistrust of cheap pretensions, and the cultivation of informed estimates, and the patience, generally, of the consciously comparative state.[22]

In this schema Henrietta Stackpole and Countess Gemini can only represent breaches of decorum. Henrietta is partly modelled on the popular caricature image of the New Woman—bluff, hearty, androgynous—which dominated the 1880s and revealed "the psychological anxieties of a society confronted by the demands of the feminists".[23] For Ralph she does so "smell of the Future—it almost knocks one down!" (1: p. 131). She compounds her vulgarity (strangely synonymous with the "originality" she compromises in her decision to marry) by being unable to enter the inner life of Europe. Too much an "emanation of the great democracy" (1: p. 130), her American sense of personal worth and morality, her loyalty and integrity, are counterbalanced by her shallow touristy reportage, her lack of a "sense of privacy" (1: p. 121), her naive wonder at the deference of English noblewomen ("In America the gentlemen obey the ladies" [1: p. 189]), her refusal to appreciate the European model. So her wish "to be treated as an American lady" (1: p. 134) can only be faintly ludicrous, can only point to the cultural insufficiency of the term. Countess Gemini, by a similar criterion, is a titular lady but cannot be a 'real' one; her surrender to the decadent morality of European nobility disqualifies her, despite an unhappy marriage, from both sympathetic treatment and a central role.

Isabel is a lady because she is not a New Woman, and because she is unlike both Henrietta and Countess Gemini. James's conception of her self is at once profoundly individualistic and inescapably social. Isabel veers sharply from being the Emersonian woman who believes in fresh beginnings, in spontaneous self-creation and development (in the manner of Margaret Fuller and Elizabeth Cady Stanton), to the American[24] and English Victorian woman, a Ruskinian defender of culture who is educated "not for self-development but for self-renunciation" and for "true wifely subjection".[25] She believes in forms and institutions, in marriage as a sanctified contract, and she represses her sexuality. The authorial voice accordingly makes a double valuation of her egoism: it is shown as both promoting a sense of self, of independence and rebellion, and as being prone to error, selfishness, and self-aggrandizement. This context makes it possible for Isabel to be offered up as an exemplary visual object—static, even frozen, in alternate postures of diffuse yearning and entrapped suffering, a woman who can be read as both agent and victim of her circumstance.

In *The Portrait* contemporary feminism is indicated as being indelicate at the level of content, and a further set of priorities is fashioned which make it tangential. Central to this process is the systematic distancing of Isabel's marriage from the realm of necessity. The unearned but merited inheritance makes it possible to remove marriage from the material realm and is analogous, at one level, to the operation of ideology as a whole in its attempt to suppress material relations. Seventy thousand pounds is Isabel's mode of access to freedom of choice, the means by which she acquires and consolidates her exceptional status—virtually an attribute of her personal uniqueness and emblematic of her distance from other women. The fictionality and ideological character of the device enable a major rearrangement of priorities: the domestic cares of everyday life, the constraints of family, are not merely suppressed but are insinuated to be unworthy. Not only does the novel carefully omit the early years of Isabel's marriage and her shortlived motherhood, it also presents her marriage as supralegal at a time when divorce was a controversial issue debated within the suffragette movement, and when legislation had brought divorce within the reach of at least upper-class women. In 1848, the state of New York passed a married woman's property bill giving women control of their own property. In England a series of legislations between 1857 and 1884 made divorce on some grounds possible, if not easy, for women, enabled them to own money and property even if married, reduced the husband's ability to enforce his conjugal rights, made him responsible for maintenance if separation was due to cruelty. Women ceased, at least legally, to be the property of the husband.[26] In practical terms, divorce was male-dominated and carried a stigma,[27] but the novel scarcely permits questions (except briefly by Henrietta) of legal recourse. The question of Isabel's marriage, subsequent oppression, and her more or less 'voluntary subjection' to it is transformed into a moral, aesthetic, and metaphysical question.

In practice, this shrinkage of the realm of necessity comes to constitute an expansion of the domain of subjectivity made up of intuition, inwardness, introspection, imagination, and the contemplative individual consciousness cogitating about personal relationships. *How* Isabel perceives and suffers is thus more central, significant, and authentic as a test of character than is social effort, and so the narrative can be structured around the anticipation, anxiety, and intervention of the other characters in *what* she will do, become, and represent. Marriage is necessary only in so far as it provides a matrix for the formation of an individual consciousness through interpersonal relationships—even while also constituting the major threat to its formation.

The shift towards subjectivity qua the female heroine is based on James's intuitive but accomplished understanding of two related facts. First, that female identity in its characteristic social construction is primarily relational and so flexible, fluid, amorphous, complex, and vulnerable—not socially fixed like the male.[28] Isabel's identity can only be enacted in relational terms, that is, through choice of suitor; the maintenance of her individual identity and what it represents hinges on the rejection of the men who define her too tightly, whether in terms of status or of sexuality. Second, that female subjectivity, both pliable in its social formation and pristine in its enforced isolation from the public world, is a prime medium through which the formation of a higher bourgeois consciousness can be enacted.

To the extent that a 'realist' vocabulary of individual motivation is inadequate to the scope of subjectivity so defined, the shift I have described is also a shift from literary realism to literary modernism, and the novel spans two historical and ideological moments. It is through the emphasis on the subjective apprehension of social reality within the confines of personal relationships that an elite 'modern' notion of individual personality and self-consciousness takes shape, and the qualities hitherto enlarged by women within the domestic realm become crucial to the articulation of this process. Subjectivity was to become an important bourgeois recourse and resource as the century moved into both more competitive and more impersonal forms of capitalism. On both sides of the Atlantic, this area of subjectivity—at once a private space demarcated *by* capitalism as an alternative to the public and so permeated by its structures, as well as a refuge *from* capitalism—had until mid-century largely been contained within and relegated to women's separate domestic sphere. Thus in its cultural definition femaleness is predicated on and indicates chiefly a mode of social being, elicits its subjective 'depth' from the sexual division of labour and the split between private and public, and is the product of a specific set of social relations. Myra Jehlen's designation of the "interior life" itself as female in the novel, wherein from the eighteenth century women become metaphors for "the female interior self in all men" is more useful as a basis for my argument than Lisa Appignanesi's definition of the feminine as a Jungian creative "feminine principle", as the mythical, mysterious, mystical other, which, in James, is a redemptive, introspective and "intense personalism" opposed to the masculine defined as "ritual, ideology, or any tendency toward a collective or transpersonal definition of self".[29] James is in fact seeking to transform the intense personalism of the female mode *into* a transpersonal, transgender definition of the self. James's novel seeks to accrue the values of femaleness qua subjectivity to an increasingly 'vulgar' commercial culture in an attempt to transcend it, just as in Richardson's *Clarissa* certain values from the private domestic female realm—"meekness, chastity, sentiment, benevolence"—had returned to "transvaluate" the political "public sphere of male discourse" in the eighteenth century.[30] What had been run down by Darwin's new scientism— namely, the greater capacity for intuition in women—as qualities of the lower species is upwardly evaluated by James as part of a higher set of bourgeois values which can include *both* men and women. Further, the trite, passive, familial, and stereotyped version of femininity espoused by nineteenth-century American sentimental fiction is transformed and recast as part of a higher literary mode addressed to a sharply defined group of people. It is worth noting that in the split between an elite and a nonelite readership James chose increasingly to write against the grain.

James's *The Portrait* and much of the fiction that follows it understand, prefigure, participate in a historical process which has created a cultural divide within the middle class, secularized a new freefloating bourgeois aristocracy by offering it ways of consuming its leisure, and formed a cultural and textual paradigm of femaleness which at its highest level includes both men and women. If men were to be sensitive their models were to come from the women's domain. James's own sensitivity to women is at bottom a sensitivity to what Jehlen calls the "metaphorical potential of the female situation"[31] rather than to the actual circumstances of women. This is the only way I can understand the similarity as well as the difference between his male and his female protagonists.

James's notion of femaleness is constructed in opposition to oppressive maleness. In Caspar Goodwood, Basil Ransom, and Chad Newsom, maleness is recognized and constituted as an unpalatable relation involving the power of sexuality, patriarchy, and money. James's scant sympathy with his conventionally rugged American heroes is in keeping with some of the tendencies in Victorian male discourse. Carol Christ demonstrates that "the ideal of the gentleman that emerges in the prose of Arnold, Ruskin, Newman also represents a more feminine ideal of male behaviour" and functions as a "retreat" from the "male world of action".[32] Ned Rosier and Gilbert Osmond claim gentlemanliness in proportion to their passivity, to how little they do. Rosier (whom Isabel sees as the "type of the useless fine gentleman" [2: p. 175]), claims that he cannot be a shopkeeper, a doctor, a clergyman, or a lawyer in America: "There's nothing for a gentleman in America. I should like to be a diplomatist; but American diplomacy—that's not for gentlemen either" (1: p. 309). Osmond says he cannot be suspected of fortune hunting because he has never "tried to earn a penny" (2: p. 80); he has renounced ambition:

> Because I could do nothing. I had no prospects, I was poor, and I was not a man of genius. I had no talents even; I took my measure early in life. I was simply the most fastidious young gentleman living. . . . The leanest gentleman can always consider himself . . . though lean, a gentleman. (1: p. 382)

Though disillusioned, Isabel still describes Osmond's social superiority as "not that of succeeding, but . . . something almost as good—that of not attempting" (2: p. 269). By this token the women who 'do' too much, Henrietta and Madame Merle, are bound to be short-changed, and only Ralph is able to rise above the imputation of vulgarity. Significantly, it is Ralph's illness which becomes "a kind of intellectual advantage; it absolved him from all professional and official emotions and left him the luxury of being exclusively personal" (2: p. 60). James's description of the feminine in Saint Beuve could equally be a description of Ralph or Isabel: "There is something feminine in his tact, his penetration, his subtlety and pliability, his rapidity of transition, his magical divinations, his sympathies and antipathies, his marvellous act of insinuation, of expressing himself by fine touches and of adding touch to touch."[33] Thus his feminized heroes—Ralph Touchett, Hyacinth Robinson, Merton Densher, Lambert Strether—will be as concerned with the intricacies of intention, motivation, and relationship as the heroines—and, *sometimes*, as vulnerable.

In *The Portrait* the main difference in James's treatment of his female protagonist lies in the pedagogic mode through which her femaleness is textualized and in the way the novel encashes the actual powerlessness of women. The notion of femaleness qua subjectivity is never let loose in the novel; it is still *bound* within a normative, naturalizing form which empowers omniscient narration, still enables the narrator to refer to the text as "our history" (1: p. 166). The omniscient narrator with his (albeit self-questioning and ironic) assumption of social authority acts as a brake, a guide, a pedagogue, a director of the 'experience' and 'subjectivity' of women. How much of Isabel's subjectivity do we really know? Isn't it more a case of asserting its value without giving up narrative authority? Isn't her subjectivity being more or less objectively inserted into the narrative frame? The spectatorial, consensual, avid paternalism of the narrative structure stems from and is reinforced by the intimate relation the omniscient narrator establishes with his surrogate, Ralph. As men they jointly endow a woman with intelligence, wealth, and vulnerability, invest her with protean potential (in some ways an idealization of her socially desirable and inculcated malleability), empower female capacity for self-realization and the ability to act without divesting her of passivity. They place on her the burden of accomplishment, challenge her to performance, but keep her 'free' of both the taint of the public role and the 'vice' of power. They constitute woman as an enigmatic subject to be unravelled, and indulge in "the boundless liberty of appreciation" and sympathy (1: p. 49). A woman not so invested—either the carefully maintained Pansy who is likened to a "sheet of blank paper" (1: p. 401), or the "too flexible, too useful . . . too ripe and too final" Madame Merle (1: p. 274)—does not stimulate or sustain the imagination or beckon the scrutiny of a man of 'calibre'. Isabel, however, continues to be "an entertainment of a high order", "a real little passionate force to see at play . . . finer than the finest work of art" (1: p. 86) for Ralph until his death. Unlike Isabel, Madame Merle is "too perfectly the social animal", since it is "difficult to think of her in any detachment or privacy", and she has none of that "tonic wildness" (1: p. 274) which invites tutelage. Rather, as a cynical schemer who believes a woman "has no natural place anywhere; wherever she finds herself she has to remain on the surface and, more or less, to crawl" (1: p. 280), she invites only punishment.

The paternal pedagogic theme is evident in "The Manners of American Women", so too is the somewhat patriarchal method by which 'empty' American content needs to be re-cased in chastening European forms. American women have grown up graceless in "conditions all preponderantly easy because preponderantly feminine"; they constitute "the great feminine collectivity asserting itself as against all interference". This cannot happen where

> the men of a community have not treacherously abjured the manly part of *real* appreciation—letting, in the guise of generosity, the whole question of responsibility, of manly competence and control, example, expectation, go by the board. . . .
>
> In societies other than ours the male privilege of correction springs, and quite logically, from the social fact that the male is the member of society primarily acting and administering and primarily listened to—whereby his education, his speech, his tone, his standards and connections, his general "competence" . . . colour the whole air, react upon his companion and establish for her the principal relation she recognizes. . . . Supreme thus in any

atmosphere of the "liberal" education the law that the man claiming to be accepted as civilized shall speak as a gentleman, and vital therefore for the maintenance of that character the testimony he so renders.

It is from his maintenance of it that the woman, as a social creature, gets her lead and her cue and her best sanction for her maintenance of hers; since she is never at all thoroughly a well-bred person unless *he* has begun by having a sense for it and by showing her the way: when—oh *then* beautifully and wonderfully and in a manner all her own!—she often improves on it and carries it, in the detail of application, much further than he. The point, at any rate, is that, if she would only take this truth as revealed to her, the wisdom of the ages has everywhere quite absolved her from the formidable care of extracting a conception of the universe and a scheme of manners from her moral consciousness alone—the burden that among ourselves she has so rashly and complacently assumed.[34]

It is clear that the subject of 'manners' is only the occasion for James to specify the place women should occupy, to commend the age-old distinction between the teacher and the taught. If women are to take on symbolic and exemplary roles, to ascend to the heights of ladyhood and femaleness, they must first accept male guidance.

James's concern in "The Speech of American Women" is also with the civilizing power of "the cultivated feminine consciousness"; he would approve of the ascendancy of this mode of femaleness, but the "authority" that uncultivated women enjoy in turn-of-century America is for him a sign of cultural decline and encroaches on the cultural authority of American men. The onus of the failure of American women falls in part on the failure of American men, overly preoccupied with the public world to take on a corrective role, to be exemplary, to be gentlemen. In Europe the men have more successfully 'made' their women: "Isn't it everywhere written that the women, in any society, are what the men make them?. . . Isn't it unmistakable in England, say, and in France, that the men have invented the standard and set the tone, and that they constitute, in the whole matter, the authority?" Unlike America, in Europe "almost the main clue in the great complexity is the number of common figures and common lives required always and everywhere to fertilize the ground for the single type of the gentlemen . . . for the type of lady." The moral advantage of American democracy is that nobody has had to pay the "penalty" for such fertilization of the social ground. The superiority of the American woman as cultural subject is precisely in the absence of social guilt, in her greater freedom and so ironically her greater pliancy: "she has grown up in an emptier, a less settled and crowded world. Her surrounding medium has not pressed upon her, as it is of the nature of the different parts of old and dense civilizations to press—and to press especially where weakness and sensibility prevail." The drawback, however, is that "the world about the American woman has not asked of her . . . that she shall have definite conceptions of duty, activity, influence; of a possible grace, of a possible sweetness, of a possible power to soothe, to please, and above all to exemplify."[35]

In what James sees as a connected failure of manners, morals, and civilization, men and women have become joint partakers in the "modern process of the apparently bland acceptance of the rising tide of barbarism", and the *majority* of American women are locked in a fool's paradise without hope of exit. He is willing, however, to grant salvation to the exceptional women: "I won't answer for it that there may not be here and there hope of escape for individuals." These exceptional women, in turn, are to be the emblems of a more generally desired salvation, for "our general hope is doubtless where the real hope almost always is, in the precious, the smallest, minority having weight."[36] Mr Touchett puts it more genially, the women will be "firm": "they'll not be affected by the social and political changes I just referred to. . . . The ladies will save us . . . that is the best of them will—for I make a difference between them" (1: p. 11).

Isabel is invested with just such an exceptionality and is so invested by virtue of what she potentially and actually signifies. She comes to have a reinvigorating role. The American Ralph, both "artist" and gentleman, produced by Harvard/Oxford, domiciled in Garden/court, dying son of a millionaire, gifted with a vicarious "imagination of loving" (1: p. 54), epitomizes the same notions of subjectivity and culture, and is transformed on his death-bed from a potential lover into a brother—the *best* of women is equal to the *best* of men. Ralph has told her "that if she should live to suffer enough she might some day see the ghost" at Gardencourt (2: p. 418). In fitting tribute she sees his. Indeed she takes her last 'role', that of fully sen-tient 'tragic' heroine, *from* him. Ralph's fear that she had become a "fine lady" who "represented Gilbert Osmond" (2: pp. 143–44) can now be banished. She has become an even finer lady who represents Ralph.

III

At the level of structure the notion of femaleness qua subjectivity is wrested from popular literature and established as a perceptual value, as a way of seeing. The suspended dialogy of the text arises from the use of the clichéd plot and character elements of popular genres—Gothic novel, penny romance, melodrama and sentimental fiction—which are then subjected not merely to a stylistic and technical transformation but to an ideological transformation. The text reveals its genealogy in its stock of common types and motifs—the victim heroine, the fortune hunters, the millionaire godfather, the magic bequest, the tyrant husband, the exiled fallen woman, the illegitimate child, the innocent young girl in love cloistered in a convent, the lover's ghost, the palace prison, the intrigue, and the death-bed scenes. The novel *draws* on these easily recognizable elements for an emotive evocation of wonder, betrayal, and horror at one level and simultaneously *relegates* them to a lower level in the following ways.

First, by making them the source of action but not the source of interest. Second, by rejecting the familiar denouement of punishing the villain. If villainy is as much a cultural index as heroism then Osmond's lineage is significant. He is both a gothicized, dandified Victorian patriarch[37] for whom daughters are "useful pawns in the game of expansion and acquisition",[38] and a pretender in the new bourgeois aristocracy of intelligent internationalism. In the conventional Gothic novel Osmond would probably have represented the feudal aristocracy. Here he represents both decadence (partly because he has no money!) and abject colonial traditionalism within the bourgeois aristocracy of choice, volition and cultivation, and therefore threatens and is opposed by the more 'vital' currents within the same. The opposition between him and Isabel is suitably "an opposition in which the vital principle of the one was a thing of contempt to the other" (2: p. 189). The defeat of Osmond seems to require not so much that he be physically vanquished but a metaphorical debasement and a displacement of his point of view. The unconventional ending, combined with the narrative interest in the individual consciousness, effectively wrests the narrative from its 'popular' origins in a predictable plot and locates it on another plane on which *knowing* the truth about Osmond is sufficient condemnation.

Third, the novel employs structures of surrogacy in which the underlying grid of similarity between various characters blurs the nature of the confrontations and develops a shifting pattern of conflicts and affinities, which, in keeping with the nature of the intra-class discriminations James is interested in making, complicate moral judgement. Thus the different possibilities latent in Isabel and her situation are actualized in the other characters and held in suspension: Pansy embodies her potential for passive suffering and martyrdom; Goodwood calls into play her fear of sexual surrender and embodies the notion of individual will in its sexually aggressive form; her temporary acquiescence to the match between Pansy and Warburton is analogous to the plotting of Madame Merle, in that both project another into choices they did not or could not themselves make; like Ralph Isabel wants to "be free to follow out a good feeling" (2: p. 73) and transfers the burden and benefit of her fortune, sets out to be Pansy's patron and ends as her "sister"; and Henrietta and Mrs Touchett also embody possible versions of American women adapting and yet not adapting to Europe. Osmond represents an extreme configuration of Isabel's concern for form and appearance: if Osmond's appealing external plasticity, the fact that his value does not seem to fit any normative standard, allows her to invent him as an object of desire and so take him at her own ideal estimate—then who is misreading whom? If, like Madame Merle, Ralph is both spectator and initiator of the plot or action, if the Isabel he believes in (like the Isabel Osmond thinks he is marrying) is partly Ralph's own creation, then why does he retain his moral value?

The point to these questions, which are commonplace in critical commentary, is not their answers but the interpretative procedure in which they are implicated. Through this procedure the areas of popular middle-class values, consensus, and imagination encoded

in the formulaic plot and character elements are first expressed and
incorporated, then deflected and made superfluous, while the novel
reassembles at a higher, more refined level of consciousness. An ideological transformation is taking place in fairly direct relation to the
conventions and readers of popular fiction, and in relation to a
particular historical moment which allows such change.

James attempts to shift the locus of power from the outer
'male' world of public action through the value he gives to femaleness
in its composite sense, but he is great enough novelist to interrogate
and recognize the self-destructive potential of the 'salvation' he
offers. In a deep sense, money continues to be the plot and Isabel's
inheritance her doom: personal relationships (of friendship and
marriage) are permeated and distorted by the commercial, and the
corporate realm of subjectivity is infused by the material forces it flees
from —even Isabel's passion is like "a large sum stored in a bank"
(2: p. 18). Money both enables this pure realm as well as marginalizes,
disrupts, and disables it; in some sense wealth is bankrupt from the
start, for the end product cannot finally be separated from the means
by which it is obtained.

And yet since James's disjunction with capitalism is only
partial, his built-in critique does not unsettle the text because it has
another structure of authority behind it. He endows this overburdened
realm of subjectivity and individual choice at once with the highest
value and the highest rate of failure, posits free will and determinism
with equal force, so that failure itself becomes a value of sorts. His
aspiring/doomed heroine becomes a gender-specific and so a socially
and qualitatively different manifestation of an evolving cultural and
historical process, deriving her paradigmatic power and persuasive-
ness from this process. Jehlen says femaleness is "by cultural
definition incapable of active fulfilment".[39] In *The Portrait* the
cultural value of femaleness is ideologically effective *only* as unfulfillable potential. Femaleness, like freedom, is experienced *as* potential: it has to be aggrandized, enshrined in 'pure' forms, to be
preserved rather than translated, and thus it encashes cultural value
from the actual powerlessness of women who are still marginal to the
real world. Donald Mull acutely points out how actual "doing
imposes a limit on the self's ability to do", and accordingly "the
maintenance of freedom" is "the suspension of its operation".[40] By its

own logic the novel must swing from aspiration to its structural obverse—failure. The 'complexity' of Isabel's failure reinforces her value because in matters of consciousness James is concerned not with the end but with the means.

The paradigm of the sensitive individual James creates is encoded in the apparent open-endedness of the conclusion—actually a retreat into privacy which reinserts and reabsorbs Isabel's social and gendered selfhood into the mystifying recesses of a transcendentalist ontology—and in the values which cluster around the word "portrait". The ambivalent conclusion actively privatizes Isabel's decision, she probably goes back to Osmond, but *why* she does so is never clearly stated. In the two crucial penultimate paragraphs the first-person voice of the omniscient narrator comments extensively on what Isabel believes and does not believe, presents and follows her 'subjective' physical sensations both discursively and imagistically, and then conveys her decision in two flat sentences:

> She had not known where to turn; but she knew now.
> There was a very straight path. (2: p. 436)

There is no breakdown of narrative authority here, authorial wisdom does not suddenly prove inadequate, the narrative voice simply skirts the task of conveying information to the reader. Isabel's achieved higher consciousness has always been presented through another narrative voice which ensured its 'correct' reception and provided a controlling hierarchical perspective. The same narrative voice now politely limits access to her consciousness, declares it out of bounds, delicately refrains from satisfying curiosity, and so ironically remains able to measure womanly discontent without being out-measured by it. If the omniscient narrator has worked on certain normative assumptions—the socializing of private life and the domestication of experience—then the ending signifies not so much a slippage of these norms as the assertion of a new one: making a public value of the private life by refusing to publicize or articulate it. Withholding information becomes an enactment of the privacy James cherished and missed in America. He deprecates New Jersey architecture for "the air of unmitigated publicity, publicity as a condition, as a doom . . . there was no achieved protection, no constituted mystery or retreat, no saving complexity".[41] The novel loops back to its beginning in Gardencourt where "privacy reign[s] supreme" (1: p. 3).

The complexity and undecipherable residue of the ending is at once the inception of a modern moment in its shift from the neat conclusions of nineteenth-century realism—of a new relation of difficulty between writer and audience—as well as the legitimation of a transcendent notion of selfhood by interlocking a notion of privacy with a notion of gender. The reticence and ambivalence create a space in which a valued ideological transformation is taking place. The secrecy ratifies at a secular level Isabel's girlish, transcendental notion of her self as something ineffable, as something which is liable to be lost under intimate gaze and public scrutiny, as something which "does not represent something other than itself but also cannot itself be represented".[42] The ending enters into a revealing contradiction with the telos of the text, for which knowing has been the final value thematized in Ralph's consuming desire to gauge Isabel's real situation and the extent of the change in her. In a precise parallel to the reader's attitude, he spends his time "fitting the facts to his theory" (2: p. 145). His curiosity not only keeps him alive but intensifies in proportion to his instinctive understanding of her situation. What Ralph obsessively wants is some outer and confessional confirmation of his understanding—precisely what the reader is denied in the end. Further, the novel has to turn back on the irony levelled at Isabel's 'naive' transcendental idealism, which is now renovated and reaffirmed as a mode of resistance to interpretation. In the interest of maintaining its value structure, wherein selfhood is deeply implicated in consciousness, the novel recreates in the end the founding illusion of the inviolable self.

Isabel's complex individuality is not at odds with her social function[43]—it *is* her social function. Since Isabel deploys her refined consciousness of unfreedom to choose unfreedom, the ending creates the paradigm of the sensitive helpless individual, encodes at one level the division of knowledge from power, and simultaneously reinvests this isolated knowledge with compensatory power. At one level the novel deepens the split between the intelligentsia and the political/economic 'doers' of the world and the split between public and pri-vate, as it confirms the historical divide between the outer impersonal world of labour or 'work' and the inner world of personal feeling or 'life'. Though moral and cultural power accrues to femaleness, political power remains where it was; the novel marks a qualitative change in the way women perceive and put up with patriarchal structures but effects no break with them. Isabel gains 'autonomy' in her subjectivity but in little else. At another level, however, the novel succeeds in redefining political (and by that token feminist) and to some extent patriarchal power in their conventional outward aspects as crude, as not worth having. The sensitive individual repeatedly chooses helplessness to preserve sensitivity, to preserve freedom as an imaginative sense of possibility. For women, the ideology of romantic love which leads to the free choice of partner and voluntary subjec-tion in marriage is overlaid with a broader ideology which asserts "the inoffensiveness of failure" (1: p. 4) and provides a refuge in the "greater happiness" of being "powerless" (1: p. 320)—or indeed in the power of impotence.

The same act of seeing which is central to James's notion of the morally elevated expanding consciousness and central to the individual's relation to experience, is also central to the visual consumption of the "portrait". Intelligent seeing is both the truest index of status and the ultimate refinement of possession. At Isabel's highest points seeing and knowing go hand in hand. When she tells Ralph all they "see" together, in a joint consummation of knowing. Culture is thus a formal value which accretes: it is the historically continuous sum of all portraits, successive viewers must qualify by being possessors of a fine moral consciousness, of the power of wealth transmuted beyond recognition, in order to appropriate it. Ironically, an incipient consumerist ethic of consciousness underlies the acquisition and deployment of such a consciousness, though it is designed precisely as a mode of overcoming commercialism. The aesthetic theory implied in the "portrait" emerges from a complex of gender, class, culture, and ideology: the spatial form of the painting, the formal structuring of experience, and the activity of the structuring consciousness are integrated in James's prefaces into a formal theory of the novel. In this aesthetic theory, as in his practice, James is offering no less than a value system by which to organize experience—a seamless persuasive model which chooses and develops certain cultural possibilities over others from a particular position, and which can be held as a set of portable attitudes both separate from and sustained by the material location of a class.

IV

In so far as James is creating a set of values through which an emergent section of the middle class and its women find a voice, he is both answering and activating a real social need, addressing a real social configuration. The tragic force of Isabel's fate and the continuing power of the text arise from this fact. In 1882 E.H. Scudder saw Isabel as representative:

> The fine purpose of her freedom, the resolution with which she seeks to be the maker of her own destiny, the subtle weakness into which all this betrays her, the apparent helplessness of her ultimate position, and the conjectured escape only through patient forbearance—what are all these, if not attributes of womanly life expended under current conditions?[44]

If nineteenth-century readings upheld Isabel's achieved consciousness as a sign of true womanhood, then contemporary readings (and often feminist ones[45]) uphold her consciousness as a sign or birth pang of mature awareness—without noting that this version of maturity is grounded in a version of experience as expanding consciousness which is ideologically constructed and informs the structure of values in which the modern reader/critic is embedded.

The Jamesian aesthetic often enters twentieth-century literary critical discourse as a way of eliciting social value from the aesthetic to assist different cultural projects. As the rebellious fraction of a professional upper class engaged in revamping bourgeois ideology, the Bloomsbury group offers the "supreme value" of the "civilized *individual*" and his/her "pluralization" as a panacea to social problems.[46] It is not surprising that they value both James's sense of "the intricacy and value of human relations" and of the helplessness of the individual will.[47] James's vision surely enters the critical theory of F.R. Leavis, who was himself engaged in a major cultural renovation in which an elite, disinterested, petit-bourgeois "clerisy" centred on literature was to become capable, by virtue of its acquired sensibility, of guiding the moral life of an aberrant society.[48] As Catherine Belsey points out, the Leavisian position "commits itself to the *scrutiny* of individual subjectivity".[49] Significantly, Leavis extols the grand synthesis of America and Europe in *The Portrait* and includes it in a "trans-historical moral order"[50] renamed "the great tradition". Symptomatically, the act of quotation for Leavis is *the* act both of critical appreciation and the appropriation of tradition— that limpid gem set in critical discourse is meant to reveal as much about the critic's ability to select sensitively as about the text or author in question. The Jamesian aesthetic coincides with New Criticism's antitechnologist claim for the text as an inherently ambiguous, privileged object providing the means for its own analysis. Lionel Trilling's early criticism derives its corrective force from the reference to an Arnoldian defence of culture and its spiritual energy from the reference to a Jamesian ethic of moral complexity.[51] James's reputation and self-explanatory status peaked during the decade of the Cold War, when 'apolitical' modes of analysis seemed so attract-ive to liberal intellectuals, and some current postmodernist defenders of his *donnee* are now entranced by the infinite possibility for the abeyance of meaning that his fiction seems to offer. The renewability of Jamesian value structures and the vocabulary he constructs for individual self-consciousness, in different ways and in different histo-rical contexts, have special implications for women who identify with the emancipatory promise of femaleness construed as a higher cultural form. They also have a special meaning in India. We too are familiar with the play of nationality versus the acquisition of culture with England as the mediatory term as well as with the complicit logics of colonial tutelage and loyalist incorporation into metropo-litan culture but not from positions of Jamesian expansiveness. Here the critical tools of Anglo–American literature are often, within universities, a coercive discourse which represents and perpetuates a far more vulnerable relation to the pedagogies of the so-called 'first' world.

Perhaps we need to identify more closely the cultural *process* which generates, limits, appropriates sexual difference in order to determine the functional and ideological aspects of gender. Some aspects of this process would be the ways in which literay texts gain authority, place and produce readers in subject positions; the ways in which literary representations enact, shape, and deflect emerging or dominant ideologies, incorporate 'lower' ideologies, and the struc-tures and assumptions of popular literature; the complex and mediated way in which they channel male and female desire, and reproduce social relations; the ways in which the same texts speak differently to different people, that is, how they encode a culturally useful plurality; and finally, the ways in which they pose the relation between discursive and social practices. We could then evolve a critical practice which aims to see the text in the sum total of its relations, of which we as women are an integral part, so that the very terms of analysis become a mode of political intervention.

This essay was presented at a seminar on Feminist Approaches to Literature held in Miranda House, Delhi University, in 1985, and at Princeton University in 1986. It was published in *Woman/Image/Text* edited by Lola Chatterjee (New Delhi: Trianka, 1986), and in *New Literary History,* 19 (1987–88). I want to thank Anuradha Kapur, Badri Raina, and Sudesh Vaid for their help in revising it.

"Not knowing, but only guessing"

a modernist resolution

... the value I wished most to render and the effect I wished most to produce were precisely those of our *not knowing, of society's not knowing, but only guessing and suspecting and trying to ignore*, what "goes on" irreconcilably, subversively, beneath the vast smug surface.

Henry James, Preface to The Princess Casamassima

The text may, it is admitted, stitch the viewer or reader into position in certain ways; it may offer the subject specific positions of intelligibility; it may operate to prefer certain readings above others. What it cannot do, it is argued, is guarantee them.

Tony Bennett, "Text and History"

How does the late Jamesian text 'position' its reader and transform each critic writing on it into a highly individual and sensitive register 'open' to the multiple possibilities inscribed in the narrative? The famous polysemy of the late Jamesian text is indeed crucial in situating the reader. This is frequently recognized in studies which locate the text–reader relation as a ludic transaction or as a willing suspension of belief: the reader postulated by the text must in effect promise not to elicit any kind of self-confirmation from the text, whether cultural, moral, or epistemological.[1] The complex 'writerly' readings of James's opacity that privilege form and celebrate the plurality of meaning are based on a notion of an autoreferential or self-reflexive literary text which anticipates both the way it will be read and the interpretations it will generate. They opt for "a total relativism" towards the text and a "scepticism towards any reconstruction of the plane of reference" based on a neo-Jamesian identification of the "vulgar" with the "literal" and of the "criminal" with the univocal.[2] In a curious circular fashion the actual reading of the text becomes almost identical with the reader postulated by the text. Such readings exemplify the persuasive power of the late Jamesian text in so far as they come to occupy the collusive reader positions 'formally' preferred by the text. Ultimately, however, the notions of polysemy, difficulty, and inaccessibility central to modernist narratives have to be unpacked not in the formal but in the cultural sphere. Epistemological difficulties are not universal—they have specifiable contours and historical locales.

The cognitive relation that the late Jamesian text prefers and establishes is produced by, and in turn produces a social relation. Both the potential of the text for reinterpretation and the difficulty of fixing meaning need to be seen as part of a social transaction involving class, politics, and ideology. Neither the fecundity of the late Jamesian text nor the way in which it seeks to position the reader in relation to itself is value free. Both are constrained by their specific ideological character which underwrites the cognitive mode they try to establish. The generative matrix (textual, formal, and social) of the text's polysemy which both enables and encourages the production and/or proliferation of meaning simultaneously determines the ideological limits of the plurality of the text. To say this is to *frame* both the late Jamesian text as a site for the production of meaning and the generative activity of the reader it implies, to argue that the text encodes the *conditions* of its reinterpretability, to claim that the *sanction* for a particular mode of plurality is to be found within the given historical moments of the text's production and consumption (which do not remain identical), and so to acknowledge the possibility of 'openness' as being a form of enclosure.

In *The Wings of the Dove* the presence of two broadly different competing epistemologies, a 'realist' and a 'modernist', creates the generative matrix of the plurality of the text, which surfaces and flourishes within a conflictive historical moment and so offers a range of "interpretative *temptations*".[3] The polysemy of the text is generated by the structures of surrogacy which unsettle conventions of character and morality only to replace them with other modes of authority, by the gathering intimacy of the narrator with

Merton Densher which signifies the emergence of a corporate consciousness, by the secrecy which underlies the weight given by characters and narrator to the unspoken and by the structure of the text to the unshown, and by the syntactical uncertainty that depends upon and 'replays' the semantic difficulty so produced. The text is both intentional and performative. It is intentional because it is a mode of address which attempts to place the reader in a preferred 'univocal' position *from* which multiple interpretations are possible. The intention of the text is not stated but performed, indeed the enacted or enactive pluralism of the text can itself be taken as the code of its unstated intention which consists in fixing the reader not to a single interpretation but to a *way* of seeing. The factors responsible for the text's polysemy instal "not knowing, but only guessing" as a primary value which in turn shuffles the reader into place, 'regularizes' plurality, and so helps to institute *undecidability* as a cognitive mode.

Even in a bare reading of the text the question of the distribution of guilt and responsibility in *The Wings of the Dove* comes to revolve around "the *similarity of the different*" and the "possibility that *the ostensibly different is actually the same*".[4] All the major characters—Kate Croy, Merton Densher, Susan Stringham, Maud Lowder, Sir Luke, and Milly Theale herself—urge the conspiracy along because it fits in various ways with their own designs. Guilt and responsibility mesh with innocence and victimization in the relationships of the protagonists. The debased and materialist Kate is also the aspiring individual trapped in sordid circumstances not of her own making. Both Milly and Maud Lowder, the American princess and the Britannia of the Market Place, manoeuvre people and relationships through the power of their money. Both Lord Mark and Densher, the impoverished aristocrat and the penniless journalist, are drawn to Milly's wealthy charm. Further, Densher does not simply shift his allegiance from Kate to Milly: he contains within himself the possibilities of *both* women *throughout* the novel. Not only is his apparent rejection of the one and embrace of the other ambivalent, but the very qualities Kate and Milly embody are fraught with grim similarity. Kate is the social being with a "talent for life", a desire for love and wealth to fulfil her potential, a dominating personality, and an uncompromising sense of reality. Milly is the weak, passive, sensitive heiress, who seeks "life" so as to actualize the potential liberty which inheres in her wealth; in seeking "life" she is prone to self-deception. If Kate is the "worker" then Milly is willing to be "worked". Her victimization is assisted by qualities within herself. And yet *both* Kate and Milly accept and enact the roles and self-images offered to them.[5] Kate becomes the family pawn who will in the process of redeeming her family's fortune somehow also find something for herself. Milly is glad to be named, to be called a "dove": she will be graceful, benevolent, and vulnerable; she will accept domination if in return she can find something for herself. Both the "selfish" and the "selfless" are at one and the same time the "workers" and the "worked".

The plastic Densher slides easily into these enveloping structures of surrogacy in which the underlying grid of similarity between various characters blurs the nature of the confrontations and develops shifting and reinterpretable patterns of conflict and affinity. Densher takes on complementary roles with Kate and Milly in so far as each woman reflects his own potential. He behaves towards Kate as she would towards him; his behaviour towards Milly is almost a reflection of her own towards him. With Kate he speaks the language of hard cash transactions, he strikes bargains, he demands returns. Money as he sees it in relation to Kate is both desirable and inevitably soiled. With Milly he functions through the passive channels of perception and retrospection. Milly's money remains pure, indeed it seems to Densher to be a perfect culmination of and "as fairly giving poetry" to her "life".[6]

Yet it is Densher who has embraced the equivocal analogy between Milly's wealth, its power, and her dove-like qualities. The dove in Milly combines the softness of beneficence with the hardness of power. The colour of the priceless pearls she wears at her party in Venice blends with the colour of the dove into a soft radiance that veils, but is synonymous with the glitter of her wealth. The chain "wound twice" (2: p. 217) around her neck faintly implies entrapment, insinuates against the free flight of the dove. Densher's comparison of this free flight of the dove to the power of wealth implicates him in the simultaneous freedom and bondage of the dove. Just as Kate and Densher state their plan unambiguously for the first time, Milly sends "across towards them in response all the candour of her smile, the lustre of her pearls, the value of her life, the essence of her wealth" (2: p. 229)—the value of her life at this moment lies, however, in the value she can bequeath with her death.

The same symbol discloses the menace of the dove and also instantaneously idealizes it: Milly is both corrupter and victimized. Kate and Densher are both conspirators and abjects cornered into desire by the power of money. For Kate, money is an escape from vulgarity, she acknowledges her guilt. Milly's money deviously takes her beyond guilt: death makes her sacrosanct, "saves" her. Her true expansion comes after death in a symbolic realm. She simultaneously relinquishes wealth and exercises power, a power which intensifies Densher's conflation of the spiritual with the material and imprisons him in memory. It is the passive Milly, too generous to confront Densher, who in the final analysis takes her revenge. The power of her wealth is the wedge which splits the relationship of Kate and Densher, her bequest calculably drives them apart. Her exercise of power is all the more effective for being covert. It is Kate, despite all her planning and plotting, who "lets off" Densher with more charity, and who is finally both undeceived and undeceiving. Densher duplicates Milly's tactics in the end, he too uses the power of wealth and the shield of virtue. In a sense he betrays both women: the active worldly principle is negated by his acceptance of the passive role; the passive "transcendental" principle is negated by his guilt, his responsibility, and his continuous aggression. But in a fundamental sense the text makes it difficult to maintain the opposition, or even distinguish, between the two.

Even as the narrative complicates the 'realistic' deciphering of motives and attitudes, the conclusion seems to put the burden of duplicity on Kate largely through the narrator's connivance with Densher. The narrator is increasingly involved and implicated in the very acts of Densher's perception, he gradually pervades Densher's consciousness further confounding the issues of guilt and responsibility.[7] Like Densher's complicity with Kate, the narrator's complicity with Densher is established early in the novel. The instances of Densher's easy compliance with the growing 'plot' are too numerous to detail, but it would be illuminating to look at a few examples of the way his consciousness blends with the narrator's. When Densher returns from America, Milly, a casual acquaintance, is fast becoming a question mark in his mind. He thinks of her already in terms of use (as a "convenience") and of premonition. Milly "popping up in his absence, occupied—he couldn't have said quite why he felt it—more of the foreground than one would have expected her in advance to find clear" (2: p. 14). The use of "one" instead of an unambiguous "he" welds Densher's premonitory unrationalized fear and desire with an authorial foreboding which must stem from the foreknowledge of a predetermined plot. Later Densher knows he is enjoying Milly's "consideration on a perfectly false footing", "soothing" though it is, but feels it would be as indelicate to "challenge her as to leave her deluded" (2: pp. 76–77). Besides, that might also mean a "betrayal" of Kate.

The fluid prevarication of the narrator assists Densher's prevarication: "It wouldn't really have taken much more to make him wonder if he hadn't before him one of those rare cases of exaltation—food for fiction, food for poetry—in which a man's fortune with the woman who doesn't care for him is positively promoted by the woman who does" (2: p. 81). The woman in this context could be either Kate, secretly engaged to Densher, or Milly, who likes him and thinks Kate does not. Later, on his return to London, his attitude to the dying Milly is strange: "He had taken with himself on leaving Venice the resolution to regard Milly as already dead to him—that being, for his spirit the only thinkable way to pass the time of waiting" (2: p. 339). In the rest of this passage the narrator does not qualify Densher's attitude but its success, which it seems is only partial. The narrator sees it as only natural that Densher should desire both to transfigure Milly and to "ignore" her "consciousness, tortured . . . crucified by its pain". This is after all structurally on par with the text's own omission of the last crucial confrontation between Densher and Milly in Venice.

In the final scene the hard choice is once again to be Kate's whereas Densher is to have the luxury of inaction. She cannot have the money except through him, and he will only renounce it through her. According to the terms of his bargain, he can remain evasive: it is to be Kate's renunciation or Kate's responsibility. She is both to possess and to exorcise the taint of the money. Whereas Kate is defined and condemned by her action, Densher's inaction blurs the edges of his guilt. Repeated justifications for his passivity are developed sometimes by him and sometimes with the narrator's help. As an accomplice who has extracted his physical due from Kate, Densher's bid for integrity must have some moral leverage before the reader can make a double judgement by which he is forgiven and she is not. The ground for such judgement is eroded by the narrator who becomes Densher's accomplice, slips into subterfuge about him, and technically condones his behaviour even as the narrative provides contrary evidence. The "moral" solution of the narrator resolves into "doing nothing" to facilitate conventional moral judgement for the reader.

The climactic moment in the narrator's relation with Densher comes near the end of the novel. After the burning of Milly's unread letter there is an expanse of things left unsaid between Kate and Densher. Densher has an added awareness of how "while the days melted, something rare went with them":

> He kept it back *like* a favorite pang; left it behind him, *so to say*, when he went out, but came home again *the sooner* for the certainty of finding it there. Then he took it out of its sacred corner and its soft wrappings; he undid them one by one, handling them, *handling it, as a father, baffled and tender, might handle a maimed child.* ... Then he took to himself at such hours, *in other words*, that he should never, never know what had been in Milly's letter. ... The part of it missed for ever was the turn she would have given her act. That turn had possibilities that, *somehow*, by wondering about them, his imagination had extraordinarily filled out and refined. It had made of them a revelation the loss of which was *like the sight of a priceless pearl cast before his eyes—his pledge given not to save it—into the fathomless sea, or rather even it was like* the sacrifice of something sentient and throbbing, *something that*, for the spiritual ear, *might have been* audible as a faint, far wail. This was the sound that he cherished when alone in the stillness of his rooms. He sought and guarded the stillness, so that it *might* prevail there till the inevitable sounds of life, *once more, comparatively* coarse and harsh, should smother and deaden it—*doubtless* by the same process with which they would officiously heal the ache in his soul that was *somehow* one with it. (2: pp. 295–96; my emphases)

The narrator and Densher are as one both in their paternalism and in their desire to consecrate the sense of loss in the stillness of memory—that realm where imagined possibility subdues the deadening "sounds of life". The narrator joins in the pledge of not redeeming the "pearl", that is, not revealing the contents of Milly's letter—to Kate, to Densher, to the reader, and by implication to himself.

The difficulty of this passage lies in disentangling the analogies, the modifying words, the parenthetical and qualifying phrases (see my emphases) that belong to Densher from those that belong to the narrator. The discretion and delicacy, the hesitation and hypothesis with which the narrator "handles" Densher's experience is an index of their joined sensibility and style, which in turn indicates the preferred attitude to the reader—not knowing, not probing, only guessing. The sentence structures incorporate various hypothetical dimensions of time: prescience and retrospection, the definite past and the indefinite past, the present moment and the indefinable present, the determined future and the indeterminable or undetermined future—all coexist in the combined consciousness of narrator, character, and reader. In this way James establishes an alternate and more expansive time-scale in which *uncertainty becomes the principle of expansion*—uncertainty blurs the edges of simple, sequential, ascertainable time and so expands it. The stylistic fiat of the narrator is to offer description as conjecture. The simultaneity with which a series of conjectures can be held and pursued is the synchronous stylistic proposition that he holds out to the reader. This betokens not so much a break with causality as a *silencing* interrogation of causality so that sequential thought appears to be both vulgar and inaccurate.

James can "work" this in formal terms because of his contradictory use of and placement between 'realism' and 'modernism': the modernist dislocations of the text are undergirded, at least in one significant way, by the 'unifying' ideology of realism. Broadly speaking, the realist novel depends on an apparent settlement between narrator and reader which claims a more or less stable and shared epistemology, while the modernist novel openly contracts to unsettle or destabilize the reader's way of knowing. In *The Wings of the Dove* the narrator is able to share his *hesitation* to fix meaning and morality with the reader in roughly the same way as the omniscient narrators of the realist novel share their knowledge and moral authority. The narrator's presence, marked in the text by the occasional use of "we" and "our", still retains some control and authority,[8] but he offers instead 'moral' assurance in uncertainty. On the one hand narrator and reader are still aligned as in the realist novel, on the other hand the partial break with realism allows the text to instal the reader in a new position, the position from which the text is 'fully' intelligible, that is, the tolerance of the vague and the acceptance of polysemy.

Tentativeness and undecidability become the authoritative measure of sensitivity and so the gauge of 'higher' morality. The text demands a 'voluntary' (as befits capitalist ideology) renunciation of certainty. Certainty is gross, a vulgar arrest of the fullness of speculation, something which can do only partial justice to reality, and can indicate only a qualitatively inferior reality. The hesitation and uncertainty appear to knit the text itself into a dense, textured, enclosing medium which offers to envelop the reader in another kind of security, and to replace the satisfaction that the closures of the realist novel provide. The narrator does not openly exhort or enlist the reader through the direct explanation and evaluation of character or event. He hesitates openly, displays his stammering lack of omniscience, avoids his 'responsibility' to retail the 'real' events of the story. Yet he manages to maintain a certain 'moral' consensus or accord with the reader: both can share, or rather the reader can come to share with the narrator, a humane and finely discriminating intelligence which depends upon and is produced by uncertainty. Uncertainty becomes both test and guarantor of the quality of such an intelligence. In this way the reader is constituted as simultaneously affiliated to the narrator (at least along an implicit axis of value) as well as an autonomous re/constructor of meaning. The reader can be both a complicit consumer of the text and also a producer of the text alert to its variability.

Undecidability is the upshot of James's own ideological position which is entangled in and encases two simultaneously present and conflicting epistemologies. Not only does the entanglement engender plural meaning but it allows him to function as author in determinate ways predicated on the shared epistemology of the realist narrative. Because James is unwilling to forego the cohesive power of an individualism that can 'authorize' and legitimate perspective or point of view, and that can bracket the proliferation of meaning by impressing a single and singular vision on the text, his modernist 'authorization' of plurality is at one level grounded on the apparently stable epistemological compact of realism. In this sense too the text offers only a single subject position[9] which has, however, the capacity to generate different interpretative strategies and various interpretations.

The formal complexity of the late Jamesian text which immediately enlists both the deciphering abilities of the reader/critic as well as his/her tolerance of plural meaning, thus expresses both an ideology and a social relation rooted in a particular evaluation of the 'real'. Not only is the "renunciation" of certainty itself an ideological position, it both signifies and requests a willingness to entertain the 'real' as subject to endless ramification and qualification. In formal terms it involves the tacit acceptance of a constant play of meaning albeit still framed by certain forms of authority. A large number of interpretations are in order as long as undecidability as a cognitive mode and its underlying assumptions are not challenged. The accommodation to uncertainty as a principle can save both reader and critic (like Densher) from the tarnish of an unmediated reality, and can guarantee the necessity of their own mediation. The critic especially is constituted as a mediator who will assist the reader to gain maximum value (of variability) from the text. And the critic can scarcely extract this maximum from the late Jamesian text unless she or he is willing to go along with its values. Margaret Walters goes even further when she says of *The Awkward Age* that unless the readers accept the novel's terms and are complicit with both its style and values, they cannot understand or even make sense of it.[10]

In this context the 'willing' readers and critics of James's later work contrast quite sharply with the 'unwilling' readers and critics. The fact that the unwilling critics were often his own contemporaries shows the different expectations of, and dramatizes the gap between, critics schooled on the so-called verities of realism from those who have matured on the fractures of modernism. In 1902 J.P. Mowbray complains that James never arrives at the story in *The Wings of the Dove:*

> How indeed can he, when he is himself the story and has come to
> believe that the constructive or co-ordinating ability to deal with
> material is of less account than the exhibition of a superb dexterity

> in keeping the material on the air. . . . His generous belief that his
> reader is gifted not only with agility but with a supernatural
> acumen to discover what he means without his saying it, is not as
> preposterous as his confidence that the reader will understand it
> when he does say it, and both these amiable qualities of the author
> sink into insignificance by the side of the superhuman faith that the
> reader will think it worth saying when he has said it.[11]

F.M. Colby ascribes the linguistic "obscurity" of the novel to "self-
indulgence", and another anonymous reviewer in 1903 who finds the
style and syntax of the novel "irritating", concludes charitably with
a gesture towards the advent of an adversary modernism: "After all,
this kind of writing, crabbed, finicking, tedious in its struggle to be
exact, intolerable when it tries, so to say, to be exact about nothing
marks a strong reaction against the kind that prevailed until twenty
years ago or even later".[12] In 1905 Tom Masson rewrites a nursery
rhyme mimicking James's idiom of parenthesis and overqualification:

> Perhaps it was providential, and yet it seemed to come, in the
> sequence of events, wholly without vagueness or sense of any
> obscurity, that is to say, quite naturally, without forethought, or
> design, or shall I say premeditation? that the girl Mary, among
> other nameless characteristics, doubtless alien and beside the
> question, so to speak, had, at the time, though it were vain to specify
> the precise hour or moment, this being a matter of debatable
> chronology, a curious illustration of nature's spend-thrift ener-
> gies, namely—a lamb.[13]

In 1923 Vernon Lee does not object to the fact that James's
style requires a special kind of attentiveness which forces a reader "to
be an intellectual, as distinguished from an impulsive or *imageful*
person"; but Stephen Spender, for whom James's style is the upshot
of his snobbery and conservatism, remarks more acerbically in 1935
that "the privilege the reader is offered is to become Henry James".[14]
Despite the occasional rumbling of discontent,[15] in recent years, the
willing critic, proficient in making vital 'modernist' commitment to
uncertainty, has been more than ready to "surrender" to James's
style. Thus Ralf Norrman believes that avoiding both faith and
disbelief, "we should stay in the Jamesian thematic mainstream of

doubt, vacillation, hesitation, and uncertainty", and Ruth Bernard Yeazell votes for a similar "susceptible" reader:

> For like the characters, we too are continuously forced to hover somewhere between ignorance and full knowledge, to struggle with intimations and possibilities which make themselves but obliquely felt. The late style demands that at every point we sense more than we are yet able to articulate; only gradually do we grow fully conscious of our own subliminal guesses.
>
> And in guessing at the facts, in trying to make conscious and explicit all that the characters themselves fear to think and speak, we may conclude by writing our own fictions—ending our search for the truth, strangely enough, where James' characters so often begin: in the realm of metaphor.
>
> Indeed the more susceptible we are to the reading of any novel—the more we characteristically surrender to the realities that words create, the more emotionally rich, if sometimes disquieting, our reading of the late James must be.[16]

James's contradictory placement between a 'realist' and 'modernist' epistemology reveals itself not just in the structures of surrogacy or in the linguistic and syntactical elaboration of the style, but is also inscribed in the structural and structuring secrecy of the text. Even a hasty account shows the polysemy of the text to be produced as much by its stylistic properties as by its plot: by both its base and its superstructure, to use a convenient, if not entirely accurate, analogy. On the one hand the text presents a 'popular' melodramatic Victorian plot of greed, corruption, conspiracy, betrayal, and death. On the other hand it constructs itself around the cogitations, speculations, and speculation on the speculations of the five centres of consciousness (including Susan Stringham and the narrator). An intricate, enormous superstructure is created from the activity of these combined consciousnesses that guess and build webs of possibility and conjecture out of the unspoken.[17] Their combined activity refines, sublimates, evades, or just ignores the facts of materiality, wealth, sexuality, pain, and death on which the plot is based. But these threatening 'facts' have to be *there* in order to be elided. It is the consistent presence and suppression of sordid fact as well as the formal emphasis on conjecture which together engender the variable text and constitute a generative matrix for plural meaning or reading. The facts and scenes pushed aside or omitted—the 'crime' of Kate's father, Kate in Densher's room, Milly on her deathbed, the origin of her wealth, the content of her letter, the nature of her disease—become by virtue of their absence the determining centre of the work. This absence, continually indicated, is what *enables* the activity of the individual consciousness and assists in the attendant dilation of time—or the spread into the unquantifiable and the uncertain. To use James's own phrase—"the margin floods the text".

There is an intrinsic structural relation in the text between the superstructure of the consciousness and its basis in plain textual and social facts. If it weren't for the crude, almost exaggerated, plot, there would be nothing to secure and ballast, or to make sensible and palatable the working of consciousness and prevent it from becoming either arbitrary or insubstantial. *Because* the factual basis is gross for James the superstructure needs to be refined; because the material foundation is powerful and determining it needs to be suppressed. Because social facts are 'real' and 'inevitable' the superstructure needs a utopian dimension. The subtle and refined superstructure of the consciousness cannot really escape its material foundation, so James develops a structural mode which discovers and builds on a tangent, rather than on the contradictions it both conceals and uncovers. And in so doing he begins to disturb its actual foundation in fact, for example, the "innocence" of Densher and the guilt of Kate. Transgressing conventional realism, he does not move towards a final unveiling in which the secrets of the narrative are disclosed. The burning of the unopened letter is literally and symbolically[18] the killing of the motive and victory of guesswork. If the letter is a sign of the process by which money is transferred, acquired, and inherited, then burning it represents an attempt to repress, even destroy, the transactive character of money. Kate is vulgar in opening the second letter; because she is ready to name the "sum," she breaks the rules of the not-knowing game, the game Densher will continue to play. In effect the rarefied superstructure begins in willed and wilful fashion to question its basis in factuality, and in turn, the ugly dimensions of the suppressed base and the submerged links between its components, such as wealth and sexuality, constantly threaten to engulf the rarefied superstructure of the consciousness. Thus Densher's passion for Kate is a bargain which displays an equivalence between sexuality and money—the one in return for the other. After Kate's visit to his rooms has converted "luminous conception into an historic truth" (2: p. 236), Densher's fulfilment communicates itself retrospectively:

> The force of the engagement, the *quantity of the article to be supplied, the special solidity of the contract*, the way, above all, as a *service* for which *the price named* by him had been magnificently *paid*, his equivalent office was to take effect—such *items* might well fill his consciousness when there was nothing from outside to interfere. Never was a consciousness more rounded and fastened down over what *filled* it; which is precisely what we have spoken of as, in its degree, *the oppression of success*, the somewhat *chilled state*—tending to the solitary—*of supreme recognition*. If it was slightly awful to feel so justified, this way by *the loss of the warmth of the element of mystery. The lucid reigned instead* of it, and it was into the lucid that he sat and stared. (2: pp. 237–38; my emphases)

The conflation of money and sexuality, of commercial success with oppression, of satiety with lucidity, and of lucidity with loss tell their own story, which in part is retold in the text's transaction with the reader.

The material and social base cannot but invade the personal relationships which are the content[19] and the catalyst of the individual consciousness, both its nourishment and reason for its activity. It is not only, as Allon White notes, "the affinity between the enigmas of sexuality and the 'play' of signification" which are "a crucial generating complex of obscurity",[20] but also the 'play' of money with the 'play' of signification the consciousness undertakes. The analogy between money and consciousness, the identicality of their fluid operations, becomes promiscuous at times; the play of money—"that perpetual passionate pecuniary purpose which plays with all forms, which derides and devours them"[21]—can expose the similarity of the superstructure of the consciousness with the base upon which, and because of which, it operates. Not only does each call into question the 'value' of the other, they also threaten to become synonymous and so continuously devalue and destabilize each other. James is caught in the vibration of these, at bottom, social contradictions which are, however, conceived as enmeshed polarities—the prolonged moment of yearning and loathing, of revealing that he is concealing, encapsulates the discursive structure of his later work. Though the narrative secures and preserves a modernist notion of the real as residing in individual perception, it is unable to deny or prevent the return of the determining real. Since rupture is always immanent in the way James conceives of these opposing forces, the defiantly infinite extension of "not knowing" becomes his line. Unwilling and unable to pay with the "lucid" he invests in a discourse of subtlety, hesitation, overmodification, and uncertainty.

The Jamesian social relation is poised in the struggle to both acknowledge and transcend its materiality. There is both a desire to cash in on a particular historical moment in which the possibilities of freedom for the materially well-endowed bourgeoisie seem vast, as well as the recognition that these possibilities are gravely endangered, if not foreclosed, by the very materialism which enables them. Thus, in the late Jamesian text there is a visible straining toward the sum possibilities of individual freedom and the startling, though usually suppressed, recognition of its conceptual and material limitations—both equally unavoidable for him in his chosen social location and in his historical moment. For James, then, the question is not one of choosing between alternatives but of making it impossible to choose between the antinomies which typify his fiction. The fatalism of James's later work (encoded in the failure, entrapment, impotence, or death of his protagonists) increases in the same proportion as does the narrative density and fecundity of the texts. The two are in fact identical, for if one side of the medal is failure the other side is success.

The radical transgression of form in its overdevelopment (in its linguistic superfluity and in the structures of surrogacy) constitutes a major interrogation of nineteenth-century juridical bourgeois morality, and is at the same time a shift of bourgeois social morality into a new field of operation—the cognitive. Here morality is based on qualitative acts of cognition and representation (qualitative in this case because suffused with a special, exfoliating uncertainty) rather than on old-fashioned semantic content. The *act* of perception itself both becomes and betokens a kind of social style. Not only is understanding seen to reside in the act of perception (whether that of the text or reader), but undecidability as a cognitive mode is infused with social value and social content. Premeditated difficulty becomes a mode of resisting certain forms of bourgeois complacency and consumerism as well as the site for forging and empowering a superior bourgeois consciousness. And, the uncertainty of the acts of cognition and representation along with the accompanying secrecy and guesswork put a premium on the multiple interpretative possibilities of the text. The positive evaluation of uncertainty and difficulty privileges criticism and exegetical activity. Critical reading is situated as both a matter of minute textual exegesis and as a 'private' transaction between text and reader. The text itself makes a public value of the private life by articulating its cognitive structures and at the same time maintains its own (and the reader's) privacy by withholding or even refusing to publish the ground of such activity. The critic as constituted by the late Jamesian text is bound to be original: the contract the text enters into with its potential critic encodes the promise of ever subtler and more individual reading—in other words, the promise of renewability. Further, the late Jamesian text presumes and creates a graded hierarchy of readers and critics which depends upon their *own* perception, sensitivity, and responsiveness to the subjectivity of the characters and the complexity of the text as a whole.

James thus succeeds in canonizing an area of experience, in letting the margin flood the text in more than a literary sense. He legitimizes a particular style of bourgeois consciousness whose characteristics are an expansive sense of self, a tortuous relation to the social, a material density so palpable it nearly becomes a purer alternative to history, a sense of confidence and of fatality, a vision of possibility, and a posture of passivity and renunciation. In fact the capacity of this consciousness to loop back on its own verities, to jeopardize the very act of perception it seeks to make primary, to be so knowing about "not knowing", makes of such a consciousness an infinitely plastic, agile, self-preserving mode whose self-doubt and self-irony serve to both preempt and subsume critique, and so ensure its own resilience. The narrator's collusion with Densher is not an instance of authorial bad faith but a modus operandi for transforming the individual consciousness so described into a *collective* one. An ideological collectivity of characters, narrator and potentially the reader, is posited through the successive alliances the isolated individual (Densher) is seen to make with the narrator's authority and with 'femaleness' (Milly).

The surface dialogy of the text in which different centres of consciousness address each other is subsumed under the broad ideological monolith of a bourgeois consciousness—a cohesive medium punctuated by its own compulsive self-reflexivity. And this corporate consciousness (as befits the ideology of late capitalism)[22] is also based on the incorporation of 'femaleness'. An influential cultural definition of 'femaleness' in nineteenth-century Europe and America was predicated on and indicated chiefly a mode of social being, it elicited its subjective 'depth' from the sexual division of labour and the split between public and private spheres. The product of a specific set of social relations, 'female subjectivity', both pliable in its social formation and pristine in its enforced isolation from the public world, was a prime medium through which the formation of a higher, introspective bourgeois consciousness could be enacted.[23] Milly's greater freedom as an American girl and heiress also ironically accounts for her greater pliancy. At one level the feminization of Densher, for whom "plasticity" has always been "within limits . . . a mode of life like another—certainly better than some" (2: p. 182), is completed only with the final transaction which occurs behind the burned letter: the absorption of Milly's femaleness which is both enshrined as unfulfillable potential and "reworked" through memory, thoroughly internalized and individualized. Milly's femaleness, qua her subjectivity, is of greater value than her money, exactly as the burned letter is of more value than the letter from her lawyers. The "faint, far wail" of the dead Milly becomes the substantive and displaced content of Densher's consciousness which along with that of the narrator begins to dominate the latter part of the text.

In this context it is worth noting the similarity of the narrator's and Densher's style to what Robin Lakoff describes as the "polite" speech of American women which (as the bearer of social decorum) is prone to "hesitancy", "uncertainty", "hedges", and euphemisms, and to what she describes as the stereotype of women's discourse: "indirect, repetitious, meandering, unclear, exaggerated", making "wider use of the properties of implicature", unlike male discourse which is "clear, direct, precise, and to the point".[24] The incorporation of femaleness, as historically recognizable and potent bearer of both subjectivity and social style, is the wider strategy of the text. Among other things, James is seeking to transfer and transform the intense personalism of the female mode *into* a transpersonal, transgender definition of the bourgeois consciousness—the absorption of femaleness is part and parcel of a larger social and ideological project.

The anxious proliferation of meaning is also tied to the renewed development of an aesthetic of hermeneutic freedom. This notion of 'freedom', itself honed on an epistemic split between instrumental necessity and a noninstrumental aesthetic domain, partly produced in the Euro–American theatres of colonization, acquires a new urgency at the turn of the century with the emerging contours of nationalist struggles in the imperialized formations and the intra-European contests over them. In this context, James's horror at the possibility of the destruction of metropolitan 'culture' (an affiliation that he, as American emigré, had chosen), his covert attachment to imperial power, and his obsessive attempt to detach epistemological modes by muffling the worlds in which the enabling surpluses were produced, now appears in an ironic light. The late Jamesian text is engaged in strenuous, extra-literary, salvage work, even in wanting the reader to perform "quite half the labour".[25] But on whose behalf?

In our context we may not only wish to reread our first and tutored relation to the late Jamesian text, but to recognize that its capacity simply to speak differently to different readers is perhaps less significant than the fact that it *still* encodes a culturally *usable* plurality, and still offers a model of literary 'competence'. It may well be the attraction of a privileged position in a hierarchy, the charm of inexhaustibility in a commodity culture, the lure of privacy, the guarantee of originality, and the promise of self-governance which continue to encourage readers to write on James.

This essay was written for a seminar on Art and Expression in Nineteenth Century American Literature at Mussoorie in 1983. It was published in *Ourstory: Indian Response to Nineteenth Century Literature*, eds Mohua Lahiri and Anand Prakash (Delhi: Academic Foundation, 1992), and in *Henry James Review*, 13:3 (Fall 1992).

Figures for the 'unconscious'
the pressures on description

This presentation has a double location: the first is my work on the formation of literatures in relation to colonialism; the second is in response to present questions about modes of access to 'indigenous' forms, the 'unconscious' as a (possibly regenerative) cultural resource, and the cultural processes which enable the symbolic empowerment or mythicization of the figure of the woman.

The issue I have chosen to discuss here is the 'unconscious' as an area of ascription. Since the unconscious is said to reside in or to occupy those parts of human consciousness which are either pre-cognitive or least directly available to itself, the logic of designating it consists of making it available by concretizing it in apprehendable forms of subjectivity or material reality, giving it 'substance'; and marking its presence through either representational practices which surface the subliminal 'depth' of individuals and/or cultures, or through scientistic 'evidential' modes. Different notions of the unconscious may intersect in any act of ascription, for example, as that which is essentially unavailable to cognition, or as the pyschologized realm of the libidinal and the repressed, or as the deep structure of collectivities/cultures through which traditions and identities are imbibed—that is, as anteriority, interiority, or depth.

There are three interrelated questions here—first, the nature of the 'unconscious' as the thing-in-itself; second, the relation that modes of ascription bear at any given time to the existence or experience of the thing-in-itself; and third, the governing histories of specific ascriptive modes which empower the act of designating the 'unconscious'. A provisional answer to all three, as perhaps to all questions regarding human consciousness, must be historically and culturally specific; this would revolve around further questions about ways of defining human agency, about the relations between the 'conscious' and the 'unconscious' and between knowledge and uncertainty, as well as about the relations between the modes which designate the domain of the unconscious and lived social relations.

I propose merely to raise some questions about the histories of ascriptive modes through a discussion of two novels written about a century apart—Romesh Chandra Dutt's *The Last of the Rajputs* (*Rajput Jiban Sandhya*, 1879) and Arun Joshi's *The Strange Case of Billy Biswas* (1971).

I

The Last of the Rajputs partakes of the Bengal *bhadralok* (middle class) valorization of medieval rajputs (including the immolation of women) in the late nineteenth century; a self-conscious parable of national 'unity', it typically transforms the chosen political affiliations of several rajput chiefs to the Mughal rulers and their antagonism towards other rajput chiefs into the classic structure of the feud, that is, into matters of revenge and honour alone. Again, in a move common in this period, the twin embarrassment of rajput alliances with Mughal rulers and the substantial loyalism of several rajput rulers (and Bengal *bhadralok*) towards the British during the 1857 revolt is sought to be resolved through the compensatory narrative devices of *sati* (widow immolation) and *jauhar* (mass immolation of women). The narrative laments the political defeat of Rana Pratap, the ruler of Mewar, by the Mughal emperor Akbar, while celebrating the 'cultural' victory of medieval rajput codes of honour and fealty. The tribal bhils and all the women characters are ranged along a triple axis of feudal hierarchy, colonial anthropology, and an evolving upper-caste/middle-class patriarchy, bound by a nascent nationalism seeking modes of unification. Inequality among Indians is presented as consenting, equable, nondestructive. The bhils, dispossessed of their land by rajputs, are said to have moved about two thousand years ago to the hills and mountains, "where they continued to enjoy complete liberty and self esteem".[1] Though they periodically raid the rajputs and Muslims, they are ritually tied to rajputs: there is a "bond" between the two, the bhils call themselves rajputs and assist them in times of war.

Once the political placement is made with this notation of
a cooperative, organic, precolonial polity, the tone shifts to one of
an ethnographic, encyclopaedic entry into that vast colonial dossier
of criminal tribes and castes, beliefs, customs, manners, and eating
habits. Like "the primitive tribes of India", the bhils have borrowed
one or two Hindu deities, claim descent from them but have no caste
divisions, and live like "birds of prey" through plunder (pp. 72–73).
In some respects, the bhils *mirror* rajputs: in courage, in that the
"uncivilized Bhil" never forgets an act of kindness or breaks his word,
in that bhil tribes quarrel constantly but unite in times of trouble or
war. The bhils are shifting subjects of a mixed genre—a romantic,
nationalist historiography, and a clumsy anthropology.

Among the women characters, a broad contrast is built
between culture and nature—its more precise delineation being between tamed nature and untamed nature. This appears to be at once
in succession to, a displacement of, and in answer to particular colonial descriptions of culture and nature. Though rajput women formally inhabit the realm of high civilization, both their "valour" and
wifely fidelity in acts of *jauhar* or in plans of *sati* are enacted not as
culture but as nature—as the untaught emanation of racial essence
which inheres in rajput blood. Race turns culture into nature; the
conjunctural, shifting histories and meanings of all these events are
blurred into an unchanging continuum. Logically, then, *jauhar*
comes to be described in the intonations of colonial anthropology as
a developed, reiterated, ancient rajput ritual, inscribed in a continuous present tense.[2] In a patriarchal inflection characteristic of late
nineteenth-century narratives, the 'bond' of Hindu indissoluble
marriage is given its ideological frontier in the ideology of '*sati*' while
its practical culmination is found in the immolation of women! Part
of a familiar Bengal *bhadralok* syndrome of infusing colonial
abjection with patriarchal dominance, the mass immolation of
women itself comes to signify an ideological victory (in physical
defeat) that is structured around a play of male sexual honour vested
in the possession of women.

Bhil women too are objects of an ethnography which places
them at the far end of this social continuum. Rajput women bond and
form a collectivity typified through rituals of wifely fidelity and
valour. Bhil women, typified through common dress and appearance,

are loosely aggregated and form a collectivity through the perfor-mance of manual labour. Where rajput women are ruled by strong behavioural codes emanating from the sanctity of marriage, bhil women are subject to more flexible, less confining, but also less highly 'evolved' patriarchal arrangements.

> The women are a little less dark and they are good-looking: for clothing they have a piece of cloth that covers their loins and a single breast; *churis* and anklets made of lac decorate their arms and legs. Their marriage ceremony is very simple. On a day fixed the young men and women of a village meet together; the men pick out the girls they like and retire into the woods where they spend a few days; they then return to the village. (p. 73)

The more specialized contrast between tamed nature and untamed nature is displayed in the narrative as a struggle for the love of the hero Tej Singh between Pushpa, the garden flower (the named, individualized embodiment of the wifely fidelity of the rajput 'race'), and the bhil girl, the wild flower (the unnamed type of the enigmatic tribal woman). Both are child-women. Pushpa was about to be affianced at the age of seven to Tej Singh when he disappeared and was believed dead. In this prototypical 'fair' romantic heroine both conjugal love and its corollary, the suffer-ings of 'voluntary' widowhood, are already in place in childhood. She assumes the garb of a widow in order to ward off other suitors; she takes patriarchal values 'innocently' on faith without reason-ing, and as such ratifies them more 'naturally' than an adult figure. The bhil girl is presented as both a type of the 'dark' romantic heroine and of a fey child-woman filled with mystery, wisdom, intuition, and gravity. Her sexual attraction is translated into the sportiveness of the child—playing with flowers, watching clouds and lightning, singing in the moonlight. Her elusive sexuality mystifies and bewilders Tej Singh.

The plot of misunderstanding is initiated by Tej Singh's unthinking promise to the bhil girl which she takes literally. Subsequently, the bhil girl lies, Tej Singh spurns Pushpa, Pushpa suffers silently, the bhil girl moved by her suffering reveals her own 'duplicity' and enables Tej Singh to marry Pushpa. In her letter the bhil girl writes that Pushpa had lost both a ring and a "precious gem", she cannot find the gem of greater value but is returning the ring; she declares that she has wrongly believed in equality, has been mistaken in her belief that she and Pushpa each had the same body, were made from the same clay, and could make the same claims (pp. 177–79). The bhil girl ends up being of service to a more 'cultured' patriarchy but herself remains tantalizingly separate—its pathetic, romantic fringe. Her letter indicates that though she has tried to learn from Pushpa, she has never understood the "precious gem" of rajput patri-archal values and upper-caste conjugality.

The tribal woman is placed in a schema in which the high-caste Hindu woman retains her moral ascendancy, indeed provides the terms for the bhil girl's 'self-recognition'. However, both women are tied into the complex of a sentimental nationalism where female agency comes increasingly to be defined as suffering and self-sacrifice. Excluded from the domestic sphere ("she could not take to domestic duties)", the bhil girl wanders unmarried, the bane of lovers, and is perceived as a restless spirit haunting the neighbour-hood (p. 178). Neither the narrative nor the bhil girl herself can locate the source of her energy. There is no self-naming even in her letter: she refers to herself as a bhil girl.

In the narrative as a whole, the bhils or tribals, though culturally semi-alien, even 'external', are ethnographically descri-bable and politically assimilable into India's so-called organic feudal past as both participants in and guarantors of rajput nobility. Bhils and rajputs remain coeval in time, inheritors of a common antiquity. Yet the bhil girl is patriarchally unassimilable. She is singled out, extracted from her tribe, but newer forms and languages of ownership and ascription have not yet developed. The novel cannot admit to the only too scrutable practices or languages of power and ownership that *did* exist—bhil women were often *paswans* (concubines) of or sexually available to rajput rulers—since they do not synchronize with the narrative's desire to fit rajputs into a *bhadralok* model of monogamous conjugality. The bhil girl belongs neither to bhil, nor rajput, nor even late-nineteenth-century middle-class Bengali men. She has tried but failed to mirror Pushpa and is thereby precluded from the embrace of nineteenth-century upper-caste male reformism. Her wild untutored nature and her sexual attraction retain a certain autonomy even as they invite and await incorporation. For Dutt, strategies of othering and complementary mechanisms of internalization were either not at hand or only falteringly so. It is only in a second move (readily available to Arun Joshi a century later) that the tribal and the woman can be incorporated, can become bearers of a cultural authenticity, and as such, figures of the 'unconscious'.

II

In *The Strange Case of Billy Biswas*, Billy, the son of a supreme court judge, is a student of anthropology in America. He returns to India, teaches at Delhi University, becomes an affluent businessman on the side; restless and disoriented, he dislikes materialist, desensualized, urban middle-class living and is unable to find solace in congregational temple worship. He finally gives up his family and disappears into the hills of Madhya Pradesh, near Chattisgarh, where he lives with Bilasia, fully absorbed into a tribal lifestyle. The tribals are subjects of a changing polity, servile and cunning in relation to bureaucracy, but unchanged, homogeneous, and pristine among themselves. The tribal here, especially the woman, is dark, inscrutable, a kind of repository of unrepressed, orgiastic, magical sexuality, therapeutic powers, and the 'unconscious', and as such a solution for the urban malaise. There are several images of Billy being "possessed", and receding into primal or primitive zones: watching an Oriya tribal dance can bring up an erotic energy which resembles the effects of a hallucinogen. He has a "primitive force" welling inside him. The primitive is at the core of Billy's self as well as one of his conscious obsessions alongside occult phenomena and other extra-rational worlds. Assimilated into tribal myth as a reincarnated king from their lost past, the tribals believe he has brought about the long-prophesied return of their immolated queen as a protective Devimata. Revitalized, Billy practises 'magical' cures, intercedes on behalf of tribals with the state government, and helps them more than the officiating collector.

Billy's story is narrated by his best friend whom he met in America. This friend later joined the IAS and is posted as a collector in the same district of Madhya Pradesh. The collector does his best to protect Billy from being found by Billy's father and wife and returned to the urban world. He doesn't manage to protect him adequately: there is a noticeable ambiguity here. In the end he becomes the cause for Billy's discovery—a discovery that leads to the accidental death of Billy at the hands of the state machinery which has embarked on a 'hunt' for him.

Billy is in a sense the surrogate self of the narrator, who in turn represents the conscience of the state. The 'tragedy' the narrative proposes rests on the failure of the middle class to recognize the value of an organic and unspoilt tribal culture and the failure of the state to preserve or guard this enclave of salvation. Tribal culture here represents the potential wealth of the state, the sole guarantee of its cultural vitality. The tribal is seen to demand a patronage that the state is unable to give. In this sense the understanding of the middle class and of the state remains, by implication, inferior to that of an anthropology learnt in America.

The state, however, in the shape of one of its functionaries—the narrator—does have a conscience; it recognizes the task that its own bureaucratic and law-enforcing structures do not permit it to undertake. Significantly, the task is not one of Nehruvian social reconstruction: the promised equal access to a democracy which would both protect and bring the tribal into the process of nation-building. Rather, it is the preservation of what appears to be a kind of cultural capital or reified heritage wherein the woman and the tribal, separately as well as together, become the 'unconscious' of the nation, the essence of a collectivity. This idea of the unconscious emerges in several ways in the text: it is definitionally precarious, unstable and dimly understood; it is apparently located in an earlier mode of production (blurring the location of tribal groups in a wider economy), threatened by capitalism, but also presented as the only mode of resisting capitalism or of filling its hollowness. It is also definitionally 'primitive', located in opposition to forms of class or caste stratification, and this paradoxically assists in homogenizing a cross-class notion of the unconscious. The 'primitive' which inhabits the tribals and Billy is a sign of the primeval or pre-civilizational 'spirit', the undefinable secret which is older than, prior to, Hinduism—its 'unconscious'. Finally it rests on a conflation of the tribal with the female or the woman. The magnetism of the woman is indistinguishable from the magnetism of drums and jungle; her sexuality, as wild and primeval as the surrounding forests, is the 'essence' of 'primitive' force; if waking and dreaming belong to a single continuum for tribals, then

Bilasia embodies the eroticism of the dream. The enigmatic sexual vitality of the woman composes in turn the essence or core of the tribal. The sexual abandon of the tribal woman claims neither the past nor the future of middle-class morality. Her sexuality occupies a substantive, undeferred present, and helps to make the fixed primordial time of her tribal identity coeval with the present. Her independence and assertive sexuality—she is said to have left her husband and to have had many lovers—is repeatedly contrasted with the nagging, effete middle-class women that the narrator and Billy have married. In Billy's boyhood tribal women were forbidden women. He has long been troubled by desire for what appear to be the many faces of the dislocated tribal woman:

> A strange woman keeps crossing my dreams. I have seen her on the streets of Delhi, nursing a child in the shade of a tree or hauling stone for a rich man's house. I have seen her buying bangles at a fair. I have seen her shadow at a tribal dance, and I have seen her, pensive and inviolable, her clothes clinging to her wet body, beside a tank in Benares. And once I saw her, loading a freight train with sulphur on a siding in one of our eastern ports.[3]

It is through the exclusion of the tribal woman from the middle-class domestic sphere, even as she maintains it through her manual labour, that she can become the object/unconscious of a middle-class patriarchy. In an evenhandedly patriarchal pincer movement, middle-class women, assiduously weaned from fairs and other public sites since the nineteenth century, are now shown to be denatured by this very division between public and private (a division that has in fact been facilitated by the domestic and wage labour of tribal women), while tribal women are eroticized by the same division and by their labour in public spaces. The constitution of the public and private rests on economic and class differentiation—the narrative transforms these into a discursive separation *between* women, with authenticity and sensuality being vested in labouring women, and sterility and deculturation becoming the attributes of middle-class women. This particular construction of sexual desire, as that which is contained or repressed by middle-class morality, in fact presumes a desire that is always there ready to be un-/dis-covered as a form of primal energy, thus facilitating a conflation of sexuality and the 'unconscious'. Further, Billy's relationship with Bilasia carries traces of popular colonial narratives of interracial romance: middle-class Indian women double for prim European women, while tribal women become a synecdoche for the attractive but 'ineligible' oriental women who were objects of white male desire. An orientalist binary is thus brought into relation with class stratification in post-independence India, a relation that not only reverses the nineteenth-century male reformist privileging of upper-caste women and patriarchal models, but also transforms the dynamic of class stratification into a static cultural formation made up of some 'deep' and some 'superficial' layers.

The narrative implicitly concedes that this 'unconscious', as a determinant of Indianness and its essential character, is also incorporated into the market economy; it is eminently saleable here and abroad. The fact of Billy being trained in America is by no means fortuitous. In this sense a form of material underdevelopment becomes a necessary correlate of spiritual overdevelopment, masquerades as the affirmation of 'ethnicity'. An exportable product, this is bought at the high price of repressing the differential incorporation of tribal groups into regional caste-stratified agrarian formations and upper-caste patriarchies, into wider, changing economic and political structures, and also by obliterating all the histories of migration and marginalization, and various forms of economic, political, and cultural struggle undertaken by tribal groups in which a range of self-definitions—class-based, Hindu, Christian or pre-Hindu—have emerged. Perhaps the middle-class anthropologist turned subject and saviour is designed to assuage the anxiety over the conversion of tribes to Christianity (which is alleged to have risen dramatically in Madhya Pradesh between 1960 and 1980) by turning the tribal into the unconscious of a Hinduism—as that which enhances the market value of Hinduism precisely because it is not assimilated into it and can be represented as recalcitrant and incorruptible. Like Dutt, Joshi too searches for 'unpolluted' aspects of culture, but re-locates the sources of authenticity. If nationalist definitions privileged the 'high' Hindu and the Aryan, here the 'pre-Hindu' is privileged and synchronizes with a more anthropological definition of culture.

The narrative constructs an interpretative grid through the

double thematic of primitivism inscribed in the by now established compendium of settler and expropriative colonialism and of colonial anthropology. The former provides tropes, fantasies, myths, and paradigms—either as breakdown or as rejuvenation—of the European who goes native, the natives who invite merchants and colonization, the deification of the colonial explorer or entrepreneur, the discoverer who travels back into the primordial history of 'man' and becomes himself an enigmatic oracle and a myth, the journey to unintelligible places by a friend/narrator to recover his voice, the primitive as projection and self-recovery, the joint investigation of the 'civilized' self and the 'primitive' in which the primitive annihilates the civilized self in epiphanic self-discovery, the body of the woman as giving access to the spiritual or cognitive wholeness of a primitive collectivity, and tropical landscape as the text of a prehistoric religion. The latter—colonial anthropology especially in its vulgarized forms—provides the figure of the ethnographer as intimate observer, as agent for documentation and destruction of the primitive, the narrative devices of initiation, autobiography, and allegory, as well as a pseudo-anthropological expectation of the unlettered, singing, dancing, drinking, transcultural, transhistorical, ontologically distinct tribal, a sign of the free play of sexual desire.[4]

Together they form a grid through which the relation of the middle class to 'tribes' and of state to civil society will be displayed. The displacement of colonial discursivities and power relations into a contemporary class relation is one of the coordinates of this distancing and 'internalization'—a peculiar mixture of subjection (to the processes of 'deculturation') and of sovereignty (over these very processes). Ironically, the narrative's attempt to project the tribal qua unconscious as a rejuvenating fullness results in an evacuation, its intended significances are drained by the pressure of such a concatenation of stereotypes.

III

How was this version of the unconscious enabled? The politics of its 'conferral' on tribals and women are evident. From where does its glibness and ease arise? Which other accumulated histories and designating discourses converge into it, or more accurately, are flattened by it? Finally, what are the methodological propositions that could emerge from such a text? The similarity of some of the assumptions and methods of this text with a whole range of more or less sophisticated, more or less popular, production in contemporary Indian theatre, cinema, and the arts is, I think, apparent. I cannot offer a systematic analysis, but will very briefly suggest the range and complexity of related, converging histories and discourses. And, notationally, indicate within these a process of garnering 'depth' which may in turn entail qualitatively different kinds of foregrounding and flattening.

One strand is composed by powerful narratives of salvation which have invested heavily in inversions of social subalternity, whether of the low-caste, the woman, or the peasant. These narratives, which have a recurring and changing history stretching back to some puranic and Vaishnav texts,[5] infused disadvantaged 'others' with regenerative value while simultaneously designating normative patterns of social and patriarchal obedience. In fact it was the stake in social stratification that produced an exorbitation of subalternity. Later reaggregated in several nationalist ideological ensembles and intersected by variants of both romantic aesthetics and colonial othering, they found a new legitimacy and new forms of generalization, as for instance in Gandhi's thought. This strand continues to find sustenance in various contemporary conservative, patriarchal, and communal ideologies. Still underwritten by a pivotal, normative contrast between women who accept forms of patriarchal authority and those who appear not to do so, it remains unable to establish the erotic in legitimate social locales.

A second strand, that of nostalgia for either past or 'other' organic agrarian societies, was a product of postindustrial romanticism in Europe from the eighteenth century and involved in an ideological range of representations that had included protest and critique.[6] It is this nostalgia which we now see in a new formation, interlocked with the sectoral development of capital in India, where certain enclaves can be 'opened' while others are to be 'protected', that is, differently exploited. A subtheme in the orientalist tendencies within this formation was of course the endowment of blacks, tribals, and orientals with a surplus of imagination or sensuality, and a corollary sterilizing of the 'west' and European women as overly rational.

A third strand is made up of the more indigenist of the multiple faces of nationalism, with its long and involuted histories in pre and post-independence India. These, among other things, not only entailed an orientalizing and 'anthropologizing' of the tribal, of uneasy creations of 'organic' communities to resist (and oblige) the colonial regime, but also produced narrow, class-based definitions of gender which either excluded lower-caste, peasant, and tribal women or found new ways of incorporating them. In fact, the prolonged coexistence of the tribal with the agricultural mode of production marked by assimilative, appropriative, and other ideological manoeuvres by state formations and elite groups (traders, landowners, brahmin 'pioneers') had produced definitions of the tribal that could now find nodes of intersection with colonial and capitalist definitions of the primitive. At another level, cultural indigenism produced the difficulty of distinguishing between the evocation of energizing myths and the evocation of enabling history: a living contradiction we often see in caricature today.

A fourth strand (which entered into active relation with the previous two) belongs to European histories of designating the unconscious. The idea of the unconscious, as it developed, was knotted into notions of 'femaleness', race, and class in ways that require an enormous amount of disentangling, especially since it was related to the fashioning and expansion of notions of character, depth, subjectivity, alterity, and epistemological difficulty. For instance, there was a curious and paradoxical movement in the psychologization of character. It moved away from 'type' in some narrative genres such as the novel, while at the same time other genres and discourses such as travelogues constructed typologies of non-European societies according to a series of abstractable traits: these in some sense divided the inhabitants of the known world once again into type and character, but this time along lines of geographical territory, racial division, and political power.

In the prolonged process of designating and enlarging the domain of the unconscious—I refer largely to England, partly to America—notions of 'depth' were wrested from the contentious and threatening spaces of class, gender, and colonial inequality. These ranged from depth of character to the depth that accrues to a community, and were often sites for the production of epistemological indeterminacy. For instance, in a number of nineteenth-century texts female subjectivity was represented as depth and sensitivity, and unlike male activity in the outer world. This particular idea of 'depth' and subjectivity only became possible through a specific development of capital, the sexual division of labour, and the ideological demarcation of the private 'female' realm as distinct from the public. It is these that enabled a notion of subjectivity in which 'femaleness' became a purer repository of cultural value and was invested with a higher subjectivity than 'maleness'. Henry James's narratives are a good example of how this notion of subjectivity qua femaleness was universalized as something both men and women could aspire to, and how it assisted in producing a residue of undecipherability or generating a resistance to interpretation within the text.[7] There are many other examples in modernist fiction in which alterity, cognitive difficulty, or outright unknowability are located in and extrapolated from those contradictory sites where class, gender, racial, and cultural differences were being formed and then attached to the interiority of a 'high' bourgeois subject. By the beginning of the twentieth century many of these accumulated notions were being systematized and the indeterminacy of the unconscious was opened to various forms of determination, collectivization, scientific enquiry, and social control, as for example in the writings of Freud and Jung.

Finally, alongside notions of depth and epistemological uncertainty, another significant facet of the history of designating the unconscious in Europe clustered around the histories of primitivization. Some of these histories worked through unilateral ascriptive procedures that could encompass non-European peoples, European women, and lower classes, while others settled into wider collaborative configurations. In the late nineteenth century the primitivization of certain categories became quite strident: most notably of female sexuality and of women who, along with 'nonwestern' societies, were placed on the scale of evolution. Popular versions of the evolution debate followed on Herbert Spencer.[8] An article in *Saturday Times* claimed that men and women in primitive societies had an equivalent size of brain and women were able to undertake hard physical labour; as society or civilization developed the size of brain began to vary, and western women who were now removed from physical labour were seen to have a smaller brain size—any rational and intellectual labour on their part now would actually upset their roles as mothers. In effect, the price western women would have to pay for the west's present place in the ladder of evolution and achieved state of civilization (read imperial power and racial purity) was to consent to be subordinate.[9] Here primitivization did double work—at home and in colonies—producing a 'fit' between the local regulation of female sexuality with racism abroad. Havelock Ellis's primitivization of female sexuality was not only equally implicated in colonial othering, but also condensed, internalized, and displaced its history. An inventor of 'scientific' sexology, Ellis was an ardent proponent of eugenics for the "regeneration of the race" and the "evolution of a super-mankind".[10] In his *Studies in the Psychology of Sex* (1898) the female is sexually primitive, and so liable to disrupt the civilization she otherwise ensures. The prostitute, the primitive, and the madwoman are a part of every middle-class woman as forms of sexuality which she must sublimate. 'Woman' is the name of a desire that is deeper, more primitive, more elusive, and more complex than man, while to be female is to contain within the self uncivilized or degenerate desires perpetually in need of control. For Ellis the woman remains a savage who is never fully civilized.[11]

The scientization of the primitive was carried out side by side with its aestheticization through a series of 'revaluations'. The 'primitive' ranged from the external and measurable to its converse—the unwritten, internal, and immeasurable. The early primitive stages of evolution were thought to be manifested physically in other races and could be measured: as by the anthropometric measurement of skulls. In India in the 1870s, caste, race, and tribe were used almost interchangeably, while aborigines did not yet have a fixed definition. In this long history of shifting classifications, 'tribes' were sought to be defined along an Aryan, a Hindu, and an evolutionary scale, and either proved to be entirely distinct as pre-Aryan, pre-Hindu, and primitive, or later, via anthropometry, as mutually assimilated into a mixed race in which there was no longer either a pure Aryan or a pure pre-Aryan. The cultural (and ideological) extensions of the latter thesis could in turn cast the primitive as the deepest substratum of Hinduism. The 'documentary' methods of social science thus lent themselves both to 'realistic' stereotyping and to mystical, symbolic, non-rational enterprises. The evolutionary myths that underwrote imperialism were replaced in later anthropology by an upward evaluation of the primitive (a development of which romanticism was a precursor) through the 'discovery' of symbolic systems and a 'scientific' primitivism where tribals were now instinctual, unrepressed, spontaneous, superior to the modern, and virtually paradisal.[12] Modernist art criticism too began to overlap with anthropology, in what James Clifford has called a "controlled migration" between two institutionalized domains, and generated an aesthetic revaluation of primitive art as a product of nature: that is, as unmediated and unreflective.[13]

The internalizations of the primitive turned measurable *surfaces* into immeasurable depth or an 'unconscious'; they derived from *both* the devalued and the overvalued primitive, imbricated evidential and metaphoric modes, and occurred in varied combinatoires. The 'primitive' could either be equated with or contained in the unconscious. A D.H. Lawrence could go to Mexico and discover there both the 'primitive' interiority of the 'western' consciousness and the elixir which could regenerate the 'west'. For him the recovery of wholeness and spontaneity came through contact with the primitive man within the self: a combination of the "old blood" of "vertebrate consciousness" of aboriginal civilization with the "white man's present mental–spiritual consciousness".[14] The terms of this combination were determined by the fact that for him the exotic east was simultaneously the object of a recurring, racist disgust.[15] For others, travel was not necessary to encounter the primitive. Since it also lay at the base of 'civilized' minds, it could be discovered by introspection, especially by the artist.[16]

A series of ideological ensembles are visible in a wide range of nineteenth and early twentieth-century narrative and pictorial invocations where the primitive becomes homologous with the unconscious as a synchronic and *spatially available* anteriority, interiority or depth, while the unconscious qua the 'primitive' or the 'irrational' is derived from imperialized formations but differently composed. This is a fascinating area of competing and overlapping modernisms. The use of the unconscious in each case and the designation of the unconscious itself, was not the same; what the surrealists assemble through their close connection with ethnography and its institutions is a professed interruption of various notions of order that was quite different from the conservative Anglo–American modernists. For Ezra Pound the expansion of the domain of irrationality via a miscellany of incompatible fragments, which included Chinese ideograms, became a correlate of the expansion of the idea of Order that in turn became the correlate of a fascist political position. W.B. Yeats, however, combined a Jungian collective unconscious with notions of the irrational, drawn partly from the hybrid occultism of Madame Blavatsky, the Theosophical Society, and the spiritualism of Shri Purohit Swami, to forge a fascist relation between elite and masses. Indeed some of the politically conservative Anglo–Americn modernists could be partially located in a transnational ideological configuration made up of different appropriations of Spengler that were concurrently reappropriated.[17] His thesis of history as cyclic in the *Decline of the West* (1918) on the one hand filtered into tropes of European decay and made possible a series of assimilations of non-European religio-mysticisms from metropolitan locations,[18] and on the other hand, opened the possibility of relegating modernity and 'western materialism' in the name of the indigenist nationalisms emerging within imperialized formations. Spengler's mechanistic conception of the cyclic birth, ascendance and decay of civilizations, inexorably subject to predetermined laws, made short shrift of causality. It could, however, be filled with an anticolonial and anti'western' content to assert a (compensatory) cultural superiority.[19] W.B.Yeats, almost uniquely, spoke from both positions.

The Conradian primitive also reversed linear evolutionary ascent; however, honed in Africa, it centred on fears of the white man's regression or relapse into savagery, of crossing the 'frontiers' of consciousness. As such, it assisted various modernist transformations of colonized territories into internalized mental landscapes or psychoanalytic spaces as well as informed popular narrativizations of the 'return of the repressed'. In India, significantly, the Conradian trope of regression was often displaced on Eurasians who did not fit into models of racial purity.[20] Unlike Africa (extrapolated predominantly from its tribal formations), repeatedly inscribed as intractable, incomprehensible depth, inherently resistant to rational explanation, in India (extrapolated more from its stratified agricultural formations than its relatively small tribal pockets),[21] the primitive had no fixed but only *shifting* locations: it ranged from high Hindu temple ritual to the tribal to the timeless and pre-Hindu (read unreformable) of E.M. Forster's caves in *A Passage to India*. Indeed even members of the middle-class intelligentsia could become the interlocutors of the lost self of both modern Indians and the modern 'west' through Theosophy or related types of religiosity. Their, in this case collaborative, constitutive procedures overlapped with many of the characteristic devices of primitivization: scientization, exoticization, the threat of extinction, the exorbitation of antiquity, the sacred, and secret knowledge.[22] The end product was an ancient India that could, in a novel twist, be recuperated as the hypercivilized unconscious of a modernity marked simultaneously by barbarism and material progress.

The Theosophical Society (which was founded in America), and Madame Blavatsky in particular, were attempting a theoretical syncretism involving Hinduism and other religions, in order to develop 'spiritual powers' and produce a more saleable salvation narrative for the 'west'.[23] The projects they undertook are quite interesting. For instance, it appears that Madame Blavatsky felt that if she presented the full cycle of rebirth in Europe this would be met with great impatience, so she reduced it to seven rebirths before salvation. This was a popularizing syncretic tendency which is significant for other reasons as well. It often provided models for or assisted in the internationalization of Hinduism later, by Vivekananda and other swamis, as a religion which could undertake to teach an ethically inferior world. Blavatsky's project also assisted the tendency to scientize 'tradition', 'ancient knowledge', and the supernatural in India by joining a form of 'scientific' evolutionary distancing to romantic forms of idealizing of the 'east'. If the scientization of 'race' through discourses of evolution and biology in nineteenth-century England was mediated by colonial relations of inferiorizing subject populations, the Blavatskian scientization of the ensemble of tradition, ancient knowledge, and the supernatural was mediated by discourses of aggrandization; given to images of contemporary decline, it rested on a reversal of evolutionary discourse and carried an anti'western' address. In a 'quest' that builds on but rechoreographs the two earlier idealizing phases of British Orientalism and German Indology,[24] she discovers an India where, charlatans aside, customs and superstitions are founded on a true knowledge of scientific principles unavailable to the west; an India which is now a pygmy but whose immeasurable, mysterious past can be recovered from all manner of fragments and extant practices (including mesmerism); an India which is irrevocably a sacred realm of hidden arcana. In an emphatic and literal conflation of the sacred and secrecy, India is cast as a scientific–spiritual enigma, and her narrative is dominated by a double search. One object is a secret master manuscript and sundry other "secret MSS" (held by Jains, rajput thakurs, and native princes) unseen by any western eye, indeed guarded jealously from western eyes by "fanatic" Hindus, the discovery of which would among other things validate Theosophy. The other object is authentic *rajyogis*, the few and select hereditary keepers of the secret of the proper training of spiritual powers, which comprises the very basis of Theosophical faith. A probable candidate is an educated rajput. This is not surprising since Blavatsky considers rajputs to be the oldest inhabitants of India, the carriers of its most ancient memory—a potentially discoverable 'unconscious'.[25] For her travelling to India is a travelling back into prehistoric time.

Blavatsky partakes of, perhaps even inaugurates, what was to become an influential transnational ideological configuration in the nineteenth and early twentieth centuries. Its key features were the construction of an arid materialist and rational 'west', an overcompensatory and preemptive scientization of ancient non-European belief systems and pseudoscientific methods for recovering the essence of such systems. Its major achievement was a fundamentally modern appropriation of the 'premodern'—that borrowed its aura from an antimaterialism purporting to be antiwestern even as it took its methods and legitimating devices from science—and the creation of a nonconflictual compartmentalized relation, even alignment, of precapitalist belief systems with modernity–rationality. The relation with science was both circular and analogical. On the one hand scientific discoveries confirmed Theosophy, the existence of the pineal gland bore out the theory of the 'Third Eye', and on the other the occultist already had the knowledge for which scientists such as Newton were only groping. Analogies were made between matter and gravity and those forces of nature which were actions of "Invisible Intelligences", between the atom and the "Elastic and Indivisible Soul", between evolution and the "Successive Races of Man".[26] And novel rapprochements were made with theories of evolution.[27]

Theosophy relaxed the tension between scientific modernity and precapitalist belief systems, thus facilitating what were in fact synthesizing or eclectic positions but which represented themselves as utterly authentic. The eclecticism of Theosophy permitted dabbling in occultisms and arcana, in reincarnation as well as eugenics, and from the late nineteenth century it entered as much into the refashioning of Hinduism as of Celtic nationalism, as much into Swami Dayanand as into W.B.Yeats.[28] This configuration proved to be a natural ally of the Spenglerianisms that followed later; it too could be anticolonial but not antiimperialist. Many of Blavatsky's ideas were not only repeated by Annie Besant but vigorously entered into the commonsense of the Hindu tendencies in Indian nationalism.[29] Besant best represents a type of interpellation in which theories for regenerating Europe interlock with the patriarchal desires and nationalist aspirations of Indian men, fuelling an antireformism alongside an anticolonialism. As such it could and did feed Hindu chauvinism of the modern communal variety.[30] Blavatsky and her followers simply presented Hinduism, the *vedanta* and even *maya* (the concept of the world as an illusion) as predecessors of modern science which had none of the drawbacks of the materialist west.[31] Her 'native informants', whom she describes as western educated Hindus, now better able to appreciate the grandeur of their ancient civilization, claim that Manu anticipated Darwin, or combining Darwin, philology, and the *Ramayana*, claim that Europeans descended from Hanuman.[32] Blavatsky derided the modernized, liberal, materialist Hindu, chastised colonial rule which had encouraged false religions among the masses; she believed, however, that for some select Hindus, western education could function as a window to the past. The naturalization of a combination of a high level of modern educational competence and/or a privileged class position with a patronage of 'non-rational' or supra-rational aspects of Indian 'culture' or 'tradition' in the nineteenth century is a process that finds a culmination in Blavatsky. She is one of the early examples of that pact between selected 'western' and 'Indian' individuals—the former will come in search of a soul and the latter will be ready to provide one.

IV

Both the unilateral and the collaborative denials of modernity to non-Europeans thus threw up versions of the unconscious: it was primarily an ideological denial and could usually accommodate, selectively, the material benefits of modernity.

There are many other histories that interconnect with the shifting designations and locales of the unconscious qua the primitive. Among those that I have not even touched are the history of aesthetic forms; 'tribes' as a colonial and contemporary administrative category in India (usually as less evolved, homogeneous, geographically and culturally isolated animists) alongside the displacement and often economically exploitative integration of tribals into administrative and economic structures and their own struggles against colonial rule; the continuities and changes in the categorization of tribals after independence; the different stages in anthropology and its relation to precapitalist social formations;[33] and the development of a 'countercultural orientalism' in the 1960s. Nor have I detailed the transpositions of the global histories of the primitive in India or the specific relation of Dutt and Joshi's narratives to the strands I have sketched.

At any rate what does an argument of this sort propose? At issue here are several different kinds of things: for me it is the attempt to write a certain kind of cultural history, for others it would be art practice itself. These are different preoccupations and it is not easy to address them together. The one thing which seems indisputable to me is that human consciousness is carved and recarved in a variety of ways, and at this moment notions of the irrational, the extra-rational and the unconscious, are being produced through a complex articulation of different histories.

In the act of designating the unconscious, ascriptions or representations may simply come to stand in for the thing-in-itself. In this sense, the unconscious does not seem to be prior to its ascription or representation in any form of cultural production, but to be constantly produced and reshaped: it is not an inalienable fixed resource but open to various instrumentalities and various anxieties, in the very shaping of it. It is as much created by different social histories, by ascriptive and representational modes, as it is believed to create them. And, even more important, from my point of view, it is often created on behalf of, as well as by, different notions of the aesthetic, of the imagination, of gender, different aspirations for social order and different analyses of social disorder. The act of designating the unconscious enters into relations with the real which are far from innocent and fraught with existing power relations.

One of the most interesting coalitions at the moment in the notion of the unconscious is between indeterminacy and determination. The unconscious is both that which is inscrutable, inevitably ambiguous, as well as that which is open to scientific analysis: it is both that which is random, in its combinations, as well as entirely structured. And it is therefore something which is open to both a reading of being infinitely resourceful and inexhaustible, as well as to various forms of control. And I think it is this kind of reading which shows that it is not a notion necessarily opposed to science but may be part of a paradigm of rationality that has its own 'other'.

How then should we deal with this idea which impresses itself upon us in different ways? Given some of the histories indicated, I think what may be at issue is a certain rethinking of the relations between gender, class, 'national' or 'cultural' differences, and capitalism. Perhaps we might begin by reflecting on two things. First, that the social, historical, and economic processes which produce 'depth' of the sort which is then accrued to the ideas of the unconscious, are also the same processes which at a later stage empty it, or threaten to empty it: certain developments of capitalism which accomplish the 'emptying' are also the same operations that produce the centrality of the notion of the unconscious—the two are not separate. It seems to me that this reflection has to *precede* any designation of the unconscious as a subversive or restorative proposition. Second, it would be useful to set out to understand how—in precapitalist, colonial or contemporary cultural products—certain kinds of 'depth' and 'surface' emerge in relation to character, which notions of the self are produced that posit different kinds of interiority and exteriority, what the relation of these notions of the self is to ideas of tradition and to social struggles, and how they are shaped at different times. I have not done so here but I would be most interested in trying to elicit the relationship between particular ideas of tradition, posited as extra-individual or as different forms of collectivity, and different notions of the self: to see whether the carving of the interior and exterior is part of a related, interconnected series, and if so, what kinds of uniformities and contradictions this produces. It may eventually be possible to open the idea of the unconscious to different forms of interrogation.

This talk emerged as an unscheduled response to the discussion at a workshop on Critique of Contemporary Culture in Kasauli in 1988, and was presented at the Centre for Studies in Social Sciences, Calcutta, and the Nehru Memorial Museum and Library in 1990. It was subsequently published in the *Journal of Arts & Ideas*, 20–21 (March 1991).

Relating histories

The central concern of this essay is the close articulation of class formation with self-designations of the early nineteenth-century colonial state and with emerging cultural categories—specifically as these categories are constituted in descriptions of gender, definitions of literature, and the situating of literary genres in India and England. This essay begins what I hope will be a series of essays sketching the movement of a complex and shifting ideological configuration centred on reform and altruism; a product of colonial rule, shot with diverse intentionalities, it interlocked with class formation, sexual divisions of labour, the political economy, and with chosen and evolving modes of governance. This ideological configuration was produced through and entered into negotiations of both confluent and contradictory material class interests including patriarchal arrangements. The intricate patterns of intersecting exploitation relations typical of a new middle class, which tends to occupy a position that is at once exploitative along one dimension of these but itself exploited on another,[1] were overdetermined by the specificities of colonization in India. Consequently, some of the characteristic relations of an emergent middle class to colonialism—antagonistic alliances, relayed subalternity and relayed antagonism, a compound of power and subjection, as well as a sectorization of knowledge—are encapsulated within this configuration.

My working hypothesis is that the colonial states and cultural formations established under the aegis of imperialism have produced specifiable ideological configurations which loop and spread across 'national' boundaries. Their 'transnational' character is itself a sign of the changes that occur with capitalism in the relations between class and ideologies and between social reality and discourses. More concretely, such ideological configurations emerge from the material conditions of colonial expansion and consolidation, as well as from the differences, contradictions, and affiliations between the colonial rulers and indigenous elites; the ideologies thus produced in turn function as a set of pressures and enter into determining the context for indigenist, anticolonial and nationalist intentions, positions, and activities. In our case the coincidences and contradictions of the consolidating British middle classes and emerging Indian middle classes were sharpened by British nationalism on the one hand and nascent Indian cultural nationalism on the other—the cultural coordinates and evaluative positions of both, whether complementary or antagonistic, were produced through a wide-ranging, interactive, and often related process. The transnational ideological configuration is assembled neither by a single hegemonic operation nor by the homologous operations of a single dominant ideology, but through the crisscrossing articulation and reproduction of dominant and emerging ideologies, in different ways and from different places in the social formation. It seems to me that this ideological configuration, itself formed in different domains and contexts, was in turn active in different ways in different contexts—but always in conjunction with other determining structures, situations, and agencies. Secondly, and nearly simultaneously, it became a cultural grid through which social practices were interpreted and notions of selfhood or culture were formed. Its substantial, and at times hegemonic, power lay not in heterogeneity but in flexibility, in the fact that its sedimented intentionalities could be reaccentuated or remodelled from many different places.

Though outlining an ideological configuration runs the risk of homogenization, I feel it may help to elicit both more *relational* and more *specific*, materially grounded accounts of different cultural projects in India and in England. 'Literature', for instance, came to be reconstituted as an object by the processes of political colonization, the formation of class and the re-formation of patriarchies in the first half of the nineteenth century; it also had an active, constitutive agency in these histories. A study of these processes in turn involves a study of the formation of 'literature' which, inscribed with intentionalities and contradictions, formed a part of as well as mediated social relations. In this essay, confined to a specific intersection between literature, literacy, and gender description in early nineteenth-century Calcutta and England, I have attempted to suggest or elicit a series of relationships between mobile cultural categories—Sanskrit, English, Hindu women, English women—as they emerged in a mesh of perception and representation filtered through institutional or other practices. However, the essay does not presume to exhaust the meanings of either these categories or the complex, constitutive social relations which they condense, and further, does not elaborate their extensive precolonial history or their location within precapitalist class relations. Even within these limits I am presenting a notational, not a detailed, analysis.

A dialectic of reform and preservation: Sanskrit and Hindu women

I   The large-scale negotiation of precolonial and precapitalist cultural practices and ideologies, first by the East India Company and later (with the steady reduction of Company monopoly and increased parliamentary control by the 1830s) in its transformed character as the early colonial state, appears to be a correlate of the political economy. The political economy of colonialism to some extent overlaid, derived, and structured its modalities around existing mercantile practices in India.[2] More significantly, merchant capital, preoccupied with extracting surplus with the help of military conquest and appropriate political alliances, did not set out to dissolve precapitalist forms in their entirety. This, as Marx has shown, was consistent with its character. Though itself formed under the aegis of a rapidly industrializing society in the late eighteenth and early nineteenth centuries, the colonial state undertook only a sectoral reorganization of the Indian economy. Many social relations were in part maintained or recreated as 'feudal' ones for reasons which were not only economic but also political and ideological.[3]

Until at least the 1830s the colonial enterprise in India

entailed several disjunctions. The most relevant are the following. First, at a time when laissez-faire dominated in England and informed British trade relations creating and maintaining favourable conditions for capitalism, India became the subject of a formal, bureaucratic apparatus of rule involving a restructuring of institutions to which laissez-faire did not apply.[4] In some sense the nature of Company rule and the colonial state coincided with the shape of colonial political economy. The mercantile entrepreneurial bourgeoisie of the East India Company and the colonial state did not, following the logic of metropolitan capital, replicate the transformation from mercantile to industrial capital in the colony. Instead, here (under the auspices of both Company rule and the colonial state) they entered into formal protective and extractive relationships and various political alliances with local feudal groups (for example, the high-caste, landowning rural gentry in Bengal or the princely regimes) in order to harness their class interests to those of the colonial state. While protecting the exploitative relationship of these groups to direct producers, the colonial state both used and transformed local class relations (for example, through the creation of a new gentry). In late eighteenth and early nineteenth-century England the discrepancy between the theoretical powers and the real powers of the monarchy was widening, and the substantive power of the monarchy was being steadily reduced by parliament.[5] However, in India, constrained in part by indigenous class structures, the colonial state undertook to preserve *selectively* the order of caste, hierarchy, and custom[6] and sought its own legitimacy in the circumscription of bourgeois modes of authority.

The second disjunction may be located in the history of British agrarian capitalism in the eighteenth century. This is a history of complex interaction and alliance between rich landed interests and industry and commerce, often making it difficult to make sharp distinctions between the landowning and the industrial classes. The predominant landowning class was politically an aristocracy in eighteenth-century England, but one that presided over the social relations of agrarian capitalism. The business classes, at their apex, were successively assimilated into the political power and social patterns of the gentry and the aristocracy wherein the acquisition of land assigned the perquisites of a social class. This process, together with the restriction of suffrage and the joint front formed by landowners and the bourgeoisie against the proletariat, ensured the social and cultural dominance of the gentry and the aristocracy, virtually unchallenged till the 1830s, throughout the nineteenth century.[7] There is thus a disjunction within the history of British agrarian capitalism between the economy and the attendant gentrified or aristocratic political methods and cultural assumptions; these were often shown to be legitimized by 'tradition', prompting a continuous negotiation of paternal values and culturally dominant aristocratic forms by an economically mobile bourgeoisie.[8] Further, the colonial ascendancy and subsequent external dependancy which accompanied the crystallization of Britain's internal social forms and class order pushed towards the retention of social hierarchy, patrician political structures, and conservative notions of stability, eventually shaping the trajectory of its industrial revolution.[9]

The third set of disjunctions which the colonial enterprise set out to manage was between direct and indirect rule in India, as well as between two rather different but simultaneous historical moments and pressures represented by the British state and the colonial state—where converging material interests often produced divergent modes of legitimization. These sharpened the contradiction between liberal ideology at home, its corollary civilizing mission, and the semblance of liberal polity in the areas under direct rule on the one hand, and on the other the image of 'ultimate' autocratic sovereignty presented as self-legitimizing device to the princely states. While both the Company and later the colonial state drew partly on indigenous structures of authority, the dominant carriers of laissez-faire ideology seem to have been the private commercial interests in India; all three, however, argued on behalf of the English 'nation'.

The negotiation of 'feudal' modes of landowning and upper-caste groups by British officials was itself problematic: it involved political calculation, maximization of revenue or profit, strategy, simulation, as well as internalization and ideological preference. An ideological preference for the values of a 'patrimonial system' (for hierarchy alongside contract) and the groups which represented it, evident in several administrators, was connected with the martial–mercantile character of colonial rule, the hegemony of aristocratic values combined with obsessive status consciousness at home, and the growing idealization of English landowning classes as part of a pastoral nostalgia exacerbated by the industrial revolution.[10] It may also have been connected to the residual but resilient precapitalist relations of production in eighteenth and early nineteenth-century England.[11] All of these combined to produce the attraction to 'martial', aristocratic, landowning, and non-commercial groups in India. Such 'paternalistic' preference was of course deeply implicated in corollary patriarchal values and often took the shape of support for the patriarchal practices of those groups whose class interests the colonial state had chosen to support. There is an open or submerged recognition in many colonial accounts of the articulation of gender roles, domestic ideologies, and family structure with economic organization and the political needs of the state (which gradually came to include education). In most accounts directed at governing India, descriptions of women function as an abbreviated mode for situating patriarchies (though not named as such) as an integral part of social structures.

British social history and the structural links of the colonial state with the indigenous ruling groups thus often produced, though by no means evenly or uniformly, ideological confluences, while the newly created Indian middle class, because of the social and economic processes as well as blockages which were a part of its formation, had its own internal compulsions to negotiate or accommodate precolonial, precapitalist practices and ideologies. This class, heterogeneous in caste origin, consisted of a new landed gentry which replaced the old aristocracy of Bengal as well as of a merchant community which invested wealth, acquired through moneylending or subordinate commercial partnerships with Europeans, in zamindari purchases and landholdings. Many of the new zamindars who in turn undertook commercial enterprises with European merchants also represented dual interests. Both groups were beneficiaries of the partition of old estates and the new proprietary under-tenures of the Permanent Settlement. Since most purchasers of under-tenures were urban, and these were the decades of deindustrialization, there was a tendency to absentee landlordism, turning much of Bengal's landed gentry into a class of rentiers rather than agricultural entrepreneurs. The range of class elements and strata between direct producers and the colonial state included less affluent groups such as small traders, clerks, teachers, and artisans.[12] The overlaps between these strata were not confined to those between landed property and regional commerce, but extended to overlaps between these and bureaucratic employment. The political affinities of different sections were made with British liberals and free traders as well as with conservatives; however, dependent on the colonial structure for jobs and often for landed interests, shaped by the processes of deindustrialization, this class was loyalist in the main and argued for liberalization, not replacement of British rule. The boundaries of its political radicalism are well defined.[13]

The redescription of gender and education was central to the emerging self-consciousness of this as yet amorphous class, setting out to make horizontal alignments and to reorder its conceptual apparatus, discursive universe, as well as its practical social organization. The intense negotiation of precolonial forms was partly a direct negotiation of colonial economy and the shift in the locus of power, and partly a self-definition in relation to changing inter-caste relations, to other classes, to existing rural affiliations, and to urbanization. For the zamindari sections whose coercive powers (economic and extra-economic) were both backed and curtailed by the colonial state—given their own reliance on both intermediaries and forms of sub-infeudation—many kinds of social authority must have been at stake. The opposing and crisscrossing positions on women and education need to be seen in this context. These were a part of class formation at a time when, owing to the heterogenous character, composition, and uneven development of the Bengal middle class, there was no readymade ground for the cultural coherence of the various elements and strata which comprised it. Both patriarchies and modes of cultural authority needed to be constituted afresh. Neither issue was a byproduct of colonial attitudes alone, but many of the specific problematics of both were produced by the contradictory pressures of colonial intervention. The question of women remained unsettled for another reason as well—a structural reconstitution of patriarchal practices was difficult to coordinate with existing local ideologies, with new bourgeois ideologies, and with the possible combinations which were becoming available.

The contradictory character of colonial rule produced *divided* readings of India as the barbaric subject of reform and as the 'civilized' repository of usable 'feudal' modes. Though never acknowledged as such, in several colonial accounts, as well as in the British Orientalists' codification of law and translation of older texts, the past civilization granted to India was conceptually inseparable from what such a civilization was a product of: the unequal divisions of labour and the extraction of surplus which had produced complex hierarchical modes for the social management of women and lower castes, as well as visible monuments and canonical texts. This precolonial past could provide models of 'feudal' governance for the purpose of colonial rule. In this sense it was, selectively, to become the usable past both for some of the colonizers and a fraction of the colonized; the traditions they invented were extrapolated from and engrafted on existing and emerging structures of inequality. For both, civilization, or at least one meaning of it, was a usable past composed of hierarchical stratifications and the cultural products and practices of upper-caste or elite and ruling groups; it was based on a joint elision of the fact that in earlier historical periods too assertions of continuity were implicated in the production of ideologies on behalf of such groups. Further, starting with Bengal, British annexation of political power from Muslim rulers in many parts of the country inaugurated a discursivity which constituted Hindus as the passive, god-fearing subjects of colonial rule, as opposed to the pugnacious, recalcitrant Muslims, complicated by the British functioning simultaneously as successors of the Mughal empire and as benefactors who had rescued Hindus from Muslim tyranny.

With cultural, communal, and patriarchal distinctions being established together, it was the *antiquity* of religious texts, patriarchal practices, and literature which became central to the assertion of a desired continuity. 'Hindu womanhood' as a compound referent for continuity and perpetuity came to serve a range of ideological purposes in the struggle for class and imperial domination. So did Sanskrit. In sum, many reasons for and ways of constituting tradition, central to how women and literature would be defined, were at work in both countries. Needless to say, the assertion of the continuity of the Indian past became a material and ideological ground for projected and selective change. Paternal and patriarchal ideologies in an interpenetrative, contradictory combination with the ideologies of liberal reform and progress (a facet of class struggle in Britain) *together* became the agencies of interpretation and of change in India. Both in the case of women and of literature, a broad dialectic between reform and preservation emerged; it is in relation to these two concepts, often entangled and equally dependent on characte-rizing what *existed*, that new definitions and institutions also took shape.

Philanthropy and altruism became a common yet conten-tious meeting ground between eighteenth-century traditions of pater-nalism and ascendant Utilitarian and Evangelical tendencies through the wider 'moral' and political imperatives of colonization. Meliora-tive charity and philanthropy, material aspects of British upper-class paternalism as well as middle-class life, were not only implicated in managing class antagonisms, in the maintenance of class order or position, and in upward mobility (an aspiration which Utilitarians and Evangelicals shared despite theoretical oppositions), but also integrated with a domestic economy involving desired roles for women commensurate with class management and mobility. The composition of the East India Company in the late eighteenth and early nineteenth centuries was upper middle class at the apex with a strengthening Evangelical component; civil servants, including Evangelicals, were connected with both old and new landed families and with banking and commercial families.[14] In India reforms were not only an agency of change, they characterized and legitimized the colonial state as altruistic—as possessed of a morality above and beyond political need. Altruism, a central element of this configura-tion, was inserted at different levels of intentionality and meaning in state policies. Narratives and discourses of reform, often actively engaged in reassembling patriarchies, became crucial to the self-description of middle-class, upper-caste Indians, as well as to the English. In fact the ubiquitous thematic of self-reform comes to encapsulate the aspirations and anxieties of colonizing and being colonized, of social transformations both actual and desired, as well as the cultural interfaces and social tensions of class mobility.

The ideologies produced about women and literature in India by the reforming colonial venture find precedents, extensions, or counterpoints in those produced in England. The definitions of women and literature which emerge at this time in India were initially produced in the *entangled* space of colonizers, local literati, and middle-class intelligentsia, whereas in England they were produced in an *embattled* space occupied by the consolidation of political classes, struggles for franchise, growing working-class militancy, and an emergent feminism. Together these definitions and ideologies made up a single, albeit complex, and shifting ideological configuration.

II

Some of the coordinates which preceded and shaped the entry of English were made in the Orientalist field, in a broader cultural semantic which developed around the policy, or more accurately, the politics of non-interference, as well as in specific institutions and ideologies related to literature. The British Orientalists' rediscovery of Indian culture was the ideological counterpart of Warren Hastings's project of rule after 1772. Hastings's ambition to reconcile British rule with Indian institutions was partly modelled on the Roman empire, a way of elevating "the British Name", and a bid to maintain his own and the Company's autonomy from British law (if introduced in India alongside British judicial processes) and the supreme court.[15] While in England religion was gradually superseded by law or political liberalism as central legitimizing ideologies, here religion was conflated with law in the early decades of colonial rule with long-term practical and ideological consequences. Despite a repeated administrative emphasis in which religion (the Koran and the Shastras) is to Indians what the constitution is to the British,[16] non-interference was fraught with contradictions. Not only was it conditional on colonial interests, and later also on the moral principles which colonial power was seen to represent, but changes in the economy altered the ideological location of social practices or their authority even where they did not alter the practices themselves. After Hastings, with the gradual consolidation of the colonial state and the need for markets, non-interference was increasingly contested and a source of tension within the colonial administration, but it did not end decisively with Bentinck's reforms. The *hesitation* to develop or use, in the full sense, bourgeois modes of authority, recurred in changing contexts and with different reasons throughout the nineteenth century. It was crucial in shaping a field of *conjoint* (indigenous plus colonial) and *fissured* authority—ideological conflicts and contradictions were structured *into* the semantic of emerging cultural categories, making them resistant to homogenization.

Earlier travel, missionary, and scholarly writing on Indian philosophy, religion, languages, and cultures provided an ad hoc field which was enlarged, systematized, and pressed into new ideological shapes by the British Orientalists. Orientalism (I refer specifically to the Indian school) inscribes its European scholars as learners and teachers adding to the store of European enlightenment. A powerful interpretative paradigm of carrying the knowledge of Asia to Europe for European improvement and advantage takes shape in which Orientalism, obsessed with antiquity, chronology, the common origins of language, mythology, science, and race—all the coordinates of the post-Renaissance constitution of 'Europe'—becomes a foundational history of the 'west'.[17] The slants and biases in the 'discovery' of India are evident enough: the relativization and romanticization of Indian mythology, Sanskrit language, drama, or poetry which are placed on a new comparative plane, measuring present 'fallen' customs against 'authentic' traditions in ancient texts, or preparing digests of law. Equally evident is the entanglement of rational enquiry with impetuous speculation: the isolation of Indian science and rational currents in Hinduism coexisted with fitting puranic time-scales into a Christian chronology, resulting among other things in identifying Manu with Noah. What is less evident about their research is that ancient India was on the one hand represented as an indivisible realm where religious and civil institutions were fused in the circularity of self-confirming faith, but on the other hand its insertion into a new historical conjuncture required methods of rationalization, a critical and selective validation of faith by reason, the disentangling of fact and history from myth, allegory, and fiction, and the selection of those elements from religious institutions which could be pragmatically adjusted with civil law. The considerable power of such relativization, a form of historicization, to unsettle the revelations in Christianity or the originary assumptions in Hinduism is implicitly acknowledged by William Jones, albeit in the form of repeated disavowal.[18]

The Orientalist field, at least initially, could only be established with local collaboration, yet Indians were not a publicly acknowledged voice in the Orientalist field, with a few exceptions (Ram Kamal Sen, Mritunjaya Vidyalankar), and even then their presence is subdued in proportion to their enormous labour. Instead Orientalist accounts are littered with references to Indian literati, named and unnamed, reliable and unreliable, especially pandits who forge, mislead, tailor texts in accordance with European demand, provide hundreds of manuscripts but seldom author or authorize translations, as well as with accounts of outwitting them by devising new methods of work and collation. The 'native' interpreter is constituted as at once the (unconscious, since he lacks historical consciousness) repository of ancient knowledge and as perennially recalcitrant or obstructive and in need of control (often through the agency of this same textual, Orientalist domain).

For Warren Hastings, Orientalist knowledge is a specific aspect of state power which can reduce the weight of "subjection" for Indians, produce "the sense and obligation of benevolence" in Englishmen, and more generally be "a gain for humanity".[19] The Orientalists who either held or rose to important positions in the government were committed to preserving British power, but erratic government funding and the serial logic and momentum of their labour gave it a degree of autonomy. However, this mild disjunction with direct utility later ballooned into a paradigm of pure scholarship and disinterested knowledge.

> The dissemination of knowledge is in all cultivated societies the worthy occupation of talent and power. Even where that knowledge may not be of generally practical application, its possession may be endowed with specific value, and much that is little essential to the necessities of life, is of high value to intellectual ambition. It may be of trifling import to the welfare of any particular community to discover and adjust the dark tradition of remote antiquity. . . . To the mind that is liberalized by studious enquiry, and elevated by expanded views, these subjects are deeply important and the studies of the scholar and the speculations of the philosopher, cannot be without effect upon the improvement of society, and the happiness of mankind.[20]

In this context, the rapid, selective appropriation of the Orientalists as bestowers of history, art, science, and literature—a composite cultural greatness cognate with their social aspirations— by upper-caste, middle-class Hindus is hardly surprising. Since

Orientalists were often accused of being unchristian,[21] it was easy to set up a false opposition between them and the missionaries. The increasing implication in and reproduction of Orientalism in both erudite and popular forms by a section of the middle class in subsequent decades (a subject beyond the scope of this essay) was not a case of mere imitation or derivation. It was determined by a number of factors including the very nature of the Orientalist field itself which condensed the new social relations between the colonial state and this emerging class, resonated with the latter's social power resting on relayed exploitation of those below as well as with the requirements and aspirations for government jobs; it reflected the historical process of colonization that was producing some cognate areas of political compatibility, congruent material and class interests, as well as specific ideological adjacencies between sections of the British and (initially) of the Bengal middle class; it provided a potentially advantageous method for constituting a largely 'Hindu' past and presenting a comparative relation, howsoever spurious, between different ways of structuring knowledge, wherein these differences could be read through a 'culturalist' grid that promised, even encoded, civilizational depth and a collaborative version of cultural authenticity.

Thus the power of Orientalism lay in the methodological field itself which, among other things, offered a *relationship* with the 'west'. It becomes potentially hegemonic *only* when it becomes a mode of self-identification for members of the Indian middle class— a parallel field of authority alongside other existing routes to Indian texts. The other source of its power lay in its contents, in the fact that it was preeminently a *mediatory* discourse. In relation to the subjects at hand, patriarchy, religion, and to a much lesser extent literature, Orientalist and related colonial positions were in some fundamental ways derived or extrapolated not only from visible and invisible informants but from more or less familiar Indian texts—in this sense they are not so much founding, or innovative, as influential mediating discourses. As a discursive field directly and indirectly related to the inequality of colonial rule, which comes to be jointly shaped by some of the colonizers and some of the colonized in complicit and contradictory ways, moulded by the local histories of each, Orientalism is the most fully developed model of *potentially dividable authority*.

The more so since it rehearses without resolving—what must at the time have been a directly experienced and daily contradiction—the split between rationality and faith.

'Tradition' was not, as it is projected, the authentic object of scholarly 'recovery' or 'renascent discovery'; rather it was an altered field in a new social formation, aligned to new configurations of exercising, aspiring to, and sharing power. Ironically, the primary object of this field—the project of cultural authenticity—was undone at its inception. This is evident in the reconstitution of Sanskrit—in the past a language of brahmin hegemony and kshatriya legitimation, implicated in expansion through settlement and conquest—now as a cultural category: a body of writing, a language, a set of associations.

The need for intermediary groups and the desire to slide into or replace existing structures of patronage resulted in Sanskrit, along with Persian and Arabic, becoming one of the first recipients of state patronage. Warren Hastings's Calcutta Madrasa was formed on local demand to train Muslim men through religious instruction for subordinate positions in civil and criminal courts. Jonathan Duncan (the resident of Benaras and a member of the Asiatic Society of Bengal, an association of elite Company officials and chief disseminator of Orientalism which invited local membership in 1829) argued in 1791 on the same lines for a Hindu college "for the preservation and cultivation of the Laws, Literature and Religion of that Nation at this Centre of their Faith", which would endear "our government to the native Hindus; by our exceeding in our attentions towards them and their systems, the care shown even by their own native princes" and provide "a nursery of future doctors and expounders" of "Hindu law" to "assist European judges".[22] The subsumption of Law and Literature into Faith requires a colonial subject for whom religious belief and cultural identity is commensurate with belief in the colonial dispensation.

The recurring official emphasis on patronage was replete with Orientalist assumptions—the decline of science and literature caused by the absence of aristocratic patronage partly explained the present condition of India and shaped the College of Fort William's ideological location of Sanskrit: preservation, cultural vitalization, the reintroduction of an indigenous elite to the 'treasury' of Sanskritic tradition. In his speech at the annual disputations of the college in 1804, Marquess Wellesley spoke of the brahmin description of Sanskrit learning as a lush virgin forest "surrounded by a strong and thorny fence"—the Orientalists had broken the fence in several places but the college had made a "highway... into the midst of the wood",[23] while Lord Minto elaborated this in his speeches in 1808 and 1813 in metaphors of "impenetrable mystery" and "pristine form".[24] Else-where Minto laments that Britain ("distinguished for its love and successful cultivation of letters") had failed "to extend its fostering care to the literature of the Hindus, and to aid its opening to the learned in Europe the repositories of that literature".[25] With parlia-ment accepting in principle government responsibility for Indian education in 1813, the Charter Act sharpened the thematic of reform in setting aside an annual sum for "the *revival* and *improvement* of literature and the encouragement of the learned natives of India, and for the introduction and promotion of a knowledge of the sciences among the inhabitants..."[26] (my emphases). The Court of Directors' despatch on education in 1814 continued the policy of nurturing the long-established usages of an existing Hindu elite (for service in judicial departments), restoring the laws and ethics of the Sanskritic tradition, and using Indian sciences while hoping they would gradu-ally improve or modernize on western lines.[27] This emphasis was retained by the despatches of 1824 and by the Committee of Public Instruction.

How indeed does one improve or cultivate a pristine trea-sury? The confusion is bred by conflicting intentions, not by meta-phors. The 1814 despatch makes of Sanskrit a meliorist moment, a stepping-stone. The resolution of the governor-general-in-council apropos the Orientalist H.H. Wilson's Sanskrit College (which admitted only upper-caste students) states that:

> ... the immediate object of the institution is the cultivation of Hindu literature. Yet it is in the judgement of His Lordship in Council, a purpose of much deeper interest to seek every practicable means of effecting the gradual diffusion of European knowledge. It seems indeed no unreasonable anticipation to hope that if the higher and educated classes among the Hindoos shall, *through the medium of their sacred language, be imbued with a taste for the European*

> *literature and science, general acquaintance with these and with*
> *the language whence they are drawn, will be as surely and as*
> *extensively communicated as by any attempt at direct instruction*
> by other and humble seminaries.[28] (my emphases)

Here Sanskrit becomes a diet which can cultivate a taste for European knowledge and a form of indirect instruction in the English language, virtually a sacral step towards secular knowledge. The lines connecting Sanskrit with English and European knowledge are drawn from this widely diffused Orientalist tendency to pose Sanskrit not only as carrier of European knowledge but also as a means for 'developing' vernaculars:

> *Upon its* [Sanskrit's] *cultivation depends the means of native*
> *dialects to embody European learning and science.* It is a visionary
> absurdity to think of making English the language of India. It
> should be extensively studied, no doubt, but *the improvement of*
> *the native dialects enriching them with Sanskrit terms for English*
> *ideas* [must be continued], and to effect this, Sanskrit must be
> cultivated as well as English.[29] (my emphases)

The complementarity of preservation and reform was most apparent in H.H. Wilson's (then secretary to the Committee of Public Instruction) merger of Sanskrit College and Hindu College in 1823. This would not only "*preserve from decay and degradation a system of science and literature held in pious veneration by the great body of its subjects, deeply interwoven with their domestic habits and religious faith*", but also open "*new sources of intellectual and moral improvements by the gradual admission of . . . European science and learning . . .*"[30] (my emphases). In a letter to the governor-general the committee expressed the hope that

> *the union of European and Hindu learning being thus quietly*
> *effected* in one case, it will hereafter be comparatively easy to carry
> the combination into other departments, and the *improved culti-*
> *vation* of science and literature may be thus successfully and
> extensively promoted.[31] (my emphases)

The contradictions of reform (involving the not always compatible processes of pruning and engrafting for this generation of Orientalists) and preservation are here smoothed in a compliant language of synthesis, equally amenable for Indian middle-class aspirations. However, the ideological difficulties of engrafting surface in practical attempts. Lancelot Wilkinson (assistant resident at Bhopal), for instance, recommends teaching science through the Siddhantas with local *jyotishis* (astrologers) as intermediaries, on the ground that "the pure and unadulterated truth" cannot be easily communicated to the masses, and further is "absolutely rejected". Adulterated truth, it seems, could be a step towards pure truth. In his editorial note to the essay, James Prinsep suggests that a moralist could similarly sift the valuable from "the dross of ancient schools" in the search for compatible elements in Hindu philosophy.[32] Similarly, the Committee of Public Instruction paradoxically describes indigenous knowledge as erroneous while *defending* its Orientalist policy: in order to lay a foundation for a group of English-knowing "translators and preceptors", "we must qualify the same individuals highly in their own system as well as ours, in order that they may be competent to refute error and impart truth, if we would wish them to exercise any influence over the minds of their countrymen."[33]

Sanskrit's claim to truth involved continuous adjudication, and the Orientalists develop what appears to be a model of knowledge as a *process* of *veiled confrontation*. Sanskrit signifies assimilation—it becomes a hybrid sign for the adulteration, erosion, overlay, synthesis, or engrafting of Indian with European knowledge—and simultaneously the space for reclaiming or maintaining indigenous purity. Structured around a series of tensions, it is at once a site for the reclamation of religious and juridical truth as for comparative study and cultural relativization; beset with problems of interpretation regarding allegory, metaphor, or figuration, it provides a body of texts for framing legal codes as well as for replenishing European poetry. The overarching tension is the simultaneous reconstitution of Sanskrit as *synchronic* and *historical*: as the composite recovery of a fixed body of knowledge from a golden age and as a capacious vehicle for accommodation or change. Sanskrit, acquiring an uneven gait in time, comes to be fraught with anxiety, striving, and complacency.

The Serampore missionary enterprises (unlike those of the Anglicists Charles Grant or Duff) which shared Orientalist modes of constructing knowledge and seeking legitimacy, if anything, sharpened the ideological strain within Sanskrit. Missionaries frequently justified the dissemination of those portions of Indian texts which appeared to accord with Christian ethics,[34] and considered knowledge of the Shastras necessary for native Christians to extend their influence. William Carey's project, homologous to the administrators, aspired to a group of informants (brahmin pandits) and an intermediary servicing cadre who could disseminate Christianity more effectively through its inwardness with indigenous culture.[35] Carey edited and translated the *Ramayana* with aid from the Asiatic Society, while the Serampore Mission's newspaper, *Samachar Darpan* (1818), employed distinguished pandits as editorial staff; in fact the practice of employing pandits for translation was common among missionaries.[36]

Serampore College seems to have functioned on the principle of simultaneously consolidating and undermining the authority of Sanskrit. Established on the understanding that, "If the gospel stands in India, it must be *by native being opposed to native* in demonstrating its excellence above all other systems",[37] the college made provisions for educating Hindus (including caste-based accommodation) and Muslims for their secular advantage without offending their respective moralities, and proposed to teach and preserve indigenous science so that the institution would have 'respectability' in the eyes of learned, upper-caste sections. Committed to a native cadre—an effective enlightenment in India "should be attempted through the *Natives themselves*"—the principles of the institution were stated in the First Report of Serampore College as

> that of laying it open to other native youth for support as well as instruction,—of excluding everything which can operate as a punishment on them for acting according to their own sense of right,—*of introducing all the science now possessed by the natives as preparatory to a wider expansion of ideas on the principles of European science*,—and of *preserving the ancient writings of India*,—and of *strengthening the minds* of all those whose time and circumstances permit *by a thorough knowledge of Sanskrit grammar*. . . .[38] (my emphases)

Along with the appointment of two professors of European science, this report proposed publication of the four Vedas! Indigenous knowledge, especially Sanskrit, is a narrow rigorous base for wider European knowledge as well as a necessary medium for its own supersession. Tendencies latent in Orientalists and administrators expressed as dissimulation, disguise, relativization, engrafting, or improvement, come to a logical fruition in this group of missionaries in so far as they propose a paradigm of inevitably *disputed knowledge*, both internally—native against native, and externally—indigenous versus European.

William Jones saw translation of the Bible into Sanskrit and Persian and distribution amongst learned groups as the only and extremely doubtful possibility for converting Hindus and Muslims.[39] The missionary newspaper, *Friend of India*, developed this and cognate Orientalist and missionary positions into an extended rationale for teaching Sanskrit. The class under consideration for being instructed in Sanskrit along with European knowledge and science is still the intellectual elite, on whom the labouring masses depend for guidance and who "regulate the opinion of the country". Pragmatically, Sanskrit is perceived as "an indispensable qualification for native students who may hereafter be placed in elevated situations". Culturally, Sanskrit is a language of antiquity, held in "unprecedented" veneration, the living repository of both instruction and the sacred, to which the people, including the "lowest class" of unlettered Hindus, are universally attached and which they treat with confidence and respect.

> When therefore men imbued with European science and ideas, go forth to instruct their own countrymen, would it be wise to deny them that which will add so much to their weight? And as they will have to combat the errors of men of high endowments, should they not be placed exactly on par with their antagonists? . . . How can we call ourselves the friends of truth, if we fail to give it [Sanskrit] the same common chance of reception with the dogmas of error? However extensive and profound may be their attainments in other respects, without a knowledge of Sanskrit, the supporters of truth will find it difficult to maintain their ground against their adversaries, and they will feel themselves in a great measure neglected by the bulk of the people. . . . *By sending forth the doctrine of true science under the protection of this venerable tongue, we*

shall meet its adversaries on their own ground; and by attaching
to the soundest truths, that consideration which is now felt
exclusively for the ancient dogmas of error, we shall accelerate the
improvement of India full half a century.[40] (my emphases)

The argument for maintaining forms while shifting contents not only
makes Sanskrit an *encasing* for European knowledge but also
suggests a method for splitting and usurping the social authority of
Sanskrit. There are supplementary arguments: along with access to
its "treasures", the advantage of learning Sanskrit lies in its difficulty;
mastering it requires memory, "close and arduous application", and
"habits of industry"—Sanskrit can become the *disciplining ground*
which arms the student for the combats of "true science". Knowledge
of Sanskrit also "imparts" "principles of refined taste in composition" which allow the student not only to write "elegantly" in the
vernaculars, but to "improve" and "enrich" the "meagre" and
"debased" vernaculars from the well-preserved "great parent of all
the Indian languages". Indeed Sanskrit is all that has been preserved
from India's civilized past, "unsullied from the touch of foreign
invasion". Finally, Sanskrit, understood over a vast geographical
stretch, will circulate widely, influence more people, function as a
carrier of metropolitan discoveries, and is proposed almost as an
early version of a quasi-national language. If for many Orientalists
the knowledge represented by Sanskrit was made, selectively, to
stand in for European knowledge, missionaries use and press this
logic to the point where Sanskrit was to be *replaced from within*, to
become capable of *self-chastisement* if not self-demolition.

III

As is evident, Orientalist scholarship, and in some sense the
field itself, was widely dispersed by the early nineteenth century
among missionaries, administrators, popular journals, and other
institutions; already in tandem with and assimilated into higher
levels of policy-making and theories of governance, it came to
provide a ready commonsense about preservation and reform. In the
writing which composed this substantially widened field, a broad
cultural semantic centred on non-interference emerged. One strand of
this was enmeshed with descriptions of Indian women and patriarchal

practices. In constituting women as subjects of partial reform, in interpreting and negotiating existing patriarchal practices of upper-caste, landowning groups in India, several colonizers used preexist-ing and emergent British patriarchal forms located in various social and ideological formations at home as an interpretative grid. Patriarchal forms were already perceived or experienced as being a part of class order or social stability, as well as open to reformulation.

This could on occasion become a play of complementary patriarchies resting on a male mutuality about the sexual division of labour. For instance, the Company official George Foster's compunc-tion for the merits of prescriptive Hinduism and patriarchal arrange-ments is such that he virtually adopts the stance of a surrogate brahmin measuring the virtue of women by the degree of their con-formity to the Shastras. He describes the illiteracy of women approvingly as an "expedient" arrangement since for Hindus educa-tion contributes neither to "individual happiness", "decorum of character", nor the domestic usefulness of women:

> They urge that a knowledge of literature would conduce to draw a woman from her household cares, and give a disrelish to those offices, in which consist the only satisfaction and amusement that she can, with propriety, and an observance of rectitude, par-take of; and such is the force of custom, that a Hindu woman would incur severe reproach, were it known that she could read or write. The Hindoo dancing girls, whose occupations are avowedly devo-ted to the public pleasure, are on the contrary taught the use of letters. . . . [41]

The contradictions between reform and preservation devel-oped in missionaries before they did among administrators. A good example is the French Roman Catholic missionary Abbe J.A. Dubois, who was in India from 1792 to 1823. The first manuscript of his *Hindu Manners, Customs and Ceremonies* was purchased by Lord William Bentinck, then in Madras, on behalf of the East India Company in 1807, in order to fill a felt lacuna in colonial knowledge. Such a work, functioning as an official handbook, would help "the servants of the Government in conducting themselves more in unison with the customs and prejudices of the natives".[42] The English translation of the first manuscript in 1816 was used among others by James Mill, and illustrates the way usable knowledge at the upper levels of administration was becoming derivative and textual. As an anti-Jacobin and a pessimistic missionary, Dubois was easy to align with conservative tendencies in the administration. Several eighteenth and early nineteenth-century administrators, Orientalists, and missionaries had already identified Hinduism and its customs with political docility, the habitual unfreedom of the 'native', and the submission of Hindu women to patriarchy.[43] Dubois' text, condensing these strands, represents a curious intersection between missionary revulsion, non-interfering tolerance, paternalistic as well as companionate patriarchal ideologies: indigenous institutions, usages, and patriarchal practices are situated as *equally* a source of libidinousness and Hindu loyalism. His account wavers between situating the policy of non-interference as a legacy of the Mughal empire and as an especial sign of British largesse.

For Dubois, "the greatest vices" common to all Hindus, "untrustworthiness, deceit and double-dealing", which make for their unprecedented inscrutability, are not "innate" but the product of prolonged subjugation by

> masters who had recourse to all sorts of artifices to oppress and despoil them. The timid Hindu could think of no better expedient with which to defend himself than to meet ruse with ruse, dissimulation with dissimulation, and fraud with fraud. (pp. 306–07)

Hindus become the wily survivor victims of a Mughal rule which paradoxically changed their character but left all their civil and religious institutions intact. The same Hindu timidity which took strategic recourse in duplicity in the face of Muslim tyranny ultimately turns out to be a product of submission to custom and religion which definitionally predate Muslim rule. And since it is "in the nature of Hindus to cling to their civil and religous institutions, to their old customs and habits", Dubois does not even think it possible to convert or modernize Hindus, for "to make a new race of the Hindu, one would have to begin by undermining the very foundations of their civilization, religion, and polity, and by turning them into atheists and barbarians"(p. 96).

> Let us leave them their cherished laws and prejudices, since no

human effort will persuade them to give them up, even in their own interests, and let us not risk making the gentlest and most submissive people in the world furious and indomitable by fighting them. Let us take care lest we bring about, by some hasty or imprudent course of action, catastrophes which would reduce the country to a state of anarchy, desolation and ultimate ruin, for, in my humble opinion, the day when the Government attempts to interfere with any of the more important religious and civil usages of the Hindus will be the last of its existence as a political power. (p. 97)

The 1806 Vellore sepoy mutiny, ascribed to missionary activities, seems to have aligned a belief in continued Hindu submissiveness—by maintaining their customs and institutions—more strongly to the policy of non-interference.[44]

Hindu male passivity thrives on a relayed subalternity: the gentle and submissive subject of colonial rule is however an 'independent' unrelenting patriarch, a "proud and overbearing master" in his home. Marriages, never companionate, are usually devoid of "sincere and mutual affection" while

in the eyes of a native the woman is simply a passsive object who must be abjectly submissive to her husband's will and fancy. She is never looked upon as a companion who can share her husband's thoughts and be the first object of his care and affection. (p. 231)

But is not the patriarchy of which women are passive victims a part of the Hindu's "cherished laws and prejudices" (p. 97)? And is not then the abjection of women essential to maintaining the customary realm? The problem of condemning and maintaining patriarchy at the same time undergirds Dubois' account. A revealing slip from the passive victim to the libidinous woman virtually justifies the practice of child marriage as the only means of controlling the sexual agency of women. Women are

subject on all sides to the moral ascendancy of man. . . . The opinion is firmly established throughout the whole of India, that women were only created for the propagation of the species, and to satisfy men's desires. All women are therefore obliged to marry, and marriages are carefully arranged before they arrive at marriageable age. If by that time they have not found a husband, they very rarely keep their innocence much longer. *Experience has taught that young Hindu women do not possess a sufficient firmness, and sufficient regard for their own honour, to resist the ardent solicitations of a seducer. Therefore measures cannot be taken too early to place them intact in their husband's hands.* Those who are unable to enter into any lawful union form a connexion as concubines with any man who cares to receive them as such. (p. 207, my emphases)

By the end of the passage Dubois' voice becomes indistinguishable from the patriarchy he sets out to describe. However, when he reverses his evaluation elsewhere, it is partly because Indian "civil and religious institutions" appear to him so libidinous that by contrast women improve (p. 308). While deploring "the special power which sexual passion exercises in India", he writes, "Hindu women are naturally chaste" and to "cite a few examples of unseemly conduct, a few lapses attributable to human frailty, is no proof of their want of chastity as a body"; he would even "go so far as to say that Hindu women are more virtuous than the women of many other more civilized countries"[45] (pp. 313–14). Their "temperament is outwardly calm and equable, and though a passionate fire may smoulder underneath, without the igniting spark it will remain quiescent". For the rest he wonders whether this "dormant coldness of disposition" is to be attributed to a secluded upbringing, to a special training, to the unbridgeable distance between them and the men, or to "climatic influence"—but he cannot quite decide (p. 314).

There is thus a double reading of women as naturally libidinous (in need of control by patriarchal institutions such as early marriage) and women as naturally chaste and quiescent. Patriarchal excesses are reprehensible and will serve as the moral legitimation of the colonial state; yet the field of precolonial custom and religion in which these excesses are implicated is the solid core of political stability that makes the Hindu an amenable subject of colonial rule and cannot be tampered with. Patriarchy is *at once* something to be *reformed* and to be *preserved*. The Hindu woman, played into the larger frames of European mistrust of female sexuality and the stereotype of a licentious orient, is simultaneously set apart as the soothing exemplum of chastity, a model for western women to emulate.

The chaste woman then is the submissive object of a generalized patriarchy, the foundation of male-dominated social structures. The passivity ascribed to Hindu men and the egoless subjection ascribed to women under patriarchal dominance are in miniature aspects of the governability of India—two favourable conditions among others for colonial rule. Whereas male passivity has to be maintained by eliminating provocation, Dubois tries to naturalize female passivity; a corollary subtext of such feminization situates the colonial state as the 'masculine' agent of a 'benevolent' patriarchy. As this account reveals, the question of patriarchies is structurally embedded in the discourse of character, governance, governability, and colonial agency.

More noticeably in Dubois' than in earlier accounts, non-intervention in the customary and religious domain assumed a prior and ongoing definition of that domain. The Sanskritic textual domain—part of the project of isolating the principles of Hinduism and the codification of law—under male, ruling-class, upper-caste, and brahminical jurisdiction, intricately knotted with utility and political control, could be identified with paternalistic inclinations and patriarchal interests in order to find a sanction for maintaining the sexual division of labour or redescribing the regulation of female sexuality. Conventionally in the control of the few, frequently construed as the opposite of popular custom and practice, it remained the resource of legislators and reformers. Women themselves, largely illiterate, had limited access either to religious texts or to defining (as opposed to maintaining) custom, or even to the reflective, philoso-phical aspects of Hinduism. By virtue of their subordination they were prime subjects to be made either subject to government by text and custom or into the *expressive* medium, the very being of religion.

The ideological locations of other positions on women differed but many of the cultural coordinates were similar. Where non-interference coincides fully with paternalism, as in Foster, women need little reform, they are *already schooled*. But when Hindu patriarchal practices are seen to resist or clash with the evolving familial ideology of the upwardly mobile British middle class which required good mothers and companionate wives, it appears to result either in direct denigration or sharpens a self-contradicting desire for change. James Mill, in *History of British India*, wonders at the inconsistency of a libidinous Hinduism also promoting chastity, and echoes Dubois in ranting at the inherent libidinousness of Hindu women but places companionate marriage as a higher stage in civilization, out of their reach.[46] William Ward, who shares Dubois' sense of abomination at libidinous Hindu religious texts and practices,[47] as well as his commitment to non-interference, describes Serampore's policy of conversion in what must be a classic accommodation of interference to 'invisibility': ". . . we have carefully avoided everything that might Anglicize the converts. We have made no change in their dress, their names, their food, their language, or their domestic habits. . . . [Otherwise] the idolators would have triumphed. . . ."[48] For Ward, illiteracy, part product of shastric injunction, accounts for the inadequacy of Hindu wives and mothers when compared with educated European mothers who are "greater benefactors to the age in which they live"; he cites Hindu male fears that women will become proud, widowed, or "engage in clandestine correspondence" if literate, but also holds the licentiousness of their texts responsible for Hindu opposition to female education.[49] By this standard good women could only, if that, be aligned to carefully expunged prescriptive religious texts. However, before the question of what women should read can be decided, reading itself has to be freed from danger for those missionaries who seem to share Hindu male fears:

> Even the present system of excluding females from a knowledge of books and men, is found scarcely sufficient to restrain them [women] within the bounds of propriety. To what extent would not immorality be carried then, if greater facility for secret intrigue were afforded them by a knowledge of reading and writing! . . . women must not read, lest they should become more vicious.[50]

Nor can women be left as they are, as H. Crisp of the London Missionary Society put it in 1828: "There must be a change here, for while the female character continues ignorant and degraded as at present, how can any great moral revolution be expected?"[51]

The British were not alone in constituting women as contradictory subjects of reform. The cultural semantic which crystallizes around non-interference had an extended political locale in the early nineteenth century with the establishment of a public sphere in semblance of a liberal polity, composed of educational, literary, and religious societies or institutions, the English and vernacular press. The debates on religious, patriarchal, and educational reform tied the consciousness of identity of *both* the British and the Bengal middle class, in part, to the redescription of gender and literature. Further, the reconceptualization of womanhood was embedded in the aspirations of the emergent but far from homogeneous middle class which needed to restructure the family, to produce ideologies for the reproduction of households, to measure patriarchal practices against emerging forms of stratification, to align personal with general class interests, to produce a common language about 'culture' as well as contest the colonial state's practised juridical rights over a newly constituted 'public sphere'. The religious textual domain, identified at one level with colonial authority, was almost simultaneously reinterpreted to challenge certain aspects of colonial interpretation.

In this period, indigenism is produced by the colonial negotiation of 'feudal' and patriarchal social relations *alongside* a liberal conception of the state interacting with local elite and middle-class groups themselves engaged in negotiating colonial power, precolonial practices and ideologies, and often implicated in the Orientalist domain. The parameters of both indigenism and the woman question, which were henceforth to be seen relatedly, were set within this constellation, and both pro and anticolonial positions took shape inside them. Women become the subjects and vehicles through whom both the retention and modernization of newly defined Hindu patriarchal forms were to be achieved. A cultural semantic is produced where the libidinous woman typifying the orient is, like other 'bad natives', given fresh legitimacy by the moral imperatives of colonial reform, while the chaste Hindu woman gets a new lease of life from the type of conservatism produced by non-interference. The chaste woman herself is a conflictual sign of either Hindu male oppression (it is men who need reform) or emblematic of the tenacity and longevity of Hinduism. In this aspect of British and Indian interaction two competing and overlapping forms of essentialism can be discerned as coinciding in the *characterization* of women (but not in the assessment of patriarchal practices): bourgeois forms of essentialism either correspond with or are themselves overdetermined by precapitalist forms of essentialism expressed in *stridharma* and *strisvabhav*, which smooths the discursive complications somewhat, but does not resolve them.

Further, since the need for control over women and the desire for schooled women is primary for almost any patriarchal arrangement, there was a much greater overlap between the British and the Bengal middle class here than over other issues. The *tutored* woman is not in question. But there were divergent views on the inherent nature of women and, accordingly, on whether literacy would help or hinder. The swing from chaste abject victim to immoral sexual agent parallels a swing between education as either redundant or an ornamental form of enlightenment versus education as an imperative for moral tutelage. Education is alternately morally harmful or inculcates morals; women are either already schooled by domesticity and shastric injunction or are in need of further schooling. The problem of characterization of course extended beyond education: reform was caught in the contradictions of innovation and restoration (which also inhabited the concept from its inception in England)[52] and of the by then old colonial themes, perfected in other theatres of European conquest, of offering similitude and exploiting cultural difference. For the Bengal middle class, reform offered a new self and similitude to Europeans as well as a purifying return to an earlier self which would maintain cultural or moral differences.

Despite similarities, the semantic of reforming women, unlike Sanskrit, was caught in a logic which was more difficult to resolve, internalize, or displace because patriarchal practices were *directly* at issue. No easy relation can be made between women and literature since gender questions have a discrete material and nondiscursive locale. However, notions of 'literature' took shape within a cognate set of social contradictions and were often made in adjacent or even overlapping textual domains. Further, the severe battles fought over patriarchal issues such as widow immolation, which I cannot go into here, resonated in the polemic over English and structured some of its meanings. Indeed the puzzling confluence of material interests and the *different* ideological positions taken about English, as well as the sharp ideological polarizations which occurred in the otherwise confused and amorphous field named 'literature', were rooted within local as well as broader class and colonial

configurations, and may have obtained some of their contours and
their energy from the struggles over describing women and reshaping
patriarchy. Before looking at some of the relationships posited
between women and literature, it will help to look at some of the
meanings of 'literature' and the constitution of English.

Literature, female literacy, colonial English: an interface

IV

    What is 'literature'? Is it possible to separate English lite-
rature from English education in this period? In the first three decades
of the nineteenth century in Bengal, 'literature' as defined through the
structuring activities of interconnected institutions, documents and
debates on education, colonial self-descriptions, and popular usage
emerged as a wide, amorphous category, fed from several directions,
including the Orientalist domain and the cultural semantic of gender
centred on non-interference. Literature was usually used in the evaluative yet generalized, class-specific, eighteenth-century sense of
polite and higher learning,[53] and general meanings of literature preceded the more precise demarcation of English literature. Literature
itself was a subset of 'knowledge' without clear boundaries developed simultaneously with reference to eighteenth-century Europe and
to a *localized* Indian or more broadly Asian context.

    For the Orientalists knowledge was local yet inclusive. In
his first address to the Asiatic Society of Bengal, the only boundaries
William Jones sets for enquiry into Asia are geographical:

> But if it now be asked what are the intended objects of our enquiries
> within these spacious limits, we answer *man* and *nature*; *whatever
> is perceived by the one or produced by the other*. Human knowl-
> edge has been elegantly analysed according to the three great
> faculties of the mind, memory, reason and imagination, which we
> constantly find employed in arranging and retaining, comparing
> and distinguishing, combining and diversifying the ideas, which we

receive through our senses, or acquire by reflection. Here the three main Branches of Learning are History, Science and Art; the first comprehends either an account of Natural Productions, or the genuine records of Empires and States; the second embraces the whole circle of pure and mixed Mathematics, together with Ethics and Law, as far as they depend on the reasoning faculty; and the third includes all the beauties of Imagery and the charms of Invention displayed in modulated language, or represented by colour and figure, or sound.[54]

The scholarly compendious knowledge of the Orientalists is contemporaneized, generalized as 'literary' by the Bombay Literary Society (1804), and put within the reach of the amateur by extending the field of writing to include forms of documenting India based on observation but not necessarily on learning. Though it also had a British membership, and many of its translation, publication, and archival activities overlapped with the Asiatic Society,[55] the Bombay Literary Society was described approvingly by the *Calcutta Journal* as an institution of a "general literary nature . . . which might direct its attention . . . to subjects beyond the range of those peculiarly Oriental".[56] While contrasting its activities favourably with those of the Asiatic Society on the ground that the definition of literature is broader, of contemporary relevance, and morally more efficacious, the *Calcutta Journal* makes a significant shift from 'learning' to a potentially more unifying or homogenizing concept of 'taste' that is identified with range: it could include Greek and Latin writing as readily as "an enquiry into the effects of polygamy on the native population of India—the causes and cure of the prevailing Epidemic—or in short any other subject suggested by local circumstance".[57] As opposed to the abstruse erudition of the Asiatic Society confined to oriental literature, its advantages are lively discussion and emulation, forming "a habit of reasoning and enquiry", and establishing a "taste" for "that which is permanently beautiful and excellent": the range of "History, Poetry, Morals, Science, Art, and Philosophy" is praised for contributing to a process of refinement through diffusion.

The president Sir James Mackintosh's (a senior administrator in Bombay Presidency and later a professor at Haileybury College) speech at the first meeting of the Bombay Literary Society, in 1804, *unifies* the diversity of literature with a militant altruism which describes "*all* Europeans who visit remote countries, whatever their separate pursuits may be, as detachments from the main body of civilized men, sent out to levy contributions of knowledge as well as to gain victories over barbarism". Like the Asiatic Society, it had to address Europe. He divides knowledge into the "Physical"—the phy-sical sciences which "display . . . the authority of man over nature" and have an undisputed utility in a country "where so many treasures must still be unexplored" and new "sources of wealth" can still be discovered, and the "Moral"—which will "chiefly comprehend the past and present condition" of the inhabitants of India. The contents of the "Moral" combine the quality of an early census with a latterday social history covering demography, infant mortality, proportion of castes and occupations and sex ratios, laws and customs, systems of commerce, wage labour, agriculture, and trade. This redefined body of knowledge is democratically opened to an average Englishman. Enquiries into the "Moral"

> have the advantage of being easy and open to all men of good sense. They do not, like antiquarian and philological researches, require great previous erudition and constant reference to extensive libraries. They *require nothing but a resolution to observe facts attentively and to relate them accurately.* And whoever feels a dis-position to ascend from facts to principles, will in general find sufficient aid to his understanding in the great work of Dr Smith. . . . They have the further advantage of being closely and intimately connected with the professional pursuits and public duties of every Englishman who fills a civil office in the country— they *form the very science of administration.*[58] (my emphases)

Though as expansive, Mackintosh's is a closer negotiation of the differential play of enlightenment in Britain and in its colonies than Jones's address. While the "Physical" is allied to the discovery and extraction of wealth, the "Moral" is the sphere for rationalizing colonial domination by developing a body of local knowledge about India identified with the "science of administration". Knowledge based on reason and observation is more conducive to colonial expansion. The continuity posited between literature and local knowledge by Mackintosh allows literature to be placed simultaneously in an explicit instrumentality, in governmental or other power structures, and an aspiration to status or 'sensibility'. The unproblematic alignment of colonial utility with social refinement appears to rest on the corollary that such knowledge acquires a degree of autonomy.

Should this useful knowledge be confined to the government or made publicly available? A curious discussion follows on *whose* province this knowledge is, centred on the choice between secrecy and diffusion, between the claims of the state and the universalistic claims of science. The contradiction between colonial rule and the wider requirements of European enlightenment seem to be related to an interesting fringe disagreement among administrators on knowledge as the province of the state as opposed to its functionaries and citizens in general, that is, on whether knowledge is to be fully integrated with the state or to be an allied field.[59] Mackintosh resolves it in the direction of publication as being more useful for the government by building a wide comparative field of knowledge, acting as a check on the dishonesty or laziness of civil servants, and in forming a corrective public opinion against possible state tyranny: "This knowledge is a control on subordinate agents for Government, as well as a control on Government for their subjects." Further, as a form of knowledge, "political economy" promotes meliorist reform and stability—of government, of property, of persons. On these principles, 'improvement' becomes simultaneously a defence of present interests. The body of knowledge structured by the requirements of the state must in turn regulate the state, thereby, paradoxically, giving the state a wider legitimacy.

The self-definition of the Bombay Literary Society established literature as a reformative apparatus in the wider and not in the specialized sense. Literature had no fixed national boundary—it became a hybrid structure of knowledge. It is not surprising that the 1813 Charter Act's usage of the term could mean either Indian or European; at the level of practice it had become a composite term in which Indian literature could almost be a subset of the wider category literature, but at other levels it was ridden with biases. With a location partly derived from the Orientalists, literature was launched as a terrain of social history, law-making et al., from within a conception of colonial utility.[60] The easy consensuality of Mackintosh's description, characteristic of the mid-eighteenth century in many respects,[61] is somewhat anachronistic given increasing class struggle in England; he appears to be engaged in a rearguard action with the assistance of colonial power. Proposing an equivalence of subject matter (Indian and European) alongside denial of equality to the ruled, he not only accommodates colonial power as a form of knowledge but naturalizes the knowledge produced under colonial auspices as 'range' or 'refinement'. Not only is his universalism ideologically pretentious, the rhetorical face of usable local knowledge, but widening 'range' both actively increases the number of those excluded from 'taste' and 'refinement' *and* provides a fresh basis for inclusion: a putative democracy for all Englishmen is proposed in relation to this expanding body of knowledge. In addition, Mackintosh's definition presents the difficulty of categorizing a non-literary realm in India—it simply ingests both past and present in their entirety. Defining literature, in the colonial context, becomes first and foremost defining a culture.

The emphasis on taste and refinement was, however, philanthropically extended by others to Sanskrit (by the missionaries and Orientalists cited earlier) and to the vernaculars. If the Asiatic and Bombay Literary Societies placed literature self-consciously in the realm of scholarly and amateur cultivation respectively, addressing cosmopolitan and indigenous elites, the College of Fort William and the missionaries it collaborated with, seeking a wider address and local readership for their vernacular translations, professionalized the field. The ambit of literature as defined by some of the faculty was as ambitious as that of the Orientalists. Gilchrist's aim in translating Aesop's *Fables* (1803) was

> to form such a body of useful and entertaining literature in [Hindustani] as will ultimately raise it to that estimation among the natives which it would many years ago have attained among an enlightened and energetic people. . . .[62]

His *Oriental Fabulist* (1803) similarly addresses future civil servants and also expects to diffuse "a taste" for "such exercises" among Hindustanis.[63] Under British patronage, with different Europeans representing specific linguistic and cultural groups, linguistic entities and literary configurations in the vernaculars were being defined by the activities of the college which demarcate language and literature as a *professional* terrain of reinterpretation and scholarly disputation, linking the proficiency of students with subsequent civil service appointments.

In popular usage literature was a portmanteau term. The 'Literature' section of the *Calcutta Journal* carried articles on Durga puja, on idolatry (by Rammohun Roy), or on the origin of the Pindaris; the phrase "literary productions" designated Warren Hastings's account of the insurrection in Benares, his review of the state of Bengal, and his memoirs, that is, a broad written oeuvre; *Friend of India* used literature synonymously with 'learning', while in 1823 the Gaudiya Samaj was set up as a literary society both to promote Bengali literature and to defend Hinduism.[64] 'Religion' was increasingly segregated in the 1830s: Kashiprasad Ghose (a product of Hindu College famed for his English verse) admitted virtually all prose (history, fables) into Bengali literature but pointedly excluded Roy's and Vidyalankar's pamphlets as religious controversy not literature, while members of the Anglo–Hindu Association, excluding "religious topics", confined discussion to "literary subjects".[65] Printed 'literature' and its new definitions of course coexisted with other extant modes of transmission, with earlier classificatory schemas and contemporary definitions of oral and written vernacular compositions as well as with the rich, diverse oral traditions of Bengal. These latter were being simultaneously reformulated in print and subjected to unsystematic* exclusion; for instance, William Ward classifies compositions popular among *vairagis* and common people as not "much superior to an English story in verse or a common ballad".[66]

The activities and syllabi of many institutions *combined* the indigeneous (qua Orientalist) with the 'western' in practice, and if anything, helped to consolidate literature as a dispersed and hybrid field. The College of Fort William concentrated on living Indian languages, published a miscellany—grammars, lexicons, history, biography, letters, translations of dialogues, proverbs, verse, tales, moral fables from older languages and oral literature, Indian epics, Tulsidas, a *barahmasa*, and the Christian gospels—while its library, opened to Indians in 1818, contained large European holdings which included history, travel writing, Greek and Latin classics, and general literature. The Serampore Mission's Bengali newspaper, *Dig-Darsan* (1818), sent to Hindu College and *pathshalas* of the Calcutta Book Society published fragments of western history, literature, and science; missionaries translated many European texts. Sanskrit College (1824), admitting only upper-caste students, offered alongside Sanskritic studies 'useful' courses in medicine and the sciences, as well as optional courses in English language which were attended by less than half the students for fear of losing caste.[67] The English class in Sanskrit College was discontinued in 1835—the year of official polarizations—because of its partial success. The filtration of English and European literature through translations or adaptations into vernaculars also occurred under the aegis of these and other institutions.

The more specialized meaning of literature as creative or imaginative, signalled by romanticism and exemplified in Jones, was also on the horizon. In India the specialized meaning of literature as 'creative' emerged as a polarization between imagination and *colonial* utility. Though the reformative capacities of a discretely defined 'disinterested' aesthetic domain distinct from gross 'materiality' had not yet been singled out, the accompanying meaning of 'sensibility' when combined with the eighteenth-century meaning of 'refinement' acquired a different inflection here from the opposition between barbarity and civilization, and so played quite readily into different notions of acculturation. The split between imagination as a higher faculty and as a lower faculty was neither evenly nor passively transposed on to Indian texts, it was muddied and contoured by colonial relations as well as by the so-called Anglicist–Orientalist controversy. The split is prefigured in Orientalists, while Anglicists and Utilitarians, bound like Bentham to the self-evident morality of fact, exaggerate the distinction between useful literature governed by reason or observation and the useless characterized as fiction or imagination. Whereas Jones's address to the Asiatic Society neatly compartmentalizes mind, memory, reason, and imagination as more or less equivalent capacities which structure knowledge, elsewhere he retains "reason" and "taste" as the "grand prerogatives of European minds" while accrediting India, like the rest of Asia, in the imaginative sphere.[68] On the other side Macaulay, with his assertive, nationalist revaluation of the vernacular, begins by situating reason and imagination hierarchically. Unlike James Mill, who in his *History* had located the arts and historical compositions in the literature of the Hindus (but not of the Muslims) in the same primitive, despotic, intellectually immature stage of civilization as Hindu women, Macaulay grants near parity to eastern poetry or "works of imagination", but in "works in which facts are recorded" (history, science) there is an "immeasurable" distance between Asia and Europe; Eng-lish literature has "historical compositions" unequalled as "vehicles of ethical and political instruction" as well as "just and lively repre-sentations of human life and human nature".[69] Conjoining a moralized utility with mimetic modes becomes more problematic for Macaulay than it was for Mill. As a historian he yearns for mimetic illusion: the palpability of the eyewitness account, the substantiation and intimate knowledge of men, an immediacy in the reconstruction of the past, "to give to truth those attractions which have been usurped by fiction". A novelistic imagination is needed to "make narrative affective and picturesque", but invention being inferior and the pres-sure of authentication by "sufficient testimony" being paramount, imagination must be "absolutely" *controlled*;[70] if retained to enhance the semantic function its epistemological potential should be curtailed. In order to combine colonial utility with mimetic modes, ima-gination had to be annexed, yet subjugated, since as yet reason and utility were the major vectors of cultural difference. To fuse them effectively required either the impoverishing moves of severing ima-gination from both mimesis and the world of affairs or, more subtly, transforming imagination itself into a site for cultural differentiation.

In sum, there was a whole continuum of meaning under the aegis of 'literature' and the 'literary'—ranging from virtually the entire field of available knowledge, to the specialized products of imaginative activity which appeared more as a subset than as a separate entity. Within these uneven notions, both functional and fluid, which provided some of the energy and produced a context for the introduction of English, many inflections, affinities, and contradictions appeared, and certain definitional contrasts and ideological polarizations crystallized, especially around English. Initially 'English literature' was embedded and diluted in the general meanings and hybrid expanse of literature; gradually it became a site of the shift from the eighteenth-century isolation of utility as a test of value for the few to a majoritarian concept of utility hailed by Utilitarians, and then moved into the narrowed space of 'colonial utility' which not only derived from both the above but was a specific contextual product of British and Indian interaction. Further, the interrelated definition of English and colonial utility became a part of the process of demarcating a new notion of culture.

In several administrative documents, the content of English literature is synonymous with British or European civilization comprising a social order, ordered knowledge, and refinement,[71] appears to include the entire field of writing, and is distinguished only from science. Falling under the general rubric of 'modernity', no steady division between literature and civilization, and later, between literature and culture, is maintained. The Committee of Public Instruction, in a passage apropos Hindu College quoted later ("A taste for English has been widely disseminated . . . "), uses the word English to designate a composite education including literature, language, and science. In Macaulay's 1835 Minute, the "literature" extant in the English language includes works of imagination, historical compositions, moral philosophy, political economy, and science. However, finer subdivisions were made in syllabi, mainly on classical or neo-classical lines, for example, at the Calcutta Seminary for British students, Hindu College or Rammohun Roy's Anglo–Hindu School.[72]

The location of English education in colonial utility was fairly specific. This education, joined to material, political, commercial, missionary aims, entered and proliferated under the triple signs of pragmatic interest, religious pedagogy, and individual philanthropy. However, there were different tendencies even among those administrators who advocated maintaining indigenous institutions, identifying knowledge with inducement, improvement with reward. Sir Thomas Munro, for instance, saw foreign subjugation and moral improvement as fundamentally contradictory unless the British shared the administrative and material benefits of power with Indians. "Our books alone will do little or nothing; dry simple literature will never improve the character of a nation. To produce this effect it must open the road to wealth, and honour, and public employment."[73] Among Evangelicals like Charles Grant, ironically a staunch defender of Company monopoly and an opponent of free trade, Christianity, like English, was allied to material benefits and expansion of the British market; his ally, Wilberforce, extended these partially to Indians:

> Christianity, independent of its effects on a future state of exist-
> ence, has been acknowledged even by avowed sceptics to be,
> beyond all other institutions that ever existed, favourable to the
> temporal interests and happiness of man: and never was there a
> country where there is greater need than in India for the diffusion
> of its general influence.[74]

English education began in an ad hoc way in the early nineteenth century; by the time it was systematized by state policy in
1835, a well-formed connection had evolved between the acquisition
of prosperity and the language of the rulers,[75] giving English the
emblematic character of choice on the part of an articulate section of
the Bengal middle class. In practice and in terms of sectional interests,
the line between administrators, Orientalists, missionaries, and unofficial British private entrepreneurs could often be thin, fluctuating,
or nonexistent. Not only did the activities and syllabi of most colonial
institutions have analogous aims as well as practical and ideological
overlaps, but different ideologies frequently converged on similar
material or political interests with Orientalists, administrators, missionaries, and the articulate section of the Bengal middle class alike.
It was partly along these lines of confluence and rift that indigenous
institutions specifically designed to teach English took shape. Hindu
College was set up at the initiative of, and financed and managed by
Calcutta's newly rich, newly urbanized elite. The nature and amount
of support they received from individual Englishmen is still difficult
to determine.[76] However, its genesis is an index of the self-perception
of choice. Though the college proposed to teach Indian literature,
languages, and science along with English language, literature, and
science, in practice the latter triad was emphasized. In 1823 Rammohun
Roy characterized Sanskrit as resembling the pre-Baconian scholas-
ticism of medieval Europe, a form of "imaginary learning" "of little
or no practicable use" with the labour being incommensurate with the
reward, and asked the government for the useful sciences and human-
ist education of "modern Europe".[77] The letter is an implicit critique
of the misguided altruism, retrogressive policy, and superfluity of the
state's educational enterprises. Why, Rammohun wants to know,

should it patronize forms of knowledge "*already* current" and "commonly taught" in India—why should the *British* teach Sanskrit?

The functionality of English cannot of course be taken at face value. Though there seems to have been a virtual unanimity among the vocal Hindu elite on the usefulness of English education, they were divided about English as acculturation.[78] Whereas in the gene-ral ambit of literature, colonial utility pushes definitions of *literature* in the direction of social history and a broad body of usable local knowledge, this same utility pushes definitions of *English* simultaneously in two mutually opposing directions—on the one hand as a language of secular universalism, and on the other hand as a lang-uage of cultural differentiation centred on 'acculturation' that also feeds a notion of 'culture'. Mill's or Macaulay's Utilitarianism as the philosophy of an ascendant, secularizing middle class had a certain appeal for the emerging middle class here; but since it reproduced and elaborated in singularly vicious ways a pejorative vocabulary of cultural differentiation, it aggravated the fissures in colonial authority, became one of the forces which pressed the moral onus of reform and preservation as an imperative on the Bengal middle class. Ironi-cally, whereas the apparent dedication of earlier administrators to maintaining cultural differences displayed areas of overlap between patriarchal assumptions, this later offer of con-structing cultural simi-litude through the processes of English edu-cation, with its assumption that no such similitude yet existed, exaggerated cultural differences.

One direction colonial utility pressed in was that of an ethical, scientific, or syncretic universalism. Here some secularizing missionary or administrative initiatives and utilitarian notions con-verged with local attempts to shape a complementary version of use-ful moral instruction which was not, in its intention, tied to any single religion. The Marquess of Hasting disputed as outmoded the Court of Directors' 1814 despatch on education (discussed earlier), pointed to changed conditions in India, emphasized the vernacular and the advancement of science and morality *before* Orientalist education since "the arts which adorn and embellish life will follow in ordinary course", and advocated the distribution of "little manuals of religious sentiments and ethic[al] maxims" to village schoolmasters without any bias in favour of a particular religious creed.[79] A similar desire to cull a universally applicable morality was evident in the fables translated in the College of Fort William, or in J.D. Pearson (of London Missionary Society) and Radhakant Deb's collaborative *Nitikatha* ("Moral Tales" based on Aesop's *Fables*) of 1821 which "drew on both Christianity and Hindu traditions and were designed to inculcate a feeling of morality without any religious bias",[80] or in the composition and rules of the Calcutta School Book Society. The first managing committee of the society, which consisted of Hindus and Muslims, missionaries, British administrators and businessmen (a composition quite similar to the Calcutta School Society), offered an explicitly secular model. Its rules stated:

> That it forms no part of the design of this Institution, to furnish Religious Books:—a restriction, however, very far from being meant to preclude the supply of Moral Tracts, or works of a moral tendency, which, without interfering with the religious sentiments of any person, may be calculated to enlarge the understanding, and improve the character.[81]

Rammohun Roy, with his bearings in Islamic rationalism[82] and other modes of relativization, finding an affinity with Unitarianism, attempted to extract an ethical universal from Christianity by sifting the "moral precepts" from the historical and doctrinal parts of the New Testament since the latter were open to doubt and disputation in India, especially the unconvincing "miraculous relations, which are much less wonderful than the fabricated tales handed down to the natives of Asia". The moral doctrines would be "beyond the reach of *metaphysical perversion*, and intelligible alike to the learned and unlearned".[83] Believing Indians to have the "same capability of improvement as any civilized people", identifying freedom with freedom from prejudice and useless religious constraint,[84] and taking a comparativist standpoint, Roy tries to extract a purely ethical definition of utility which cannot be challenged on the bases of mimetic accuracy or convincing fabulation.

Together, these various emphases comprised a tendency attempting to produce a syncretic ethical universalism which could not only forge a consensual, relatively secular, bourgeois morality grounded in uncamouflaged pragmatic interest, but also manage the contradictions of colonialism for this class. The fact that various sections of the Bengal elite could unite across differences about women or education on issues related to revenue, judicial matters, and freedom of the press reveals a common interest in demarcating an area of civil life separable from religion. But lines were being drawn differently—the frequent recall of religious sanction to define the civil added to the confusion. The attempt to shape a secular ethic floun-dered either on veiled proselytizing ambitions, or in other areas on the conflation of religion and civil law (partially derived from Islamic and Hindu religious texts). Thus the Marquess of Hasting in the same despatch cited above suggested to missionaries that moral instruction may be regarded as an intermediary step to Christianity; Radhakant Deb, protesting the abolition of widow immolation, later became a founder of the Dharma Sabha; and Roy found it necessary to recall the Shastras while arguing against customary malpractice regarding property rights for women.

The difficulty of forging an ethical universalism in which utility did not frequently slip into acculturation was evident in the problematic reliance on certain kinds of elimination. The Calcutta School Book Society translated western science, history, and litera-ture into the vernacular, and obtained permission to reprint books published by the London Society for the Diffusion of Useful Knowl-edge in 1830; all religious texts—Christian, Hindu, Muslim—were omitted on the ground that fairness consisted in either full inclusion or total exclusion.[85] Yet the difficulty of compiling an adequate body of secular knowledge through the practice of elimination remained; one complaint was that most "English Literature", "from the speller to the most abstruse works on moral and political philosophy, con-tains repeated admission of the divine authority of Christian faith".[86] Further, lines drawn on the basis of elimination often wavered when secular intention had to be translated into practice. The acculturative aspect of colonial utility could undo its secular claims as in Hindu College. The founders had wanted government patronage for encour-agement of "a more classical knowledge of English language and lite-rature" and "the English system of morals" as well as a "liberal edu-cation" from which they could eliminate whatever "they could not reconcile with their religious opinions".[87] All the rules were written by conservative, upper-caste Hindus; there was to be no religious study. With Derozio's dismissal for 'iconoclasm' by the management committee of the college (which included Radhakant Deb but not Rammohun Roy) it appears that the secular principles of the college, when tested, meant silent conformity to Hinduism. The management committee's 1829 resolution asked the headmaster to "check as far as possible all disquisitions leading to unsettle the belief of the boys in the great principles of national religion", and it directed teachers in 1830 to "abstain from any communication on the subject of Hindu religion with the boys, or to suffer any practices inconsistent with the Hindu notions of propriety. . .".[88]

Paradoxically, even as colonial utility and acculturation became *mutually* contaminating, an effective opposition between instrumentality and acculturation was in place for both British and Indian, cutting across vernaculars, Sanskrit and English, by the 1830s. As early as 1804, the College of Fort William served for Marquess Wellesley the conservative impulse of forestalling the effects of the French Revolution (at the time also a motive force for many Evangelicals) on Company servants as the "best security" for "British power".[89] The college intended to model ideal civil servants, to put them on par with a similar bureaucratic stratum in Europe, and to have an acculturative function which balanced necessary knowledge about India with European education and British interests:

> Their education should be founded in a general knowledge of those branches of literature and science which form the basis of the education of persons destined to similar occupations in Europe. To this foundation should be added an intimate acquaintance with the history, languages, customs and manners of the people of India, with the Mohammedan and Hindoo Codes of law and religion, and the political and commercial interests and relations of Great Britain.[90]

At the same time, since British students had to be protected from excess 'foreign' acculturation, the suggested counterbalances were the "Christian religion" and the "wise laws and constitutions of Great Britain": an oath of loyalty to both was to be taken by teachers.[91] The opposition set up here—pragmatic on both sides—is between a potentially 'Indianizing' Orientalist scholarship or study and a Christianity allied to a 'western' education. The college eventually foundered on this very opposition, resolved through a *spatial* division of European education (which was to take place at Haileybury College established in England in 1806) from training in the Indian languages at Fort William. Another example is the pervasive discourse on character and governability: 'native' ignorance, the necessary scaffold of altruism, was proposed alternately as making for the good queiscent subject or the barbaric and potentially inflammatory subject. Evangelicals like Charles Grant proposed for Christianity the role of a pacifier making for governability just as Dubois and others had done for Hinduism.[92]

Colonial utility could not simply be a question of straightforward expedience, even when the mismatch between education and government employment was at issue. In 1834 several former students of Sanskrit College addressed a petition to the secretary of the Committee of Public Instruction, complaining of unemployment after having studied "Hindoo literature and science, more especially Law" for a decade or more.[93] Yet, once battle lines were drawn in 1835, and the government proposed to distinguish between "artificial encouragement" and genuine need when funding Orientalist institutions, a 'memorial' with 10,000 signatures was sent to the Court of Directors in 1837 by Hindus asking for the preservation of Sanskrit College and for the encouragement of Sanskrit language and literature.[94] Artificial needs and internalized needs were already entangled while economic needs found their coherence within an emerging set of cultural definitions.

Each notion of colonial utility was not only informed by prior characterization of a culture but engaged in creating an 'accultured' space. Utility was alternately placed inside or displaced from Indian institutions and texts: every definition of utility became an attrition or creation of cultural value. Sanskrit texts were alternately a source from which ethical instruction and juridical 'truth' could be culled (with or without the help of a golden age) or irredeemably profligate. In the tussle over distinguishing correct from incorrect Indian literature, antiquity became the contested source rather than a fixed guarantee of morality, eventually leading to increasingly 'nationalist' definitions of utility. Whereas Lord Minto had ascribed crimes, especially of perjury and forgery, "both in Mahomedans and Hindus, to the want of due instruction in the moral and religious tenets of their respective faiths",[95] the 1824 Court of Director's despatch to the governor-general of Bengal opposes "useful learning" to indigenous learning. With a Utilitarian contempt for poetry, it upbraids the Committee of Public Instruction for not distinguishing and retaining only that which was "useful in Hindu and Mahomedan literature"; by establishing institutions

> for the purpose of teaching mere Hindoo or mere Mahomedan literature, you bound yourself to teach a great deal of what was frivolous, not a little of what was purely mischievous and a small remainder indeed in which utility was in any way concerned.[96]

This implicit piecing together of specific intellectual, religious, and aesthetic production with a particular way of life and bringing both under fresh cultivation itself heralds a new notion of culture.[97] The committee (which contained H.H. Wilson and H.T. Prinsep but had no Indian members yet) in its own defence upheld poetry as a "very important part" of Sanskrit and Arabic literature, as "the source of national imagery, the expression of national feeling, and the repository of the most approved phraseology and style".[98] An alternative version of utility based on 'national' value is offered which also interrelates moral, social, and aesthetic judgement—contemporary vitality depends on a 'classical' repository identified with a set of 'national' feelings and images. Here the aesthetic and the instrumental, 'culture' and utility, are explicitly formulated as a set of interdependent categories.

Even the practical affinities and structural similarities between English and Sanskrit—apart from the relation of Sanskrit to European knowledge already discussed—which at one level eased middle-class alignment with English, simultaneously pressed up issues of acculturation or pushed in the direction of nationalist definitions of 'culture'.[99] Despite the practical and ideological overlaps in terms of class and colonial rule, education in this period had some of the ideological coordinates of a constituency education—directed at Hindus (according to caste), Muslims, Christian converts, would-be converts, civil servants, et al.—and worked through a system of exclusions. English, at least up to 1835, was a 'Hindu' subject. Neither Sanskrit College nor the Madrasa was able to fully establish a bilinguality combining Persian, Arabic, or Sanskrit with English. The Committee of Public Instruction's suggestion in 1826 of establishing

an English college in Calcutta open to both Muslim and Hindu
students went unheeded. Hindu College with some improvements
was felt "capable of answering the purpose". Only in 1835 was the
committee, acknowledging that "the Mahomedan community at the
capital labours under great disadvantages from the little encouragement which has as yet been held out to them to cultivate English
literature", able to resolve to emphasize English at the Calcutta
Madrasa.[100] Apart from uneven economic development, it is not very
clear why Muslims were slower than the Hindu elite to invest in English education[101] or what part the uncertainty caused by the projected
shift from Persian as an administrative language was playing,[102] but
for all practical purposes both English and Sanskrit virtually excluded Muslims. From the demand to deprivilege Persian it is evident
that English was perceived as such: in 1835, a memorial signed by
6,945 Hindus (including all the managers, students, and parents of the
students at Hindu College) asked Lord Bentinck to remove existing
restrictions on English in the law courts and give it the same privileges
as Persian, on the ground that Persian was as foreign as English, and
English was now the language of "all the principal functionaries of
the state".[103] This perception seems to have cut across the 'conservative–radical' divide. The Derozian Krishnamohan Banerji, describing Persian as an antiquarian language, wrote: "It sounds very odd
indeed that a language neither of conquerors nor of the conquered
should be the medium of administering justice in a country."[104]

The contradictions of education based on a system of exclusions became sharper when 'identity' could not be rapidly established
as with Eurasians—where neither language, loyalty, nor acculturation was an administrative issue but cultural disparity was assumed.
Their letters to *Calcutta Journal* are eloquent. 'An Anglo Briton'
wants to know why "the Country born, or descendents of Englishmen" should "*alone* be excluded from a Collegiate education, *in
Calcutta*" while "Colleges are founded and endowed for Civil, and
Military, the Mahomedan and the Hindoo".[105] 'Benevolus', an
'Anglo Briton', asks for a respectable seminary for the children of
"such officers who may not have the means of sending them to England"; after all "Country-born children . . . by their upright, honest
and virtuous conduct do more honour to their parents than many of
those who have fairer faces."[106] A 'Country-Born' seeking to make

"useful and not dangerous Scions of the mother Stem" proffers the Roman model of colonization to the British.

> ... it was their [the Romans'] first endeavour to colonize, so as to have a stronger tie than mere conquest upon their new subjects— these colonists intermarried with the natives, and by the learning and useful arts introduced by them, the conquered gloried in the name of being Romans; and when in the course of events the mother country fell into decay, her colonies rose up and flourished in the form of the Governments which now diversify the present map of Europe.[107]

The Derozian journal *Kaleidoscope* asked for patronage, educational, and employment avenues for the "distinct class" of "half-castes"—children of Europeans by Indian women—who though less robust than the British, were equal to the "natives" and "remarkable for their docility and intelligence".[108] Using the semantic of non-interference, Eurasians represent themselves as an intermediary, if not successor group, combining a 'Hindu' docility with innate loyalty and intelligence; but the combination of physical difference and cultural similitude seems to have weakened the administrative will to reform.[109]

English was recognizably a successor of Sanskritic studies in the means of alignment with colonial power and at this level the opposition often set up between the two was more ideological than material: both were possible modes of present affiliation as well as of potential resistance to colonial rule or its cultural paraphernalia. Further, with the classicization of English which crystallized with Macaulay's 1835 Minute, another structural similarity with Sanskrit developed—both could be invoked for cultural nationalisms, whether British or Indian. If European literature is to be placed above Indian and Arabian for Macaulay, then English literature is to be placed above that of the entire world. It is the ideological relocation and re-entry of English literature, the accumulation of three hundred years, as discrete and synchronic which, like Sanskrit, facilitates its insertion as a seamless tradition. The insertion allows Macaulay to upgrade English from an imitator of the classics to *itself* becoming, comparably, a classic: it can be a sign of venerable antiquity for present-day Indians just as Latin and Greek were for the sixteenth-century English. Here, having become identical with its own antecedents, it can function as an 'autonomous' category. Legitimizing modernity with the patina of antiquity, Macaulay implicitly situates English literature as both an object of recovery as well as a mode (the regulated study of English literature) of recuperating tradition.

Oppositions between English and Hinduism and/or Sanskrit were set up by the British and Indians across the political spectrum throughout this period. For instance, the same Committee of Public Instruction which defended Indian poetry and was committed to the engrafting model of combining indigenous learning with scientific knowledge,[110] noted the progress made by Hindu College with pleasure, identifying English with a loftier morality which could not but undermine Hinduism:

> A taste for English has been widely disseminated, and independent schools, conducted by young men, reared in the Vidyalaya, are springing up in every direction. The moral effect has been equally remarkable, and an impatience of the restrictions of Hinduism, and a disregard of its ceremonies, are openly avowed by many young men of respectable birth and talents, and entertained by many more who outwardly conform to the practices of their countrymen. Another generation will, probably, witness a very material alteration in the notions and feelings of the educated classes of the Hindu community in Calcutta.[111]

A new conflation of liberalization as represented by English education, and loyalism partly representing the growing influence of free traders, emerged, and in some sections of the administration, superseded the earlier emphasis on non-interference, as for instance in the debates on widow immolation.[112] Even William Ward had approved of English education in Hindu College for a leisured elite, as it would enable them to "unite" "most intimately with the government" and philanthropic Europeans, though he considered it impractical for the masses for whom he recommended "transfusing European language" into the vernaculars.[113] After Derozio's dismissal which polarized Young Bengal from so-called orthodox Bengal, British reactions ranged from conservative fear of anarchy to triumph over the newfound prowess of an English placed in frontal combat with Hinduism. A missionary newspaper re-presented the Derozians as

> that small party of educated Hindoos, *who have made the highest*
> *attainments in English literature and the highest advances in*
> *liberality of sentiments*; who, alive to the inefficacy of half-
> measures and scorning the hypocrisy of double-dealing, have at
> once renounced in theory and practice the whole system of
> Hindooism, pure and impure, ancient, modern, Vedantic and
> Pouranic; and who, being thus left in a region of vacancy as
> regards religion, have announced themselves to the world as free
> enquirers after truth.[114] (my emphases)

Macaulay proclaimed: "No Hindu, who has received an English
edu-cation, ever remains sincerely attached to his religion."[115]
However, a libertarian English could not unproblematically guarantee loyalism; he also wrote: "We have to engraft on despotism those
blessings which are the natural fruits of liberty."[116] If English is an
authoritative harbinger of a new morality it is also naturally seditious;
disrupt-ing indigenous authority, it can be potentially disruptive of
British authority. Educational reform must ensure that English be a
structure of withholding liberty while offering knowledge and
minimal power. Further, the very triumph of English lays it open to
the double-edged logic of hybridization—the seduction of the market
and the dangerous prospect of infinite reproducibility. For Macaulay
English produces the ability to *consume*—he prefers that Indians
were "ruled by their own kings, but wearing our broadcloth and
working with our cut-lery"[117]—but he cannot bear to surrender
Shakespeare, whose reading he recommends, to Indian reinterpretation. Shakespeare *per-formed* is anathema; he can "conceive nothing
more grotesque" than seeing "Portia represented by a little black
boy" in a Calcutta col-lege.[118] Indeed the simultaneous entry of
English into a market economy and a 'national' culture produced
unresolvable anxiety: the influential, recurrent British trope of
English in India as a *failed imi-tation* was a symptom of this fear that
English on assiduous export may not remain quite English.

The Derozians themselves, who represented a brief moment
of scepticism, elaborated the opposition, deploying English as seditious in a freedom-versus-enslavement rhetoric—with English education standing for potential and prescriptive Hinduism for constriction. Partly in reaction against these celebratory accents, English

literature was identified by some others in the same period with cultural amnesia: 'One decidedly against superstition' recounts his family brahmin priest's condemnation of English literature as responsible for the present ignorance about the customs and manners of fore-fathers.[119] If this represented anxiety about closure of existing modes of access into indigenous culture, there was an equal if not greater anxiety among the 'new orthodoxy' about the recovery of sceptical traditions through what were perceived as interpretative modes rela-ted to colonial education. *Samachar Chandrika*, which in the same years was protesting against the abolition of widow immolation, pointed to atheists and admirers of Charvak among the Hindu Col-lege boys and asked for government intervention![120]

The acculturation debate over English acquired its energy from the semantic of non-interference and from the Orientalist elaboration of an influential field of 'reculturation'. Hinduism increasingly comes to be proposed as prophylactic or antidote for acculturation just as Christianity was in Fort William College, accentuating some of the ideological tendencies of non-interference at a time when British rule was consolidating on altered lines. If knowledge introduced as an apparently self-identifying cultural totality could become a form of sectional class power, then this was *as* important for new orthodox tendencies as the pressure of existing orthodox norms in their search for modes of resisting, regulating, or effecting change. The self-definition of the new Hindu orthodoxy relied on a new notion of culture dependent on volition and conscious cultivation in which reform and preservation could become virtually identical. A letter to the editor of the *Soodhakar* by 'A Friend to Religion' bemoans the fact that students of Hindu College have become exactly like the English in knowledge and customs; he considers this a not unnatural "fruit of their education" and their exposure to English since childhood: "For how can he that is eminent in any kind of learning shew his eminence, unless he adopts accordant custom?" He proposes a sequential compartmentalization of 'culture' and utility as a solution:

> . . . children first be made to attend somewhat in their childhood
> to the Sanskrit Shastras and afterwards be taught English for the
> purpose of business, so that *the means of attaining both holiness
> and wealth* may be secured. In this way, their parents, at a small

> expense, will see the young people advancing *both in religion and*
> *opulence* and are not to suppose that all the cost is for religion.[121]
> (my emphases)

Ironically, the Hinduism proposed as a model of 'reculturation' was
symbiotically related to English proposed as a model of 'deculturation':
it was because the former could provide a usable past and 'culture'
that English could be confidently assimilated as utility, and acculturation could seem so scandalous. In fact the noise about deculturation
in this period tends to blur its actual imperatives—that it was
happening due to massive changes in a number of areas ranging from
the political and economic to the familial—as well as to efface the
real nature of reculturation. The new orthodoxy attempted to separate or protect the acquisition of power (which had well-defined
boundaries in relation to the British) from the experience of loss—or
to preempt loss by honing or holding ready modes of 'recovery' and
new modes of social authority. In counterposing English to Sanskrit
and/or Hinduism, the new orthodoxy proportionately increased the
power of English making it commensurate to the longevity or
entrenchment of the inert customs or beliefs it was seen to erode or
destroy. Increasing the power of one term enlarged the power of the
other—and thereby bestowed the aura of an exaggerated transformative capacity on English.

   English, still emergent, could be inserted into the fabric of
middle-class lives in different ways, and the struggle seems to be
about regulating the modes of its insertion. Depending on political
affinities, its representations as destructive of the familial, customary, or metaphysical, became ways of defining antagonistic, exclu-
ded/exclusive areas, or incompatible, undesirable elements in Indian
society. In this process not only were the familial, customary, and
metaphysical effectively reconstituted but the meanings of *both*
English and Hinduism were often *reduced*. English became a form of
alienation, partly from its class location, and partly from the reduction of both English and indigenous culture to a reciprocal system
of blockages. In order to understand the range and implications of
this process it may help to connect it with other pressures on this
class—alignments with familial, caste, and rural structures, attitudes to agrarian unrest and lower-caste conversion—for making

modes of legitimacy and social authority. Its own vulnerability and confidence are apparent both in relation to existing 'orthodoxy' and to the new orthodoxy being made: ideological affinities crisscross, individuals speak from the contradictory, often bewildering possibilities available.

As a cultural category English was multiply and irreconcilably constituted as *choice, colonial imposition, cultural threat,* and *class power;* it condensed the political, economic, and social relations of the Bengal middle class but with differing implications for different sections. At one level no genuine cultural relativization of English, as one language among others, could occur within the political economy of colonialism. For this tiny minority English opened limited service opportunities at a time of deindustrialization and blockage of certain forms of economic mobility. Whereas liberal sections sought links with British free trader groups, the force destroying Bengal's production economy,[122] and developed assimilative tendencies, the new orthodoxy transposed this wider obstruction on to 'culture' and sought to circumscribe colonial power by synonymizing it with English. If Sanskrit, in one sense, is already conceptualized as a means for displacement of indigenous knowledge, English conversely becomes a medium for displaced struggle. In the first three decades of the nineteenth century English emerged from a general notion of literature, identified with a composite notion of civilization, and became attendant on a specialized voluntarist notion of culture resting on volition and cultivation which later could in its weaker forms be attached to liberal syncretic Indian nationalism, and in its stronger variants be either attached to British nationalism or counterposed by a nascent Hindu chauvinist nationalism. Though the transformation was fed by the comparativism of the Orientalists and the paternalism of non-interference, it crystallized with the acculturation debate accelerated, ironically, by the 'philistine' Utilitarian Anglicists and the new orthodoxy of Bengal.

Macaulay's Minute of 1835 becomes somewhat illusory as a historic moment. There is little that is new in it except the insistence that the government must recognize a new class in India and amend its policy accordingly: the utility of Sanskrit and Persian for compiling the law was nearly at an end, while British rule, local needs, and the 'state of the market' had altered. The Minute condensed and simplified a complex field of institutional and class interaction, contradictory and collusive tendencies, into the language of fiat and racist imposition. An ironic postscript on Macaulay is that the British government sought and received support from the affluent new orthodoxy—many of whom were prominent members of the Dharma Sabha—for its Anglicist education policy, and when the government stopped releasing money for the printing of Oriental works, with drastic effects on the Asiatic Society of Bengal, a missionary news-paper, the *Friend of India*, suggested that the Dharma Sabha pass a vote of censure on the council![123]

V

Whereas in the case of English the argument was over controlling its insertion into the social fabric, controlling women was at issue in the debates on female education. Not surprisingly, female knowledge, unlike male knowledge, was usually demarcated quite strictly within the purview of domestic serviceability.[124] However, the corollary insertion into the moral, tackled in different ways, took place under the indirect aegis of colonial utility and an emerging notion of 'culture'. Women were seldom represented as partakers of literature—whether Sanskrit or English—and arguments hinged on the practical issue of access to literacy while literature had a more or less symbolic location. Though advocates of literacy ranged from the new orthodoxy to the Derozians, the nature of women's inscription into literacy, which must encode a demarcation of knowledge, was uncertain.

Here the influential, contradictory, and often intractable logics set up in the overlapping or common ascriptive, denominational fields of womanhood, literature, and Hinduism are of some significance. The debate on female education is conceptually informed by the oppositions between women as chaste victims and as libidinous agents, between embodied knowledge and acquired knowledge, between English and Sanskrit and/or Hinduism, between essential selves and selves that could be refashioned, and between reform and preservation. In the accounts of paternalist administrators or missionaries discussed earlier, embodied knowledge is knowledge of subjection to patriarchal norms coincident with Hinduism in its prescriptive aspects. The chaste Hindu woman is the primary type; her chastity is an embodied knowledge substantiated in behaviour, evinced in lack of choice, identified with *stridharma* (duty). Illiterate yet governed, the Hindu woman, if chaste, herself becomes a pedagogical category. But since patriarchy is reintroduced as simultaneously Hindu uniqueness and Hindu male stigmata, this pedagogic principle of embodied knowledge—the chaste woman—is self-divided. Torn between civilization and barbarity, representing both the longevity of a prescriptive Hinduism successfully translated into domesticity as well as Hindu male oppression, such a principle also situates men as in need of reform, thereby both reinforcing and casting male pedagogic authority into doubt. However, chastity, a synecdochic representation of the sexual division of labour, legitimate patrilineal inheritance, class and caste boundaries, remains the substratum of womanhood and was never disputed by middle-class reformers.

In a second related logic, deriving from early missionary and Orientalist accounts, implicated in the civilizational 'values' selectively extrapolated from upper-caste patriarchy, 'Hindu womanhood' must be preserved as symbolic and opposed to the definitional threat of English, especially for the new orthodoxy. But if opposed to literature as higher learning per se the symbolic nature of womanhood itself is jeopardized. The illiterate woman who has no means of access to the past is difficult to square with the Orientalist recovery of a Hindu golden age, the Anglicist snatching back of the same, the liberal ideology of improvement or missionary proselytizing. Nor is there a simple resolution by which education for Hindu women can be cast as a *return*. The persistence of the licentious woman of missionary accounts, of the perfidies of *strisvabhav*, and the presence of unregulated women in the home willy nilly situate education as the fashioning of a new self, alternately raise fears that women will become worse and the hope that they will improve. A part of the debate on female education thus became a discourse on women's faults (indicative perhaps of the fragility of the family), resembling the discourse on 'native' character and governability. The debate in fact teetered between two notions of women's character and male agency. The figure of the errant woman formed in the confluence of an extant misogyny and the discourse of the 'bad' native recurs, in part, in order to argue for the necessity of women's education, male governance, and male-initiated reform. However, when women are presented as also victims of patriarchal arrangements, the emphasis shifts to male error, splitting male agency into self-reform and reform of women.

The irreconcilable logics of this field were compounded by at least two other difficulties. Firstly, the Hindu woman's ideality had to be measured against caste distinctions, existing patriarchal practices, and emerging class arrangements. The surrounding models of literate or educated women, past and present, were bewildering in their heterogeneity: learned women in ancient Hindu texts, women from princely (especially rajput) families, the odd brahmin woman, the occasional widow, female mendicants, that is, *vairaginis* and *sannyasinis* many of whom know Sanskrit, dancing girls or prostitutes, low-caste converts, and European women.[125] The literacy of the Hindu woman had to be freed from semantic adjacency with other women, except the first three, by ballasting her education with a weightier morality—the confines and contours of knowledge had to begin to mark out a middle-class private sphere. For instance, *Stri-shikshavidhayak* (1823), printed for the Calcutta School Book Society, included the famous courtesan Chitralekha in its roster of learned ancient Indian women but did not elaborate with episodes from her life. Since learning was being presented as preventing bad deeds and absorbing women in *dharma*, and knowledge as capable of controlling desire—*mun ke matvaare haathi* (the wild, drunk elephants in/ of the heart)—a courtesan could only be an embarrassment. The only respectable examples to be found in contemporary Bengal and its neighbourhood were: Rani Bhavani, a benevolent brahmin ruler, along with all the women of her household in Murshidabad; all the women in the raja's household in Calcutta; Hati Vidyalankar of Kashi who studied in the leisure time left after housework and became a pandit of such calibre that she now taught the Shastras; Shyamsundari, the wife of a learned brahmin in a village in Faridpur *zila* who had read some of the Shastras; and the two daughters of one Bhattacharya of Ula village.[126] Significantly, the agency of these women is bounded by the norms of good conduct guaranteed through upper-caste and/ or aristocratic birth, the responsibilities of regency or of domestic labour.

Secondly, what superficially appear to be concepts which should be particularly amenable to 'orthodox' Hindus—women as embodied knowledge or education as a return to the golden age—in fact faced powerful opposition from within, that is from existing patriarchal *practices*. One strand in the debates on widow immolation, for instance, was related to questions of knowledge and pedagogy. In 1818, Rammohun Roy, drawing on Mritunjay Vidyalankar, opposed widow immolation on the basis that chastity and abstinence leading to philosophical wisdom and beatitude were a higher goal for the widow according to the Shastras; the attainment of knowledge was superior to "the performance of rites", and the existence of learned women in ancient texts proved that women could attain divine knowledge.[127] Though the lines between choice and duty are vexed and the widow remains under family supervision, austerity composes a prescribed, behavioural form of embodied knowledge which Rammohun attempts to resituate as volition or acquired knowledge. An anonymous, untitled, answering pamphlet in Bengali (with English translation appended) attributed to pandits and also drawing on the Shastras appeared. Stridently advocating widow immolation, this argued that though beatitude may be a higher goal, women lacked chastity, intelligence, and learning, and would never attain it; so

> to discipline them in the Sacred Wisdom . . . would be attended
> with no other success than to *condemn* them for both the one and
> the other. . . . It is therefore very improper that the women who
> have never been conscious of so much as the meaning of the
> word wisdom, should be desired to follow the system of sacred
> knowledge.[128]

Immolation is said to be necessary because women are immoral and incapable of acquiring knowledge; it not only prevents potential breach of chastity but can atone for scolding as well as adultery on the part of the woman; nor does it conflict with her self-interest since it is immaterial whether the widow's motive is "amours [concupiscence], wrath, fear or affection". The pamphlet rationalizes the use of force and blatantly situates widow immolation as an external, expiatory, and punitive regulation of sexuality: at this level it is committed to the practice rather than to its legitimizing ideology. The editor of *Calcutta Journal* was quick to seize this: "Then a suttee at once loses both its name and nature. It is no longer the effect of chaste affection."[129] Ironically, in this interchange, the chaste woman as pedagogic principle is proposed in two different ways by those opposing widow immolation, but *altogether* denied by those advocating widow immolation. The latter's defence of this violent practice on the grounds of its antiquity cannot be reconciled with other images from antiquity—the chaste widow and the learned woman—and reflects two crucial disjunctions sharpened by the entry of bourgeois patriarchal values: firstly between construing women as *sources* and as *subjects* of (patriarchal) pedagogic authority, and secondly between wanting to continue *specific* patriarchal practices and constituting women as emblems of a desired, composite, *symbolic* continuity.

Yet the new orthodox supporters of widow immolation were not all opposed to female literacy—partly because of their own social location and partly because such a deep commitment to women's innate immorality or *strisvabhav* by middle-class men had to waver between punishment and reform; a conservative recognition of the nece-ssity of reproduction and socialization would call for less drastic, internalizable forms of ethical instruction. For instance, Radhakanta Deb—whose grandfather largely owed his enormous wealth, lands, social and political power to collaborative and profitable relations as well as employment with the East India Company—was a multilingual scholar, Persian interpreter, champion of English education, and compiler of a Bengali–English dictionary. He had received an English education and became a director of the Hindu College managing committee in 1818 (voted for Derozio's dismissal), was an active member of the Calcutta School Book Society and the Calcutta School Society, had connections with both Serampore missionaries and Sanskrit College Orientalists, and was invited to join the Asiatic Society of Bengal. It is unclear whether the family was kayasth or the hierarchically lower subarnavanik by caste, but Radhakanta seems to have followed his father and grandfather in becoming a self-styled, quasi-brahminical spokesman for the kayasth community and affluent zamindars; politically, his steadfast loyalism culminated in public support for the British during the 1857 revolt.[130] He wrote to the president of the Calcutta School Society in 1821 opposing *direct* instruction of women of his class by missionaries as discordant with Hindu "social practices and customs", but promised that "the Hindus will arrange to educate their daughters before their marriage by engaging tutors at home". He wanted women missionaries to train women belonging to "respectable" but "poor" families; these 'native intermediaries' could then be appointed as tutors by affluent families: "At this there would be no encroachment on the time-honoured customs and practices of the Hindus, but there would be spread of edu-cation among women."[131] Women had not been sequestered before Muslim rule and now they needed education before they could be given liberty like European women; he urged the education of women in domestic skills in *Stri-sikhar Bidya* (1822), and in order to dispel the superstition that literacy spelled widowhood for women, claimed support from corroborating scriptures and Puranas.[132] In the 1824 version, the dialogue between two girls goes:

> Question: But old men say that a girl who reads and writes becomes a widow.
> Answer: Nonsense. It is not supported by scriptures and our Puranas refer to educated women. Take, for example, the European ladies. They are educated but not widows.[133]

I do not know if he was associated with the first pamphlet, but he became one of the chief patrons of the Dharma Sabha; significantly, with the exception of two brahmins, its committee consisted of kayasths and subarnavaniks—caste groups struggling with brahmins to claim ritual status in the 1830s.[134] Radhakanta was involved in drafting the 1829 petition of "Conservative Hindus" against the abolition of widow immolation. The petition makes a significant shift from the first pamphlet, a shift that betokens a selective appropriation of Orientalist and 'liberal' Hindu positions. It argues for the influence of Hinduism as "proportionate to its antiquity". It describes Hinduism as successfully resistant to Muslim "proselytism", yet accredits the otherwise fanatic Muslim or Mughal rulers with non-interference in this practice. And finally it claims widow immolation as at once based in the *volition* of women *and* as their "sacred *duty*" and "high privilege" accruing from shastric "precept" and "religious usages".[135] Radhakanta's newspaper, *Samachar Chandrika*, also supported both educational reforms and widow immolation: it argued against foreign interference in the culturally unique fidelity and heroism of the Hindu wife who climbs onto the pyre "without the least sign of pain or symptom of reluctance, to the utter astonishment and discomfiture of her enemies".[136]

It is worth noting here that the triangular language of 'communal' differentiation centred on the so-called destructive Muslim interregnum and forged in the politics of a comprador loyalism was shared by new orthodoxy and liberals alike, thus revealing its own contradictions as well as their bad faith even though their assessment of Mughal policy on widow immolation was not identical. While Mughal policy on widow immolation was one of limited regulations, the supporters of widow immolation, from the old and new orthodoxy, not only recast Mughal policy as one of 'non-interference' but also upheld it as a salutary *example* for the British to follow. The liberal opponents of widow immolation joined them in asserting the constitutional opposition of Muslim or Mughal rulers to Hinduism, but paradoxically, from about 1818 onwards, the liberals presented Mughal 'non-interference' in widow immolation as a sign of the cruelty, caprice, and indifference of Muslim rulers towards Hindu subjects![137] Apart from the strategic nature of these arguments, a central, unstated issue here is the differing perception of patriarchies associated with Muslim and British rule. For the old and the new orthodoxy, Muslim rule constitutes a nonantagonistic, even a conducive patriarchy as opposed to that of the British, while for the liberals Muslim rule constitutes an antagonistic patriarchy as opposed to British benevolence.

Radhakanta, who is not opposed to the British in proposing a more 'competent' private sphere via female education, simultaneously stakes a claim for the self-adjudication of patriarchy by aligning women to religious prescription. The sheer bad faith of representing the continuation or tightening of patriarchy hinging on the physical control of women as a form of resistance to British rule, which still dogs us, should be apparent. His position mimics the self-exempting structures of colonial reform—withholding freedom yet offering minimal knowledge to women. Further, in attempting to form a reinterpretative field from which to negotiate the relation between household authority and 'community' authority, Radhakanta self-interestedly rehearses the Orientalist split between rationality and faith, drawing on the colonial conflation of religion and law. Rational and selective, he will challenge Shastra with Shastra but at the same time redefine the obligatory for women on the ground of faith.

The debate on education in the *Reformer*, managed and

edited by Prasanna Kumar Tagore (a supporter of Rammohun Roy and later trustee of the Brahmo Samaj), and the plea for reform by Mahesh Chunder Deb (a former student of Derozio from Hindu College) are significant for their overlaps and differences from the new orthodox position, for the range of definitions of companionate marriage, morality, and reform, as well as for the comparative relation posited between women and literature. Unlike Radhakanta, in the *Reformer* the danger of education is usually dispelled not on shastric authority but on the basis of some form of equality—natural, divinely ordained, or human.

An editorial attempts to establish companionate marriage as an ancient 'Hindu' practice, identifies education not with literacy but with a cultivated moral sense. Attributing the present situation of women to the Muslim interregnum, it contests the popular notion that education is dangerous for women since nature has not discriminated against women in forming their minds: "By education we do not here mean a knowledge of letters or any particular science: but the culture of the mind in general, the improvement of the moral sense." In such moral education women can be equal to men, for the *improvement* of future generations of men. The education of men must begin in infancy through imitation and example (of women) so that Indians can achieve the degree of civilization European nations enjoy. The companionate model of a "rational interchange of ideas" is upheld as a desirable one, and the writer laments that so many Hindus have "adopted the unnatural Mahomedan custom of considering women rather as slaves than as companions". The essay ends on a note of dis-approval of the Native Female School in Simla which is educating low-caste women primarily in a knowledge of Christianity.[138] Ano-ther editorial comment on a letter upholding the domestic utility of women's education in supervising the education of daughters adds that it will also direct the career of sons to a "happy goal". Women must be responsible for the early moral education of sons as well as for their physical education so they can bring up sons of robust con-stitution, remove their "physical inferiority" as a "weaker race" in comparison to other races.[139]

One 'Lunar Complexion', in a letter preoccupied with the faults of women, defines the function of female education as primarily moral. Education will remove their malice, envy, overconsumption, disobedience, and instigation of "frequent domestic broils", all of which are caused by ignorance:

> I have witnessed myself, Mr Editor, that it is impossible for any man to convince them of the truth of anything, or persuade them to virtue and to make them obedient to the duties they owe to their husbands by the virtue of sacred marriage. And further their godly reverence to gold creates frequent breach of peace between the wife and the husband; whose income being inadequate to meet his family expenses, cannot fulfil her desire by furnishing her with her fancy ornaments. Thus the Females of India being deprived of all the advantages of education, become subject to the vices which render their lives unhappy forever.[140]

Though his discourse of the erring woman resembles the orthodox pamphlet, what emerges more sharply is an unregulated, inadequate middle-class woman. Appropriately, in a second letter Lunar Complexion contests the waffly editorial position on moral and physical education as implying no more than oral instruction for women. Neither oral instruction nor literacy alone is sufficient. "Literary education" is necessary to develop a moral, evaluative faculty:

> because how is it possible that minds unseasoned without the cultivation of literature will be susceptible of receiving any impression of the sublime truths of morality; when they cannot comprehend their meaning and appreciate their value, what will the moral lectures and instructions be to them but idle jargons and nocturnal dreams, and further where is the country that has been freed from the shackles of ignorance by this phantastical mode of physical education. . . .[141]

Here the resonant discourse of the 'bad', uncivilized 'native' results in privileging acquired knowledge above an embodied knowledge ballasted by a golden age. This equalizes Indian and European literature in educative value, anchoring the future securely in the past.

> . . . in another part of your letter you say that the habits of frugality, temperance and chastity and other female virtues do not require the aid of letters, in answer to this I simply beg to ask you what then creates the difference between a civilized and uncivilized people,

and is it not an undeniable truth that the more illiterate a nation, the more they are subject to vicious feelings, manners and customs ... on the other hand observe from the commencement of the tenth century since Alfred the Great, the harbinger of the intellectual day, appeared in the west, with what progressive steps the nations of the western regions have reached the present perfection of civilization *in proportion to the gradual approach of the literary sun* to its intellectual meridian! And further let us take a retrospective view of our common mother India; what had obtained her so much celebrity in point of civilization in the rhymes of the poets, the annals of history and in the speculations of the philosophers of antiquity? Why was she called paradise of the world; what had gained her that celestial home. Nothing but *the benign influence of literature raised her to the aggrandizement.* . . . (my emphases)

The contents of a moral education could also be syncretic and/or religious, drawing on different existing or developing sanctions. A letter by 'Zarian', imbued with the notion of progress, argues for a 'return' routed through syncretic modernity: god made women not as drudges or sexual objects but as companions, the dignity women enjoyed in ancient times should be restored by educating them and selecting what is good from other cultures. Education is not mere literacy and will not lead women to fall into the "gulf of vice".[142] Sreeman Chatterjee's letter to the *Reformer*, scoffing at those who consider female education to be useless and productive only of "mischievous needs", plunges into a rhetoric of equality. Surely women possess the same "thirst for knowledge", human feelings, desire for changing their sad condition as men, and are "made from the same dust". His rhetoric flounders on the question, "Do they not possess a real desire of examining worldly happiness as the others?" "Worldly happiness" is apologetically glossed as "I mean the reading of those books which are formed by God, as Bible in English, Mahabharat and Poorans in Bengalee."[143]

The identification of religious with moral education could paradoxically constitute a break with brahminical and maybe even new orthodox positions in permitting women to *know* what they could *embody*. An 'Instructor' writing to the *India Gazette*, is ready to challenge shastric interdiction only if he can transport women, as yet wholly errant, into an ethically instructive Sanskritic domain divorced from direct utility.

> It is not my opinion that women should study English, Persian, Arabic, or Arithmetic, and acquire the desire of displaying their attainments, or of making money for their temporal support by them: but I merely wish [them to study] that *by which their stupidity may be removed, and they may be able to distinguish between good and evil, holiness and unholiness.* Those women who formerly gave themselves to learning acquired the knowledge of Sanskrit, in which they also wrote poems. Through the helps to the acquisition of the Sanskrit which now exist, *women who have but a little leisure* in the course of the day may easily attain it, *in the same manner as it is studied by foreigners.*[144] (my emphases)

This correspondent suppresses as well as acknowledges Sanskrit as a complex category functioning simultaneously as node of assimilation and of resistance to colonial utility. He claims Sanskrit for his class by distinguishing its mode of acquisition: recommending study of Sanskrit in the European "manner" implicitly opposes it to other extant ways of learning Sanskrit (that of the *vairaginis?*).

The Derozian Mahesh Chunder Deb does something similar for English. The "physical, moral and social improvement of India", its "civilization and refinement" depend on the amelioration of the condition of its Hindu women.[145] Addressing men who have broken the "shackles of prejudice and superstition . . . whose understandings have been cultivated, and whose feelings have been refined by education", he seeks to unsettle their "apathy" (p. 91). He believes the affective, mimetic portrayal of the condition of women to be the job of the male reformer which in turn will produce reforming zeal; he has himself therefore

> undertaken to embody in language the miseries of our countrywomen and to paint them in vivid but faithful colours. . . . The only way therefore that seems to me calculated to direct our attention to her degraded and miserable condition and to enlist our sensibilities in favour of the companion of man in this country, is to depict as often as we can her sufferings with all the eloquence of truth and feeling. (p. 91)

He contrasts English literature, European science and philosophy with Hindu women. The two are severely, sorely incompatible. Of the "truly deplorable" condition of Hindu women, he says:

> The more we meditate upon it, the more we are induced to forget the divinity of our nature, the more powerfully are we persuaded to think that Newton, Laplace, and Milton, Bacon, Shakespeare and Socrates —beings who "have actually exalted the nature of man above its destined sphere" were of a higher and superior order. The contrast is powerful. While one class [women] leads us almost to lose sight of the dignified rank we hold in the scale of being and tempts us to believe we were made to pass our days in misery and ignorance and in all manner of imperfections, the other [the composite world of European culture] furnishes us with the most exalted notions of human capacity, affords the most satisfactory evidences of the degree of perfection which is accessible to us, holds out the most pleasing prospects of human bliss and yields the most incontrovertible proofs of the preeminence of our nature. (pp. 91–92)

The illiteracy of women which confines them to a lower world does not match the higher world of literature and universal reason. The world women inhabit is one of "ignorance . . . credulity, superstition, bigotry, envy, jealousy, and all the wild passions of the human heart unrestrained by self command or the placid influence of education". The other world, from which because of their limited range of mind they are debarred, contains "enjoyments beyond the gratification of the senses", "pleasures of novelty of imagination and of intellect", "contemplation of the sublime and the beautiful" and "the field of nature which is at once calculated to please and instruct", as well as "aspirations to fame" (pp. 95–96). Attached to this individualism and part neoclassical, part romantic aesthetic, is the dream of companionate wives endowed with "refined intellectual attainments", "a delightful refuge from the thrall and tedium of business" (p. 96).

A major obstacle to women's ascent to this world of potential are the Shastras which enslave them to men. Prescriptive Hindu texts oppose the world of enlightened knowledge and literature; however, their prescriptions regarding women have to be mitigated or relocated, not dismissed.

> By this I do not mean to condemn that refined piety which every
> female ought to show towards her husband and which it is her
> bounden duty to maintain not only because it is one of the highest
> recommendations and one of the brightest ornaments in a woman
> but it is ordained by nature. (p. 97)

Female fidelity or chastity is the unquestioned substratum of his castigation of social evils. Hindu women, basically good, attentive,
"pious and dutiful" in conduct, and "submissive" towards their husbands, are sequestered in the home, occupied in degrading household
drudgery, victims of cruelty and neglect (p. 93). Their seclusion and
consequent lack of education are a product of Muslim rule. If
arranged marriages produce "incongruous matches", prevent "conjugal love" and "domestic felicity", and lead to male adultery, then
polygamy destroys domestic happiness, companionate conjugality,
and leads the "slighted wife" to the "unlawful pleasures" of adultery
or to suicide (pp. 99, 102). Child marriage leads to a proliferation of
widows, and increases misery because "the loss of her lord to a
Hindoo woman is the greatest calamity which can betide her", while
the prohibition of widow remarriage leads to sexual promiscuity and
infanticide on the part of those widows who are "young and beautiful
and unable to subdue nature" (pp. 103–04). The in-forming contrast
between chaste victims and libidinous women balances out since *strisvabhav* or female libidinousness is partially externalized and relocated as a product of male behaviour and social conditions. Character
is both a set of inborn traits and qualities moulded by education and
circumstance; knowledge may be embodied or acquired.

Not only was this an early attempt to discover the degree of
compatibility between the higher values of literature and the shaping
effect of literature on women, but the nature of the demand here
for a different kind of private sphere based on expressive qualities in
domesticity and women instead of on the actual, existing seclusion of
women, is also significant. With Mahesh Chunder, English literature
is a male domain dragged down by the lack of a complementary
domestic sphere and 'compatible' women. The opposition between
women and English literature is iterated not as an ideal but as a
lament. Women reformed will cease to conflict with literature while
literature will isolate the undesirable elements of Hindu patriarchy.

In building a companionate private sphere, by partially splitting patriarchy from religion, he seeks to base patriarchy in a *moral* realm which is nonreligious and in that sense relatively autonomous or voluntary. The insertion of literature facilitates the split and conversely literature and women together make up a compound referent—culture. Relatively speaking, he tries to form a 'radical' field replacing consensual or 'community' authority as represented by the (confining) Shastras with voluntaristic modes which acquire their authority from English literature. Another issue here of course was the struggle to define the relation of the new middle-class male to his kin or caste group: should it be the caste group (a cohesive corporate patriarchal unit that also binds men) which is empowered, as Radhakanta implies, or the individual, as Mahesh Chunder implies? The former sees a caste group newly magnified as a religious and 'Hindu community' as the primary ground for (male) consensus and as a means for generalizing sectional interests, whereas the latter seeks to commit himself initially to a nonreligious but moral definition which allows greater male mobility and individuation. Though individuation cannot yet be presented as a new form of sociality, for Mahesh Chunder patriarchy is on the way to becoming a matter of *self* adjudication.

The *Reformer* displayed an uneven, mixed consciousness, oscillating between religious and literary education, return and progress, but its overlaps with both the new orthodox Radhakanta and the Derozian Mahesh Chunder are apparent. In different ways all were looking for a homogenizing model of a middle-class patriarchy where the 'private' could be situated as a mediatory realm accommodating as well as reacting to British rule, and simultaneously function as a mode of *partial* alignment with colonial structures and polity easing male entry into the public sphere. Though placing the stresses differently, they pressed the reform–preservation dialectic of colonial rule into a sphere of self-adjudication and sought to retain and revamp newly defined patriarchal forms. Patriarchal forms and norms were a site of struggle, yet a basic consensual unit was the patriarchal obedience of women, which was sought to be partially relocated by the more liberal Roy and Mahesh Chunder attracted to companionate marriage, as individual volition or acquired knowledge. The undisputed, common, and naturalized ground of empowerment, whether of the individual male or the caste group, was as yet the chaste woman.

The conflictual constitution of a 'Hindu' patriarchy and the chaste woman was addressed in the Orientalist idiom of the 'fall', more markedly in the liberal tendencies. The onus of male self-reform was elided or mitigated by the recurring device of transforming this otherwise tenacious 'Hindu' patriarchy into a gift of the invader: the choric reliance on the Muslim interregnum absolves both antiquity and 'Hindu' men of responsibility in another act of bad faith which persists today. Ironically, by equating conquest with causality and abdicating from historical agency, these 'Hindu' men not only identified with the passivity ascribed to them in colonial accounts but wilfully defined the patriarchal oppression they inflicted as emasculation, both disguising and jeopardizing their agential capacity. As in the relationship of the new orthodoxy with English, so in the relationship of liberal tendencies with patriarchy: power and abjection, generated from the same contradictory structures, come to be garnered from the same sources. However, in a broader sense, *both* the new orthodoxy and liberals construed patriarchal practices—either past or present—as an indigenous response to external threat. The history of patriarchal practices coagulates into the spurious assertion of a 'Hindu' male unity. Forms of patriarchal oppression (illiteracy, seclusion, widow immolation) were interpreted as forms of protection for women. With their own social relations structured by a series of 'antagonist alliances', the location of these sections of the middle class in the social formation (as exploiters and exploited) was particularly conducive to conceiving patriarchy as an exercise in relayed and compensatory power. 'Hindu' here is not so much a coherent community or a consensual denomination as a name for a specific set of existing and desired social, political, and patriarchal relations.

Broadly speaking, a general ideology took shape in which women emerged as the subjects in whom the unity of a composite culture—customary, religious, moral, intellectual—was sought to be projected by constituting them as emblems of continuity and objects of reform. The difficulties of such unification which can be simultaneously *evoked* and *recultivated* are evident. There is no 'fit' between the symbolic ideality of the Orientalist field, the general ideology which sustains it, specific patriarchal practices, and women themselves. If status quo must be maintained on the ground of antiquity, whether customary or textual, then antiquity itself falls short producing contradictions rather than coherence. Prescriptive texts are inconsistent and disputable, may be used to advocate widow immolation, female volition, or companionate marriage respectively. The same general ideology may be used for refashioning or restructuring a range of practices. Women themselves can scarcely be educated without granting them volition, and even though the problems of a new self may be glossed by casting it as return, their access to volition has to be carefully negotiated. Middle-class 'Hindu' women have *not* as yet been given moral power of the sort ascribed in bourgeois domestic ideologies. Though, significantly, it was the liberals not the orthodoxy or the new orthodoxy who first became interested in claiming moral power on behalf of women, the primary struggle was over the sources of male moral authority, and patriarchal reforms were conceived as a process of removing *male stigma* (even by Rammohun Roy).[146] Even for Mahesh Chunder, who associated moral power specifically with English, the articulated issue as yet was moral *parity* for women and moral *power* for men. Middle-class women cannot have access to moral power unless they have relatively undisputed theoretical access to some forms of volition and agency. Even embodied knowledge, in so far as it rests on religious prescription, is inadequate as a form of agency because it still represents duty and obedience.

Significantly, in a letter by 'Women of Chinsura', the authors claimed neither moral agency nor moral superiority. Nor did they speak as 'Hindu' women. The letter follows the etiquettes of male paternalism but reforms are sought only on the grounds of male injustice, the sexual double standard, and in the interests of companionate marriage. They demanded education and free social intercourse with other men and women comparable to "women of civilized countries", the freedom to choose compatible husbands under family supervision, the right to keep bride price as *stridhan*, and the right to conjugal sexual satisfaction made impossible by male polygamy and the prohibition on widow remarriage.[147]

Women may have been an axis of seeking class unification but not necessarily of achieving it. In the first four decades of the nineteenth century in Calcutta, women, the private sphere, moral power, and literature emerged not as contiguous but as unevenly related categories. Not unlike Sanskrit, women were shuttled back and forth in time. Though past and future could become compatible, the present remained recalcitrant.

The gender of ignorance and altruism: English women and empire

VI   The particular interlocking ideological configuration centred on altruism and reform which I have been describing extended into the formation of ideologies about English women as well as notions of knowledge and literature in England at this time—a time when women's entry into the labour market was at issue. As I argued earlier, preexisting British patriarchal attitudes entered significantly into the negotiation of Indian patriarchal forms mediated by the political economy of the colonial state and the nostalgia for 'organic' agrarian societies. The extended field of operation and reinforcement for paternal–patriarchal ideologies which India provided for the British upper and middle classes renovated their contradiction with class mobility and laissez-faire. The process of colonization simultaneously split the (ideological) trajectories of sections of the British ruling classes as well as rejoined local developments to its wider imperatives. Not only did the landed gentry and the middle class have common interests in empire but they gradually evolved a class order in the stable form most appropriate for colonial exploitation, breeding an undue respect for hierarchy and deference and honing special modes of compromise and con-tainment.[148] The accompanying over-identification by the middle class with 'morality' and social stability in its attempted translation of social mobility and new wealth into paternalist, aristocratic, or patrimonial idioms, cast reform as an emphatic discourse of *restoration* endowing women with unsustainable moral power, presenting the odd spectacle of a middle class confronting its rise through imageries of moral decline. It also *exacerbated* the division between the public and private spheres and inscribed emerging familial ideologies tightly into the language of empire. As existing or emerging British patriarchies were drawn into new and significant relations with colonialism, the private sphere acquired a range of *performative* attributes and functions while corresponding and related modes of gendering knowledge emerged. Whereas in Bengal middle-class women seem to have virtually no voice, in England by this time middle-class women were both being reconstituted and constituting themselves even as demarcations of knowledge were being structured into notions of female agency. If, as James Mill argues in his *History*, the standard and level of civilization was to be judged by the status of its women, how then were English women to become emblems of national superiority and cultural difference without threatening the family as a unit of social stability? Some conservative negotiations of this question by Jane Austen, Sara Ellis, and John Ruskin develop notions of female knowledge as forms of ignorance, affirming the unequal play of the Enlightenment vis-à-vis both colonies and English women but from *different*, developing positions of class consolidation.

Within the relationship Austen establishes between hierarchy and class mobility, between a paternalist landed gentry and trade interests partly located in new forms of wealth,[149] the selective assimilation of the middle class into the gentry rests on the peculiar pact of mutual reform. Unlike Burke, her interest in the nationalist project of improving the ruling classes takes the shape not of addressing their excesses in the colonies but of transforming their unscrupulous profit into scruple and 'value'. *Mansfield Park's* (1814) discourse on native character, governance, governability, and colonial agency hinges on successful and unsuccessful pedagogy. Sir Bertram attributes his pedagogical failure with his own daughters to their innate lack of "active principle", inadequate instruction in "duty", "self-denial", "humility", and self-discipline, as well as their inability to translate religious instruction into "daily practice".[150] Fanny, a beneficiary of upper-class philanthropy, product of his and Edmund's tutelage and approval, is a better pupil in part because class differences are assiduously maintained until she graduates, upon which she can assume moral guardianship of the class to which she has ascended. The unreformed middle class is especially deficient and unfit to rule. Fanny's parents, who have shown no desire to learn from or ingratiate themselves with their well-connected daughter, are symptomatic: her father has coarse manners, "no curiosity, and no information beyond his profession"; her mother "was a partial, ill-judging parent, a daw-dle, a slattern, who neither taught nor restrained her children, whose house was the scene of mismanagement and discomfort from beginning to end, and who had no talent, no conversation, no affection towards herself" (pp. 706–07). Susan, who looks up to Fanny for guid-ance, has "an innate taste for the genteel" (p. 725), is a natural refor-mer, wins her approval, and is cast as her unschooled replica.[151] It is a measure of the consolidation of Fanny's upper-class consciousness that she should place Susan in the same patriarchal structure of dele-gated authority that she herself has been placed in. The division into separate spheres is at one level described by a colonial relation in which patriarchy is reconstituted as a system wherein men can con-centrate on maintaining order in the savage world outside while women, the beneficiaries of this activity, must learn to maintain order by taming the barbarians within.

Power delegated to women is based on a different kind of knowledge. Fanny self-deprecatingly recounts to Edmund her question to Sir Bertram; a colonial proprietor in Antigua, his financial stability depends on his Caribbean profits.

> "Your uncle is disposed to be pleased with you in every respect, and I only wish you would talk to him more. You are one of those who are too silent in the evening circle."
>
> "But I do talk to him more than I used. I am sure I do. Did you not hear me ask him about the slave-trade last night?"
>
> "I did—and was in hopes the question would be followed up by others. It would have pleased your uncle to be enquired of farther."
>
> "And I longed to do it—but there was such a dead silence! And while my cousins were sitting by without speaking a word, or seeming at all interested in the subject, I did not like—I thought it would appear as if I wanted to set myself off at their expense, by showing a curiosity and pleasure in his information which he must wish his own daughters to feel." (p. 588)

In the decade of intense public agitation about slave trade (centred on abolition, illicit trading, atrocities by plantation owners, fears of the corruption of British politics, and degradation of British manners by returning adventureres and West Indian planters, and also entangled in questions about the working poor and factory reforms in England), Austen's Evangelical affinities impel her to insert the question but *only* to mark those boundaries of decorum which Fanny will not transgress.[152] In a judicious act of evaluation and exclusion, slave trade is disarmingly placed in a structure of conversational equivalence, as one drawing-room subject among others. Moral emphasis falls on curiosity, a quality which distinguishes good learners, not on accountability. We do not know if the question was answered, we know why Fanny would not insist that it be; her gentility, a product of the subtle play of class difference, forecloses the issue. It is Fanny not Sir Bertram who is put to the test. Working within a similar constellation of refinement and utility as Macintosh's address to the Bombay Literary Society, Austen reverses his expansion of knowledge, whittling down its relativizing potentials, but to a roughly *similar* end. The male equation between knowledge, power, and refinement must be complemented by a female equation between self-narrowing knowledge and refinement before female knowledge can become answerable to the broad imperatives of colonial utility. Macintosh offered himself as "the representative of the *curiosity* of Europe":[153] male curiosity settles into a *drive* for capitalist expansion while female curiosity remains a partially self-cancelling *attribute* content with its own *display*. *Mansfield Park* hones a mutually structuring yet sundered epistemic relation between a system of colonization functioning on an instrumental epistemology of information and use, and an apparently non-instrumental female domain based on forms of deflected agency which partly involve learning not to know. Fanny's canny 'knowing' ignorance becomes a version of femininity eligible for upwardly mobile marriage. The integration of self-censorship with manners and morality must have eased considerably the problem of processing the quantity of 'bad' knowledge produced by an expanding empire! More pertinently, *willed ignorance*, a form of voluntary divestment, becomes a sign of *instructability* and *capacity to instruct*, the site of new forms of investment. Through the ability to *learn* to preserve ignorance in the face of politically undesirable knowledge which can corrode class complacency, colonial profit is transformed into a series of values—domestic comfort, status, social grace—which enter the minutiae of the daily life of the gentry. With remarkable mutuality, female willingness to know less enhances male agency and converts male power into female propriety. Politeness as distilled power helps in turn to insert the private sphere into the wider expanse of empire.[154]

The narrative's unrelenting display of social error counterpointed by an opaque Antigua, the barely mentioned site of undisplayed error which Sir Bertram goes to 'correct', rechannels sexual desire and entrepreneurial ambition. The tendency of Austen's narrative form "to disown at an ideological level what it embraces at a constructional one"[155] seems to be related to her gendered discourse of knowledge and morality which rehearses colonial social relations and is embedded in cognitive modes of colonial self-legitimation. The display of the immoral manipulations of most of the characters anxiously hopes thereby to consolidate the substantiveness or finality of the 'truth' Fanny represents: a truth which will occlude its own nature as *value* produced from *opacity*, or as a *contract* of partial ignorance committed to unfulfilled 'curiosity' about immoral British manipulations in Antigua.

Austen's enterprise produced new contradictions: the chastening power of female moral autonomy fashioned for wider purposes also exceeds the local paternalist context in which it is meant to 'fit'. When Sir Bertram and Fanny with stunning unsentimentality and self-righteousness relegate erring members of their respective families redefining the family as a *moral* union subject to ruthless improvement, they ironically drive a wedge into the heart of domestic ideology. In fact Fanny shows more grit than Sir Bertram in re-moulding the will to power as a claim to conscience. In the teeth of its own investment in continuity the narrative plants a species of contractual individualism, projected as moral autonomy, for nurturance within paternalistic structures. At the same time, the selective recreation of patrimony—with the help of female knowledge—frees it from the simpler logics of succession, undifferentiated emotional investment, straightforward utility, and the equivalence of the market, so making a modality for the *consumption* of a now 'exclusive' patrimony as a means of social differentiation.

By a multiple irony, for at least one nineteenth-century

reader Austen's novels helped to reconcile militant conquest with virtue. 'Rajah' Brooke of Sarawak's career of mercenary conquest and private trade represents the entrepreneurial aspect of colonization which needed constant chastening and regulation by the British state even though its gains were seldom relinquished. Brooke is portrayed by his loyal secretary-cum-biographer as ruling Sarawak with "mild despotism", spreading "civilization, commerce and religion" with the aid of philanthropy, altruism et al., introducing "better customs and settled laws", extirpating piracy, correcting the "native character", and of course defending himself against charges of corruption and brutal massacres: his favourite reading consists of "Miss Austen's novels".[156]

In *Mansfield Park* there is a conjunction of the mobility of selected women with selective knowledge. Where the consolidation of middle-class women as a *body* was at issue then female knowledge was defined more often through expressive roles and opposed to literary, intellectual, or instrumental ones. The Evangelical Hannah More says: "Their knowledge is not often like the learning of men, to be reproduced in some literary composition, nor even in any learned profession, but is to come out in conduct."[157] As altruism and philanthropy entered into 'creative' relation with gender ascription, class division, and capitalism in England and with the colonies outside, they were not only internalized by women but middle-class women were increasingly constituted as reformers—of prostitutes, servants, lower classes, and whether directly or by extension, of colonial subjects—that is, as bearers of class power in an imperial arena. More than men, the domestic sphere itself came to be cast as a benign pedagogue. Further, the patriarchal family unit and domestic ideology tend to be explicitly articulated with political order and national interest since the site for the formation of male character was at home while other countries were an operative space where it had to be maintained or represented.[158]

In Mrs Sarah Ellis's (brought up a Quaker, became a Congregrationalist and married the well-known missionaryReverend William Ellis in 1837) popular manual, *Women of England* (1839), middle-class *women*, not upper-class *ladies*, uphold the "moral worth" of the country.[159] When England's national and "*moral characteristics*" are judged "in the scale of nations", "the justice of her laws, the extent of her commerce, and the amount of her resources" become the "boast" of her "patriotic sons", while its celebrated "domestic character"—"the home comforts, and fireside virtues"— depends upon the "moral feelings and habits of women" (pp. 13–14). Lamenting the decline of the estimable moral character and influence of English women with "false notions of refinement", overcultivation of "mental facilities" through improved education and dissatisfaction with the divinely ordained sphere of domestic duty, she advocates a "fresh exercise of moral power" (pp. 15, 20, 24, vii).

This restorative task is addressed to the commercial middle class constituting the majority or, given the difficulties of reconciling fixed demarcation with social mobility, "to that portion of it who are restricted to the service of from one to four domestics,—who, on the one hand, enjoy the advantages of a liberal education, and, on the other, have no pretension to family rank" (pp. 24–25). While affirming the class divisions which make England the most "beauti-fully proportioned" of countries, she debars aristocratic and poor women as bearers of the "strong features of nationality"—the former because of their leisure and international lifestyle, the latter because in their lack of privilege they resemble the poor of any country in "social feelings and domestic habits" (pp. 18–19). Only this section of middle-class women have

> the highest tone of moral feeling, because they are at the same time removed from the pressing necessities of absolute poverty, and admitted to the intellectual privileges of the great: and this, while they enjoy every facility in the way of acquiring knowledge, it is still their higher privilege not to be exempt from domestic duties which call forth the best energies of female character. (p. 26)

The true source of benevolence is the character of women *as formed within* an expressive domesticity requiring disinterested rendering of "personal services" (pp. 21–22). Not only does the insulated private sphere have an educative function, but Ellis, wishing to retain women's capacity for manual labour as a safety net for a class with fluctuating incomes, tries to dignify domestic labour as a "kindness". The daily lives as well as the sexuality of women are brought under the dominion of altruism.

Female benevolence in turn transforms the home into a

hierarchical, harmonious enclave; an ensemble which enables women to cleanse the body politic and maintain orderly class relations through the "promotion of public and private good", "benevolent institutions", and the succour of the "unfortunate and afflicted" (pp. 33–34). The propriety and reserve of English women preserves their "purity of mind", guards the country's "moral worth", and exercises a supervisory class function of sorts, extending "to every sphere of action in which they move, discountenancing vice in every form, and investing social duty with that true moral dignity which it ought ever to possess" (pp. 40, 42). Though women of the nobility have and are "devoting their time and property to objects of benevolence", their domestic life and upbringing makes them "less fitted for practical usefulness" than middle-class women who have "advantages in the formation of character" (p. 35). The aristocratic, landowning traditions of benevolent paternalism are sought to be usurped by the commercial–manufacturing middle class on the ground of the domestically inculcated benevolence of their women, and this new class is sought to be defined according to the quality and efficacy of its altruism.

Women, being "strictly speaking, relative creatures", are bound to feel inferior in relation to men (p. 155). However, the ethical, religious, experiential, and nonintellectual character of woman's intelligence and training make her an honest "fireside" companion, give her insight into human nature, access to "unvarnished truth", the ability to reason and apply received ideas despite her microscopic "sphere of observation" (pp. 35, 37–38); in any case a "more extended vision" would distract her from minute attention of domestic detail (p. 40). Relative ignorance is to be compensated by a lively imagination and sound judgement, making for a freshness in conversation. The diminution of woman, cast as a wise ingenue, expands her moral power. The more "*moral power*" is cultivated "independently of all personal attractions, and unaccompanied by any high attainments in learning or art", the more the influence of women and "their power of doing good" will increase (p. 59). Moral power is the *sum* of a narrow domesticity and a desexualized, egoless, antiintellectual femininity. In this drastic reform, which began as a project of reclamation describing women as repositories of long established custom, women are made to renounce their essential errant nature and become estranged, dematerialized creatures tethered to 'values' alone and expected to *enact* their attributes. In Ellis's own words, "woman *herself* is nothing in comparison with her attributes" (p. 36). For woman to

> be *individually* what she is praised for being in *general* it is necessary for her to lay aside all her natural caprice, her love of self-indulgence, her vanity, her indolence—in short, her very *self*—and assuming a new nature, which nothing less than watchfulness and prayer can enable her constantly to maintain, to spend her mental and moral capabilities in devising means for promoting the happiness of others, while her own derives a remote and secondary existence from theirs. (pp. 52–53)

In disclaiming any desire to encroach on male preserves Ellis confronts the mercantile and martial pursuits of the class addressed: women do not "*possess* more moral power", but their upbringing and domestic circumstance makes their "moral feelings" "less liable to be impaired by the pecuniary objects" which preoccupy men (pp. 46, 50). Further, the ethical power of women is in the service of men engaged in the marketplace and the battlefield (pp. 52–53). The "potent consideration of worldly aggrandisement" and of expediency belongs to men (p. 50). The woman is his secret, subordinate mentor, who while herself staying in one place travels into the public sphere as his peripatetic conscience:

> Nay, so potent may have become his secret influence, that he may have borne it about with him like a kind of second conscience, for mental reference, and spiritual counsel, in moments of trial; and when the snares of the world were around him, and temptations from within and without have bribed over the witness in his own bosom, he has thought of the humble monitress who sat alone, guarding the fireside comforts of his distant home; and the remembrance of her character, clothed in moral beauty, has scattered the clouds before his mental vision, and sent him back to that beloved home, a wiser and better man. (p. 62)

The scope of conscience is determined by the *size* of British empire: the empire *is* the extended public sphere.

> The sphere of their direct personal influence is central, and
> consequently small; but its extreme operations are as widely
> extended as the range of human feelings. They may be less striking
> in society than some of the women of other countries . . . but as far
> as the noble daring of Britain has sent forth her adventurous sons,
> and that is to every point of danger on the habitable globe, they
> have borne along with them a generosity, a disinterestedness, and
> a moral courage, derived in no small measure from the female
> influence of their native country. (p. 63)

No wonder Ellis began with the urgent exhortation: "You have deep
responsibilities, you have urgent claims; a nation's moral wealth is
in your keeping" (p. 17). As bankers of national wealth women have
joint stock in the colonial enterprise.

Ellis tries to forge a commercial–manufacturing class, or in
her own terms, a representative nationalism, and inscribes gender
(hers) into the processes which have brought the new middle class
into power. It is only by a more stringent ascription of gender difference and male and female roles that she can claim a special
authority for women: the self-abnegating woman is the deep centre of
nationalist class consolidation, the benevolent or altruistic woman
and domestic ideology nestle at the core of empire. The private sphere
is integrated as the inspirational centre, the heart and conscience of
colonial rule. Together, nation and empire inscribe female gender as
a constellation of sacrificial and preserving attributes. The very
excesses of empire necessitate the continuance of the private sphere,
and in turn the private sphere is vindicated by the presence of colonialism. As in Austen, domestic space both resists such excesses as
well as enfolds them—negotiates the discrepancy between the colonial state's ideological constitution of itself as Christian and altruistic
and the brute facts of conquest and rule. To claim female authority—
at the cost of abnegating sexual agency as well as direct economic and
political power—and simultaneously to retain empire, it becomes
necessary for her to exaggerate the split between public and private
while covertly entering them into a relation of mutual dependency
and legitimation.

If in conservative formulations female moral authority was
construed as a *lack* of certain forms of power and agency, or as acquir-

ed through a voluntary divestment of these, it was simultaneously inserted into other agential structures of patriarchal delegation or surrogacy. Altruism not only structured the entry of English women into the public domain, it offered them both class mobility and—conditionally—a position of imperial dominance. If English women were distinguished from Hindu women described as victims of a grosser form of patriarchy needing reform, they were also read along the same continuum of value as Hindu women—chaste, self-sacrificing, egoless, secluded (afresh) in the home, repositories of custom and religion. Hindu women were apparently always so, but English women (at least for Ellis) must willingly become more so. William Henry Sleeman (who came to India in 1809 as a soldier in the Bengal army, then joined the Indian Political Service), dedicating his book to the sister(s) at home in appreciation of her valuable letters, wrote in 1844:

> ... and while contributing so much to our happiness, they [English women] no doubt tend to make us better citizens of the world, and servants of government, than we should otherwise be, for, in our 'struggles through life in India', we have all, more or less, an eye to the approbation of those circles which our kind sisters represent—who may, therefore, be considered in *the exalted light of a valuable species of unpaid magistracy to the Government of India.*[160] (my emphases)

Paradoxically, policing an (usually) unseen colony, known aurally or textually, can only further the disjunction between the private sphere and the wider relations which structure it even as it constitutes domestic ideologies as a mode of empowerment for some women. The bestowed and claimed virtue of English women becomes part of the moral right to rule; their consent to be reforming vigilantes, good sisters and wives enhances the moral power and patriarchal benevolence of the colonial state. The proclaimed altruism of the colonial enterprise thus coincided and intersected with the investment of women at home with unprecedented moral power, forming simultaneously a backward female subject and a 'high' civilized female subject, the latter distinct in that she was both tutelary and self-correcting. (The tension between the two is latent in Mahesh Chunder Deb as an unarticulated disparity.) Both Hindu women and

English women were subject to the tension between 'received' and 'refashioned' women, but whereas in Bengal literal prescriptions were being negotiated as alternately 'law' or 'culture', in England the tension entered a developed bourgeois framework. Altruism, a colonial model of dominance, is not only internalized as female attribute, but also becomes a local as well as imperial construction of female 'desire'. The paradigmatic heroines of the domestic fiction of moral worth take on the onus of self-improvement as well as the role of reforming others, becoming both self-punishing learners and teachers. The empire folds back into the home—the conscious surveillance of oneself and of others becomes naturalized as a mark or model of female subjectivity.

The ideological configuration I have described shifted decisively after the challenge to the state represented by the 1857 rebellion. The events of 1857 simultaneously established the vulnerability and military superiority of the British and became the occasion for both the heroization and chastisement of British rule. (1857 also inaugurated a new phase in the politics of non-interference that is discussed in the next essay.) Further, India now became a full-fledged crown colony while England, a predominantly agrarian society in the time of Hastings, had become a predominantly industrial society. The relationship of a section of the British intelligentsia to the middle class also entered a new conservative phase centred not on class consolidation but on forming elites to counteract the democratic enlargement of franchise and mass literacy, in part by pressing the state to represent higher values. It is in projects which both recognized the necessity as well as feared a generalization of the emancipatory ideals of the Enlightenment that the categories honed in the colonies and in the private sphere through a *sectorization* of Enlightenment values, now became useful for defining culture. Ruskin achieved one of the most complex articulations of the private sphere, female knowledge, literature, and empire. Mediated by his Christian Socialism, medievalism, aristocratic leanings, and critique of Victorian materialism, it was made possible by a unifying anticapitalist organicism.

In "Conventional Art", the "bestial acts of the Indian race" in 1857 confirm Ruskin's worst suspicions of India as primitive and despotic. Exceptionally offensive because "examples of decency and civilization" exist around Indians,[161] the mutiny represents "cruelty stretched to its fiercest against the gentle and unoffending, and corruption festered to its loathsomest in the midst of the *witnessing presence of a disciplined civilization*" (p. 90, my emphases). In "Unity of Art" (1859), Ruskin proposes a choice between two paths with corollary dispositions for the artist: art which seeks pleasure and art which seeks truth first and then descends to pleasure; the former is "the gift of cruel and savage nations" like India and Arabia while the latter indicates the "peculiar gentleness and tenderness of mind" of European artists (p. 127). In "Conventional Art", he defines "Tenderness" as an inherent "disdain towards base things" (p. 107). Comparing the "national capacities" of Scotland and India, he perceives "an extreme energy of virtue" in the Scottish philistines (who avenged the mutiny) and "an extreme energy of baseness" (pp. 89–90) in the Indian lovers of art (who were responsible for the mutiny).[162] However, art cannot be shunned, only certain kinds: Indian art, an ungodly "ignorant play. . . of heartless fancy" (p. 113), "cut off from all possible sources of healthy knowledge or natural delight", is purely imaginary and "evil" because "*it never represents a natural fact*" (p. 92, my emphases).

> It either forms its compositions out of meaningless fragments of colour and flowings of line; or, if it represents any living creature, it represents that creature under some monstrous and distorted form. To all the facts and forms of nature it wilfully and resolutely opposes itself. . . . (p. 92)

Such art produced "for its own sake" in which the "delight of the workman is in what he *does* and *produces*, instead of in what he *interprets* or *exhibits*", destroys "*intellectual power and moral principle*" (p. 95). The growth of heuristic (not imitative), mimetic modes capable of intuitively grasping underlying, higher truths yet based on observation—or as Ruskin puts it, "veracity" designed and arranged by "*the visible operation of human intellect in the presentation of truth*" so as to make facts "serviceable" and "beautiful" (pp. 110–12)—secure the growth of a nation.

The supposed lack of history and utility in 'Hindu' literature had been already attributed to the absence of mimetic modes by Mill and Macaulay. Ruskin, who supported the spread of Christianity, shares their ideological posture about India although unlike them he opposes philistinism, and wanting to give art, selectively, an agency in social regeneration, cannot relinquish the special place of imagination in his quasi-romantic aesthetic. Besides, empire demands its due from a nation:

> The dominion of the sea seems to have been associated, in past time, with dominion in the arts also: Athens had them together; Venice had them together; but by so much as our authority over the ocean is wider than theirs over the Aegean or Adriatic, let us strive to make our art more widely beneficent than theirs, though it cannot be more exalted. . . . (p. 135)

Together, these positions propel him into producing a tutored or principled imagination, both militant and virtuous, filtered through the 'apolitical' domestic sphere, good literature, and a singular definition of female knowledge.

The private sphere which crystallizes in "Of Queen's Gardens" (1864) is not only central to an efficient "disciplining civilization" but the abnegation of the pleasure principle in great art and good women seem to be related—while the pleasure principle itself places the colonies as the space which the private sphere will police and transcend. Representations of good women are a criterion through which past civilizations are to be judged, and the 'value' of literature ascertained. Literature in turn (Shakespeare, Scott, Dante, Greek literature, medieval chivalric romances) provides models of this lasting good in women which thus stretches back to 'European' antiquity. With some circularity, women are said to be good if they read good literature, and literature, constructed on a principle of moral representation, both shapes and represents female subjectivity. Classics are safe while even the best romances are dangerous if they lead to an impatience with daily life and a thirst for unattainable novelty and excitement. Good novels are grudgingly admitted because they have in the abstract, though seldom in practice, "serious use, being nothing less than treatises in moral anatomy and chemistry; studies of human nature in the elements of it" (pp. 65–66).

Through the medium of chivalric love Ruskin inserts a notion of woman-created, honourable "manhood" (appropriate to a martial nation) morally subject to women, effecting a transformation of adulterous chivalric romance into domestic ideology (p. 57). "True wifely subjection" is reconciled with chivalry by giving women "a *guiding*, not a determining function" (p. 58). The woman is placed simultaneously at the top and bottom of what is virtually a feudal hie-rarchy—queenliness is the attribute of the willing slave. The eternal pupil is the eternal guide. The companionate, comple-mentary terms of subordination are established as the permanent substratum of the "queenly power" of the *reformed* woman— "incorruptibly good", "infallibly wise . . . not for self-development, but for self-renunciation"—and of the home as a sanctuary (pp. 49, 60). Conversely, the sacralized home is not only where the "true wife" is, but identical with her: she carries home as a portable aura. In this epitome of dom-esticity as an expressive mode, indeed *as* the subjective essence of women—woman's place becomes identical with her power. The per-fect loveliness of a woman, a combination of "majestic peace" and a "majestic childishness", is the product and promise of cheerful ser-vice and endless pliancy (p. 62). Housewives who covet the benign power "to heal, to redeem, to guide, and to guard" become self-made queens holding "the stainless sceptre, of womanhood"—part of his projected middle-class aristocracy of "labour" and "merit" (pp. 72, 74, 9).

The essay solidifies a developing tendency in the ideologi-cal formation of the private sphere—the division of epistemolo-gical functions and pedagogical labour. The woman's education should provide an intuitive and expressive, not an instrumental or abstract knowledge. Where the man's "command" of knowledge should be "foundational", "progressive" and thorough, hers should be "general", "accomplished for daily and helpful use", and suffi-cient only as it may "enable her to sympathize in her husband's pleasures" (pp. 64–65). Geography is unnecessary, theology tabooed. Her knowledge should be "given, not as knowledge, —not as it were, or could be, for her an object to know; but only to feel, and to judge" (p. 62). The woman's moral superiority rests on knowledge which cannot be used as power within a rational–scientific universe, that is, on an evaluative, nuanced, empathetic epistemology: "She sees the qualities of things, their claims, and their places" (p. 59). She is to *enter* the public sphere through empathy and imagination, but her imagination is carefully distinguished from the imagination of the Indian or Arabian artist. First a chastening attentiveness to history which heightens altruism:

> She is to exercise herself in imagining what would be the effects upon her mind and conduct, if she were daily brought into the presence of the suffering which is not the less real because shut from her sight. (p. 63)

In this schema altruism is more a function of female subjectivity then a question of practical help! Second, education in empathy:

> she should be taught to enter with her whole personality into the history she reads; to picture the passages of it vitally in her own bright imagination; to apprehend, with her fine instincts, the pathetic circumstances and dramatic relations, which the historian too often eclipses by his reasoning, and disconnects by his arrangement; it is for her to trace the hidden equities of divine reward, and catch sight, through the darkness, of the fateful threads of woven fire that connect error with its retribution. (p. 63)

The essay shifts from limiting her information to demarcating a cognitive mode, from an externally discriminating pedagogy to a different and internally striated epistemology. The especial cognitive faculty and subjectivity of women is coextensive with a companionate, subordinate domesticity, while the favoured epistemological mode is novelistic, a moral, magisterial understanding of the personal dramas of impersonal history. In a further development from Austen and Ellis, Ruskin situates women in relation to *imagined*, not merely opaque or unseen, realities.

Ruskin ends, contradictorily, by identifying women, the family, and the private sphere with the state (internally stratifying the state into a composite of public and private). The woman's "queenly office with respect to the state" is an "expansion" of her domestic "duty"—moral, advisory, and ornamental (pp. 71–72). Women must take the blame for the "misrule and violence" of men (p. 74). There is not an injustice or a war that women are not "answerable" for— not for provoking but for not hindering them. Men are deficient in "sympathy" and "hope", only women can "feel the depths of pain"; men "by their nature, are prone to fight" and it is up to women to "choose the cause" or to forbid (p. 75). The family here becomes a microcosm of the state; the private sphere till now upheld as an alternative to the public now appears to be a compression of the public sphere. In retrospect, the 1857 uprising appears to represent both the failure of the queenly power of women and a primitive defiance of the altruistic colonial state. In order to reconfirm and resuscitate the (weakening) civilizing powers of women and the state, the private sphere must be simultaneously narrowed and its duties expanded, the actual agency of women restricted while symbolically their very subjectivity—embedded in home, state, and in expressive, adjudicatory, mimetic modes—is 'enlarged'. Both the soul of women and the soul of the nation is at stake.

In a parallel essay, "Of Kings's Treasuries", Ruskin undertakes a critique of greedy and exploitative capitalism. A nation cannot last if it concentrates "its soul on Pence": philistinism must be curbed, England's innate virtues preserved and the state must assume an extra-economic role supporting literature and art rather than "unjust wars" (pp. 28–29, 45). Elsewhere Ruskin clarifies that he does not oppose "necessary" or "noble" wars (p. 221)! A critique of capitalism can be combined with support of empire if the British state *maintains* its altruism, partly because this critique itself is based on values—beneficent paternalism and monitored progress—commensurate with those which the colonial state has been using in self-legitimation. And the definition and internalization of altruism depends, in part, on defining women, the private sphere, female knowledge and literature, as producers of required values.[163]

In so far as domestic ideology is paradoxically a scheme of social reform used to teach acceptance of social strife in Ellis[164] or Ruskin, it also builds a spectacle of male immorality essentialized to the degree that status quo and fixity of gender roles are sought. Perfecting English women, demarcating a private sphere, investing both with moral power, not only rest on a recurring, risky acknowledgement of male fallibility but magnify male culpability and public corruption. Though male error is often mitigated by shifting the 'feminine' values of the private sphere to the public or into revised notions of masculinity,[165] its inescapable presence exacerbated the mid-Victorian chasm between moral and material utility. Moral power and other bourgeois claims to moral value, implicitly or explicitly refracted through the split between the instrumental and the non-instrumental honed in domestic ideologies and ascriptions of female agency or female knowledge, increasingly come to be based on deflected agency or voluntary divestment. Deflected agency as it interlocks with a female knowledge, contradictorily structured by delegation of patriarchal authority and by moral autonomy, can act on *behalf of* as well as on its *own* behalf. Similarly, altruism, from being based on a coincidence of self-interest, utility, and value in the late-eighteenth and early-nineteenth centuries, comes to look for legitimacy in forms of (apparent) self-denial while claims to other kinds of higher value begin to seek 'autonomy' through stressing disinterest in material utility.

Ruskin's characterization of a 'secondary' female knowledge—moral empathy, a principled imagination, ajudicatory mimetic modes—resembles late-nineteenth century descriptions of domestic realism, the fictions of moral worth. This is not surprising considering that such narratives could play into the ideological configuration describing women, the functions of the private sphere, and female knowledge. In these narratives, more complex and less consistent than my description suggests, subjectivities formed in relation to colonial altruism in turn come to moderate, interiorize, rework, or translate the contradictions of empire—unbridled unsettling individualism, aggrandized founding moments, the submerged dramas of imperialism—into the yearnings and restrictions of British class society, into the voluntary or necessary recognition of pressures and limits. In other words, into the dramas of everyday life. Like female knowledge, they do so circuitously, claiming moral identification yet disclaiming direct knowledge. Exempted from direct utility, they set out to be the obverse of popular genres of travel and adventure, which through different narrative conventions, overt forms of othering, and heroic masculinist paradigms, aggrandize the founding moments of political and economic power and engage assertively with some of the material aspects of colonial rule. The absence of direct address in domestic fictions is only a comforting illusion since conservative modes of bourgeois civility and individuation, underwritten by contracts of patriarchal subjection, colonial subjugation, and sectoral knowledge, have already saturated discourses of character and morality with colonial social relations and corollary cognitive modes. Domestic fictions transform the by now geographically wide, inalterably looping, spatial logic of 'character' into local, linear narratives of individual growth.

I will conclude, somewhat summarily, with noting the structural and semantic adjacency of the private sphere, female knowledge, and domestic fictions—despite obvious dissimilarities and contradictions—with certain definitions of 'English literature' at a later and different historical conjuncture which were made first informally then institutionally. All of these four bear a common relation to an agential, self-critical historical knowledge. In an influential, still extant but increasingly discredited definition, English literature comes to be affective, experiential, the opposite of analytic thought or conceptual enquiry, with cognitive modes distinct from science; apolitical, feminine, redemptive, civilizing, it becomes a moral discourse which must "invigilate the political domain" without entering it.[166] Literature evaluates and controls the quality but not the political or material contours of experience. The category 'English literature' depends on a courteous compact to control its own potential seditiousness as a useful 'export'. It also depends on and ratifies that preeminently ideological splitting of an 'autonomous' terrain of metropolitan art and 'culture' from the brute materialities of the imperialism which sustained it. Revolving around the experienced antinomies of female, class, and colonial agency, English literature comes to be positioned on the side of self-containment, non-instrumentality, moral efficacy, deflected agency, and 'passivity' at a time when increased feminist militancy in Britain and political resistance to British rule in India were prising these values apart from the social terrains in which they were initially fashioned. It is perhaps such a curbed, self-limiting, furtive relation to historical knowledge which is consolidated when canons come to be settled, selectively upgrading the status of domestic fictions of moral worth in relation to other popular genres. Literary institutions, implicated in a wider ideological configuration, refract, crystallize, or condense social and ideological tendencies, protracted historical processes.

Afterword

The transnational ideological configuration I have described continued to be active in several domains, in conjunction with other determining structures, material interests, local histories and agencies, and was remodelled and reaccentuated from different class and institutional terrains. Shifting yet anchored in specificities, looping back and forwards in a two-way traffic, marked by recursivities, transformations, and resistances, it involved a continuous interdependent circuit of production, circulation, and consumption. This is a complex matter beyond the scope of a single essay. English literature and literary canons in fact represent its most sophisticated transmutation—wherein certain modes of thought that had been visible on textual surfaces until the 1860s went 'underground' in a later phase of canonization because they were already embedded in the grain of writing and in definitions of 'value'. And literary canons were only one such terrain.

The tense interplay between the *proffered* class and colonial agencies embedded in this configuration and the *enacted* agencies of women was another terrain. Structured around philanthropy, altruism, the private sphere, and female knowledge, active in different trajectories of embourgeoisement and at different nodes of class formation and class consolidation, this configuration had, in the decades of its initial formation, interpellated English women as well as Bengali *bhadralok* men. Not only was it amenable for class mobility and class differentiation based on diverse forms of othering, it reinforced domestic ideology for both in different ways, that is, from positions of social and imperial power/patriarchal subjection or of colonial subjection/patriarchal power, simultaneously allowing some forms of agency while forbidding others for both. Even more significantly, domestic ideologies as they were formed within this configuration were not only constituted by class and colonial relations and imbricated in imperial expansion, but also replete with both specific repressive functions and agential capacities. And it was this wide formation that generally underwrote and deepened the oft-noted relation between domestic ideologies and nineteenth-century British feminism—itself mediated by the prolonged implication of European women in colonization as missionaries, nurses, teachers, and wives of administrators.[167] More specifically, it also shaped those now embarrassing connections between early, organized feminism and the constellation of domestic ideologies, eugenics, biological theories of race, Social Darwinism, and civilizing missions.

In northern India too its repertoire expanded and its locations proliferated later in the century. Moral power was first proffered to and then claimed by middle-class women only from the 1840s in Bengal and from the 1870s in the United Provinces. As two other essays in this volume show, in the United Provinces this configuration was not only overdetermined by the post-1857 politics of loyalism and non-interference, but also by middle castes appropriating upper-caste prescriptive texts and patriarchal practices in a general bid for class differentiation. In addition to defining class and colonial 'others', domestic ideologies became a site for differentiating between women on the ground of caste and religion, and produced a new model: the *missionary Hindu woman*. Assiduously nurtured and educated in the ubiquitous trope of the Muslim interregnum, her compliant domesticity gave her a social purpose beyond the home.[168] It was this figure that was later endowed with cross-class valences by some tendentious nationalist currents, and thus endorsed, became one of the discursive precursors of present-day communalized Hindu women. Communal Hindu women have bought into this sedimented, even congealed ideological configuration, now a package of domestic ideology, 'Hinduness', anti-Muslim rhetoric, and 'cleansing' of the corrupt public sphere that, despite its claims to empowerment, in fact sharply delimits the forms of social power and political agency for women in new ways.[169]

The presentations on which this essay is based were made at Northwestern University, Department of Modern European Languages, Delhi University, Miranda House, University of California at Santa Cruz and at Berkeley, Jadavpur University, Instituut Kern, Leiden, and Transnational Institute, Amsterdam between 1987 and 1991. It was published under the title of "Relating histories: literature, literacy and gender in early nineteenth century Calcutta and England" in *Rethinking English*, ed. Svati Joshi (Delhi: Trianka, 1991).

Women against women

Women suspecting, fearing, excluding, controlling, repressing, punishing, annihilating 'other' women. Women staged as plotting and scheming against 'other' women. These recurrent scenarios in textbooks, tracts, and fiction of the 1870s turned most social tensions into conflicts between women, blocked other interpretative possibilities. How did they manage to create and disguise similarities in the subjection of women, maintain and exploit class or other existing distinctions, as well as institute new differences between them? Such quadrangular ideological operations after all still characterize patriarchies and continue to have political consequences for feminist collectivities.

Patriarchies had become the object of reform and preservation in the early decades of colonial rule. Ideologies of altruism had become integral to gender formation, and helped to establish a compact for obtaining female literacy that guaranteed piety and domestic labour, structured women's access to knowledge, and curtailed their agency. The transnational ideological configuration described in "Relating histories" was central to this process; it travelled from Bengal to the North West Provinces and Awadh (later known as the United Provinces), and proliferated after the 1857 uprising; here the contract of women's vernacular education stretched to the new politics of loyalism and religious identity that involved consent to represent and police symbolic boundaries. The persistent re-establishment of this configuration in new locales in the latter half of the century can partly be explained by its own capacity for functioning as a naturalizing discourse for both inequality *and* social mobility. The other reasons were conjunctural and lay in its contextual interplay and alliances with a new set of material interests, a renewed and politically expedient discourse of loyalism in the United Provinces (UP), an expanded vernacular educational apparatus, the vernacularization of the ensemble named 'English', a hardening vocabulary for making religious differences and defining 'communities' engendered by the state. At its inception in early nineteenth-century Bengal this configuration had a 'Hindu' loyalist character. From the 1860s the more liberal Muslim sections in UP entered it through a constellation of class processes and government policies that brought them into the fold of English education. Their participation in this configuration re-confirmed its patriarchal and loyalist premises but unsettled its 'Hindu' indigenist ones. It was at once consolidated and fractured by the mirroring structure of religious divisions, crosscutting popular practices and the diversity of emerging print formations.

By the late nineteenth century, the domestic sphere, far from being a private retreat or a sanctuary from the public, became an undisguised partisan in the colonial venture—an instrumental, even expedient site. And domestic ideologies became a political field on which caste, class, 'community', religious, and linguistic contentions were reconfigured, managed, or played out. Indeed the importance of the early 1870s in UP for me lies in the contradictory functions that domestic ideologies were acquiring at this time. They simultaneously carry *universalizing* imperatives that blur or undercut religious boundaries, act as a *particularizing* force in the production of caste and religious difference, and function as *homogenizing* agencies in the erasure of syncretic popular culture. As such they could occupy different political locations ranging from the secular to the communal. In the latter case, the production of 'others' in domestic ideologies either preceded or coincided with emerging communal discourses. And, domestic ideologies not only gathered a significant potential to differentiate between women on the ground of class and primordial identities, but also to authorize aggressive projects beyond the home. Their capacity to mark and maintain a field of everyday behaviour, practices, and discriminations that could translate into consent to caste or communal violence and give women access to some forms of power, is not a matter of historical excavation alone but a pressing contemporary issue as well.

From my point of view, what makes this period in UP

especially significant is the way in which class processes assisted in the formation of patriarchal consensualities *across* religions at the same time as quasi-political Hindu and Muslim identities were being constituted. In fact patriarchies raise two crucial isues that are both theoretical and conjunctural: their specific articulation of class with non-class factors, and the nature of the challenge they present to identitarian boundaries since they cut across primordial principles of social organization.

Social conditions conducive to mutually congenial or over-lapping patriarchal arrangements across denominations had existed prior to colonial rule. Coexistence and local interaction produced structural similarities, corresponding practices, and common customs at every class level from the uppermost to the lowest. The self-definition of upper-class/caste groups, regardless of religion, had rested in part on possessing 'exclusive' and more stringent patriarchies. The inception of modern class formation, community claims, and bureaucratically redefined personal laws (that placed the community above the individual) instituted new axes of political differentiation, but they also *added* to this long history of overlaps.

The political economy of capitalism overdetermined by colonial rule manufactured matching obsessions with protecting 'traditional' enclaves which included patriarchies. Class processes generated mirroring community claims and reform agendas. Ironically, the desire to mark class/caste boundaries and particularize primordial communities through domestic ideologies produced women as similar 'types' of class subjects. In a further irony, the patriarchal class imperatives that inhered in the seclusion of women and in the wider pressure to distance or exclude lower-caste/class men and women, served to undercut the production of broad-based unified 'Hindu' or 'Muslim' communities. The processes of desyncretization— often coterminous or synonymous with islamicization and hindu-ization—were also linked to class formation, as is evident in the near-compulsive proscription of popular worship and customs, and the attack on the denominational ambiguities of nomenclature and social practice that were especially marked among the lower castes and classes. Though lower and middle-caste mobility did to some extent assist in defining the boundaries of muslimness and hinduness, broad 'community' identities were diffused even as they were made because class processes undermined their ability to incorporate those below.

The issue here is not one of using class as an analytic category to subsume non-class features and oppressions within it, but to see how class governs and/or re-invests, re-orders, articulates with non-class processes in a specific social formation. Whereas class processes are imaginable without community or identity claims, the community and identity claims made in this period are unimaginable without class processes. It may then be useful to work towards a relational analysis between different systemic structures of class, cross-class, and non-class oppressions, and an understanding of the junctions between them at particular historical moments.

Given the possibilities within this conjuncture, my own attempt here is a preliminary exploration of some interrelated themes bearing on the formation of class, patriarchies, caste distinctions, and religious identities through a small cluster of popular tracts in Hindi and Urdu printed in the early 1870s. With the exception of economic and political histories, much writing on these themes tends to concentrate exclusively on one 'community', on the reform agendas of either 'Hindu' or 'Islamic' sects, or to reconstruct discrete symbolic–sacrolegal complexes. I have resisted such enclavization and tried to approach the 'Hindu' and the 'Muslim' as an interdependent and material field of *sociality* with equivalences, cross-connections, parallels, and disjunctions. Again, instead of confining the argument to overprivileged canonical 'literature', I have assembled a wider reading configuration that can reveal the interfaces between the high and low, orality and print. The essay is structured around Maulavi Nazir Ahmad's *Mir'at ul'-Arus*, Pandit Ramprasad Tiwari's *Ritiratnakar*, Munshi Ahmad Husain's *Istri Updesh*, and the multiauthored *Chhabili Bhatiyari*—narrative, prescription, and romance—to elicit the play of similarities, the constitution of differences, the making of a casteist patriarchal consensus across religious lines, the resolutions *and* ruptures in this consensus.

Mirroring trajectories:
the fortunes of English, the logics of class

"O brother! the religion of Hindoos and Mahommedans is all one—therefore all you soldiers should know this."

Letter from a mutinous regiment to two
disaffected regiments, 18 May 1857

The itinerary: from Bengal to the United Provinces

The interaction of class processes in Britain and Bengal within a set of unequal power relations in the early nineteenth century had produced an ideological configuration centred on altruism. The state's own exploitative accommodation of precapitalist social relations under the rubric of 'non-interference' articulated with existing patriarchal arrangements and set the parameters for the adjustments with colonial power that were being made by internally hetero-genous, contentious, 'feudal' elite, and new middle-class groups. The political, economic, and discursive coordinates of this process engendered ideological contradictions as well as confluences between the two. Many of the patriarchal paradigms that dominated the colonial period were installed through this history of complicity. Existing Indian languages of ruling group hegemony, upward mobility, and conservative retrenchment combined or collaborated with languages attendant on colonial rule to create new vocabularies of entitlement centred on women and religion.

The new politics of official 'non-interference' instituted in the decades following the 1857 uprising was the second major shaping moment in this configuration. While marking a shift in the self-legitimation of the state from an altruistic to a reluctant reformism, it remained, however, just as hesitant about bourgeois authority, as manipulative, and as implicated in ideologies and policies of governance. The now absolute power of the British crown came in the guise of religious tolerance and an abnegation of cultural authority that disclaimed any desire to interfere in 'native' customs and beliefs. The queen's proclamation of 1858 offered at once to maintain India as a feudal society and to modernize it. Victoria's 'housewifeization' in England and her new title of 'Empress of India' not only situated her as a 'successor' of Mughal rule but gave a maternal, monarchical, feudatory aura to what was in fact an imperial state. The logics of non-interference dovetailed into those of indirect rule, and the maintenance of 'backward' princely enclaves as "a bulwark of British prestige and influence" provided a fresh ideological resource; in the presidencies too, religious neutrality was increasingly interpreted to mean support for conservative elements and pulling back from reformism.[1] Even as the state shifted the full onus of loyalism from the middle classes to a 'hereditary' elite of landlords, taluqdars, and princes in India,[2] a new conservatism emerged in England centred on forming elites to counteract mass literacy and the enlargement of franchise. Consequently, the application of liberal principles became even more selective. Secular education especially for women was represented by some administrators as a threat to political stability![3]

The promise and premises of such 'non-interference' and the emergence of new nodes of interaction between the state and consolidating groups and classes after 1857 contributed to the further development of this configuration and the spread of its indigenist vocabulary from Bengal to the north. In the interests of its own consolidation, the state re-discovered a pragmatic interest in the respective merits of Hinduism, Islam, and Sikhism, and in the value of castes, tribes, sects, and religious 'communities' who could be played off against one another through selective and sectional recruitment.[4] At the same time, previously well-placed groups in UP—ashraf, rajput, kayasth, khatri, brahmin, bania—were being refigured as a petty-bourgeois intelligentsia in the new dispensation. Unlike Bengal, the ideological insertion of this urban and *mofussil* (small town) intelligentsia into colonial reformism in the 1860s and 70s took place under the aegis of explicitly divisive policies. As far as Muslims were concerned, the state veered between suspicion and paranoia—about their role in the 1857 revolt and the more recent Wahabi uprisings—and conciliation and incorporation, but it made a concerted bid to separate Hindus and Muslims into two distinct entities of victim and oppressor in order to erase the memory of 1857 where both had fought under the same banner.

From its inception this configuration had been encrusted with a distinct language for othering Muslims. Early administrators had represented Hindus as timid, god-fearing subjects more amenable to colonial rule than the refractory Muslims from whom they had annexed political power, while Stewart's *Historical Anecdotes* (1825) had established that British altruism was directed towards Hindus and necessarily entailed Hindu antagonism towards Muslims.[5] Now prominent colonial administrators and historians, like H.M. Elliott in *The History of India as told by its own Historians* (1867), exploited religious differences and sought Hindu loyalty by reiterating sagas of Muslim tyranny—sagas that were replicated in school textbooks such as Babu Sivaprasad's *Itihasa-timirnasak* (1871). India was identified with 'Hindus' and Hindus with an essentialized religiosity.[6] W.W. Hunter in *The Indian Musalmans, Are They Bound in Conscience to Rebel Against the Queen?* (1871) went even further and claimed that Hindus were "the real natives of the country" and Muslims, a discrete religious "community" or "nationality", were "their deadliest ene-mies".[7] Almost in tandem, most late nineteenth-century Hindu refor-mism within this configuration (which gradually seeped into many middle and lower-caste associations) framed its self-representations in an externalist 'historical' narrative of 'foreign assaults' on reli-gion and culture, and thus substituted causality with interruption. The projection of Muslim rule as a dark interregnum elided many histories of aggression by representing Hindus as victims alone and recast the forging of new social relations in the language of self-defence. In fact this ideological configuration, as I will show, had precise and demonstrable relations to the process of 'hinduization' and the weakening or suppression of syncretic elements in the nine-teenth century. It provided an arsenal for the attack on common customs and forms of worship.

'Religion' was already an object of joint definition by administrators, Orientalists, missionaries, sections of the old literati and the new middle class from the early nineteenth century in the regions under direct rule. At the same time it was a 'cultural' space for veiled political argument. After the 1857 uprising, however, religion also came to be seen as an arena for forging a singular 'nativeness' and a special zone of immunity from colonial interference demarcated by Queen Victoria's proclamation. Religion, particularly Hinduism, was thus becoming a paradoxical terrain, at once collaborating with the political domain and being situated outside it. Islam too was being pulled into a similar logic of 'compatibility' with the colonial economy—as that which could, like Hinduism, procure loyalism, ensure desirable limits to anglicization, and guarantee political stability. Thus in UP the state made a bid to attach Muslims to British rule through education by teaching them "modern science" combined with their "own literature".[8] Hunter too urged that the "sober and genial knowlege of the West" which should be encouraged by the British amongst Muslims must be accompanied by "sufficient acquaintance with their religious codes to command the respect of their own community".[9]

Even as religious rationales for inequality were becoming difficult to sustain, these post-1857 redefinitions pulled both caste and patriarchies more forcefully under the rubric of 'religion'. The queen's proclamation of non-interference was commonly interpreted as supporting the maintenance of caste distinctions.[10] The welding of selected patriarchal practices with reformed hinduisms also carved new social spaces for this ideological configuration which was already imbricated in domestic ideologies. It now carried a settled pedagogical repertoire: middle-class male tutelage and uplift of women, reform and preservation of ancient 'tradition', 'national' regeneration through domestic reform, the double recourse to textual authenticity and the force of custom. With intermediary castes appropriating brahminical texts and upper-caste patriarchal ideologies, and some lower castes adopting higher-caste patriarchal arrangements in bids for class differentiation and class mobility in UP, it was reformulated at various reformist sites and most of its legitimating devices were rehearsed. Those reforms that seemed desirable or obligatory were often conveniently established as ancient 'Hindu' practices interrupted by Muslim rule. This indigenism, a joint product of colonial and Indian reformism, largely functioned as a gendered rationale for preserving systemic asymmetries of knowledge, labour, and power. In fact, the frequent difficulty of drawing a line

—on either the reproduction of a glorious past or on fundamental issues such as domestic labour, marriage, prostitution, differential education, methods for containing the effects of modernity on women—between conservative British commentators and dominant local groups seeking to assert alternate or antagonist traditions, illustrates not merely their interlocking formation but also their overlapping patriarchal interests.[11]

In Bengal, contests over reform had produced a wider range of ideological tendencies and political positions, and more ambivalent or hybrid categories. UP had a history of piecemeal annexation, shifting administrative boundaries, uneven political and cultural change, and no comparable reform movements. Here the acquisition of new privileges, prestige, and functions by socially dominant groups from different castes, the entry of middle castes into reformist configurations, the interlock between reform and renascent 'scriptures' proliferating through print, and the availability of books translated from Bengali (largely by Bharatendu Harishchandra and his circle), worked together to attach a pre-formed, simplified ideological conservatism to women's education that was, however, refracted through a set of regionally specific contradictions.

The material and ideological conditions in which a section of the respectable Muslim gentry or ashraf entered colonial reformism were different from Bengal. The permanent settlement in Bengal had broadly speaking expropriated the Muslim gentry, already numerically smaller, in favour of Hindu zamindars.[12] There was hardly any class formation among Muslims corresponding to that among Hindus. Not only were the bulk of landowners Hindu but Muslims also had a weaker base in commerce and the new professions; their entry into English education as well as their formation of voluntary associations were belated and sporadic.[13] The gains and losses of colonial rule could not be measured by denomination in UP. Here a section of the Mughal ruling elite of administrators, warriors, scribes, and courtiers who had consolidated their positions between state and agrarian society, had been transmuted into a landlord bureaucrat class to provide a system of political control and a social base for British rule. Hindu and Muslim tehsildars benefited from British political control while both Hindu thakurs and Muslim landholders lost land due to revenue arrears. After the 1857 revolt, some sections of the old landed gentry (rajput, jat, and Muslim) were destroyed by confiscations, some were restored or created by government rewards in grants of land, while some remained unaffected.[14] The state no longer characterized the Awadh taluqdars as upstarts or parasites but as respectable men of ancient lineage ruling over a stable, deferential society; and some large landowners, now termed the "native aristocracy", were even given magisterial powers.[15]

The pace of embourgeoisement was not as discrepant in UP as it had been in Bengal. Whereas Muslims had been swept out of administration by land and later linguistic reforms, and collaborated relatively less with the British in Bengal, here they were relatively better represented in influential government posts until the 1880s.[16] There was not only an elite section that was not very distant from political power but many more UP Muslims were urban, articulate, and serious contenders for government jobs. The contest over jobs thus was relatively more equal, direct, and immediate. What is more, the actual number of government posts available amounted to a tiny fraction of the literate population, and the route to them was still controlled by social, kinship, and state networks of patronage.[17]

The conditions in which a section of the ashraf entered the linguistic and ideological ensemble of 'English' under British patronage also differed from Bengal. Hindus predominated in English education in the rest of the country. This was the only region—NWP, Awadh and the Delhi zone—where the percentage of Muslims was proportionate in government schools and relatively high in English education; though even here Muslim girls were not given a formal English education.[18] The diffusion of English in NWP was, however, weaker than Bengal. The General Report for Public Instruction (1843–44) traced this to the absence of a full-fledged colonial state apparatus, European residents, merchants, and sailors, as well as to the conduct of most public business in the vernacular.[19] Up to the mid-nineteenth century madrasa or school graduates qualified for government service and till the 1860s English was not absolutely necessary for many levels of service.[20] The proportion of Muslims fell sharply at higher levels of education in Awadh and their percentage in schools and colleges declined in the 1870s in NWP, but they remained along with the traditional literati—brahmins, many of whom had also entered professions, and kayasths, scribes who had moved from Mughal to colonial service and professions—ahead of other groups till the 1890s.[21]

Unlike Bengal, English was introduced within the parameters of Anglo-Vernacular education. Woods' Despatch (1854) had sought to extend "European knowledge" through vernacular languages, a sentiment that determined the government's institutional policies and was supported in the 1860s by the British Indian Association which, however, wanted to combine the vernacular with education in English. The choice of vernacular became an object of contention among the Urdu-speaking elite and burgeoned into the Hindi–Urdu controversy. Government recognition of Hindi and Urdu as separate subjects and the printing of textbooks in both the Nagri and Urdu script from the 1850s also heightened differences and helped create opposing "vernacular elites".[22] Shifts in institutional power accompanied these new linguistic ensembles. There was an institutional cutback in Orientalist education in classical languages (Arabic, Sanskrit, and Persian) after 1857, and an increase in government control of vernacular education and state patronage of textbooks; by the 1870s Anglo-Vernacular education began to diminish the authority of pandits learned in Sanskrit; and Urdu, which initially accounted for the largest number of books, was outstripped by Hindi by the end of the century.[23]

While the process of reconciling English education with Persian, Arabic, and Islam had only just begun, a set of ideological affinities and rapprochements between the categories of English, Sanskrit, and 'Hindu womanhood' had already been crafted in early nineteenth-century Bengal. The latter were replayed in UP in this context of competing vernaculars and a bilingual Anglo-Vernacular education that was directly linked to monetary advantage in the colonial regime. All these factors, along with the more limited and more monitored access to European texts, mediated the entry not only of Muslims but of the urban and *mofussil* literati as a whole into state education and the service sector, and configured the 'private' education of women differently.

Whereas 'Hindu' and *bhadralok* (genteel middle classes) had been more or less synonymous in Bengal, the dominant class of landlords and government servants which comprised the Urdu-speaking elite in UP extended beyond Muslims to upper (Kashmiri brahmin, rajput) and middle castes (bania, khatri, kayasth), many of whom were perceived as being 'islamicized' in varying degrees. Conflicting centres of interest between land, trade, and government service pulled Hindu and Muslim groups into both ideological antagonisms and alliances. A number of voluntary, parallel, often short-lived associations proliferated, formed both independently and collaboratively with British administrators, directed at social and educational reform, religious purification, caste uplift, or lobbying with the government. There was no single pattern, some were exclusive, others either had members from different denominations, usually part of the Urdu-speaking elite, coming together on common issues or were even intended to promote Hindu–Muslim friendship.[24]

In UP, then, the issue was the religious and linguistic *splitting* of an Urdu-speaking elite that was unified at many levels in terms of class, clientage, and culture and had a long if uneven history of religious syncretism. The new ideologies and techniques of 'communal' othering honed in Bengal ripened here in an accelerated logic of mobility (upward and downward), de- and re-gentrification (with brahmins and trading groups like khatris and banias becoming landowners), and in a situation where there were far greater potentials for intra-class conflict.

In the early 1870s, the communalism that pervaded the state and was incipient at these upper levels had begun to seep into political processes, public and educational sites, but it was by no means firmly embedded.[25] Even the communitarian frameworks of the Deobandis and loyalists like Harishchandra and Sayyid Ahmad Khan that emerged in this decade were not accompanied by exclusive concepts of the nation.[26] Poised in a historical moment partly concurrent with the entry of organized nationalism and communal organizations (such as the Arya Samaj with its vicious polemic against Islam and Christianity) but prior to their consolidation, this configuration had a formative role in the founding of an urban and *mofussil* intelligentsia and reading public in UP. However, its vocabulary was undercut by several contradictions—if there were receptivities to communalization there were also resistances. Significantly, the cross-cutting contours of communal and syncretic tendencies were now being actively shaped not only by colonial intervention but also by this intelligentsia. And as I see it, the crucial relationship here is not between modernity and tradition (read 'communities') but between the dynamics of *partial* embourgeoisement and the logics of communalization. Embourgeoisement was clipped as much by the petty rentier character and ideological convergence with landed interests within this intelligentisia, as by the ideological configurations and peculiarities of class formation within the colonial economy. Class processes both assisted and deflected communalization. Even the indigenist claims inscribed in this configuration could, paradoxically, double as an ideational matrix of partial embourgeoisement and disperse religious unities as they were enunciated.

Between women: Mir'at ul'-Arus and Ritiratnakar

Mir'at ul'-Arus (1869) and *Ritiratnakar* (1872) were part of the discourse of female literacy. Printed under government patronage, they became curricular reading and represented a field of aspiration for government service that was much wider than the actual number of jobs available. Maulavi Nazir Ahmad, born in 1836 in a village in Bijnor district, educated in Delhi, rewarded for his loyalty with the post of deputy inspector of schools, became a deputy collector in 1863 and was a prominent figure in the Aligarh movement. Pandit Ramprasad Tiwari, born in village Lehra near Prayag, was the author of *Sutaprabodh* (1871), another government-sponsored textbook for girls' schools.[27] But they had more in common than loyalist ashraf and brahmin interests in service, patronage, reward. Male reformers across denominations had already internalized the premises of colonial moral authority and could simply graft its ideologies of altruism with the regional specificities of class formation and the reformulation of patriarchies. The creation of near-singular communities in *Mir'at* and *Riti* mimicked divisive colonial policies but their *mirrored* constitution of reformed women displayed a remarkable patriarchal overlap.

Both books revolve on dyads of misogyny and reform. The introduction of *Mir'at ul'-Arus* (lit. the bride's mirror) notices the misogyny in prevailing attitudes as well as in the Koran, but the onus of self-correction, proving their ability, and reversing their social inferiority rests on women themselves. The introduction of *Riti* sets out to destroy the demoness of stupidity and ignorance, *murkhta rupini pishachini*, who dogs women (p. 2). Both narratives participate in the misogyny that held together much contemporary prescription: 'bad' women infringe all marital and familial codes. They are ignorant, illiterate, disobedient, quarrelsome, insult their husbands, fail to cook and sew, go out on any pretext, desire independence, love jewellery excessively, steal or appropriate the mother-in-law's wealth, try to separate from the joint household—in *Riti* a wicked daughter-in-law even sets fire to her mother-in-law's hair. Ironically, the narrativization of unreformed women in *Mir'at* is far more compelling than its own pedagogic intentions can sustain. The 'bad' sister Akbari exemplifies a textbook misogyny: lazy, unskilled, self-pleasuring, wilful, brought up without suitable fatherly or parental tutelage in the protection of her doting maternal grandmother, she disobeys all patriarchal authority, refuses to cook or celebrate festivals, and sleeps too much. The heavy punishments she is given do not, however, fully cancel the pleasure of subversion or the spectre of autonomy.

Both writers have a stake in homogenizing customs and gear decription to selective change. *Ritiratnakar* (lit. digest of customs), explicitly situated at an intersection between the medieval compendium and the by now full-blown, travelogue-inspired colonial genre of 'customs and manners', sorts out *ritis* or customs in terms of their familiarity, relevance, and adaptability. The form of both narratives hovers between tutelary discourse and novelization. A claustrophobic pedagogy is produced through their self-projection as exemplary reading for girls and women, a series of self-confirming, matching and mutually corroborative voices, the geometrical balancing of cautionary and exemplary events, punishments and rewards, heroines whose voices resonate with authorial positions and who function as links in what become seamless, circulating chains of relayed prescription.[28] Both books are obsessed with self-duplication. Women narrate exemplary stories to other women. In *Mir'at* every story they read had to instruct, admonish, carry a *nasihat* (p. 147). Their heroines Asghari and Maina are, respectively, the voice and emblem of consenting women. Literate daughters-in-law, wives of salaried men, they have common objects of reform: women of the same class, husbands, and more unevenly or ambiguously, lower-class and caste women.

Both teach other women. In *Mir'at*, Asghari is born into an eminent Delhi family, *khandaan*, with a tradition of service in princely states, but her father has moved into British employment as a tehsildar; she is married to the son of a maulavi learned in Persian and Arabic who looks after the estates of a rich landowner, *rais*, in Lahore. Asghari sets up a free *maktab* or primary school in her home, carefully selecting students from ashraf families, and her altruism is eventually the vector of family mobility. She is able to arrange a marriage for her personally tutored sister-in-law Mehmooda with the brother of her wealthy and aristocratic student (whose uncle is divan of the ruler of Patiala and whose father was administrator in the Indore ruler's government and now lives on rents from his extensive urban properties), a relationship that is cemented later when her own son marries Mehmooda's daughter. Altruism combined with educating women becomes a form of female entrepreneurship which renews and enlarges the network of social acquaintance, *wakfiyat*, through existing and emerging structures of patronage and tutelage; it builds a meritocracy of women through which the impoverished, genteel, educated, salaried ashraf can *reunite* with the landowning, wealthy aristocracy by offering them, in an upward flow of moral worth, talent, and managerial skills, *hunar* and *intizam*, reformed and reforming women in marriage (p. 178). This desired mobility and ashraf consolidation are in part effected by exorcizing poor 'Muslim' women, a feature I will return to. An authorial statement dividing the world into male labour in the public sphere and female labour in the domestic domain is accompanied paradoxically by a significant conflation of domestic management and worldly affairs, *khanadari* and *duniyadari* (pp. 21–22)—a recognition of the emergence of new forms of domestic labour as producers of social credit and symbolic value. The resourcefulness and networks of women provide barricades against male failure, produce status and family prosperity. Altruism virtually becomes an obligation for women as members of a class.

In *Ritiratnakar*, once individual mobility is assured, higher-caste consolidation and group mobility structure the narrative. The narrative invests in a generalized 'Hindu' model around which upper and middle castes can cohere, affirm brahmin superiority, and underscore lower-caste inferiority. Unlike *Mir'at*, marriages in the same economic strata, though in nearby regions, are preferred. The heroine Maina is not a brahmin. Her references to her husband as *lalaji* and the fact that they socialize with mahajans (merchants) indicate a nebulous amalgam of bania and kayasth, mercantile and scribal castes. She laments the lack of education among all high castes. With the help of Shuklaniji, a learned brahmin woman, she starts literacy lessons for neighbourhood women. In both narratives structured teaching is combined with lengthy conversational tutelage of female relatives and neighbours while religious books *and* arithmetic have a special place in their syllabi. A consensual model of the new woman, naturalized as a relatively secluded, home-based teacher of other women, seems to emerge in both books and signifies a shift in the status of such teaching: respectable middle-class women take on a task earlier performed by widows, poor upper-caste, or impoverished well-bred women. Further, unpaid teachers had more status than paid ones; *ustanis* who taught the Koran and other Arabic scriptures seem to have been regarded mainly as a higher class of domestic servants.[29] Education, then, was to be the voluntary work of reformed women, resting neither on profit nor on state institutions but on informal, civic initiatives by suitably *deprofessionalized* women. Asghari does not use the money from the *maktab* (except as loan) since women are not meant to earn and provide:

> *Aurato ki kamai bhi koi kamai hai. Agar aurato ki kamai se ghar chala karen to mard kyo ho.* (*Mir'at*, p. 165)

In this regard the narratives echo, extend, and transform into female altruism, a prevailing philanthropic tendency in private education conducted without profit, salary, fees or government aid, as well as the desire for independent educational institutions that informed madrasas like Deoband in 1867, the plans for the univerity in Aligarh in the 1870s and later for the Benares Hindu University. However, such private schools, whether *maktabs* or *pathshalas*, were by no means as exclusive in terms of class and denomination as these two narratives suggest.[30]

Both women reform their husbands, underwrite their professional success, and manage social relations. It is their agility and surveillance that guarantees male eligibility for government jobs. In *Mir'at*, Asghari encourages her husband to stand on his own merit, study diligently, learn accounting and arithmetic in addition to the increasingly useless Farsi and Arabic, and to seek a job, *naukari*, with the colonial regime rather than with the declining aristocracy who have been ruined by the British and cannot afford to pay their employees for years. She instils in him the thrift, hard work, moral rectitude, social decorum, and scruple against taking bribes that will make him both a fit servant of the British and a steady provider. She is a mine of information and advice about existing social techniques for securing a job in the *kachahri* through informal apprenticeship and establishing personal ties with better-placed Indians (competitive qualifying examinations had not yet been instituted), as well as about how to deal with British employers.[31] She rescues him from corrupt sycophants, expensive entertainment, and the nautch or *naachrang*, arranging his life and safeguarding his job as naib sarishtadar in far-away Sialkot. If Asghari knows how to 'work' the colonial system, she is also conversant with the etiquettes and tactics required for 'native' employment, and indeed even of situations where the two intersect! She virtually moulds her father-in-law's relations with his *rais* employer: when he should retire, how to ensure that his elder son will be the successor for his job, how to obtain a *sifarish* (recommendation) from the *rais* for his younger son's British employer (which results in a tripled salary), how he can obtain a gift for his daughter's wedding (pp. 162–63). The authorial voice describes British supremacy as a product of superior education and the colonial administration as an altruistic, universalizing apparatus that benignly rewards educated Indians with jobs. However, taken as a whole, this is a narrative of *female intercession* in which the domestic sphere is an indispensable adjunct of the public domain. It marks the entry of the UP ashraf into an ideological configuration conjointly produced by British and Indian in Bengal, but now in the rescue of dispossessed or declining upper-class groups, in the mobility of a new service strata of verna-cular intelligentsia, and in the self-description of middle classes.

In *Riti* too women seem to maintain networks of stable family and neighbourhood relationships while men are projected as mobile career makers, in a new relation of complementarity designed to con-trol or at least to enter emerging configurations of social and political power, including new linguistic ensembles. Maina's husband has a government job in Prayag, squanders his salary on *naach rang*, osten-tatious clothes, hordes of guests, and sends no money home (p. 6). She is compelled to join him in order to police his expenditure.

The intensity of Maina's reformism, however, hinges on a crusade against Urdu and Farsi. She turns her Farsi-educated, Urdu-loving husband into a Sanskrit learner. For him Urdu is the language of wit and repartee, for her it is the language of abuse and invective. Diffusing his initial anger about the Sanskrit lessons she herself is taking, she also argues that Urdu is difficult, contains no *gyan* (knowledge) as compared to Hindi, and cannot be understood by women, villagers, and common people (pp. 19–20, 22). Farsi alienates Hindus from their own religion and holy books: *dharma, granths,* and Dharmashastras. She represents the English as rulers of the world who have never forsaken their mother tongue, finds it shameful that Hindus should have adapted to a Muslim language, and insists that a Hindu who cannot speak his *deshbhasha,* national language, has no *hindupan* or hinduness (pp. 20, 24). The ground for religious and linguistic synonymity had in part been prepared by the language controversy which began in the 1860s. In a memorandum of 1868 advocating the Nagri script, Babu Shiva Prasad of Benares, an Oswal bania*, had declared the antiquity of Hindi, designated Persian as a "Semitic element" that alienated Hindus from "Aryan speech", turned them into "semi-Muhammedans", and destroyed their "Hindu nationality".[32] Since Sanskrit and Hindi are identified with primordial faith, Maina's reform of her husband virtually amounts to a conversion!

Asghari and Maina are loyalists deeply invested in the emblems of British modernity: technology, medicine, hygiene, education, English women. If the author of *Mir'at* is fascinated with trains, then his heroine earnestly explains to her pupils the virtues of modern communications—letter, telegram, camera, newspaper, ship, herself uses medicines as part of good mothering, and introduces a superior hygiene. The logic of loyalism involves praising and explaining how a woman became monarch of the largest known empire. Since no commensurate Indian examples can be remembered, some effort is needed to explain Victoria's succession as that of a niece rather than of a wife, that her husband is royal but not a king, that she is an efficient ruler not a pawn, that she has sons but they do not rule, that women can do everything men can do. Asghari,

---

* Oswal bania: traders.

who owns a photograph of Queen Victoria, eulogizes her *amal-dari*: her rule is marked by the absence of bribery, corruption, force, violence, war, and unlike tyrannical monarchies in other parts of the world, by benevolence and care for Indian subjects (p. 152). Unsecluded English women are defended on the ground that purdah or seclusion is not customary in England as indeed it was not in a village Asghari took shelter in during the 1857 revolt. The modesty, *lihaaz*, of these rural women, she claims, was superior to that of secluded women. She endorses the commitment English women have to their children's education even if it involves sending them to England, and contrasts it with the unwillingness of ashraf women to part with their children. In *Riti* the author praises the political stability and rule of law of the colonial regime. Maina too showers praise on British lifestyles, edu-cation, architecture, hygiene, hard work, urban development, their wonderful transformation of the city of Prayag.[33] English women are courteous, virtuous, linguistically proficient in several languages including Farsi and (conflating script with language) *nagri*, educate both sons and daughters. Maina's own son was cured by a memsahib.

For Maina too women can participate as intercessionaries in the colonial regime. The brahmin Shuklaniji, a veritable goddess of learning, *sakshaat Saraswati*, and her two *chelis*, disciples, become the native informants of an English memsahib (p. 26). This memsahib is a widow, has two sons in government service, and spends her time distributing medicines and charity. Shuklaniji's hatred of Farsi and Arabic, ardent propagation of Nagri and Hindi, and description of the fall of Hindu women create an instant rapport with the memsahib. The delighted memsahib says she has not yet met a *kulin*, well-born, learned upper-caste woman but only her low-caste servants, women whose accounts are untrustworthy and unreliable: *unki baat kucch vishwas ke yogye nahin hai* (p. 95). Shuklaniji and her disciples willingly provide a detailed digest and calendar of festivals, fairs, and fasts. Shuklaniji wants a return to the Dharmashastras including the *Manusmriti*, defends polytheism and the worship of cows on 'practical' grounds, argues for irrigating the field, *khet*, of English with the water, *jal*, of Sanskrit-Hindi, and pleads for state patronage of learned brahmins (p. 146). The convinced memsahib wishes the British would rule India according to her own customs or *ritis*, commit

themselves to protecting cows, shift their official patronage to Sanskrit and English to lighten the burden of Hindus, and promises to
intercede with friendly administrators.[34] Shuklaniji too concurs with
the memsahib's modest proposal for modernization—the need to
rationalize customs and reduce the number of festive occasions:
*dhanya mem sahib dhanya mein tumhaari buddhi ki kahan tak
saraahna karun* (p. 144).

In what is a neatly gendered complementarity, Shuklaniji
not only displaces low-caste female informants but becomes a
successor of the male brahmin as native informant, supplicant, and
interlocutor. The early Orientalists and missionaries had projected
'Sanskrit' severally as a passage, vehicle or pragmatic encasing for
European knowledge, a means for 'developing' the vernaculars, and
as a model of potentially dividable authority; early administrators
had singled out Hindus for their religion-induced docility as the most
pliable subjects and special beneficiaries of colonial rule. It is from
these histories of loyalism and conferral, of the secret kinship of
'Sanskrit' and 'English'—a relation of substitution, affinity, assimilation, and antagonism—honed in the 1820s and 1830s, that a weapon
is forged by the urban UP intelligentsia for its politics of representation in which the relation of Sanskrit and English not only becomes
licit and explicit but fits effortlessly and unthreateningly into the
increasingly self-conscious 'Hindu' claims to class and culture.[35] Further, this configuration had already imbricated the class-based logics
of domestic ideologies in England and India with those of race and
empire, and interpellated English women within a constellation of
moral power and national identity that offered them an altruistic
social agency. Now it similarly interpellated an increasing number
of Indian women creating consent, however, more often for a 'Hindu'
than an Indian identity.[36]

Ritiratnakar seems to be infused with a dream of brahmin
hegemony now suitably modified to the dream of being permanent
intermediaries who can attach 'native' female knowledge of customs
and manners to modern British knowledge. The semantic of non-
interference that emerged in the early decades of colonial rule identified the authority of Indian religions with colonial authority and
had given a quasi-divine aura to the colonial state as interpreter,
preserver, and 'ameliorator' of the higher-caste, religio-patriarchal

domain. *Riti* elaborates this indigenist semantic, refurbishes colonial authority by turning high-caste women into conduits of 'first-hand' ethnographic data, and English women into generators and evaluators of this information. Religion becomes at once a private or domestic arena imbricated in text and custom, a public arena within which political agendas and vocabularies can be formulated, and a product of transnational female collaboration.

Mir'at ul'-Arus stands at an intersection between Deobandi and Aligarhi reformism. The Deobandi ulema did allow women the same potentials as men but positioned them inside the home and outside the ambit of 'western' contamination; their cultural antagonism to the west did not however include hostility to government service. The Aligarhi model developed in Sayyid Ahmad Khan's limited reformism combined a quasi-anglicist model of efficiency, order, discipline, and secular rationality with a reformulated Islamic theology but was initially quite conservative about women's education: this had to be postponed until men were educated. Sayyid Ahmad's loyalism represented post-1857 pacificatory adjustments by a section of propertied UP Muslims; it was geared to rescuing the fortunes and status of the ashraf and reconciling the aristocracy to British rule. 'Hindu' loyalism however drew on a longer ideological history of adjacencies encapsulated in the mediatory field of British Orientalism which had produced collaborative versions of 'Hindu' cultural authenticity, discourses of preservation or revitalization, and functioned as a conduit in the transformation of a section of the pre-colonial literati into a new intelligentsia in Bengal. Some of this trickled into NWP through the Calcutta School Book Society in the early nineteenth century while comparable enterprises for restoring Hindu culture and Sanskrit within this Orientalist configuration had been undertaken first by Benares Sanskrit College, then by the Benares Institute in the 1860s, and later in Harishchandra's publications in the 1870s.

The overlap between old and new, Hindu and Muslim histories of loyalism found a common local ground in UP in the materialities of collaboration (in government service, military contracting, trading, and banking[37]) prior to the 1857 uprising and in the confiscations, rewards, and restorations of land after it. In a broader sense, loyalism also represented a more general understanding that with most aspects of civil life having come under the jurisdiction of the government, the only way to participate in political decisions about allocation or control of social resources after 1857 was to make some accommodation with it.[38] The ideological relocation and convergence of these vectors of loyalism produced new bonds and new fractures. In so far as it worked as a form of ideological cohesion in class and patriarchal terms, it cut across religious lines but distanced both the rebellious and the gendered history of 1857. And in so far as it was cast in a 'Hindu' language of religious difference, it blurred the cross-denominational cooperation or Hindu–Muslim unities forged during the revolt.

The loyalism that *Mir'at* and *Riti* conferred on women mediated and softened imperialism. It went beyond placing UP women in the same ideological configuration of education, altruism, domesticity, and upward mobility vis-à-vis colonial rule as their predecessors and counterparts in Bengal. The loyalism of these 'new' higher-caste and ashraf women covertly put the well-known (though unrecorded and uncollated), actively *disloyal* participation of ordinary and aristocratic women in the 1857 uprising under erasure. And, it confirmed the delegatory powers of male reformers, shaped a grammar in which the ubiquitous memsahib could both be othered and assimilated to their own domestic agendas. The Bengali Keshub Chander Sen pleaded for the service of "well-trained, accomplished English ladies" to elevate "Hindu women" and give them "an education free and liberal and comprehensive in character, calculated to make Indian women good wives, mothers, sisters and daughters". Harishchandra, whose abject loyalism took the shape of panegyrics to the royal family—in which British rulers featured as the rescuers of Hindus and a fallen India—and whose journal *Balabodhini* obsessively recuperated model *pativratas* (faithful wives) in the 1870s, went on to counterpose "the sad plight of Indian women" who had fallen into "darkness" because of Muslim rule to the companionate freedom of English women, in the preface to *Nildevi* (1881). Indian women were not of course to "mingle with their menfolk merrily and freely" like them or to "change their ways of modesty and womanly dignity", but only to be "alert and enlightened, so that they know how to run their homes efficiently, to educate their children, to carefully decide what is good for Indian society."[39]

Female loyalism also performed other functions. It verna-
cularized the constellation of English and feminized the raj. Unlike
men, women were not expected to learn English as a language but to
enter 'English' as an ideological ensemble *through* the vernacular, to
learn *about* England and to learn *from* English women. In this reconfiguration, the vernacular (Hindi, Urdu) is posed as an intermediary and mediating category poised between the transregional and
'cosmopolitan' languages of belief (Sanskrit, Arabic) and rule (Farsi,
English). And Hindi is far from being a full-bodied language or a sign
of tradition. Hindi becomes the node at which its parent, Sanskrit, the
repository of Hindu culture, meets 'English', the fount of real
knowledge, and itself sets out to either displace regional dialects
(Bhojpuri, Awadhi, Braj) or to bifurcate a lingua franca (Hindustani)
into incommensurate and antagonistic languages (Hindi, Urdu).[40]

The only languages women learn in *Riti* are Sanskrit and
Hindi. Pandit Gauri Datta's *Devrani Jethani ki Kahani* (1870), obviously modeled on *Mir'at*, describes a shopkeeping Agrawal bania
family living near Meerut. One son is taught English on the advice
of a relative who works in a madrasa while the daughter learns *nagri*
from a *misrani*, the daughter-in-law of the *purohit* or family priest,
Dilla Pande. She runs a neighbourhood school for girls in her home
patronized by a British *mem*, who encourages and rewards good students with trinkets. The son obtains British employment, and in what
is represented as the epitome of companionate conjugality, marries
a Nagri-knowing girl.[41] Datta, a Saraswat brahmin and a teacher till
the age of forty, later became a *sannyasi*, ascetic, dedicated to the
cause of the Nagri script!

Khwaja Altaf Husain 'Hali's *Majalis un-Nissa* (1874),
influenced by *Mir'at*, also condenses many of these tendencies. His
ancestors were in Mughal service, his father moved into British service, he himself took a clerical job in Hissar; later, traumatized by
the 1857 rebellion, he became a tutor in the employ of a Delhi nawab,
then shifted to Punjab Book Depot in Lahore revising Urdu translations of English textbooks. He started two girls' schools in Panipat
that were run by women of his own family. He is said to have known
no English and to have resisted the valorization of government service.[42] Yet *Majalis* was even more committed to the details of British
modernity and monarchy than *Mir'at* or *Riti*.[43] An exemplary mother

praises Queen Victoria for learning, compassion, lack of arrogance, altruism, a paternalist benevolence which can raise the deserving poor from rags to riches. Imagining Britain as a monarchy without a parliament, she places Shahjahan's daughter Roshanara alongside Victoria. 'English' becomes the site of conjugality and Victoria a model of conjugal love, indissoluble marriage, and good widowhood. The most powerful ruler was the best and most loving of wives who went into "perpetual mourning" when her husband died and even wrote a book about him: she knew that "husbands have a higher position" (p. 86). The recasting of Victoria in the image of an ideal upper-caste/class wife then proceeded simultaneously with, if it did not actually precede, her housewifeization in England; and she appears as an empress of India in the full sense of the phrase some years before she actually had the title! However, the mother in *Majalis* also teaches her daughter that men are not superior, and the very logic of her eulogy heads subversively in the direction of greater equality and power:

> Knowledge is something that permits the woman who possesses it to have hundreds and thousands of men as her subjects. You see as an example our ruler, Queen Victoria. . . . Because she is so learned she can rule over two countries. (p. 55)

Her reformed daughter Zubaida is, like Asghari, a miracle of management and the centre of several networks of relationships which enable her to 'influence' the behaviour and improve the status of the family. While girls are taught Arabic, Urdu, and Persian, Zubaida's son learns Urdu, Arabic, English, and a very small amount of Farsi (since it is no longer the language of rulers) and ends—a hybrid of the precapitalist picaro and Samuel Smiles—with the job of translator in the household of the Sultan of Istanbul.

How would this modernizing female adventure in which women routinely rescue family fortunes be contained? *Mir'at* had difficulty in foreclosing certain agential possibilities. Asghari runs her natal home from the age of eight; a paragon by thirteen, her reformism peaks within a few years of marriage. She organizes family finances with her father-in-law, reunites her husband's extended family, arranges the affairs of her sister-in-law Mehmooda and her husband, and on the departure of Mehmooda's father-in-law for pilgrimage to Mecca, she becomes the chief adviser and manages their extensive affairs. The meteoric increase in Asghari's power effectively makes all but men's earning redundant. Women in households where men are living and earning in other towns can manage without male surveillance, direct or supervise male comportment in the public world, and accumulate power in the absence of men. Even fathers-in-law become superfluous in the face of their managerial skills and can only take to piety and pilgrimage. How then would the power of the reformed and reforming woman be circumscribed? After all the optimal model now was Queen Victoria! Nazir Ahmed's answer was to limit her reward to fame, to constrict her agency within the frame of male tutelage (that of her father), and finally to subject her to the blows of fate and undeserved suffering. Asghari loses all but one of her children to death. Similarly in 'Hali's *Majalis* good deeds do not win more than honour, prestige, and the benediction of the family, servants, and neighbours for women. *Riti*'s mode of containment was to seclude Maina and restrict her agency to self-duplication among family and neighbourhood women.

Ironically, it was domestic prescription that conferred manipulative powers on women: their reformism could be socially acceptable and contained only if they were vectors of indirect agency and schooled into structures of indirect reward. Yet the contradictory class logics of secluding women whose networks were increasingly valuable as well as the contradiction between the passive wife and the quasi-bourgeois reformer remained. These could only be neutralized by reinstating female obedience, the familiar constraints of family, labour, and marriage, in effect, by combining emerging companionate bourgeois ideologies with extant patriarchal ideologies and arrangements. Both *Riti* and *Mir'at* emphasize the bride's obligation to the entire family and are preoccupied with the economic imperatives of the joint family as being both cheaper and a buffer for unemployment. Both participate in the cross-denominational consensus on the necessity of women's domestic labour which dominated prescriptive writing in this region and period.[44] And finally, a shared and unshakeable marital ideology lay beneath the modernizing venture of both narratives. Though there was an obvious difference between cousin marriage and exogamy, no sharp distinction obtains between so-called Muslim contractual marriage and Hindu sacramental marriage in practice. Contractual marriage as defined by Islamic law made it easier for widows to remarry but among the northern ash-raf widows were seldom remarried.[45] *Mir'at* confesses that it is impossible to dissolve ashraf marriages: *ashrafon mein kahin bibiya bhi choot ti hain* (p. 56). Asghari's father advises her to maintain a respectful and deferential civility, *adab*, towards her husband, cites a *hadis* (somewhat unconvincingly) which declares that if it were permissible to worship anyone other than god then husbands would be worshipped:[46]

> *Maine hadis ki kitab mein padha tha ki agar khuda ke sivai kisi doosre ko sijda karna rava hota to paigambar saheb farmate hai ki mein bibi ko hukm deta ki apne miya ko sijda kiya kare.*

And adds that since regional customs (*mulki rivaj*) have also made marriage unbreakable she should regard it as life-long (pp. 76–78). This *de facto* indissolubility is not too far from the *de jure* position of *Riti*, which stresses husband service, *patiseva*. Shuklaniji gives a departing bride the classic lesson of subservience to her husband thinly camouflaged in metaphors of 'mutual' dependence between the land and the king: *Stri purush ka sambandh aisa hai jaise prithvi aur raja ka, ki yeh dono paraspar ek doosre ke aadheen hai* (p. 185).

Subjugating women 'below'

Reformed women had to control and/or reform servants. Their chief struggle was not with patriarchal arrangements but with lower-caste/class women and the ways in which the domestic and customary domain was structured around the services they provided. The acquisition of moral and wifely power for reformed women rested not on othering women from different denominations but on othering women 'below'. However, *through* this, women were being used to mark more generalized enclosures of 'hinduness' and 'muslimness'.

Mir'at is structured around a parallel emplotment of unre-formed and reformed women: the downfall of the former ensues from close relations with lower-caste and class women, while the success of the latter rests on the ability to outsmart and defeat them. Akbari's circle of friendship is composed of women from urban artisanal, servicing, petty vending, or trading families who may have seemed

more threatening because they did not fall wholly within relations of
clientage with the gentry and were moving gradually into an
independent sector of the economy. Before marriage she had fond
sisterly relations with Banno, the daughter of a panihaari* to whom
she gave food, clothes, and money stolen from her grandmother and
who she misses after marriage. After her marriage Akbari chooses to
establish companionate and near-familial relations with other women:
Chuniya the bhatiyari, Zulfan who is connected to the qalaigar,
Rahmat the sakkani and *kaali-kaali* Salmati, the jet-black daughter
of a local kunjra* (p. 38). Predictably, the narrative instantiates its
own accusations against these women—giving bad advice, dividing
families, being predatory, defrauding ashraf women.[47] On his sister's
information, Chuniya's brother robs Akbari of her household goods.
While Akbari is punished with impoverishment, Asghari is praised for
her lack of intimacy with women and especially for her rejection of
low-class women. Asghari's success is related to her ability to expose
and expel *mama* Azmat, the old family servant.

In both *Mir'at* and *Riti* lower-caste/class women are *controlling* intermediaries and much-needed buffers, dreaded spies and
indispensable informants. Their importance is related to the seclusion
(whether relative or absolute) of higher-caste/class women whose
relationship to the public domain they mediate and whose 'homes'
they insulate by dealing with the outside world. They carry information in and out, and this knowledge has effectivities both in the working world outside and for women confined to the home. In *Riti* Dasiya
acts as messenger, reveals the character of women neighbours and
neighbourhood secrets, *mohalle ke bhed*, to Maina (p. 12). An ayah
functions as the conduit to the memsahib for Maina. Migrant women
in domestic service carry back accounts of urban life and British
households to upper-caste/class rural women. In *Mir'at* Azmat is a
vector for the circulation of gossip and information. Zulfan runs to
inform Akbari's parents of their daughter's unhappiness in her marital home. It is her lower-class women friends who help Akbari to move
house. Even Asghari needs the help of other servant women to
ascertain prices and the extent of Azmat's cheating. But it is Azmat

* panihaari: water carrier.
* bhatiyar: inn keeper; qalaigar: tinner; sakkani: bhishti or water carrier;
  kunjra: fruit and vegetable seller.

who unveils the full structures of dependence. She shops for every domestic need including food, clothes, and jewellery, arranges and regulates the household economy like a man: *mardo ki tarah is ghar ki muntzim thi* (p. 85). The maulavi's remittances arrive casually at intervals of six months and the household runs on loans and debts, *karz*. Only Azmat has the ability to secure loans and prevent shop-keepers from claiming them. Each time she is dismissed, the house is beseiged by kunjra, bania, bazaz, sonar, and kasai* clamouring for money, and she has to be recalled to deal with them. Azmat boasts openly that she is not easy to dismiss, if she leaves it will only be after bankrupting and auctioning the house. The family too fears her ability to incite shopkeepers. Azmat possesses sufficient financial expertise to put the household in her control; she in fact signifies a dangerously *mis-located* worldly power. If Akbari was punished for her infringement of desired domesticity, Azmat is punished for the threat she poses to the very image of that desire. Azmat is made to pay for her share in the *karz* on Asghari's suggestion; this involves giving up all her daughter's jewellery and mortgaging her home to shop-keepers: in effect total impoverishment compounded by being dis-owned by her daughter—the prime beneficiary of her theft!

The access that low-caste and class women in *Mir'at* have to the public world is denied to secluded ashraf women. The problem of controlling these women without giving ashraf women the commen-surate ability to undertake those tasks assumes acute proportions. Purdah could not end, men were either physically absent or when present left *khanadari* to the women. Azmat's power grows in direct proportion to male absence or neglect and since it rests on perform-ing 'male' tasks, her dual role, indeed her very existence, challenges and demystifies the gendered division of space and labour made in domestic ideologies. As a corollary the battle of wits occurs *between women*. Setting up the servant as the main class enemy of both reform-ed and unreformed women could also displace class conflict, absorb-ing it into the seemingly innocuous logics of thrift, domestic manage-ment, and status production on a limited budget. In fact, the conjoint logic of Asghari's thrift and Azmat's expulsion directly benefits the finances of absent men (the father-in-law gets the lion's share of his

* bania: provision vendor; bazaz: cloth merchant; sonar: goldsmith; kasai: butcher.

income for his own use), and assuages general male anxieties about refashioning women to run households in a strata where the search for native or British employment frequently involved male absence.[48] At the same time social status did accrue from servants: even one was a sign that the household and its women had not lost their gentility. *Mir'at* proves that social status of the old sort can be maintained through employing only *one* servant by increasing the managerial efficiency of the housewife. And, status production can be conjoined with thrift precisely because the servant's 'share' is being reduced.

At one level, Azmat represents the old type of 'feudal retainer' thriving on oral transactions, the largesse of the employer and the *barakat* or benign plenitude of the household—all marked by the absence of close calculation—now in mortal combat with the thrift, efficiency, and domestic accounting system designed for surveillance represented by Asghari. Azmat contrasts favourably the generosity of Asghari's mother-in-law, a saintly person, *aulia admi*, with the miserly, penny-pinching daughter-in-law (p. 95). Azmat obviously recognizes that paternalism is part of "a studied technique of rule", while deference is a part of "necessary self preservation or calculated extraction".[49] She nevertheless resents certain changes in paternalism and labour relations—especially because the gradual removal of perquisites from the orbit of reciprocal social relations between persons, the transformation of these into purely economic relations as measured payments for service, are working to redefine her own perquisites as theft.

At another level Azmat is a petty entrepreneur, disenchanted with the discourse of paternalism which demands a denial of self-interest, and seems to be shifting into a discourse of rights. In this she is an analogue of the salaried class that had a foot in two worlds: the paternalist model of mutual obligation and the self-interested contractual view of the 'free market' of labour. The new mode of altruistic enterprise that Asghari represents is pitted against Azmat's entrepreneurial style that consists of buying triple the quantities needed, one to support her daughter and one to sell, a candid thievery she is not afraid to confess to shopkeepers. Azmat perceives her cheating as compensation for being grossly underpaid and overworked. She is not content with the routine tip from shopkeepers for bringing in custom. She claims that she does the work of four people, indeed *all* the work *both* inside and outside, *andar bahar mein akeli admi*, and should get the equivalent of four salaries (pp. 87–88). Azmat's location may be ambivalent but its consequences are not. Everything that she brings about is reversed: the agential or 'causal' powers of the lower orders are fully undone by the reformed woman leaving not a trace behind.

The contest with the family servant also replaces the more classic conflict with the mother-in-law. The servant fulfils some of the same functions: misrepresenting the bride, creating dissension between her and her husband and mother-in-law, generating a family politics. Asghari thinks of Azmat as equivalent to having a rude and bad-tempered mother-in-law and sister-in-law. There is a curious substitution here too. Since the bad servant is a product of the faulty domestic management and complaisance of the uneducated mother-in-law, in effect the latter is dethroned along with Azmat. Expelling the servant becomes a way of re-delegating domestic power to the reformed daughter-in-law and *nominalizing* the mother-in-law without directly challenging the latter or the joint family. The domestic servant provides a buffer that absorbs some of the tensions produced in the transition from older to newer patriarchal forms as well as a means for bypassing the vexed question of nuclear households that was implicit in emergent bourgeois domestic ideologies.

Significantly, women employing servants were cast in a managerial model that was complementary to the emerging capitalist economy while the ideal servant was modelled on a complete and abject dependency whose material coordinates were rural migration, urban dislocation, the absence of resources as well as of supportive kinship and neighbourhood networks. These 'qualifications' for employment not only intensified exploitation but, ironically, replicated higher-caste patriarchal arrangements. Thus the rationale for choosing a new servant in *Mir'at* is: she must have no family in the neighbourhood whom she may support, provision, or spend leisure time with; she must not love good clothes and jewels; she must not be a local woman who can trap them in networks of power and local knowledge; she must not have children and increase the mouths to be fed. In effect the desirable servant is a woman who is *maximally vulnerable*, amenable to patriarchal and class control, an analogue of the uprooted, patrilocally resident, lonely bride, the deserted, destitute wife, or the childless, 'ascetic' widow.

In *Mir'at* poor women are chastised but excluded from reformist tutelage. Ashraf women are ready to mete out physical punishment to servants while spoilt girls routinely ill-treat them. There is also a marked authorial anxiety that the increasing literacy of menial classes will diminish ashraf dignity, authority, and prestige: if *dhobi-sakke-mazdur** learn to read and write there will be no honour or esteem, *izzat*, for illiterate ashraf men and women (p. 28). Nazir Ahmad, otherwise influenced by Sayyid Ahmad, was ahead of him on the question of women's education but behind him on the question of the extension of literacy. Sayyid Ahmad, who initially shared the ashraf and upper-caste scorn for English-educated persons from middle or lower classes—sons of bania, bazaz, khansaman (domestic steward in British household), jamadar (peon or petty official)—later expressed the need to educate not only Muslims who looked to government service or religious occupations but also shopkeepers, artisans, peasants, and labourers.[50]

Whereas *Mir'at* refused to ideologically incorporate poor women into new familial models save paternalistically as honest, pliable servants or as objects of charity, *Riti* worked through a double process of exclusion and selective incorporation into emerging modes of 'community' paternalism. The pincer logic of male absence and women's seclusion in *Mir'at* turned the home into a space for battle with indispensable yet threatening lower-class women. *Riti's* project was more complicated. If *Mir'at* moved towards a 'Hindu' concept of marriage as part of the brahminical model of propriety, achieved mobility, and general strategy of containment, *Riti* moved towards a more stringent seclusion of women in emulation of the regionally settled ashraf model of refinement and gentility. But paradoxically, relative seclusion and restricted mobility were now the preconditions of a militant public surveillance: women had first to be pulled further back from the public domain into the home and then propelled into a combat that extended into public spaces.

If Asghari is overadept at manipulating class codes then Maina is a skilled manipulator of caste and religious differences. Maina reforms low-caste servants and subjects the kaharin, Dasiya, to lengthy tutelary discourses but never loses sight of her inferior

---

* dhobi: washermen; sakke: water carriers; mazdur: labourers.

caste, *neech jati* (p.25). Dasiya's husband is ailing, foul-mouthed, useless, a *nikamma* who does not work. Until she becomes Maina's personal servant, Dasiya has been forced to eke out a subsistence through daily wage labour, *majuri*, spinning, hauling water, gathering edible leaves for her family: *mein tiriya jaat kya kar sakti hoon* (p. 9). Maina symbolically *renames* the kaharin when she gives her domestic employment: Dasiya becomes Ramdasi. The narrative is almost prescient. Kahars, the highest caste for domestic service in Hindu homes, were largely palanquin bearers and carriers who supplied water to Muslim and Hindu homes; they practised widow remarriage and some even ate pork.[51] In the following decades, kahars were to take on a Vaishnav-centred model of upward caste mobility, adopt the suffix *das* (lit. servant) or 'Ram' as a surname, claim kshatriya identities and the practice of widow immolation as a sign of status, and use the language of loyalism in parts of UP and Bihar.[52] It seems new possibilities of collusion and appropriation (as well as conflict) between higher, intermediate, and 'clean' lower castes were already being opened in the expanding and accelerating claims to brahmin, kshatriya, vaishya and Vaishnav origins. And as is evident in *Riti*, the older etiquettes of sanskritization were now to be combined with a new form of hinduization, that entailed communal othering, and the wider diffusion of higher-caste patriarchal ideologies against an equally new ideological horizon of intra-class conflict revolving on competing identities and colonial investment in definitive 'communities'.

In *Riti* the renaming of Dasiya not only imposes a name but also institutes a competence, functions as an imperative—it signifies how she should conduct herself. The nominally incorporated kaharin is therefore given the voice of a self-deprecating, consenting woman: *mein abhaagi is naam ke yogya kahan hoon* (p. 9). She is simultaneously made to invest in the upper-caste rajput landowning paternalism to which she owes her literacy, the altruism of the urban woman who employs her, a claim to cultural superiority resting on antagonism to Farsi, and a belief in the rewards of Sanskrit combined with English as a contemporary model for mobility and prosperity. As mark and seal of her reformed condition, Dasiya too sets up an allegorical binary in which the Sanskrit and English-educated Hindu gets a good job with the British while the Farsi-educated Hindu gets his comeuppance. She narrates the life of a village thakur, Subansh, unparalleled in paternalism, charity, duty, *dharma*. Unlike another local thakur, Abhimaan, who is usurious, extortionate, violent, and hires a julaha* to teach his son Farsi, Subansh's son, Chiranjiv, is given a Sanskrit education *followed* by English education, English being the language of the law, *kanoon* (p. 41). Chiranjiv's English tutor, one Swami Paramhans, combines professional success and mercantile acumen with piety: a brahmin born in Bengal, he learnt English at a Calcutta government school, became first a visitor of schools then a deputy collector, earned lakhs from a printing press that published English, Sanskrit and Bengali books, ensconced his sons in government jobs and finally renounced the world, took *sannyas*! Subansh's wife, the thakurani Daya, educates neighbourhood girls including some from lower castes: she teaches Dasiya to read and write. Chiranjiv, by virtue of his Sanskrit–English education, became first a favourite of the collector sahib, then a tehsildar, and has now been promised a *diputi collectori* (p. 44). He opens a Sanskrit–English school for boys and a *nagri* school for girls in his village, gets a good wife, Sampatti, and has fine children. Rosha, the wife of thakur Abhiman, beats the servants, deprives them of customary food and clothes. Their Farsi-educated son is islamicized by the julaha, chases away the Shia maulavi who replaces the julaha, and gets an untutored wife, Vipatti. Worse than Akbari, on whom she is modelled, she is arrogant, violent, consorts with *neech jati* women—kurmi, kacchi, kol, khatik, nai*—who relieve her of her money, give bad advice such as selling the grain from the thakur's granaries, connive in the theft. On her mother-in-law's death, Vipatti hires five personal servants and four *pisanharis* for grinding grain who eat her out of house and home; a pandit and a fakir (religious mendicant) defraud her of money and jewels; the household goes bankrupt and the family breaks up.[53] Dasiya's story is designed to extend full, subservient approval to the altruistic thakurani and to Maina, her urban counterpart and successor, and implies that the

---

* julaha: mainly weavers, some cultivators.
* kurmi: higher-ranking cultivators; kacchi: low-ranking cultivators, some artisans and some turning entrepreneurial as market gardeners; kol: wood cutters and sellers, water carriers, fishermen; khatik: cultivators, dealers in vegetables and fruit, poulterers, goat butchers; nai: barbers.

uplift of lower-caste women servants must come through a sanskritic hinduization—acts of ideological (self)incorporation. Significantly, the family retainer in 'Hali's *Majalis* was modelled not on the Azmat of *Mir'at* but on the incorporated servicing women in *Riti*: Atiji not only canvasses zealously for female literacy but transmits the same moral tutelage as the upper-class women who employ her.

The politics of language in *Riti* is triple-edged. Women's lack of access to languages of rule—"Urdu–Farsi" and "Farsi–Angrezi"—is denounced for excluding them from the precincts of male knowledge, denying men and women a common language and creating a public–private division on linguistic lines; at the same time, the propagation of Sanskrit and Nagri splits the colloquial lingua franca of women, dividing them along communal lines but uniting them across caste lines. Shuklaniji recommends Nagri and Hindi on the ground of domestic harmony and gender equality: if men and women have the same language it will make women's education easier. In fact, even disapproving accounts written at this time, including those of Harishchandra, acknowledged that women commonly spoke and felt more comfortable speaking Urdu or the mixture known as Hindustani rather than *nagri* at home: *Urdu se mile jule shabd unko saral aur apni boli jaan padte hai.*[54] *Riti* blends the kaharin's voice with that of the learned brahmin woman; Dasiya too adopts the language of othering, replays the trope of the Muslim interregnum, and identifies reform as a recognized technique for removing practices that obstruct social mobility in the colonial dispensation. And jobs were singularly important in the language controversy. The single reference in *Mir'at* to Farsi is Asghari's assertion that a maulavi's Farsi is always superior giving him a natural eligibility for jobs, unlike the superficial knowledge of Hindus who merely read any three Farsi books and get jobs in a *kachahri* (p.170).

In Dasiya's story the combination of Sanskrit and English becomes a fully crystallized conduit of desired mobility and commensurate patriarchy: *jobs* and *wives* match each other. If lower-caste women must reinforce higher-caste patriarchal ideologies in acts of (self)insertion, then higher-caste women must wean their men from Farsi in a familial, intra-class struggle and linguistically *disaggregate* the Urdu-speaking elite. One reference was to the contemporary investment of Kashmiri brahmins and kayasths in Farsi.[55] According to Maina, there is just *one* corrupt branch among kayasths, the Srivastava, who having learnt only Farsi from childhood have lost their *hindupan*; she attributes their immorality and opulence, *aishwarya*, not only to Farsi but to the company of the *miyaji* or Mus-lim who teaches it (pp. 176, 178). The second reference in Dasiya's story was to the dominant class of landlords. Within this rajput thakurs were not only important collaborators of Muslims but the reluctance of this class as a whole (along with some of the ashraf) to equip their sons with English was well known.[56] Compared to middle-class professionals they had less interest in the vernacular and little commitment to formal education for women; yet the combi-nation of English and Sanskrit did bear some relationship to taluqdari patterns of philanthropic investment in education.[57] The wider and more dominant pattern of education among Awadh taluqdars could however, at its most extensive, combine Arabic, Persian, Hindi, Sanskrit, Urdu, and English.[58] This catholicity became a target of de-islamicization by the end of the century. The third reference may have been to the potentials in and through British employment for low castes. In this region, from the early nineteenth century, kahars along with chamars, telis, and kalwars* had found jobs with Europeans as cooks, stable boys, bearers and domestic servants, while other low castes were employed in servicing jobs at military stations. A section of kahars called dhanuk had specialized in serving Europeans.[59] Telis, some of whom had become merchants, and kalwars, some of whom had advanced from selling liquor to wider trading and money-lending activities, were upwardly mobile while kalwars had even staked a claim to vaishya identity.

A now-perfected semantic alliance of 'Sanskrit' and 'Eng-lish' is made to wrestle with Farsi by playing on the gendered access to language in *Riti*. From their inception in Bengal, the categories of 'Sanskrit' and 'Hindu womanhood' had been multivocal: at once *assimilative* nodes of affiliation to colonial rule and hybrid signs of *reclaiming* an indigenist authenticity. They were vehicles for change *and* referents for continuity. Whereas for the Bengal middle class Hindu womanhood was also opposed to the acculturative ensemble named 'English', and like 'Hinduism', intended to undo its alienating

---

* chamars: leather workers, weavers, agricultural, menial and day labourers; telis: oil pressers, manufacturers and sellers; kalwars: liquor distillers.

effects, in UP the two simply become natural allies against a common enemy. Similarly, the transgressive potentials that English acquired in Bengal, as seditious vis-à-vis British rule or liberatory vis-à-vis constricting shastric prescription, are absent in *Riti* or *Devrani Jethani*.[60] Here English is fully loyalist, readily accommodates tradition, and signifies a 'containable', gender-segregated choice rather than a disruptive imposition.

The ideological rapprochement of Urdu, Arabic, and Islam with English was weaker, institutionally less entrenched, and relatively ungendered in that it did not enter a symbiotic relation with Muslim womanhood. The combination of English with Urdu, Persian, or Arabic did predominate at higher educational levels in this region.[61] Yet the positions of even Sayyid Ahmad, who worked hardest to propagate English knowledge within an Islamic context and fuse the two in the educational institutions he founded, were inconsistent and shifting. They neither rested on a univocal Islamic identity for Urdu nor created deep ideological affinities with English. Initially he described the combination of English and Urdu education as anti-religious since Urdu was *secular*, that is, not a carrier of religious instruction like Arabic, and dismissed Urdu as an appropriate medium for higher education because it was insufficiently developed. Later he asked for Urdu alongside English on the ground that the vernacular was more *democratic*, accessible to more people. In 1868 his response to the Hindi campaign was to argue that Hindi and Urdu were in fact the *same* language, a position also taken by some supporters of Nagri, including Harishchandra, in the early years of the controversy over scripts. In 1873, even as he opposed Hindi, Sayyid Ahmad maintained that Urdu was a joint or *shared* and not an inherently 'Muslim' language.[62] As far as English was concerned, he claimed it would make Muslims "better citizens and better British subjects", lead to progress and uplift, provide access to the richest treasures of modern thought and knowledge. However, like some of the early Bengal *bhadralok*, he compartmentalized the utility of English to prove that it could be compatibile with Islam: English would not erode faith if religious education was given side by side from primary school.[63] And even when he explicitly located English as a desirable cultural ensemble in the 1880s, he segregated rather than synthesized it with Islam.[64]

Unlike 'Hindu' womanhood then, there was no settled model of 'Muslim' womanhood that could fuse language, religion, and culture. From the early decades of colonial rule in Bengal, the trope of the Muslim interregnum had been formed and replayed most effectively on patriarchal terrains. It had helped to bond *and* absolve Hindu men who could attribute the present state of their women to it, and in loyalist, self-exculpatory gestures transpose their own patriarchal excesses onto Muslim invaders. And, more signficantly, it had enlarged the symbolic endowment of 'Hindu' women, which could now assist in identifying women with language in UP and *resituate* intra-class conflicts as tensions between *women*. Pieced together on the sites of domestic ideology, this identification with language was to be elaborated later. The growing conflation of Urdu with the sensuous decadence and rampant sexuality associated with Wajid Ali Shah's court was sealed by Harishchandra's sexualization of Urdu as the language of fallen women. By 1882 his positions had hardened enough to claim that Hindu men who supported Urdu did so from a "secret motive": it was "the language of their mistresses and beloved one"—prostitutes, dancing girls, harlots, concubines.[65] Ironically, he himself was multilingual, a personally extravagant scion of the persianized elite, and visited courtesans regularly. The plays of Pandit Gauri Datta and Munshi Sohan Prasad personified Urdu, Nagri, Persian, English as women. Prasad's *Hindi aur Urdu ki Larai* (1885), featured Urdu as a low-caste/Muslim prostitute, and fol-lowing *Ritiratnakar* which had sought confirmation from an altruistic English woman, presented English as adjudicating the quarrel bet-ween Hindu and Urdu.[66] Its representation of English as favouring Nagri did, however, duplicate existing administrative biases.[67]

Dividing and excluding women

Maina also engages in an inverse task in *Riti*: belittling the customary and ritual roles of low castes at higher-caste ceremonial occasions, especially weddings. These practices are attributed, on the one hand, to the fall of brahmins who have lost their *vidya*, *gun*, learning, merit, and tutelary ability for reasons that remain unspeci-fied, and on the other, to the ubiquitous Muslim interregnum which

* Dhobis were untouchables and washing clothes considered degrading.

produced Hindu degeneration and syncretic customs (p. 173). The faultless *ritis* of ancient India deteriorated when low-caste and Muslim popular cults emerged: for instance, dhobins, a *neech* and polluting caste*, acquired an indispensable ritual role as bestowers of *suhaag* (the good fortune of never being cursed by widowhood) at the weddings of both rich and poor, *bade aur chhote* (pp. 170–71). She has heard an ancient story about one Soma dhobin of Singaldeep who miraculously restored a woman's husband to life, but surely all dhobins do not have these powers as is evident from the fact that women continue to be widowed. She does not know why such customs emerged but believes that they have become foolish, blind traditions, *andh parampara*, which education can expel (p. 173). Maina, whose intense admiration for Shuklaniji borders on religiosity, prefers the latter's advice at childbirth to the services of the dai (midwife) who she refers to as a *rand* or widow (p. 38).[68] The censoriousness is not however accompanied by radical alterations. Sticking to custom, Maina avails of the services of chamarins to cut the umbilical cord, oil the infant, and that of the nain from the sixth day.* When the birth is celebrated the nain oversees the preparation of food and serves it, the bhatin plays the *dhol* and sings, the tamolin makes *paan*, and the *chudiwali* or manihaarin distributes bangles.*[69] Nain, bhatin, kaharin, malin, baarin* participate extensively at family weddings while the dhobin continues to give the *sindur* (vermilion) from her own forehead.[70] What is more, Maina procures tea for the English memsahib from a *musalmani nain* (p. 90).

Both Asghari and Maina advocate reforms in dowry, but within this constellation of educated women, status production and upward mobility, reduction in dowry amounts to a choice between one-off status marking and the long-term status production that a reformed woman could bring to the family. In *Mir'at*, Asghari also inveighs against ostentation, debt, too many clothes, jewels, and ritual occasions. Her mother-in-law wishes the British would legislate against these. Asghari assures her that according to the newspapers

---

* chamarin: wife of chamar; nain: barber's wife.
* bhatin: wife of a bhat or bard; tamolin: wife of tamboli, betel-leaf manufacturer and seller; manihaarin: bangle seller.
* malin: wife of mali or gardener; baarin: wife of baari, leaf cup and platter makers for weddings, torch bearers, domestic servants in Hindu homes.

they are about to do something, having already set limits on expenditure and *mehr* (wife's marriage portion) and invited the rich men of Delhi for discussion (p. 184). However, despite Asghari's reformist claims, Mehmooda ends up with a huge dowry, fulsomely described, acquired with money that Asghari herself arranges from family contributions and other sources. Similarly, for all Maina's strictures, her daughter has a lavish wedding and gets a substantial dowry.

Marriage expenses including dowry were at this time in fact the joint object of administrative, upper and middle-class/caste reform, and visibly linked to whittling down customary lower-caste roles. Charles Raikes, magistrate of zila Mainpuri, exhorted kshatriyas to save their properties by curtailing marriage expenses and eliminating bhats* from weddings; he wrested an agreement to do so from zamindars and taluqdars at a Kshatriya Sabha formed for the purpose in Agra in 1852; if *purohit*, bhat, nai, and baari made extortionate demands they were to be punished and arrested.[71] The British Indian Association of Oudh (1861) to which all taluqdars belonged made some half-hearted attempts to curtail lavish expenditure and dowry for rajputs while the Benares Institute (1870) set out to reduce marriage expenses among several castes, especially rajputs and kayasths, both of whom had traditions of Mughal service and were often steeped in nawabi ways.[72] Munshi Pyarelal, formerly in British service, organized several meetings and committees of administrators, local notables, and Indians in the upper echelons of British service, and sought agreement from major *biradaris* (extended clan brotherhood or patrilineal kinship group) to cut down marriage expenses. *Paddhati Prayagshetra* (1870), printed in Hindi and Urdu, describes one meeting at Prayag that included scribal (kayasth), agricultural (jat) and commercial groups (khatri, Agrawal bania, baraseni, dhusar*), and another held especially for kayasths.[73] In *Jagopkarak* (1871), an Urdu tract in Nagri script, Pyarelal described his activities in helping to make and popularize a set of rules from Delhi to Patna for the benefit of the *Hindu kaum*, in practice kshatriyas, brahmins, bhuihaars*

---

* bhats: hereditary bards and genealogists who visited homes two or three times a year.
* baraseni: bankers; dhusar: clerks, traders and commercial men who had prospered under Muslim rule.
* bhuihaars: mainly landholders and agriculturalists.

and kayasths.[74] Significantly, kayasths, khatris, and Agrawal banias had begun to claim kshatriya ranking in this decade while bhuihaars, who were degraded brahmins, were soon to claim brahmin status.

The chief fears in *Paddhati* were loss of property and female infanticide leading to corruption of caste through marrying low-caste women and paying bride price. In *Jagopkarak,* unnecessary extravagant expenditure, *fazul kharchi*, was not only the cause of the decline or indigence of landed and upper classes through the destruction of *khandaans*, noble families, loss of zamindaris and reputations, recourse to bribery and crime, but also linked to national reform and issues such as child marriage and sale of daughters (pp. 1–2, 46–47). Pyarelal even feared that ostentatious marriages and inflated dowries would lead to *kaum badla*, conversion to other religions or loss of caste of the *Hindu kaum* through intermarriage with bhar and kanjar *kaums** (p. 46). *Kaum* here implied religion, caste, and tribe. *Riti* also traced the deterioration of kshatriyas to excess dowry, female infanticide, and bride price. Harishchandra, himself an Agrawal bania with an active stake in caste mobility and kshatriya regeneration, made a similar diagnosis and presented the education of women as a means for reforming customs, reducing excess expenditure, and lessening the deterioration of caste, *jati ka kshay*.[75]

Gifts to bhats and *naach* organized by the bride's parents were proscribed in *Paddhati* and the amounts to be paid to mali, sonar, dhobi, bhangi, *chudarin* (probably churihaarin)* were fixed. In *Jagopkarak*, each caste group and *biradari* was recognized as being class stratified while rules for expenditure were fixed differentially for four grades within each according to caste ranking, capacity, and income. Significantly, though the text condemned dancing by prostitutes, *randi nachaana, naach* was rationed according to a hierarchy of wealth and social status, and had no connection with ritual caste ranking. Proscribed altogether for brahmins, forbidden to kayasths at the wedding but allowed before or after it in their own homes, *naach* was merely limited for kshatriyas and bhuihaars. Even as *Paddhati* gave to panchayats and *biradaris* the power to punish infringements and boycott offenders, *Jagopkarak* enjoined benevo-

---

* bhar: lower agriculturalists, ploughmen, village guards, labourers, some
   of whom ate pork; kanjar: thread and rope makers and sellers, pork eaters.
* bhangi: scavengers; churihaar: glass bangle makers.

lence: the rich of every *biradari* were to help the poor either individually or through a locally and institutionally organized paternalism.

Rasala Kharch Kam Karne ke Vishay Mein (1874), brought out by the Anjuman-i-Ajmere, followed on the heels of *Jagopkarak* but represented a wider cooperative enterprise. The attempt to reduce wedding expenses was also initiated by British administrators, but here involved Hindu and Muslim notables, *rais*, in equal numbers. The writers were kayasth, brahmin, Muslim, and the proceedings published in Hindi and Urdu. Though located in Ajmer (a princely state that was part of NWP until 1871), the tract projects itself as join-ing an all-India movement and cites all previous attempts at limiting excess expenditure including Charles Raikes, Pyarelal, Sayyid Ahmad Khan, Awadh taluqdars, Allahabadi kayasths and reformers from other provinces. For Munshi Harnarayan what are considered old rites are in fact invented ones and need to be changed while the kayasth Ramji Sahay considers it better to spend on the education of children than on marriages. Hafiz Muhammed Husain's essay, *mazmoon*, seeks legitimation from both the Koran and Dharma-shastras, and points out that none of the present marriage customs were mentioned in these or even in the Bhagwat and Vedas. Countries that are not mortgaged to these harmful *ritis*, such as England, have a higher, enviable standard of living. Unlike the congested homes of Hindus and Muslims which double as kitchens and godowns, the English live in furnished bungalows with separate rooms for eating, sleeping, cooking, bathing, entertaining, and storage.

> *Unke ghar bangla aur bagicha bangle mein naukaro ke baithneke liye baramda sone ka kamra alag khane ka alag baithne milne ka alag nahane aur cheez bast rakhne ka alag phir pratyek kamre mein konch, chowki, mez, dari, kadh, handi, lagi hui hai...tumhare ghar do teen kotdi ek aad chaubara ek do dalaan usi mein sona usi mein baithna naaj noon tel sab usi mein yahan tak ki lakri bhi usi mein bhari hui...rasoi ka sthan juda kahe ko ho jo musalman hai to ghar mein kisi jagah chulha rakh liya jo hindu hai to itna ki chhatwale ghar mein rakha . . . dari bicchone ka kaam hi kya dharti aap hi pavitra hai konch chauki ki jagah do ek purani tooti si khat.* [76]

All the writers ask for laws curtailing and prohibiting excess expen-

diture and recommend British intervention. Harnarayan compares
state intervention in this matter to the abolition of widow immolation: both have the consent of Indian subjects and are not intrusive.
Muhammed Husain cannily points out that if the subjects are poor,
the treasury of the king will also be empty. Extravagant expenditure
should be legally punishable like gambling and debt, since it has the
same destructive consequences. What is more, he argues, laws are
needed where customs are difficult to change, and especially necessary where even literacy is superficial or half-baked: Muslims learn
a fraction of the Koran and become maulavis while Hindus learn a
bit of the Shastras and the *gayatri* (a Vedic mantra) and become
pandits, and the word of both becomes law.

   Rasala Kharch suggested different levels of expenditure
correlative to levels of income within *biradaris*. It asked for general
limits on some things especially *sevak logon ka kharch*, disbursement
of money to menials for services, and *naach tamasha*, dance and
drama (p. 78). Harnarayan rails against vulgar songs at weddings
while Husain condemns dancing women, *naachnewalia* (p. 34). The
elite of each *biradari* were to fix the amounts to be spent at each
income level, the less wealthy who imitated the expenditure levels of
the rich were to be punished by the *biradari,* and infringements were
to be fined.

   The reforms proposed both in *Rasala Kharch* and *Jagopkarak*
were obviously addressing a contradiction in marriage expenditure:
the potential for mobility gathered through a display of status could
be lost because of the dissipation of wealth in that display. In calculat-
ing dowry and expenses according to income, caste associations
sought a balance between present status and future security by making a *fixed* equivalence between marriage expense and status that
would be both consensual and safe from inflation. The older economy
of nawabi ostentation identified social being with its representations,
expenditure could be justifiably dictated by the rank one *wished* to
hold. Both these tracts, however, distinguished between being and
seeming, between class distinction and pretension or imitation, and
were poised between a middle-class *commitment* to the symbolic and
an accurate assessment of the level of representation that available
resources could stretch to. *Jagopkarak* guards the exclusive claim of
the rich to some (already discriminatory) precapitalist modes of dis-

play. In *Rasala*, which is more invested in maintaining and marking
class differences and hierarchies, the contradictions are also more
explicit. It simultaneously seeks to define impediments to upward
mobility, accommodate social aspirations, build complicities that
disguise or mitigate what could be conflicting class positions within
biradaris, put a brake on the appropriation of higher-class modes of
consumption by those below, and compensate with paternalist aid.

Some of the same themes were to reappear more prominently
in tracts setting out to reform upper-caste men. In these, the fact that
reforms of dowry and marriage expenditure had also signalled a
change in the customary or ritual roles of those below became even
clearer. Already in *Riti* an archetypal Farsi-educated kayasth, Lala
Dharmachyutdas, is chastised for drinking, spending money on
naach tamashe, employing bhands, consorting with lower castes—
julaha, dhuniya* (pp. 177–78). *Riti* proscribes dancing by *veshyas*
and performances by bhands at weddings (p. 200).[77] Similarly,
Munshi Ramlal's *Banitabuddhi-Prakashini* (1871), a textbook for
girls, opposed lavish outlays on weddings and other ceremonies as the
cause of impoverishment, recommended limits on expenditure, perquisites and customary payments to servants, dependents, beggars,
nai negi bhat bhikari, and the institution of a low-cost religious
wedding, *dharma vivah*.[78] A later tract, *Kshatriyakul Timirprabhakar*
(1893), advised rajput men to stop going to prostitutes or women other
than wives, indulging in alcohol, dance and music, or enjoying the
company of dom, *kalaar randi* (probably a kalarin), *bhaduya* (procu-
rer and/or bhand) and mirasiya.* All of them are the primary agents
of dissipation and causes of bankruptcy. The tract not only censures
excess spending on marriage which could lead to sale of zamindaris
but also giving money to brahmins or bhats. The dancing of *veshyas*
at weddings was not an ancient custom, corrupted young people, and
was to be substituted with the lectures of the learned, *vidwaano ka*

---

* bhand: jesters, entertainers at births, weddings; dhuniya: cotton carders
  and combers with butcher and sweeper subcastes.
* dom: lowest of castes, involved in burial and cremation, scavengers,
  sweepers, labourers, village menials, makers of small handicrafts from
  leaf, cane, and bamboo, some had become carpenters; kalarin: wife of a
  kallar, a group of rajput converts who distilled and sold liquor; mirasi:
  teachers of music and dance, mirasins were occupational jesters in
  zenanas, women's apartments.

updesh. Nais and other such *murkh*, stupid, and illiterate low castes were no longer be allowed to continue as go-betweens in matchmaking for they could not suggest compatible unions; parents, especially fathers, are advised to arrange marriages personally or advertise in newspapers.[79] UP rajputs are being propelled into a self-reform that will remove the degeneracy and decline of ruling groups. In a text where the reform of men is a conduit of the return to past glory, one key element is weaning them away from prostitutes and low castes. A decade later, the Deobandi reformer Maulana Ashraf 'Ali Thanawi condemned the dancing of domnis,* all the ritual roles of the nai in marriages, gifts in cash and kind to nai, nain, bhangis, and singing women, on the ground that giving gifts to menials was wasteful and a 'Hindu' practice, quite ignoring that 'Hindus' themselves were arguing against the same practices! [80]

It seems that in such texts a crucial feature of even partial embourgeoisement was reducing and/or cutting free of reciprocal, patterned, and ritual relations with low castes combined with a belief that group organization and group prosperity could be the vectors for class mobility and maintenance of class power or status. The menial and ritual functions of artisanal, servicing, and untouchable groups, often through structured relations of clientage (*jajmani*), had till then *maintained* the status of those above. And it had given them some leverage too. Bhats could intentionally distort family history at public recitations and subject any member to general ridicule.[81] Dhobins could obstruct a marriage until their demands were fulfilled, and in *Riti* the family resents having to wait for a dhobin because she is in the midst of a busy wedding season. What was worse, status depended on the *words* of those below and displays of dissatisfaction *mattered*. *Banitabuddhi* excoriates the voracious greed of bhat, kahar, chamar, and *gadiwan* (coachman) at weddings who eat, loot, and sell the food and yet complain they went hungry (p. 32).

Now these relationships were being rationalized while the very sites, means, and modes for the production of status were changing. There was a partial shift from forms of power based on sumptuary display to new forms that included professional enclaves, the generation of a new subjectivity for women structured on the labour

---

* domni: wife of dom, domnis were professional entertainers who performed for women in the *zenana*.

of representation, status production through women's domestic work and social skills, as well as public philanthropy. Customary relations of clientage with servicing lower-caste/class groups, along with the relatively modest redistribution they entailed, were sought to be replaced by meliorative charity and a competitive philanthropy that could manage class antagonisms, maintain class positions, and sig-nal upward mobility. In *Banitabuddhi* the money saved from perfor-mers, *bhand bhagtiyo*, is used to dig a well and make a public garden (p. 38). Muhammed Husain provides a vivid yet sour description of the undervaluation of actual expenses and dowries by the in-laws in *Rasala Kharch*. He argues for expenditure on more appropriate objects that also ensure salvation: building mosques, *sarais* (inns), schools, funding students, hospitals and pilgrims, digging wells, charity to the poor and maimed. *Kshatriyakul* recommends a similar shift in objects of charity to the poor, maimed and orphaned, genteel widows and poor relatives, helpless old persons and victims of fam-ine, learned brahmins, religious and educational institutions. This transition corresponded with the acceleration of competitive philanthropies among landed gentry and taluqdars by colonial rule, and interlocked with the partial shift in religious patronage to emerging service elites, merchants, and newly-rich rural gentry. These old and new forms of charity or religious endowment often became a part of caste solidarity and advancement and could even feed assertions of religious identity.[82]

In such a context the self-reforming logic of *Mir'at*, though strictly limited to the ashraf, was not different from that of the bur-geoning bania, khatri, kayasth, rajput, and brahmin caste associa-tions that were combining localized self-reform agendas with wider symbolic assistance from 'Hindi', 'Sanskrit' or *hindupan*.[83] All were major landholding groups in NWP and Awadh, competing for jobs, investing in common models of status indication and upward mobili-ty, identifying impediments to mobility or professional advancement, and trying to decide which older forms of ostentation or conspicuous consumption were still socially necessary investments and which ones actively conflicted with new professional social relationships—and usually, they straddled or combined the old and the new. Some of them were ideologically closer, especially ashraf, kayasth and rajput; and as landed ruling groups often dispossessed either by the British or by sale or transfer of land to banias, brahmins, khatris, or even prosperous though low-caste kalwars, they were equally prone to a sense of 'fallenness' and visions of recapturing past prestige or power.[84]

The political economy of colonial rule *simultaneously* introduced logics of *individual* and of *group* mobility. This double logic in fact created the nodes for the articulation of class processes with caste or religious affiliation. Group mobility offered internal bonding, a security from outside interference, minimized risk; it was related to existing modes of social cohesion and intensified by both the unevenness of capitalist development and the bureaucratic definitions spawned by colonial rule. Caste and religious grouping could function as levers for acquiring class identity: upward mobility required networks of dependence, protection, patronage, control and self-conscious organization. Class processes thus were both based on shared interests or solidarities and relied on caste or religious affiliations. At times, community claims were barely distinguishable from the enhancement, retention, or formation of class. Further, 'community' could not rest on religious affiliation alone since there were crosscutting class relations in the determination of entitlements, place, property, authority, education, jobs.[85] A subsumption of class by community leaves no theoretical space for relationships of mutuality at different class levels between persons of diverse religious affiliations. Nor for the fact that though cross-class 'community' bonding could undercut individuation and did imply a certain levelling, it could at the same time foster a species of paternalism that reinforced stratification within the 'community'. This is evident in the way reforms of marriage expenditure maintained class distinctions within *biradaris*. 'Community' then cannot be abstracted from class nor used to displace class with 'culture'. The difficulty of synchronizing class with the inclusive concepts of 'community' that were appearing is evident from the fact that none of the upper and middle classes, whether ashraf or higher caste, wanted to own the lower castes and classes.[86] In practice muslimness and hinduness were being defined on desired, lost or newly achieved class terrains, and the pressure to exclude the lower classes was equally compulsive for both.

The consensus on caste discrimination too cut across English and vernacular education, *mofussil* and metropolitan intelligentsia, Hindu and Muslim, upper and some intermediary castes. At one

level, class status still coincided with caste difference: the term ashraf
in its broader meaning of well-born and cultivated could extend to
include any of the non-labouring, landowning, non-Muslim upper
castes or kayasths, but not the *razil* (lit. low, base) which included
Muslim and Hindu clean castes and unclean labouring or artisanal
castes.[87] Caste affiliation often did not bear a single or straightforward relation to religious belief (a question I will return to), and even
when it did, it could not produce homogenous communities because
of internal distinctions and hierarchies. Vertical caste norms existed
in contentious relation with the horizontal ties of religion, howsoever
broadly defined. In this period, sanskritization was in fact not a facet
of tradition supporting modernity, as is commonly believed, but a
vector of class formation that relied on a caste-based vocabulary of
status.[88] This type of activation of caste identities was, like religious
identities, tied to class interests, and as such more committed to stabilizing a higher-caste patriarchy and finding 'others' below than in
universalizing a set of common patriarchal arrangements.

These double logics of class and 'community' can be seen in
the contradictions within patriarchal aspirations. Reformed women
and their educational altruistic activities enlarged *wakfiyat*, helped
to build an effective 'community' through sets of relationships in
which various kinds of affiliations providing status, mobility, even
money, could be forged and maintained; these were essential because
they determined class networks and resources above and beyond *naukari* and which indeed were a precondition of *naukari*. Conversely,
the interrelated imperatives of containment, patriarchal control, and
eligibility for such activities necessitated that women be secluded,
withdrawn from 'dubious' public places and association with lower-
caste/class women in all except tutelary or supervisory capacities—
all of which were class imperatives that worked against the creation
of unified 'Hindu' or 'Muslim' communities. In effect, women as
either *jati* or class markers could not, except symbolically, be markers of a broader religious community at the same time.

There was in fact an astounding coincidence between class
formation and partial embourgeoisement on the one side, and desyncretization and attempts to control, proscribe, or remodel older *and*
emerging forms of women's sociality on the other. The latter involved
curtailing individual freedoms in a period when the number of women

going to *melas*, fairs, and pilgrimages was in fact increasing. It also
entailed withdrawing women from formal institutionalized gatherings at wedding and death rituals sanctioned by custom, and the informal gatherings and gossip networks which had provided supportive
structures in both artisanal and urban formations. Through these
women exchanged information, schooled or monitored each other,
but also shared and determined the significance of personal experiences, publicized patriarchal excesses, sifted as well as generated forms
of social classification of ordinary life—all of which seem to have unsettled desired decorums.[89] The fact that virtually identical interdic-
tions were being made by reformers in Bengal, Maharashtra, Punjab,
as well as by Christian missionaries indicates that these were an integral aspect of a wider, transregional process of class formation.[90]

Diverse faiths, shared customs, composite beliefs

Purifying customs

The attempt to constitute these tenuous 'communities' interlocked with upward mobility and class consolidation, and also with
the parallel logics of ashraf islamicization and brahminical hinduization. Both of these rested on a common project of 'purifying' religions, bore the same animus against popular festivity, worship, syncretic and low-caste cults.[91] *Riti* and *Mir'at* too were engaged in
splitting off a private sphere that was tied as much to class processes
as to desyncretization. They simultaneously privileged religious texts
and textualized customs in order to purge women's belief systems.
The ease with which women's education was annexed to agendas for
conceiving religious 'communities' came from the fact that patriarchies were already central to rewriting the past and education could
now play a material role in the selective critiques of custom.

Ritiratnakar, assisted by the combined powers of 'Sanskrit'
(which could reverse the 'fall') and 'English' (which could dispel
superstition), made a two-pronged attack against low-caste cults and

women's involvement in syncretic modes of worship. Maina's valorization of (male and female) brahmin tutelage, along with a syllabus
of reading structured around Vaishnav piety and fasts centred on
suhaag and *pativratas*, helps to exorcise non-brahminical forms of
worship amongst neighbourhood women. The main targets of *Riti*
were the interlinked practices of *bhoot pooja* (propitiating ghosts
and evil spirits), going to *dargahs* (tombs, shrines) and *melas*.
Maina's method for weaning women from undesirable practices is
by branding these as low-caste and fake. *Bhoot* cults, she claims, are
the pre-serve of the kurmi, chamar, mali, dhanuk and pasi,* and
neech jati women merely pretend to be possessed by *bhoots* to cover
their crimes (p. 33). In order to screen her theft of grain, the bad
Vipatti of Dasiya's story fakes possession with the help of an ojha
(exorcist, diviner).[92] *Melas* are denounced as crowded with thieves
and base castes, *chhoti jatian*: kunjra, dhuniya, chamar, julaha, ahir
(an ahirin is a domestic servant in *Riti*), gadariya, khatik, pasi* (p.
34).[93] Though julahas, who were mainly Muslim and often ranked
as low as the untouch- able chamars, are the object of special
interdiction, it is significant that clean and unclean, Muslim and
non-Muslim, agriculturalist and pastoralist lower castes are lumped
together and that many of these have been, equally, objects of scorn
in *Mir'at*.

　　　The joint production and mutual assimilation of customs
were wide-ranging.[94] And middle-caste/class urban groups were
clearly quite eclectic in their religious practices, particularly the scribal and mercantile, whom Maina singles out for censure.[95] It seems
that *all* Maina's 'Hindu' neighbours except the brahmins wear black
at Muharram, worship *tazias*,[96] offer *fatihas* to Ghazi Miya, believe
him to be their *kuldevta* or family god, call themselves *Pachpiriha*
(pp. 27, 29). Some Hindu women of the city offer flowers, sweets, and

---

* mali: higher cultivators, vegetable and flower growers and suppliers to
markets; dhanuk: menial cultivators, village watchmen, drummers at
weddings, archers, palanquin bearers, water haulers; pasi: toddy palm
tappers, liquor collectors, watchmen, petty agricultural, menial, and day
labourers.

* ahir: cowherds, graziers, a 'higher' group; gadariya: shepherds, blanket
weavers and manufacturers, agricultural occupations; khatik: a degraded
group, often considered untouchable.

* Agrawal bania: traders originally from Rajasthan and Punjab; khatri:
traders originally from Punjab.

fatihas or prayers for the dead at Muslim graves; they, particularly Agrawal women, are entranced by the power of male martyrs: *shaheed mard se bahut darti hai* (p. 29). Agrawal women have even been spotted standing around a grave while a Muslim boy offered a *fatiha* near Chipolia (pp. 29–30). The shameful sign of the especial degeneration of urban women, kayasth, khatri and Agrawal bania,* is not only going to *melas* which no respectable village women frequent, but particularly to the one held for Ghazi Miya. The *mela* becomes a composite sign of the loss of gentility and religious purity in which casteism slides into, even fuses with, othering Muslims. Ghazi Miya becomes the object of a vendetta especially since belief in the syncretic Panchpiri cult cuts across class and caste lines: he is worshipped by the wives and daughters of lawyers, dhuniyas, pathaars, and barhais* (p. 32).[97] Believers are denounced for *pretending* that he has granted them boons, *murads*, or cured their diseases (p. 36). Maina persuades a woman neighbour, Neta, that Ghazi Miya is *not*, as she believes, a *devta* or a deity, but a Muslim invader killed by Hindus in Bahraich and now worshipped by ignorant Hindus. Neta, convinced, recounts a matching incident: one year the Ramlila and *tazia* processions fell on the same day, there was a fight between Hindus and Muslims, a Muslim boy was killed, Muslims made a grave for him, pronounced him a martyr and great saint, *shaheed aur bara aulia*, and gradually people began to worship there.[98] Maina says graves are impure anyway, clinching the argument and converting Neta to *parameshwar puja*, worship of the ultimate creator, the god above all gods (pp. 35–36).[99]

There was nothing singular about *Riti's* attempt. *Strivichar* (1876) by Hariharhiralal, a Bhatnagar kayasth, derogates *totas* and *bhoot* cults. *Banitabuddhi* also condemns exorcism, magic spells, formulae, charms, amulets, strings, *jhaad phunk*, *totka tona*, *ganda taveez* (pp. 65, 69). It states that unlike the south which had less to do with Muslims and so the Hindus have managed to follow the Shastras and practise ancient or *prachin ritis*, the north has become the home of *musalmani*. Barring a few exceptions, the majority of Hindus have been corrupted and remain Hindus only in name. Their worship of *pir*, *miya*, and *sayyad* is destroying Hindu *dharma*:

---

* pathaar: makers and sellers of *rakhis*, ceremonial wristbands; barhais: mainly carpenters, some blacksmiths.

*Parantu yahan to musalmani ne apna ghar sa bana liya is karan
hinduon ke bahutere achran bhrasht ho gaye keval naam ke hindu
rah gaye. . . . Bahuda aise dekhne mein aata hai ki log apne sarva
shaktiman ishwar ko bhul kar pir ko malida chadhate hai aur miya
ko gulgule khilate hai aur sayyado ko chadar udhate hai par yeh
vichar nahin karte ki piron ki jhutan khane se hindu dharm ki kya
dasha hogi. . . . In baaton se birle hi bache hai shesh to ghar ghar
yahi dekhne main aata hai.* (p. 69)*

Women are especially quick to give up their own *dharma* to adopt
new and false faiths, *nanakpanthi kundapanthi aadi naye naye mat
angikar karti hai,* and believe in local godlings, animist cults, Muslim saints, ghosts, demons, *bhuiya bhootela pir madar aur bhoot
pishach* (p. 69). Too many new non-shastric customs are being followed and some of these have been invented by *murkh* women (p. 2).
In *Devrani Jethani* too *tone totke gande taweez* is considered the
'work' of *murkh* women (p. 84). *Banitabuddhi* is more abusive than
Riti about *neech jati* women—malin, kaharin: they are not merely
accused of faking goddess possession but called *mlecchniya*, a term
that carried the triple innuendo of non-Aryan, low-caste, foreign and
Muslim (pp. 63–64). *Stridharma Saar* (1892), a later prescriptive
tract written under the auspices of the Khatri Hitkari Sabha, Agra, by
the *Hathras nivasi* Munshi Jivaram Kapur Khatri, participated in the
by-then wider move to proscribe syncretic worship, and added Christianity to Islam. Women are told that they will go to hell in punishment for worshipping Muslims or being duped by Christian women
into believing that Christ is a deity and singing Christian hymns, *miya
ko poojna aur Isai aurato ke phande me aakar Isa ko devta maankar
uske bhajan gaana* (p. 23). Ironically the desyncretizing techniques of
hinduization were synonymous with those of christianization. A missionary text, *Ratnamala or Reading Book for Women* (1869), warns
against belief in *jyotishis* (astrologers), *bhut pret, tone totke, jhaad
phunk,* and superstitions about auspicious days, even as it offers the
pativrata as an ideal and advises women to reform husbands through
their own exemplary behaviour (pp. 76, 87, 101, 144–45).

The disparagement of women's belief systems, then, was
part of the wider devaluation of syncretic culture: most women clearly did not occupy orthodox or discrete 'Hindu' or 'Islamic' or 'Christian' spaces in their religious practices. Though *Riti* does not name

Muslim women, forms of non-textual religious worship, animistic and 'superstitious' practices including *bhoot* possession, belief in shrines, magic, and *nazar* (evil eye) were evidently common to Muslim women.[100] Unlike *Riti,* which creates the spectre of endangered public space, *Mir'at ul'-Arus* is centred on an enclosed space intermittently invaded by pedlars, hawkers, traders and shopkeepers. However, *Mir'at* also rejects *jhaad phunk, nazar, utara, bhoot, chudail,* for curing the sick, all *tone totke* including those for securing a husband's love and obedience, and recommends the simplification of festivals by discontinuing non-koranic, customary forms of celebration (p. 174).[101] Among the practices that it prohibits as accretions are *bibi ka kunda,* the feeding of married women in the name of Fatima; *mannat,* boons from the dead; *chadar,* offerings on graves of the dead; *basant mela* and offerings at graves; *phulwalon ki sair,* the *mela* at Hazrat Qutubuddin Bakhtiyar Kaki's shrine; *satarvhin,* the *urs* of Hazrat Sultan Nizamuddin at his shrine (p.106). In 'Hali's *Majalis,* the singing of domnis (who were also exorcists) to cure barrenness, obsessions with spirits or the evil eye are censured; so too are oblations to various figures who intercede with the deity, especially those revered by women and associated with rituals of spirit possession—Allah Baksh, Sayyid Ahmad Kabir, Bale Miya, Nanhe Miya, Darya Khan, Sheikh Saddu—on the ground that none of these were sufis.[102] Other Muslim reformers, including Deobandis, were also opposing *pir* worship and syncretic cults such as Ghazi Miya in the drive towards ashrafization, islamicization or 'de-hinduization' in this period.[103] The list of popular practices interdicted for women in Thanawi's *Bihishti Zewar* was very similar to that of *Ritiratnakar.*[104]

These syncretic and other shared religious practices had varied ideological locations. Non-textual or non-theological practices, popular worship, magic, and animism often merely assuaged the insecurities generated *by* patriarchal inequities, and could be equally implicated in the reproduction of patriarchies. However, they could only have taken effect in a normative context of social tolerances and suggest the predominance of regional formations over class, caste, and denominational identities. There was a crisscross between well-defined sects such as the Vaishnav and popular religions or animism in the upper strata, but the overlaps were widest among the lower strata.[105] Of the forty million "Hindus" returned by the 1891 Census in this region, classified by "striking out the members of fairly recognisable religions" such as Islam and Christianity and naming "everyone else a Hindu", one and a half million were "unable to record the deity they worshipped", two and a half million worshipped Muslim saints, and about four million practised varieties of animism and "superstition", or worshipped special deities.[106] In both colonial classification and prescriptive literature, religious contrasts were built between transhistorical textual systems—biblical, koranic, and shastric—rather than between different and overlapping contemporary social systems. The privileging of texts, then as now, systematically obscured how far similar or *common* patriarchal practices can be theoretically governed by *different* religio–textual laws. In *Mir'at* and *Riti* superstition, animism, and popular religion came to be defined as all that fell outside the realm of high textuality: as not-Muslim, not-Hindu and of course as signs of credulity and sacrilege. This was linked to the withdrawal of patronage from a host of non-textual religious intermediaries and local sites that were patronized across castes, classes, and religions. The new middle-class and higher-caste women were to be made by purging their religious practices, forbidding access to the public and social terrain of religion, commerce, and entertainment represented by shrines and seasonal fairs.

A second layer in the production of religious difference was the casting of religious reforms as a return to or restoration of either the 'pre-Islamic' or the 'pre-Hindu' through a break with the customary domain, a domain that had blurred too many distinctions. Reforms at one level were mimicking projects of religious differentiation, with each seeking freedom from the 'other's' corruptions through identical methods. The customary—that they sought to repress or exorcise—was misperceived on both sides as merely a site of the 'fall' to be reversed through hinduization or islamicization, whereas it was in fact a mutually shaped and frequently patriarchal realm of consensuality. In fact the whole discourse reveals how far women actually were *outside* high textual regimes and governed by shared customs (whether or not these now seem desirable). That is why, despite their strictures on non-textual practices, custom not only remained a primary referent in *Riti* and *Mir'at* but custom was textualized. Both enumerated pilgrimages, *yatra* and *hajj*, lucky or auspicious dates, *mahurats*, marriage and birth rituals, calibrated familial transactions of gifts and money, *lena dena*, the correct cele-bration of festivals and performance of seasonal chores. Though some of these were structured around discrete religious texts or practices and a generalized female piety, the remarkable similarity in the pat-tern of women's lives, "domestic habits and institutions", and the tenor of patriarchal aspirations noticeably cut across denomina-tional differences.[107] So did the transformation of a wide expanse of narra-tive repertoires and cultural practices into textualized and printed pedagogies for women.

Instead of being recognized as a field of mutual patriarchal accommodation, custom became an arena of 'religious' challenge. Neither *Mir'at* nor *Riti* was adding up customs to affirm an existing identity but changing them in order to forge one. Every attempt at purification in fact involved an acknowledgement, albeit pejorative, of syncretic worship and eclectic mixtures of customs and rituals, while in every rejection of joint culture impure customs had to be 'named'. In *Riti* kayasths are vilified most as the agents of such adul-teration: Lala Dharmchyutdas employs Muslim servants, celebrates the festivals of Id and Bakrid, distributes alms to *musalmani fakirs* on Friday, entertains Muslims and irreligious, *dharmahin Hindus* at Muharram, spends a fortune on *tazias*, gets the *marsiya*, an elegiac account of the tribulations of Husain, read; Lala Islamdas's family has observed the *roza* fasts for several generations, and other than marrying sons and daughters to *Hindu kayasths* all their *ritis* are like those of Muslims (pp. 177–78). Later, in Prasad's *Hindi aur Urdu ki Larai*, Hindi and Urdu, that is Hindu and Muslim, accuse each other of mimicry and mutual corruption. Urdu rebukes Hindi/Hindus for observing Ramzan, worshipping the *tazia*, *pirs*, and frequenting 'Muslim' holy places. Hindi chides Urdu/Islam for Muslims playing music at weddings, failing to arrange remarriage for widows, Mus-lim women using *sindur* and singing during marriage ceremonies. Significantly, English, the so-called arbiter of the dispute, actually incites Hindus against Muslims by accusing them of passivity, lack of unity, worshipping grave, *tazia* and *pir*, and not protecting cows![108] In sum, both sides othered the same customs, abdicated shared spaces and practices. In the selective extraction of 'pure' Hinduisms and Islams from the extant matrix of shared faiths,

common superstitions, syncretic cults, it was unclear who this contaminated matrix would now belong to if it had become each one's
'other'. Nor is it clear how far such islamicization and hinduization
actually changed shared practices or closed the gap between religious
beliefs and customs.

The marked resemblances and greater patriarchal consensus
between ashraf and higher castes than of either 'within' their respective religious 'communities' stemmed in part from the difficulty
of managing the question of lower castes and classes. Further, the
ashraf and higher caste were as yet *openly* similar, complementary,
or over-lapping and had not been ideologically recomposed as
competing patriarchal systems. Thus the characteristic theme in
which a number of caste and class issues could also be subsumed was
that of *women* against women. Later, the dominant model in
twentieth-century communal Hindu discourse came to rest on *male*
rivalry in which the excessive patriarchal privileges of Muslim men
were chastised; women were figured as property endangered by men
of 'other' groups, men as proprietors governing competing patriarchies, communal tension as between Hindu and Muslim men.[109]

However, the remarkable conferral of patriarchal agency on
women did bear the seeds of the articulation of domestic ideology,
new models of 'womanhood', a redefined religion and political
agency for women. At bottom, class processes, patriarchal imperatives, linguistic and regional particularities, religious and caste differences or 'communities' remained difficult to synchronize. The *symbolic overextension* of Hindu and Muslim women as boundary
markers was increasingly used to blur or resolve this difficulty. The
flip side of such symbolic overextension was an overcommittment to
detail, and minutely defined, stringent controls on women's behaviour.
In these fluid spaces of class formation, the manipulation of social and
gendered signs thus was immensely important for both *Mir'at* and
Riti. Both endowed women with new powers of persuasion, manipulation, othering, and evaluation of the public world from within
specified ideological parameters. Both tried to produce women whose
dispositions were commensurate with emerging forms of charity and
religious patronage. Asghari actively engages in all the standard,
institutionalized forms of Islamic charity, builds the colony of
"Tamizgunj", and is individually memorialized through philan-

thropy. Unlike her, Maina does not indulge in any of the parallel forms of Hindu charity.[110] Her piety is a more mundane matter of observing correct *ritis* at birth, marriage, death, obedience towards learned brahmins rather than false *gurus* or spiritual preceptors, and upholding the petty charities of upper and middle castes to the poor particularly in the form of education—an activity exalted as *vidyadaan* in other brahmin-authored textbooks.[111] Though Asghari's philanthropy is wider, it is Maina who is a fledgling instance of the Hindu woman as *missionary* and *crusader* whose compliant domesticity gives her a social purpose stretching beyond home, *jati,* and class. The precondition was being a good wife, the possibilities began from persuading, exhorting, and 'converting' husbands and stretched into a capacity to invigilate the public domain without entering it—a Ruskinian model of indirect female agency that is relocated and deployed for new purposes.

    Mir'at remains a loose conglomeration of elements that were tightly knotted in *Riti.* The unifying trope of the Muslim interregnum in *Riti* assisted in positing a 'community' extrapolated through local contests, in making Hindi, educated Hindu women, and purified *hindupan* (ancient and Aryan) synonymous, and in opposing them to a single metonymic continuum of Urdu, Muslims, 'fallen' women, syncretic worship, despicable low-caste customs, and extortionate customary practices. Unlike 'Hindu' womanhood, then, 'Muslim' womanhood did not become either a fully developed source of patriarchal pedagogic authority or of a composite symbolic continuity that could be extended into a wider social field or put in active service of communal othering. At this stage political Hinduism was more *aggressively* gendered than political Islam. It was *Riti*'s insidious model of womanhood that was the discursive precursor of the militant Hindu woman, a figure that was to function as a significant proselytizing force in the communalization of religious identity in later decades.

Istri Updesh: A composite 'Indian' woman?

This configuration remodelled an earlier anti-Muslim and indigenist constellation into a middle-class commonsense and ripened it for 'Hindu nationalist' interpellation. However, the very existence of patriarchal commonalities opened it to significant re-

combinations which later converged with the more secular tendencies in nationalism. The same insistence on caste and class differences
that prevented a universalization of patriarchal arrangements, paradoxically, also locked into a middle-class patriarchal consensus cutting across religious differences, and created the conditions for the
emergence of a composite 'Indian' woman. This consensus was not
entirely compartmentalized. That is, it was not separately constituted or enforced on two sides of an impermeable religious boundary
as it appears to be in *Riti* or *Mir'at*.

The confluences were visible in the composite woman that
took shape in Munshi Ahmad Husain's *Istri Updesh: Do ladkiyon ki
kahani* (1873), a collaborative and hybrid textbook.[112] While patriarchal commonalities have to be extracted from *Mir'at* and *Riti*, *Istri
Updesh* is a text of explicit patriarchal bonding. Prepared by Husain
on the order of Pandit Gokulchand, headclerk, for use in a Farsi
madrasa, the book has the air of a brahmin–ashraf collaboration, not
merely in its commissioning but as a partnership in a joint prescriptive enterprise. Situated outside high textuality, the text invokes
neither shastric nor koranic authority and is a complex compound of
acceptance, adjustment to, and resistance of religious difference. It in
fact actively negotiates and resolves the contradictions between this
middle-class patriarchal consensus and the Hindu cast of the ideological configuration I have described.

In formal terms *Istri Updesh* bears the mark of a nineteenth-
century 'Hindu' ancestry, as is evident in its title and its recourse to
the expansive tutelary and symbolic powers of Hindu women established through Bengal *bhadralok* enterprise in the preceding decades.
The 'Hindu' Deva has accumulated enough moral power to speak on
behalf of all women. The textbook is structured as a 'dialogue' between two schoolgoing girls—Deva lectures her good friend Sukhwanti
who is not too keen to study—a familiar pedagogic device of cloning
and reproduction through conversations between women.[113] *Riti*'s
term for elevating this new female discourse was *satsang* (lit. the
society of pious men).

In other respects *Istri Updesh* was innovative. Obstacles to
a collaborative patriarchal reformism were transmuted or removed.
One impediment was the trope of the Muslim interregnum which had
by this period burgeoned into a loyalist metadiscourse on woman's

education reiterated in textbooks for girls such as Ramlal's *Banita-buddhi*, Vamsidhara's *Sutashikshavali* (1865), Pandit Ramkrishan's *Strishiksha* (1871), and Harishchandra's journal *Balabodhini* (1874). The 'fall' of 'Hindu' women, attributed to Muslim rule and its so-called effects (child marriage, purdah, widow immolation), had become the classic and often primary rationale for female literacy; and it was usually followed by a near-canonical list of exemplary and learned ancient women (read prelapsarian Hindus). In Bengal, this historiographical trope had served to push the 'break' with indigenous culture backwards in time to Muslim rule salvaging colonial rule for the English-educated middle class and carried a structural relation between Muslim othering and loyalty to the British. After the 1857 uprising, which was frequently identified with Muslims alone, this emphasis became much sharper for the *bhadralok*. Bireswar Sen's comparative work, *Influence of English Education: Bengal and the North West Provinces* (1876), begins with the self-congratulatory proposition that Bengalis *invited* the British to deliver them from Muslim oppression and so do not, like the population of NWP, look upon them as conquerors and oppressors. This text encodes a triple entailment for Bengalis: to be loyal to the British they must hate Muslims; they must redescribe their own betrayal of the country into foreign hands as the birth of freedom, the entry of education, and the improvement of women; and they must ensure that loyalism does not mean crass westernization, especially of women. For Sen, Bengali women, already superior to NWP women, were being emancipated but not anglicized: they had as much "liberty" as was consistent with their "nationality".[114]

In post-1857 UP, the section of the Muslim intelligentsia which had acquired an uneasy investment in British rule fractured this discourse, and reconfigured the ideological formation centred on loyalism and altruism in ways that underplayed religious divisions or antagonisms. For Sayyid Ahmad the 'fall' of the ashraf was a result of their neglecting to cultivate the virtues that were commensurate with their status: social duty and acquisition of knowledge.[115] Muhsin ul-Mulk, who was close to him, claimed in 1873 that Muslim civilization had reached its zenith in the eighth century, was now completely decadent and could be rejuvenated only by assimilating western civilization.[116] Husain's *Istri Updesh* too relocated the 'fall', implicitly, in some unspecified post-Mughal yet pre-British moment while the canonical undergirding of the Muslim interregnum was dismantled. Overendowed ancient 'Hindu' women line up with ancient and medieval Muslim women, Muslim and Hindu aristocracy rub shoulders with merchants' wives and fictive characters from Arab stories.

The textbook constitutes a non or pre-nationalist 'Indian' woman by internationalizing the canon within the loyalist meta-discourse of literacy. It sets out to establish that the status of *all* women has deteriorated and they have to learn from a common model: English women. Deva's roster of exemplary learned women from "olden times" begins with Gauri and Parvati with their capacity for *bhakti*, Sita and Mandodari as depicted in Tulsi Das's "Ramayan", Rukmini, Raja Bhoj's wife and Lilavati. It extends to Ayesha of Samarkand who taught other women and composed poetry, and Lala Khatun, daughter of the king of mulk Kirman. In ancient times, Deva concludes, both Hindu and Muslim women were learned and now both have fallen; they must therefore look to English women who can manage everything in the absence of husbands. So can the women of Arabia, Rome, France, and Persia. Only the women of India are ignorant; they spy on or fight with each other and do not want to part with their children so that they can be educated, unlike English women who even send their children to England to study. Education can improve women's behaviour, access to religion, and ability to distinguish between good and evil. The maxim that educated women are equal in intelligence to men is illustrated by the Arabian *begum* who manages to stay alive by telling the emperor stories every night! And of course by the lives of real queens. The story of the "Irani" who migrated to Hindustan with his wife, gave birth near Kandhar to Nurjehan, who went on to become very learned, married first Sher Afghan then Jehangir, is followed by that of Raja Ratnaroop's daughter, Chandraswaroopa, who became a valiant queen.

This 'Indian' woman was involved in other settlements too. Deva's lecture is versatile enough to recommend conventional Hindu morning prayer and take in widow remarriage in a spirit very far from both upper-caste orthodoxy and reformism. The textbook assumes that remarriage is both customary and correct and seems to be addressing its practitioners rather than its opponents. Girls are told not to rely on remarriage *alone*, but to become proficient in some form of skilled labour which they can fall back on if widowed, since remarriage was not always possible especially if a woman was neither young nor beautiful nor wealthy. The inability of widows to remarry thus is tied to the necessity of literacy and artisanal skills as well as to the spectre of impoverishment. Deva says uneducated, virtueless, *nirgun* women can only be dependents, and if their sole option on being widowed is remarriage because they are unequipped to do anything else, they can even become destitute (p. 70). She narrates the story of a noble *amir's* daughter, a spoilt girl who inherited her parents' wealth and married a merchant, *saudagar*. Looted by dacoits while travelling with her husband and a group of people, her face is injured and her husband is killed. She loses her beauty and her property. The others manage through their labour and skills, she has none. She wants to remarry but is so unattractive that that no one wants to marry her and ends up becoming a beggar. Prescription, like narration, relied on stories of jeopardized status.

This particular accent on remarriage seems to indicate a lower strata intersection occupied as much by Muslims as by middle and lower castes. Levirate and widow remarriage were customary among many of the lower-caste groups that *Ritiratnakar* scorns.[117] Higher-caste groups who felt too constrained by custom to practise remarriage could however assent to it in theory. The Agrawal family in *Devrani Jethani* pities a child widow who is spending her time in piety and prayer and concludes that the bania *jati* is cursed because, even though the Dharmashastras allow it, its customs forbid the remarriage of virgin widows. Significantly, they find salutary models not merely among Muslims, British, and reformed Bengalis but also among lower castes:

> *Patthar to hamaari jati mein pade hain. Musalmano aur sahib logo mein doosre vivah ho jai hai aur ab to Bengaliyon mein bhi hone laga. Jat, gujar, nai, dhobi, kahar, ahir aadiyon mein to doosre vivah ki kuch roktok nahin. Aage dharm shastra mein bhi likha hai ki jis stri ka uske pati se sambhashan nahin hua ho aur vivah ke peeche pati ka dehant ho jai to vahan punarvivah yogya hai ar-that us stri ka doosra vivah kar dene mein kuch dosh nahin.* (p. 85)

Along with widow remarriage, *Istri Updesh's* general preoccupation with restricted consumption, artisanal labour, and the fall from class indicate that the author, or at least the address, belonged to a relatively lower strata or petty bourgeoisie—the ashraf poised on the imperilled brink of gentility, insecure traders or the small-scale salariat who had to fall back on artisanal skills and cottage industry in times of need.

Apart from these nuances, the textbook is replete with most of the characteristic themes of contemporary prescriptive writing. Thus the major benefit of education is not merely that it is a form of wealth but that it safeguards wealth. Literacy and arithmetic prevent women from being duped, teach them to manage a husband's property in his absence, and not be swindled on his death. Deva narrates stories of Muslim and Hindu wives including that of a wealthy *seth*, who are either cheated of all their property in the absence of their husbands or defrauded of everything on being widowed. Deva, in behaviour-book fashion, lectures Sukhwanti on daily routine, housework, hygiene, hospitality, the vice of anger, the virtues of truthfulness, modesty, humility, courtesy, softness, submissiveness, pliancy, *lajja*, *namrata*, *komalta*. Sukhwanti is told to never be stubborn, *dheeth*, waste time in play or in sleep during the day or in the evening, habits which will be unacceptable later in her father-in-law's household, *sasural* (p. 70). Daytime sleep produces sadness and lethargy, she is to pray or tell stories to the younger ones instead. Diligent work and the sexual repression of women's bodies go hand in hand. Deva embeds values in the minutest gestures, the body establishes equivalences between posture, class, and gender divisions. The finer points of genteel comportment are: eating in a decorous way without talking or laughing, table manners, letting guests eat first, walking straight without sticking the chest out or swinging hands or shoulders, *kandha matkana*, neither too slow nor too fast, talking little and speaking correctly (pp. 64–68).

As in *Riti* and *Mir'at*, here too error is the principle of readerly interest, essential to desired moral outcomes, and underpins the misogyny in the text. Good wives keep husbands happy, lack of greed helps women to adjust to poverty, tyrannical in-laws, as well as to the absence of choice in marriage. A wicked, *kharaab*, and *nikkammi* woman is one who fights with her husband, abuses him to other women, misuses his money, cheats him, does not share his difficulties, or spoils his reputation (p. 73). Good women should stay away from such women.

This then was the 'core' set of patriarchal arrangements—involving female literacy leavened by chastity, piety, efficient domestic management, good wifely service, an exorbitated male tutelage, dowry, and some degree of seclusion—acceptable to all denominations among the propertied and salaried classes, small entrepreneurs, perhaps even the wealthier artisans. The emphasis on male absence situates the address in part to people in salaried *nau-karis* and merchants away on business. There is a remarkable fluidity in a class identity that can be shared substantively as well as through fear and aspiration.

A more precise area of consensuality was the location of the textbook within a loyalist configuration. The author begins the book with praise for the British and Deva follows in his tracks. In her exemplification of English women as civilizing agents, no distinctions are made between missionaries, teachers, or wives of administrators. They are simply compressed into an abstract moral-pedagogical category with which Indian women must enter into a subordinate, emulative relationship. When Sukhwanti is convinced and ready to study (after 44 pages), Deva deals with her awakened curiosity about England by giving her a 'geography' lesson. This consists of a eulogistic discourse on England's government, calendar, customs, manners, architecture, miraculous buildings, London city and museum, books, unknown toys, extensive educational and charitable institutions, and the arithmetic its women learn. But geography is carefully separated from utility—in this respect women's knowledge had to be non-instrumental.

For Deva education helps women to travel only *through* books. This then was the exhilarating romance of education for colonized, secluded, and immobile women: reading offered an illusory yet compensatory nomadism, a chimerical relation with and a vicarious investment in colonial power seen to rest on omniscient, omnipotent knowledge. The imaginative possibilities such second-hand female knowledge of history and geography, *taarikh aur jugrafiya*, gave for entering otherwise unseeable public spaces were present in *Mir'at—Padhna seekho ki purde main baithe baithe tamaam duniya ki sair kar liya karo* (p. 27)—and elaborated in 'Hali's *Majalis* where a eulogy to Queen Victoria is followed by the prospect/daydream of a magical mobility:

> Daughter! If you read all those books, you will be able to travel to every corner of the world while sitting at home, up in the sky, under the earth, across rivers to the tops of mountains. Whatever exists, you will experience it. (p. 55)

The broad similarities in the patriarchal assumptions, aspirations, and generalizing attempts of *Mir'at*, *Riti*, and *Istri Updesh* confirm that there were no separate patriarchies belonging to hermetically sealed religious 'communities', and that within the wider political economy it was easier for patriarchal arrangements to cut across religions than across all classes. Male bonding too seems to have been not only common to prescriptive literature but a necessary precondition of its misogyny! However, in *Istri Updesh* Hindu and Muslim women were unselfconsciously presented in the same structure. This unquestioned assumption of commonality was not merely induced by shared class interests but also a shared history of patriarchal privileges and arrangements in UP. If higher-caste/class narratives of their 'fall' and loss of power were attached to long historical memories, then practised patriarchal commonalities carried a far more sedimented history. Like *Riti* and *Mir'at*, *Istri Updesh* too speaks for the structural reorganization of many groups, but in an interdependent rather than a competitive way. Though the lowest castes and classes remain outside the ambit of its composite woman, the class address of *Istri Updesh* is much wider than *Mir'at* and *Riti*, and perhaps for that reason there is less intra-class conflict, a relatively weaker and more eclectic reliance on religious legitimation, and the textbook is not mortgaged to the parallel logics of hinduization and islamicization. It is of course ironic that this shared patriarchy can disengage from denominational exclusivity or communal differentiation only when it is stripped down to its prescriptive core.

The same class and colonial processes were consolidating and dissolving religious unities. In the dialectical process of class and 'community' formation mediated by caste distinctions, domestic ideologies thus had a contradictory location. If they played a significant role in marking each one of these boundaries, they were also caught in the struggle to particularize *and* universalize, mark differences *and* unities. As particularist projects domestic ideologies were to provide a language and a fertile soil for later communal organizations. But in their universalizing imperatives they undercut religious boundaries and provided (ironically) a consensual social base for nationalist positions that were committed to a conception of com-posite culture and sought to address both Hindus and Muslims and a wide range of castes and classes. Deva's catholicity in a period also marked by religious othering speaks then not only of a pre-history but of a history to come. Indeed the patriarchal modalities of male reformism and everyday domestic ideologies may well have been a model and a resource for nationalist self-fashioning. Women had already been constituted as monitored yet regulatory socializing agents, as reformers of deviant husbands, relatives, neighbours, and servants. Henceforth nationalist agendas could attach, encash or appropriate female domestic authority, substantively expand women's participation, and continue the effort to limit their agency.

The prism of caste: Chhabili Bhatiyari

Scheming women

If the expansion of educational institutions and printing presses in the 1860s made for an unprecedented diffusion of religious texts, classical languages, and pedagogical literature making indigenist possibilities widely available to new groups for investment, it also allowed for a proliferation of romances that threatened to undo the ideological compacts for female literacy. Not surprisingly, most prescriptive writing, including *Mir'at* and *Bihishti Zewar,* condemned such reading. *Stridharma Saar* proscribed women from even listening to *qisse kahaniya* (p. 24). Amanat's *Indar Sabha* and the multiauthored *Chhabili Bhatiyari* were among the depraved books, *kharab aur buri kitaben,* which the julaha taught to the bad thakur's son in *Riti* (p. 45).

The form of the qissa, a short *dastaan* in which the real and the marvellous interpenetrate, traversed 'downwards' from Persian to *dakhani* Urdu, from royal courts to bazaars, from persianized 'elite' to Fort William College publications and thence to the 'popular'—popular in terms of its mobility and multiple locations and in the sense of being preferred listening, watching, and reading. Qissas also moved from verse to largely prose, from oral narratives to the written and printed, and in the late nineteenth century circulated back and forth between oral narration, print, and performance. Oral narration continued till the 1920s.[118]

Chhabili Bhatiyari was one such qissa. First printed in Agra in 1864, it went through virtually continuous reprinting, initially as a qissa then as a *sangit* (a nineteenth-century musical form performed by itinerant troupes), in Agra, Hathras, Kanpur, Meerut, Delhi, Benares, Aligarh, and remained in print till 1977. *Chhabili* had six *sangit* editions between 1920 and 1933 and there were at least three reprints in the 1970s.[119] The 'authorship' of various editions ranged from being initially and intermittently anonymous (1864, 1873, 1884, 1927), to Muslim (1868), khatri, bania and brahmin (1920, 1926, 1928, 1943). The 1928 version was in Urdu.[120] The term author in different editions could mean compiler, translator, editor, or even plagiarist.

Chhabili Bhatiyari: Sikandar Shah Badshah ke Shahzade Raman Shah ka Qissa (1873) narrates the jealous contest and battle of wits between a rajput woman and a low-caste woman over a Muslim prince.[121] Like others in the genre, this qissa too stood outside the pressures of linguistic and 'religious difference' and the grammar of domestic prescription. And the anonymous versions that I have discussed were not even constricted by the pressure of an authorial identity. Thematically, it falls into the outer cluster of the genre centred on clever, untrustworthy female protagonists or trickster women that became prominent after mid-century. In the formal scale of qissas it occupies that end which had the fewest nonmimetic devices or conventions. It has no heroic quests or marvellous events, very little magic (spells and counterspells) or romantic love and adventure. It does, however, carry some characteristic motifs: undisguised sexual desire, imputation of a magic gaze, *nazar*, the execution of 'guilty' women, a woman with whom sexual relations cause death, a plot structured around an implausible ruse and improbable masquerades. Though there is recorded evidence only for a few performances, the form of this qissa and its typical combination of verse and prose suggest the likelihood of continuous theatrical performance and oral narration, or at the very least a fluid borderline between print narratives and performances. The verse it carries is suited to musical rendition, the plot has the chronological, climactic sequence and abbreviation of drama rather than the copious convolution characteristic of the *dastaan,* while the verse repartee and verbal contests suggest a playful, conversational relation to an audience.

Chhabili is a panhari or water carrier by occupation and a bhatiyari by *jati.* Prince Raman, son of the emperor, *badshah* of Dilli, sees her when she is filling water, loses his senses when their eyes meet, and goes to her dwelling, *dera.* She serves him on the instruction of her *saas* (lit. mother-in-law) who encourages a liaison when she sees the quantity of money the prince is paying (p. 8). Chhabili responds to his attentions and agrees to do what he says on the condition that whenever he is in Dilli he will live in her *dera.* He begins visiting every day. The *wazir, amir,* ministers, and courtiers find out and tell his father; they suggest marrying the prince to a girl of his choice to detach him from Chhabili.

The hunt for a beautiful wife begins. Fifty *dootis* (female messengers and go-betweens) with access to the *zenankhanas* (women's quarters) of noble families contrive to get eligible women to stand in an unsecluded place or at a window so that waiting artists can sketch their faces. The prince is to choose from these portraits which are plastered on a wall on his daily route to the palace. At first nobody seems as good as Chhabili, then the portrait of the daughter of a Hindu jagirdar, Mansingh, catches his eye. The *badshah* first makes the "raja", Mansingh, promise to give him anything he asks for, then proceeds to ask for his daughter. Mansingh agrees but says he needs to consult the people of his *kabeela,* his brothers, family, and clan (p. 17). He goes home and tells his wife who says he must abide by his promise. He then consults his daughter, Bichitra Kunwar, telling her he had to say yes because the *badshah* was king of the world. Bichitra says if her father has agreed then so does she, but Hindus and Muslims have a different *rasm,* rites and rituals, and she will consent to the marriage if it is performed by Hindu *rasm*:

Hazrat musalman ki aur hindu ki rasm judi judi hoti hai isliye jo musalman ki rasm karo to mere nakabul hai aur hindu ki rasm karo to kabul hai. (p. 19)

Mansingh's advisers say the wedding should be performed in Chauhdere and not in Dilli. Mansingh tells the *badshah,* he agrees to both conditions. Chhabili discovers what is going on through a woman spy she has sent to the palace, and asks the prince to take her with him when he goes to get married. The prince agrees and says she can accompany him in his *mahadol,* a closed litter, but she does not want to be a laughing-stock and prefers to travel secretly cloaked in a *chadar* atop the *bawarchikhana* or 'kitchen' camel (p. 22).

Chhabili persuades the prince that she will go and look at his future wife. He cannot refuse and she plans to go with a flower garland disguised as a malin. When she sees the beauty of Mansingh's daughter she loses her senses, then weeps, for it spells the end of the prince's attraction to her. Chhabili tells the prince that his future wife has the face of a *shankhini* and a demonic gaze, *nazar,* that dooms whoever looks at her to lose his life, and that this marriage is part of a conspiracy to kill him—the heir to the throne (p. 26).[122] She tells him that if he wants to save his life he must never look at his wife and keep his eyes bandaged on the pretext that they hurt. The gullible prince gets married with his eyes bandaged and keeps them so on his wedding night. After the wedding he goes to meet Chhabili while his wife apprises his mother of her marital difficulties and in turn is told about his relationship with Chhabili.

Bichitra Kunwar now disguises herself as a gujri* selling curd, *dahi* (p. 31). Even her mother-in-law cannot recognize her. Verses about reclaiming her husband follow. On reaching Chhabili's house she sells curd to the prince. Chhabili is angry, especially about the *dahi* seller not wearing a veil, *ghunghat.* An acerbic, vituperative verse dialogue takes place between the two women in which each accuses the other of being a wily, immoral, money-grubbing, brazen seductress. The prince agrees to take the curd, and asks for the price. In versifying on the cost of this priceless curd, *lakh taka dahi,* the gujri indirectly suggests that he unbandage his eyes and eat the sugar, *khaand,* in his own home instead of *paraya gud,* molasses in a stran-

---

* gujri: wife of gujar, manufacturers of dairy products.

ger's house (p. 34). This too angers Chhabili; she replies in verse that
the gujri wants the death of the king, sells curd but is herself on sale.
The gujri answers in kind. The prince is still ready to buy the curd but
has no money; he gives her his jewels and says she can use them to
claim her money the next day. As the gujri is about to leave he praises
her beauty to Chhabili who complains that his heart is beginning to
go astray. She abuses the gujri again as vulgar, boorish, a *gavaar*,
accuses her of exploiting her youth, and reiterates her demand that
the gujri wear a *ghunghat* (p. 35). Chhabili sits on the prince's bed,
this makes the gujri jealous and angry and provokes a verse on the
revenge she will take: twist Chhabili's nose, pull out her tongue,
squeeze her in an oil-press. The titillated prince asks Chhabili to get
up from his bed. This pleases the gujri who now versifies about her
own disloyal husband who is not unlike the prince in appearance and
behaviour. The prince wants to know where she lives. He leaves early
on the pretext of wandering about Chandni Chowk but cannot find
the gujri since the address she gave him, *paaeen ki sarai*, is fictitious
(p. 38). He goes home again with bandaged eyes. As is her daily wont,
Bichitra does *solah singar*; adorned and beautified in sixteen ways,
she stands by his bed. He ignores her. After *chaar ghadi* (ninety-six
minutes) she asks where she should sleep. He tells her dismissively to
remain at his feet—*paaint pad raho* (p. 38). Bichitra marvels at his
stupidity in not understanding what occurred despite its transpa-
rency. He returns to Chhabili the next day.

His wife now disguises herself as a *shahzada*, Bichitra Shah,
a strange yet wonderful prince, and proves attractive to her husband
again in this guise (p. 40). They go hunting together. She is injured,
the prince bandages her foot, and she gives him the same fictitious
address again. The prince relates how attractive he found the gujri
and how he wants to meet her. Bichitra Shah says the gujri lives
beneath his palace and promises to help. At the last moment, however, the disguised Bichitra gives him the slip. The prince tells
Chhabili of his love for the gujri and then goes home again with bandaged eyes. His wife is once again disappointed by his obtuseness.
She says her foot hurts. He wants to know why since she does nothing
but loll on carpets or the bed. She says why do his eyes hurt if he can
hunt with them. She tells him she is both the gujri and the wonderful prince, offering him the jewels as proof. He is afraid to open his

eyes in case he is blinded by her sight and loses his kingship, then
compromises by deciding to open one eye, so that he will be only partially blinded. The proof of her statement being established, he looks
at her. Bichitra brandishes a dagger, threatens to plunge it into her
stomach unless he fulfils her conditions.

The prince wants to know what is to be done with this *randi*
(prostitute), the courtiers recommend throwing her out of the city.
He holds a durbar, sends for Chhabili, publicly abuses her for her
dupli-city and fraud, *kapat* (p. 48). Chhabili says she has sinned and
bet-rayed her love but that she sinned from love, so he should punish
her as he pleases. The prince is divided. Bichitra wants Chhabili to
first be made to embrace a red-hot log in the same way that she used
to embrace her husband's body, then be half buried in the ground
with it, and finally to have her head battered by the prince—this
sequence of actions alone can cool Bichitra's heart.

> *Jis tareh isne mere khavind ki deh se deh milai hai, use garam
> garam khambh kar isko chipkaiye phir zameen mein aadhi gaadh
> upar shahzada uske sir mein tiron ki chot kare to mera ji thanda
> hoi.* (p. 49)

The prince agrees. Two descriptions follow: first, how the deceitful
woman, *dagabaazini*, is killed during the day, and then, the union of
wife with impatient husband the same evening. The description of
this union is lyrical. The metaphors used—two separated deer meeting and mating, *sona* meeting *suhaag* [sic], singer meeting melody
(*raagrang*)—are in stark contrast with the cruel extermination of
Chhabili (p. 50).

> *Sundar saras ati dampati karat rati kalidhunibhashan hai haru
> bari*
> *Kelki kalaan mein prasidh dou aise mile rasriti priti rachi ami
> surdhari.* (p. 51)

The qissa proceeds to celebrate married love and sexual pleasure,
describes the congratulations offered by all the courtiers.

> *Jab is tareh saari aish mein guzri tab fazar ke waqt sab darbar ke
> admiyon ko is khabar ke sun ne se bahut khushi haasil hui.* (p. 51)

It ends on the promising note that after this the *shahzada* began to fulfil his princely duties as a future ruler. Husbandliness, kingliness, and wifeliness are built on the battered and burnt body of a low-caste woman.

While the victorious Bichitra Kunwar has power, the consent of the prince's family and of the courtiers, the low-caste Chhabili only has her wits and her 'love'. Her death is barbaric and it is the rajput wife who wilfully decides on its nature, insists that the prince participates in killing Chhabili with his own hands. The immediate celebration and consummation of the marriage, and the 'public' participation in both the gruesome spectacle and in the legitimate sexual union through offered congratulations are equally disturbing. The narrative has elaborated the parallel entanglement of two women in wit, versification, adventure, jealousy, espionage, and self-making through disguise. Chhabili is as inventive, intelligent, and 'meritorious' as the prince's wife. Both women exercise an active agency, desire an exclusive attachment, 'defend' it in the face of competition; both practise deception and use similar strategies. Their parity undermines the moral binarism of good and evil that the denouement seems to demand. Further, both women are individualized to some extent (jealousy is an individualizing passion) and go beyond the flattened typicality of characters in romances. These similarities, along with the style and verve of the story, the romantic–comic contexts it establishes for Chhabili's ingenuity, make the closure uneasy, gratuitous—it exceeds narrative expectations. It creates a tension between what seem to be disjunct generic formulae and unsettles (at least my) readerly anticipations. Despite her conniving Chhabili appears very vulnerable in the end, punished because she struggled against being discarded. Her attachment to the prince has been extended, intense, 'singular', and resembled an informal marriage. Why then is her stake in exclusivity fraudulent, her desire *so* illegitimate? Why is her claim to upward mobility inadmissible?

The narrative, unpunctuated by adjectives, explanation, elaboration, severed by print from the inflections that would enter performance and oral renditions, gives few reading clues. Listening would be governed by verbal nuance, mimicry, gesture, precise dramatizations of each character's speech, and watching, in addition, by body language and other visual codes, while both would be punctuated and renuanced by audience responses. The 'temporal' distance

of the qissa, as in all romance, could carry none of the immediacy of
prescription but the immediacy of oral narration or performance
would be poised against the pedagogical distancing of prescriptive
texts. Prescription is 'actionable' and aims to produce bodily, behavioural practices. The printed qissa assumes an immanent sequence
of bodily, behavioural practices. That is, as an acted and enactable
text it assumes that its performative history is already inscribed within it, as the ever-present memory of listeners and watchers, and thus
neglects or erases it from the printed form on the guarantee that it
would be encoded in readerly preknowledges. At one level, the
missing clues are an effect of this thoroughly unmarked transition
from orality to print, the fact that the qissa ignores the descriptive
possibilities of written narration and relies on the parataxis (or
absence of causal connections) found in many oral traditions. But at
another level, the missing clues indicate social consensualities that
needed no explanation. The breathless, notational, unnuanced style
may have presumed on certain familiarities that were not merely
generic. A grid of interpretative possibilities then could be assembled
by refracting the narrative through its reading horizons—the social
relations, literary competences, readerly contexts, and preknowledges
of narrative as well as other formal codes in the decade of its first
printing—alongside the meanings which circulated around interreligious marriage, desire, conjugality, and caste.

Shared aspirations, discrete rituals

The readiness with which both parties assent to the wedding
of a Muslim prince and a rajput mansabdar's daughter as long as it
is performed with Hindu rituals is interesting. This was a period in
which rajput men and women were being discursively reconfigured
and communalized as historically and congenitally anti-Muslim
Hindu nationalists in an increasing number of narrative encounters,
especially in Bengal, while the trope of the Muslim interregnum embedded in a sexually repressive model of Hindu women was spreading to new locales.[123] What then would account for the fact that the
tendency to *display* rajput cooperation and investment in Muslim
rule was still at least as strong as this emerging stake in representing
them as the most determined antagonists of Muslim rule? Or indeed
for the naturalization of interreligious marriage in the qissa, for

Bichitra's desire for her Muslim husband, the celebratory consum-mation which obliterates the reason for the marriage and the status inequality that governed it, as well as the common constitution of a target in a low-caste woman?

The political, patriarchal, and cultural bonding of ruling groups in Awadh and NWP offers the most obvious vantage point. As a warrior and landed elite, leading members of rajput clans had col-laborated with Muslim rulers and sometimes gave daughters in marriage to Muslim ruling families; however, chieftains and rajas in this region did not enjoy the martial and political power of their Rajasthani counterparts, and their relation to Delhi had been much more one of fealty.[124] Rajputs and Muslims had severally, both rebelled against as well as cooperated with the British in 1857. They remained the most influential groups in the association of large landlords and usually worked together to promote landed inte-rests.[125] The ease in dealing with discrepant rituals in the qissa not only presupposes cooperation and overlap between their respect-ive marital ideologies but also assumes these shared ruling class interests. The unity of ruling groups seems to postulate forms of co-existence, mutuality *and* hierarchy: though its political other could be anywhere, its social other had to be below. The 'commonsense' about low-caste/class women was evidently cross-denominational. Other rajput and Muslim convergences could be located in the proximity and compositeness of upper-class and taluqdari culture,[126] in fluid zones of syncretism and common worship without conversion,[127] as well as in histories of conversion.[128]

The term rajput however, signfied an uneven semiotic of desired and achieved power. The normalization of rajput–muslim marriage can be related not only to these aspects of extant regional history and culture, to historical memories centred on political and marriage alliances in UP and medieval Rajasthan, but also to current aspirations. Apart from landowners, some of whom had been impove-rished through dispossession, rajputs were sepoys in the army and in the service of rajput chiefs; some were engaged in cultivation or agriculture, a few in trade, artisanal manufacture, and domestic ser-vice.[129] They were both of local origin and migrants from other regions with many gradations and hierarchies within and between clans. There were several unverified or fictitious claims to descent from clans in Rajasthan or to a rajput identity while some upwardly-mobile middle castes were claiming kshatriya ranking at this time.

The insistence on Hindu *rasm* or *rivaj* along with *barat*, the demand that the marriage procession should go to the girl's home, traverse more disparate possibilities. Hindu rites could mark a religious plurality, that is, the ability to retain respective religious rituals or practices in cross-denominational marriages. Similarly it could, relying on Mughal precedents, simply expect that a rajput–muslim marriage could be performed with Hindu rituals without fear of repercussion even in a situation of unequal power.[130] Conversely, the demand could be perceived as drawing a sharper line between converted and unconverted rajputs. Intermarriage between Hindu and Muslim rajputs still took place. Conversion had produced localized pockets of syncretic or shared rituals among rajputs that persisted till the late nineteenth century.[131] The condition of Hindu *rasm* may encode a resistance to such 'incomplete' conversions or to other forms of syncretism. There may have been an ease with overlaps in the customary and patriarchal domain but an investment in distinctive rituals. And these rituals may in part have been a mark of class status to distinguish them from the impure customs of low-ranking rajputs, as well as from non-rajput groups below whose marriage customs had either simply multiplied on conversion or had not changed entirely.[132] Were the meanings of 'Hindu' and 'Muslim' then restricted and only applicable to the ritual domain?[133] And did the Hindu rites signify non-conversion? Or were the *barat* and Hindu *rasm* merely a device to keep rajput honour intact—a play of establishing high rank and a form of political bargaining? Again, the implications could be retrospective, since the qissa entered print only after the formal end of the Delhi *badshahi* in 1857.

At any rate, the qissa seems to have been disengaged from the major contentions around religion at the time, and a positively defiant genre when compared to the prescriptive. Linguistically, a mixture of melodramatic Urdu and euphemistic Hindi, it makes no pretence to piety and does not actually raise the subject of religious conversion. The distance and defiance cannot be separated from the *mofussil*, urban, cross-denominational history of its readership or its continuous reprinting. Contemporary contentions may however have shaped contrapuntal readerly horizons and interpretations. For

instance, the Special Marriage Act of 1872 allowed, albeit selectively, for civil marriage between people of different faiths or castes
or those who did not profess any of the 'major' religions. In the controversy that preceded it, the opponents invoked scriptural authority,
raised the spectres of interference in or degradation of religions, and
the propagation of a 'European' form of love marriage that would
undermine religious, caste, and family authority. They quite ignored
the fact that contemporary preferential sexual alliances and marriages across castes and religions may have been based on 'love'.
Paradoxically, even as this act legalized transgressions and imbued
'love marriages' with new meanings related to a secular modern, it
also engendered a discursive logic of defending ritual Hindu marriage. This heightened concern with rituals, through which the
demand for Hindu *rasm* in the qissa could also be read, may have
dovetailed with the similar concerns of Vaishnav and Sanatani
dharma sabhas who at this time were questioning the shastric vali-
dity of simplified Brahmo marriage. And both may in turn have blen-
ded with the increasing symbolic significance as well as adoption of
rituals among upwardly mobile sections in lower and intermediary
castes.

Masculine plots or women's wiles?

However, in the high melodrama and theatricality of the text
the rajput–muslim marriage becomes almost peripheral. The narrative is centred on a wife trying to win her husband from the other
woman in a play of female possession that sets out to match, outwit,
and corner vagrant male desire. In the passional universe of the qissa
'love' is neither the antecedent of jealousy nor the projected motive
of either woman—except in a song sung by the gujri, and in a
defensive and self-exculpatory moment by Chhabili in the last scene.
The semiotic is one of relocating *male* desire in marriage by making
it the space for sexual pleasure and instituting the exclusivity of the
wife's claim. Within this, female jealousy and male fickleness can be
read in several registers that knot into the interrelated questions of
male regulation, female transgression, and misogyny.

The reconciliation of duty and desire for men and the proper
institutionalization of monogamous marriage were part of the problematic of patriarchal sexual regulation, and key themes in nine-

teenth-century reformism. Male decadence, especially nawabi and rajput, was a recurring concern and one item on the agenda was to wean them from the company of prostitutes and low castes. In the qissa the emphasis falls not so much on reforming as on repositioning male desire and vanquishing the 'other' woman. It resolves the decline and fall of the landed aristocracy through a salvage narrative that proposes to domesticate male sexuality. In the wider transition from the masculine ideal of a hereditary, patrilineal aristocrat whose status was authorized by the father and who bore a promiscuous sexuality to the self-made man in a colonial and capitalist economy, the qissa only makes a single move. It tames this older masculinity, identifies royal authority with sexually regulated masculinity, and though it participates tacitly in the desired shift of male status from prostitutes or 'other' women to wives, it does not link marriage to new forms of status.[134] Rather, ordered marriage is simply a royal duty and the foundation of the state.

In premodern romances and devotional traditions love was often associated with transgression or rebellion but could still occupy, in common with prescriptive traditions, emotional structures that were monogamous, enduring or permanent for women, polygamous, transient or sequential for men.[135] However, in emerging nineteenth-century definitions love marriage was associated with monogamy for women *and* men, privileged the choice of partner, and promised an end to male promiscuity. Thus *Kshatriyakul Timirprabhakar* argued for male monogamy and the installation of love and sexual desire within marriage on the ground that these would produce better progeny and end family conflicts; it even praised the ancient practice of *swayamvara*, a princess choosing her husband in public assembly, for having ensured mutual attraction and compatibility. Such notions of conjugal love that rested on ideologies of complementarity rather than prescriptive arrangement, and offered some leverage for wives in extended families, also carried new forms of interiorization, exclusivism, and anxiety for women. The qissa is poised between the old and the new. In a vocabulary of sexual desire, it plays out a (female?) fantasy of redeeming the arranged marriage by falling in love with the husband or wife—an unrebellious, politically and socially ratified love that could double as a pragmatic rapprochement with bourgeois notions of conjugality.

Female jealousy both signifies and is engendered by the mobility of *male* desire: it must then be emplotted between women. Both women occupy the same structure of insecurity—Chhabili as fear and Bichitra as umbrage—in which male desire is naturalized as insatiable and unreliable and can be withdrawn at any time. Female sexuality, even its aggressive expression, is described in/by a masculinist ethos and structured around the politics of polygamy. Polygamy was not religion-specific (it was, for instance, practised by rajput and Muslim taluqdars in Awadh), and here the sexual competitor of the elite woman is ranged across caste and class rather than denominational lines. A characteristic motif in the structure of intrigues of women subject to polygamy was to 'wish' death on the rival wife. Here fantasy becomes fact: it *is* possible to inflict death on the other woman, the unofficial *saut* (co-wife), if she is low caste. Chhabili wants to blind the prince, literally block the 'sight' that triggers romance—desire enters through the eyes—but she can only do so provisionally and does not have the power to do more. Bichitra however, rejects the suggestion of banishing Chhabili, a provisional punishment, and insists on the finality of death, the 'sight' of a spectacularized body. A degraded and violent end is reserved for the 'statusless' woman.[136] The burial and burning involved in Chhabili's death, which forge a perverse connection between illicit sexual pleasure and mortal pain, in fact suggest an inversion of the ideology of *sati*—the noble death reserved for the loyal upper-caste wife.

Love, hatred, and sexual desire are not even 'formally' committed to moderation, accuracy or realism, especially in a romance. They make their objects as a totality, engulf them whole. That is why romance and adjacent genres can rely on a 'signal' to put love, hate or desire into motion. Strangely enough, this is not dissimilar to the way social stereotypes function: they represent a more or less casual consensus regarding 'others' on the axes of class, caste, gender or race, and function as a commonsense signal that is followed by the appropriate prejudice. The lower-caste woman has a social and generic typicality and can be rolled back into a stereotype who deserves her end. But unlike the social arenas of stereotypes, some of these very differences of class, caste, and denomination have a far more ambiguous, even equivocal, life in romance. Romance after all also signifies a desired incorporation of the 'other', makes the whole social spectrum open to/available for appropriation as objects of love and pleasure. Though denouements may underscore the limits, restore the barriers, love/desire is itself narrativized as intrinsically knowing no boundaries. Perhaps that is why Bichitra's own transgressions centre on both unsettling boundaries and re-enclosure through cross-dressing and masquerade.

The prince clearly has a glad eye or rather a disposition for low-caste women, and it is this disposition that is sought to be altered. And fittingly, his wife disguises herself as a gujri. The wife must *become* both a low-caste woman and, in a reversal of gender, a prince, in order to defeat the 'other' woman and to displace and app-ropriate, simultaneously, conventional male bonding (in the mas-culinism of the hunt) and homo-erotic desire (as the 'feminine' man). The guise of the prince helps her to escape female weakness, gives her access to male power (in tropes of chase, gamble, mysteri-ous assign-ation), to the potent energy of the female rajput warrior (male cloth-ing, riding on horseback), and a homo-erotic frisson that in fact sta-bilizes gender distinctions and augments heterosexual desire. The narrative fixation on heterosexual consummation cuts short and rapidly subdues the potentials for celebrating the more indeterminate sexualities that it has itself engendered. The guise of the gujri gives Bichitra access to a new, theatrical sexuality, the 'erotic' powers of the low-caste woman. Both guises set up a flirtatious chain of acco-mmodation and denial, have practical motives, and allow her an adventurous mobility. Gujars, considered to be a mixed caste sprung from unions between rajputs and vaishyas, sudras, or chamars, were occupied in manufacture and sale of dairy products, grazing, petty vending, and cattle theft.[137] Gujar women certainly had many kinds of mobility denied to secluded rajput or Muslim women. 'Disguise' thus tacitly acknowledges that low-caste women occupy public spa-ces. Traversing lower-class/caste 'freedoms' and male privilege, Bichitra moves freely up and down vertical hierarchies. Chhabili's disguise as a malin, relatively speaking, only allows lateral movement.

If in its easy readability, disguise still signified the social rigidity of classification, it was also becoming a sign of the social in-stabilities released by a new economy, and beginning to mark an extendable range for the 'self' through serial re-expressions. Both dis-

guise and cross-dressing were complex signifiers with differing contemporary valences for women: transgressive reversal, corrupt custom, skill, performance, crime, sin, heroism, victimage, escapade,
reform. *Riti* describes the Kajri festival in which women adopt various guises and play-act, *aurate anek prakar ke swaang banaati hai*:
the well-built and *dheeth* women cross-dress and act as men, wear
soldiers' or *sipahis'* uniforms, speak in *khari boli* dialect like them,
harass sons-in-law caught in their *sasurals*, anoint them with *kaajal*
(collyrium) and *sindur*; those who go too far in their practical jokes
on men are condemned as *dusht*, vicious (pp. 120–21). The bhands
and bahurupiyas, storytellers and impersonators, wore male and
female disguises of persons of various ranks and castes for the amuse-
ment of their patrons.[138] In Wajid Ali Shah's musical entertainments
and *rahas natak*, women sang, danced, adopted the guises of Krishna,
jogins (female mendicants), and *gwalans* (milkmaids).[139] Some of the
commercial melodramas of Parsi theatre staged flamboyant scenes of
cross-dressing. The perception that criminal castes committed crimes
disguised as either affluent citizens or religious mendicants was common to the middle classes and colonial administrators;[140] a *kutni*,
trickster woman, passes off for a pilgrim returned from Mecca
(*hajjan*) in *Mir'at* and relieves Akbari of her jewels (p. 67). The Deobandi reformer Thanawi declared that it was sinful for women to
dress like men or wear men's clothes.[141] However, the protonationalist and militant figure of Rani Laxmibai of Jhansi was not far
behind. In *Dastan-e-Amir Hamzah*, Mihr Nagar dresses as a man to
escape male cruelty in the palace. Pandita Ramabai retailed the
experience of an eleven-year-old brahmin widow who, battered by
her in-laws, escaped on a train dressed first as a boy and then as a
Muslim girl.[142] In Balakrishna Bhatt's farce, *Shikshadana*, the
heroine, neglected by her husband for another woman, persuades the
barber's wife to dress as a man and wear a false moustache obtained
from a local *natak mandali* (drama troupe) in order to teach her
errant husband a lesson—the husband catches them in bed together.
(Incidentally, the nain decides to rename herself Govardhan Das
Bhattacharya but is told that brahmin men never use the suffix
das![143])

If the qissa evokes male fantasies of access to many women,
it also evokes female fantasies of adventure, masquerade, 'finally'

possessing men. And, if there was a tension in *Riti* and *Mir'at* between obedient, passive, pliant women and determined, combative, refor-mist women who stabilize the family and control their men, then the qissa only plays out the submerged possibilities of female assertion. Bichitra's name—literally *vichitra*, many-coloured, variegated, curi-ous, odd, fantastic, surprising, singular, wonderful— sets her off from women of her class. Here too mobility is related to 'sight', a romance motif on which the narrative revolves. (Indeed love at first sight has a certain literalness in contexts of female seclusion.) However, for Bichitra, the implications of 'sight' instantaneously transforming into male desire are not the same as for Chhabili. The upper-caste woman can be *unveiled* only in the guise of a man or a low-caste woman. There is a play on being low caste, sexually available, and arousing male lust: a triadic configuration the wife can only enter through dis-guise. Not surprisingly, the only defence the bhatiyari can think of is to insist that the gujri wear a *ghunghat*! The wife is 'sexualized' through her disguises, she must emulate the 'other' woman or capture her identity in order to activate the chemistry of male desire, insert illegitimate longings into legitimate connubial pleasure. The play of female jealousy—now as a sign of *women's* sexual desire and active agency—defines the sexuality of both wives and other women in reciprocal relation to male propensities.

The production of sexuality, masculinity, and femininity was also related to the production of social difference and constituted in a field of social relations and political conjunctures that were far wider than relationships between men and women. Sexuality was produced in a way that intensified and encashed class and caste differences. Upper-strata masculinity and male sexuality conventionally relied on three structured domains: sanctioned access to women whether through polygamy or otherwise, the routine transgression of marriage, and the appropriation and enjoyment of women 'below'. The qissa's definition of a deceitful woman as one who exploits male sexuality is in fact a generic ruse which screens or 'saves' male lust from scrutiny.

In this qissa, however, female sexuality also enters the fray of appropriation and exorcism in the name of conjugality, and perhaps that is another reason why the thematic of women against women becomes primary. Bichitra is properly married through the death of 'other' (erotic) possibilities, the instantiation of her claim to exclusivity. Conjugality, of the sort favoured by reformers, is relegated to a secondary position: it is a device of narrative closure and that too as consummation, not as the pleasure of a companionate marriage. In fact the pleasure of consummation here could be related to much older prescriptive and narrative traditions, partly still extant, that valorized fertility, procreation and the conjugal happiness on which they depended, acknowledged a wife's desire as legitimate, and considered it wrong if a husband did not satisfy it.[144] A standard nineteenth-century argument against polygamy was that it destroyed women's right to sexual satisfaction in marriage.[145]

Instituting monogamy for husbands of course implied sexualizing wives, ironically, at the risk of blurring the lines between wives and 'other' women. Shuklaniji's description of a wife who joins the dutifulness of a *pativrata* to the responsive sexuality of a *ramni* in *Riti* remained somewhat veiled: following her womanly nature, the good wife complies with her husband's inclination and engrosses him in various kinds of comforts, joys, and pleasures, *stribhav mein pati ke anukul hoke bhanti bhanti ke sukh aur anand mein magan kar deti hai* (p. 190). Munshi Ramlal's *Putrishikshopkari Granth* (1872), however, unselfconsciously endowed the *pativrata* with an overt sexuality: it seems the wife of a worthy kayasth in ancient Pataliputra entertained her husband with pleasurable conversations about sexual dalliance, *ras krida ki manoranjan baaten*, while the good wife's *dharma* entailed being a *kulta* in *premriti*, a 'fallen' woman in love making.[146] In Pandit Sitaram's *Stri Updesh* (1871) too the wife is exhorted to be as technically adept in the sport of love as a prostitute, *rati mein veshya samaan.*[147]

For upper-strata women the power of conjugality and the proximate skills of wives and 'other' women in the qissa could read as a prophylactic against the certainty of male fickleness. So naturalized was the model of the faithless, capricious male that Thanawi spelt out the danger a wife exposed herself to if she praised unknown women or even *described* the appearance, clothing, or jewellery of any woman to her husband:

What a disaster for you if your husband's heart inclines towards one of them, and he starts thinking about her![148]

Female precautions were the mundane face of the permanent, jealous anticipation of loss and the unending dream of discrete, exclusive bonding. The qissa, which plays them out as phantasmatic revenge, marks an imaginary zone of slowing down, or even blocking, the circulation of women between men.

Common prejudices, diverging realities

By the 1870s caste relations were changing in Awadh and NWP. Occupational diversification and upward mobility were posing a challenge, albeit small, to systems of gradation, while the colonial state was introducing changes in occupations and remodulating classificatory schemas. The 1857 uprising, in which lower castes also participated, had uncovered agrarian and urban tensions between artisanal or petty entrepreneur groups and commercial or landlord groups.[149] Gujars, for instance, who as day labourers and guards, *chaukidars*, had a peripheral role in the urban economy, were condemned for looting and burning during the 1857 revolt.[150] From the late eighteenth century, bhatiyars, traditionally keepers of *sarais* or roadside inns, who relied on the passage of imperial notables down the main routeways did not fare as well as those who lived near shrines. In fact, prolonged royal patronage may well have been connected to the curious dual classification of bhatiyars in NWP: the Shershahi and the Salimshahi, "the women of the former wore petticoats, of the latter drawers".[151] British collectors themselves reconstituted bhatiyars in the early nineteenth century and made use of them as servants of travellers or agents for police information.[152] Later they diversified further, and by the early twentieth century had become vendors of cooked meat and tobacco in addition to innkeeping.[153] Diversification did not, it seems, improve their profile for those above. In *Rasala Kharch*, Muhammed Husain says the unhygienic cooking habits of Hindus and Muslims make their homes as filthy as an innkeeper's shop, *bhatiyare ki dukaan* (p. 38). In *Saas Bahu ka Qissa* by Lakshmanprasad of Fatehpur, bhatiyaris and kunjris are quarrelsome shrews, precisely what women from respectable homes must never be: *Nahin acche ghar ladti nari / ladti kunjri aur bhatiyari*.[154]

There were no strong anti-caste or non-brahmin movements in the region; however there were subterranean contests, otherwise neither the state nor the upper and middle classes would have had to work so hard to fix power relations and invest so much energy in typification. By the 1870s the upper castes, brahmins and rajputs, as well as Muslims were seen to be losing ground to vaishyas, sudras and other lower castes among whom there was a relative increase in literacy and prosperity in UP.[155] Almost in tandem, the state categorized a number of low, out-caste, and itinerant or nomadic groups as habitual criminals (Criminal Tribes Act, 1871). Chuniya who helps her thieving brother in *Mir'at* is, like Chhabili, a bhatiyari. In *Riti* chamars are accused of looting a wedding party and angrily condemned as chandals.* The fact that Chhabili's end was 'fitting' speaks for this normalization of prejudice based on caste, class, and gender.

The lack of correspondence between the *consequences* of Chhabili's crime (fraud) and the brutality of her punishment also traverses a number of state and upper-class/caste punitive regimes: a differentialist brahminical legality based on minute caste and gender discriminations; a late Mughal state legality where women/slaves were subject to differing punishments and public *display* was part and parcel of rendering exemplary justice; the colonial appropriation of these punitive styles (public flogging, hanging) into its own spectacular traditions in the early decades of rule, and later the excessive severity and ritualism of post-1857 punishments meted to Indians in the name of avenging English women; the non-court jurisdictions of zamindars, panchayats, rural elites which directly related infliction of pain to exercise of power and used ordeals, physical mutilation, and other methods in public spectacles of humiliation; the power of upper-class men *and* women to subject servants suspected of theft to fire ordeals; the patriarchal power that circulated in lower-caste arbitration procedures—among the nomadic kanjars, women suspected of immorality were subjected to the ordeal of holding a "hot iron weeding spud" in their hands.[156] What is more, the qissa couples regulatory power with sexual appeal and pleasure. Bichitra's proficient

---

* chandal: out-caste, traditionally the offspring of brahmin mothers and sudra fathers.

assumption of the guise of a *shahzada* could also function as a sign of the authority that she can call on to dictate Chhabili's death and later fold back, keep in reserve as it were. Only centuries of sedimented patriarchal and casteist callousness could code this as a just or a happy ending under the insignia of romance, could allow a dystopic denouement to pass as a dystopia averted.

The qissa was not as fantastic as the genre permitted. It not only entered a number of punitive regimes and existing biases into the expansive punitive possibilities offered by the 'form' of the 'romance' freed from 'realistic' constraint, but also fused them with the formal structures of misogyny. At one level, the qissa merely replays or ex-tends the misogyny already present in this genre and other literature of this period. For instance, in *Simhasan Battisi* Vikram kills his six adulterous wives and marries new ones. Pandit Rangilal's popular *Qissa Tota Maina,* printed in the 1870s, introduces a gratuitous, cruel ending and male violence in keeping with a frame story centred on the wiliness of all women: the stubborn queen is whipped, blin- ded, abandoned.[157] In the prescriptive texts discussed earlier, *error* was the principle of misogyny. The tension in these texts, especially *Mir'at,* came from the contradiction between the moral absolutism and the narrative amplification of misogyny. If misogyny systema-tizes error and thereby de-individualizes women— all bad women are the same or bad for the same reasons—then the very elaboration of error in narrative individualizes women. At this level the harsh, exce-ssive punishment in the qissa is designed to neutralize what could be possibilities of identification or subversive spectacles of dominant, individualized women. It shares a familiar topos of misogyny—the overcoming of a female obstacle enroute to narrative completion, the woman as a figure of the delay or obstruction of ultimate closure.[158]

In all prescriptive texts 'bad' women come to a deserved end; here however, the end is positively celebratory. The pleasure sets up a community of affect that bridges the gap between Chhabili's tor-tured death and the beginning of a marriage. The resulting consensual definition of a connubial sexuality in terms of violence against 'other' women is masculinist but not exclusively male. The play of jealousy between women in a masculinist ethos of substituting, replacing, what are interchangeable women, also signifies female consent to being given a place in the seriality of male desire, always imagining oneself to be the one who will never be replaced, be loved 'forever'. Chhabili's burning marks the (mis)fortune of this 'forever' which causes and coincides with death. Female jealousy also stands in for a *consent* to male (self)typification: the banal series in which women change but patterns are repeated and repertoires recycled—in the kindling of desire, the constitution of its objects, the confirmation of dispositions, the duplication of affective vocabularies. Indeed it is Chhabili and Bichitra's desire for exclusive possession that *gives* the prince a universal value—a value that is not instantiated in the narrative since he is not shown to have any intrinsic worth. Chhabili's death which conjoins male indifference for the relegated object of desire with female fantasy, then, is the sign of a consensual misogyny which women—neglected or deserted for rivals—can be persuaded to share.

The qissa's misogyny is also based on the classic dyad of license and containment. Male instability and concupiscence were sanctioned both discursively and in practice as male nature and male prerogative. Female self-interest and license had no socially legitimized field of operation and were naturalized only as stigmata, that is, through the disparaging discourse of a voracious female 'nature'. The sexuality that both women project in the qissa is not restricted to procreation; it is in equal danger of encroachment by men from 'above' or 'below', and has the power to draw the prince to their respective dwellings—*dera* and Chauhdere—Chhabili through her own attraction, Bichitra through the negotiation and status of her clan. The initial encounter of both women with the prince is 'supervised'— mediated by a *saas*, arranged by a father. Yet Chhabili's sexuality is more threatening and more amenable to being read as a cautionary tale precisely because it raises the spectre of female upward mobility not subject to regulation by marriage or conventional familial arrangements. Perhaps that is why over time Chhabili came to be emphatically recast as a prostitute in what otherwise seems to have been a more or less stable text. The 1884 version, *Qissa Chhavili Bhatiyar*, is similar to the one I have discussed, though the language is slightly different.[159] The 1927 version is essentially the same except that here Bichitra calls Chhabili a *veshya* and the prince calls her a *randi* publicly in his durbar even as Chhabili seeks to explain her actions as stemming from love.[160] The punishment Bichitra devises is further refined, now the prince had to shoot an arrow into Chhabili's head after she was half buried stuck to a burning log. This is done and the prince cannot even wait till the evening to consummate his marriage. In all three versions Chhabili's *saas* encourages what seems to her to be a profitable liaison and the monetary transaction with the prince is briefly mentioned in the beginning, but it is only in the 1927 version that Chhabili is abused as *veshya*. In the early versions it is unclear whether Chhabili is a widow with a mother-in-law or whether *saas* merely refers to an older kinswoman; in this one the *saas* acquires the air of a brothel keeper.

Were the variations in relationships unconnected to formal marriage now subject to a more homogenizing morality and nomenclature? Some redefinition of such relationships was evidently taking place under the combined pressure of hardening class ascriptions, hinduization and islamicization that condemned or proscribed relationships unmarked by ritual marriage, the attempts to generalize standardized forms of marriage, the ideal of monogamous conjugality, and the new authority bequeathed to the legally married wife gathered from nineteenth-century reformism. The pressure to repress or eliminate the graded relationships—secondary marriages, informal liaisons, concubinage—between legal marriage and prostitution may have subjected these relationships to a more systematic renaming. Taken together, these would place prostitution in a starker opposition to marriage, widen the ideological split between the two even as the sexualization of the wife (following on monogamous conjugality) in fact created a new semantic adjacency between wives and prostitutes, and thus make the prostitute the object of a more intense misogyny. At the same time pressures from 'below' may have threatened to denaturalize the ending of the qissa. Was the 1927 version seeking to *justify* Chhabili's punishment by presenting her as selling her sexual services? Did the shift to *veshya* bring the ending further into the realm of social approval? Indeed does misogyny become more consensual when it provides reassuring assertions of social hierarchy in times of change?

In sum, the social contract of the romantic qissa as a genre did intersect at some levels with the domestic ideologies carried in other genres. If in prescriptive pedagogy, fidelity and domestic management were normalizing class assumptions, then in the qissa wifely desire normalizes caste distinctions and misogyny. If in *Riti* and *Mir'at* the contest with women below was played out through disavowal, displacement, suppression, projection or incorporation, in the qissa it works through substitution, appropriation and fantasy. If reformist discourses expected women to concur with their misogyny through engendering self-division and self-hatred, then the qissa extracts consent through pleasure. In fact it relies on the capacity of ideology to yield enjoyment, that "surplus" which lies beyond its own rationalizations, and can elude the most severe decoding.[161]

Classification confounded or what's in a name?

Yet it may be worth pushing the question of caste somewhat further. Why, as the title indicates, is Chhabili, a panhari, the protagonist (heroine and villain) rather than the princess Bichitra?[162] Lower-caste characters had choric and secondary roles as servants, panharis, *gwalans*, *makkhan walis* (butter sellers) in a *rahas* performance at Wajid Ali Shah's court called *Pahla Qissa Radha aur Kanhayya Ke Izhar Halat aur Ta'shuq Mein*.[163] Later, even as local songs and narratives recorded the militancy of lower-caste women in 1857, protagonists from humbler strata gradually entered the qissa.[164] *Chhabili* begins with an early-morning encounter between a *bhangin* and the *badshah* of Dilli. Despite meeting his eyes, she fails to do a *salaam* and only raises her eyebrows. The *badshah* attributes her 'sadness' to his own lack of progeny and becomes, temporarily, a *fakir*. The titles of three *sangits* printed in the 1910s feature gujar, dhobin, and banjara* as protagonists. Qissas were performed at fairs and festivals in the nineteenth century as well as daily at street corners in some cities.[165] The famous Qaiser Bagh *mela* with its juggling, song, dance, and acrobatic feats that began in 1853, had rural and urban visitors from all classes; the women included kaharins, panharis, prostitutes, "impudent bhatiyaris" who prepared food for travellers at inns, and wives of nats*.[166] Ironically, even as these very spaces were being prohibited to middle-class and higher-caste women,

---

* banjara: wandering traders, cattle dealers, grain carriers, with a cross-caste composition.
* nats: dancers, performers, the women also sang and danced.

the interdicted performances were re-emerging in printed forms on an unprecedented scale after mid-century.

What was the nature of low-caste participation in narrating, listening, watching, performing qissas, and to what extent did this mediate the printed texts? The mobile qissa may in fact be seen as a linking genre between Hindu and Muslim, upper and lower caste, literate and illiterate, urban and peri-urban women, as well as between secluded women and the servicing women who functioned as their intermediaries. If lower-caste women could listen and watch, higher-class/caste women could read and listen. Upper-class women had private storytelling sessions and kept their own female storytellers who could be well-bred but impoverished women acting as companions, tutors, general factotums, and attendants such as *ustanis* or *mughlanis*.[167] At a time when popular oral forms and their formulae were being sucked into print, with different levels of mediation, and in the absence of a social history of *qissa-khwani*, storytelling, the question of female and low-caste 'coauthorship' cannot by any means be foreclosed.

Did such cross-caste/class participation play a determining role in some aspects of the story, and if not in its violent ending, then at least in its classificatory schemas or lapses? I wish to suggest that the denominational flexibility of this qissa may have emerged as much from the amorphous denominational status of low castes as from confluences among ruling groups. The printed qissa seems to have been a point where the 'literary' experience of the older elites and the 'cultural' experience of those below converged on a fuzzy, fluctuating middle-class ground. As such, if the qissa has integrative aspects regarding caste, class, and patriarchal arrangements, it also has oppositional ones regarding caste and religious distinctions.

What would the name Chhabili (lit. graceful, beautiful) signify? If names are any indication, then the degree of muslimness or hinduness of some lower castes and classes was unclear. An 1854 textbook, *Vidyarthi ki Pratham Pustak*, attempts to differentiate between Hindu and Muslim women on the basis of names. In the list of names it provides there is a relatively clear demarcation of upper-caste/class names: some Hindu women have the appellation of Kunwar or the names of rivers and goddesses, and similarly some of the names of Muslim women are derived from Persian or Urdu. However, the names of other 'Hindu' and 'Muslim' women occupy an identical spectrum. These other 'Hindu' women are named Chhabili, Dhaniya, Chinna, Totiya, Dhamkan, Jhamma, Khaliya, Umrani, Rukiya, Gulabi, Jhalariya, Dabaliya, Pisni, Rangili, Basanti, Chhitiya, Minda, Budniya. And the other 'Muslim' women are named Gulabo, Chameli, Chhammo, Bela, Chando, Laccho, Sundar, Chandiya, Rajo, Sitaro, Jhanni, Roopa, Chunni, Champa, Sajni, Lalli.[168] Not only did these names belong to a common colloquial pool but low-caste names were as yet denominationally indistinguishable. Nor, it seems, were these names entirely confined to low castes. In *Riti* Shuklaniji's presumably higher-caste disciples are called Chhabila and Rangila. What is more, bhatiyars themselves were a mixed group and included Hindu converts to Islam. In this region and period then, nothing about Chhabili's name is incontrovertible, it could denote either or neither religion.[169]

Syncretism of course existed at every level in UP: landholding elite, satellite court culture, merchant, artisanal, and labouring groups.[170] It extended beyond worship to social practices including marriage as, for instance, among kurmis or gadariyas.[171] There were histories of conversion and mixed rituals not only among rajputs but also among parts or entire subgroups of lower castes such as churihar, dhuniya, kunjra, gujar, and bhat.[172] Among lower castes several caste ascriptions either encompassed multiple faiths or were occupational and did not necessarily disclose their religious affiliations. For instance, some of the castes jointly denigrated by *Riti, Mir'at,* and other prescriptive texts could consist of both Hindus and Muslims (gujar, ahir, kunjra), or have separate Hindu and Muslim branches and subdivisions (kalwar, ahir, gadariya, teli, banjara, nai, julaha, dhobi, bhangi, chamar), or club Hindus and Muslims together under a single occupational category (barhai, dhuniya), or the same occupation could have discrete Hindu and Muslim caste groups (qalaigar, bhat).[173] Performing castes were largely configured as occupational groups. Bahurupiyas, drawn from several castes and classes, had no specified religious affiliation; the nomadic nats who came from different strata were both Hindu and Muslim but also had separate Muslim subdivisions in Awadh; bhats, who recited poetry, had Hindu and Muslim branches, and Muslim bhatins sang in public on certain occasions unlike their Hindu counterparts; bhands, formerly Hindu and Muslim, however, were recorded as becoming mainly Muslim by the 1870s and entirely so by the twentieth century.[174] Both Muslim and non-Muslim nats practised burial, as did other groups that were not officially Muslim along with some religious sects that had mem-bers from several castes.[175] At the lowest end of the scale, untouch-ables could formally be Muslim, Hindu, or Christian but in practice they were the most difficult to classify. It was often hard to distinguish between the Hindu and the Muslim, while bhangis, chamars, and doms could not be defined as self-evidently Hindu even within the crudely overencompassing schemas of colonial categorization.[176]

There was then a very wide field of overlapping practices and faiths 'below' which confounded classification. Census returns from UP also show that in the nineteenth century depressed classes were exploring a variety of 'religious' avenues in a volatile way. In some districts larger numbers of untouchables returned themselves as Christian in a census than all the missions put together claimed as their adherents. A census or two later the official figures fell dramati-cally and the same people were returning themselves as Muslims, Hindus, or Arya Samajis.[177] By the early twentieth century, more castes seem to have become predominantly Hindu or Muslim while a few were said to have lost their mixed character altogether; thus bhatiyars were recorded as being entirely Muslim.[178]

This mixed or syncretic culture has to be situated in a context of neighbourhood, local, and occupational solidarities. Several occu-pations were obviously common to lower classes—as carpenters, weavers, bangle makers, cotton combers, tinners, oil pressers, inn-keepers, spirit sellers, petty traders, itinerant pedlars, performers, clothes washers, barbers, manual labourers, watchmen, water haul-ers, sweepers—whether they were technically Hindu or Muslim. Menial, artisanal, and servicing jobs could take them to both Hindu and Muslim homes. Prostitution too, into which Chhabili was even-tually assimilated, had a cross-caste and cross-religious composition from the lowest level to the highly cultivated tawaifs.[179] Though over time tawaifs came to be identified as mainly Muslim, the attempts to make distinctions between prostitutes on religious lines were not yet as emphatic in this region as in the older presidencies where Muslim prostitutes were being accused of adopting Hindu names,[180] or of treating prostitution as a stage in life from which they could move easily into marriage.[181] In sum, 'castes' were not homogenous entities. And where the appellation marked an occupation, it marked *class* more sharply than any other kind of homogeneity. Further, the longstanding processes of fission (leading to subdivisions and sub-castes), fusion and formation (leading to new castes or affiliation to higher castes within upwardly mobile sanskritizing logics) were *severally* produced in this period by ostracism, adoption of different customs, change in worship, conversion, change of occupation, and prosperity.[182]

The fact that the qissa did not bother to mark Chhabili's denomination though it underlined Bichitra's, and that bhatiyari, panhari, and gujri remained occupational categories, may have a wider significance. Caste prejudice was as generalized as lower-caste religions were fluctuating or amorphous. In fact one of the threats of low castes and untouchables, who could be shunned by both Muslims and Hindus, was their denominational indistinctness or ambiguity, visible not merely in syncretic worship or the fact that many could not be comfortably docketed within the emerging definition of Hinduism and Islam, but also in that they occupied a mixed social field of overlapping faiths, nominal or 'incomplete' conversions, and religious volatility which unsettled denominational categories too profoundly.[183] Socially practised discriminations from 'above' were more definitive than any definitional clarity from 'below'. And even from above who, as yet, wanted to 'own' low castes and untouchables?[184] Or even to claim that indeterminate mass of shared or syncretic popular religious practices that was left behind once pristine Hindu and Islamic identities had been disaggregated?

The qissa's silences then can provoke a rethinking of the categories 'Muslim' and 'Hindu' historically, as they were played out in the early 1870s, as well as in my own usage in this essay. Both iden-tities were plucked out of a potentially radical plurality which they either sought to marginalize or suppress. 'Hindu' and 'Muslim' did not signify coherent communities or consensual categories; rather, they followed an early nineteenth-century normative trajectory of redefining religion and became names for a specific set of existing and desired patriarchal, class, caste, and political relations.

In conclusion

This essay can be seen as provisionally isolating a cluster of texts that made up a history of borrowing, selecting, appropriating, resisting, and responding to circulating thematics. These texts both confirmed and contradicted each other in a number of areas: domestic ideology, widow remarriage, sexual pleasure, female adventure or mobility, interreligious marriage, religious identity or 'community,' religious pluralism, syncretism, and so on. Various standardized repertories—oral, written, Persian, Sanskritic, brahminical, ashraf—intermingled, clashed, were partly transformed. Their mutually corroborative and disconfirming relations, the lack of self-identity between authorial intentions, formal discursive mechanisms, and readerly receptivities are central to understanding the tensions within even wider reading configurations in a period where print formations came into being.

The reading configuration I have assembled is part of an expanding archive—as in more of the same, as in the numerous other types of texts that could be added to it, and as in itself leading out to whole clusters of other reading. It indicates broad ideological similarities as well as contrasting utilizations of common conventions, references, themes, and codes by individuals or groups with different dispositions, in relationships of distance and sharing, competition and imitation. The social effectivity or otherwise of prescription lay not in any single text but in the wider conditions of reading and its organization in formations that shaped relationships between texts, in the multiple and conjunctural relational possibilities between genres. The unstable relation between textual production and consumption can be traced to this relation each text bore to others as well as to readerly horizons governed by different preknowledges, class competencies, caste and gender locations. The propositions the qissa carried, for instance, were neither univocal nor universal but faced different interpretative expectations, horizons, and contexts embedded in the social conditions of its production. It is at the fluid intersection of oral narration, performance, print, the old bazaar and the new market economy that the contours of the social space occupied by the qissa, the determinants of its popularity and proliferation, the social relations it abstracts and condenses, can be glimpsed. The simplicity of its form has to be counterposed to its complex relation to listeners, watchers, readers, where the shared regularities of reception may have been quite different 'above' and 'below'.

The fluid relation between orality and literacy that moved in and out of each other's domains bore some relation to the (re)production of commonsense, and in this respect reading can be thought of as part of a process of re-familiarization. It also made for continuous transmission through different oral and printed vectors which make it difficult to trace neat or single transmitting lines, or to establish influences and sources. Prescription, and partially the qissa, were pre-print genres, only the novel was a print genre from its inception. The uncertain novelization of *Mir'at, Riti,* and *Devrani Jethani* may in fact stem from their double relation to orality and prescription.

In formal terms it would be artificial to pose this cluster merely as textbooks versus a romance or to make oversharp distinctions for at this time prescription could be printed in formats other than that of the school textbook. Popular treatises, tracts, and textbooks could be interchangeable, shift from one to the other, or occupy multiple reading sites while an inchoate reading public and market together blurred some of the lines between fiction and textbooks. If *Riti* is to be believed, *Chhabili Bhatiyari* was in the 'corrupt' syllabus of a Farsi-educated rajput male. *Mir'at* was to be canonized as the first Urdu novel but drew severally on the didactic and *adab* literature of ethics and etiquette, techniques of oratory, and the narrative devices of qissa, *kahani*, and *dastaan*. The circulation of reformism did however have a gendered logic. All the authors were men and more likely to know both Urdu and Hindi than women readers.

These texts were also members of "semantic chains".[185] Significantly, though most chains shift and recombine, misogyny was the most repeated, the most 'reliable' and relied upon principle of semantic cohesion. The regularity with which women were pitted against women to contain or close their agential possibilities widened into a misogynist discourse that bonded disparate genres into a singular fraternity. The recurrences and interdependences that united these texts were not merely signs of an intertextuality but of the social relations they *refracted* or tried to *institute*. The plotting of antago-nisms between women in the narrative sequences of genres, that otherwise made different claims upon the 'real', resituates domestic ideologies themselves as points of intersection between patriarchal compulsions and many other social pressures.

Qissa, prescription, and novelization had equally complex relations of desire, affirmation, and negation to social reality and none is open to a literal rendition. They did not so much enact pre-existing divisions of class, caste, gender, or religion as remake them. However, within this cluster the qissa is a moment of collision, inter-section, and confluence with the prescriptive—at once a traversal of the transgressive, a destabilization of the prescriptive, and a reaffir-mation of consensus. Clearly the formation of a middle-class culture was tense, complex in its relation to that 'below' and never entirely disjunct from it, or 'complete' in itself, while what lay below was a set of disparate possibilities for incorporation and resistance. 'Popu-lar' consciousness too was neither a symptom of age-old 'tradition-alism' nor of the inertia of the masses, rather it was part of a lived cul-ture being dynamically reconstituted from both precomposed and recomposing commonsenses, from new contests and aspirations.

If the reading cluster generates both contradictions and con-sensualities, even the latter signify latent, possible contests. The texts partially undid each other, interpellated women in ways that were often mutually irreconcileable, and even marked the points at which women's literacy could gradually alter the very hierarchies upheld in prescription. They revealed not merely the closures but also the gaps in the shift from an unreconstructed paternalism to an equally patriar-chal and paternalist reformism. These were some of the reasons why the agency of women was never entirely predicated on domestic pres-cription or communal positions, and some were able in subsequent decades to question the ideological limits placed on their literacy and demand new principles of collectivity.

More significantly, there *were* many possibilities in the early 1870s. There was no genuine class, religious community, or caste group consensus—different tendencies were in play. Within the broad dynamic of class formation, castes, region, languages, reli-gions, and patriarchies made up an interdependent field of sociality replete with tension, division, and contest but without political assistance divisions could not have congealed on any one of these lines. If class pro-cesses relied on caste or religious 'community' identities they also broke and regrouped them. 'Hindu' and 'Muslim' were shifting, un-settled, conjunctural categories. 'Popular' religions were an inter-section of many denominations that implicitly called the discreteness of each into question. And the very stringency of emerging caste and religious classifications reveal that these were not all that fixed or consensual.

The logics of religious diversity, syncretism, unclassifiability, and volatility below may have offered no self-conscious answer or opposition to the hinduization and islamicization that came largely from above. Nor were these logics transformed into ethical or heretical principles that were named as such and could be politically articulated later in concerted opposition to communalization. They remained a practical disposition within a dense social ground, an often composite culture or shared structures of feeling. Yet these logics were not produced by the porosity or fluidity of popular belief-systems alone. They were also generated *within* a profoundly contradictory dynamic: the *compartmentalizing* mechanisms of caste, class, and gender discrimination and the social *solidarities* created by these very same inequalities. And as such, as a field of historical variation, social constriction *and* indeterminacy, the logic of religious diversity carried numerous asymmetries and disjunctions that could serve as points of entry or a base for a secular, transformative politics. This dynamic demands both more nuanced formulation as well as more work on the *connections* between the segmentation, inequalities, and solidarities that govern religious diversity. Yet I will risk the claim that the recurring cleavages between processes of patriarchal and casteist bonding and communal differentiation 'above' and 'below' did have the potential to produce a space for women to jointly resist patriarchal, caste, and religious oppression.

The early 1870s, then, were an active junction of causally interrelated, specific class, cross-class, and non-class features that were not open to any single resolution—not because there were utopian alternatives at hand, but precisely because of the contradictions they generated *between* different structures of oppression. The possibilities that came to be realized at the expense of others did not only follow on the shape of organized politics in subsequent decades. They left a legacy—a politics carved out of neat primordial identities, a privileging of so-called religious communities, whether from Hindu right-wing or other culturally differentialist positions—that still threatens to foreclose more complex historical understanding and radical political intervention today. However, the multiple locations of women in contradictory structures of oppression can generate a situated critique of *all* these locations. A simultaneous challenge to patriarchies, class inequality, caste discrimination, and religious particularism may still be the only answer to the interdependent constitution of misogyny, class, caste, and religious difference.

This began as a brief essay called "Differentiating between 'Hindu' and 'Muslim' Women—on Domestic Sites" presented and circulated at a seminar on 'Appropriating Gender: Women's Activism and Politicization of Religion in South Asia' (Bellagio, August 1994). As it grew, either sections were read out, or its arguments leaked into presentations on other subjects made in seminars at Nehru Memorial Museum and Library, Indraprastha College, Indian Social Institute (Delhi), and Miranda House between 1995 and 1998. I am grateful to the participants, especially Ravinder Kumar, for their comments on my presentation, and to Anuradha Kapur, Amit Gupta, Rajendra Prasad, Shakti Kak, and Kokila Dang for their comments on the script.

The 'amenities of domestic life'

The sexual division of labour remains the basis of most feminist critiques and agendas. Domestic labour, however, is still a somewhat segregated, underanalysed subject, and in India much more information has to be assembled before it can be constituted as a field. Therefore I have set out to offer only some loosely connecting ideas about domestic labour in the first section: as culturally specific and changing, the way in which it structures and is structured by social practices, the labour market, and by other institutions that regulate labour and inheritance. The nature of its imbrication in lasting personal relations has suggestive consequences for thinking about patriarchal ideologies and processes of class differentiation. The second and third sections explore some of the possibilities for re-reading nineteenth and early twentieth-century reform agendas and controversies through the prism of domestic labour. Wives, widows, domestic servants, and prostitutes were all defined in relations of service; their labour and consumption not only constituted the underside of reformist prescription, but existed in a tense relation with emerging notions of conjugality. If in classical Marxism the concept of class hinged on the production, extraction, and control of surplus through the exploitation of labour, then by extension, I will argue, domestic labour was not only one of the many determinants of class but central to class formation in this period. This leads to a question that it would be premature to answer but important to pose: to what extent is unpaid domestic labour a *necessary* condition for class formation?

The governing social assumption that domestic labour should be done by women combined with the fact that it is largely though not exclusively performed by them, underwrites its social,

economic, and ideological locations. Unpaid and usually unacknowledged, undertaken in the constricting confines of the home, domestic
labour exists socially as a gendered category; however, it is difficult
to discuss as an abstraction because, theoretically, it could be
performed by anyone. The substantive content and ideological registers of domestic labour are determined by class and social locations—
tribal, urban, rural, different practical arrangements for sharing,
which women are freed from it and which men drawn into it, and
whether it is or is not a renumerated service.

At present, domestic labour mediates women's choice of,
capacity for, and control over paid labour, interlocks with the proliferating sexual division of labour in waged work, and is structured by
the labour market. It is part and parcel of the 'dependable' social relations in which the market is embedded. Yet the apparent location of
domestic labour outside the domain of the market and unacknowledged in the realm of exchange—for reasons that are part ideological
and part structural—facilitates its rapid, recurring transformation
and absorption into symbolic and ideological systems of valuation
based on the constellation of non-dissoluble, non-contractual marriage, service, and nurture. Carried in domestic ideologies, these systems of valuation structure social practices, and indicate not only a
recurring relation of reciprocity and simultaneity between labour and
ideologies but also the fraught location of patriarchal arrangements
in base and superstructure. Since domestic labour and domestic ideologies coexist and mutually presuppose each other, rather than fall
into a linear sequence of cause and effect, they are open to joint
reproduction.

There is a rich and unresolved Marxist and socialist–
feminist debate on domestic labour as part of the sexual division of
labour, especially in relation to capitalism, and on whether it can
qualify as productive labour.[1] On this latter question, studies on India
foreground its 'economic' nature but have rarely discussed its 'productive' dimension in strict theoretical terms; they have, however,
challenged both the customary and the state's official devaluation of
the constellation of domestic labour, subsistence labour, and house-
hold-based production as 'non-economic activity.'[2] These interroga-
tions have thoroughly denaturalized the terrain of domestic labour.
Clearly, domestic labour does possess the capacity to produce surplus

value, assist in capital accumulation, and subsidize wage labour. Further, any analysis that sets out to disaggregate domestic labour in order to underscore its significance must simultaneously analyse the ways in which the ideological and other features that impede such disaggregation emanate from *both* state and family, and are embedded in economic processes. However, several knotty questions remain. Can unpaid domestic labour be assimilated into classical Marxist notions of work and labour without a substantial reformulation of the latter? What are the relations of procreative, domestic, and subsistence labour to each other and to a particular political economy? Are shifts in domestic relations propelled from without and a result of capitalist development, or does capitalist development take place through changes occurring within household relations? Have preindustrial sexual divisions of labour shaped the disposition and definition of labour in capitalism and determined the region-specific nature of transitions?

These questions can be sustained at a level of abstraction and a level of historical density only when much more contextual information about domestic labour in particular social formations in India becomes available. Here I will attempt a preliminary discussion that may assist in a wider conceptualization and historicization of the field. And, I will work from what could be, provisionally, a minimal consensual definition: domestic labour as socially necessary labour —necessary for both production and reproduction. The unavoidability of socially necessary labour as such for survival, albeit in class-differentiated ways, in situations where men will usually not undertake it, may itself be an axis of women's consent both to domestic labour and to its (apparently compensatory?) symbolic transformations.[3]

'On our work there is no blessing': questions on labour

I   For women there is greater servitude in outside employment than
     there is in married life. There is no reason why women should not
     choose the servitude of love to that of money.
               Parvati Athavale, *Hindu Widow: An Autobiography*, 1928

        Colette Guillamin (though I do not agree with her theory of
sexage) makes two significant observations: that unpaid household
labour is given the framework of lasting personal relationships
which are not and cannot be measured in terms of time and money,
and that consequently women's instrumentality is applied to other
human beings.[4] This suggests that patriarchies build personal relationships *into* exploitation, operate *inside* the sphere of relationships of love, nurture, and sexuality, are indeed inseparable from
them. It is not surprising, then, that women themselves find it difficult
or impossible either to separate the personal from the structural or to
see themselves outside the orbit of such relationships. Nor is it surprising that most domestic ideologies prescribe, elevate, and idealize
those personal relations of mother, wife, daughter, daughter-in-law,
into which unpaid domestic labour and services are packaged. Perhaps it is because these latter cannot be measured in time or money
and are implicated in questions of human reproduction and survival, that women persistently, and at certain historical conjunctures
emphatically, become the natural subjects of ideologies of selfless
devotion, sacrifice, altruism. An affiliation between domestic labour
and this complex of sacrificial ideologies is structured both into the
nature of the work and into its positioning within familial relationships. In other words, not only are the boundaries between work and
familial relationships unclear, but the function of domestic ideologies
is precisely to dissolve them. The religious and cultural rationales for
motherhood, wifehood, and nondissoluble marriage thus may be seen

as trying not only to underwrite this source of labour but to guarantee a private domain of non-alienated labour, or rather, what can often be made to *appear* as a domain of non-alienated labour, being itself unmeasurable and occurring in the frame of lasting 'non-contractual' personal relationships.

Marx wrote:

> Suppose that we had produced in a human manner; each of us would in his production have doubly affirmed himself and his fellowmen. I would have
>
> 1) objectified in my production my individuality and its peculiarity and thus both in my activity enjoyed an individual expression of my life and also in looking at the object have had the individual pleasure of realising that my personality was objective, visible to the senses and thus a power raised beyond all doubt.
>
> 2) In your enjoyment and use of my product I would have had the direct enjoyment of realising that I had both satisfied a human need by my work and also objectified the human essence and therefore fashioned for another human being the object that met his need.
>
> 3) I would have been for you the mediator between you and the species and thus been acknowledged and felt by you as a completion of your own essence and a necessary part of yourself and have thus realised that I confirmed in both your thought and your love.
>
> 4) In my expression of my life I would have fashioned your expression of life, and thus in my own activity have realised my own essence, my human, my communal essence.[5]

If we go by his definition of unalienated labour, it is possible to see the discordant and equivocative nature of domestic labour (child-care, service, cleaning, house maintenance, food preparation): it can carry elements of affectivity and individual confirmation even as it is shot through with relations of power, entangled with ideologies of 'non-alienated' labour, and can often deindividuate women, reducing them to their 'functions.' Though forced to mimic 'non-alienated' labour, these activities would only genuinely approximate it, in Marx's sense, if power relations were erased inside and outside the home.

Its imbrication in lasting, 'non-contractual' personal

relationships in turn helps to preserve domestic labour as an unsullied domain 'outside' the market economy and the circuit of exchange. If the reproduction of this ideological matrix is recursive, it simultaneously occupies a space subject to constant threat of rupture under capitalism where the tasks of domestic labour enter a comparative schema on a hitherto unprecedented scale—they can be carried out unpaid in the sphere of the home, or some of these tasks can enter the market economy and be tied to exchange value.

Since the same tasks—child rearing, cooking, cleaning, care of the sick, etc.—also *coexist*, to varying extents, as services that can be purchased,[6] the same labour is subject to two distinct evaluative systems.[7] Just as the double insertion of many women into wage labour and domestic labour creates contradictions that are showing up in the pressure on family forms,[8] so too the dual placement of certain forms of labour as an evaluated and a 'non-evaluated' set of services may be the source of contradictions that show up in the pressure on ideologies. The increased possibility of buying and selling parallel services as well as of computing the market cost of domestic labour implies that services offered free in the home have become theoretically convertible into 'costs'—such as of replacement, opportunities for employment, market equivalents of products prepared in the household. This makes it more difficult to produce ideologies that can traverse smoothly across these two discrepant terrains or naturalize the gap between them. Does this dual placement of labour *dilute* those nineteenth-century middle-class domestic ideologies which represented marriage as a complementarity of male provision and female labour and, at the same time, *increase* the need for such rationalizations of unpaid work? What is the nature and extent of the threat that possibilities of evaluation in the capitalist marketplace hold out to the unquestioned rendering of unremunerated services in the home? And does the threat extend to the ideological representation of the lack of remuneration for domestic labour as *inherent* to this particular type of work? If so, then the tensions and contradictions created by the dual placement of this labour may partly explain the burgeoning of reformulated domestic ideologies under capitalism (including those that present women as naturally altruistic or as supplementary wage earners), as well as the parallel growth of antifeminisms in reaction to feminisms' perceived attempts to evaluate housework and democratize the sexual division of labour. They may also help to clarify why capitalism cannot afford to emancipate women fully though it socializes precisely some of these tasks; and why domestic work is the site where the fiction of disinterested labour is sought to be maintained long after the precapitalist economies which gave it birth have ceased to exist.

II

> If the institution of marriage did not exist, all amenities of domestic life will come to an end. None will serve another.
>
> Swami Dayanand Saraswati, *Satyarth Prakash*, 1875

My argument so far builds largely on studies of capitalism in Europe and America. However, it needs to be reformulated to confront the specificities of the Indian situation, marked by the sectoral entry of capitalism, segmented transitions, uneven development, and the play of precapitalist ideologies overdetermined by colonial rule. Within such a social formation, the question of domestic labour, especially when posed in relation to the recurrence of patriarchal ideologies, has different historical contours and theoretical implications,[9] which if taken together can rupture the respective exclusivisms and closures of both an economic determinism and a narrow culturalism.

If the combinatoires of precapitalist and capitalist domestic ideologies are analysed in relation to changing and/or stable forms of domestic labour, this labour, and not merely the tenacity of tradition as is commonly maintained, may turn out to be a basis for the long duration, recurrence, and reformulation of patriarchal ideologies. For instance, if the confluences of familial ideologies in the nineteenth century between the upper caste/class strata of precapitalist India (which had already naturalized and elaborated the sexual division of labour) and the British middle classes (also shaped by several patriarchal traditions) were to be seen as underwritten by a common conception of the household as a site for women's labour, then the question of labour would be relocated. To begin with, the settled affiliation between women as subjects of sacrificial patriarchal ideologies and unpaid domestic labour could be seen as having provided a *ready* ground for the new ideologies of altruism emerging from the twin locales of class consolidation and colonization.[10] More significantly, the question of labour would inscribe both the *longue durée* and the colonial conjuncture, and the entry of capitalism could be seen as setting out to alter several forms of labour without erasing the broad sexual division of labour. I would go so far as to argue that this 'non-market sphere' of domestic labour was, and persists as one of the spaces or meeting grounds where some of the adjustments bet-ween precapitalist and capitalist ideologies and practices are made, where precapitalist patriarchal ideologies and practices—with their underlying essentialism and characteristic pressure against women's individuation—come to acquire a new domain of effectivity and, in the process, are themselves reshaped.[11]

This wider argument would call for a re-reading of labour processes and the relations (conflicting or interdependent) between different kinds of labour[12]—taking as a given that labour processes and ideologies are not only conjointly reproduced but that ideologies produced at the site of labour may re-enter the social formation in different ways at different conjunctures, that the *same* ideology may be able to intertwine with a different labour process, or that a *continuing* labour process may be able to mesh with emergent ideologies. It may then be possible to see how the domestic organization of labour articulates with the mode and relations of production, that is, with class stratification, wage labour, and the market, as well as with the confluences and contradictions of the values and structures produced by unpaid domestic labour itself. If existing forms of work— for example, caste-based, agricultural, factory and other waged labour—are analysed conjointly with the imbrications of the market and 'non-market' sphere, it may suggest how labour processes congeal at different conjunctures into specific *systems* of patriarchal regulation.

The connection between domestic labour and sacrificial domestic ideologies persists partly because of the continuous need to produce social rationales for forms of unpaid labour. This connection could be analysed both in relation to other forms of unpaid work (as in bonded labour or subsistence production) and to structures of dependence or extra-economic coercion in precapitalist and capitalist social formations. For instance, did domestic labour and the tasks and services performed by women in broader structures of 'feudal' exploitation mutually shape each other? Did the wider coercive extra-economic imperatives in hereditary clientage (*jajmani*), caste-based, and bonded labour systems in-form or even condense into domestic labour?[13] What was the interrelation between other labour forms and women's 'specialization' in domestic labour?

Further, unpaid domestic labour draws attention to the nature of the institutions that make it possible—marriage, family, household—as being not only central to relations of production[14] but as institutions that organize and regulate productive, reproductive, and socially necessary labour, though differently in terms of class or conjuncture. Patriliny, lower-strata polygamy, forms of 'secondary' marriage, exogamy, and patrilocal residence may be particularly amenable to analysis as institutions that maximize the extraction of female labour. For instance, among upper castes and classes in the north, exogamy and patrilocal residence have functioned to dislocate women, restrict their entry into wage labour, and relegate them more firmly to domestic labour and reproduction.[15] Unexpected connections as well as disjunct layers of historical change may emerge if different forms of cohabitation and marriage in pre-capitalist and capitalist social formations are seen in relation to labour processes. The articulation of labour systems with these other systemic repertoires—of residence and inheritance—may also provide a more thorough and specific account of those distinct yet overlapping sets of arrangements that I have elsewhere called multiple patriarchies.[16] What is more, it may enable a periodization of these patriarchies along lines of intersection and segmentation, rather than *en bloc*.

There may be possibilities here for understanding not only historical change and transitions in a social ensemble constituted by uneven capitalism, but also how women's unpaid labour can function as a contemporary mechanism for softening the force of disparities and dislocations. Domestic labour, even as it invisibly picks up the slack of 'development' and absorbs the pressures created by lack —of medical and social services, security, education, employment, adequate wages, access to goods and services—now intensified by the new economic 'liberalization' under the aegis of the state, simultaneously interlocks with and reinforces the inequities of the private, non-state, and informal sector, creating conditions in which women's rights can remain restricted or become even more residual and contingent.[17] The articulation of relatively 'unchanging' forms of women's labour—domestic, household, subsistence—with the new economic order, along with the proletarianization of women entering wage labour and the variations in marketization and mechanization of housework, is too vast an area to explore here. However, it is becoming evident that deregulation, privatization, cuts in public expenditure, and the roll-back of welfare programmes by the state as an agency of globalization is intensifying the casualization of women's wage labour, increasing their burden of household labour (in areas such as fetching fuel or water, food processing and health care), magnifying the (double-edged) dependence on kin-support networks, and setting up the home once again as a servicing institution where women's labour will provide the buffer against the depredations of the market. Both the state and the non-state or private sector are also adapting or intensifying older gendered forms of exploitative labour such as subcontracting and home-based production, and introducing new ones, while many forms of women's labour are being resituated as a flexible resource for transnational exploitation. The World Bank and International Monetary Fund in fact explicitly, and approvingly, see 'third-world' women's unpaid labour (household and subsistence) as subsidizing global capitalism.[18]

Foregrounding domestic labour can also provoke a rethinking of the production, content, and locales of ideologies. The close articulation of precapitalist domestic ideologies with religions needs sustained attention. For instance, the frame of lasting personal relationships goes beyond the death of the husband in some upper-caste ideologies, situating the wife's domestic labour in an extended time-frame if not in a continuum with eternity. This, in contradictory fashion, pulls against, rationalizes, and even trivializes daily domestic labour, and simultaneously seeks to bestow on its daily repetition a more elongated temporality as well as the aura and density of ritual —suggesting the asymmetrical ideological transformations occurring at the quotidian site of the everyday. Further, caste distinctions are embedded in the gradations of domestic labour. The shastric classification of pure and impure work, initially related to the formation of servile castes and classes, meld labour into birth, substantiating the status of upper-caste women and determining their relation to the labour of lower-caste women and men.

If defined in relation to domestic labour, the paranoid dispro-portions of misogyny would indicate that area of the social beha-viour of women that defies desired ideological transformation, those recalcitrant moments that cannot be translated into univocal def-initions of 'women' or their character or their duty. Thus domestic labour would also be a site for the social production of 'bad' women in direct, indirect, or inverse relation to the utilization and control of their labour, with the misogyny itself signifying a punitive ideological transformation of the naggingly persistent, though historically changing gap between the desired unity of the norms and the hetero-geneity of social practices.

Yet misogyny is only one of the several disparate relationships between the desired of familial ideologies and the existing organization of households at any given moment. In practice the relation between domestic labour and familial ideologies is also far more contextual and complexly mediated than my discussion so far indicates. In detailed reconstructions, both historical and sociological, the household appears as a space for the continuous negotiation of male authority which is seldom stable, uncontested, or uninfringed.

Similarly, the notion of domestic labour as being at once un-measurable, socially devalued, and socially unacknowledged can be remodulated. I broadly agree with Guillamin that domestic labour, unpaid and socially devalued, is relatively obtuse to the rational time–money reckoning of work under capitalism. The difficulties of measurement partly lie in the diffuse nature of the work (relatively unregulated, multiple and overlapping tasks), in the inapplicability of existing paid labour and market-derived categories, in the very lack of a terminology (for tasks involving the minutiae of maintenance, thrift, status production or socialization of children to maximize their earning capacity), in the familial relationships in which it is mired, and the situations in which it is performed.[19] However, it is socially acknowledged in direct, indirect, and inconsistent ways: as a negativity, as that which must be rendered faceless, and as that concrete necessity which should be ensured and regulated. Domestic ideologies prescribe and exalt it, selectively incorporate it as the 'reality' of the dominated, and disperse it into discourses of women's entitlements and rights. In the customary (as distinct from the legal) sphere, domestic labour is palpably acknowledged and calculated into the systemic social and familial structuration of hierarchies of gender, caste, work, and consumption, into collective regimens of stricture and control.

These practised forms of acknowledgement display the tension in the ideological transformation of domestic labour into symbolic values centred on 'good' women, a transformation that seeks at the same time to actively *block* precise time–money measurement. They display the difficulty, as it were, of practical management of the recalcitrant, interstitial spaces created between the labour and the symbolic value by discrepant practices, heterogenous or conflicting needs, affective and contentious personal relationships, as well as by the demystificatory potentials that inhere in the set of relations within which domestic labour is carried out. That is, those spaces of resilient and ineffaceable materiality that resist the conjoint reproduction of labour and ideology, and which must be contained, absorbed, elided, if ideological translation into symbolic value is to continue.

This tension appears vividly in personal relationships. The ubiquity of household friction—including that between women— seems to rest partly on the facts that women's customary entitlements (usually contingent, situational, and built over time) depend on the family, and that interpersonal relations in both the natal and marital home are the sites where women's customary entitlements can either be maintained *or* abrogated. It also rests on the fact that these natal and marital interpersonal relations have increasingly come to structure women's access to statutory rights in so far as they constitute either the set of coercive pressures which forcibly prohibit access to legal rights, or the set of potentially supportive kin networks in order to maintain which women often have to 'voluntarily' forego their legal rights.

Distribution is another source of household friction because the ideological and practical constitution of hierarchies of labour intertwines with entitlement to consumption of food, goods, and services. The correlation of right to consumption and labour in/for the family as well as surveillance of consumption from both dominant and subordinate positions has been a persistent feature. Differential consumption as it is built into domestic and social hierarchies is not confined to India.[20] However, the social consensus about the value of specific categories of persons that entitlements in the natal or marital household represent in India rests on specific cultural and religious rationales. These can only be dismantled by a *joint* critique of labour, consumption, and ideologies. Women can seldom control or bargain about the value of their unpaid labour precisely because it is over-ridden by an inhibiting array of factors working through ideologies seeking to minimize their rights. A study of contemporary patterns of male and female authority and consumption in a Rajasthani village reveals a *perceived* and *practised* correlation between consumption and labour within the family: the right to food emanates from past/present/future labour. Even women themselves perceive the rights of consumption of women who work in the fields as greater than those who do not work in the fields due to purdah restrictions. However, labour contribution as a demarcator of rights to the products of labour is superseded by interpersonal relations, income contribution, and the parameters of agnation and ownership of property. The very fact that women's labour is used by both the natal and marital family through the practice of shuttling between the two households (*aoni–jaoni*) functions, perversely, to devalue it and to reduce their right to con-sumption in both places.[21] It is evident here that though the notion of differential rights to consumption carries a demystificatory potential poised to undercut the unifying ideologies of the family, it is simul-taneously revalidated by the lack of social acceptance of domestic labour as a producer and/or guarantor of such rights, even in women's *own* perception.

III

A jat peasant woman: "We work hard and [the men] work hard, but on our work there is no blessing. On the work of men there is great blessing: from it comes much produce; but from women's work comes nothing that can be exchanged." "Yet," interposed a zamindar, "if a man has no wife, he cannot cultivate. For who will cook for him and prepare the fodder and lay it before the cattle?" Malcolm Darling, *Wisdom and Waste in a Punjab Village*, 1934

What are the ideological registers and precise relations between the class differentiation of domestic labour within house-holds, and between domestic labour and wider processes of class differentiation in the social arena?

The agency of unequal divisions of labour in the creation of hierarchies among women within households depending on age, status, and quality of belonging has been widely established. Familial hierarchies are of course responsive to wider social changes. The entry of new coordinates and status markers—such as new avenues of waged labour, consumption, or education for women—can disturb or reassemble existing hierarchies. However, since the household is a space for the daily production and recreation of social inequality not only on gender but also on class and caste lines, the crosscutting class relations *inside* households would themselves severally mediate the ideological translations of labour. The identical affective structures or the same ideology of service cannot be produced or easily naturalized when women of the household take the full burden of domestic work, when domestic labour is done as a renumerated service for others by poor and/or low-caste women, or when higher-class women pay for and supervise these other women to do domestic chores—in *each* the social relations within which labour is performed are different.

The low-paid domestic service sector releases some women from the lower middle class upwards for work in other sectors of the economy, enables leisure or more choice for others, constitutes middle-class status, marks the point where racial and ethnic hierarchies are forged, and serves to maintain wider patriarchal relations especially in countries where women predominate in domestic service. The dependence of patriarchal authority on female service too becomes more transparent since the domestic service sector tends to bolster both male public roles and the domestic division of labour.[22] Significantly, it is not the wealthiest countries that have the highest servant ratios but those with the largest income differentials.[23] In India, wider ranging 'customary' forms of appropriating women's labour are replicated in households hiring 'servants', with the relentless and daily demarcation of class, caste, and pollution boundaries (re)producing a lived 'inwardness' with and investment in systemic classification, oppression, and othering. Seen from below, as it were, one woman's 'home' is another's workplace. And yet precisely because it is a home, the domestic worker is recruited informally, sequestered from public scrutiny, her work invisibilized, and her employers protected from public accountability. Redefining the home as a workplace would make the managerial, class–caste location of women who can hire domestic help and consume their services more visible. Perhaps domestic labour so rarely becomes the object of collective contestation because it is embedded in *both* familial hierarchies and class relations. An increase in cash resources or women's control over property seldom unsettles the division of labour and seems mostly to lead to the purchase of domestic services or to their delegation to women lower in the family hierarchy. Ironically, the nature of servants' work shares some of the features of unpaid domestic labour: ranked below other waged work, it partakes of the general devaluation of domestic labour, consists of diffuse tasks related to service rather than to the market, resists standardization and measurement, lacks precise evaluative criteria, is subject to on-site job definition, and is performed within quasi-personal relationships.

If higher caste/class status and ideologies can be directly or indirectly maintained by women in the domestic service sector, what of the ideological location of their *own* domestic work?[24] Is the labour of women in the domestic service sector—encashable outside but unpaid inside their own homes—thereby open to double evaluation, and does it make the (re)production of ideologies of service more tense, volatile, or fragile as compared to women who only labour inside the home? Again, though it can prop middle-class ideologies, the option of domestic service in other homes may provide an independent income, and some degree of autonomy and control in their own homes for lower-class women. And what of the large number of men and boys in the domestic service sector in India?[25] Does their presence 'degender' the labour or lower the wages of women in domestic service? Does it 'feminize' the men or produce a different set of class and gender tensions?

The class maintaining/maximizing function of domestic labour, precisely like the personal relationships it is imbricated in, is also an arena for varying degrees of women's agency and consent. As 'class work' domestic labour, thrift, consumption, and socialization of children maintain several aspects of social status,[26] and enter the logics of social mobility; failure leads to loss of status in terms of children's marriages, jobs, skills. These need not however be read mechanically. Women's stake in either class solidarity or status is a complex issue. Gender inequality in the home can undermine class

solidarity among non-propertied women.[27] Women of the propertied classes can have a precarious position because of the discrepancies between ascription or status and access to class resources
including the law; between educational levels and actual position in
the labour market; between the expansion of job opportunities and
the limits imposed by domestic responsibilities on job options or job
mobility; as well as from the gap between existing legal rights of
inheritance and actual or effective control over property often
exacerbated by the absence of natal family support.

The role of property and inheritance systems in creating
gendered class and intra-class divisions is fairly direct.[28] The relation
between labour and inheritance is not only less direct but heavily
mediated by the conditions of transfer and control which may
undermine the inheritance. This is most evident in the partial devo-
lution of property as dowry in contemporary northern exogamous,
patrilineal households. Dowry has been related to the invisibilization and devaluation of women's labour,[29] but it has no single correlation to women's wage labour. Paid work has not by itself eroded
patriarchal arrangements though it has determined the nature of their
operation. Dowry is simultaneously a part of the structural tension
between status and patrilineage (as status maintainer and as part of
pre-mortem inheritance) as well as a part of the systemic dispossession of women from mortem inheritance.[30] It can function both as part
of reciprocal long-term transactions as well as coercive and expropriative ones. Most women have little or no control over it and are
in a situation where distance from the natal family and overcommit-
ment to the conjugal family doubles their weakness.[31] Their insecurity makes domestic labour nonnegotiable, necessary to their own
survival, and for legitimating their dependent existence. When domestic labour can be parcelled to other women in the home by senior
women, it is from positions of consent, access to, and delegation of
patriarchal power.

Finally, class ascription cannot be mechanically interpreted. Social status accrues to declining class groups (especially from
upper castes) long after the actual class ascription may have changed;
it is actively sought and in urgent need of consolidation by emerging
class groups, and it has to be constantly renewed by stable groups.
The *mobility* of the processes of class location, formation, and

differentiation is itself a determining feature in the content and changing organization of domestic labour. In other words, women's labour and stakes may also differ at different levels and junctures of mobility.

Though similar in terms of responsibility, the contemporary middle-class woman's assisted labour, often geared to family status production including activities related to high consumption and elaborate maintenance of property, is not comparable to poor rural or urban women's survival-oriented domestic labour, essential to the bare existence of the family. There is, however, a relation between different types and definitions of domestic labour along the joint axes of class differentiation and mobility.

Relationships between domestic, agricultural, and artisanal labour are regionally specific. However, available information suggests that with the exception of women from substantial landowning families who can pay others to do the housework, rural women—whether in households with subsistence plots, in those where wage labour supplements small landholding, or in landless households—are almost entirely responsible for domestic labour. The content and definitions of domestic labour vary according to strata, occupation, and caste only *within* this wider overlap. Women, especially from lower castes, may carry a triple load of unpaid agricultural labour, wage labour, and domestic labour.[32] The labour of rural women, both in small producer and subsistence households, spreads into unpaid agricultural tasks or other gainful activities which become continuous with subsistence labour. Since little of this latter is dignified as 'work' in either state or customary perception, it slides soundlessly into the fold of domestic labour, either by default as 'non-work' because unwaged, or because, as has been argued, of the partial commoditization of rural societies, the blurred lines between production for home consumption and for the market, and the difficulty of disaggregating domestic work from productive work in subsistence households geared to self-consumption.[33]

When the logics of seclusion overdetermine the economy of domestic labour in households functioning as productive units, inhering power relations become starker and the process of class differentiation and mobility more visible. In poorer upper-caste sections, women often never enter waged work but perform domestic labour and those agricultural tasks that can be done within the household.[34] In green-belt Haryana, *ghunghat* or veiling has become a mobile form of seclusion that enables a much wider exploitation of women's paid and unpaid agricultural labour, reducing the need either to confine them at home or to withdraw them from work in situations of upward economic mobility.[35] An extension of domestic labour, with its privileged class location being determined by the 'seclusion' of the *place* where it is performed, can also obtain in poorer non-agricultural households or those with supplementary occupations, both rural and urban. Here 'domestic' labour can stretch into arti-sanal work, home-based production, informal sector activities inclu-ding piece or 'out' work, or petty family enterprise. These are often excluded from the category of 'work'.[36] What is more, women's pre-dominance in home-based production, especially in the lowest in-come categories, strengthens higher-caste ideologies, forms an elastic pool of labour regulated according to the needs of the market, preempts unionization and control of wage work, 'disguises' wage workers, cuts the capital investment of employers, and displays the "adaptive dexterity of capitalism".[37]

The withdrawal of women from waged agricultural work and other income-generating labour outside the home that accompa-nies improvement in a rural household's economic position in terms of access to land or income is a well-known phenomenon, increas-ingly though unevenly prevalent in north India,[38] and involves chan-ges in the organization of labour. The labour of women withdrawn from waged work is, like the labour of poor upper-caste women, dev-astatingly entrapped in a spatial logic of 'seclusion'. Waged labour is substituted with economic activities geared to household con-sumption ranging from animal husbandry, collection of fish, small game, wild fruit, firewood, cowdung, cattlefeed, maintenance of kitchen garden/orchard, work in household poultry/dairy, sewing, tailoring, weaving, and fetching water from afar. These activities, carried out in households with subsistence plots, rise systematically as landholding and access to resources and per capita expenditure increases; except for fuel foraging and fetching water they hardly exist in rural households without land and resources.[39] Beyond a point, improvement in resource position leads to women performing fewer of these tasks and concentrating on domestic labour alone.[40]

The reduction or elimination of better-off rural women's agricultural tasks is enabled not only by the existence of a large class of landless men and women whose labour is cheap enough to be available even to middle peasants, but also by 'traditions' of seclusion.[41]

Sole involvement in domestic labour is the preserve of affluent rural women, thereby altering at upper levels the economics and substantive labour *content* of spatial seclusion, without however altering the social signification of seclusion. Finer and more nuanced distinctions thus need to be made between the extended, inclusive definition of domestic labour in situations of subsistence and in situations of upward mobility. The reduced content, demarcated boundary, and narrower definition of domestic labour in this economic logic is either a class prerogative or, ironically, the product of poverty and landlessness, where however scarcity rather than ownership can again magnify the time and work involved.

Some implications of the 'seclusion' of women by withdrawal from waged labour have been noted: it operates as a strategy for further mobility, and meshes the removal of labouring women from the direct class dominance of larger landowners with the restrictive patriarchal norms of upper castes;[42] it reinforces customary, caste-linked forms of appropriating women's labour and shaping their entitlements;[43] and it functions to maintain a segregated labour market.[44]

There are also some other significant implications. At the social level where the withdrawal of rural women from wage labour is highest their overall labour also peaks (since family labour is more economical), an inverse correlation obtains between the use of female family labour and hired labour, and the *spatial* definition of women's labour becomes most acute. It is thus at this level that domestic labour becomes optimally coextensive with subsistence labour, petty commodity production, and other household production.

Since withdrawal of women from waged labour is partly a strategy of upward mobility, women's own stake in that mobility would seem to be an axis of their consent. Mobility, however, occurs at the cost of women's individuation. The *same* domestic and agricultural tasks performed for wages in relations of exchange by women from landless and assetless households as hired labour in affluent rural households, are performed unpaid by women withdrawn from waged work. Thus, for women, direct relations of exchange and access to the market economy are weakest at this upwardly mobile juncture of class formation, ensuring a reduction of their *individual* mobility: the same unpaid activities that generate a surplus and bring economic gain to the household function to reduce women's own access to cash incomes. Their underestimated productive work and devalued household labour guarantees family survival, enables men to be mobile and look for other cash incomes, and helps to create a process of male-controlled accumulation.[45] Rural women in crafts or other family enterprises too are consigned to traditional systems of customary exchange, while men tend to specialize in commercial operations.[46] The combined performance of domestic labour with agricultural, artisanal, or other labour within the household not only shapes a continuum between domestic and agricultural/other labour, but collapses the market into the 'non-market' sphere. Further, if there is an increasing correlation between cash income and 'rights' in a market economy, then women's own sense of rights, already tenuous and at the mercy of customary interpretation and enforcement, can become even more precarious.

Is it a coincidence that a conjuncture—where women have only 'recently' withdrawn from waged work and households are not yet able to hire others—should also be the fiercest space for establishing patriarchal arrangements and ideologies closer to those of the higher castes and classes? And that subsumption into the 'non-market' domain should be the *means* by which women are chained to family mobility? Women's 'domestic' labour even in this, its most 'inclusive' form, neither accumulates into capital, translates into right to property, nor allows access to cash incomes or the market; it enters *no* system of accounting. The extended definition of domestic labour enfolding subsistence, agricultural, and artisanal activity, embeds women's labour into the family economy and actively presses against their individuation. The preemption of any potential individual mobility for women can structure a contradiction between status aspirations and survival. It can also structure determinate social weaknesses, reducing women's ability to negotiate their position in the family, and opening women deprived of family support to destitution. The consequences are borne by women disgorged or cut off from the family unit—widowed, deserted, separated—who are forced to provide subsistence or earn a wage.

The combination of a devaluation of women's paid labour with a relatively higher social estimation of domestic, agricultural, or other labour when it is confined to the household, has become a justification for a series of 'new' patriarchal claims, a vector of class differentiation and aspirations, a means for making hierarchies within women's labour and deprivileging some women. And now that the World Bank and International Monetary Fund have put their seal of approval on women's unpaid domestic and subsistence labour as a vital and *elastic* resource, the spread of upper-caste domestic ideologies to new social locales will be sustained severally by the pervasive division of labour, the emergence of new classes, and the articulation of domestic and subsistence labour with the new economic order.[47]

However, there are a number of unanswered questions here regarding the household as a productive unit both in subsistence production for self-consumption, and in the small-producer economy where commodities are produced for either the informal sector or for sale. Does the formation of the household as productive unit in and of itself widen the definitions of domestic labour to include tasks related to cultivation and petty commodity production increasing both women's labour and dependence? Is the region-specific continuation and recurrent formation of households as productive units in combination with the commercialization of agriculture determining the *manner* of women's participation in surplus production, and providing a base for the reformulation of patriarchal arrangements? How is women's labour in the household as a productive unit affected by 'unmediated' and restricted monetization respectively?[48] Many more integrated accounts of the emergence of new classes, ongoing changes in the household as productive unit, and redistributions of waged and unwaged (domestic, household, subsistence) labour are needed to understand why hitherto upper-caste patriarchal ideologies are finding new social bases.

IV

Prostitutes belong to the class of Those Who Will Not Work.
Henry Mayhew, *London Labour and the London Poor* (1861)

Forms of depriveleging certain categories of women and organizing the unremunerated labour of women in the household together govern the type and conditions of their paid labour, differentiate the labour market, and thus enter the wider process of class differentiation. There is an interlock between familial and social patriarchal arrangements while gendering and abjection are structured into the processes which constitute a segmented workforce. This dual process connects women on the 'margins': working class, migrants both rural and tribal, unsupported widows, deserted or destitute women, and low-caste women in commensurate occupations.[49] Their relegation to specific kinds of work—in factories, mines, plantations, domestic service, construction, prostitution—that in turn reinforces their marginalization, is a recurring phenomenon. At another level, women hailing from *both* upper and lower strata can be crippled by higher-caste/class ideologies and unequal relations in households: many, unqualified and inexperienced, enter paid work in the worst possible conditions;[50] their choices are narrowed and determined both by enclosure within the family and ejection from it. If widowed, deserted, abducted, or outcasted, they are stigmatized in ways that undermine their bargaining capacity and ensure that they can do only 'unprotected' forms of work.[51] For instance, the depriveleging accompanying nineteenth-century upper-caste widowhood as well as the ideological construction of widows as a potential 'underclass', undoubtedly bore some relation to their availability for paid domestic service and prostitution while their under-classing was related to stepping 'below' or outside caste boundaries. In other words, familial relations and ideologies were, and are, part and parcel of the process of the production and reproduction of class differences.

This wider process of class differentiation mediating women's entry into, withdrawal, or prohibition from wage labour, is assisted by the consensual construction of binary oppositions between procreative and nonprocreative sexuality—good wives and 'others' such as widows or prostitutes—creating a hierarchical differentiation of labour and services. It is not that wives do not offer both, but that 'other' women provide a pool for the collective appropriation of labour and services wherein sexuality is unfenced by marriage. The same tasks that are taken for granted and invisible when done inside the home for the family, become the object of calumny when performed outside by poor and /or low-caste women in the public gaze. The othering and sexualization of women who worked outside the home was a marked feature both of class consolidation in nineteenth-century Britain and in the drawing of the boundaries of class difference in India, producing a series of ideological confluences between the two that opened women such as domestic servants and factory workers to near-consensual allegations of perennial promiscuity and sexual misconduct.[52] In Britain and Europe, where urbanization was perceived as undermining patriarchal authority especially for migrants, prostitution became a composite metaphor for the whole new regime of urbanism: mass production, commodification, disordered hierarchies and institutions, the rise of the masses.[53]

In nineteenth-century India, uneven and condensed class formation, self-definitions assisted by available earlier ideologies, combined with economic processes producing large numbers of 'in-between' women, threatened existing boundaries and also made it imperative to draw new lines determining which women were available to whom and which women were *not* available—especially since the clientele, both rural and urban, came from different classes. Anxieties were compounded by the caste/class/religious composition of prostitutes that ranged from low-caste women to upper-caste widows and daughters sold in distress sales, from indigent married women to women who had abandoned homes due to ill-treatment or polygamy.

Do poverty and indigence, putting as they do the strain of survival on both men and women, threaten to disrupt gender norms? And are stigmatizing, sexualizing, and othering ways of preempting any possible 're-ordering'? At any rate the sexualizing of other *women* enhances and legitimizes their sexual availability, while sexualization and othering of *men* on race, caste, or religious lines 'justifies' 'retaliatory' violence on them and their women. In other words, patriarchies produce a potentially hospitable space where racism, casteism, and communalism could meet.

To a large extent, 'prostitution' functioned as a class

ascription. Two essays on the practice by Ratnabali Chatterjee and Kokila Dang reveal that in both nineteenth-century Bengal and Awadh, prostitution was constructed in binary opposition to middle-class Hindu domesticity and married respectability.[54] Performers, religious mendicants, working-class women, domestic workers, agricultural labourers, women whose occupations straddled the town and village divide, were all labelled deviant. In Awadh, distinctions between prostitutes were made according to the class of their clientele; not only were many widows prostitutes but the line between prostitution and destitution was thin.

The location of prostitution in the political economy is marked by broad similarity and regional specificity. In Bengal, according to Chatterjee, it centred on surplus and cheapening of labour, widening class gaps in rural areas, peasant and artisan migration to urban areas where sufficient employment was unavailable, strong discrimination against working-class women, and women being forced to support themselves because of male death or desertion. According to Kokila Dang, prostitution, like other labour forms, was determined by specific crises in rural society and rural women's transactional relations with towns. In Awadh, widening social gaps, pressure on rural areas through famine, indebtedness, increase in rent and prices, accompanied by urbanization, new labour opportunities insufficient to make up for economic displacement, new demographic patterns consequent upon industrial development, made prostitution a recourse for women, among whom were milk sellers, coolies, and *pankha* pullers, who all had economic relations with cities.

It is possible to speculate that the *same* broad features of an uneven penetration of exchange relations in the transition to capitalism—nature of industrialization, massive displacement and destitution of artisans, commercialization of agriculture, increasing differentiation in the peasantry, pauperization of poorer peasantry and indebtedness leading to landlessness in some rural areas, urbanization and 'unskilled' rural to urban migration, emergence of employers and clientele from new urban and rural class formations—were contributing *both* to the growth of prostitution and of the domestic service sector. This process relocated many women and produced overlaps between them in terms of their vulnerability and the absence of familial protection as well as in their recourse to shifting or part-time occupations. The overlap between women in domestic service, wage labour, and prostitution intensified with ageing or penurious prostitutes taking to manual occupations including domestic service in their downward trajectories.[55]

The labour and production of women in the nineteenth century thus roughly settles into a quadrangular formation and inscribes a contrapuntal process which goes some way in explaining the 'sexualization' of the work of lower-class women outside the home. Though censuses did not classify it, there is sufficient evidence that lower-class women continued as before to perform domestic labour, undertake some form of household, artisanal, or agricultural production, and participate in corollary market-related activities.[56] They also continued to occupy a visible place in the bazaar economy as pedlars, hawkers, food vendors, sellers of vegetables, dairy products, baskets, or bangles. Some women from these sectors were being withdrawn from publicly visible forms of work under the imperatives of class and caste mobility, while others were subject to labour migration, pauperization, and proletarianization that pushed them into new forms of visibility in the emerging industrial sector or into occupations such as prostitution and domestic service. At the same time, house-bound women from relatively settled middle-class positions were making a conditional entry—under the shelter of education and male reformism—into altruistic and women-related professions or public activities percieved as coterminous with their domestic role.

This contrapuntal process made the disentangling of different types of female labour imperative to the formation and marking of class identities and aspirations at different points in the production process. The generation of punitive ideologies about the work of lower-class women outside the home served to 'morally' bifurcate the *same* economic process that was opening new avenues for middle-class women, leading to the withdrawal of women from better-off peasant and working-class families, and dispossessing many others. By classifying the different levels of entry for women into the labour market within a comparative schema, this moral bifurcation played a powerful and material role in the production of internalized limits and social stigmata. From the late nineteenth century, it restricted the avenues for waged work open to middle-class women by marking them as signs of low status, pauperization, or vice. The withdrawal of some women from work outside the home also functioned to denigrate those who could not withdraw, and made them more vulnerable to sexual abuse in the workplace. Since the differential entry of women into the labour market rested in part on spatial definitions of labour, it had to be accompanied by the gendering and reconfiguration of public/private and rural/urban space in line with emerging social relations. The growing entry of women into waged labour partly shifted the site of sexual use and exploitation into public, usually urban, spaces. These urban spaces had to be demarcated while others were set aside and sanitized for middle-class women. Some homes became workplaces with the expansion of the domestic service sector, some became workplaces of a different sort either with the withdrawal of women's labour from the public gaze or with the reorganization of middle-class households in keeping with new class and professional structures. That is, this process entailed wide-ranging reorganizations and shifts in forms of domestic labour in relation both to women's prohibition from wage labour *and* their entry into it. Finally, workplaces were sought to be 'privatized' for women who continued to perform agricultural labour.[57] We do not however know enough about these transitions. What was the process of reassembling domestic labour as many households became partially or fully delinked from production? How did earlier institutions for the regulation of labour fare? Were there changes within existing forms of entitlement and in the construction of domestic service?

At any rate, earlier and present constellations of domestic labour, familial inequalities, life-cycle variations in position in the family, deprivileging of many women, and the gendered constitution of the workforce do unsettle easy assumptions of class homogeneity and women's class location. I disagree, however, with arguments that represent women as a separate class and/or altogether negate women's own stake and class agency. If class is seen not as a fixity but as a process—changing, reforming, losing, recouping—and, at any given moment, an *uneven* crystallization of a number of power relations, then *within* this process the class location of women has been, and is, even more uneasy, fraught and unstable.

The servitude of love
and the science of denial

V   But the women's power is not for rule, not for battle,—and her
intellect is not for invention or creation, but for sweet ordering,
arrangement, and decision.

John Ruskin, *Of Queen's Gardens,* 1864

Seen from this perspective of labour and inequality, how
little nineteenth-century reform agendas took into account and how
much they suppressed. And how little the predominant historiographical narratives of nineteenth-century reformism—as a bold
rejection of patriarchal excesses by male reformers or as a series of
compromises in the face of 'orthodox' resistance—have set out to unpack them. In fact reform agendas, which were themselves part of the
process of class formation,[58] embedded in the materialities of both
patriarchal arrangements and different types of mobility, encoded
and effaced this other history. Unwilling to contest the gender-based
division of labour or marriage as an institution regulating it, and
faced with the difficulty of making domestic labour congruent with
emerging class formations, reform agendas foreclosed many possibilities for substantial social equality. They functioned to *school*
women as status markers and class agents—signifiers and producers
of class power through their manual or supervisory domestic labour—
and simultaneously to either make women subjects of destabilization
or to *maintain* the instability of their class location. A major social
function of many types of debate and reform became that of opposing
female individuation—in the interconnected arenas of labour power
and sexuality—by fixing women within conjugal, family, or caste
units often inflated as metaphoric correlates of the nation.

In part this structuring oscillation was a product of their own
uneven, contentious, overdetermined history. The double process in
which different social elements came together as classes in the

nineteenth century while local communities and castes became class stratified, made patriarchal as well as other types of consensus difficult and produced an inordinate degree of intra and cross-class ideological contest. Cross-class ideologies, practices, and affiliations (either those associated with prior cultural histories of languages, castes, religions, patriarchies, or those attached to the emergence of a centralized state and a nation), and intra-class or lateral conflicts (either based on political affinities, or related to and fought out on issues of caste, religion, women, property), not only existed in a dynamic relation but were written *into* this history of class formation.

The ideological definitions of public and private in the nineteenth century, in appropriative and contentious relation with liberal concepts, created a segmented world by restricting individual proprietorship and active citizenship. In practice even this sectoralization worked differentially, for though patriarchies overlapped in some ways, they were divided in terms of class and region, producing the intractable problem of desired and competing universalities each based on its own set of exclusions and hierarchies. Caste, with the different labour forms and patriarchal arrangements encoded in it, also continued to be a major impediment in the universalization of patriarchal practices though the boundaries of patriarchal ideologies were becoming more permeable. If individuation was inherently problematic it became more so in these historic crosshatches. While the possessive, proprietorial male operating in the public sphere—the cornerstone of capitalism and liberal thought[59]—was not fully in place, the woman as proprietor of either her own person or of property or indeed of her labour power, was (and is) even less so.

And yet an astonishing consensus on the continuation of women's domestic labour amongst reformers, that cut across denominational and political differences and included Deobandis, Christian missionaries, Arya Samajis, other Hindu revivalists, colonial administrators et al., emerged in both regional and pan-Indian middle-class formations straddling at least Bengal, Punjab, Maharashtra, Gujarat, and the Hindustani belt of Awadh and the North West Provinces. Conjugating domestic labour with class was both an explicit and a subliminal concern, fraught with the tension of re-entering existing practices into new evaluative systems and pulling back women's widening social agencies into normative modes. There were of course distinct registers among different constituents of the middle classes—merchants, landlords, rural rich, new professionals, and those with backgrounds in courtly service—who had no single relation to the means of production and differing capacities to exploit those below. There were gaps between individual locations or trajectories and the consciousness of an emerging class as well as between class practices and class aspirations. However, they not only shared prejudices and pedagogic desires but there was a broad structural and ideological similarity in *fixing* the *social relations* within which domestic labour was to be performed. This visible consensus around domestic labour that was being made available as a common ideal of family life, probably helped to bring about horizontal affiliations among middle classes with otherwise disparate origins, and inside which conflicts between class fractions predominated on other reformist issues. At one level, it seems to have created a patriarchal community of interests that compensated or substituted for the lack of a class consensus in other areas. At another level, women's unpaid labour played a formative role in the creation and disposition of the middle classes: it materially assisted in class formation.

A symbiotic, non-contradictory relation between the education of women and their domestic labour was beginning to be established in Bengal in the early decades of the century. An anonymous Calcutta School Book Society textbook in *khari boli* (*Strishiksha-vidhayak*, 1823) extrapolated women's aptitude for learning from their visible domestic skills and declared that education would result in better domestic labour. Education was however to be imparted in 'leisure' time and was not to be allowed to interfere with housework and husband service, *ghar ke kaaj kaam* and *swami seva.*[60] This stance prevailed in Bengal throughout the century and proliferated in the *mofussil* or small-town middle and upper caste/class intelligentsia of the Hindustani belt after the 1857 revolt—my primary source here. Dozens of textbooks, reformist tracts, treatises on women, and conduct books displayed a choric unity of brahmin and kayasth literati, Deobandi and Aligarhi reformers, petty government officials and diwans or sadar amins of princely states, khatris and banias, missionaries and schoolmasters, merchants and landowners. Written and printed in Allahabad, Bareilly, Balrampur, Benares, Lucknow, Agra, Gaya, Mirzapur, Meerut, and Lalitpur, by writers who often lived in or came from other towns (Hamirpur, Hathras, Fatehgarh, Panipat, Fatehpur, Kanpur, Thana Bhawan—a qasbah in Muzaffarpur district) and villages (Lehra near Prayag), the textbooks were intended for town and village schools in princely estates (Kotah, Benares, Indore), zila schools, Farsi madrasas and government-aided girls' schools. A majority of the textbooks were published under British patronage and are explicitly loyalist. They address the constituencies they individually 'represented' as well as each other.

These textbooks and tracts, with their parallel structures and obvious interplay, function formally as a cluster. The authorial principle is scarcely primary—prescriptions have the air of insertion into a prior/ongoing and supraindividual discourse. They make available a connection between the material and discursive in the very intensities of the consensus and structures of anxiety they generate: pushing towards univocal interpretation, they are nevertheless jagged by the anxiety of at once contesting shastric and popular prohibitions on women's education, sketching domestic utopias to elicit consent for it, prefiguring and containing its disruptive effects. Thus counterpressures to literacy were built into the very semantic of educational reform. Education could neither be allowed to individuate women nor alienate them from manual labour. Just as superstitions made a causal connection between literacy and widowhood, so too the reading of prescription was believed to be directly causative: it would transform the behaviour of women. The texts posed as surrogate patriarchs whose tutelary powers could now combine with the new authority of print and schoolbook. They also partially aligned with colonial polity in the sense of easing male entry into the forms of waged work it had engendered. Domestic labour thus became a node of condensed articulation between new agential spaces in the economy and the amenities of domestic life.

Education was to produce proficient domestic labour (Pandit Ramaprasad Tiwari, *Sutaprabodh,* 1871; Pandit Sitaram, *Stri Updesh,* 1871; Maulana Ashraf 'Ali Thanawi, *Bihishti Zewar,* c 1903; Gauri Datta, *Devrani Jethani ki Kahani,* 1870; Christian Education Vernacular Society, *Ratnamala,* 1869),[61] as well as strengthen desired though somewhat inconsistent patriarchal ideals. But was domestic labour to be authorized by conjugality or by the extended family? Some opted for conjugality, even to the point of excusing inefficient housekeeping. In his retrospective defence of the ladies of Lucknow in pre-1857 Awadh, *Guzishta Lucknow* (1913–20), Abdul Halim Sharar wrote:

> The tradition of Lucknow women is to sacrifice everything for their husband. They consider their existence to be incorporated in his. ... They may not be so accomplished as some women elsewhere and may not be able to compare with them at housekeeping. They may be extravagant, wasteful and even self-indulgent, but they are unequalled in helping their husband and giving up their lives for him.[62]

Here an upper-class, ex-ruling group perspective seems to be struggling to come to terms with emerging middle-class norms. Who after all were these "women elsewhere" who were better housekeepers? Other writers opted for both: education combined with women's selfless domestic labour was to feed an older servicing ideal of *patiseva,* or a new model of companionate, even intimate, conjugal complementarity and, simultaneously, make women more respectful or obedient to the extended family (*Bihishti*; Pandit Ramkrishan, *Strishiksha,* 1871; Gokul Kayasth, *Vamavinod,* 1875; Munshi Ramlal, *Putrishikshopkari Granth,* 1872 and *Banitabuddhi-prakashini,* 1871; Bharatendu Harishchandra's journal *Balabodhini,* 1874).[63] Such obedience would also bind extended families together (*Banitabuddhi*; Manmatha Nath Dutt, *Heroines of Ind,* 1908).[64] Khwaja Altaf Husain 'Hali' recommended expert home management in *Majalis un-Nissa* (1874) to prevent in-laws from criticizing the natal family or alienating the husband's affections from the wife, and of course to make both families "happy".[65] Some texts simply set conjugality aside, made the daughter-in-law's subservience to her *entire* marital family mandatory, and attributed partitions of the joint family to female illiteracy (*Stri Updesh*; *Devrani*; Munshi Jivaram Kapur Khatri, *Stridharma Saar,* 1892).[66] Nuclearization threatened to destroy the family networks which provided assistance or security in times of need, and must have seemed especially perilous to those landed, commercial, and professional families who had joint holdings.

Conflating literacy and labour, textbooks and tracts routinely glued images of women's domestic labour, education, and 'virtue'. From the age of seven till and through marriage girls were to be first learners, then practitioners and teachers of housework (*Stri Updesh; Majalis; Bihishti; Putrishikshopkari; Banitabuddhi; Stri-shiksha*—Ramkrishan, the author of *Strishiksha*, was a sub-deputy inspector in pargana Fatehpur Sikri and Farah zila). Most texts detailed the nature and division of domestic labour, daily routines, and schedules, aligning them to male commercial and office time-tables. Time management was a common preoccupation and produced acute anxiety. Pandita Ramabai's treatise *Stree Dharma-Neeti* (1882), which also became a textbook in government-run and aided schools in Maharashtra, advocated a daily listing of tasks followed by assessment at bedtime.[67]

In *Banitabuddhi* by Munshi Ramlal (a senior teacher at Hamirpur zila school), the daughter of a respectable brahmin family, educated and tutored in housework, is married below her caste to the son of a rich sudra merchant. By encashing their superior caste status and representing her education as her dowry, her parents are able to avoid paying a large *dakshina,* or cash donation, which is beyond their means. The legitimation of a cross-caste marriage and the partial substitution of dowry by education were only possible because of the *guarantees* offered by this running compact between education and efficient domestic labour.

The daughter's education, however, conflicted directly with her labour. In a textbook addressed to boys and produced for madrasas under the Holkar government by the Hindi master of an Indore *pathshala*, an overly playful brother and sister make a compact of mutual 'reform': the brother will go to school and the sister will do the housework (Shambhulal Kalurama Sukla, *Hindi Pahila Pustak*, 1876).[68] 'Hali's *Majalis*, which won a prize of four hundred rupees and was adopted as a textbook for girls' schools in Punjab and United Provinces, condemned this labour and bondage of a daughter in her parents' home if it was at the expense of literacy and ignored her rights:

> She kneads the flour, cooks the bread, grinds the spices, puts pots on the fire, spins thread, gins cotton, minds her brothers and sisters, serves her parents. [Her parents] only fulfilled their minimum obligation to her. They taught her how to cook so they wouldn't have to hire a maid servant. They taught her how to sew

> so they would not have to give their sewing to a tailor. They
> thought, first of all, that [to teach her how to read and write] would
> do them no good, and secondly, if she were studying, who would
> do the housework. (pp. 37–38).

He himself, however, advocated that girls should begin to practise
cooking the entire meal from the age of eight![69]

If the labour of the outgoing daughter was sought to be
maximized before marriage, exogamic displacement and patrilocal
residence were the sources of maximizing the appropriation of the
incoming daughter-in-law's labour. In addition, the *bahu* or daughter-in-law was the site of an eventual transferral of domestic power
that was sought to be deferred for as long as possible. *Putrishikshopkari*
by the schoolmaster Ramlal was one of many tracts which, prescribing complete obedience to/dependence on husband and in-laws, also
explicitly upheld the familial hierarchy of labour among women and
the authority of the mother-in-law. In Vamsidhar's *Sutashikshavali*
(1865), a Reader for Female Schools in Agra, the *purukhin* was to
control the women, divide the food, and allocate the work among all
the women according to the age and rank or *maryada* of each; the
mother-in-law or *saas* was, however, advised in a small aside to treat
her daughter-in-law well.[70] Pandit Lakshmanprasad in *Saas Bahu ka
Kissa: Gyan Updesh* (1895) shows a direct physical confrontation between a *saas* and *bahu* over the apportioning of domestic labour: the
good *bahu* must to do all the work while the *saas* is urged to be gentler
in her teaching and supervision.[71] The set moves of provocation and
retaliation in women's antagonisms, especially those between the
bahu and her mother/sister-in-law, then, encode a long and contentious history of the distribution (not the necessity) of domestic labour.

Education was represented as the means for reforming
unsatisfactory wives and daughters-in-law, and one tract even forbade marriage for illiterate girls (*Putrishikshopkari*; Pandit Tarachand
Shastri, *Stridharma Sangreh*, 1868).[72] At the same time, the education of some women obviously threatened to undo and reassemble
the familial hierarchy of labour (including the dominance of the
mother-in-law) along lines of literacy or the 'leisure' time it required.
There are indications that uneducated women resisted this new and
unprecedented ground for the redivision of domestic work. Heavier

jobs such as drawing and fetching water as well as cooking were customarily given to younger women.[73] However, in the school-teacher Gauri Datta's *Devrani* (which got a hundred-rupee prize from the lieutenant governor), the mother-in-law allots *all* the heavy work to the illiterate older *bahu* or *jethani* who comes from a village: she milks, grinds, spins, processes fuel and flour, and stores up to twenty maunds of grain singlehandedly in a day. The urban, educated younger *bahu* or *devrani*, whom the *saas* favours, being untrained for heavy work, is given lighter, 'skilled' jobs such as cooking or embroidery. The *jethani* not only complains about unequal distribution of goods in the house, but taunts the *devrani* for her inability to do the heavy work.[74] The bania author also makes a ledger of the *labh* and *haani* (profit and loss) of domestic labour according to the literacy of its practitioners (pp. 4, 84). The villainized *jethani* is quarrelsome, dirty, lazy, unorganized, and a rotten cook who never gets the salt, water, or *rotis* right. A related and recurrent contradiction, then, in the normative drive of these narratives and tracts was the new pressure to constitute the illiterate woman as aberrant—underplaying or eliding the gruelling labour of uneducated women in the same households, denigrating it as 'unskilled', and uncomfortably blocking their ideological incorporation into new familial models.[75] How would the 'bad' woman's labour be recuperated?

The etiquettes of domestic labour included observation of festivals alongside socialization of children, service of menfolk, and management of money. So settled became this unwritten code that domestic labour was absorbed into the daily and seasonal frames of different *kulnitis* or family/caste practices related to birth, marriage, and death, cuisines, *len–den* transactions with kinsfolk, gifts to menials, religious rituals, fasts and festivals, giving to these, whether as continuations or revisions, a suprafamilial 'community' authority (*Stridharma Saar*; *Banitabuddhi*; *Sutaprabodh*; *Devrani*; Bhavani Devi, *Agrawal Riti Chandrika*, 1922).[76] Pandit Ramprasad Tiwari, author of *Sutaprabodh*, a textbook for girls' schools, and of *Ritiratnakar* (1872), explicitly set out to homogenize these customs.[77] Domestic labour could be, and was, elevated beyond duty to scholarly learning and scriptural status later by women too, as in a book on cooking and home remedies entitled *Grihini Kartavya Shastra* by Yashoda Devi, that formed part of a series called *Nari Kartavya Mala*.[78]

The theme of piety in and through domestic labour was com-monly iterated across religions. The Kanpur-based Deobandi teacher and reformer Thanawi came from a section of the service gentry known for Islamic learning and drew on earlier religious and refor-mist tracts; he interpreted a *hadis* as follows:

> The rank a man attains by extraordinary acts is attained by a woman through obeying her husband, looking after her children and managing the house. (*Bihishti*, p. 310)

In Thanawi's discourse, as in that of the more liberal Aligarhi reformism of 'Hali', stitching and learning to cook were interleaved with studying the Koran, prayers, calligraphy, Persian, and arith-metic in the routine of girls, while in the latter's *Majalis* hard work was said to banish idling, complaining, abusing, quarrelling. In *Domestic Manners and Customs of the Hindoos* (1860), Babu Ishuree Das, a "Native Christian" of Fatehgarh, enumerating the heavy dom-estic chores of Hindu women, added that women continued to do these jobs even after they had been educated and converted: household duties were "very proper and scriptural", the Christian scriptures enjoined housework along with "submission and obedience to hus-bands" (pp. 173–74). In sum there was to be no escape from house-work for 'Hindu' women: conversion came enfolded in domesticity! Christian missionaries too identified household cleanliness with moral merit and religious knowledge, and believed that learning housewifery and home-based crafts would bring native women nearer god. The missionary text *Ratnamala*, though it was addressed to all women, in fact explicitly located the meeting-point between biblical and upper-caste norms. Praising both Bible and Dharmashastras, it offered the *pativrata* (devoted wife) as an ideal to Arya women, and the Bible as exhorting respect and obedience to husbands; the good *grihasthin* or housewife's daily routine only had to punctuate dom-estic work with prayer (pp. 145, 204).

The 'Hindu' model was bolstered by the Shastras, as for instance in *Stri Updesh* by Pandit Sitaram, a master in zila school, Lalitpur. In fact the ventriloquist male reformer frequently spoke through the 'voice' of the Shastras. Thus, Pandit Tarachand Shastri's *Stridharma Sangreh*, authorized by the Rohilkhand Literary Society (which had both Hindu and Muslim members), simply *substituted* housework for religious observance: women cannot take to *sannyas* (an ascetic life) or even indulge in morning prayers because that would interfere with *swami seva* and conflict with the husband's breakfast, while literacy in the Vedas and Shastras would produce better domestic labour, that is, knowledge of medicines, cooking, and rituals (pp. 11–12). Munshi Jivaram Kapur Khatri, whose manual was authorized by the Khatri Hitkari Sabha of Agra, cited the Shastras as forbidding *any* independent or *swatantra* action by women (*Stridharma Saar*, p. 28). The reformist trope of continuity with the past in fact encoded a desired continuity of the sexual and caste-based division of labour. Significantly, the Shastras, on which they drew, had also tried to ensure through facilitating ideologies that women's labour (productive, reproductive, domestic) need never be withdrawn from the household at any age, primarily by withholding the options of renunciation, mendicancy, or asceticism, by expecting a woman to lead her religious life within the householder stage and by eternizing marriage for the widow.[79] The *Manusmriti* had also placed the service of sudras to upper castes under the regulatory regimen of religious duty or *dharma,* and made it equally difficult for them to withdraw their labour.

The domestic service enjoined in the Shastras and Smritis sat comfortably with emergent bourgeois ideologies. The citation of *Manusmriti* with some of its proscriptions urged quite literally, in contexts of both upper-class consolidation and upward mobility, *resacralised* domestic labour as *dharma* (a process to which waged labour could not be subjected), and turned the *Manusmriti* into a primer for embourgeoisement and class management. A product of early class stratification, compressing domestic, ritual and reproductive labour into salvation for women, debarring them from most other religious activities, instituting controls at a time when practices were probably more flexible, the *Manusmriti* was later selectively universalized for castes and regions beyond its own intentionality and historical spread by colonial law. By now it was a heavily mediated, semantically overladen text that evoked different contemporary structures of authority. Its use represents a particular articulation of conservative versions of western organicism, brahminical orthodoxy, the refiguring of upwardly mobile middle castes into a new class configuration, and the combined weight of ancient prescription and colonial power. Like nineteenth-century scripturalism as a whole, the fixation on the *Manusmriti* can partly be seen as an attempt to produce a text-based patriarchal consensus by groups beginning to assert a 'Hindu' identity. It could function at once as a source of self-identification and share in the colonial authority that had enshrined it as a supposedly encompassing and continuous set of 'holy' laws. Not surprisingly, then, it became an ur-text invoked by ideologically disparate reformers (such as the Arya Samaji Dayanand) throughout the colonial period.

At a time when male provision through cash incomes or wage earning was coming to be associated with masculinity and more direct control of the wife's labour (and the surplus value it produced) by the husband, the *Manusmriti's* prescriptive–injunctive model of manhood could be usefully recycled. Obsessed with male-controlled, upper-caste women, it had enjoined submission to the will of the husband, classified personal service to the husband as service in the religious sphere, exhorted husbands of all castes to keep their wives under "lawful restrictions" and preserve them from vice.[80] What is more, the text had privileged procreation and, tacitly, the labour that this included.[81] Brahmin, khatri, bania and kayasth tracts reiterated its ideology of *pati-parameshwar*, the husband as *devta* or deity, submission to a husband of *any* kind, the virtues of serving him, *pati ki chakri*, and made housework and service of this husband-god directly equivalent to prayer (*Stridharma Saar*, p. 20; *Stridharma Sangreh*, p. 63; *Stri Updesh*, p. 16; *Vamavinod*; Hariharhiralal, *Strivichar*, 1876).[82] Harishchandra's *Balabodhini,* which paraded exemplary *pativratas*, ancient and contemporary, and claimed that the highest *dharma* for the wife according to the Shastras was her husband, reproduced the *Manusmriti's* model of obedient, worshipful wives and even praised widow immolation.[83] In fact, the tension within the *Manusmriti* between conjugality and repression, between giving women a rightful 'place' within its patriarchal schema and outright misogyny, was often resolved in these tracts into a conjugality predicated *on* repression. Further, the *Manusmriti* also partially helped to gloss over one problem in printed prescription: its limited readership. Howsoever strategic the use of domestic labour to sanitize literacy may have been, its very correlation with literacy circumscribed the proliferation of new domestic ideologies to only the few who could afford education—while ancient law with its inbuilt concessions to custom could be manipulated into providing a universally applicable sanction.

Finally, the *Manusmriti* was especially useful in confirming specific regimens of labour. The woman had to always be "cheerful", clever in the "daily superintendence of domestic affairs", careful in cleaning her utensils, economical in expenditure, and occupied in the 'production' and nurture of children (5.150; 9.10–11, 27). Swami Dayanand Saraswati, who was a vehement proponent of patrilocality and the greatest possible geographical distance between the natal and the marital home, cited these passages to enjoin dextrous household management, thrift, cleanliness, pure and healthy cooking, and exacting "sufficient work from domestics and menials" (*Satyarth Prakash*, 1875).[84] This too was to be repeated verbatim in several tracts until the 1940s. Pandharinath Prabhu (*Hindu Social Organization*, 1940), retained *Manusmriti* as the primary text for management of household affairs, collection, and economic expenditure of the husband's wealth; and with the nonironic reflexivity characteristic of this popular genre—a compendium or compressed digest, embellished it with a copious collation from the Smritis and epics. From *Vyasa Smriti*: a daily itinerary conjoining caste purity, servant management, budgeting, and service. From the *Mahabharata*: Draupadi's feat of serving five husbands and exemplary domestic management that included manual labour, perfect cleanliness, offering religious oblations and worship, hospitality to guests, and *full* knowledge of the royal establishment. From Vatsyayana's *Kamasutra*: the wife's duty as manager of the household's work, arrangements, purchases, and as accountant of income and expenditure. From the *Sukraniti*: a blend of domestic routines and clock-time with the wife getting up before her husband, cleaning utensils, sweeping the home, paying respect to the elders, cooking and so on.[85]

Control of labour has been related to control of sexuality in other social formations.[86] Here too the abilities of domestic labour to restrain women from immoral pursuits or illicit sexual activity were valued. Domestic labour virtually had the purifying effects of ablution; the constant activity it required interleaved with scriptural reading was intended to prevent women from becoming vulnerable to bad company, save them "from a thousand vices" (*Majalis*, p. 77).

Sharar, with his disapproval of the courtesan culture of Lucknow, was more explicit. The 'morality' of Lakhnavi women deteriorated less than men precisely because male debauchery had intensified their household duties, curtailed their leisure, and saved them from male corruption (*Guzishta*, p. 192). The *Manusmriti* had offered domestic labour as a form of surveillance: wives could not be wholly restrained by "violent measures"; domestic and ritual labour—saving and spen-ding money, "purification and female duty", cooking and house-work—were expedient methods for the regulation of sexuality (9.10–11). Prabhu, who taught at Bombay University, approving entirely of this desire to keep women engaged in household affairs so that "they may not get idle moments for thinking of or doing any undesirable or shameful act", merely sociologized the genre and elevated the autho-rity of the 'modern pyschology' of the female hysteric above that of religious ritual. His source was Charles Cooley's *Social Organization*, which it seems had urged the value of routinized labour and claimed that its absence "among women of the richer classes is a chief cause of the restless, exacting, often hysterical spirit harassing to its owner and everyone else, which tends towards discontent, indiscretion and divorce" (*Hindu Social*, p. 238).

In subtle and unsubtle ways domestic work was resettled into the tighter upper-caste ideological mould of *pativrata dharma* and pulled into an emerging Hindu middle-class configuration. Redefining its content and ideological locales became part of the selective welding of emergent bourgeois models of the 'new' middle-class housewife with older forms of abjection. The way domestic labour was woven into daily routines of family service, bathing, prayer, enumerated proper tasks and correct times, placed it in structures of a functional religiosity and of worship in the Hindustani texts (*Strivichar, Balabodhini*), while the veiled, praying, nursing, labouring Hindu wife fetching water from the village well became a more *sentimental* icon with the Bengali *bhadralok* (as in *Heroines of Ind* by Manmatha Nath Dutt, rector at the Keshub Academy).

Domestic labour was of course defined in class differentiated ways. Moving downwards as it were, consumption, thrift, and the cultivation of home-based money-earning skills were the axes of differentiation. The translation of wealth into prescriptive and regu-

lated consumption patterns regarding food, money, clothes provided
full-time work for women in mercantile groups, as is evident in the
account of Bhavani Devi, the wife of a banker and zamindar (*Agrawal Riti*). Where financial security was assured, as among the mahajan women described in Harishchandra's *Balabodhini* (he was himself an unusually wealthy and aristocratic Agrawal bania), stitching
and embroidery accompanied by the display and distribution of these
articles indicated the status of the family and the 'leisure' of its
women. Here the substitution of women's labour for purchase of such
commodities could also function to blur status disparities and class
differences.

Thrift, manual and artisanal skills, especially stitching and
embroidery, in addition to housework, were enjoined for women from
upwardly mobile but financially less secure groups, as an insurance
for bad times even among the more secure, and as a means of survival
for widows (*Sutashikshavali*; Munshi Ahmad Husain, *Istri Updesh*,
1873).[87] In Gokul Kayasth's *Vamavinod*, the good wife had to help
to increase her husband's *sampatti* or property and wealth, as well as
learn to manage through her thrift in times of *vipatti* or adversity (pp.
192, 201). Thanawi recommends saving out of the housekeeping
money, while the good *bahu* in the bania family in *Devrani* saves a
hundred rupees out of her housekeeping money and loans it out on
interest. In 'Hali's *Majalis*, the mother believes that a woman should
not rely too heavily on a man's earning but should learn some skill
or profession; the English, she points out, are very considerate to their
wives, very powerful, yet no woman in England is without "a skill or
craft"—even Queen Victoria can draw pictures (p. 68). Her well-
trained daughter Zubaida marries a merchant, looks after his stores
of merchandise, and her careful management helps to repay the
family debt. ('Hali' himself moved from a clerical job to becoming
a tutor in the employ of a Delhi nawab to an editorial job for Punjab
Book Depot in Lahore.) In *Mir'at ul-Arus* (1869), Maulavi Nazir
Ahmad, who had a good government job but had, like 'Hali', wit-
nessed the decline of many families after the 1857 uprising, insisted
that girls had to learn to cook and sew since anyone could suffer
financial distress and a *hunar* or skill would help in times of misfortune.[88] In the schoolmaster Ramlal's *Banitabuddhi*, the daughter
of respectable but not rich brahmins is taught sewing and embroidery,

so that if ever in a state of poverty—*daridrata ki dasha*—she can be spared the ignominy of *dasi kaam*, that is, cooking, scouring, and grinding (p. 22). Ramlal opposed, however, any private loaning of money for interest by women as a gross sign of independence. At the bottom of the ladder, women seem to have been given more cash-earning responsibilities even when they were secluded or in purdah. For instance, education in cooking and housework and specific artisanal crafts such as dyeing cloth and wool was in the curriculum for village women in the *deshi pathshalas* of the family domains of the Maharaja of Benares (Munshi Gangaprasad, *Kumari Tattva-prakashika*, 1871).[89]

Husain's *Istri Updesh*, a textbook prepared on order of Pandit Gokul Chand for a Farsi madrasa, recommended the cultivation of skills in braid and lace making, embroidery, knitting, making small articles like drawstrings, handkerchiefs, caps, baskets, *gota, kinari, belboota, chikan, lace, moze dastaane, phita, roomal, topi, tokri banaana*, as safety nets for widows in times of need (p. 73). Thanawi, who was an advocate of strict seclusion for women and opposed to their westernization, also recommended manual and artisanal work for poor widows in *Bihishti Zewar*. He claimed that it was only the "ignorant people of Hindustan" who condemned manual work—the prophets and elders themselves had worked the land, ground flour, baked bread, engaged in trade or animal husbandry, dyed cloth, were carpenters, tailors, weavers, masons, ironsmiths, though these were not their main occupations. He provided detailed instruction in "light and easy jobs" through which women could make a living. Since he considered many of these enterprises useful for all women, his list not only gives some indication of extant household production—embroidery, knitting, sewing (on machines if possible), making soap, ink, medicines and toothpowder, dyeing, keeping poultry, painting, spinning, weaving, processing cotton, tobacco and rice, binding books, making handicrafts, rope, and edibles for sale, tinning utensils, printing cloth, trading in petty items, teaching girls (pp. 354–57)—but virtually suggests a means of extending domestic labour into home-based production for the new economy, as a respectable artisanal adjustment of possible indigence with the need for seclusion, the exigencies of the market, and the political fortunes of the petty gentry.[90] It is worth noting that Thanawi came from one of the epicentres of the rebellion, and many aristocratic women from the nawabi Lucknow court had indeed been forced to eke out a living as humble embroiderers after 1857.[91] Perhaps the seeds of a limited economic independence for women lay within this common fear of pauperization.

And perhaps it also heightened the dystopia of female idleness. Idleness was univocally condemned. There were frequent tirades against *alasi* (lazy) women (*Vamavinod*; *Mir'at*; *Stree Dharma-Neeti*; *Bihishti*; Henry Chavasse Pye and Raghunath Das, *Bharyahit*, 1883).[92] *Stridharma Saar*, in a diagnosis that was to be frequently repeated, described the Indian woman, *Bharat ki naari,* as 'fallen' because she was neglecting children and housework and in need of reform (p. 34). *Bharyahit* offered housework as the answer to both boredom and leisure; women who rose early would set an example for servants while idle women would have idle servants. In *Majalis* idleness has these and other consequences: houses fall into dirt and disrepair while servants become good-for-nothing and loot the house. The profound fear of female idleness then arose from the perception that it led to the loss of class markers—a well-maintained house, rigorously supervised servants, adequately socialized children—and created a perennial threat to property from servants.

VI

Political economy, this science of wealth, is therefore at the same time the science of denial, of starvation, of saving . . . of ascetism, and its true ideal is the ascetic but rapacious skinflint and the ascetic but productive slave. . . .

Karl Marx, *Economic and Philosophical Manuscripts*, 1844

The definition of thrift was not univocal. Waste was not consensually defined: status-related expenditure was a necessary expense for some while for others older definitions of status—customary gifts, large dowries, ostentatious expenditure—were being called into question and new ones were emerging. As yet thrift could both represent profound insecurities as well as denote a regularity of income and social relations within which saving could take place. It could be related to petty accumulation or signify orderliness in household management. However, it always combined the minimization of expenditure with the maximization of the unpaid labour, restraint, self-denial, and self-discipline of women.

Domestic ideologies set out to create a new middle-class woman whose labour supported men but whose own relation to the market as consumer (or as waged worker) had to be strictly regulated, even curtailed. These texts simultaneously indicate changes in concepts of consumption, the necessity for negotiating new market forms, and what were, at least experientially, unstable class positions. Consumption became, at once, an essential part of the domestic curriculum and a ground for misogyny. Women had to be schooled into patterns of skilful purchase: judge quality, estimate quantities, acquire techniques of daily shopping and seasonal bulk-buying when prices were down; the husband's labour lay in the toil of earning, the wife's in housework and judicious spending (*Stridharma Saar; Heroines; Majalis*). Accounts became the mirror of thrift. Women were to keep detailed accounts of income, expenditure, salaries, and payments for services, and not to spend money without consulting husbands (*Stree Dharma-Neeti; Bihishti*). In *Majalis*, a mother teaches her daughter intricate stratagems by which women in purdah could monitor cash purchases and outwit servants who "think it is their birthright to keep aside four annas out of every rupee":

> Now I am going to tell you how to get things from the bazaar day by day, so that those wretched people don't pilfer. . . . You should ask all those who come to the house from outside (the water carrier, the sweeper woman, the vegetable seller, the miller woman, the bangle seller) what the current market prices are. Ask them periodically and when you detect a discrepancy between the reported price and what you should have spent then chastise the person who did the shopping . . . fresh vegetables, meat, yoghurt, milk have to be bought on a daily basis. For those, it is not good always to send the same person. . . . Vary the person whom you send to do the shopping. That will keep the servants on their toes (pp. 71–72).

Paradoxically, even as more women were being trained to handle cash incomes, the activities of women from middle-caste, upwardly mobile, and emerging middle-class groups were being curtailed through prohibitions on going to places where commercial transaction took place such as bazaars or fairs, and on dealing with poor women—vendors, pedlars, hawkers—who made doorstep sales (*Stridharma Saar; Sutaprabodh; Mir'at; Devrani*). Were these too in part a way of reducing and controlling the sites of possible cash expenditure?

Strictures on women's overconsumption were fairly routine (*Strivichar; Istri Updesh; Stree Dharma-Neeti; Devrani; Banita-buddhi*). According to the missionary text *Ratnamala*, Arya women were to be neither greedy for jewels nor make any demands that their husbands could not afford to fulfil. For Thanawi, extravagance was not only a "sin" but reduced that capacity for fortitude which could withstand the inexorable process of levelling:

> Do not cultivate the habit of fine food and drink. The times do not always remain the same, at some point everyone has to suffer. (*Bihishti*, p. 352)

Too much expenditure on clothes or jewellery could lead a husband astray and even to taking bribes. But he did not give husbands the right to deprive their wives:

> A wife may take money secretly if her husband is a person of means and does not provide resources adequate for her expenses. It is not right, however, to take from him for foolish expenditures or for carrying out worldly customs. (*Bihishti*, p. 183)

Husains's *Istri Updesh*, however, excoriates wives who cheat their husbands. It condemns *chatorpan* (the mixture of pleasure, desire, excess in eating) on the ground that lack of greed helps women to adjust to poverty, protects them against future privation in the marital household. One young girl admonishes another: what would she do if she was married to a poor man, and even if she were to marry a rich one her husband's family would hate her for it and never let her eat her favourite foods! Ramlal's *Banitabuddhi* condemns the self-pleasuring nature, *chatora svabhav*, of women who obtain and eat choice foods—*manmaani vastu*—secretly (p. 44). Similarly, one of the sins of the wilful Akbari in *Mir'at* was buying ready-cooked snacks and sweets from the market instead of eating home-cooked food. In *Strivichar* by Hariharhiralal, a Bhatnagar kayasth and nazir or petty subcourt official in Meerut, *chatorpan* is said to be associated with the character and disposition or *svabhav* of prostitutes (presumably prone to gluttony and undeferred gratification), not with housewives or *grihi striyan* (p. 55). Kapur Khatri, perhaps with the extra vulnerability of merchants to financial ups and downs, extended the regulation of appetite to the whole family.[93] Good food was to be confined to festivals, *chatorpan* or the avid uncontrolled love of dainty foods ate into savings and capital and led a family into impoverishment and bankruptcy: *jiski jeebh chatori hoti hai uske ghar se daridra kabhi nahin jaate (Stridharma Saar*, p. 120). He did not however object to women acquiring jewellery since this was an investment that could be encashed in times of need. By and large the actual acquisitiveness of this class was in stark contrast to the altruism and self-privation required of its women.

Images of women as emblems of unmitigated, unearned consumption (eliding their labour) abound in Bengal and the Hindustani belt in the nineteenth century. These seem to have functioned at once as a latent critique of mercantile capitalism and as an adjustment to it.[94] The decrease of subsistence-related activities, household production and food processing in urban homes, and increased dependence on cash purchase of preprocessed staples, food, and other items may have had some relation to the attempt to restrain women's consumption. Rich and poor urban women, among whom were migrant rural women who had hitherto engaged in subsistence labour, were entering new logics of cash purchase and consumption. Women then had to be simultaneously turned into consumers, taught to handle cash incomes, and castigated for potential excesses, while one of the functions of domestic labour was to reduce cash outlays. The arrival of manufacture and cash markets had not however rendered housework superfluous. As in the early stages of industrialization in other countries, here too unremunerated domestic labour worked as a resource that bridged the gap between cash incomes and the actual labour value of household activities.[95] As is evident from the prescriptions, much of this labour in fact went into conserving food, clothes, and household items. It would appear that female consumption became an emotive issue as more households became dependent on *both* cash income and unpaid labour: if only women consumed less and laboured more then there would be no gap between income and family survival.

Perhaps it was not coincidental that domestic labour was

pulled into a discourse of health at this juncture. *Bharyahit*, a health manual, recommended exercise for women in ways that would not interfere with housework and seclusion—secluded women were advised to climb stairs twenty times a day, while housework, care of children, the old and the sick, supervision of servants were presented as forms of healthful activity. Housework produced a robust, energetic body, prevented insomnia, indigestion, and other illnesses (*Majalis*). The discourse of health also appeared among salaried, mercantile, and affluent landowning groups who had more access to food bought from the market, and food processing, especially grinding and husking grain, no longer *had* to be done at home. Good health and hard labour not only became synonymous with each other but with *grinding*:

> Women's most laborious work is that of husking and grinding grain . . . it is healthy work and produces a fine physical development in those accustomed to the excercise.[96]

Grinding was not pulled into this logic when the household economy was configured differently in relation to status concerns and the market. In the bania household described in *Devrani*, where male incomes come from shopkeeping and petty government service, the mother-in-law *costs* the market price of the illiterate *jethani's* grinding at two paisa a day, and the educated *devrani's* gold and silver braids, fringes, borders, and lace or *gota-kinari* work at eight annas a day; she settles for the higher market price and status-producing value of the latter and ignores the invigorating properties of the former (p. 41).[97] However, in *Bharyahit* health and labour melt down into acute class anxiety. This collaborative manual represents a colonial and princely service elite configuration: the diwan bahadur of Kotah state adapted Pye's *Advice to a Wife*, selecting what he considered to be useful and relevant. It was so popular that the twelfth edition of 1883 ran to one lakh and ten thousand. The manual fiercely chastizes *dhanwali alsi*, or rich idle women, for not lactating and attributes it to their bad habits. They are contrasted to poor women who make better mothers because they are in the habit of working hard—*kangaal striyon se jo balakon ki acchi raksha hoti hai, uska ek karan yeh bhi hai ki unko kaam bahut rahta hai* (p. 244)—and for the same reason lactate profusely even though they do not get enough to eat. The end result of the laziness of affluent women, unless they improved their habits, would be that poor women would have rosy, healthy, happy children, the rich would have to hire poor women as wet nurses, and would themselves be frightening creatures: diseased, yellow, emaciated, and dependent on physicians.

> *Kangalon ke nirog chhote mote gulab ke phul jaise hasmukh balak*
> *hone do aur apne dhanwalon ke rogi, sukhe, peele daravane stri*
> *purush dekho, jo bahudha vaidya ke hi adhin rahte hain.* (p. 245)

And, the lazy woman would not only get dyspepsia and apoplexy (*ajeen rog, murccha rog*), but her children would either fall ill or die (p. 246).

Ensuring the labour of women while restricting their consumption, replete with misogynies and practical consequences in unequal resource distribution in families, suggests not only an accommodative defiance of the market but also a perceived precariousness of class positions. This sense of precariousness appears most emphatically in what may crudely be called the 'proletarianization' or 'peasantization' of women. The healthy body of the *dhai* or wet nurse in *Bharyahit* is a product of having to work daily in order to eat:

> *Dhai aati kahan se hai? Kangalon mein se, jinko dhandhe ki kami*
> *nahin, nit uth pet ko kamaati hain aur isi se unke sharir acche rahte*
> *hain.* (p. 245)

Indigent women then possess the inherent virtue of hard work which affluent women would do well to copy. In *Majalis*, a mother tells her daughter to accustom herself to hard work as a natural way of being. Hard work will not only prepare her for the ups and downs of life but bring the same happiness that poor labouring women enjoy:

> The miller women who sit and grind all day, the water carriers who bring two big vessels of water from the well, the bangle sellers who use their eyes all day, the cowherds who make dung all day, and the peasants and labouring women who, in the extreme heat of May and June, spend the whole day cultivating and harvesting—if you could look into their hearts, you would find that they are happier than the grandest of queens and noblemen. (p. 75)

Axiomatically, "leisure and ease are illusory" while those "who work hard are happier than the rich" (pp. 76–77). In what approximates a proletarianization of domestic labour, women, even from land-owning families, are being asked to model themselves not on the aris-tocracy but on the classes whose labour they appropriate. This was only partly a metaphorical move; it had a material basis in so far as the physical labour involved in domestic tasks did cut across classes. All women could be practitioners of true poverty: through lack of greed and an abundance of labour. The logics of self-exploitation, so characteristic of the petit bourgeoisie, were thoroughly gendered.

The trope of the obedient wife in this literature then can be read as a signifier of that flexibility which a woman had to maintain in order to adapt to her class circumstance imposed by fluctuating fortunes or by marrying below—a constantly renewed ideological preparation for downward adjustment through curtailed consumption and images of proletarianization. Women *had* to be pliant in order to be content to make do with very little in times of need. This preoccupation, as I will show, also partly determined the respective location of the labour of the servant and the housewife.

There are many unanswered questions here: did the family become the primary unit of social mobility (overriding the caste group to some extent), and if so what kind of actual or definitional flexibility was sought? What precise changes occurred for women and in familial ties with the insertion of the family as a locus of consumption in the market economy, an insertion essential to the circulation of commodities under capitalism? Were there new possibilities in this transition to capitalism for the conversion of female labour into male wealth?

VII

The remnants of their [brahmins] food must be given to him [the sudra servant], as well as their old clothes, the refuse of their grain, and their old household furniture.

Manusmriti, 10.125

The question of hired domestic labour and techniques of supervision hinged both on class management (and exploitation) and on the management of anxieties about unstable class positions. New models of supervision were conjoined with literacy and in some of these texts conceived as essential to upward mobility. Education would help women in keeping accounts, preventing pilferage and cheating by servants (*Stri Updesh; Mir'at; Majalis*). Thanawi assured women that

> Account-keeping will also give you control over servants. If they take something, they cannot deny it. (*Bihishti*, p. 364)

At the same time, supervision was presented as *work* and designed to ensure that hiring servants would neither release housewives from domestic labour nor permit any abdication of household chores by them. It was *meant* to occupy women's time (*Bharyahit*).[98] And if the formidable list of tasks for close and detailed supervision presented in *Majalis* (and corroborated in *Mir'at* and *Bihishti*) is to be believed, then it did. The domestic calendar consists of tasks which were to be performed and overseen on an annual, seasonal, fortnightly, weekly, biweekly, daily, and even hourly basis:[99]

> From time to time you should go to the kitchen and taste the salt, or peel vegetables, or fry the spice or something. This too keeps the servants on their toes, so they will not get careless in their work, and they will cook better. You too will get into the habit of keeping track of things. (*Majalis*, p. 71)

Supervision entailed a considerable amount of measurement—itself a measure of 'distrust,' the daily negotiation of class conflict from 'above' and continuous subversion from 'below'. Since the family described in *Majalis* owned land, supplies of grain did not have to be purchased, but this grain along with all other produce and supplies had to be calculated, weighed, and allocated every day.[100] Clothes had to be counted and recounted for the washerwoman, and each item was to be examined before she took it— "so that if she brings it back torn, she can't claim it was already torn when she got it" (p. 73). Servants' consumption had to be rationed: "You should also send ordinary food out to the menservants and feed the maidservants inside" (p. 72). Old and torn clothes were to be set aside for them. The ability to exercise the class prerogatives of a land-owning family and call upon a large number of artisanal and menial services increased the supervision of the mistress, even as it decreased her manual labour.

Supervision and surveillance were a full-time job and could position the housewife as both manager and worker. From Sharar's *Guzishta*, it seems that in wealthy households which employed various types of maidservants to do all the work, women were 'released' for more status-producing activities: Lakhnavi women sewed, embroidered, ran and decorated the house, and of course supervised. Servants were to allow for a redistribution but not a withdrawal of their labour. Unsupervised servants only created filth and chaos (*Ritiratnakar*). The housewife's own labour was seen especially by middling groups as a safety net for economic fluctuations; she had to know everything so as not to be dependent on servants and in order to teach them (*Majalis; Bharyahit*). *Mir'at*, which became a government-recommended textbook, presented a list of jobs that women should do *even* when they had servants; women had to remain in the habit of doing domestic work so that they would always be prepared for the times when there were no servants. An early cookbook intended for all castes and classes of women, rural and urban, simultaneously addressed women who cooked and those who taught and supervised servants (Jaishankar, *Vyanjana Prakar*, 1867).[101] In *Bharyahit*, self-cooked food came in for high praise accompanied with examples of French and Swedish women.[102] For many the aim was to *divide* work between housewives and servants—houswives were still to cook, serve, stitch, care for children, now a rapidly expanding task that demanded constant vigilance. The price of inefficient mothering and lack of alertness could be death. *Banitabuddhi* carries an episode that excoriates both negligent mothers and lower-class ingratitude; a *pisanhari* employed to do the grinding repays the benevolence of a *seth* with theft and the murder of his grandchild. *Bharyahit* railed against the useless or *nikammi* housewife who left all the work to servants—it would surely make her ill and barren (pp. 79–80). But middle-class mahajan women without servants had to *appear* as if they left it to them: *Balabodhini* made a formidable list of dawn-till-early-morning tasks—dusting, making beds, cleaning the kitchen, scouring utensils, and so on, and pointed out that the advantage of doing the dirty jobs, *maile kuchaile kaam*, so early was that no one outside the family would find out whether or not a woman servant, *tahalni*, was employed by the household.[103] Understandably, then, sometimes there was a slippage between wife and servant. The good wife is as a servant in housework (*Stri Updesh*), while in a more euphemistic Bengal *bhadralok* account she is the mistress *and* "the servant of the house, who does all the work without being told" (*Heroines of Ind*, p. xi).

The models of supervision and class management occupied a spectrum ranging from 'feudal' or landowning patronage to colonial tutelage. The older models seem to have relied on paternalism and were barely concerned with reforming servants. The punitive underside of this paternalism can be glimpsed in the practices of physical punishment that were now being reordered. A textbook for a village girls' school in the family domains of the ruler of Benares, written by the principal sadar amin, Munshi Gangaprasad, provided a list of what were now regarded as public crimes *by* women so that women would not commit them in "ignorance". These included beating a maidservant suspected of theft to death and the "fire ordeal" of all servants by putting their hands in hot oil to find the thief, and give some indication of the aggression and punitive supervisory powers of upper-strata rural women (*Kumari*, pp. 31–32).

A more 'rational' paternalism was also emerging which did not condone such breakdowns of etiquette. Thanawi presumed that the class he addressed hired servants, but opposed tyrannical behaviour and overharsh or oppressive treatment, especially by the employers' children. The emphasis fell on guarding possessions so that occasions for theft and punishment could not arise (*Bihishti*, p. 342).[104] Thanawi occupied a middle-class configuration poised against the upper-class decadence of the nawabi elite as well as liberals and anglicization, though not against government service. He condemned work extracted by force and/or without fixed wages and the arbitrary terms of work imposed on menials (such as kahars) in traditional relations of clientage as a sin. He insisted that there should be no underpayment of labourers for services and wanted to rationalize expenses on servants by cutting out useless status-maintaining gifts to menials on customary and ritual occasions. These gifts, he felt, substituted for wages and even prevented the proper fixation of wages.

The new model of class management was unabashedly

reformist. The reform of middle-class women was predicated on the presumed, unquestioned labour of unreformable 'servants'. Shirking, lying, cheating, thieving, their profile still does not change, but they become the objects of reform by middle-class women within a colonial configuration centred on altruism in which British modes of domestic governance intersected with the Indian and class turned into caste and race.[105] *Mulsutra* (1823), a Hindi Spelling-Book written by Mrs Rowe of Digah and printed for the Calcutta Book Society, is a remarkable instance of the uncertainties of the incipient model of altruistic tutelage in the early decades of the century. Tiny vocabulary lessons leavened by injunctive anecdotes narrate sentimental stories of poor young girls: a blind *garib chokri* makes baskets day and night and donates the money she earns to missionaries for the education of *Hindu baba log*; another poor girl, hearing of the pitiable illiteracy of Hindu girls, makes hats for dolls and gives the money from their sale to missionaries to construct a school; one *choti ladki* saves an *adhela* (small copper coin) every week from her *majoori* (wages for manual labour) for the missionaries to educate the daughters of *Hindu log*, and once being unable to find work she delivers a basket of hand-picked potatoes instead; an eight-year-old daughter of indigent parents learns to stitch in order to make her weekly donation to this cause! [106] From the blanks in these anecdotes it would seem that these girls are neither 'Hindu' nor literate nor candidates for literacy; they are presented as already moral, selfless, self-punishing assistants of reformers, while missionaries become the conduit between the profit from the poor girls' labour and the education of 'Hindu' girls. The constituted altruism of the poor combines with the altruism of the missionaries; the unrelieved labour of the poor is intended to inspire Hindu girls and bears no relation to accumulation, mobility, prospect of future leisure, or change in caste hierarchies.

A Christian Vernacular Education Society textbook of 1875 shows a now settled understanding of the directionality and class location of tutelage and takes the labour of domestic servants for granted; they are the objects of surveillance, reform, and religious conversion by the British mistress of the home (*Lara Lari: Panch Jhagralu Striyon ki Katha*). Caste hierarchies now have a glutinous fixity even among servants—ayah, khansama (steward), bawarchi (cook), dhobi (washerman) and mihtar (sweeper). The mihtar is the only one for whom the sahib does not construct a good home and his children are singled out as dirty. The top-ranking ayah has a deep scorn for the mihtar and has even employed an old woman, a *budhiya*, to cook for her.[107] Low-caste servants are presented as quarrelsome and undeserving of their employers' charity. The dissension and physical violence between the ayah and the wives of the other servants begins because the ayah, a loyalist, sees herself as singled out for special benevolence by the sahib. Their conversion to amiability, though not literacy, is effected by the mistress through the curious expedient of making the ayah, who already believes herself to be highest in the pecking order, the sole personal object of her Christian reform. The khansama chooses to play 'native intermediary', independently punishes his 'quarrelsome' wife for not living up to the British ideal of a servant.

By the middle of the century, class and colonial processes had established the Victorian home as a tutelary–pedagogical complex centred on status, education, and control. They positioned women's class work in the management of servants and their 'influence' on those below as a 'spontaneous' yet passive counterpart of male political power.

> Unwittingly, you are exercising in your own families, a vast social and political power; you are educating the poor under you. . . . the female servants in your household, whom you have . . . instructed in their respective duties—whose manners you have softened—who have learned from you how to manage a household—who have caught up from you, insensibly, lessons of vast utility, lessons of order, lessons of the management of children . . . carry into a lower and very extended circle the influence of your teaching and training.[108]

Women's magazines rehearsed the 'servant problem' while child-rearing manuals carried instructions on how to guard the children from nannies, maids, and servants who were to be suspected, watched, and taught.[109] Though India was low on the list, from the 1860s, domestic service in the white settler colonies was recommended for single middle-class Englishwomen (as nannies or governesses) and for poor women (as maids) to save them from a life of vice.

Flora Annie Steele belonged to a colonial family and herself became an inspectress of female schools in Punjab and first woman member of the Punjabi Education Board.[110] She dedicated *The Complete Indian Housekeeper* (1888) to those "English Girls to whom Fate may assign the task of being Housemothers in our Eastern Empire". The book was intended as a practical guide for memsahibs who could not find "the familiar landmarks" of efficient housemothery, and ran into ten editions. The chapters on the duties of servants were issued sepa-rately in the form of pamplets in Urdu and Hindi and priced from one to two annas: if illiterate, servants were expected to get someone to read them aloud. A regional inventory of work and wages, the book also marks a shift from the old colonial style of domestic service that drew on Indian courtly models to a new bureaucratic pattern. The rules of empire were now routinely replicated and miniaturized in the home: servants had to wear uniforms, live only in allotted quarters which were regulated and inspected; servants caught lying had to henceforth produce a witness for the smallest detail; they had to be "caught and trained young" and none employed for "*too long*". What is more, this "skulking savage with a reed broom" or the infantilized "child in everything save age" was to be treated with "a system of rewards and punishments" and educated into "some sense of duty"; the most obstinate needed to be dosed with castor oil "on the ground that there must be some physical cause for inability to learn or remem-ber". Supervising women had to be exemplary in their own disci-pline, solve disputes, inspect and distribute stores daily, keep professional accounts (detailed *forms* were to be filled), and were advised to guard the *ghi*. In Steele's hierarchy low castes were pref-erable to Muslims because they were cleaner, while the ayah even if she was an untouchable, was to be given pride of place. However, along with finicky rules of cleanliness for servants who had to keep their "fingers" out of the food they cooked, she recommended the high-caste horror of contamination and purity–pollution taboos as having "hygienic benefits" that the "Westerns" might do well to "follow".[111]

Here, the very conditions of the subalternity of Victorian women were internalized and reproduced as the strategems of dominance, while higher-caste and class Indian women, themselves invested in the class relations of domestic labour, began to speak of the home as a "school" for servants and children in which the mistress and master were the principal teachers (Parvati Athawale, *Hindu Widow*, 1928).[112] Women had already been produced as 'classed' subjects by this discourse *before* they began to reproduce it. The altruistic missionary model of supervision is visible in Gokul Kayasth's *Vamavinod* (a textbook written on order of the loyalist, philanthropic Sri Digvijay Singh for his riyasat Balrampur, the largest estate in Awadh), and crystallizes in Tiwari's *Ritiratnakar*, where a low-caste woman servant is hinduized.[113] Ramabai's *Stree Dharma-Neeti*, largely used the voice bequeathed by male reformism, but also expressed some of the vulnerabilities, inconsistencies, and stresses of her insertion into this model of female tutelage. She attributes the behaviour of servants who are disobedient, make fun of the house-wife, or give her orders, to the fact that:

> The persons who perform lowly jobs are usually not from a good family and not deferential. Constant bad company makes their minds totally inferior. (p. 91)

Thus the improvement of servants and the inculcation of deference become the task of the mistress. However, the 'moderation' that Ramabai recommends to women is a compound of a class behaviour that encodes distance, decorum, distrust, and an acute fear of financial viccissitudes that may at *any* time *reverse* the class positions of mistress and servant.

> One should talk to servants in moderation, that is, only when necessary. One should never jest and joke with them, laugh without reason or discuss shameful things with them. Nor should one go to the other extreme and talk to them all the time with an unpleasant face, angrily, harshly, or as if giving orders .... If the servant commits an error, it should be explained to him properly and sweetly, with slight contempt. . . . One should never be arrogant and show them disrespect. By the grace of God, one is enjoying good days and is able to keep servants who are forced to serve others because they have fallen on bad days. But all days are not alike; it cannot be foretold who will acquire wealth and who will be in distress. It need not cause surprise if those who are

> one's servants today become wealthy, while one is visited by misfortune oneself and is compelled to serve them in order to earn a living. . . . Always show servants pity and compassion. Console them in their grief. When they are ill, nurse them as a mother nurses her children, with affection. . . . One should not trust servants fully and entrust everything to them. . . . One should treat servants affectionately, knowing that one's relationship with them is like that of a mother with her children. (p. 91)

The altruism of maternal tutelage and compassion, though essential to the production of the reformed servant, sat uneasily with this generic mistrust as well as with Ramabai's own class anxieties that had been heightened by her experience of poverty and widowhood.

Even as the *jajmani* system was breaking down with the growth of commercialization in rural areas, domestic ideologies were seeking to relocate its paternalism in the altruism of higher caste/class women and its deferential relations in domestic service. (*Jajmani* consisted of customary, even ritualized, 'exchange' of 'reciprocal' services and duties, or shares in the produce of the land, and was governed by caste functions and hereditary clientage.) How far the relation between employers and employed in the late nineteenth century was indeed paternalistic and/or familial and generational, and how far market-determined is unclear.[114] Thanawi's rationalizations and shift from the customary perquisites and relationships of *jajmani* to work for wages does suggest the ascendance of market-oriented relationships.[115] A few lower and intermediate castes were beginning to refuse to act as domestics and withdraw from customary forms of menial labour and *begar* (forced and often unpaid labour) as a corollary of either conversion or upward caste mobility through education or claims to higher ritual status. In 1872, Harishchandra's *Kavivachansudha*, satirizing a mehterani's ambition to study and give up sweeping, advised her to keep her place:

> Oh oh if people such as these take to reading and writing, who's going to clean the streets? The hapless good folk can't be expected to do this work.[116]

However, many of the women and men who migrated from rural areas recreated urban variants of the *jajmani* system.[117] Further, as the self-deprecating and ventriloquist discourse of the servant in *Ritiratnakar* sets out to enact, they may still have carried the internalized hierarchies and service patterns connected to *jajmani*: acceptance of constituted authority and marks of precedence, and direct appeal only to the employer's personal benevolence. Together these groups seem to have provided a new field for the suppressions and assertions of a colonially constituted altruism.

Privacy became a governing feature of the Victorian management of servants. In *The Gentlemen's House; or How to Plan English Residence, from the Parsonage to the Palace* (1864), Robert Kerr redefines upper-class homes in order to distinguish them from the homes of lower classes such as tradesmen and farmers, where employers and servants lived in close proximity. The house is separated into two departments that represent separate communities: Family and Servants. The "essential privacy" of the former was to be ensured by obscuring everything that passed on the other side of the "boundary". This was to be achieved through the proper location of kitchens, windows, and gardens (to prevent being overheard or seen unexpectedly and to block out unsightly labour), and also by separating entrances, sleeping-rooms, routes of "traffic" through staircases and corridors.[118] Servants had to be inaudible and invisible in inverse proportion to the tangibility of the services they rendered and their lives were to intersect with that of the family at no point other than service—that is, outside ritualized transactions. The deliberated spatial gap and the amount of privacy wrested *from* servants determined class status more than the possession of servants, while the cultivation of distance in a situation of physical proximity turned the home into a training ground for class relations.

This fraught colonial question of 'privacy' appeared in north-Indian reformist texts as a tension between supervision and sequestration: servants had to be prevented from *both* "loitering and listening" (*Majalis*, p. 70). However, it was not so much a recessive bourgeois privacy as family and class solidarity which was at stake in the common advice that servants must not be privy to family secrets: "never tell servants confidential things about your ... family members or malign them in front of servants" (*Stree Dharma-neeti*, p. 91). Girls had to be taught to "avoid fraternising with servants" and not be "informal with persons of low status" (*Majalis*, p. 49;

Bihishti, p. 352). Tutelage too demanded face-to-face relationships, as is evident in the colloquies between women and servants in *Ritiratnakar* and *Majalis*. Except in the case of low and 'polluting' castes, rules of proximity tended to be behavioural rather than spatial. In spatial terms the home was much more a training ground for caste relations.

The relation between caste and domestic service was spelled out by none as crudely as Swami Dayanand in *Satyarth Prakash*. This consisted of a partial reformulation of existing practices, many of which still prevail in north-Indian homes. He argued for *varna* classification by "merit" rather than by birth but, like the *Manusmriti*, still considered sudras (that is, the "ignorant") as naturally suited to manual labour and rendering service to upper castes (pp. 135, 155). He advised that upper castes could and should eat food cooked by sudras, because men and women of twice-born castes had better things to do than "cooking, cleaning and scouring utensils": they should be engaged in "teaching, conducting affairs of government, tending cattle, cultivating land and commercial enterprises" and other "higher virtues" (p. 288). Apastamba had authorized the service of sudra men and women to Arya families "to cook and do other menial work":

> But they should keep their person and clothes scrupulously clean. When cooking food at the houses of Aryas they should bandage their mouth to prevent salival particles and outbreaths from getting mixed up with food. They should shave and pare their nails every eight days, cook food after bathing, and eat after the Aryas have taken their food. (p. 285)

Dayanand not only 'feminized' sudras but clung to pollution categories. Food prepared in sudra homes or served in their vessels was polluted and could not be eaten by Aryas *except* in the "time of misfortune" (p. 284). The sudras he referred to were clean castes with whom restricted contact could be made. Where untouchables were concerned all talk of merit vanished and a naked biologism appeared. Food could not be taken from or prepared by castes such as sweepers, shoemakers, and chandals because

> the sperm and the ova produced in the bodies of a low caste man

and woman are not so pure and free from impurity as those of a brahmin and his wife's bodies which are nourished with the pure articles of food. For the body of a low caste is full of the atoms and stench and other noxious matter. But it is not so with the brahmins and other higher castes. (p. 287)

This biologistic discourse not only melted principles of purity and pollution into a modern scientistic discourse of hygiene, but also steered both into a vituperative communalism. The kitchen of the "Mahomedan", unlike the cowdung-purified kitchen of the Arya, was filled with

> scattered charcoal, ashes, fuel, broken earthen pots, unclean plates, bones, limbs, confusedly in all directions and flies are hovering in swarms. The place looks so bad and filthy that it is possible a gentleman may vomit who goes there to sit. (p. 286)

At bottom, Dayanand's loosening and reformulation of a brahminical taboo took place on pragmatic 'modern' grounds: what was the logic in preventing sudras from cooking food when sudras along with "shoemakers, sweepers, Mahomedans, Christians" had already "touched" or processed agricultural products such as cornflour, sugarcane, tubers, fruits, roots, and milk with unclean hands. And worse they had contaminated the food they processed with "drops of their sweat", "urine, filth, dung and dirt" and even faeces (p. 284).[119] Stronger taboos might involve starvation or even manual labour for the Aryas!

A cogent critique of caste did come from Phule in Maharashtra. He set out to build a community of labour among the toiling masses who worked on the land, and attempted to anchor his polemic against those who consumed the fruits of this labour in the caste and professional mobility already at work in the maratha–kunbi complex. He upgraded the work of sudra women alongside their husbands in the fields and contrasted it with the life of ease that brahmin women led. He did not of course include their housework in his category of labour:

> These brahmin women sleep on late in the morning, get up at leisure and do their hair; sweep and wash their houses and do a bit of cooking and washing, and then sit around all day listening to old

religious tales and puranas being read to them.[120]

However, the semantic adjacency between illiterate women, servants, low castes, and Muslims had already created a space in which gender, caste, and religious discrimination could flow into each other, meld into housework, infect daily labour, and insert women into multiple structures of inequality. Domestic labour, then, had become a politicized field in which its systematic routines, produced 'below' the level of self-conscious political discourse, were being forcefully articulated with emerging discourses of caste and communal difference.

In sum, domestic service became a site for 'othering' poor and low-caste women and men, a reformist field for the self-adjudication of patriarchies, and a way of bestowing a limited agency on better-off women. The employment and supervision of domestic servants carried a double entailment: as prescribed work and as a form of patriarchal surrogacy in which 'managing' women could replay the unequal, gendered relationships to which they were themselves subject. On one level, except at the uppermost end of the class scale, the managing woman was also a worker who along with servants provided the labour that maintained the home; though the one exploited the other, both were enmeshed in social divisions of labour and service. At another level, the downward relay of social divisions by managing women relied on a play of substitution, displacement, and identification: in the creation of a hierarchy of workers (the servant's labour ranked below their own); in the redistribution of work (the most heavy and menial tasks were shifted to servants); in the production of status (as through wives so through servants); in the recreation of hierarchies of consumption (through giving even less to 'others'); in making spatial distinctions and boundaries on class/caste lines (that mimicked the public/private boundaries which controlled their own lives); in maintaining paternalism and allied structures of deference; in tutelage and 'acculturation' of those below (including migrants from rural areas); and in structuring the labour of servants in ways that replicated their own (schooling into the routines, personal habits, expectations, and idiosyncratic requirements of particular households). If patriarchal bargains allowed women to assist in the achievement of status and exercise some power within the home, they did so at the cost of women consenting to remain subservient and unsullied by contact with the public domain. In return, as it were, all the marks of patriarchal *restriction* simply became the marks of caste and class power, and   the public mechanisms of class superiority were transformed into   domestic assertions.

VIII

Your mouths are full of talk about reform but who actually does anything? You hold these great meetings, you turn up to them in your fancy shawls and embroidered turbans, you go through a whole ton of *supari* nut, cartloads of betel, you hand out all sorts of garlands, you use up a tank full of rosewater, then you come home. And that's it. That's all you do.

Tarabai Shinde, Stree-Purush-Tulana, 1882

Reading this literature then must have entered the logics of both novelty and recognition. The meanings of these tracts and textbooks were produced within wider communicative systems that included social practices. Printed prescription was a recent and limited urban form; oral transmission was still the norm for rural, tribal, artisanal, and many urban households. Here, unlike print, the transmission of norms would have precise contextual frames, be less explicit, trickle through social practices mostly as either perceived regularities or interpersonal relationships, and as such would probably have more space for situational modifications and choices. Forms of women's sociability would accompany labour and even be linked to certain types of domestic work such as spinning or sewing. Further, oral transmission would take place not only in lived contexts of subordination but also of subversion and transgression.

The printed texts rely for their fitting reconstruction on evoking an extant oral, patriarchal commonsense, even as they extend its reach through a new technology of diffusion and give it the finality of the textbook. They carry the marks of oral culture (proverbs, stories, digressions, amateurish division of subject matter), confirm oral knowledge and work patterns, ratify what women should be, that is, indicate existing practices and name a desire. But what print reframes or suppresses are precisely the inconsistencies, questions, idiosyncrasies, ruptures, that surround and inhabit oral prescription. Significantly, the near-universal attempt of these texts to erase earlier (or at least existing) forms of women's sociability and reciprocity under the signs of idleness and gossip—characterized in *Devrani, Stridharma Saar, Majalis,* as superstitious, uneducated, uncivilized, ill-tempered, cavilling—stemmed from the fear of the 'corrupting' effects of women's conversations. *Banitabuddhi* recounts one of these abhorrent conversations in which women share their resistance to domestic labour and marital relationships: they tell each other how on the pretence of being ill they refused to do any housework or fetch water for their husbands, how they refused to eat until their demands were fulfilled, and how they were able to be disobedient because of support from their natal families. In fact the 'aberrant' practices condemned by prescription now open them to an 'unauthorized' reading as a threatening language of female secrets, vicarious pleasure and angry complaint, or as cathartic 'reverse' discourses. A song sung by women while filling water at the well characterizes men as lazy and profligate:

> *Ek sakhi kahti hai ki piya mera tambaku pita hai*
> *Kaam na kuch ghar ka para rahta sota hai.*
> *Dusri sakhi kahti hai ki piya hamara randibaaz*
> *Ghar ka maltal sab khokar rahe raat din randi saath.*
> (Said one woman to her friend: my husband smokes and drinks, does no work for the house and sleeps all the time. Said the second: my husband spends all his time with prostitutes and gives them everything we own.)[121]

These texts were then neither part of a primary or residual orality nor of high literacy, but of an intermediate orality that tos and fros with print, and characterized the uneven locations of a *mofussil* intelligentsia in the colonial economy. The printed was drawn from and re-entered orality, and this movement was formally encoded in the texts in the ubiquitous devices of dialogue and conversation.[122] Comprehension and retention depended on what Roger Chartier has called preknowledges. Again, the orality that print relied on had to varying degrees and effects itself interacted with earlier textual traditions. Customs too depended on the continuous renewal of oral traditions; thus the repetition, exhortation, and intertextuality of these printed tracts have both a purposiveness and a sociology. Perhaps the incontrovertible evidence of the reentry of print into oral transmission and as reconstituted practices can be found in the childhoods of north-Indian women of my generation who heard much of this from grandmothers and older women and watched some variant or other of these practices in our own homes. If these texts played out the anxieties of a *mofussil* intelligentsia, they were also spaces where the *moffusil* and the metropolitan converged.

The organizing social locales must have ranged from schools and neighbourhoods to homes, blurring the lines between school textbooks and popularly read books, between formal and private reading. But the excessive normativity and regularities of their content usually preclude the solitary reader or an 'individual' subjectivity. Thus the texts emphasize the sociability of reading as opposed to its 'privatization' precisely to the extent that they oppose the individuation of women. And, they wish to transform homes into schools, refine all relations between women as preceptorial, recast all their gatherings and conversations as hortatory and edifying, in *Ritiratnakar's* phrase, as *satsang*. Texts set up chains of female tutelage. A learned *vedvidushika* converses with a woman anxious to learn about the *dharma* of women; drawing heavily on the *Manusmriti*, she delivers shastric injunctions and emphasizes the procreative role of women (*Stridharma Sangreh*).[123] In what is only apparently a 'dialogue' between two schoolgoing girls, Deva lectures her good friend Sukhwanti who is not keen to study (*Istri Updesh: Do ladkiyon ki kahani*). The *bahu* in *Ritiratnakar* returns to her village after a long stay in Prayag and converses with her childhood friends, now grown women with married children, *about* her conversations with several women in Prayag, passing on the wisdom she has acquired there from a brahmin woman teacher, Shuklaniji. Her home in Prayag, under the auspices of Shuklaniji, was in fact a school—for herself, her women friends, and neighbours—while her village home becomes a school for adult women under her own auspices. In *Majalis*, where the title indicates assemblies of women, the text is structured around nine such conversations between middle-class women—relatives, friends, visitors—in Delhi, while the circulation of the mother's teachings to her daughter ends in Atiji, the old family retainer, who in turn recounts them to other women. In this case female and maternal tutelage is an effect of purdah, indeed a form engendered through the exigencies of female seclusion and internalization of the public/ private division of roles. In *Banitabuddhi*, the brahmin Kalawati, trained by her learned *mahapandita* and *pativrata* mother Lilawati (who also narrates edifying stories to her husband and neighbours), goes on to teach her daughter and women neighbours; this better-educated daughter then becomes the preceptor of her older sister-in-law and children.

The reconstitution of mothers as teachers here is significant precisely because it was *not* a regular feature of these texts. This seems to indicate a related set of anxieties about allowing maternal instruction to fully supplant male tutelage, the relevance or apposite-ness of mothers in a situation where the norms for women's obedience were being made afresh in a changing economy, and where education was diversifying and dispersing the sources of pedagogic, patriarchal authority into new terrains. Since the discourse of domestic labour was tied to the discourse of female literacy, there would be serious difficulties in recuperating the mother as a teacher. In a situation where few mothers were learned and most were not only illiterate but themselves the unnamed objects of prescription, could the teaching of domestic labour be left entirely to them? The absent mother may also have signified fears about the breakdown of generational transmission: she emblematizes precisely that *gap* in generational transmission which these texts seek to fill even as they set out, through a play of old (prescriptive) and new (curricular) forms of control, to ensure that a new generation of women will not be estranged by education.

Again, these texts were in fact partly heard and partly 'taught'. The overlap between oral and written cut against the pri-vatization of reading, made for a sociability composed of pre and post-textual oral formulations that framed the written. This empha-sis too is miniaturized in those texts that are structured around the device of 'conversation' between women. The device in fact not only encoded the simultaneity of two modes of circulation but condensed another newly emerging form of sociability. Women's reading com-munities were being formed for the first time. Here women are framed as reading in pairs, groups. Women read *for* other women. Their reading acquires a representative supraindividual quality of a special kind—that of a generic learner whose own teaching will replicate the male reformist model. Women are represented, seductively, as both subjects and sources of patriarchal authority. Women teaching other women, dialogues between women, also function as tropes for the desired sharing and proliferation of as yet circumscribed knowledge.

The use of women's voices 'feminized' the genre. The male projection of pedagogic women and women's consenting voices *preceded* any writing by women in this genre; in later decades it would either powerfully undercut the voices of dissenting women or shade into women's own consenting voices. Almost all the male-authored Hindustani tracts and textbooks I have discussed were dotted with women's voices agreeing (with shastric gurus or husband–teachers) or avowing that domestic labour was the precondition of the project of literacy. *Stri Updesh* stages a dialogue between a pandit and his *pativrata* wife anxious to know why women remain impure and ignorant while men become clever and learned: she consents to every prescription. The form of *Sutashikshavali* is a patriarchal conversation between Arundhati and the sage Vasistha; set up as a woman apprentice asking a learned man for moral instruction, *shiksha*, she seeks answers to questions on domestic and worldly behaviour and avidly asks for prescriptions for women.[124] Datta claims, on the title page, to have written *Devrani* with the approval, advice, assent —*sammati*—of an unnamed educated woman. Harishchandra's eponymous Balabodhini introduces herself in the first issue of the journal as the newly born sister and friend, *bahen*, *sakhi*, of her women readers. In *Putrishikshopkari* and *Ritiratnakar* too, the chief propagators of domestic ideology are the voices of women. In exceptional cases, the voice of a girl (Yamuna, in dialogue with her brother Vinayak) could be used to agree to recieving *no* education and to confine herself to domestic labour (*Hindi Pahila Pustak*).

The youthful voices of consenting women setting the terms of their eligibility not only make a bridge between the new education (and companionate ideology) and selected prescriptive, textual norms, but become an intermediate zone where volatile social changes are domesticated and naturalized even as patriarchies are refurbished. The woman's voice, here a sign of the *limits* of female agency, seems to be a structural necessity of these texts and was clearly becoming indispensable for the reproduction of patriarchies.

IX

The woman who knows and fulfils her duty realises her dignified status. She is the queen, not the slave, of the household over which she presides.

M.K. Gandhi, *Harijan*, 1934

It was not till Gandhi that this freshly essentialized constellation of domestic labour was taken altogether out of the discourse of literacy. Domestic work was simplified, dignified, revalued, loosened from overt class differentiation, split off from supervisory functions, caste and communal hierarchies, and entered into a nationalist configuration articulating women's labour and consumption with swadeshi, where it acquired the potential of becoming the substratum of a cross-class patriarchy that could incorporate poor, rural, illiterate, and fallen women. Not only did Gandhi fail to challenge the division of labour, but he was also deeply implicated in the wider class logics that governed women's work.

Handspun *khadi* signified resistance to colonial rule and an identification (which urban women had to seek) with the great rural tradition.[125] The spinning of *khadi*, a subsistence activity for rural women under the auspices of swadeshi, became the means for economic and moral regeneration. What was a way of earning a livelihood for poor women became a "duty" and *dharma* for women of the upper strata.[126] Through the *charkha* and swadeshi, the upper-class woman as consumer (who would boycott foreign cloth) and the poor woman as producer were brought into the same fold.

This wide sweep was possible not only because spinning could cut across castes and religions, but also because the properties of spinning and *khadi*—prolonged labour, nonviolence, sacrifice, chastity—were identical in their characteristics to those that Gandhi ascribed to womanhood. Spinning, "essentially a slow and comparatively silent process" was naturally coextensive with woman, "the embodiment of sacrifice and therefore, non-violence" as well as with "her occupations" which were and must be "more conducive to peace than to war".[127] More significantly, though men were advised to spin, women had "a natural advantage over men" in spinning because it was "part of an essential division of labour" that had existed from "the beginning of time".[128] Finally, as an activity that could

rehabilitate or purify prostitutes and keep rural women off the fields
and in the home, spinning was a form of *Ishwarbhakti* to be
accompanied by devotion:[129] "Each of you should spin for an hour
daily, singing devotional songs the while."[130] Equivalent to chastity,
it even carried undertones of surveillance. So if middle-class women
reformers wished to "protect the chastity" of their "poor sisters" they
must take a "prominent part" in the swadeshi campaign.[131]

The domestic sphere which Gandhi carved for his projected
nation-state was not only class differentiated but depended on a sharp
distinction between the political and the economic participation of
women in the public sphere. Like Ruskin, he located the mechanisms
of social order and integration inside the family, and saw it as the
stable pedagogical unit upon which state formations rested.[132] The
family was further remodelled as the micro-institution that would
both mediate and facilitate the political participation of women in
nationalist struggle even as it would make women economically
noncompetitive and unthreatening by ensuring that their primary
affiliation was to the home. In effect, his graft of bourgeois familial
ideology and extant patriarchal modes worked to restrict quite
severely the entry of women into wage work and production. For a
rural woman the home itself was to be the site of labour via *khadi*,
and it fell to her to 'familialize' rural India by folding what was in fact
her 'non-domestic' productive labour into the structures of domesticity. The working-class woman was simply asked to return to the
home, not only because it was not right for women to work in factories
for "an extra income of three or four rupees", that is, their wage was
supplementary, but also because:

> They have plenty of work in their own homes. They should
> attend to the bringing up of their children. They may give peace to
> the husband when he returns home tired, minister to him, soothe
> him if angry and do any work they can staying at home. It is not
> for our women to go out and work as men do. If we send them to
> the factories, who will look after our domestic and social affairs?
> If women go out to work, our social life will be ruined and moral
> standards will decline.[133]

The middle-class woman, already given the job of reform and
cultural diffusion which was in some sense continuous with her

domestic role, was also to be primarily a housewife. Thus, all "women in the new order will be part-time workers, their primary function being to look after the home".[134] On the one hand, he claimed that by and large only urban and high-caste women lacked "economic independence",[135] and said that "the husband's earnings are the joint property of husband and wife, as he makes money by her assistance, if only as a cook".[136] On the other hand, he made it clear that economic restriction was to be practised by *all* women as self-restriction in compliance with the sexual division of labour. "Equality of the sexes" simply "does not mean equality of occupations". No legal bars or laws discriminating against women in the job market were necessary because woman "instinctively recoils from a function that belongs to man".[137]

Gandhi's constitution of womanhood, at one level, provides a religio–national imperative for maintaining the rural household as a productive unit (in keeping with his antiindustrialization stance) and women inside a subsistence economy that could be doubly exploitative of their labour. At another level, it seeks simply to debar women who were caught halfway between the productive rural household and middle-class respectability from the new industrial sector. Gandhi virtually rehearsed the ideology of the 'family wage' (a wage high enough to permit male workers to withdraw their wives from paid work). This gained ground in the 1920s and prominence in the 1930s, and was able to cast men as proper breadwinners and women as natural dependents by resolutely ignoring the fact that the majority of women in the industrial labour force were neither embedded in families nor supplementary wage earners. Designed to preclude or push women out of waged work, it reinforced the social disadvantages of women workers.[138] Gandhi's pastoralization of working-class women's housework positioned them in a mode of passive benevolence, and extended to working-class men a middle-class ideology that linked masculinity to the man as *sole* wage earner.[139] The partial erosion of the household as a productive unit, and the substitution of factory for home-made goods which made the working classes economically less independent, also made it easier to forge a cross-class ideology and draw working-class women into the same fold as middle-class women.

Gandhi's advice has to be understood in a context where the

proportion of women had increased in agriculture but declined in industry, partly due to retrenchment. In addition, many of the women pushed out of villages due to immiserization or out of agricultural, traditional, and artisanal occupations (including spinning) in the preceding decades had been proletarianized.[140] They were facing the hostility towards women working outside the home engendered precisely by ideologies related to female sequestration, a hostility that governed and even inhibited their entry into the labour market. Could 'voluntary' acceptance of patriarchal codes in the Gandhian sense, then, have the same meaning for women of different classes subjected to different patriarchal arrangements and with differing stakes in the reproduction of class identity? How would it profit working-class women to be ministering angels rather than work for wages? Gandhi's solution of keeping women at home scants inegalitarian class, gender, and familial relations in favour of a familiar form of ideological control. He virtually replicates Ruskin's elevation of the existing division of labour and echoes his language of duty, queenliness, domestic bliss, and complementarity: "It is a woman's right to rule the home. Man is master outside."[141] Was the rural household, structured around the productive work of women, a 'private' sphere over which women could 'rule'? And what indeed would this rule consist of—if it was over production (*khadi*) and curtailing consumption alone, but not over sale and distribution? As home-based out-work, would not *khadi* become a means of restricting women's direct relations to exchange, blurring definitions of work and remuneration, and sustaining the biases of the labour market, all so conducive to the seclusion of women in upwardly mobile sections? In effect what would the 'restoration' of spinning mean within the new framework of accelerating rural class formation, consequent de-peasantization, changing urban class divisions, and the gender segmentation of the labour market?

Given such a context of continuous class formation in which not only had differentiation in the peasantry deepened, but mobility frequently took the shape of claims for higher status by a wide range of caste groups—claims that were accelerating and intensifying with the censuses, the question of *who* Gandhi represented on the issue of women's paid and unpaid work has to be recognized and delinked from both a sentimental populism and his own antiwesternism.

Structured on a negotiation of emergent bourgeois patriarchies, Gandhi's version was closer to the patriarchal resolutions being sought by upwardly mobile sections than to poor peasants or landless labourers. At another level, keeping women at home was an economic solution that interlocked *both* with intermediate caste models of upward mobility and with the upper and middle caste–class insignia of long-held or achieved status—withholding or withdrawing women from waged work, curtailing their access to the market, and imposing restrictions even when they were central to agricultural production. In both cases it ensured a captive unremunerated domestic labour force. In restricting women's entry to the economic domain, then, he was able to address the 'needs' of better-off peasant, landowning, mercantile, and professional groups, paradoxically locking a model of antiindustrialism with the patriarchal logics of class differentiation and upward mobility.

There are interesting indications of how swadeshi and self-denial could simply be reabsorbed into the existing etiquettes of hinduized domestic labour, proscription of female leisure, and restriction of women's consumption. In a collection of verses set to music, edited by Kapurchandji Jain (*Nari Ratna Singar*, 1931),[142] a *bhajan* addressed to women enumerates the benefits of *charkha*: national reform, accumulation of wealth, protection of female chastity, and instruction in wifely duties.

> *Charkha striyon ki laaj bachayega*
> *Charkha pativrat dharma sikhlayega*

One *ghazal* entitled "*Fashion ki Ninda*" opposes *charkha* to *shringar*, ornamental toilettes, satin and London velvet. Women urge husbands to wear swadeshi in another. An adjacent *updesh* to "Hindu" women exhorts complete obedience to husbands while another addressed to ignorant, *agyan,* women asks them in rapid succession to serve their marital family, abjure Pears soap, German combs, lavender, and read the *Gita*, then chastises them for not looking after the home efficiently. A gruelling daily itinerary is itemized, not very different from that in *Balabodhini*:[143] wake, wake the husband, excrete, clean the wheat, heat the water, purify the utensils for *yagna*, wash the kitchen utensils, layer the courtyard with dung, bathe, pray, perform the *havan* (fire ritual), wash and feed the children, chop the vegetables, grind the spices, cook with love, serve and feed the entire family with respect, eat last, dry the wet clothes. Over and above this, women were to spend spare time in studying, teaching children, keeping household accounts, and spend two hours on stitching and painting. Swadeshi, and even *charkha*, identified as a weapon to defeat the British, become legitimating patriotic *additions* to mandatory daily labour. *Mahila Gitanjali* (1930), edited by Sushiladevi, a commander of the Mahila Hindustani Sewadal in Muradabad, also virtually reconstitutes women as home-based artisans.[144] Women promise to spin *after* they have finished their housework in a *dadra*: *Sab kaam kaaj karke mein charkha chalaungi*. A *geet* and a *dadra* identify Indian products, swadeshi, with the auspicious married state, *suhaag*, and *videshi*, or non-Indian ones, with "fashion", ignorance, bothering the husband, and wasting money; they also insist on service of the husband, female learning, and hard work. Both collections resettle by now generic wifely voices into a nationalist mould. They project women as cajoling husbands to renounce foreign goods to protect the modesty and honour of their wives:

> *Mere swami vilayati na laya karo* (Nari Ratna)

> *Laaj angon ki mere bachao piya*
> *Kahi maano videshi na lao piya* (Mahila Gitanjali)

Both use the occasion to redefine women's leisure activity by proscribing storytelling, watching *nautanki* performances, gossiping, reading 'bad' books, and wasting time. Leisure time in effect becomes work time.

The promise and retreat of conjugality: widows and prostitutes

X   In the unknowable mystery of destiny [the wife] often becomes a
widow and widowhood is but another shade of Hindu marriage
because she believes marriage is for eternity.

Manmath Nath Dutt, Heroines of Ind

The logics of domestic labour underwrote the marked preoccupation with *eternizing* marriage in relation to wives, upper-caste
widows and prostitutes in most colonial reformism. 'Endangered religion' could be a canopy for perceived threats to patriarchal arrangements. For instance, the near-hysterical debates on the appropriate
age of consent for consummation of marriage (twelve years instead
of ten)[145]—in which a sacramental, nondissoluble marriage was pitted against a civil, contractual marriage, making the former homologous with a nationalism itself represented as non-contractual, and the
latter with the colonial state's sporadic and piecemeal appropriation
of the right to determine what constituted legal marriage—were in
part related to maintaining and reconstituting a private sphere of
non-alienated labour. This is evident from the fact that most reformers committed to delayed consummation did not oppose early,
'non-consensual' marriage.[146] The lines between 'reform' and 'orthodoxy' were blurred. Non-consensual marriage preserved natal and
marital family authority, and family authority was in part assembled through control of women's labour. Keeping marriage, ideologically, out of the market economy simultaneously defined women's
labour as outside the circuit of exchange. Higher-caste practices and
ideologies that negated women working outside the home not only
assisted this process but could only conditionally incorporate peasant, artisanal, tribal, low-caste, and other working women. In liberal
democratic discourse the private realm was to be freed from the illegitimate interference of the state; in India, the 'anticolonial' and

sacrosanct connotations given to the family after the 1857 revolt worked primarily as an alibi for patriarchal privileges. The family and non-contractual Hindu marriage were even represented not as institutions but as acts of faith and effects of the Hindu wife's labour and ideality (*Heroines of Ind*). The very attempt to 'free' *this* private realm from state intrusion, contradictorily, pressed further against the individuation of women, sharpening the coercive edges of some precapitalist patriarchal prescriptions and arrangements. 'Sacramental' marriage thus bound women more than men!

Even though as an object of reform, the 'Hindu widow' was usually posited as undifferentiated in terms of region, caste, and class, and derived from generalizing the situation of upper castes, widowhood proved the most difficult of patriarchal relations to consensualize through either earlier or emerging familial ideologies. By the turn of the century the widow occupied too many spaces in the ideological spectrum—the possible legatee to her husband's property; the desireless, ascetic, altruistic, and even self-immolating widow attached to a commensurate nation; the object of missionary conversion; the sexually debased agent or victim of predatory male (increasingly Muslim male) lust always at the brink of prostitution; the already degenerate corrupter of all unmarried and unwidowed women; and the criminal guilty of infanticide. But racked by desire, how could she provide an ideal of chastity for the wife? As a type of *strisvabhav*—a trope for unregulated sexuality—how could she be made to evoke womanly duty, *stridharma*? The epitome of upper-caste norms, she was at the same time a potential agent of 'dehinduization', prone to running away with low-caste or Muslim men. The 'widow' was a profoundly unstable signifier and barely adequate to the tasks she was given: namely, fixing domestic ideologies and policing caste, class, communal boundaries. She was simultaneously a victim of patriarchy, a transgressive agent requiring external regulation, and a desired exemplum of self-regulation!

This instability was related to, or at least significantly accompanied by, an enhanced mobility of her labour. The widow's labour could now be utilized unpaid in the home or in the service of the nation; unlike wives, except when deserted or ill-treated, many more widows, including brahmin ones, had entered the domestic service sector (often as cooks, a job in which belonging to an upper caste became an advantage) or the service market of prostitution. Many of these, marginalized by families, had been forced to migrate from villages or prised out of artisanal occupations, and some were later to cluster in industrial sectors such as the Calcutta jute mills.[147] In fact the voluble propagation by many male reformers of the 'eligibility' of higher-caste widows for 'respectable' professions such as teaching, was often no more than a means for preventing their entry into such 'degraded' and/or waged work.[148] However, whether in domestic service or pushed by near-destitution into the workforce or in altruistic, women-related professions, the venue for the higher-caste widow's labour had partly shifted outside the home.

The eternizing of marriage in the upper and middle-caste ideologies of widowhood were addressed as much to wives, and partially underwritten by similar anxieties about domestic labour. The *object* of much popular prescription was the production of the good widow: it centred on a repression of her needs, curtailment of her consumption, and maximization of her domestic work. Harihar-hiralal, a kayasth, advocated stringent proscription of gossip, merry-making, self-adornment (*shringar*), any food, drink, perfume or conversation that might kindle sexual desire (*kaam*), and prescribed a death-like life (*mritak samaan*) of piety and concentration on the dead husband (*Strivichar*, pp. 71–72, 77). Jivaram Kapur, a khatri, cited the *Manusmriti* as prescribing austerity and manual domestic labour for widows. He expressed with unusual clarity the underlying misogynist fear of the widow's unrestrained consumption, freedom from domestic labour, and social license, especially through gossip or institutionalized occasions such as the *syaapa* where women congregated for mourning:

> *Yeh nahin chaahiye ki pati ke marne se ghar ke kaam kaaj ki to fikr gayi aur dar kisi ka raha nahin, savere se dopahar tak to acche khane peene mein khoya aur dopahar baad chadar odhi aur syaapon ki sair ko, jahan gayi chaar baat jhoothi sacchi idhar ki udhar lagayi jodhi, do chaar se ladai kara shaam ko ghar aayi or apne kiye ki khushi manayi aur phir khoob tan kar khaa neend bhar soin, baras roz ek jagah baithne aur raat ke khaane ka badla chukaya, kahan ka pati aur kahan ka parmeshwar, uske jeeteji*

to vaise anand manaya aur marne par swatantrata ka sukh paya.
(*Stridharma Saar*, p. 27)

Even the resistance to widow remarriage among higher
castes in the nineteenth century could be recast as an issue about who
would have access to the widow's labour. However, neither of these
squared neatly with the total situation of the emerging middle classes.
Retaining control of women's labour after the marriage through
which it was recruited had ceased to exist materially, but was kept
alive symbolically, may have come into contradiction with the
financial difficulty of absorbing social dependencies within new
urban middle-class households, especially in families relying solely
on male wages. The pressure to marry widows stemmed from changes in urbanization, kinship, coresidential patterns, methods of surveillance, and notions of conjugality. This conflicted with other
imperatives that forbade widow remarriage—upper-caste hegemony
that also determined modes of upward mobility, the increasing
proscription of widow remarriage by non-brahmin lower and middle
castes, taboos on marriage to a non-virgin, the consolidation and
male control of property. Sanctifying marriage to ensure domestic
labour was also at odds with widow remarriage. The resulting range
of positions suggests both the conflicting pulls on the middle class
with its heterogenous origins, and the heterogeneity of 'family
arrangements' interacting with a new economy. In this context it is
significant that the first generation of north-Indian women reformers
who hesitated in proposing remarriage for widows, vehemently
opposed the remarriage of widowers and the expendability of women
that it implied. Perhaps this was a latent recognition of the fact that
serial marriage for widowed men often amounted to a form of labour
replacement.

But eternizing marriage or a constitutive address rhetori-
cally extending from widow to wife could not suppress the complex
relation of widowhood to conjugality, and the way its contradictions were structured by labour and inheritance. The *presence* of
wives and widows in the same household, all of whom would depend
on interpersonal relations to safeguard their customary rights,
threatened conjugality as a *practised relationship* and also made it
difficult to sustain emergent bourgeois companionate conjugal

models, especially since these models presumed a simple house-hold.[149] Nor was there a natural or easy 'fit' between the widow and emergent bourgeois ideologies centred on the wife. Indeed the domestic economy of unequal labour and consumption, and the fact that establishing an affective conjugality would marginalize all other women in the household, may have been among the forces arrayed against the new conjugal models and in favour of the more dispersed relationships of the extended family.

In part the widow's work was governed by the broader imperatives of domestic labour, and its heaviness stemmed from an exacerbation of the familiar logics of sexual surveillance, patrilocal residence, and enforced isolation from the natal family in the name of 'conjugality'. But whereas a wife gained some status in exchange for her labour, the higher-caste widow 'exchanged' her increased labour with a fall in status within the home. Her reconstitution as a source of servile, unpaid labour not only exposed the inequality among women in the family but also the way in which other women in the family could acquire a stake in maintaining this inequality: the deprivileging of the widow could after all entail a redistribution of domestic labour. Further, if the widow was the ideological lynchpin of eternized marriage, in practice she was also the one most likely to enter domestic labour into the logics of the market. In what was a profound historical irony, the widow was the first among higher castes to have a concrete cash value assigned to her domestic work.

The sexual and economic vulnerability as well as the labour of the upper-caste widow in late nineteenth-century Maharashtra are evident in the life-histories of the women who entered Pandita Ramabai's home for widows. Natal families either abandoned them to their fate or, like marital families, exploited their labour and cut their consumption. (Significantly, one of the targets of criticism against the Sharda Sadan was that Ramabai "spoilt her widows with a diet of milk and butter".)[150] Marital families frequently extracted labour from widows through physical violence, defrauded them, tried on occasion to sell them to pimps, and often farmed them out as cooks, situations in which they were vulnerable to both sexual threats and temptations. In one instance, an eleven-year-old brahmin widow worked eighteen hours a day on domestic jobs for the family, and as cook and general drudge at a hotel for Hindus run by her brother-in-law. In another, a vaishya widow who did menial work in many people's houses "fell into bad company" and tried to sell her daughter into prostitution. Others took to prostitution themselves.[151] A recent essay on Maharashtra shows that the widow's labour was performed without full belonging or proprietorship; though primary in her own perception, it was in 'return' for maintenance, supposedly a 'right'. Further, ideologies of asceticism and systems of purity–pollution interlocked with differential labour in the household and with depri-vation in terms of distribution. The widow constituted 'mobile' labour sent out to work in and manage different households either in support of young and sickly wives, to replace dead ones, or to run communal kitchens; households sometimes competed for her labour, and in one instance its withdrawal was acceptably compensated for with money by Ramabai.[152]

The marginal status of women in general, and more so of widows with their 'threatening' sexuality, thus not only bore an inverse relation to their labour output but determined their entitlements to consumption and both the conditions and supervision of their labour. The conditional maintenance of the upper-caste widow, the competition for her mobile labour, and the accepted compensation suggest not only forms of acknowledging and computing its value according to the cost of replacing her with hired domestic help, but also a continuum between unpaid domestic labour and hired domestic labour, with widows performing the one or the other, depending on whether they were 'maintained'. This blatant transformation of familial into menial relations suggests a latent, always possible slide in situations where the solid structuring of kin relations by status differences can simultaneously activate a process of the hollowing of affective claims.

Further, the structural location of the widow in propertied families could demystify and jeopardize conjugality both as a *joint material interest* and as an emergent *ideology* of companionate marriage and affective complementarity. Wherever the widow could not control her husband's property, the 'joint interests' of conjugality ceased on his death. Religious rationales, customary stigmata, and patriarchal ideologies could barely naturalize or compensate for their apparent ephemerality, or disguise the incompatibility of patrimonial succession with the joint interests of a conjugal couple.

The nineteenth-century upper-caste widow was such a contested figure partly because male death in the absence of well-defined and imple-mented rights laid bare the unwritten contractual nature of suppo-sedly non-contractual 'Hindu' marriage, its material under-pinnings in inequality and exploitation of labour, and the extent of women's vulnerability. Male death could be the paradoxical site where both women's consent and crimes against women were at their starkest—withdrawal of maintenance, dispossession, even immolation. Since the widow—as object of disinheritance, sexual abuse, and violation inside the family, and as subject to hard labour, poverty, or enforced vagrancy—often represented the miserliness and breakdowns of patriarchal, paternalistic protection, her life was bound to stand in uneasy relation with her symbolic constitution as the ultimate ratifier of the institution of sacramental marriage. Indeed she stood as the constantly suppressed challenge to *both* traditional family paternalism and the new companionate domestic ideal.

Women's inheritance bore an inverse relation to their labour, but nowhere as starkly as in the case of the upper-caste widow. In fact a revealing history of protracted struggle against even the widow's limited right to property, since the passing of the Hindu Widows' Remarriage Act in 1856 up till and after the passing of the Hindu Succession Act in 1956 which gave her full and absolute ownership, could be assembled. Apart from coercion, the modalities deployed in different regional practices included invalidating customs that sanctioned a lower or middle-caste widow's entitlement to property despite remarriage, foisting levirate remarriage, or using and bypassing state legislation to undercut her claims and chain her to the contingencies and whimsicalities of maintenance.[153] The controversy over Sarda's Bill (which was supported by many women's organizations) rehearsed the tensions between social practice and symbolic constitution. The Arya Samaji Rai Sahib Harbilas Sarda first introduced the Hindu Widows Right of Inheritance Bill in 1929, proposing to make widows who were debarred from parental property and often ill-treated because of the "disintegration" of the joint family in the colonial economy, the sole owners of their deceased husbands' personal property. The arguments against it were numerous: "grave disturbances would occur in Hindu society", life interest in property was preferred to absolute right, absolute right would deprive sons of property, widows were secluded and illiterate and incapable of managing property, their share should not equal that of the members of the late husband's family since a woman's, especially a widow's, requirements were less than a man's.

Sarda's bill projected the Hindu widow as first and foremost a wife and proprietor. For him the conjugal couple constituted "one entity" of which the wife was a half (*ardhangini*) and thus entitled to be a co-owner of her husband's property; whereas for those who either argued for a life interest or opposed it altogether, she was first and foremost a subsidiary member of a family, and her interests and needs were less than those of men, children, and the rest of her husband's family. Here, a notion of the companionate wife on quasi-bourgeois lines wrestles with a conception of the extended family as an emblem of 'precapitalist' harmony.[154] The model of the 'ascetic' widow was used in a pragmatic and exculpatory fashion: her *needs* were fewer, the family could not be blamed in giving her less. Ideologically, this pragmatism dovetails, indeed blends indistinguishably with a suspicious ease into the euphemism of nationalist constructs. For instance, Gandhi, though he put the widow more into a husband-centred model of companionate marriage rather than a family or caste-based one, argued for a *voluntary* instead of an enforced curtailment of needs: a model ascetic widow was above worldly comfort and sensual pleasure, offering labour to households and social service to the nation. In other words, he simply set aside all that governed (and demystified) widowhood—dispossession, curtailed consumption, and enforced labour. The spinning he recommended for widows in fact was already a compulsory part of their domestic drudgery.[155]

This pragmatism reaccents a curious preoccupation of nationalist thought: the extreme agency bestowed on the ideal widow. She is a product of pure volition, whether as a self-immolator or as an ascetic—a self-regulating woman in full control of her desires even in the absence of the direct patriarchal control of her husband. The voluntarism exists in proportionately inverse relation to the customary, collaborative, familial, and social control sought and exercised over her labour, sexuality, and property. Could she guarantee good motherhood, chastity, or asceticism without extra-familial institutional structures to support them?

Like the higher-caste widow, the prostitute, signifying the failures of familial protection, stood poised to demystify marriage and its ideologies. She too represented the potential slide from the domestic economy of labour to the market economy of labour, from customary structures of availability (in which the widow was embedded) to public availability through exchange. Her over-sexualization and villainization, usually in the name of reform, similarly deflected this set of relations by positing a voluntarist relation to familial ideology. If the good widow eternized marriage through voluntary self-restraint and curtailed consumption, marriage was withdrawn from the reach of even the 'good' prostitute who at heart subscribed to these values (a favoured narrative denouement).[156] The 'bad', licentious widow could, however, be exorcised or even granted social salvation through a stable narrative device that fused female volition, the ascetic Hindu widow, domestic service, and familial ideology within a constellation of upper-caste and bourgeois patriarchal norms.[157]

The ideological opposition between marriage and prostitution could also be seen as both springing from and attempting to blur the confluence and contradiction between these two different but related institutionalized grids for obtaining labour and services. Indeed moral disapproval of prostitutes seems designed to suppress its structural coordinates, while ideologies of women entering the profession for gratification of sexual desire were often explicitly intended to delink prostitution from labour.

The semantic adjacency of higher-caste widows, prostitutes, and domestic servants in reformist literature, then, was not gratuitous. It replicated the interconnected grids through which their labour was appropriated even as it sought to suppress or displace these. Curiously enough, these adjacencies could emerge in the very stringencies of prescription as it strung together the multiple duties of a wife. Brahmin-authored textbooks recommended that the good wife's *dharma* was to be as a servant—*dasi* or *cheri*—in work, as a mother at mealtimes, and as a prostitute or *kulta* in *prem riti* or love making, *rati mein veshya samaan* (*Stri Updesh*, p. 17; *Ritiratnakar*, p. 189; *Putrishikshopkari*, p. 31).

As prostitution came more explicitly to be a service determined by the labour market and the role of women in it, and acquired an increasingly emphatic location in the domain of exchange in the nineteenth century, the intensity of social opprobrium escalated with the extent of women's visible agency in exchange of services for money. Wealthier prostitutes in control of gifts/incomes raised the spectre of unfettered female individuation: possibilities of individual accumulation and upward mobility *not* subject to marriage or familial patriarchal control. The common figuration of the prostitute as an emblem of mercantile capitalism—a type of wilful self-commodification rather than a product of patriarchal arrangements—encoded the intense resentment of individual mobility through beauty or sexuality.

The borderline between domestic service, concubinage, and prostitution was also threatening: it signified a survival-oriented move by women into a cash nexus that exposed the limits of paternalist protection and also uncovered the other pretences of paternalism. Male employers could not only sexually exploit servants, but north-Indian households sometimes hired women servants for the sexual initiation of sons—a practice seldom acknowledged in print. The popular disapproval of the commodification of prostitution and the emphasis on the financial insecurity of prostitutes as compared to wives, simply erased the fact that marriage was no guarantee of maintenance, security, or inheritance, especially for secondary or informal wives. Both marriage and prostitution unilaterally guaranteed the availability of many women to one man, along a range of fluctuating monetary arrangements. The discourse of the good wife was not only fractured by a variety of practices, but wives, widows, domestic servants, and prostitutes were positioned in similar structures of abjection.

There was, then, a continuous and even threatening tension between conjugality—as a practised relationship, as a joint material interest, as an emergent ideology in the nineteenth century—and the extended, propertied household, producing a curious oscillation in emerging familial ideologies between the promise and retreat of conjugality. This may also have had some relation to uneven processes of capitalization that can simultaneously produce nuclearization of family forms and increase the utility of kinship links as a resource.[158]

As usual, a number of questions remain. Was the unprecedented obsession with the widow's chastity in urban discourses related to the loosening knot between productive labour and sexual surveillance, or even to the breakdown of earlier forms of surveillance? Which practices—the objects of prescription and spaces for negotiation—were threatened by the changing economy? Precisely how did nationalist projections of the ideal–typical family coincide and contradict with the variety of familial needs? Did the partial transition from customary to legal jurisdiction in the disposition of property and new forms of property ownership reduce the importance of kin, aggrandize the male proprietor/head of household, and produce more families, simple or extended, structured around conjugality? Did the very concept of property for women remain *de facto* more embedded in social relations, enabling male individuation to exceed the female? New notions of conjugality among the middle, and later the working classes, may have been linked to the constitution of men as independent wage earners, distinct economic agents on their *own* account, capable of sustaining a livelihood and supporting a family— as implied for instance in the concept of the family wage or the Hindu Gains of Learning Act (1930) that reduced the importance of joint family enterprise. Significantly, the act provided for individual ownership of the money a person earned by virtue of his "learning" even if acquired through the funds or support of the joint family, it no longer had to be pooled into the coparcenary. The 'value' *of* education then could enhance male individuation even as the values propagated *by* education actively impeded female individuation.

XI

. . . the supposed advantages of licensed prostitution accrue to the upper social classes, which are, in fact, the lower moral classes. The crusade against licensed fornication is a war between respectable daughters of the poor and rich and powerful men and women. . . . when so-called 'Christian England' took control of 'heathen India' and . . . Cantonments were staked for the residence of the British soldiers and their officers, full provision was made for the flesh, to fulfil the lusts thereof.

Elizabeth Andrew and Katherine Bushnell,
The Queen's Daughters in India, 1899

The constitution of north-Indian middle-class familial ideologies and the colonial state's regulation of family, marriage, and property relations were a related process. Contradictions beset British administrators regarding state intervention in marriage or family, but they displayed a sharper understanding of their constituent classes. In nineteenth-century Britain, the state's legislation was governed by and secured the continuation and redefinition of specific pre-existing patriarchal forms that it did not necessarily create; it drew on, modified, and transformed particular sets of patriarchal relations in tandem with specific contemporary historical, economic, political, legal, and ideological developments, contests, and struggles.[159] In India the colonial state created a bourgeois state appa-ratus to enforce prebourgeois ideological forms and institutions based on the sexual division of labour. The state was committed neither to the idea of women as having interests independent of their menfolk nor to the idea of marriage as a purely civil contract; rather, it main-tained precapitalist 'moral' and ideological configurations and played an active role in reproducing the position of women within the family.

The colonial state seems to have had a differential, class-specific relation to women's domestic and productive labour along the different *available* socially sanctioned grids for organizing it and the regionally different class formations it supported. A blend of upper-caste and bourgeois domestic ideologies, with their characteristic mix of domestic labour and 'educated' nurture of children, was seen as appropriate for upper-caste and new middle-class women.[160] The state supported not merely separate education or gender-determined syllabi but helped to make religious instruction, domestic labour, and the social relations in which it was performed a part of the curriculum. Innumerable administrative reports from the 1860s on public education in the north stressed the importance of instruction in cooking, housekeeping, and morality over book-learning for girls. However, agricultural or lower-caste women were evaluated as a labour force on the understanding that their labour was not commensurate with companionate marriage: for instance, the hard labour of rural women had to be accompanied not by companionate conjugality but with old-fashioned "female submission".[161] The state therefore sanctioned those family forms that could provide the basis of an agricultural economy and secure its revenues, regardless of whether these diminished or upheld women's right to property.[162] Slave-born domestics as well as *begar* labour by women and men persisted in a large number of princely states, while some even legally enforced hereditary labour; the colonial state condoned this as "a service of affection"![163]

The state not only supported *different* familial and patriarchal labour arrangements, it also ensured its own access to another pool of labour, the 'extra-familial' one of prostitution. The fees and fines levied in Awadh show that it was put into a structure of labour and work for wages by the state which controlled their income and dictated the "terms and conditions" of their service.[164] Ironically, in this regard the market posed as much of a threat to them as it did to the guardians of nondissoluble marriage.

There was a tendency from the inception of British rule to admire prostitutes under state control. In 1782, George Foster expressed unstinted approval of such 'customary', socially sanctioned prostitution, with women living under the protection and daily regulation of the government and being taxed according to their incomes.[165] Direct state patronage exempted it from condemnation or stigma, and prostitution was seen as seamlessly integrated into the organic social and religious structure of India: an orderly custom within a hierarchical society. Outside this structure and such patronage 'voluntary' prostitution was disorderly and licentious.[166] A century later this consoling opposition between customary and voluntary profession was severely traumatized by the market, even leading to laments about the degeneration of the former institution. With prostitution forming an intermittent and/or supplementary recourse determined by women's position in the labour market, and with the state stepping into the role of patron, it was no longer easy to maintain a distinction between orderly prostitutes and the disorderly ones outside its direct control.[167] Significantly, the civilizational scale that Mayhew was constructing in England rested precisely on the possibility of maintaining such distinctions: the most superior civilizations were those that set the highest value on female chastity, relied on the internalization of chastity by women rather than on surveillance, and among whom prostitutes were a *distinct* class segregated from other women.[168] In India, an administrative paranoia about the supposed existence of an uncontrollable "multitude of unchaste women" which rendered state regulation marginal, clashed violently with earlier administrative positions that continued to produce soothing rationalizations about a contained, caste-based profession overtly sanctioned by pub-lic consent, hereditary custom, and ancient texts.[169] Paradoxically, the newly discovered multititude of un-chaste women also constituted a hidden sanction. The ideological conundrum—as customary profession, sanctioned and not immoral, prostitution could be patronized by the state, but as voluntarily adopted trade it was disreputable—was partly resolved in practice. In both capacities the state retained the right to regulate it. In the case of the profession it had inherited the right to do so from the 'Hindu' law books and by virtue of its own sovereignty. In the case of the voluntary trade the women, being immoral, deserved if not called forth regulation, and the state could also intercede on its own behalf as client in a market economy.

Perhaps present theories which homogenize colonialism in the name of the anti or postcolonial and characterize national elites as either politically derivative or culturally exceptional, need to be rethought. The political and the cultural cannot be split. The charge of derivation masks the *similarity* and intersections of class proce-sses across the colonial divide in metropolitan and imperialized social formations, as well as the specificity of the non-class features with which they came to be articulated. The anticolonial claim to cultural exceptionalism not only blurs this specificity but can also double as an alibi for several undesirable, patriarchal, and quite mat-erial arrangements. What is more, the claim to cultural imposition can suppress the fact that colonialism mediated the extant as much as it invented the new, and that British culture and patriarchal ideolo-gies were themselves shaped 'abroad' as it were.

This essay was first read at a seminar at IIAS, Shimla, in 1992 and published in a shorter and differently organized form in *Social Scientist*, 244–46 (Sept.–Nov. 1993). As it grew, parts of it were presented at the Humanities Institute, State University of New York at Stonybrook, University of Cornell, Kurukshetra University, a seminar organized by the Centre for Transcultural Studies (Chicago) in Delhi, and trickled into presentations on other subjects at Jawaharlal Nehru University and Indian Social Institute, Delhi, between 1994 and 1998. I am deeply grateful to Amit Gupta, Rajendra Prasad, Kokila Dang, Shakti Kak and Vivek Chhiber for their comments on this essay.

Consent, agency, and rhetorics of incitement

Women's agency being a contextual question, there are dangers even in modest generalization. Nor is any generalization feasible about Indian women. This essay is confined to posing a few problems about a working notion of women's agency or transformative capacity, which may help in more rigorous contextualization. The centrality of the question of agency for feminists, both in relation to practical organization and to historical reconstruction, needs little elaboration. Marxist and socialist feminists have worked with a notion of *direct* agency, at the point of its emergence into self-consciousness and its transformation into collective political will. However, women's agency remains problematic in both theory and practice: because women are simultaneously class differentiated and subject to the frequent cross-class expansion of patriarchal ideologies, their agency is not open to historically self-evident modes of collectivization. I think more attention needs to be paid to the existing definitions and constitution of agential structures for women in order to forge interventionary possibilities adequate to a thoroughgoing politics of change.

In this essay I will discuss an area seldom taken into account, that of socially structured and often sanctioned forms of *indirect* agency, in their specific articulation of *consent* and *resistance*, as significant signs of the ways in which men and women make their history or are inhibited from doing so. Indirect agency, as I see it, also comprises of agency as it is ascribed to, conferred upon, and delegated to women within patriarchal structures, characteristically functions through 'feminized' agential modes such as convolution, disguise, displacement, deflection, surrogacy, or manipulation, and signals some degree of consent to patriarchies. A feminist politics needs to account for women's consent to patriarchies, but without giving theoretical and political primacy to women's consent to forms of oppression *over and above* their will to contest these, since such a primacy has already been on offer by standard forms of male conservatism which attribute the persistence of patriarchal practices to women's 'own' will or volition.

In order to understand consent, a major impediment to organized resistance, we need to work with a notion of materiality which can extend from minuscule arrangements of daily life to broader features of a social formation, as well as work towards a sharper understanding of the differences between the nature of change brought about through individual acts of resistance and through collective, organized resistance. This will help in defining consent as an axis of division among women who could potentially unite in a common opposition to patriarchies; consent to class, caste, and patriarchies can enable some women to exercise power over other women and men. It will also help in preventing confusion between women's agency deriving from consent and a politically interventionist feminist agency. (For instance, the active role of women in right-wing Hindutva politics has produced in some analyses an alarming conflation of consent with feminist agency, forgetting that consent to patriarchies has and still does empower women for selected forms of social agency, that this consent works through appropriating available hegemonic or legitimating languages, and that in the present conjuncture this includes a partial appropriation of the language of feminism.) Feminist agency consists of the organized initiatives of women and men committed to gender justice within an egalitarian framework: this definitionally excludes women committed to a right-wing politics with its accompanying set of permissions to 'other' women and men from different religions.

Feminist recognitions of systemic regularities and 'generic' similarities—both in and across historically and socially specific contexts—have been a poignant and revealing enterprise which have persistently renewed the question of structures. Conceptions of individual or collective transformative agency and struggle are vacuous without an accompanying understanding of their dialectical relation with determining material, epistemic, institutional, and ideological structures which they both reproduce and transform. Perhaps structures are best seen as multiple, intersecting, at some levels interactive[1] and at other levels in dialectical contradiction, and structuration grasped as a continuous, renewing, changing, unresolved historical process. At once determined and determining, the condition and outcome of human agency, structures are not a fully fixed a priori—some may be in place, others being evolved by or displaced through the conscious collectivization of agencies.

In indirect ways . . .

Women's agency: some current definitions

It may help to begin with two broad definitional tendencies which inflect a great deal of contemporary writing on Indian women, and which have made it difficult to situate, understand, or evaluate women's agency. In liberal schemas (often carelessly incorporated into mainstream history of different political persuasions), a historical process which has *produced* the split between the political and the economic as well as an ideological division between the public and the private as discrete domains, is unquestioningly analysed in its *own* terms. This has led to conceptually identifying women's agency with only direct or conscious political action, and direct participation in the capitalist labour process. Not only does such such a conception of agency usually devolve on narrow notions of political or economic participation, but it is based on a devaluation of certain categories of women's labour and an overvaluation of their social passivity. The work of several socialist and Marxist feminists has shown that the domains of both the political and the economic expand considerably when they are gendered, and has challenged the notion of women being either peripheral or passive in any social formation.[2] However, procreative activity, household labour, subsistence labour, and other forms of the sexual division of labour are seldom integrated into the political economy. The division of public and private into discrete domains, when taken as an a priori instead of as a changing historical variable, functions as a form of obfuscation. It has served to block off enquiry into the nature of earlier precapitalist divisions that were named and experienced differently—along lines of social mobility, spatial demarcation, or as specialized 'masculine' domains—as well as their coincidence or interaction with subsequent divisions between public and private under the aegis of capitalism. Further, the *effects* of this division at a given historical moment—women's lack of direct access to the 'public' sphere or to direct forms of social action, as well as the production of corroborative patriarchal ideologies—are used not only as an *indice* of women's existing agential capacity but become the theoretical grid through which their agency or emancipation is defined. This has had at least two consequences. It not only theoretically reproduces, even reinforces the division, but naturalizes what were in liberal theory, explicitly normative distinctions serving to mask and perpetuate several patriarchal arrangements.[3] The production of a public sphere was in fact integral to class formation, based on exclusions (such as of lower classes and/or colonized peoples) and many of the 'conditions' for entry were gendered (such as altruism for women), while the production of the private sphere was also implicated in the minutiae of class differentiation and heavily invested in the reformulation of patriarchies.[4] In practice, 'public' and 'private' not only interpenetrate in varied and often systematic ways, but are *produced* together, connected in relations of condensation or displacement, and display different levels of articulation. In this sense too the 'private' sphere is a distinct 'political' site for the tangential and direct formation of the gendered subject.

A second consequence has been the foreclosure of a rigorous historicization of the categories of the private and the public.[5] From the nineteenth century, definitions of public and private have been produced along a number of concurrent lines that are both material and discursive, spatial and ideological, based in prescription as well as in divisions of labour; further, the meaning of 'public' and 'private' varies in different theoretical grids, for instance, in demarcations of a 'political' arena and as a correlate of the distinction between state and civil society,[6] in legal classification (compartmentalizing 'work' from 'family' matters), or in structurally linked 'public' and 'private' patriarchal institutions (such as prostitution and marriage). These definitions and divisions may overlap but may not fully coincide, nor need they entail the physical presence or absence of women. The equation of women's agency with women's entry into the public sphere has been especially problematic in most histories of the colonial period. Not only do these carelessly rehearse a typical theme of early nationalist historiography, present the private and the public as mutually exclusive rather than jointly formed, but they are elitist in so far as they centre on the emergence of home-bound women—from the upper and middle classes and castes—into the public arena, ignoring the vast mass of women below who already laboured outside the home, who were entering waged work in increasing numbers, and whose labour was determining both the definitions and the conditions of the 'private'. Further, the simplistic translation of public and private into world and home both replicates and is analogous to the modernity and tradition binarism that predictably and ideologically identifies women with tradition. From this it has been but a short step, taken by many, to identifying colonial rule and its legal paraphernalia as invasive of 'traditional' and 'private' familial spaces—thereby turning a particular concept of the home into a fixed transhistorical entity. (This is a questionable assumption since several premodern legal systems in India opened both family and sexuality to detailed inventory as well as to a 'public' gaze.[7]) Within this deployment of the public–private schema the home is usually projected as a site of male autonomy from colonial rule and/or female passivity and incarceration. In practice, however, homes were entangled in the colonial political economy, and domestic ideologies structured women's agency in undesirable ways, but did not deny it altogether—if they proscribed some forms, they made available other forms.

A major obstacle to the theoretical expansion of the political and the economic is the virtual absence of family histories even of nineteenth and twentieth-century India, with the notable exception of some field studies by feminists. Without histories of the articulation of families with political structures and the economy, we can only speculate about the following: the differential ways in which divisions between the public and private have been made both in terms of class and in terms of a sectoral development of capitalism in the past two centuries; the diverse household structures which sustain a specific mode of production, or indeed the nature of the household structures which sustain the complex articulation of surviving and emerging modes of production; the changes in the definition, corporate power, and affective relations of kin groups; the structural changes which occur for women with the insertion of families as a unit of consumption in the market economy and with the introduction of land as private property and commodity; the reorganization of labour patterns (including the sexual divisions of labour) with individuals beginning to replace family units or kin-based groups; the loosening of family ties amongst migrant labour, or the extent to which the household remains a unit of production thereby giving a different leverage to the 'private' sphere. Apart from the complacent neglect of feminist issues and the consistent evasion of their capacity to alter our understanding of history as a whole, the changing and contingent histories of families have also been neglected because mainstream historians scarcely acknowledge other forms of productive activity or labour outside the designated spheres of artisanal labour, agricultural labour, and the working class, and virtually refuse to acknowledge gender differentiation as an *integral* part of class formation. In the political domain it is becoming possible to indicate, at least superficially, how the state, implicated in familial ideologies, intervenes in the ordering, valuation, and gendered definition of labour, as well as legally in marriage, inheritance, sexuality, procreation, and other areas—at one level endorsing and reproducing some extant divisions of public and private, while simultaneously making the distinction between public and private untenable at the level of state and civil society.[8] However, at least three significant areas remain obscure: the way at any given time the state changes the wider context in which local and kin-based power structures operate; the degree to which state structures penetrate local power and authority structures and so become involved in the manipulation of marriage, caste, or kinship rules, or, in other words, the nature of the complicity of family and community with the state and its juridical institutions; and the range of actions which take forms that are difficult to fit into commonly understood typologies of organized political activity.[9]

On the other side, a side often more alert to feminist issues, an equally narrow culturalism has emerged in which the subjectivities and perceptions displayed in literary or cultural production are projected as the privileged, if not sole, forms of women's agency. The creative activity of women is not only pitted against an amorphous notion of patriarchal restriction but also posited as a separate

transgressive space—a space for overly individualized 'private' resolutions. These resolutions, howsoever worthy of attention and respect,
seem to make any direct, collective confrontation of material power
structures redundant. One problem in such analyses is the exorbitation
of ideology: patriarchies are seen as either ideological constructs or
as a set of more or less customary constraints in the 'priv-ate' sphere,
and as such become either a singular or an inverse deter-minant of
women's creative activity. Where they are a singular deter-minant,
the other material and historical coordinates which suffuse even the
formal properties of literary and cultural production are ignored,
while discursive and ideological constructions are presented as if they
operate outside the play of other determinations. Ironically, this only
functions to circumscribe the wider social agency of the very modes
of cultural production being valorized. The projection of pat-riarchies
as an inverse determinant is underwritten by the curious assumption
that patriarchies preclude creativity per se. All forms of social
inequality undoubtedly block off a great deal of human poten-tial,
but equally we know that in precapitalist social formations, divisions
of labour by caste, class, or gender produced specialized enclaves of
creativity, including artisanal forms, which often made for the
'aesthetic' deepening or enhancement of certain forms of daily
labour. A characteristic fallout of the writing within such a framework—which displays different degrees of investment in the 'necessary non-correspondence' of the ideological and the material—has
been the naive separation of 'cultural' from 'material' agency, whereas since patriarchies are in fact sustained in both base[10] and superstructure in ways that mark the reciprocity of the two, the material
factors which shape women's agency are seldom separable from the
cultural forms or practices which embody them. Indeed the issue here
could well be that of the ideological determination of women's access
to either socially accepted languages for expressing, or political modalities for constituting individuated and collective interests.

A related tendency is visible in reviews of the spheres of
'power' reserved for women in so-called 'traditional' and 'semi-
traditional' societies like ours. Quite apart from the frequent rehash
of the tradition–modernity binarism, here such spheres are read as
signs of women's agency or as spaces for their subjectivity within
recognizably unequal societies, or even as signs of a transgressive

excess by which women escape being fully contained by social structures. Often written from avowedly anti-Enlightenment or anti-colonial positions, they display an inordinate and helplessly 'modern' respect for 'traditions', especially religious traditions—somewhat ironic in a country which is both renowned for its many coercive and oppressive traditions as well as rich in lesser known strands of irreverence. (The respect for tradition is in fact part of an indigenist tendency that extends beyond questions of gender; this valorizes a critique of traditions from 'within', wherein belonging not only gives a special right to speak but bestows an 'authenticity' that can serve as a weapon against the rationality and the 'alienations' of the Enlightenment.) This contemporary reverence for transgression and alternate spaces, howsoever feminist in its orientation, leaves little space for making alternatives outside traditions. Further, this reverence is but a short step away from interpreting women's access to all forms of power— even in conservative, indigenist, or communal right-wing forma-tions—as self-legitimizing and/or inherently subversive. In political terms it amounts to a capitulative tendency and that too in a cha-racteristically 'feminized' mode, that is, working through a play of compensations. Transgressions or subversions can perpetuate power structures unless they are linked to other collective, confrontative, radical forces of change.[11] On the whole, in evading the precise social content and ideological location of these valorized spheres of female 'power' and so of their subversive potential, this tendency implicitly refuses to recognize how patriarchies function.

Patriarchies—I use the term broadly to denote systems of sub-ordinating women—function *simultaneously* through *coercion* or the threat and practice of violence, through making a wide social *con-sensus* drawn from and dispersed over many areas of social life and through obtaining in various ways, different degrees of *consent* from women. Women's agential capacity within so-called 'traditional' societies and accompanying discursivities may actually be one of the ways by which consensual elements in patriarchies are often made— for unless certain distributions of power are made within patriarchal arrangements it is difficult to imagine how any degree of consent from women can be obtained.[12]

When women agree: redefining consent

In the following paragraphs I will sketch a working notion of patriarchal systems within a class-differentiated social formation—referring only to patrilineal, patrilocal systems prevalent in the north and not to either matrilineal or tribal systems. While the terms of my discussion are too general to be useful for specific analyses, and my reference to different patriarchies is merely notational,[13] I hope that it will help in moving towards a more precise definition and identification of 'consent'. My emphasis will be on consensual elements which are usually neglected but are important in building an understanding of agency, and my attempt will be to shift the locus of consent from victimization and/or the ideological misperception of their own interests by women to the wide social processes in which patriarchies are embedded.

Women's agential capacity is distinct in so far as women are subject to the determination of patriarchal structures.[14] Patriarchies are resilient not only because they are embedded in social stratification, divisions of labour, other political structures, religious and cultural practices, institutions, and categories, but also because of the 'contractual' and consensual element in them which along with patriarchal systems is open to constant and consistent reformulation. These elements, stretching across a continuum from acquiescence or passive acceptance to active collusion, need to be analysed not only as produced through the coercive and ideological operation of patriarchies but also as specific articulations of patriarchal ideologies and material factors: the bases of these elements, which lie in the social structuring and particular material base of a patriarchal system, also seem to inhere in the very mechanisms of its reproduction—a process to which women are subject but of which they may also be agents. The persistence of these elements may have some connection with the fact that the modalities of the reconstitution of a patriarchy work through both overlap and reformulation: over a period of time, the various constitutive elements of a patriarchy may have different durations and tempos of change.[15] Women's consent is neither an essential nor a historically frozen category, but a part of this uneven process of the reconstitution of patriarchies.

The question of consensuality is a complicated one. Since patriarchal systems are linked to others, neither the consent nor the resistance of women can be interpreted as a manichean drama with an enveloping patriarchy alone. So when women tolerate, accept, con-sent to, are complicit with, or invest in patriarchal values, practices or arrangements, and assume their obligations, it need not be con-strued as consent to these alone since the patriarchies they are sub-jected to are simultaneously located in specific modes of production, in class structures and mobility, in particular forms of caste–class status and inequality, and intersected by specific forms of self-identification with custom, tradition or religion. Indeed it is this very range of determinations of patriarchal systems that also creates the tolerance of patriarchal power within all social domains. Conversely, patriarchies help in inculcating an acceptance of social inequality in different historical periods and in making structures of deference that are wider than the relations between men and women. In other words, patriarchies are not only laterally related to other structures of legitimation but enter the wide dialectic of social legitimation, thereby needing commensurate broad-based forms of collective resistance.[16] (However, while patriarchies are variously related to other structures of social inequality, they remain distinct and are not collapsible into them.) Though the relation between classes and patriarchies is complex and variable, being both direct and indirect, and class formation and social differentiation are themselves uneven and contradictory processes, even so, women's consent or investment may extend to those structures in relation to which that particular patriarchy operates and is open to a class-differentiated analysis. Further, consensual elements may either be gathered from without or honed from within patriarchal arrangements. Consequently, the problem of evaluating the hegemonic power or social effectivity of a so-called determinant is knotty, entangled with many other questions about the role it plays in the reproduction of patriarchies and other related structures, as well as about the nature and degree of the articulation of particular patriarchal structures with others. I would go so far as to say that just as the conditions which govern women's consent are wider than patriarchies, so women's consent may itself be one of the nodes of the condensed articulation of patriarchies with other social structures in specific historical conjunctures.

The means by which a degree of reciprocity is established for consensual and 'contractual' elements in patriarchies may be both material and ideological; careful analytic distinctions would need to be made between consent resting on material arrangements which guarantee women rights, compensations, or protection (despite the usual asymmetry between rights and obligations), consent resting on ideological ensembles which offer at best precarious, at worst illusory rights, compensations, or protection, and consent resting on forms of coercion which push women towards normative behaviour.[17] The consensual, 'contractual' elements combine agential power with subjection for women and produce a mixture of consent and resentment. They would seldom produce just consent. Nor is there anything straightforward about the element of consent since it may rest on a series of factors ranging from wide social consensualities, economic dependence, social pressures congealed into structural necessities or dispersed as moral systems, the pull of affective relationships, and the perceived legitimacy of the offer to 'protect' women from the patriarchal violence of other individuals or groups.[18] The particular articulation of consensual and coercive elements within patriarchal systems would also be shaped by a range of other factors, including the nature of women's access to resources and insertion into the labour market, as well as the interplay between women's productivity or participation in 'recognized' forms of labour and in 'invisibilized' forms of household or domestic labour. Even so, women's implication in the 'contractual', consensual elements of a patriarchy not only puts them in a contradictory relation with that patriarchy itself, but also tends to situate their social agency in fairly contradictory fashion as both complicit and transgressive. There is not much to be gained in valorizing one term over the other, both need to be seen in *relationship* to each other and to the *reproduction* of any given ensemble of social relations.

A class-differentiated analysis of consent would need to bear in mind that while patriarchal arrangements differ and sexual divisions of labour occur within a specific set of social relations, patriarchal ideologies have more fluid, permeable boundaries. Women from the propertied classes or the upper layers of social hierarchy should especially be looked at in the full range of complicities and extracted compensations. Women may often derive their class status from men but they conjointly live out class relations and participate in their reproduction.[19] They share to some extent the structural capacities derived by the class as a whole by virtue of its position in the relations of production. The modalities of their oppression deny women from the upper and middle strata many of their interests and rights (both *de facto* and *de jure*), but do they deny *all* those which accrue to a class? Does their consent rest on the pincer logic of bondage produced through caste–class affiliations and privilege or power exercised over others? We have to think quite seriously about the class, caste, and communal assertion which is built into patriarchal norms, as for example in the chaste upper-caste hindu woman or the dutiful wife in middle-class domestic ideology. Both carry a set of aggressions and are not as innocuous as they seem; they have not only been persistent models of status indication and upward mobility but also have social implications that stretch beyond the home. In other words, the question here would be about the forms of social agency which can accompany normative patriarchal ideologies, and the degree of customary or class or otherwise institutionalized power they provide some women over others—whether men or other women.[20]

Women from the labouring classes who, broadly speaking, are not in a position to exploit the labour of other individuals or classes, are subject to different patriarchal arrangements, though some aspects of these are structurally related to the patriarchal practices and ideologies of the upper strata; their 'consent' is nuanced differently, often even centred on the facts of their wide-ranging social subordination. Tied to the family unit in an economy of survival, subject to the coercive patriarchal practices of their own class as well as to the exploitation of their labour and sexuality by upper castes–classes, women's 'acceptance' is poised at the nodes where at least two contradictions are at their most acute: first, between the economic and ideological dimensions of the family, and second, between the myth of the responsible male protector–provider (which men are either unable or unwilling to live up to) and the reality of women's labour as the indispensable and sometimes primary source of family subsistence.[21]

Given the complications of consent, our starting point could well be to formulate the questions which are latent in just this insistent, structural pressure produced by women's contradictory location in patriarchies: who or what women's agency is on behalf of, the quality and precise nature of the combination of power and subjection, the *cost* of either such power or of subsistence within compensatory structures for women. Do we want them at all? Are *all* modes of empowerment for women equally desirable? Do we prefer to define ourselves not merely as we are but also as we would wish to be? Are the rights or compensations on which consent rests structurally available to all women of that group or to some? How would collective struggle affect them? How far do 'contractual' and consensual elements persist because of the absence of external support structures for women and how far do they actually inhibit their formation?

As far as the question of the contradictory structuring of women's agency within families is concerned I think analyses need to be reinflected in at least two ways. Firstly, we need to attend to the gap between familial ideologies and the family as a social entity or a concrete constellation of relationships, and resist the tendency to conflate the desired ideals of familial ideologies with the existing structure and organization of households at any historical moment.[22] Given the plethora of ancient and modern prescriptive texts which have functioned as modes of ideological homogenization disguising both the contests undertaken and the actual heterogeneity of family arrangements, it is misleading to read prescriptive texts as unproblematical descriptions of family forms: familial ideologies are not reproduced mechanically in the family as a material institution. For instance, legal and religious texts recognized a number of living arrangements and forms of marriage, through description and classification, even as they proscribed them. Caught in the logics of existing reality that may not match with prescriptive desire, normative discourses only indirectly (if at all) indicate the extent of women's leverage or agency, and the nature of family conflicts.

Secondly, families need to be seen not merely as an undifferentiated site of women's socialization and oppression, but also as a site of struggle and of the daily recreation of different types of gender, caste, and class inequality in which women participate. In at least the nineteenth and early twentieth centuries, class formation and emergence were not only overdetermined by caste but were not tantamount to class solidarity or a singular class consensus; given the range of intermediary strata between direct producers and the state, horizontal affiliations have continuously been made in part through reconceptualizing the family as a social unit, a unit for the social reproduction of caste and class inequality. From the 'middle-class' writing of this period, there is evidence not only of the contentious relation between existing or emerging ideologies and actual household arrangements but the family also appears to have been a self-conscious arena of heated battles about regulating sexuality, defining gender roles, controlling marriage and reproduction. At the same time, familial ideologies—compounded of romantic love, female nurturance and self-sacrifice, masculine protection and financial support—were becoming a way of distinguishing between classes. With upward mobility being uneven, significant differentiation emerged within families even generationally. There is ample evidence of the differential enactment of class as a *relation* by individuals within a family: whether in nuclear units identifying with wider kin networks, in extended families, or in the nucleated units of semi-extended families. Different external class locations being played out by individual members *within* a family surface in memories and descriptions of conflicts, resentment, rivalry, shifts in power, and were sought to be resolved in a fixing of status through various kinds of family narratives. Further, in these narratives individuals appear as the complex bearers of past, emergent, and desired class positions. How were women located in such intra-family class divisions? What was the nature of the contradiction between the moral onus on women to hold family units together and the actual suspension of morality in such friction or abrasions within the family? One facet of this may be the creation of hierarchies of labour and consumption, and the evident struggle over control of available resources. Women seem to have been as much a party to this as men, especially where household resources were concerned. The politics of the household seem to be structured according to the degree of access women have to patriarchal power (as for instance the mother-in-law), in the form of some control over the redivision of household labour among women—daughters, daughters-in-law, unmarried women, and especially widows—over marriage alliances, over sons, and in other forms accruing from an acceptance of delegated or surrogate patriarchal roles which included the surveillance of other women. Not only did these produce tension among women but ensured that in family situations women were only able, if at all, to form an uneasy collectivity. Is it that consensual elements in patriarchies functioned to *divide* women both within the family and in a broader sense? Is the differential access to patriarchal power for women and women's implication in patriarchal consensuality to be interpreted only on generational lines? Did the degree of incorporation of women into the marital family increase both their leverage and their subjugation? Did the struggles for power within 'middle-class' families open avenues of 'compensatory' power for women, though they seldom altered their position in other ways? Did the invisibilization of women's household labour also push them into compensatory structures?[23] What was the precise nature of the articulation of affective relationships and material factors in families as well as the nature of the bonding which took place across this range of contradictions?

Towards a feminist historiography

The question of feminist historiography is an extensive one and my discussion here is confined to a few aspects related to agency and consent.

The historical constitution of notions of 'female agency'—as offered cultural abstractions—have a special bearing on the problem of historical reconstruction, and constitute another reason for discarding the simplistic notion of a woman acting for 'herself'. Who is she? So thoroughgoing is the social constitution of notions of femaleness, self, or identity that the question of women's agency is inescapably linked to or determined by other available histories—family, class, religion, existing notions of moral order, extant modes of individuation and collectivization. Patriarchies themselves are relational, subject to a wider political economy, occupy changing historical configurations, and are frequently reformulated; that is, there is no historical essentialism available to women. Further, with patriarchies being tied into cosmological or bourgeois moral notions, women's consent may not always be instrumental or 'rational'.

The question of dispersed social 'identities' also arises; women's identity, like other social identities, need not be sought along a single unified axis. It may be useful to interpret multiple identities through several crisscrossing ideologies rather than a single one. However, these multiple identities may exist not as atomized entities but in significant *relation with each other* at other levels of the social formation (for instance as structured differences), especially since hegemonic ideologies may themselves operate at different sites. Further, identities are neither merely discursive nor infinitely plural but produced in determinate historical conditions and may involve choices between multiple, competing interpellations.[24]

One problem of historical reconstruction then hinges on understanding the particularly complex relation which obtains between social practices and representational forms. Since patriarchies function in and through relations of production and divisions of labour as well as through diverse forms of discursivity, the material and the discursive are mutually implicated—but there is no *single* relation between the two. Material and discursive modes of constituting women's agency may coincide or conflict. The connection between the material and the discursive may not always be open to direct description; it may be more available through the contradictions and consensualities generated, which serrate both offered ideologies and enacted agencies. Indeed, the peculiar emphases of consensualities is one way of marking a possible or latent contradiction. For instance, prescriptive condensations and narrative elaborations pose, blur, or 'resolve' social 'deviances' differently and also play out consensualities in different ways. Prescriptive texts may be as much histories of dissent and conflict—since patriarchal ideologies too are formed through processes of social contestation within and between caste, class, or religious groupings—as of achieved cohesion, hegemonic ideologies, and the naturalization of inequalities. Their desired ideals are open to being measured against the social 'imperfections' or 'aberrations' which they seek to contest or eradicate, and they require sustained analysis as thematized, mediated, often contradictory documents. Especially since their own logic of modification and accommodation of customary variation has made them amenable to conjunctural use.[25] Further, though they function as pressure and produce structures of anxiety, their prescriptions and ideologies, however stringent, are seldom identical with enacted agencies or the actual range of possible choices.

Nor can a straightforward opposition between prescription and agency be maintained. Rather, for feminists it remains important to see women as evaluative agents even as simplistic and essentialist notions of women as passive bearers of prescribed norms are rejected, and a sense of how deeply women are embedded in ideological and epistemological structures is retained. Even when evaluation is not articulated or part of an explicit political, collective self-consciousness on the part of women, there may be an implicit evaluation of patriarchal structures acting as both horizon and limit (enabling certain forms of agency while restricting it in other forms), as well as of the forms of agential power available or denied within patriarchal consensualities.[26]

Narrative elaborations, each bearing their own social and formal histories, refract, work out, extend, or repress *potential* social agencies; they can play a significant role in making relationships between offered and practised agencies and in re-entering the latter into evaluative systems of ascription, and so may even attempt to refold widening social agencies into normative modes. Narratives themselves need to be evaluated in a matrix of social practices, especially since they may, situationally, acquire direct agential roles. Perhaps the degree to which a narrative or prescriptive unit (or for that matter any particular structure) is implicated in *both* base and superstructure will effectively increase its capacity to determine, as indeed will the degree to which a particular structure is dispersed in the social realm as well as over time as a culturally consolidated or sanctioned unit. That is why in looking at the sedimented histories of prescriptive and narrative forms, an understanding needs to be developed that they bear not only the histories of patriarchies but of many different social tensions. Indeed reading prescriptive and narrative forms through each other or making them collide may be a way of locating social tensions or contradictions. The specific intersection between the narrative and the normative is a space for looking for the 'possibles' of agency.

The coordinates of women's agency need to be established— the interplay between structural constraints and conjunctural opportunities, the conditions of possibility, of proscription, of loopholes, of contradictions—before racing to conclusions about it. How is agency, female and male, being defined or redefined at that moment—in the range of material factors, historical circumstances, and ascription? Thus, a history of women's 'volition' may turn out to be as much a history of the politics of male conferral. Or, a transitional historical moment, for instance medieval *bhakti* or the nineteenth century, may open possibilities unforeseen in 'discourses' alone; these possibilities emerge in social disjunctures, from inconsistencies or even schisms between women's agency as it is represented and as it is practised, from qualitative shifts in the historical constitution of volition, subjectivity, and female knowledge, as well as through changing relations between moral strictures and affective structures.[27] The conjunctural sites of underdetermination are also of some importance: the points at which agencies slip through structures—in new situations, at transitional moments, or in liminal areas; those factors which allow individual women to act differently, independently, or even contrary to the demands of other structured relationships; and the situational ability of individuals to act against their own immediate interest to maintain structured relations of collective power—such as family, caste, community—leading to complicated forms of 'self'-oppression and/or oppression of others. The female voices of oppression and 'resistance'—victimage, moral power, self-sacrifice—shaped and bequeathed by patriarchal ideologies are also significant. These may carry some normative values, may not challenge material power relations, or more disturbingly, work out the agential possibilities of discontent, compromise, and reform that are offered by or written into patriarchal structures. In each reconstruction the delicate and variable relations between ideologies and agencies come up.

Historical reconstruction then becomes a matter of provisionally eliciting structures, through the aggregation of actions, events, and agencies, of narrative, prescriptive, and other discursive genres or performative modes, of divisions of labour, mechanisms for the generation of surplus and the distribution of resources, family forms and household arrangements, and so on. Through the juxtaposition, collisions, contradictions of these not only could practised agencies be reconstructed to some extent, but a recursive relation between structures and agencies may be tentatively established.

At one level, 'structure' is an approximation through analytic abstraction, a cognitive grid of a social terrain more complex or dense than the sum of structures which may be seen to constitute it. Not only may a social formation contain a subjectively valid underlife of forces and events for which there may not be decisive evidence, and where the nature of these events or forces may preclude even immanently objectified traces,[28] but there may in social practices be inflections, asymmetries, interpretative possibilities, cultural densities, a

range of actions and choices available to individuals which cannot be
mechanically read off from structures. The underexplanation of social
theory combined with the scarcity of information (which accompanies
the history of all but ruling groups) compounds the problem of
historical retrieval for feminist historiography. Feminist historiography then *exceeds* normative rules of evidence in looking, as it must,
at the frontiers of articulation to locate the less visible props of
patriarchal structures and the *potentials* for women's agency (that is,
for more than its practice).

    This search and the selection of such potentials is inevitably
marked by our own contemporary historical location in feminism.
However, feminist projects of retrieving the agency of women from
past historical periods have often suffered from a degree of simplification produced through the anxiety to recover a roster of independent or rebellious women and enter them into liberatory schemas. But
surely we cannot expect to find either a bourgeois self or a political
subject replete with ideas of autonomy and concepts of rights who
unequivocally challenges political authority and patriarchal institutions; 'her' agency can only be approximated through our reconstitution of a set of 'possibles' within the complex articulation of a number of *determinate* factors and horizons. It may be more useful to
begin by retrieving the nature of existing potentials and constraints,
in other words, a sense of the struggle. The case of Mirabai is
paradigmatic. 'Mirabai' *can* only be a history of potentials and of different constellations named 'Mirabai': she may or may not have
existed, and if she did, then only on the basis of much later reconstructions. However, the several versions of a rebel saint which have
been offered for decades are embarrassingly literal and psycholo-
gized accounts of unequivocal defiance. They ignore the difficulties of
reading the content of several discrepant hagiographies as a single
biography, the difficulties of establishing even her substantial presence as a historical figure, and the difficulty of labelling a woman
who occupied and altered a female voice and a devotional language
already shaped by many others. They also suppress questions about
the materiality and social spread of metaphoric interpretations of
religion, as well as about an adequate methodology for analysing the
multitemporal sedimentation, overlaps, and variations of oral traditions in which the ideological baggage of the compositions may be

quite different from the events described in hagiographies. Oral traditions are sustained interpretations by a number of unnamed persons belonging to a roughly specifiable historical period. The nature and quality of this sustained interpretation have to be explored in order to understand the potentials for women's agency within it, holding in tension the double possibility of 'individual' and 'collective' or 'serial' inscription. For instance, do images of manual labour never assume the primacy in Mira's songs that they do in compositions of lower-caste women saints in medieval Maharashtra because her location as a rajput princess inhibited such reinscription? Or, why is the patriarchal or even misogynist content in compositions signed in the names of male poets heavier than of those signed in Mira's name? Was it that certain kinds of patriarchal values were difficult to attach either to a woman's name or to the intractable Mira figured by the legends, but they could be easily attached to a male signature using a female voice within the same devotional tradition? What does this say about the consensuality of patriarchal values not only in oral traditions but in social practices? Given the processes of selection and addition that work in oral transmission, Mirabai represents as much a set of *attributed* agencies as of *enacted* agencies. Further, the agency that is sought to be reconstructed here may turn out to be not just of this one woman but of whole collectivities with variations of caste, class, gender, region, who reproduced, extended, 'corrected', and transformed her corpus over centuries, an agency which speaks also of the *limits* of that recomposition. Indeed these limits may well be the mark of some of the numerous, barely decipherable contests inscribed in oral *bhakti* compositions. Orality is an 'open' social relation because of the continuous possibility of re-inscription; but the latitude or possibilities of reinscription are not for that reason *infinite*. If there are openings there are also closures which may be generic, ideological, produced by the emotional logic of an *oeuvre*, or tied to the hagiographic and popular significations attached to a particular signature. The mechanisms of these openings and closures, the overlap and distinction of *oeuvres* and signatures could be the subject of retrieval, and yield a far richer notion of women's agency than has hitherto become available.

Boons, entitlements, obligations:
Kaikeyi and Manthara

Symbolic attribution, social ascription, ideologies, and narratives interact in an emphatic way in maintaining the sexual division of labour and in structuring women's reproductive role; this combined with women's marginality in ideologically defined 'public' domains, has often pressed the practised and ascribed agency of women into *convoluted* shapes, into shifting and displaced intentionalities. Discursivities in turn have been important in determining the cultural forms which these convoluted agencies will, can, or should take.

Female incitement, a significant and recurring narrative or discursive unit of convoluted agency, is dispersed in many social spaces as well as across time; it occurs as biography, autobiography, orality, cinematic type, political discourse of nationalist and now communal parties, and functions variously as trope or prescription, as fable or exhortation. The instances are numerous and many are common knowledge, from Surpanakha, Manthara and Kaikeyi in the *Ramayana*, Kunti, Vidula and Draupadi in the *Mahabharata*, to several rajput women in nineteenth and twentieth-century narratives, and now to party ideologues like Sadhvi Rithambara. A history of the proliferation and change of this unit in different 'formal' structures, its crystallization as a culturally consolidated or sanctioned unit, the sources of its social intelligibility and its relation to specific structures of value, could be an undertaking in itself. Here I will discuss it briefly, not as an illustration of the foregoing discussion, but as a way of raising further questions.

Female incitement—women calling upon men to act—is a politically charged discursive unit which marks the entry of women (who may sometimes be under threat of sexual violation) into surveillance of a male 'public' domain by calling a paternalistic patriarchy to account in recognized forms of surrogate action, or it may even mark the entry of women themselves into a 'public' domain. It may exist at the tense interface of agency as it is ascribed to or proffered to women and as it is, often within these terms, represented in narratives or taken up by women in their lives and used, often unsettlingly, in ways which may reproduce or transform it. Incitement exists at an intersection between the 'political' and the 'domestic', between gender relations and other power relations, occupies an uneasy boundary between the respective logics of women's consent and resistance while rearticulating their relationship in different ways.

If, as a convenient entry point, a generalized semantic is extracted, it reveals three related features. First, that women share the *values* for which men are being incited and have a stake in the *social relation* which is sought to be preserved. Second, that they cannot act independently and directly on behalf of these but must act through men: they can be the active custodians of particular values and social relations but they cannot usually take action (generally militant or public) themselves. Third, that if incitement is to carry an inspirational connotation, women must neither *name* the social relation they are trying to preserve nor present it as a personal or material interest; they can only name the *abstraction*—family, honour, religion, nation —to which that social relation is either directly attached or which mediates it. If women name it (or rather give it no other name?) and/ or state their own personal stake in it, then incitement acquires a malignant connotation: the women become status-conscious materialists who lead men astray, conniving intriguers, or wicked manipulators.[29] In the naming and the not-naming resides the distinction between villainous and heroic inciting women. Since men are usually perceived as having both rights and duties, and women as having primarily duties, any claim to rights, unless effectively disguised, becomes a sign of women's evil nature. The same structures which push women into forms of convoluted agency also produce or ratify misogyny, in this case as a system of representing and characterizing that agency as malignant. Though 'good' and 'bad' inciting women reflect a consensuality of values, the distinction between the two also rests on the fact that in relation to both the constitution of social values and of material structures of inequality, patriarchal structures are part of a connected series. 'Undisguised' material or personal interests can be designated as illegitimate or malign female agency because by staking a claim to these women may interrogate or 'expose' not only the material bases of a patriarchy but also of a large number of social values, thereby endangering the entire dense imbrication of patriarchal structures with the other related social structures. Conversely, in its inspirational forms incitement can be legitimate—even be a sign of female strength—because it may actually assist in either integrating patriarchies with or reformulating them in relation to other ideological coherences or consensualities, for instance, those of 'community' or 'nation'.

At another level, the inciting woman may represent a temporary control over male sexuality: she is putting male honour—ineluctably tied to male sexual potency and to the protection of women from sexual violation—at stake. Though she relies on a consensual value structure, at that moment she may stake male sexuality in a way calculated to *wrest* consent. For instance, if at *that* moment the man does not want a confrontation, he will be branded a coward by others. Here a woman is exercising some situational control over a man's status (in a masculinist hierarchy) by laying him open to social castigation for being unmanly. She can, through setting up a structure of incitement—which polarizes success and failure, effect his social standing, insist on patriarchy as a structure of public accountability, and so throw it into jeopardy. At this level incitement may be poised at moments of the perceived breakdown of the 'reciprocal', consensual element in patriarchies. It gesturally ties men down by invoking the potential humiliation of *publicity* (a mode of redress?), temporarily denaturalizes patriarchal arrangements by displaying them as social and 'contractual', and points at the precariousness of the guarantees offered to women by 'contractual' and consensual patriarchal elements.

I would suggest that precisely *because* incitement involves an exercise of power from a 'dependent' position, it is socially 'dangerous' for those men, whether as individuals or as groups, towards whom it is directed. That is why it becomes acceptable if women incite in the name of something else, even when they represent themselves as victims, rather than if they incite in their own name. It is also on this issue that the line between a benignly inspirational and a malevolent female agency is drawn. Though the good woman is seen to inspire and the bad merely to incite, the semantic structure is the same. In one she becomes the excellent custodian of value, in the other wanton with male sexuality and replete with self-interest, even though she may be risking men in both. Ironically, since women suffer from the successes of a patriarchy and also from its breakdowns (especially in obtaining protection from 'other' men) the stake in 'inspiration' is double-edged. Inspiration builds an ego, incitement threatens symbolic castration. Both produce social guilt, the one from transcendence, the other from 'exposure'. Both are agents. In practice of course the line between the two may be thin or fluctuating.

Any instance, such as that of Manthara and Kaikeyi in the Valmiki *Ramayana*, even when read cursorily, is considerably more complicated than the generalized semantic described above and raises its own specific set of questions. The contested nature of socially approved languages for embodying the interests of women, definitions of individual agency and of 'character', the nature of institutional forms, interpretative schemas, and tacit consensualities which structure the episode of incitement in the epic are difficult to contextualize. The epic not only covers a protracted period of centuries and an extended, even variable, social space, but is also internally fissured by the different versions layered into its composition and by social difficulties that were barely acknowledged in extant prescriptive texts. Given the growing emphasis on chastity for women alongside the emphasis on primogeniture which was still contested as a norm for succession,[30] the partial shift from a tribal to an agricultural mode of production and substantial alterations of social configurations, the transition from lineage-based systems to monarchical states,[31] the shifts in sources of authority and of legitimation,[32] the epic's incorporation of a whole continuum of social and economic forms,[33] the different coexisting forms of marriage, the implied shifts from matriliny to patriliny,[34] and the traces of polyandry among the Ikshvakus and the *vanars* (monkeys) which exist in the epic,[35] how do we begin to conceptualize the reformulation of patriarchies and the shaping of convoluted agential modes for women? Are these produced through the contradictions of these transitions as they are encapsulated in the epic which compresses several layers of time?

The episode of incitement makes a signal omission. There is no reference to Dashrath's promise to Kaikeyi's father in a 'bride price' agreement or stipulation made at marriage, that her son would inherit the throne.[36] Whatever its historical coordinates may prove to be, the omission *functions* ideologically: as a transmutation of contradictions that shifts the coherence of the narrative from women's customary entitlements, or more specifically a woman's 'rights' stemming from a specific type of marriage transaction, to the marital obligations of (all) women. This structuring evasion controls the reception of the epic: it delegitimizes and villainizes first Manthara then Kaikeyi, makes a 'victim' of Dashrath, and inflects both the evaluation of the 'character' of the inciting women as well of the mode of redress they plan. Though the marriage agreement simply does not enter the chain of causality or sense of motivation in this episode, it is not fully suppressed in the early part of the *Ayodhyakhand*.[37] It lurks in the conspiratorial air about the coronation: Dashrath in his haste omits to invite Bharat, explicitly tells Ram that it is better to perform it in Bharat's absence since Bharat may begin to entertain evil thoughts and cease to be the good brother he is at present, and tells Kaikeyi after telling his other wives and after the entire city has begun its preparations and crowds have collected, thinking that she will not know since the news has spread only that day. All of these amount to a subdued recognition of Bharat's claim to kingship. Almost at the end of the *Ayodhyakhand*, when the marriage agreement is mentioned by Ram, it is in order to persuade Bharat of his eligibility for kingship! It is given no weight as a causal or motivating event. Ram does not say anything about Dashrath breaking his pact and promise, or anything to exonerate Kaikeyi. His brief, bland *description* neutralizes the significance of the promise, impeding its social proliferation, deflecting the energy encapsulated in Kaikeyi and Manthara to disrupt desired social harmonies.

Manthara, Kaikeyi's nursemaid from her natal family, appears to speak the language of material interests: she implies that Kaikeyi's son Bharat has an equal right to the kingdom and should have been given at least half of it; Ram's coronation will mean a final disinheritance since only sons inherit from fathers; Ram is selfish and once crowned will be vindictive enough to exile or kill Bharat; Kaikeyi, the proud, beautiful sexual favourite of the king who has spurned her senior co-wife Kaushalya, will find her status changed since Kaushalya as Ram's mother will not miss the opportunity for revenge; the status of Bharat and his wives as well as the fortunes (and suffering) of Manthara are tied to Kaikeyi, and will be downgraded along with Kaikeyi's own who will now have to serve Kaushalya. Manthara peels away Ram's ideality—which the larger design of the epic obsessively establishes since his goodness is a validation of his right to kingship—calls Dashrath ungrateful, hypocritical, the betrayer and enemy of Kaikeyi, perceives the domestic situation as inherently conflictual, even factional, with Ram and Lakshman ranged against Bharat and Shatrughna. For her both fraternal and polygamous relations are the inevitable site of 'fission'. Her challenge to all forms of ideality goes against the grain of the epic.[38] The epic in turn is unequivocal about her wickedness, she is described as the producer of *vishaad* (sorrow), *bhed-bhav* (dissension), the *paapdarshini* who leads Kaikeyi to the road of sin. And yet even such a Manthara does not bring up the stipulation made in the marriage agreement. Is the unstated the assumed of consensuality, the inertia of commonsense, or does it exist at some frontier of articulation as the unsayable, even the unthinkable?

The plan hinges in part on what seem to be customary modes of expressing anger, presenting a grievance and seeking redressal or almost routine features for 'framing' women's discontent: the shedding of finery, the recourse to a display of suffering in an established *krodhagar* (literally abode of anger), extracting a promise from the king before asking for the boons. One verse sympathetically describes Kaikeyi's lying on the floor as the action of an *abala* or helpless woman, who has taken the only form of action available to her. The *krodhagar* speaks of an externality, assuageability, and excess of women's emotion—women, it seems, require theatres to play out emotions; as an institution which acknowledges polygamous relations as problematic, it organizes the release of emotions at a point where they do impinge on the domain of the king and state, but in a place which is still private and contained.

Manthara understands material interests as material and as related to 'rights' (not of course in the modern meaning but as socially acknowledged entitlements and rightful claims resting on birth, ascription, and context); however, she does not advocate that Kaikeyi claim them as such but rather as boons granted in return for her two earlier acts of bravery in saving Dashrath's life on the battlefield. Once she has made the plan her own, Kaikeyi adds to it a vow that if baulked she will starve herself to death in the *krodhagar*, and later also uses the language of *dharma* or duty with Dashrath and Ram.

Why does a justifiable claim or a 'right' warranted by a transaction change into a boon? What are the realities of the social world which the epic refracts? Is it that since Dashrath has already broken his agreement with her father and fixed Ram's coronation, there is no likelihood of his changing his mind? Or is it that he cannot publicly reverse his decision except under stronger pressure? Or that only fathers and not daughters can seek to enforce the provisos of such 'bride price' agreements? Or that the epic seeks to flatten the obvious conflict between the marriage agreement and primogeniture? Is a boon a consensual method of redress and the only way to counteract male deception? What is the nature of women's access to a *language* for expressing individuated interests in relation to the power of emerging prohibitive systems of moral classification? Is it that a king's boon is more binding, obligatory, and imperative? Is his boon coming to acquire more social legitimacy than a woman's rightful claim in the emerging language of *dharma* which Ram seeks to establish, and do Manthara and Kaikeyi use this knowledge?[39]

The semantic of the boon itself forces us to reconsider what agency may mean here. A boon, granted for good deeds or behaviour (bringing in the huge question of the social constitution of morality), is a highly personalized, legitimate way of gaining power. So for Kaikeyi a boon could signify *merit earned* in her *own* capacity rather than as a daughter given in a specific marriage arrangement. As merit earned it may even be perceived as a special and unique, yet rightful and enforceable claim. The boon, though non-contractual, rests on a tacit mutual agreement in which the giver, in a position of power relative to the grantee, must obey his own generosity. And if the content and terms of the boon are not specified by the giver or specified in the grantee's request at the moment of granting, then it becomes a *content-unknown* boon which makes the giver quite vulnerable—he does not know what he will be asked, he cannot withdraw without losing face, the sense of his own munificence, or perhaps even his power to grant.[40] However, for the grantee a deferred boon becomes a way of covering any future contingency which may arise: Kaikeyi describes it as *dharohar*—trust or deposit.

Finally, unlike a boon asked from the gods, a boon asked from a king would have to be commensurate with his capacity to give: it would occupy the material domain of resources under his control or fall within the purview of his political power. Though a king's boon recodes what is rightfully due as a favour or as bounty, it may be the only way open for a subject to express her *will* in relation to the king. If the boon is interpreted as a figurative trope (rather than as an evidential event) for exceptional, relatively unstructured and uncodified transfers of goods and power, then it hints at the social location, uneven distribution, and mechanics of power, albeit power practised as 'beneficence'. Kaikeyi's convoluted agential mode, based on an understanding of hierarchy among women in the palace, may after all not be all that indirect. She can and has been refused a 'right' conferred by an agreement, but she *cannot* be refused an already-granted boon, unless Dashrath undoes his kingly status and sacred appointment. And yet what if this understanding is based not merely on the internal semantic of the boon but on the fact that the social location of the boon itself has changed from the time when it was granted? An auratic, non-contractual, personal transaction, an unequal exchange, arbitrary in the sense that it is embedded in its own formal and social codes but not governed by enforceable laws, is sought to be encashed at a moment when the failure to grant the boon would *now* be involved in a dangerous ideological delegitimization of the state. This is a state that hinges both on the king's obligations towards and the 'contractual' rights of a choric, faceless *praja* (subjects) encoded as *dharma* and *satya* (truth)—together these amount to what is virtually a system of legitimation above the king.[41] Is the marriage agreement redundant in the changed context? Are Kaikeyi and Manthara investing in the new order for their own protection, but uncertainly using a mixture of old and new methods?

Is that why for the boon to be honoured it has to be shored up, even encircled by a promise on one side and a threat of suicide on the other? All three appear to draw on existing and emerging structures of public acceptability. The three levers—the promise, the boon, the threatened suicide—draw respectively on the power of the favourite wife's withheld sexuality, the *dharma* of a king, that is, a structure of public approval and stricture, and making a grievance public while placing the burden of guilt on the king. The first—withdrawal of favour—a form of sexual coquetry, builds a context for asking and is based on the only *personal* form of leverage Kaikeyi has.[42] The latter two rest on the application of moral pressure and production of guilt in a situation where she has no access to political power, and also play on Dashrath's own repeatedly expressed fear of public perception, infamy, and the opinion of other *men*.[43] It is this fear that makes him recast his desire for Kaikeyi as a sign of weakness. There is an element of misogyny in the public opinion which acts as a virtually juridical pressure on him; the recurring description of Dashrath as transfixed by the spell of *kaama* (carnal desire) ironically confounds desire and *dharma*—the very existence of *kaama* falsifies *dharma*. Kaikeyi's threat of making his breach of promise public by telling the *rajarshis* (royal princes who had adopted a life of devotion and become sages such as Ikshvaku and Viswamitra) could suggest traces of earlier jural systems of checks on the power of tribal chieftains that also carried notions of women's entitlements; but it explicitly invokes a new system of public arbitration of a king's *dharma* which is related to the sources of authority that were being popularized in the monarchical state—a triad of king, brahmin, and *rishi* (sage).[44] Her threat amounts to a recourse to genealogical principles and moral authority which encompass and transcend kingly authority, especially since the *rajarshis* can also signify a movement from kshatriya to brahmin.[45] Indeed there seems to be an altogether uneasy relation between different structures of authority, between multiple jural sites, and between male authority and male obligation, that becomes visible in both customary and evolving modes of redressal.

The tense relation of Kaikeyi with emerging 'rules' is evident, she is complicit with them in one sense but not 'knowing' or compliant enough in another. She argues in the name of abstractions and values that the epic itself exorbitates—*satya*, men's *dharma*, clan honour—in order to hold the weakening Dashrath to his word and later to put the onus of preserving or salvaging Dashrath's *dharma* on Ram. This enables her to taunt and fasten Dashrath and Ram to their self-representation, but does not prevent her from being villainized. And that seems to be because she has not learnt a corollary rhetoric of self-characterization—*naridharma* or woman's duty—which may be an emerging mode of negotiation based on an apparent 'exchange' of women's entitlements and men's obligations.[46] Sita and Kaushalya self-servingly confirm *naridharma*, play it as the basis of conjugal affectivities, mimic Ram both in ideal self-representation and in *displaying* virtue.[47]

Indeed *naridharma* is presented as a possible resolution of the running contradiction between patriarchal *dharma* and women's agency: unless male *dharma* is accompanied by female self-abnegation its values cannot be socially ensconced. Ram tries to resolve this contradiction before leaving for the forest telling first Kaikeyi, then his mother Kaushalya, who is claiming extreme ill-treatment by her husband, to remain, as a *pativrata* (faithful wife) should, with her husband, while asking Dashrath to show greater respect for his mother who has proved her virtue. He tries to establish a reciprocity between male duty and wifely virtue. Female incitement partly serves to set up a rationale for the necessity of *naridharma*. With Kaikeyi as foil all the other wives of the Ikshvakus not only appear good but become self-righteous, while two different rhetorics and modes of presentation, one externally planted and the other internally experienced, assist in making a villain of Kaikeyi and a victim of Dashrath. Kaikeyi's is a coached performance, while Dashrath's is a spontaneous outburst. Since the marriage agreement is never mentioned, her motives are reduced to domestic jealousy, fear of lowered status, an almost arbitrary cussedness, a product of maltutoring. Dashrath presents an exhaustive range of reasons, both 'public' and private', is 'humanized' as a nearly tragic, broken old man, torn by irreconcilable truths. The power of Dashrath's anguish becomes an argument against women's agency, pitting his suffering and proclamation of Kaikeyi's guilt against her demands. The mode of presentation magnifies her crime: Dashrath's anguish and pleading, the descriptions of the goodness and beauty of Ram, the expectations and congratulation of the crowd and of other women offered to Ram, Ram's rhetoric of filial obedience, Kaushalya's anguish at hearing the news of the exile, the description of the luxury of the palace Ram must forsake for the hardship of the forest are interleaved at great length with Kaikeyi's stubbornness, her disobedience, and lack of doubt. Similarly, Dashrath's silence puts the onus of telling Ram of the decision on Kaikeyi. She is left only with the coldness of a stance, everyone else suffers, has emotions. No one mitigates anything for Kaikeyi. Eventually she becomes the object of everyone's hatred and anger.

One latent contradiction is that a boon granted to her in the

capacity of a wife who has been extraordinarily 'good' and courage-
ous is sought to be encashed as a 'mother' securing her future when
Dashrath's *grihasthashram* (stage of life as a householder) is about to
end, thereby shifting the locus of exercising power in a way which
dramatically opposes husband to son. Bharat's rejection of his mother
—a denial of an affective, primordial bond—functions as a statement
that wifehood and motherhood should *not* contradict.[48]

Ironically, the epic in fact highlights the precariousness if
not failure of male protection and the way it interacts with dependency: women—neglected, deserted, rejected—cannot rely fully on
the protection of the kin group, while protection and even reciprocity
from a husband is uncertain.[49] At one level protection seems to be
given only if the wife is good. But even obedient wives lose out as with
Kaushalya and Sita.[50] Despite its anxiety to establish a male ideality
(extending into exemplary kingship), the contradictions are not
resolved in the Valmiki *Ramayana*, both Dashrath and Ram die of
grief.[51] Nor do changing modes of male authority and royal legitimation square easily with existing and emerging patriarchies. If
protection is to be one of the 'contractual' elements within a patriarchal ensemble of obligations and entitlements, then it is not fully in
place. Is this because protection conflicts with *dharma*, duty, and
public consent, that is, with other social forms of consensuality which
are *simultaneously* sought to be instated?[52] Or is the epic showing not
the failure of protection but trying to establish, somewhat inconsistently, the conditions under which it can work?

Women themselves seem to have different degrees of inves-
titure in the old and the new; involved in the reformulation of a patriarchy, they use and waver between two *different* axes of consent. The
definition of women's agency is also problematic both in relation to
the mythicization of the plot and the individuation of character. The
convoluted agential modes of women interact with direct male political agencies to propel the plot. Is this too a trace of an earlier, more
dispersed form of decision-making among men and women, being
reinterpreted in a new morality of the good wife and the new centra-
lization of state power in men? In the later vaishnavizing interpolations in the Valmiki *Ramayana* the events acquire the additional
gloss of being preordained.[53] Character exists at the ambivalent node
of two different causal sequences—motivation and preordainment.

Yet if Kaikeyi and Manthara are also serving the purpose of the gods in assisting Ram's preordained task, then why the severity of the condemnation?[54] If Kaikeyi and Manthara set in motion a whole series of events starting with Ram's exile and his mythic deification, which are however an offshoot of Kaikeyi's *presence* on the battle-field, then how do we define 'political' and 'domestic' domains? Does this device signify the 'domestic' origin of a massive myth of male valour? Or did women's agency have both political origins and conse-quences though its own modes and the changes that were occurring curtailed social acknowledgement?[55]

The individuation of agency is also problematic. Since Man-thara incites Kaikeyi to incite Dashrath, in one sense they form a sin-gle agential unit.[56] However, the relation between the two itself appears to form a set of mutually displaced agencies. First, Kaikeyi is presented as good until 'converted' by Manthara—her very nature is said to have altered. Manthara as evil incarnate and Kaikeyi's con-version together undercut any full sense of motivation on their part, their actions retain an edge of arbitrariness. The second remarkable fact is that once converted, Kaikeyi metaphorically *beautifies*, even sexualizes, the hunchback Manthara's body almost in the language of love—even the hump is no longer a deformity but an object of love, a unique, integral part of her. The hump is where Manthara's intellect, inclination, recollection, jurisprudence, wisdom, sagacity, statecraft, knowledge of fraud and delusion (*mati, smriti, buddhi, rajniti,* knowledge of the *mayas*) are stored; if Bharat is crowned Kaikeyi will ornament the hump with a gold necklace and anoint it with sandal-wood.[57] Admiration or gratitude takes the form of a fulsome acknow-ledgement of Manthara's person which becomes implicitly equal to or even surpasses Kaikeyi's own. What is the significance of endow-ing Manthara with a beauty that is a full complement to her intelli-gence? It may be a sign of the suppressed potentials for reversal of the hierarchical relationships between women, coded here as 'beauty' and 'ugliness'. In that case, Shatrughna's dragging of the bedecked, bejewelled Manthara across the floor breaking her ornaments, until Kaikeyi intercedes with Bharat to save her, would be the symbolic inverse of the beautification. The now speechless Manthara sits at Kai-keyi's feet looking at her for protection with *kaatar* eyes, that is, at the brink of unspecified emotions.[58] Third, though Manthara dictates the

strategy, she resents having to do so: she even suggests a disingenu-
ousness on Kaikeyi's part in suddenly choosing to forget a story—of
the two boons granted her by Dashrath—she has often retold,
thereby 'setting up' Manthara as the schemer. In this virtual 'exposure'
of Kaikeyi, Manthara appears to understand Kaikeyi's contradictory
location in this patriarchal system. Manthara recognizes the springs
of Kaikeyi's resentment as well as her capacity to extract compensations from and enter into 'contractual', consensual settlements while
she herself, personalized only by her 'abnormality', has neither a
socially consolidated identity nor a set of consensually accepted capacities from which to 'work' the system, and can only hope to sustain
the pressure of individual incitement.

Finally, the wavering misogyny of the epic is a curious
feature. Here 'character' hovers between the personalization of individual error and the depersonalization of misogyny which system-
atizes female error. Dashrath veers between blaming Kaikeyi personally and representing himself as a man trapped by the lure of *a*
woman. He reminds himself that in condemning her he must not
condemn all women as selfish. This may be an indication that misogyny was already consensual enough to be considered as an explanatory mechanism. Bharat's abuse of his mother, though the most
vindictive,[59] is personalized: all women appear good to him in contrast with Kaikeyi.[60] However, both he and Dashrath fear that the
consequences of her action will bring total social perversion, break
the bonds of conjugality, reverse orderly familial and social relations—a dystopian vision which may be a precursor of the conflation
of the dark age of *kaliyug* and *strisvabhav* later in some puranic
texts.[61] Sumantra, who like the others berates Kaikeyi as a woman
who has courted widowhood[62] and destroyed the honour of the lineage, claims she has inherited her *svabhav* (disposition) from her
mother![63] Though a strict binarism between s*tridharma* (the duty of
women) and *strisvabhav* (the essential nature of women) is not in
place, this does become one of the sites where misogyny is produced—
a site marked by the tenuousness and fading of one language and set
of sources authorizing women's 'rights' and guaranteeing their legitimate claims, as well as by the strong presence of an emerging notion
of the good wife's duties as the qualifying condition and desired basis
upon which women's entitlements should be sanctioned.[64] Does

misogyny originate in the crystallization of specific hierarchical social forms? Produced in this instance through a set of ideological manoeuvres, in part to ratify female self-abnegation, what does it say about the existing social agency of women? How does the move from the individual errant woman to the universalization of misogyny and its subsequent placement in schemas of good and evil, occur? Is Dashrath's split between patriarchal *dharma* and sexual desire, between the *'dharma'* of instituting primogeniture and the *'dharma'* of keeping his word, an indication that misogyny was produced from the *contradictions* between a patriarchy and other social structures?[65]

Under institutional sanction: the discourse of violence

Incitement in the Valmiki *Ramayana,* then, is one version of a female agential mode in the making, a mode which is involved in the production of misogyny, replete with unresolved contradictions, some of which are compounded by our historical distance. It may be pertinent to conclude the discussion with a contemporary instance which, though it invokes the sedimented histories and repertoire of female incitement in its narrative and cinematic forms, is a different phenomenon and part of a very different problematic.

Sadhvi Rithambara, the Bharatiya Janata Party (BJP) ideologue, is placed squarely within a militant, communal, hindu rightwing formation. She affiliates herself to and speaks from two interconnected sites of institutionalized power: a 'community' of *sadhumahants* (religious mendicants and heads of *maths* or religious centres), and the organizational cluster of the BJP, Vishwa Hindu Parishad (VHP), Bajrang Dal (BD), and Rashtriya Swayamsevak Sangh (RSS). The explicit staging of herself as an inciting woman emanates from an organized public domain; female incitement here is a unit of political discourse but works through a complex set of refractions.

This right-wing formation shares with other patriarchal

ideological ensembles the desire to simultaneously consensualize women's investment in patriarchal values and introduce or confirm a number of conditionalities; but unlike some other ensembles, it seeks to do so by invoking women's agency in the cause of *hindu rashtra* (hindu nation). The heritage of communal positions emerged out of the matrix of the nineteenth century and one of its many features was the attempt to square 'traditional' or existing patriarchal forms with emerging bourgeois patriarchal forms;[66] its present arena is a social formation in which the issue of 'acceptable' bourgeois rights for women of the middle and even upper strata is far from having been settled. Rithambara, a part of the new negotiations underway, is engaged in both a reassertion and a reformulation of patriarchal values, most notably in their *coercive* aspects.

Rithambara's public speeches reproduce a hindu-communal patriarchal history hinging on male sexual honour, *izzat* (honour), the values of patriliny and patrimony. She describes the future of the country, a future that hindu militancy must prevent, as a *repetition* of the rape and pillage which supposedly characterized medieval India. The underlying notion of rape as a norm, even an accepted rule in the complicit codes of both victor and vanquished, is in fact a typical feature of masculinist ideologies and invokes a broad *male* consensus on 'retribution' by violence on 'other' women as just. Rape here is emphatically not a routine exercise of patriarchal power practised through and existing in family, class, caste, or state structures that cut across all religious groups; rather it is the unique history of hindu women's sexual vulnerability, and since hindu women represent 'community' identity, rape represents a violation of the 'community's' proprietorship of its woman by 'other' men. Implicitly legitimizing the masculinist ideology of rape as 'normal' through the consenting voice of a woman, her discourse suppresses resistance by women in the name of anything other than 'community' or communal hatred, thus pitting hindu women against muslim women and men, while her persona of the inciting woman simultaneously produces a specific masculinity revolving on competition and retaliation, in which protection of one's 'own' women involves violation of 'other' women. Rape cannot be challenged as an institution from such a position since its entire rhetoric is already patriarchal; decrying the rape of hindu women alone in these terms can imply accepting similar assaults on non-hindu women. The march of this patriarchal history is punctuated with corroborative masculinist ideologies of male emasculation and impotence, and redeploys colonial images of effeminate men and lazy natives as a rationale for female incitement. In the process there is an obsessive reenactment and reclaiming of male honour which first plays on male fears of dispossession, and then on women's anxieties by displaying all hindu women as past and future victims of sexual violation,[67] and finally equates male sexual honour with the projected *hindu rashtra* itself. 'Masculinity' acquires a single axis of social determination. The ability of hindu men to protect their women, in a singular cross-caste/class universalization of the (usually kshatriya) claim to martial valour, becomes the basis of their right to self-government and their claim to monopolize a nation.

The nation, so defined as a condensation of the sexual honour of men of a single 'community', is intended to cut across and neutralize the contradictions of caste and class. Rithambara's incitement involves the social production of guilt and anxiety; in the address to men—*bhaiyon aur hinduon*, brothers and hindus—the play on sexual honour carries the implicit threat of emasculation in the name of the violated mother(land), acquiring an additional frisson from her persona of the '*sadhvi*' (literally, a chaste woman). 'Celibacy' is played as political theatre. Within the stage-managed presence of the *sadhvi*, she uses sexual innuendo and jokes, exhorts in breathless *chaupais* (verses with four-line rhyme pattern), projects a latent sexuality; the performance encourages a specific sort of male bonding as well as titillates middle-class women in the audience. These devices work together to legitimize not only patriarchal but also communal forms of violence, which both in her own rhetoric and in her invocations is presented as a continuous, reiterated narrative of zealous women and flagging men.

At one level hindu identity remains patrilineal—*ragon mein hindu baap ka khoon daur raha hai*, the blood of hindu fathers is flowing in their veins—while hindu strength (*shakti*) is presented as a divided patrimony, which can be reclaimed only if they unite.[68] At another level history is presented as 'family' history—as a system of correctly *claimed* family lineages—and functions as both a device of conditional assimilation and exclusion. Muslims who claim Babur or Aurangzeb as an ancestor are at once treacherous enemies and cowardly eunuchs, *napunsak*—while those who claim Rahim and Raskhan can be addressed as uncles, *tau* and *chacha*. Muslims are asked to recognize that four or five generations ago their ancestors were the same as hindus. Family history is also the history of good and evil—hindus have not worshipped their villainous relatives like Kansa, and if a Ravana or a Kansa is born then a god arrives as an *avatar* (incarnation) to destroy him. Ram is claimed as a father and his birthplace defended on the basis of custom, ancestry, and emotional affiliation. The separation of wheat from chaff within the family not only implies that muslims lack family feeling and have an inadequate schema of good and evil but draws on a masculinist ideology of the family feud.[69] This 'family' history can acknowledge kinship with (some) muslims and simultaneously exorcize the guilt of murdering kin through the device of the family feud, which makes violence admissible by irrevocably turning kin into foes. At a historical and political level, an ancestral lineage is also presented as a product of selection rather than of birth to enable a selective appropriation of the history of nationalist reforms, and to make a distinction between 'good' and 'bad' hindus: thus hindu defeat is a product not of "Islam" but of the power hunger of medieval kings and contemporary politicians, while hindus are divided between the Ramvanshis and the Ravanavanshis.[70] At a social level, the family appears as the unit of social cohesion and Rithambara's speech builds a fear of hindu family relations breaking down, with a concept of rights and the greed for inheritance replacing duty towards parents on the part of children. The family, then, as a set of associations, appears in a contradictory light—it is essential to communal identity, patriarchal practice, and an honest polity, while itself remaining above the law and outside history.

Who is Rithambara herself? In the effort to carve a constituency, she must name herself as an individual in relation to a collectivity and its interests. Incitement in its inspirational forms found a fertile soil in certain nationalist tendencies where endangered masculinity, endangered women, endangered religion and nation were key themes. Numerous popular narratives related the 'adventures' of rajput women either inciting or assisting their menfolk in battles with muslim rulers or themselves engaged in direct combat. Valorized transformations of unworldly ascetics into patriotic militants as well as nationalist interpellations of hindu women as uncorrupted were also common. Further, even though several nationalist ideologies relied on and recycled convoluted notions of women's agency, they also succeeded in conferring a direct political agency on 'good' women who could act on behalf of the nation. This repertoire of nationalism becomes the opportunist preamble to Rithambara's self-location.

She names herself not as a woman but as a *sadhvi*, one of a community of *sant-mahatmas* or saints and holy men (shades of Bankim's novel *Ananda Math?*). *Sadhus* are presented as epic figures, a composite Viswamitra come to rescue India from Ravana. The content of this claim is not very different from other BJP MPs who are also offering self-images as *sants* engaged, now as in ancient times, in purging or cleansing a criminalized body-politic.[71] Rithambara seeks to present *sadhus* as the uncorrupt new Mr Cleans of Indian politics who, however, must now stand for unmitigated violence against minority groups. The language of these hitherto peaceful men has become *ugra*, militant, but, she claims, it is only the corruption of the polity which has brought them to the streets (that is, unworldly ascetics have perforce turned into contemporary communalists). Not only do they now constitute a supreme court of saints, *santon ka nyayalay*, which has decreed that the claim to Ram Janmabhumi is valid, making all other proof redundant, but they will also provide weapons for the crowds who are exhorted to fight like Indra and Chandragupta.

One subset of the social relations which inform these self-descriptions becomes visible. The agency of *sadhus* is offered as both direct and surrogate (not unlike that offered to women); their real interests are said to lie elsewhere, in the assured attainment of spiritual monarchy. Rithambara challenges misguided hindus who think they are playing a political game or looking for political power, all they want is Ram and his supposed birthplace:

> *Are hame vote chahiye? Ham sadhu mahatma Vyas gaddi pe baith ke poori kaynat ke badshah ho jate hai. Hame tumhaari Delhi ki satta nahin chahiye. Hame hamara Ram chahiye. Hame Ram janam bhumi chahiye.* (Do you think we want votes? We saints can become emperors of the universe simply by virtue of our claim to the omniscience of Vyas. We do not want political power in Delhi. We want our Ram. We want Ram's place of birth.)

Through the very energy of her disavowal *sadhus* emerge as they are: heads of decayed priestly groups locked in internecine battles, seeking new sources of political, electoral, and institutional power, and being sought as subsidiary allies by those emergent classes and class fractions investing in the ideology of Hindutva.

The persona of the *sadhvi* is clothed in self-abnegation, that abstraction which is the property of the body of *sadhus* to whom she belongs. This identification along with that of the past militancy of 'good' women—Durgavati, Rani of Jhansi—authorizes, empowers, and becomes the rationale for present incitement. By apparently giving up her entitlement to the material, Rithambara not only acquires an exemplary, exceptional, personal upward mobility, but is able to shift the level of political discourse from the challenge of material reallocations to an ideological plane.[72] As a woman 'saint', she can assimilate the legacy of reform into communal reformism, vindicating the vicious call to communal violence on the ground of removing the inner taint of hindus. Secondly, by joining the band of the desireless, she not only gains the authority to play with the discourse of desire and male impotence/sexuality (rather than confine herself to the conventional advocacy of celibacy or *brahmacharya*), but produces a volatile intersection between male sexuality and militant political agency—sexualizing both the *hindu rashtra* and communal violence, achieving an effect quite different from the male use of similar discourse. The demand for aggression which follows accusations of male impotence is publicly made by a woman; it not only welds men's capacity for violence with 'proof' of their sexual potency, but these have now also to be displayed *to* a woman whose mantle of celibacy and discourse of desire at once neuter and provocatively emphasize her own female presence.

The simultaneous interpellation of men as hindus who desire a *hindu rashtra* and bear the burden of a corrupt polity, as protectors of women and 'true' nationalists, as the goaded and insulted victims of history, as men whose past *bhaichara* (brotherliness) and *sharafat* (decency) towards muslims having been read as unmanly cowardice must now prove their masculinity through warlike violence, offers them the prospect of reversal. The "awakened hindu" slides metonymically into a pantheon of armed gods—Bajrang with his *gada* (mace), Ram with his *dhanush* (bow), and Shiv with his *tandav* (dance of destruction). The devaluation of morals and ethics, public corruption and blackmarketing, the breakdown of familial relationships, as well as male degeneration into laziness and effeminacy, or the loss of *purusharth* (valour, energy), can all be *spectacularly reversed* through a three-point programme of reform: voting BJP, reclaiming Ram Janmabhumi, and killing muslims.

Violence is explicitly linked to communal rioting—a major site for the crystallization of communal identities—and familiar riot-centred ideologies of hindu retaliation with their settled discursive moves of provocation and revenge are replayed.[73] One of the specific targets for instigation is the PAC (Provincial Armed Constabulary)—of whose notorious, partisan, and aggressive role in riot violence we need no reminder.[74] The PAC are said to have hindu hearts beating beneath their secular uniform, *PAC ne vardiyan pehni hai lekin dil hinduon ka dharak raha hai*, and are asked to fire at dissenters and muslims.[75] Rithambara's personal identification with violence as the only decisive political solution is remarkably bloodthirsty. Drawing on the Durga and Kali genres of female militancy, she repeatedly argues for bloodshed, *khoon-kharaba*, on a large scale, if not for outright genocide:

> *Tum baat karte rahte ho ki ham balidaan denge. Are ham balidaan dene se pehle ham hazaaro balidaan lenge. Ab yeh khoon bahayenge hi nahi, auron ka bhi khoon bahayenge.* (You keep saying that you will sacrifice yourselves. But before we sacrifice ourselves we will compel 'others' to sacrifice themselves. We will not only shed our own blood but we will also make the blood of 'others' flow.)

As an inciting woman she seeks to produce a series of clones. Stories of mothers or wives inciting sons and husbands to militancy are ritually invoked: Bhagat Singh's mother who wept when her son was hanged not because he was dying but because she had no more sons to offer to the nation, rubs shoulders with the wife of a *seth* (merchant) who repeatedly tells her husband that thieves are entering the house, emptying the money box, and leaving with the loot. The merchant's wife tries with these taunts to prod and activate her husband's virile masculinity—*is tareh patni ne pati ke purushtva ko phir kureda*—and failing, bursts out with an irate demand for action from him. Women in families need to protect male *izzat* and nurture male valour. Ironically, the ideology of *izzat* is open to such cross-class universalization precisely because it mimics those actual practices of patriarchal violence against women which in fact cut across caste, class, and communal distinctions. Here *izzat* is presented as a structuring principle both in daily life and in times of crisis. *Izzat* is in fact placed at the intersection between patriarchies and communalization—two axes of inequality—and underpins other claims to family, religion, and nation. Women are offered agential roles only as the implicit subjects of a communal history of sexual violation and their consent is sought in the interests of their *own* protection.

The literal effects of Rithambara's incitement should not be underestimated. Her speeches are reported to produce delirium and male hysteria among listening crowds[76] and there are instances of men taking up the proffered role: after one of her speeches some BJP supporters reportedly beat up muslims in an adjacent *mohalla* (neighbourhood) before going home.[77]

The agency of such literalization is not a spontaneous but an institutional one, one which also gives Rithambara the 'protection' to instigate. Her speeches constitute a small part of the general instigatory activity and propaganda produced by these institutions. The communal violence that her speeches leave in their wake or return to legitimize is not propelled by ideological mobilization alone—but erupts, rather, in specific conjunctural combinations with the operations of a growing institutional infrastructure, forms of political mobilization, local histories, and the wider contradictions of social processes, creating spaces vulnerable to communal differentiation and violence. That is why her speeches 'work' at some times and in some places but not in others. Rithambara herself is 'controlled' by communal organizations and seems to have been assigned a conjunctural role: she is moved from backstage to centrestage at strategic moments. The men who engage in communal violence do not do so literally at her behest but on the understanding, which she *represents*, that violence has an institutional sanction, organizational protection, a degree of popular consent, and consequently immunity from subsequent legal action. Participation in violence in turn builds both complicity and danger, reinforcing the need for party or other organizational protection.

Before turning to some of the specificities of her institutional agency and her function as an inciting woman, I will try to situate

Rithambara in relation to the broad ideology, flexibility, selective
appropriation, and current location of this cluster of right-wing
organizations, especially the BJP. The BJP not only has different caste–
class, urban–rural constituencies in different regions, but shifts are
taking place in its social base.[78] The right-wing needs to renegotiate
its basis of legitimization both internally with its cadres and externally
in relation to desired constituencies. As such there is now a whole
spectrum of right-wing ideologies and practices while a range of mul-
tifaceted positions, local as well as general, are being produced. Their
eclecticism as well as appropriative procedures have to be seen both
as a part of the wider imperatives of this spectrum as well as in relation to their present political location.

At the ideological level, the eclecticism within this formation
is partly a product of using different existing modes of legitimization—
mythic, empirical, historical, customary, religious, experiential.[79]
Indeed this multifacetedness has helped to multiply the axes of communalization which extend beyond religion, as well as to create
flexible mechanisms for the inclusion into or exclusion from the
hindu fold of some minority and tribal groups in tandem with the
demands of changing situations.[80] However, though in some senses
the accommodative capacities of this right-wing formation make for
an internal pluralism, they also *unify* it and make it monolithic in
relation to what it is opposed to. Given the unsettled nature of class,
caste, and gender issues, communalization has become a major axis
of internal unification and public consensuality, a vector for the interested reinterpretation of social contradictions.

There has also been a selective appropriation of left, liberal,
civil liberties, and feminist platforms, which are then deflected, controlled, condemned. In this process *blocks of existing social consensus
are being shifted rightward*. Present consciousnesses are appropriated, re-coordinated, achieving new consensual patterns. Liberal positions in particular have been either massively taken over or evacu-
ated.[81] Rithambara achieves the shift from the liberal to the militant
right by presenting political choice as a temporal–historical movement ('we were once liberal, tolerant and selfless but now . . .'),
making a sliding continuum from liberal to right along which it
becomes *natural* to move. Even the classic image of secular coexistence (*mandir, masjid, gurudwara*) is used first to promote a liberal

self-description and then, in this historical schema, turned into a rationale for communal violence.

A parallel process is at work with feminism. Certain aspects of bourgeois feminism, women's advances and own efforts to redefine their social agency or sexuality, are selectively acknowledged but only in order to curb them, roll them back, or to monitor women's entry into the public–political domain, or more broadly to control the ways in which 'public' becomes 'private' and vice versa. However, contradictions between domestic ideologies, patriarchal practices, and independent public–political roles for women are rampant within this formation. The package on offer ranges from the defence of 'voluntary' widow immolation by Vijayraje Scindia, the blatant antifeminism of Bal Thackeray interested in pushing women back into the home, to K.R. Malkani's claim that though inequalities exist Indian women are by and large "queens" in their homes,[82] to Rithambara's explicit appeals to certain kinds of initiative on the part of women. Significantly, right-wing women's support for Thackeray is said to be dwindling, while though Rithambara's claim to inspirational agency appeals to both men and women, she has been criticized by some BJP men and women.[83] Neither Thackeray nor Rithambara singly represents the fully consolidated or consensual voice of the hindu communal right. At other sites the BJP has been taking certain aspects of bourgeois feminism on board; for instance, their *stri-shakti* versus *stri-mukti* (women's strength versus women's liberation) programme in Gujarat and Maharashtra continues some aspects of middle-class reformism and presumes the existence of working women while attempting to denigrate other aspects and types of feminism as deviant.[84] Rithambara's position needs to be seen in relation to this conflict of interpellations, as a singular variation among a whole range of ideological positions being produced within this right-wing formation.

The eclectic and appropriative strategies of this cluster of right-wing organizations allows them to insert themselves into different regional and political conjunctures, gives them the ability to absorb and replay conjunctural gains, situational exigencies, contingent attitudes, to use religious faith as well as to bypass it, in order to bind unconsolidated urban masses into collectivities and to achieve new, smooth relations between verbal rhetorics and conflicting social practices.

The concatenation of voices (male and female) in this rightwing formation, in some sense, corresponds with its current political location. The development of multiple organized addresses alongside broad general ideologies, as well as of different, locally accented ideological positions and institutions drawing on different class–caste and experiential clusters, is related not only to the range and to changes in class–caste constituencies in different regions, but also to the overall strategy of simultaneous insertion into existing rural–urban power structures while making new avenues for political mobility. The coordinated, quadrangular political formation of the hindu communal right—the BJP as a parliamentary opponent of the central government relying on nonparliamentary activity, as itself a contender for central state power in search of appropriate legitimacy, alongside the steady, systemic infiltration of the institutions of state and civil society, and the development of fascistically organized militant wings in the RSS, BD and Durga Vahini allied to the 'fanatically' religious VHP, with their ready recourse to communal violence in specific electoral or other conjunctures—is making for an oscillation between parliamentary forms and fascist methods. This, combined with its overall location, make it possible to understand both the internal heterogeneity of ideological positions as well as the specific modalities of holding ideologies as a persistent pressure, as a sign of political power, as a reminder of the organizational capacity for violence, and as trigger for violence in specific conjunctures.

If we look at Rithambara as one such pressure point, then apart from the overlap between the content of her speeches and organizational positions, at least two of the special functions which female incitement serves can be demarcated. Here it is once again significant that Rithambara does not name herself as a woman. Her function is not to represent other women in relation to the problems of inequality, but to reiterate and represent women only in terms of a specific set of patriarchal consensualities which are particularly conducive to conjunctures of communal violence. (From these she also extracts a singular discursive and political power for herself.) It is not that she blocks off all change for women on the hindu communal right, but rather offers them the combination of direct and convoluted agency that is also vested in her own person: a particular sort of militancy drawing on nationalist models which infuses her with a quasi-patriarchal authority combined with two facets of bourgeois domestic ideologies, self-abnegation and women's surveillance of the public sphere.[85] This offer of male protection is accompanied by the usual codicil, that protection from the threat of male violence be accompanied by submission to patriarchal norms in the home. In other words, women are yet again asked to become the consenting custodians of patriarchal values in order to be eligible for certain forms of protection and agency, but this time with the implicit guarantee of becoming participants as instigators in hindu male communal coercion and as sharers of the power which may accrue from it. Female incitement becomes a compensatory structure for women to *police* men while it is at the same time poised and *held* at the brink of militancy in its own right. However, the question of the precise nature of the needs and interests of different sections of women which the hindu communal right is *producing* and *encashing* is much bigger and as yet unanswered. How, for instance, is Rithambara's offer of male protection articulating with different existing or desired class positions within the constituency of Hindutva?

Secondly, Rithambara performs the function of drawing *wide consensualities* of values, including that of male coercion, through which patriarchies function, into a *new* relation with organized hindu militancy. She elicits consent for patriarchal values on the basis of defence of 'nation' and 'religion', and simultaneously uses existing social consent for patriarchies to get consent for *hindu rashtra*.[86] In her own combination of institutional power with normative patriarchal ideologies recast as a challenge to male sexuality, she ratifies both. She thus draws on and increases areas of consent, enlarges fronts of recruitment. The issue here is one of the very *modality* of the production of new ideological constellations. What is the nature of the articulations, transformations, as well as displacements between the political, the economic, and this ideological constellation? Which are the mechanisms by which performative political rhetorics reappropriate media and cinematic forms, relate them to 'commonsense', and then encash the resonance of both? What is the precise relation of these cultural forms of articulation to their own respective histories and of the specific ideologies generated by this hindu communal right-wing formation to its existing and desired social base? These broad questions still need to be addressed but one conclusion is inescapable. This discourse is antifeminist in its attempt to re-instate patriarchal consensualities that have been fractured by feminist struggles, while female voices of consent and incitement enhance the capacity of communal ideologies to be shifted about *en bloc* and reattached to different social tensions produced by gender inequality, unequal distribution of resources, developmental deformations, and an increasingly delegitimized state.[87]

Lectures and seminar presentations based on this essay were given at INDRA, University of Amsterdam, Chandigarh University, Vikas Adhyayan Kendra, Lonavla, and IIAS, Shimla in 1991 and 1992. It was first printed as a Nehru Memorial Museum and Library Occasional Paper in August 1992 and subsequently in *Economic and Political Weekly* 28:18 (1 May 1993). I have used muslim and hindu in lower case in this essay in an attempt to neutralize the demonization, exorbitation, and encashment of religious identities in Rithambara's oratory. I want to thank Ram Bapat for his enthusiastic and detailed discussion in Lonavla, Uma Chakravarti for sorting out numerous queries, and both of them along with Aijaz Ahmad for their comments on the first draft.

Notes

Between the lines: in introduction

1 The discourse of postmodernism, it is suggested, though established in a "Eurocentred 'First World'" is "the discourse of the periphery" which "decentres the centre" by revealing that "there is not one world" but many worlds "being lived at different speeds, according to different rhythms, producing contradictory histories" ("Introduction", *Postmodernism: A Reader*, ed. Thomas Doherty (New York: Columbia Univ. Press, 1993), p. 445).

2 Specificity has been the vector of ontological difference based on structural stasis, ethno-racial and religio-cultural typology bestowed on nonwestern societies by orientalisms and refurbished by neo-orientalist sociology. Anowar Abdel-Malek was among the first to point out that the accepted concept of specificity was developed mainly to deal with nonwestern, nonindustrial societies, travelled from "colonial sociology" to the "sociology of development", "underdevelopment", and the "third world", resulted in an exceptionalism that was mortgaged to an ethnocentric, often racialist, notion of "authenticity" and a form of "cultural irredentism". It permitted a recognition of difference between these societies but also posited an "unbridgeable gap" between them predicated on structurally different particularities and not on historical development. See *Social Dialectics: Civilizations and Critical Theory* (Albany: State Univ. of New York Press, 1981), pp. 166–68.

3 As the continuous self-transformation into kshatriya (warrior) groups seems to indicate. Sheldon Pollock suggests that central Asian and Iranian immigrants may in fact have expanded the discursive domain of Sanskrit and turned it squarely into an instrument of polity. See "Literary History, Indian History, World History", *Social Scientist*, 269–71 (Dec. 1995), p. 127.

4 The implications of the absence of a perfect pattern of industrialization or uniform transitions, uneven capitalist development and simultaneity of modees of production in European countries have been well understood. (See Ernst Bloch, *Heritage of Our Times* (Oxford: Polity Press, 1994), pp. 90–91; Fernand Braudel, *Afterthoughts on Material Civilization and Capitalism*, trs. Patricia Ranum (Baltimore: Johns Hopkins Univ. Press, 1977), pp. 88–102; Amiya Kumar Bagchi,

"From a Fractured Compromise to a Democratic Consensus", *Economic and Political Weekly*, 26:11–12 (March 1991); Colin Mooers, *The Making of Bourgeois Europe* (London: Verso, 1991), p. 31; R.S. Neale, "Afterword" in *History and Class*, ed. R.S. Neale (Oxford: Basil Blackwell, 1983), pp. 278–80; Raymond Williams, *The Politics of Modernism* (London: Verso, 1989), pp. 44–45.)

Ellen Meiksins Wood points out that there was a coherent conjunction of monarchy and Christianity with capitalist property relations in Britain and therefore the polarities between bourgeoisie/aristocracy, rationalism/religion, contract/hierarchy are false in English history. They cannot stand up against the fact that capitalism, conventionally represented as the fruition of 'bourgeois' values and practices, emerged and flourished first under the auspices of the English aristocracy and monarchy, not, for instance, as the historic project of a revolutionary bourgeoisie in France or a republican commercial patriciate in Italy. She proposes a different set of polarities for defining England's passage to modernity: rentier mentality versus productivism, politically constituted property versus economic modes of surplus extraction, the state as a form of property versus the separation of the state and civil society, production and property relations circumscribed by communal regulations and customary rights versus the laws of competition and market imperatives. See *The Pristine Culture of Capitalism* (London: Verso, 1993), p. 143.

5 See Rosa Luxemburg, *The Accumulation of Capital*, trs. A. Schwarzchild (New York: Monthly Review Press, 1964), pp. 368–418; Lionel Cliffe, "Class Formation as an 'Articulation' Process: East African Cases" in *Sociology of Developing Societies*, eds Hamza Alavi and Teodor Shanin (London: Macmillan, 1982), p. 269.

6 The phrase is derived from Althusser's formulation of social formations as simultaneously concrete wholes and as multiplicities of determinations. Though his model cannot be mechanically applied either to the Indian subcontinent or to the wider arena of colonization, his rejection of a continuous and homogenous time in favour of a structural history that can grasp the uneven, indirect efficacy of different structures within a given social whole remains suggestive in thinking about types of dislocation and torsion. See Louis Althusser and Etienne Balibar, *Reading Capital* (London: New Left Books, 1970), pp. 99–104.

7 On the significance of the qualitative rather than linear dialectics of time that Etienne Balibar discerns in Marx's writing, and Ernst Bloch's reflections on the asynchronicity of global history see Darko Suvin ("Two Cheers for Essentialism and Totality: On Marx's Oscillation and its Limits", *Rethinking Marxism*, 10:1 (Spring 1998), pp. 75–76). On the usefulness of positing more than one historical trajectory and thereby more complex patterns of decomposition and recombination of elements of modes of production see Henry Bernstein, "Industrialization, Development and Dependence" in *Sociology*, eds Alavi et al., pp. 231–32; Eric Olin Wright, "Class Analysis, History and Emancipation", *New Left Review*, 202 (Nov.-Dec. 1993), pp. 24–25; Alex Callinocos, *Theories and Narratives: Reflections on the Philosophy of History* (Durham: Duke Univ. Press, 1995), pp. 161–63.

8 For instance, in both missionary and administrative accounts, virtually opposing views emerged of India: stagnant/changing, a feudal class stratified society/a conglomeration of regional, caste or discrete religious communities/an ambiguous mess; of Indians: barbarians/an ancient high civilization, one they should eradicate/expropriate, restore/exploit; of Muslim rule: chaotic, barbaric, object of villainization/an imitable model; of British rule: as affiliated to Mughal rule and even its successor/as liberating oppressed Hindus from Muslim tyranny; and of the colonial mission: reform/preservation, non-interference/conversion of heathens, reproduction of precapitalist ideologies/enlightenment.

9 On the crucial difference of precolonial from colonial classification and between its operations in Britain and India in the production of ethnic, race, religious and caste difference, group identity, and majoritarianism see Arjun Appadorai, "Number in the Colonial Imagination" in *Orientalism and the Postcolonial Predicament*, eds Carol Breckenridge and Peter van der Veer (Philadelphia: Univ. of Pennsylvania Press, 1993), pp. 314 –31.

10 Albert Memmi's phrase in *The Colonizer and the Colonized* (Boston: Beacon Press, 1967), p. 88.

11 Jan Nederveen Pieterse's phrase, "Fictions of Europe", *Race and Class*, 32:3 (1991), p. 3; see also J.M. Blaut, *The Colonizers' Model of the World: Geographical Diffusionism and Eurocentric History* (London: Guilford Press, 1993), pp. 41, 59.

12 On English and French nationalism see Nigel Leask, *British Romantic Writers and the East: Anxieties of Empire* (Cambridge: Cambridge Univ. Press, 1993), p. 86; Ann Stoler, "Sexual Affronts and Racial Frontiers: National Identity, 'Mixed Bloods' and the Cultural Genealogies of Europeans in Colonial Southeast Asia", manuscript (1994).

13 Karl Pearson, "The Ethic of Free Thought" (1888), and Herbert Spencer, "Principles of Ethics" (1892–93), cited in Lorna Duffin, "Prisoners of Progress: Women and Evolution" in *The Nineteenth Century Women*, eds. Sara Delamont and Lorna Duffin (London: Croom Helm, 1978), pp. 63, 68, 85.

14 Rita Felski has pointed out that in Europe the figure of woman served as "a recurring cipher of the premodern within modernity itself" (*The Gender of Modernity* (Cambridge: Harvard Univ. Press, 1995), p. 56).

15 On these exclusions see Samir Amin, *Eurocentrism* (London: Zed, 1989); Joan Landes, *Women in the Public Sphere in the Age of the French Revolution* (Ithaca: Cornell Univ. Press, 1988); Felski, *The Gender of Modernity*; Paul Gilroy, *The Black Atlantic: Modernity and Double Consciousness* (Cambridge: Harvard Univ. Press, 1993); Sabina Lovibond, "Feminism and Postmodernism" in *Postmodernism and Society*, eds Roy Boyne and Ali Rattansi (New York: St Martins Press, 1993). Ironically these very excluded constituencies, women, blacks, the colonized, whose critiques were also affirmations, are the ones in whose names the (post)Enlightenment is being rejected today.

16 Reverse projects of indianizing Europe maintained the terms of eurocentrism. For instance, the counter-diffusionist thesis forged by a section of the Indian middle class in the crucible of British Orientalism, Indology, and Theosophy claimed that Hindu-Aryan India supplied the world with culture, wisdom, language, spirituality, and science-and indocentrism that pushed science and modernity backwards into ancient India, a cornucopia that prefigured modernity and so discounted derivation and preempted rupture.

17 See for instance, Kwame Anthony Appiah, "Postmodern, Postcolonial", *Critical Inquiry*, 17 (Winter 1991), p. 348; Nestor Garcia Canclini, "The Hybrid: A Conversation with Margarita Zires, Raymundo Mier, and Mabel Piccini", *Boundary* 2, 20:3 (1993), pp. 77–85; Ella Shohat, "Notes on the 'Post-Colonial'", Social Text, 31–32 (1993), p. 110; Gilroy, *The Black Atlantic;* Shalini Puri, "East Indian/West Indian: Discourses of Race and Place", mansucript (1994); Geeta Kapur, "*Dismantling the Norm" in Traditions/Tensions* (New York: Asia Society Gallery, 1996); Terry Eagleton, "Where Do Postmodernists Come From?" in *Defense of History: Marxism and the Postmodern Agenda*, eds Ellen Meiksins Wood and John Bellamy Foster (New York: Monthly Review Press, 1997), p. 21; Bart Moore-Gilbert, *Postcolonial Theory: Contents, Practices, Politics* (London: Verso, 1997), pp. 181–84, 193–95.

18 On neo-modernisn see Jeffrey C. Alexander, "Modern, Anti, Post, and Neo", *New Left Review*, 210 (March-April 1995), pp. 92–93.

19 M.M. Bakhtin has made a useful distinction between intentional hybrids that create internally conflictual structures, are divisive, contestatory or ironizing, and organic hybrids that make no conscious contest or opposition, are mute or opaque but produce new modes through unintentional mixing and fusion, and are profoundly productive historically. See *The Dialogic Imagination*, trs. Caryl Emerson and Michael Holquist (Austin: Univ. of Texas Press, 1981), pp. 358–61; and William Rowe and Vivian Schelling, *Memory, Modernity: Popular Culture in Latin America* (London: Verso, 1991), p. 201.

20 The Indian subcontinent was part of wider precapitalist constellations and 'cultural spheres' with southeast Asia, Europe, and the Mediterranean that involved cultural interchange, circulation of ideologies, and even patriarchal arrangements. Precolonial European culture too was itself a Eurasian and Euro–African phenomenon that drew substantively from the non-European. See Martin Bernal, *Black Athena* (London: Free Association Books, 1987); Jack Goody, *The Ancient, the Oriental and the Primitive* (Cambridge: Cambridge Univ. Press, 1990); R.I. Moore, "Europe as a Eurasian Phenomena", *Modern Asian Studies*, 3:3 (1997).

Politics of the possible: or the perils of reclassification

1 Gabriel Garcia Marquez, 1982 Nobel Lecture, "Latin America's Solitude", *Le Novel Observateur* (8 Jan. 1983), p. 60.

2 Irlemar Chiampi Cortez, "In Search of a Latin American Writing", *Diacritics*, 8:4 (Winter 1978), p. 7.

3 Gabriel Garcia Marquez, *The Fragrance of Guava*, trs. Ann Wright (London: Verso, 1982), p. 31.

4 "But Saenz de la Barra had made him note that with every six heads sixty enemies are produced and for every sixty six hundred are produced and then six thousand and then six million, the whole country, God damn it, we'll never end, and Saenz de la Barra answered him impassively to rest easy, general, we'll finish with them when they're all finished, what a barbarian" (Gabriel Garcia Marquez, *The Autumn of the Patriarch*, trs. Gregory Rabassa (London: Picador, 1978), p. 162. Further citations from this work will be included in the text).

5 Octavio Paz, *Alternating Current*, trs. Helen R. Lane (New York: Viking Press, 1967), p. 21. Geoffrey Hartman describes the "cultural supermarket": "a liberation not of men and women, but of images, has created a *theatrum mundi* in which the distance between past and present, culture and culture, truth and superstition is suspended by a quasi-divine synchronism" (*The Fate of Reading* (Chicago: Univ. of Chicago Press), 1975, p. 104).

6 Gabriel Garcia Marquez, *One Hundred Years of Solitude*, trs. Gregory Rabassa (Harmondsworth: Penguin, 1970), pp. 52–53. Further citations from this work will be included in the text.

7 During 'The Violence' or *La Violencia* in Columbia between 1946 and 1953, certain techniques of torture and death were so common that they were given names; thus *picar para tamal* referred to cutting up a living person into small pieces.

8 In an interview with Gene Bell-Villada, Garcia Marquez discusses the strike sequence in *One Hundred Years*: "That sequence sticks closely to the facts of the United Fruit strike of 1928, which dates from my childhood. . . . The only exaggeration is in the number of dead, though it does fit the proportions of the novel. So instead of hundreds dead, I upped it to thousands. But it's strange, a Columbian journalist the other day alluded in passing to 'the thousands who died in the 1928 strike'. As my Patriarch says: 'It doesn't matter if something isn't true, because eventually it will be!'" (*South* (Jan. 1983), p. 22).

9 It is illuminating to see how Garcia Marquez can be read in Latin America. When he decided he would not publish another book until Pinochet quit as Chile's president, political prisoners at a detention camp near Valparaiso decided to give him a gift: "They would recreate *One Hundred Years of Solitude* in popular verse— the traditional form of verses of ten lines each. The book would be illustrated with woodcuts, a technique used by Chilean popular engravers since the nineteenth century. The wood came from used tea chests. The only tool was a small knife made from an old metal saw. The inking roll was an empty shampoo bottle filled with sand." One woodcut, done by historian Leonardo Leon, shows Innocent Erendira's wicked grandmother being carried by skeletons who represent "the exploitation of the ill-fed, ill-clothed masses" (ibid., p. 23).

10 Garcia Marquez says, "I know very ordinary people who've read *One Hundred Years* . . . carefully and with a lot of pleasure, but with no surprise at all because, when all is said and done, I'm telling them nothing that hasn't happened in their own lives" (*The Fragrance of Guava*, p. 36).

11 Garcia Marquez claims that "the multiple monologue allows several unidentifed voices to interrupt, just as it happens in real history. For example, think of those massive Caribbean conspiracies, full of endless secrets which everyone knows about" (ibid., p. 86).

12 I owe this point to Ruth Frankenburg who develops it in her essay "The Challenge of Orientalism for Feminist Theory" (1984, unpublished).

13 Edward Said, "In the Shadow of the West", *Wedge*, 7/8 (Winter-Spring 1985), p. 4.

14 Alejo Carpentier describes hearing an illiterate black poet recite "the wonderful story of Charlemagne in a version similar to that of the *Song of Roland*" in a small fishing village on the Caribbean coast, and points out how the search for an "authentic" regional essence reveals that a "particular folkloric dance was only the contemporary manifestation of an age-old ritual or liturgy which . . . had travelled from the Mediterranean to the New World via Africa", or that "a peasant folksong was almost word for word an old frontier ballad from the days of the Moorish occupation of Spain", or how a researcher recently heard "peasants deep in the Cuban interior reciting past Hindustani eulogies to Count Lucanor and even a version of *King Lear*"("The Latin American Novel", *New Left Review*, 154 (Nov.-Dec. 1985), pp. 100, 106).

15 Geeta Kapur, "Art and Internationalism", *Economic and Political Weekly*, 13:19 (May 1978), p. 803.

16 Garcia Marquez, interview in *South* (Jan. 1983), p. 22.

17 Francoise Grund also discusses the artistry of many 'third-world' performances that "rests assuredly in the interpretative quality of repetition" in contrast to western theatre which is "based on the sudden discovery of the unknown, the 'taking' of the spectator by surprise. The western artist and dramatist must be a master of surprise, must be a perpetual innovator, a novelist" ("Ali Baba's Cave", *Semiotext(e)*, 4:3 (1984), pp. 55–56).

18 Like a slowed-down whirl of the leaf storm, the story revolves around the death of the doctor through repeated narratives. The arrival of the banana company is perceived as a leaf storm which rearranges the human and material "dregs" and "rubble" of other towns into a "different and more complex town" (Gabriel Garcia Marquez, *Leaf Storm and Other Stories*, trs. Gregory Rabassa (New York: Harper and Row, 1979), p. 1).

19 C.V. Subbarao writes: "It is through oral traditions that the peasants preserve their history. . . . History is for them not discontinuous. Each insurgency brings not only fresh history but also fresh ways of remembering and preserving it. And it is a history as remembered by them that can help change history. The peasant is thus not only the subject of history but also a historian, presumably with his own historiography" (unpublished review of Ranajit Guha's *Elementary Aspects of Peasant Insurgency*, 1984). See also Jean Franco on the radical role of oral narratives, especially for the Indians in Latin America in "Dependency Theory and Literary History: the Case of Latin America", *Minnesota Review*, 5 (Fall 1975), pp. 68–69.

20 Gabriel Garcia Marquez, *The Chronicle of a Death Foretold*, trs. Gregory Rabassa (New York: Alfred Knopf, 1983), p. 96. Further citations from this work will be included in the text.

21 See James Clifford, "Power and Dialogue in Ethnography" in *Observers Observed: Essays in Ethnographic Fieldwork*, ed. George Stocking (Madison, Wisconsin: Univ. of Wisconsin Press, 1983), p. 147.

22 For instance, the representation of gender in the female nude is a crucial site for the management and mystification of class and cultural differences. Thus in the 'everyday' nudes of Degas, only the covert voyeurism of the painter's eye can ensure and establish the 'naturalness' of the woman, her pristine self-absorption. Degas aimed in his bathing, dressing women to show "a human creature preoccupied with herself—a cat who licks herself; hitherto, the nude has always been represented in poses which presuppose an audience, but these women of mine are honest and simple folk, unconcerned by any other interests than those involved in their physical condition. . . . It is as if you looked through a keyhole" (*Post-Impressionism* (London: Royal Academy of the Arts, 1979), p. 64).

23 Tzvetan Todorov, *The Conquest of America*, trs. Richard Howard (New York: Harper and Row, 1984), p. 19.

24 Ibid., pp. 111–12.

25 Vyacheslav Ivanov, "Correspondence from Opposite Corners", quoted by Renato Poggioli in *The Theory of the Avant-Garde*, trs. Gerald Fitzgerald (Cambridge, Mass.: Harvard Univ. Press, 1968), p. 75.

26 Nicos Hadjinicolaou, "On the Ideology of Avant-gardism", *Praxis*, 6 (1982), p. 56.

27 For a more detailed discussion see Kumkum Sangari, "The Changing Text", *Journal of Arts & Ideas*, 8 (July-Sept. 1984), pp. 73–74.

28 Raymond Wlliams, *Writing in Society* (London: Verso, 1984), pp. 221–23.

29 K.V. Akshara has demonstrated how "traditional Indian theatre techniques were exported from India and are now being imported in the form of postcolonial influences" in "Western Responses to Traditional Indian Theatre", *Journal of Arts & Ideas*, 8 (July-Sept. 1984), p. 54.

30 For a documentation and critique of some aspects of this process, see James Clifford, "Histories of the Tribal and Modern", *Art in America*, 73:4 (April 1985), pp. 164–77, and Hal Foster, *Recodings: Art, Spectacle, Cultural Politics* (Port Townsend, Wa.: Bay Press, 1985), pp. 181–209.

31 See, for example, Fredric Jameson, "Literary Innovation and Modes of Production: A Commentary", *Modern Chinese Literature*, 1:1 (1984), p. 76.

32 This is in fact the resounding note on which Hal Foster concludes in *Recodings* (p. 208).

33 To borrow a phrase from Jean-Christophe Agnew's "The Consuming Vision of Henry James" in *The Culture of Consumption: Critical Essays in American History*, eds. Richard Wrightman Fox and T.J. Jackson Lears (New York: Pantheon, 1983), p. 74.

34 James Clifford, *review of Orientalism* by Edward Said in *History and Theory*, 12:2 (1980), p. 220.

35 See Arturo Escobar, "Discourse and Power in Development: Michel Foucault and the Relevance of His Work to the Third World", *Alternatives*, 10:3 (Winter 1984–85), p. 387.

36 Jean-Francois Lyotard, "Rules and Paradoxes and a Svelte Appendix", *Cultural Critique*, 5 (Winter 1986–87), p. 216.

37 See "Of ladies, gentlemen, and 'the short-cut'" in this volume.

Of ladies, gentlemen, and "the short-cut": or choosing unfreedom

1 Elizabeth Allen, *A Woman's Place in the Novels of Henry James* (London: Macmillan, 1984), pp. 5, 7–8.

2 Eileen Power, *Medieval Women*, ed. M.M. Postan (Cambridge: Cambridge Univ. Press, 1975), pp. 24, 30–32.

3 *Oxford English Dictionary*, 1961 edn, emphasis added.

4 See M. Jeanne Peterson, "The Victorian Governess: Status Incongruence in Family and Society" in *Suffer and Be Still: Women in the Victorian Age*, ed. Martha Vicinus (Bloomington: Indiana Univ. Press, 1973), pp. 10, 17.

5 See Harold Perkin, *The Origins of Modern English Society, 1770–1880* (London: Routledge and Kegan Paul, 1969), p. 59.

6 *A Dictionary of American English: On Historical Principles*, eds. William Craigie and James R. Hulbert (Chicago: Univ. of Chicago Press, 1942); *Webster: An American Dictionary of the English Language*, 1970 edn.

7 Ann Douglas, *The Feminization of American Culture* (New York: Alfred Knopf, 1977), pp. 55, 60.

8 Francois Bedarida, *A Social History of England 1851–1975*, trs. A.S. Forster (London: Methuen, 1975), pp. 128–29.

9 Barry Supple, "The Governing Framework: Social Class and Institutional Reform in Victorian Britain" in *The Victorians*, ed. Laurence Lerner (New York: Holmes and Meier, 1978), p. 94.

10 Henry James, "The Question of the Opportunities", *Literature* (1898), collected in *Henry James: The American Essays*, ed. Leon Edel (New York: Vintage Books, 1956), p. 202.

11 Henry James, *The American Scene* (1907), intro. Leon Edel (Bloomington and London: Indiana Univ. Press, 1968), p. 66.

12 *Henry James: The American Essays*, p. 202.

13 Letter of 20 Sept. 1867 in *Selected Letters of Henry James, 1843–1875*, ed. Leon Edel (Cambridge, Mass.: Belknap, Harvard Univ. Press, 1974), vol. I, p. 77.

14 Allon White, *The Uses of Obscurity: The Fiction of Early Modernism* (London: Routledge and Kegan Paul, 1981), p. 52.

15 "The Manners of American Women", *Harper's Bazaar*, 41 (April-July 1907), collected in *Henry James, French Writers and American Women: Essays*, ed. and intro. Peter Buitenhuis (Branford, Connecticut: Compass Publishing Company, 1960), p. 68, emphasis added. John Ruskin had written in mild protest against the common arrogation of "Lady" by English women instead of the more appropriate "gentle-women". The assumption of the "title" ought to go together with a taking on of the duties signified by ladyhood and with a claim to merit: "I wish there was a *true order of chivalry* instituted for our English youth *of certain ranks,* in which both boy and girl should receive, at a given age, their knighthood and ladyhood by true title; *attainable only by certain probation and trial both of character and accomplishment,* and to be forfeited, on conviction, by their peers of any dishonourable act" ("Of Queen's Gardens" in *Sesame and Lilies* (1865), revised edn (New York: John Wiley and Son, 1875), p. 111, emphases added).

16 Henry James, *The Portrait of A Lady* (1908: Fairfield, New Jersey: Augustus M. Kelley, 1977), vol. I, p. 271. Subsequent references are to this edition (vols. III and IV of the New York Edition) and appear in the text.

17 Jules Zanger, "'Consider the Lilies of the Field': The Inheritance Theme in American Literature", *The Antioch Review*, 41:4 (Fall 1983), p. 485; *The American Scene*, p. 11.

18 Quoted by Leon Edel in *Henry James: The Middle Years, 1882–1895* (New York: J.B. Lippincott Company, 1962), p. 21.

19 See Fred Reid, "The Disintegration of Liberalism, 1895–1931" in *The Context of English Literature 1900–1930*, ed. Michael Bell (London: Methuen, 1980), pp. 95–98; Carol Dyhouse, "The Condition of England 1860–1900" in *The Victorians*, ed. Lerner, p. 78.

20 James, *The American Scene*, pp. 12–13, emphasis added.

21 Ibid., pp. 77, 465, 54.

22 James, "The Manners of American Women", *French Writers*, p. 72.

23 Carol Dyhouse, "The Role of Women: From Self-sacrifice to Self-awareness" in *The Victorians*, ed. Lerner, p. 189.

24 Elizabeth Allen points out that "the freedom of the American girl was in reality the freedom to behave well of her own accord rather than by compulsion" and this "freedom" was present in New England morality which as "the embodiment of individual conscience rather than of established religious custom was a more sophisticated form of restriction" (*A Woman's Place*, pp. 32–33).

25 Ruskin, "Of Queen's Gardens", pp. 92, 89.

26 See Bedarida, *A Social History*, pp. 121–22.

27 Estelle B. Freedman and Erna Olafson Hellerstein, "Introduction to Part II" in *Victorian Women: A Documentary Account of Women's Lives in Nineteenth Century France, England and the United States*, eds. Erna Olafson Hellerstein, Leslie Parker Hume and Karen M. Offen (Stanford: Stanford Univ. Press, 1981), p. 132.

28 See Nancy Chodorow, *The Reproduction of Mothering: Psychoanalysis and the Sociology of Gender* (Berkeley: Univ. of California Press, 1978), pp. 175, 109–10.

29 Myra Jehlen, "Archimedes and the Paradox of Feminist Criticism", *Signs*, 6:4 (1981), pp. 596, 598; Lisa Appignanesi, *Femininity and the Creative Imagination: A Study of Henry James, Robert Musil and Marcel Proust* (London: Vision Press, 1973), pp. 10, 15, 24.

30 See Terry Eagleton's analysis of Richardson in his *The Rape of Clarissa: Writing, Sexuality and Class Struggle in Samuel Richardson* (Oxford: Blackwell, 1982), pp. 13, 95.

31 Jehlen, "Archimedes", p. 597.

32 Carol Christ, "Victorian Masculinity and the Angel in the House" in *A Widening Sphere: Changing Roles of Victorian Women*, ed. Martha Vicinus (Bloomington: Indiana Univ. Press, 1977), pp. 160, 158.

33 Henry James, "Saint Beuve", *North American Review*, 130 (Jan. 1880), p. 53, quoted in Appignanesi, *Femininity and the Creative Imagination*, p. 21.

34 James, "The Manners of American Women", *French Writers*, pp. 78–79.

35 Henry James, "The Speech of American Women", *Harper's Bazaar*, 40–41 (Nov. 1906-Feb. 1907), collected in *French Writers,* pp. 38, 39, 35, 33, 35, 46, 53.

36 James, "The Speech of American Women" in ibid., pp. 46, 53; "The Manners of American Women" in ibid., p. 74.

37 Willam Veeder, *Henry James-The Lessons of the Master: Popular Fiction and Personal Style in the Nineteenth Century* (Chicago: Univ. of Chicago Press, 1975), pp. 121, 124–45.

38 Jenni Calder, *Women and Marriage in Victorian Fiction* (London: Thames and Hudson, 1976), p. 82.

39 Jehlen, "Archimedes", p. 599.

40 Donald Mull, *Henry James' "Sublime Economy": Money as Symbolic Center in the Fiction* (Middletown, Connecticut: Wesleyan Univ. Press, 1973), pp. 50, 61.

41 James, *The American Scene*, pp. 9–10. James goes on to claim that "highest luxury of all, the supremely expensive thing, is constituted privacy" (p. 11).

42 Mull, *Henry James' "Sublime Economy"*, p. 91.

43 As Allen claims in *A Woman's Place*, p. 10.

44 H.E. Scudder, *Atlantic,* 49 (January 1882), collected in *Henry James: The Critical Heritage*, ed. Roger Gard (New York: Barnes and Noble, 1968), p. 109.

45 See Allen, *A Woman's Place*, pp. 80–83.

46 Raymond Williams, *Problems in Materialism and Culture* (London: New Left Books, 1980), pp. 165–67.

47 Sydney Waterlow, "The Work of Mr Henry James", *Independent Review*, 4 (November 1904), collected in *Henry James: The Critical Heritage*, pp. 370–71.

48 Francis Mulhern, *The Moment of 'Scrutiny'* (London: New Left Books, 1979), p. 33. There are imperial inclinations in Leavis's 'minoritarianism'. He wrote in *For Continuity* (1933): "The minority capable not only of appreciating Dante, Shakespeare, Donne, Baudelaire, Hardy but of recognising their latest successors constitute the *Consciousness of the race (or of a branch of it)* at a given time. For such capacity does not merely belong to an isolated aesthetic realm: it implies responsiveness to theory as well as to art, to science and philosophy in so far as these may affect the sense of the human situation and of the nature of life. Upon this minority depends our power of profiting by the finest human experience of the past; they keep alive the subtlest and most perishable parts of tradition. Upon them depend the implicit standards that order the finer living of an age, the sense that this is worth more than that, this rather than that is the direction in which to go, that the centre is here rather than there" (my emphases; cited in Chris Baldick, *The Social Mission of English Criticism* 1848–1932 (Oxford: Clarendon, 1983), pp. 164–65). See also ibid. pp. 220–21.

49 Catherine Belsey, "Re-Reading the Great Tradition" in *Re-Reading English*, ed. Peter Widdowson (London and New York: Methuen, 1982), p. 129.

50 Mulhern's phrase, *The Moment*, p. 264.

51 See Mark Krupnick, "Lionel Trilling, Freud and the Fifties", *Humanities in Society*, 3:3 (Summer 1980), pp. 265–81.

"Not knowing, but only guessing": a modernist resolution

1 See, for example, Susan Kappeler, *Writing and Reading in Henry James* (London: Macmillan, 1980), pp. 52, 55.

2 Ibid., pp. 55, 74, 163; and Shoshana Felman, "Turning the Screw of Interpretation", *Yale French Studies*, 55/56 (1977), pp. 115, 155, 107, 166, 176.

3 Fredric Jameson's phrase in "The Realist Floor-Plan" in *On Signs*, ed. Marshall Blonsky (Baltimore: Johns Hopkins Univ. Press, 1985), p. 382. Jameson points out that Flaubert's fiction, located in a transitional historical moment, can offer different kinds of "interpretative *temptations*" which appear to "retain an objective existence" in the text.

4 Ralph Norrman, *The Insecure World of Henry James' Fiction: Intensity and Ambiguity* (London: Macmillan, 1982), p. 160. Norrman attributes this structure of chiastic inversion found in the language and characters of the late fiction to James's personal insecurity.

5 For detailed discussions see John Goode, "The Pervasive Mystery of Style: *The Wings of the Dove*" in *The Air of Reality: New Essays on Henry James*, ed. John Goode (London: Methuen, 1972); and Elizabeth Allen's reading of the novel in her *A Woman's Place in the Novels of Henry James* (Basingstoke and London: Macmillan, 1984).

6 Henry James, *The Wings of the Dove*, New York Edition, vols. 19–20 (Fairfield: Augustus M. Kelley, 1976), p. 341. Further references are cited in the text.

7 Ruth Bernard Yeazell shows how the language of the late novels does not allow the reader to "keep the minds of the narrator and his characters properly distinct" (*Language and Knowledge in the Late Novels of Henry James* (Chicago: Univ. of Chicago Press, 1976), p. 12); Leo Bersani demonstrates the difficulty of distinguishing precisely the characters' expression of their thoughts from the narrator's presentation of them, or even from his comments, in "The Narrator as Center in *The Wings of the Dove*", *Modern Fiction Studies*, 6 (Summer 1960), p. 131.

8 Mark Seltzer says in a somewhat different vein of *The Golden Bowl* that "the organic regulation of plot allows for a recession of narrative authority and makes for a dispersal of narrative control that is nonetheless immanent in every movement and gesture of character and plot" (*Henry James and the Art of Power* (Ithaca: Cornell Univ. Press, 1984), pp. 87-88).

9 Terry Eagleton also points out that James does not "explode" the realist form to the extent of calling the "spectatorial ego into explicit question" (*Criticism and Ideology* (London: Verso, 1978), p. 145).

10 Margaret Walters, "Keeping the Place Tidy for the Young Female Mind: *The Awkward Age*" in *The Air of Reality*, p. 202.

11 J.P. Mowbray, "The Apotheosis of Henry James", *Critic*, 41 (Nov. 1902) in *Henry James: The Critical Heritage*, ed. Roger Gard (New York: Barnes and Noble, 1968), pp. 328, 331.

12 F.M. Colby, "In Darkest James", *Bookman* (America), 16 (Nov. 1902) in *Henry James: The Critical Heritage*, p. 340; unsigned review, *Saturday*, 45 (Jan. 1903) in ibid., pp. 332–33.

13 Tom Masson, "Mary's Little Lamb. In Different Keys", *Life* (4 May 1905), in E.R. Hagemann, "'Unexpected Light in Shady Places': Henry James and *Life*, 1883–1916", *Western Humanities Review*, 24:3 (Summer 1970), p. 247.

14 Vernon Lee, *The Handling of Words* (London: John Lane, 1923), p. 244, cited in Seymour Chatman, *The Later Style of Henry James* (Oxford: Blackwell, 1972), p. 58; Stephen Spender, *The Destructive Element* (London: Jonathan Cape, 1935), p. 197.

15 See, for example, William B. Stone, "Idiolect and Ideology: Some Stylistic Aspects of Norris, James and Dubois", *Style*, 10:4 (Fall 1976), pp. 416–17.

16 Norrman, *Insecure World*, p. 180; Yeazell, *Language and Knowledge*, pp. 35, 36, 130.

17 On "verbalized unuttered utterance" in the late fiction see Norrman, *Insecure World,* pp. 119–29.

18 Allon White says apropos the unopened letter that throughout the novel "James has signalled his rejection of that kind of narrative certainty, with its concomitant public affirmations-the novel begins to exclude the type of reader who expects and demands these things in his reading: the refusal to open communication is fundamental to the narrative and authorial positions in it" (*The Uses of Obscurity: The Fiction of Early Modernism* (London: Routledge and Kegan Paul, 1981), p. 21).

19 Raymond Williams does not see James's fiction as solipsist, "since consciousness is social, its exploration, its rendering as a process, is connecting, inevitably" (*The English Novel from Dickens to Lawrence* (London: Chatto and Windus, 1970), p. 135).

20 White, *Uses of Obscurity*, p. 133.

21 Henry James, *The American Scene*, intro. Irving Howe (New York: Horizon Press, 1967), p. 111. See also Jean-Christophe Agnew's discussion of the way James's writing restructures feeling and perception "to accommodate the ubiquity and liquidity of the commodity form" ("The Consuming Vision of Henry James" in *The Culture of Consumption: Critical Essays in American History, 1880–1890*, eds. Richard Wrightman Fox and T.J. Jackson Lears (New York: Pantheon, 1983), p. 68).

22 It is corporate too in the sense that it is "generated by the pervasive power of enormous corporation wealth". See Eagleton, *Criticism and Ideology*, p. 142.

23 For a detailed discussion of James's incorporation of 'femaleness', see "Of ladies, gentlemen, and 'the short-cut'" in this volume.

24 Robin Lakoff, *Language and Woman's Place* (New York: Harper and Row, 1975), pp. 66, 73–74.

25 Henry James, "Novels of George Eliot" in *Views and Reviews*, ed. Le Roy Phillips (Boston: Ball, 1908), p. 18.

Figures for the 'unconscious': the pressures on description

1 Romesh C. Dutt, *Pratap Singh, The Last of the Rajputs: A Tale of Rajput Courage and Chivalry*, trs. Ajoy Dutt (Allahabad: Kitabistan, 1943), p. 71. Further citations are included in the text.

2ˋ "When defeat, dishonour and loss of religion are inevitable, Rajput women preserve their chastity in this manner" (p. 125).

3 Arun Joshi, *The Strange Case of Billy Biswas* (Bombay: Asia Publishing House, 1971), p. 93.

4 Adam Kuper points out that the anthropologist as romantic reactionary who wanted only to preserve, segregate, and museumize tribals was a caricature that did however have some truth. Those who indulged most in nostalgia—traders, administrators, missionaries-were themselves agents of change and "corruption" (*Anthropologists and Anthropology: The British School 1922–1972* (Harmondsworth: Penguin, 1973), pp. 141–42). For a critique of salvage or redemptive ethnography, see James Clifford, "On Ethnographic Allegory" in *Writing Culture: The Poetics and Politics of Ethnography*, eds. James Clifford and George E. Marcus (California: Univ. of California Press, 1986), pp. 112–16.

5 See Kumkum Sangari, "Mirabai and the Spiritual Economy of Bhakti", *Economic and Political Weekly*, 15:27 and 28 (July 1990).

6 As Raymond Williams has shown, local pastoralisms were not only infinitely regressive in their location of lost organic moments but also interlocked with global binaries such as that of the civilized and the primitive. See *The Country and the City* (1973; Frogmore, St. Albans: Paladin, 1975), pp. 9–12.

7 In the essays on Henry James in this volume I have discussed the growing investment of 'high' culture in 'not knowing'.

8 For a discussion of Spencer, see Lorna Duffin, "Prisoners of Progress: Women and Evolution" in *The Nineteenth Century Woman: Her Cultural and Physical World*, eds. Sara Delmont and Lorna Duffin (London: Croom Helm, 1978), pp. 61–68.

9 This newspaper article faced the prospect of the growing mental inferiority of English women as a part of advancing western civilization with cheerful equanimity: "The lower we go among the savage tribes, the less of this diversity there would seem to be; so that it appears to be a direct retrogression to assimilate the work of highly-developed woman to that of her mate; and if perfection is to be the aim of our efforts, it will be best advanced by further divergence of male and female characteristics. . . . To discourage subordination in women, to countenance their competition in masculine careers by way of their enfranchisement, is probably the shortest method of barbarizing our race. . . . Slight checks may seriously affect the prospect of a race in the severe struggle of humanity, and if our better halves alter the conditions which have raised us from the condition of orang-outangs, a relapse into savagery is quite possible" ("The Possible Retrogression of Women", *Saturday Review*, 32 (1871), p. 11). See Duffin, "Prisoners of Progress" in *The Nineteenth Century Woman*, eds. Delmont and Duffin, pp. 66–67, 84.

10 See Shiela Jeffreys, *The Spinster and Her Enemies: Feminism and Sexuality 1880–1930* (London: Pandora, 1985), pp. 134–35.

11 See Anita Levy, *Other Women: The Writing of Class, Race and Gender 1832–1892* (Princeton, New Jersey: Princeton Univ. Press, 1991), pp. 119–21.

12 Johannes Fabian has critiqued the symbol as a unifying system that allows one to discover in primitive culture a universal, transhistorical mode of existence; he questions whether it is the primitive whose way of thinking is symbolic or whether anthropology itself is symbolic in its projection of symbolic meanings and understanding on the other; he asks too whether the attribution of symbolic systems helps anthropology to place its other in a time different from our own. See *Time and the Other: How Anthropology makes its Object* (New York: Columbia Univ. Press, 1983), p. 125.

13 James Clifford, "Objects and Selves-An Afterword" in *Objects and Others: Essays on Museums and Material Culture*, ed. George W. Stocking Jr. (Madison: Univ. of Wisconsin Press, 1985), p. 243. A primitive unconscious was constructed through descriptions of primitive art as possessing a direct relationship between vision and representation, between artist's sensibility and its expression, as being a product of nature that was as unreflective as dreaming, as ruled by the functions and conventions of magic and religion, and even as maintaining social cohesion. These ascribed qualities were often extended to tribal social practices. See Julian Stallabrass, "The Idea of the Primitive: British Art and Anthropology 1918–930", *New Left Review*, 103 (Sept.-Oct. 1990), pp. 100–01, 103–04.

14 Quoted in Jean Franco, *The Modern Culture of Latin America: Society and the Artist* (Harmondsworth: Penguin, 1970), p. 119.

15 He wrote: ". . . it is ridiculous to look to the East for inspiration. . . . One always felt irked by the East coming it over us. It is sheer fraud. The East is marvellously interesting for tracing our steps back. But for going forward, it is nothing. All it can hope for is to be fertilised by Europe, so that it can start on a new phase." And apropos his visit to Ceylon: "Those natives are *back of us*-in the living sense *lower* than we are. But they're going to swarm over us and suffocate us. We are, have been for five centuries, the growing tip. Now we're going to fall. But you don't catch me going back on my whiteness and Englishness and myself. English in the teeth of the world, even in the teeth of England. How England deliberately undermines England. . . ." (Letter to Lady Ottoline Morrel, 24 May 1916, and letter to Lady Cynthia Asquith, 30 April 1922 in *Letters of D.H. Lawrence*, ed. Aldous Huxley (London: Heinemann, 1937), pp. 350, 546, quoted in Alex Aronson, *Europe Looks at India* (1946; Calcutta: Riddhi, 1979), pp. 120, 122).

16 See Stallabrass, "The Idea of the Primitive", p. 101.

17 The transnational ideological configuration centred on scientism and a regenerative India is the flip side of the one centred on altruism and a fallen India; it is described in "Relating histories" in this volume.

18 T.S. Eliot, for instance, recuperates a regenerative salve from India for a supposedly disintegrating Europe. Art is given the role of salvage and order, 'oriental' philosophy and mysticisms are inserted as a panacea for disorder and incorporated into conservative notions of wholeness, while the trope of decay in his poetry functions to blur the ideological and material determinants of this monumentalist Europe.

19 If western civilization was in its death throes, as Spengler diagnosed, the implication that could be extracted was that other cultures might have been, and could become, the equals or superiors of western culture. For such a reception of Spengler by some Latin American writers see Franco (*The Modern Culture*, p. 118). In India too Eliot and Yeats have been popularly read and applauded by two generations of literary critics for their recognition of India' s spiritual grandeur!

20 In Alice Perrin's *The Stronger Claim* (1903) the protagonist, son of a well-born English father and a feckless Eurasian mother, is brought up in England. When he returns to India he is "claimed" by the east; he dies calling "his gods" in Hindustani against the clamour of the bells and conches of a religious festival. See Benita Parry, *Delusions and Discoveries: Studies in British Imagination* (Delhi: Orient Longman, 1972), p. 77.

21 According to Kuper, the British used their anthropology mainly in Africa while in India ethnology never meant much more than the development of the census to include social and cultural data, and to a limited extent, the study of tribal peoples. See *Anthropologists*, p. 127.

22 The scope of this particular collaboration was wide, stretching across a variety of discourses and including differently located Indians and Europeans. Significantly, in tandem with Theosophy in the 1880s, there was an upward evaluation of Indian spirituality in popular British fiction in India. See Allan J Greenberger, *The British Image of India* (London: Oxford Univ. Press, 1969), pp. 124–25.

23 Blavatsky envisaged the Theosophical Society as a noninterfering overlayer on existing religious sects in India. If primitivism was partly assembled through spatialization, synchrony and modernist juxtapositions, then the constellation clustered around Theosophy suggests a supermarket of religions from which to choose and assemble new ones.

24 For a discussion of British Orientalism as a model of potentially dividable authority, see "Relating histories" in this volume.

25 In fact she goes to great length to dispute the theory that bhils were the original inhabitants and that rajputs were newcomers of Scythian origin who defeated them. This *Rajyogi* claims that "gymnastics" for the soul exist and that these are his own secret. Like other *Rajyogis* he can foresee the future, heal all diseases, understand all languages, read thoughts, witness events anywhere miles away at will, understand the language of animals and birds, abandon his own body to enter any other body, tame wild animals with his eyes, and subjugate anyone with his mesmeric powers. See Madame Blavatsky, *From the Caves and Jungles of Hindustan* (London and Madras: Theosophical Society, 1892), pp. 289, 316.

26 See, for instance, Annie Besant's review of Madame Blavatsky' s *The Secret Doctrine*, *Pall Mall Gazette* (25 April 1889), rpt *The Theosophical Journal*, 15:6 (Nov.-Dec. 1974), pp. 3–5.

27 For instance, in one effort to reconcile cyclic epochs with the theory of the four *yugas* and prevalent scientific notions of the earth's age, different races were placed in concurrent *yugas*; the present was designated as a dark *kaliyug* only for Aryans on the basis of ascending evil and materialism while other races, at present in their childhood, were said to still be in earlier *yugas*; that is, the *yugas* or ages started and finished differently for different races: races inhabited different ages while living in the same time on the globe. See W.Q. Judge, "The Kali Yuga", *The Path* (Nov. 1894), rpt *The Theosophical Movement* (Feb. 1991).

Vivekananda claimed that evolution was a mere reiteration by European science of the ancient discovery of non-duality or *advaita* in Indian philosophy according to which all living species were closely interlinked. (See Tapan Raychaudhuri, *Europe Reconsidered: Perceptions of the West in Nineteenth Century Bengal* (Delhi: Oxford Univ. Press, 1988), p. 280.) At its crassest, the type of antiwesternism that Theosophy engendered could become a veneer for modernization, a typical mix of economic subjection and cultural uniqueness.

28 Blavatsky initially sought out Dayanand as a partner for the Theosophical Society in India. The alliance did not materialize but the parallels are striking enough to suggest a confluence. Dayanand's itinerary is marked by eclectic borrowing, a return to the most ancient sources of knowledge—the vedic, the search for a true *yogi*, a comparativist stance towards Hinduism via orientalist routes and Indology, the desire to forge a pan-Hinduism, the interest in patronage from princes as well as newly educated middle classes, and a belief in racial superiority that involved recommending eugenic solutions.

Yeats was looking for hermeneutical resources to interpret ancient Ireland and legitimate his own brand of Celtic, anti-English nationalism. Ironically, he settled on India and the semitic east through orientalist routes that were determined by his simultaneous identification with Anglo-European culture. He believed Arabs to be the oldest, least conquered, and still almost unchanged race. From Spengler he derived a version of cyclic history. He structured his 'quests' around lost manuscripts in *The Speckled Bird* (1897) and *Vision* (1925, 1937). Arab culture would give the rejuvenating gift of sexuality while India, initially mediated through Blavatskian Theosophy (closely connected with romantic Celtic nationalism in Ireland), would provide eternal life through rebirth. The semitic East, India, and Ireland could be conjoint saviours of the 'west'. The scientism of Theosophy probably assisted his later dabbling in eugenics in *On the Boiler* (1938). (For his Arab fictions, see S.B. Bushrui, "Yeats' Arabic Interests" in *In Excited Reverie*, eds. A. Norman Jeffares and K.G.W. Cross (London: Macmillan, 1965), pp. 280–92.)

Significantly, Yeats thought he had realized the dream of the Theosophists in 1931—he found a yogi and a manuscript. His identification of an ancient Ireland— a compound of part-pagan exuberance and part-Christian piety—with contemporary India intensified with his discovery of Shri Purohit Swami. The latter's autobiography became an object lesson in 'premodern' collectivity: it displayed a holistic pattern of life shared by commoners and the elect in a quasi-medievalist complex of aristocrat-peasant-anchorite-bard in which all "popular literature" was also "religious". Purohit Swami, a representative as well as a "minstrel" and "story-teller" of this collective life, became the exemplar of a spirituality that did not need to renounce its social obligations. Typically, Mokashi-Punekar, who documents Yeats's relationship with the Swami, is himself invested in this configuration: he is delighted that a narrowly focused 'Hindu' refinement finally came to moderate Yeats's earlier eclectic mysticisms derived from neo-Platonism and an overly universalizing Theosophy! (See Shankar Mokashi-Punekar, "Shri Purohit Swami and W.B. Yeats" in *The Image of India in Western Creative Writ-ing*, eds. M.K. Naik et al. (Madras: Macmillan, 1971), pp. 129–31, 133, 137–41.)

Like Lawrence, the combination of the libidinous with the sacred turns Yeats's 'quests' into a journey into his own unconscious, of which the sacred is the hitherto 'undiscovered' part. The 'secret' enters into a different relation with the 'sacred' here—the sacralized realms of non-European societies function as the innermost reaches of or the repositories of 'western' 'male' sexuality. In this both Yeats and Lawrence reformulate a romantic theme. Novalis, the German romantic, wrote: "In the temple of Sais, a man once lifted the veil of the goddess / And found—O wonder of wonders!—and found concealed there—himself" (quoted in Michael Edwardes, *East-West Passage* (New York: Taplinger, 1971), p. 154).

29 The word Aryan had already come to signify an exalting relationship chiefly through Max Mueller whose theory of Aryans had turned Europeans and some Indians into cognates. Annie Besant combined this Mueller-centred Aryan constellation with Theosophy. Ancient India had been a nation; its unity, imposed by Aryans (who possessed every virtue), was disrupted by Islam. Ancient Hindu philosophy and rituals had either carried the foundation of or coincided with modern science or even exceeded it. Indeed *varnashrama dharma* virtually preempted every discovery of modern medical science while yoga-practising Hindus could still compete with the west on its own ground and even become its scientific mentors. Now India, still synonymous with Hinduism, was degraded, fallen from ancient glory; "this widowed Mother of the Aryan race, this discrowned Queen" required re-spiritualization; once regenerated she would nourish the west, uplift the whole world, and evolve a world culture based on spirituality. Unlike India, the evolution of "man" in the "west" had brought about a rapid growth of the "lower mind"—the "reasoning, questioning, scientific mind". Besant opposed English education, advocated a religious nationalism and a limited 'nonwesternizing' reformism, especially for women. Typically, Hindu women had a high status in the past; the sexes were biologically different but lived in harmonious complementarity. See *Hindu Ideals* (London: Theosophical Publishing Society, 1904) pp. 11–15, 164–66.

30 Besant's theories were euphorically received and rapidly elaborated. See Raychaudhuri, *Europe Reconsidered*, pp. 34–35.

31 The erasure of this conflict between Hinduism and modern science and rationality was later enhanced by the general commodification of religions and the development of particular brands of Hindu spirituality for export.

32 Swami Vivekananda's insertion into Theosophy allowed similar extensions of Indology as well as reversals of some of its claims. His attempt to visualize a cultural synthesis between east and west and to forge a universal religion involved claiming an Asian (Indian and Arab) role in creating and civilizing Europe, a Hindu influence on Greek thought, and finally Hindu origins for Christianity. See Raychaudhuri, *Europe Reconsidered*, pp. 272–75, 291, 296.

33 For changing descriptions of Africans and other shifts in anthropology, see

Kuper, *Anthropologists*, pp. 132–44; George Stocking, "Philanthropoids and Vanishing Cultures" in *Objects and Others*, ed. Stocking, pp. 114–16.

Relating histories

1 Eric Olin Wright, *Classes* (London: Verso, 1985), p. 87. For instance, Bengal zamindars who, as rentiers, formed a sizeable section of the new middle class in the early nineteenth century, combined political subordination to the colonial state with systemic social power over the peasantry exercised through a number of intermediaries.

2 See C.A. Bayly, *Ruler, Townsmen and Bazaars: North Indian Society in the Age of British Expansion 1770– 1870* (Cambridge: Cambridge Univ. Press, 1983).

3 Amiya Kumar Bagchi, "Colonialism and the Nature of Capitalist Enterprise in India", *Economic and Political Weekly*, 23:31 (July 1988). For examples of local studies see Jayati Gupta, "Himalayan Polyandry: Bondage among Women in Jaunsar Bawar" in *Chains of Servitude: Bondage and Slavery in India*, eds. Utsa Patnaik and Manjari Dingwaney (Delhi: Sangam, 1985), pp. 279–80; Virginius Xaxa, "Colonial Capitalism and Underdevelopment in North Bengal", *Economic and Political Weekly*, 20:39 (Sept. 1985). By 'feudal' I am referring very broadly to precapitalist economic and extra-economic structures for the appropriation of surplus from the peasantry by the existing ruling classes.

4 E.J. Hobsbawm, *Industry and Empire* (1968; Harmondsworth: Penguin, 1984), pp. 230, 148–49.

5 M.S. Anderson, *Eighteenth Century Europe 1713–1789* (London: Oxford Univ. Press, 1966), pp. 98–100.

6 The 'customs' preserved were often those of local elites whose political support was valuable or, as in the case of the transformation of slavery into indentured labour, served the needs of British capital. See Manjari Dingwaney, "Unredeemed Promises: The Law and Servitude" in *Chains*, eds. Patnaik and Dingwaney.

7 Raymond Williams, *The Country and the City* (1973; Frogmore, St Albans: Paladin, 1975), pp. 78, 226; G.M. Trevelyan, *English Social History* (1942; Harmondsworth: Penguin, 1967), pp. 287, 325, 386–87, 321–22, 413; Hobsbawm, *Industry and Empire*, pp. 168, 80–83; Barry Supple, "The Governing Framework: Social Class and Institutional Reform" in *The Victorians*, ed. Lawrence Lerner (New York: Holmes and Meier, 1978), pp. 95, 103–05; Tom Nairn, *The Break-Up of Britain: Crisis and Neo-Nationalism* (London: New Left Books, 1979), p. 29.

8 Williams, *The Country*, pp. 143, 221–22; Hobsbawm, *Industry and Empire*, pp. 18–19.

9 Nairn, *The Break-Up*, pp. 23–32.

10 In a provocative reversal of usual explanations of pastoral nostalgia, Ellen Meaksins Wood argues that far from being the sign of a 'backward' antiindustrialism, the attraction of the English countryside owed a great deal to its long domination by concentrated wealth and agrarian capitalism, and that it bespoke both the dynamism and prosperity of English agriculture and the long-standing culture of 'improvement'. See *The Pristine Culture of Capitalism* (London: Verso, 1991), pp. 109–11.

11 R.S. Neale characterizes this as a period of uneven economic development in "Afterword", *History and Class*, ed. R.S. Neale (Oxford: Basil Blackwell, 1984), pp. 277–80.

12 B.B. Misra, *The Indian Middle Classes* (1961; Delhi: Oxford Univ. Press, 1978), pp. 133–34; A.F. Salauddin Ahmed, *Social Ideas and Social Change in Bengal 1818–1835* (1965; 2nd edn, Calcutta: Riddhi, 1976), pp. 7–17, 117; Asok Sen, "The Bengal Economy and Raja Rammohun Roy" in *Raja Rammohun Roy and the Process of Modernization in India*, ed. V.C. Joshi (Delhi: Vikas, 1975), pp. 126–27; S.N. Mukherjee, "The Social Implications of the Political Thought of Raja Rammohun Roy" in *Indian Society: Historical Probings*, ed. R.S. Sharma (Calcutta: People's Publishing House, 1974), p. 364.

13 Sumit Sarkar, *A Critique of Colonial India* (Calcutta: Papyrus, 1985), pp. 10–13, 30, 47; Ahmed, *Social Ideas*, pp. 116–18. According to Pradip Kumar Lahiri, the wealthy Hindu intelligentsia served as a buffer section between the government and anti-British risings such as the Wahabi and Faraizi movements in Bengal. (See *Bengali Muslim Thought 1818–1947* (Calcutta: K. Bagchi, 1991), p. 13.) The Wahabi sect formed in the late 1820s, composed of Muslim *ryots* and of weavers pauperized by deindustrialization, was rebelling against increased rents, unauthorized imposition of collections, illegal exactions, and arbitrary arrests; their immediate targets were the extractive and juridical powers of the Hindu and Muslim zamindars, zamindari collusion with police against peasantry, extortion by rural moneylenders, and exploitation by European indigo planters; the movement assumed an anti-British government character and culminated in an uprising in 1831. See Abhijit Dutta, *Muslim Society in Transition: Titu Meer's Revolt* (1831) (Calcutta: Minerva, 1987), pp. 69, 140; Narahari Kaviraj, *Wahabi and Faraizi Rebels of Bengal* (Delhi: People's Publishing House, 1982), pp. 33–34, 52–60.

14 Bernard Cohn, *An Anthropologist Among the Historians* (Delhi: Oxford Univ. Press, 1987), pp. 430, 519–21.

15 Keith Feiling, *Warren Hastings* ...(London: Macmillan, 1954), p. 236; Michael Edwardes, *Warren Hastings, King of the Nabobs* (London, 1976), p. 74, quoted in David Musselwhite, "The Trial of Warren Hastings" in *Literature, Politics, and Theory*, eds. Francis Barker et al (London: Methuen, 1986), p. 83.

16 For example, see Thomas Twining, *A Letter to the Chairman of the East India Company on the danger of interfering in the religious opinions of the Natives of India* ... (1807), pp. 29–31, in P. J. Marshal, *Problems of Empire: Britain and India 1757–1813* (London: Allen and Unwin, 1968), pp. 189–90.

17 Romila Thapar points out that the ancient Indian past was virtually perceived as "a lost wing" of early European culture, as for instance in William Jones's discovery of the affinity between Sanskrit and Greek and Latin. See "Interpretations of Ancient Indian History", *History and Theory*, 7 (1968), p. 319.

18 William Jones, "On the Gods of Greece and Italy", *Asiatick Researches*, vol.

4, in P.J. Marshal, *The British Discovery of Hinduism* (Cambridge: Cambridge Univ. Press, 1970), pp. 242–43. The relativization of both Christianity and its claim to a unique revelation was a byproduct of the field and can be seen even in earlier European comparativists.

19 4 Oct. 1784, Letter to Nathaniel Smith, Chairman of the East India Company, in Marshal, *The British Discovery*, p. 189.

20 Farewell address to the Marquess of Hastings by the Vice-President of the Asiatic Society, 6 Feb. 1822, *Proceedings of the Meetings of the Asiatic Society in Bengal,* quoted in O.P. Kejriwal, *Asiatic Society of Bengal and the Discovery of India's Past 1784–1838* (Delhi: Oxford Univ. Press, 1988), p. 138.

21 Kejriwal, *Asiatic Society,* pp. 230–31.

22 *Selections from Educational Records, 1781–1839,* ed. W.H. Sharp (Calcutta: Bureau of Education, 1920), part I, pp. 8, 11–12.

23 29 Sept. 1804, *Primitiae Orientales* (1804), p. 114, in David Kopf, *British Orientalism and the Bengal Renaissance* (Calcutta: Firma K.L. Mukhopadhyay, 1969), p. 90.

24 *Public Disputations of the Students of the College of Fort William* (Calcutta: Hindoostanee Press, 1808), p. 23, and *Public Disputations of the Students of the College of Fort William* (Calcutta: Hindoostanee Press, 1814), p. 14.

25 6 March 1811, *Minute on Native Education in Raja Rammohun Roy and Progressive Movements in India,* ed. J.K. Majumdar (Calcutta: Art Press, 1941), pp. 224–25.

26 6 Sept. 1813, in ibid., p. 227.

27 3 June 1814, in ibid., pp. 227–30. This project of engrafting western on indigenous science was widely elaborated. See for example "Scientific Knowledge of the Hindoos", *Calcutta Journal,* 12 March 1820, in *Selections from Indian Journals,* ed. Satyajit Das (Calcutta: Firma K.L. Mukhopadhyay, 1963) p. 65; further references to this journal are from this volume.

28 20 Aug. 1821, *Selections,* ed. Sharp, part I, p. 79.

29 H.H. Wilson to Sen, 20 Aug. 1834, in Kopf, *British Orientalism,* p. 242. See also ibid., pp. 151–52.

30 C. Lushington, *The History, Design and Present State of the Religious, Benevolent, and Charitable Institutions Founded by the British in Calcutta* (Calcutta: Hindoostanee Press, 1824), p. 133, in Kopf, *British Orientalism,* p. 179.

31 6 Oct. 1823, Sharp, *Selections,* part I, p. 87.

32 Lancelot Wilkinson, "On the Use of the Siddhantas in the Work of Native Education", *Journal of the Asiatic Society of Bengal,* 3 (Oct. 1834), pp. 504–19.

33 18 Aug. 1824, General Committee of Public Instruction to Court of Directors, in *Raja Rammohun,* ed. Majumdar, p. 258.

34 "Review of the [Serampore] Mission addressed to their Society at the close of the year 1813", *Calcutta Journal,* 23 May 1819.

35 Kopf, *British Orientalism,* p. 93.

36 See Ahmed, *Social Ideas,* p. 93; Kenneth Ingham, *Reformers in India 1793–1833* (Cambridge: Cambridge Univ. Press, 1956), p. 106.

37 *Prospectus of a College for the Instruction of Asiatic Christians and Other*

Youth in Eastern Literature and European Science at Serampore (Serampore: Serampore Mission Press, 1818), p. 5, quoted in Ingham, *Reformers in India,* p. 74.

38 *First Report of Serampore College,* 1819, *Calcutta Journal,* 26 Sept. 1819.

39 William Jones, "On the Gods of Greece, Italy, and India", *Asiatick Researches,* vol. I (1789) in Marshal, *British Discovery,* p. 45.

40 "Sanskrit Language. On the Importance of Sanskrit to the Future Improvement of India", *Calcutta Journal,* 14 May 1820. The Boden Chair of Sanskrit was founded in 1832 in Oxford as a means to speed conversions. See Kejriwal, *Asiatic Society,* p. 229.

41 George Foster, *A Journey from Bengal to England,* 2 vols. (London: R. Fauldner, 1798), vol. I, pp. 59–60.

42 Abbé J.A. Dubois, *Hindu Manners, Customs and Ceremonies,* trs. and ed. Henry K. Beauchamp (3rd edn, Oxford: Clarendon Press, 1906; rpt 1959), p. xv. Subsequent references are cited in the text.

43 An implicit correlation is made between religion and political docility in *A Code of Gentoo Laws* (1776) by Nathaniel Halhed (a writer in the East India Company), and a more forthright one in Alexander Dow's *History of Hindostan,* in which Hinduism is described as "productive from its principles of the greatest degree of subordination to political authority" (London, 1768–72, vol. 3, pp. xiii, lxxviii).

Connections between Hinduism, the submission of the 'natives' and the submission of women to patriarchal arrangements were forged simultaneously. In his attempt to produce a politically usable account of the "revolutions in Bengal" in *Reflections on the Government of Indostan* (1763), Luke Scrafton (who played an active role in the pre-Plassey conspiracy along with Clive) fashioned a submerged link between the patriarchal domestic economy of the Hindus and the political needs of an emerging colonial state. The subsuming organizing principle is changeless religion while *child marriage* is said to produce not only the fidelity and conjugal affection of the wife (as evinced in widow immolation) but also the early mortality, passive virtue, easy conquerability, and political governability of the average Hindu male! See *Reflections,* rpt, London: W. Strahan, 1770, pp. 2, 10–11, 16–17.

44 Significantly, this early constitution of Hindu political passivity cum religious inflammability later played neatly into and was pulled into several Hindu communal arguments.

45 Such a comparative exorbitation of Hindu female chastity was common to several British accounts in this period. For instance, James Forbes saw the women of Gujarati revenue office and landlord families as untainted by the vices of public life that corrupted their menfolk: "Mild, gentle, and affectionate, they seemed formed to make good wives and mothers: ignorant of the world, and the various temptations to which European females are liable, religious and domestic duties engross their chief attention" (*Oriental Memoirs: Selected and Abridged from a series of familiar Letters written during 17 years of Residence in India,* 4 vols. (London: n.p., 1813), vol. 2, pp. 518–19).

46 James Mill, *History of British India* (London: J. Madden, 1848), ed H.H. Wilson, vol. I, pp. 294, 312–14, 447.

47 William Ward, *A View of the History, Literature and Mythology of the Hindus: including a minute description of their manners and customs*, 4 vols. (3rd edn, London: Black, Kingsbury, Parberry and Allen, 1820), pp. xxxvi-xxxix.

48 William Ward, *Farewell Letters to a Few Friends* (New York: E. Bliss and E. Whitney, 1821), pp. 166–67.

49 Ward, *A View* (1820), vol. 3, pp. 279–80, and vol. 4, p. 503; *A View of the History, Literature and Mythology of the Hindus* (2nd edn, Serampore: Serampore Mission Press, 1818), p. 598.

50 "On the State of Female Society in India", *Friend of India*, 1:2 (1820).

51 Quoted in Ingham, *Reformers*, p. 86.

52 Raymond Williams, *Keywords* (Glasgow: Fontana, 1976), p. 221.

53 See Raymond Williams, *Marxism and Literature* (Oxford: Oxford Univ. Press, 1978), pp. 47–48.

54 William Jones, "A Discourse on the Institution of a Society", *Asiatick Researches*, vol. I (1788), pp. x-xi, rpt *Calcutta Journal*, 1 Jan. 1820.

55 *Calcutta Journal*, 8 July 1819. In *Calcutta Journal*, 17 Sept. 1819, a report of the meeting of the Asiatic Society enumerates gifts of a collection of fossils and a botanical description of plants alongside documents on archaeology and old manuscripts. See also Kejriwal, *Asiatic Society*, p. 116.

56 *Calcutta Journal*, 6 Oct. 1818.

57 *Calcutta Journal*, 11 July 1819.

58 "A Discourse on the Opening of the Literary Society of Bombay, by Sir James Mackintosh, President of the Society, Read at Parel, 26 Nov. 1804", *Calcutta Journal*, 11 July 1819.

59 In 1826 eleven members of the Asiatic Society, including William Carey, asked the government's permission to publish in the *Asiatick Researches* the valuable information gathered and extensive field reports written by administrators on hitherto unexplored parts of the country, since once they became official documents they were liable to "become official lumber, and to moulder on the shelves of a department, and perish and be forgotten". The government agreed to let them inspect "papers, maps, plans" and give them "copies or extracts" of any papers not of a secret nature; later the motion was self-censoriously vetoed at a meeting of the society as injudicious and improper despite its novelty and good intentions. See *Proceedings of the Meetings of the Asiatic Society of Bengal, 5 July 1826*, cited in Kejriwal, *Asiatic Society*, p. 150.

60 The Madras Literary Society, conceived on similar lines, among other things, read on Hindu law, constitution of Hindu courts, oaths and ordeals (*Calcutta Journal*, 11 Dec. 1818). Both societies merged with the Royal Asiatic Society of Great Britain in 1828.

61 See Terry Eagleton, *The Function of Criticism* (London: Verso, 1984), pp. 12–21.

62 Quoted in Kopf, *British Orientalism*, p. 83.

63 Quoted in ibid., p. 84.

64 *Calcutta Journal*, 13 Oct. 1818, 20 Nov. 1818, 11 April 1819, 5 Sept. 1819; Ahmed, *Social Ideas*, p. 28.

65 "Kashiprasad Ghose on Bengali Works and Writers", *India Gazette*, 27 Jan. 1830, cited in *Raja Rammohun*, ed. Majumdar, pp. 276–78; *Sambad Kaumudi* in *John Bull*, 20 Sept. 1830, ibid., p. 271.

66 Ward, *A View* (1820), vol. 4, p. 502.

67 Ahmed, *Social Ideas*, pp. 169–70; Kopf, *British Orientalism*, pp. 183–84.

68 "The Second Anniversary Discourse", *Asiatick Researches*, vol. I (1789), p. 407, in S.N. Mukherjee, *Sir William Jones* (Cambridge: Cambridge Univ. Press, 1968), p. 120.

69 Minute, 2 Feb. 1835, in *Macaulay: Prose and Poetry*, ed. G. Young (Cambridge, Mass.: Harvard Univ. Press, 1967), pp. 722–23.

70 Macaulay, "Hallam", and "History", in *Critical, Historical and Miscellaneous Essays and Poems* (New York, 1880), vol. I, pp. 310–12, 303, 307, cited in Mark Philips, "Macaulay, Scott, and the Literary Challenge to Historiography", *Journal of the History of Ideas*, 50:1 (1989), pp. 118, 121, 132.

71 Williams, *Keywords*, pp. 48–49.

72 *Calcutta Journal*, 15 Jan. 1820; Sushil Kumar De, *Bengali Literature in the Nineteenth Century 1757–1857* (1919; 2nd edn, Calcutta: Firma K.L. Mukhopadhyay, 1962), p. 488; *Bengal Hurkaru*, 28 Feb. 1829, in *Raja Rammohun*, ed. Majumdar, p. 269.

73 Minute, 31 Dec. 1824, *Parliamentary Papers*, 1830.

74 Speech, 22 June 1813, in Eric Stokes, *The English Utilitarians and India* (Oxford: Oxford Univ. Press, 1959), p. 33.

75 De, *Bengali Literature*, pp. 458–61; Ahmed, *Social Ideas*, p. 161.

76 Ahmed, ibid., pp. 203–04.

77 Letter to Lord Amherst, 11 Dec. 1823, in *Raja Rammohun*, ed. Majumdar, pp. 250–52.

78 These themes were to be repeated by the liberal section of the Muslim intelligentsia in the United Provinces half a century later. See "Women against women" in this volume.

79 Minute on Native Education, 2 Oct. 1815, in *Raja Rammohun*, ed. Majumdar, pp. 232–36. Though it has an obvious christianizing bias, the missionary Marshman's *Hints Relative to Christian Schools* (1816) is not dissimilar, with its anticlassical tendency, desire to educate the masses, model of the European renaissance, emphasis on utility and morality through a teaching of history, science and ethics, as well as the proposal to integrate useful knowledge into the vernacular. (See Kopf, *British Orientalism*, pp. 156, 158–59.) In England, however, William Godwin had taken the secular argument further *in An Enquiry Concerning Political Justice* (1793). Criticizing national public education for replicating prejudice and conservatism, stifling truth, diversity, independence and genuine improvement, as well as for its alliance with the government which would use it to expand its own power, institutions and political base, he argued against any creed or catechism, moral or political, in education.

80 Ingham, *Reformers*, p. 13; Kopf, *British Orientalism*, p. 195.

81 *Report of the Provisional Committee of the Calcutta School-Book Society* (Calcutta, 1817), p. iii, quoted in Ahmed, *Social Ideas*, p. 24.

82 See Sarkar, *A Critique*, p. 3.

83 *Raja Rammohun*, ed. Majumdar, p. xxiii.

84 Mukherjee, "The Social Implications" in *Indian Society*, ed. Sharma, pp. 384–85.

85 *Calcutta Journal*, 23 May 1819.

86 *Calcutta Christian Observer*, 3 (1834), p. 359.

87 Sir Edward Hyde East to Sir Charles Trevelyan, Calcutta, 18 May 1816, in Ahmed, *Social Ideas*, pp. 211–12.

88 De, *Bengali Literature*, pp. 490–91.

89 *Minute on the Foundation of a College at Fort William*, 10 July 1800, rpt in *The Despatches, Minutes and Correspondences of the Marquess Wellesly, K.G.; during his Administration in India*, ed. M. Martin (London: W.H.Allen, 1837), vol. II, p. 346, in Kopf, *British Orientalism*, p. 47.

90 *The Despatches*, edited by Martin, vol. II, pp. 329–30, in Sisir Kumar Das, *Sahibs and Munshis: An Account of the College of Fort William* (Calcutta: Orion Publishers, 1978), p. 6.

91 Section 11, Statutes, *Admission of the Superior Officers and Professors*, in Das, *Sahibs*, p. 7.

92 Grant, *Observations on the State of Society among the Asiatic Subjects of Great Britain particularly with respect to Morals; and on the Means of Improving it* (1792), pp. 105, 116, in Francis G. Hutchins, *The Illusion of Permanence* (Princeton: Princeton Univ. Press, 1963), pp. 13–14.

93 *Bengal Hurkaru*, 19 March 1834, in Ahmed, *Social Ideas*, p. 177.

94 Resolution of the Governor-General-in-Council on 7 March 1835, *Selections*, ed. Sharp, part I, pp. 130–33; *Revenue, Judicial and Legislative Committee. Miscellaneous Papers*, vol. 9, in Ahmed, *Social Ideas*, p. 195.

95 *Minute on Native Education*, 6 March 1811, in *Raja Rammohun*, ed. Majumdar, pp. 224–25.

96 18 Feb. 1824, in ibid., p. 255.

97 Williams, *Keywords*, p. 80.

98 18 Aug. 1824, General Committee of Public Instruction to Governor-General-in-Council, in *Raja Rammohun*, ed. Majumdar, pp. 259–60.

99 The naturalization of a combination of English and Sanskrit as the ideal education for men appears in more developed form with the urban and *mofussil* Hindu intelligentsia in the United Provinces in the 1870s. See "Women against women" in this volume.

100 Ahmed, *Social Ideas*, pp. 164–65, 170–71; *Letter from Bengal*, 27 Jan. 1836, in ibid., p. 166; *Despatch to Bengal*, 29 Sept. 1830, in ibid., p. 167; *Report of the General Committee of Public Instruction*, 1835, p. 28, in ibid., pp. 171–72.

101 See Ahmed, *Social Ideas*, p. 167; Sarkar, *A Critique*, p. 64; Amalendu De, "Roots of Separatism in Nineteenth Century Bengal" in *Essays in Honour of Prof. S.C. Sarkar*, ed. Barun De (Delhi: People's Publishing House, 1976), pp. 321, 327–28. Some of the reasons given for this unevenness are: the wide class and linguistic gap between the small urban Muslim elite and the majority of Muslims who were rural artisans and peasants; Hindu predominance in trade, commerce, revenue jobs, and zamindaris in the pre-British period that continued after the conquest of Bengal; the differential effects of the Permanent Settlement on Muslims and Hindus; the effects of the collapse of Mughal power; relatively less collaboration on the part of Muslims with the British; and agrarian uprisings that had a religious character. (See A.F Salahuddin Ahmed, "Muslim Thought and Leadership in Bengal in the Nineteenth Century" *in Essays in Honour of S.C. Sarkar*, pp. 633–41.) Other commentators have stressed the effects of the Permanent Settlement: it ruined many rural landed aristocracies, especially Muslims whose estates were often purchased by affluent Hindu speculators; Muslims were worst affected by the resumptions of Mughal land grants; and not only were new zamindars usually Hindu but more Hindus obtained government employment. See Dutta, *Muslim Society in Transition*, pp. 87–93; Kaviraj, *Wahabi and Faraizi Rebels*, pp. 33–34.

102 See, for instance, the *Reformer* editorials of 19 May 1833 and 2 June 1833, in Benoy Ghose, *Selections from English Periodicals of Nineteenth Century Bengal 1815–1833* (Calcutta: Papyrus), vol. I , 1978.

103 *India. Public Consultation*, 10 Feb. 1835, nos. 27 and 28, quoted in Ahmed, *Social Ideas*, p. 175.

104 *Enquirer*, 1831, in Ahmed, *Social Ideas*, p. 173.

105 Letter to *Calcutta Journal*, 23 Oct. 1819.

106 Ibid.

107 Letter to *Calcutta Journal*, 12 Sept. 1820.

108 "Remarks on the Condition of East Indians", *Kaleidoscope*, 5 (Dec. 1829), *in Bengal: Early 19th Century, Selected Documents*, ed. Gautam Chattopadhyay (Calcutta: Research India Publications, 1978), p. 89.

109 'Reform' and state-sponsored 'constituency' education were of course closely tied to government jobs. Some of the East Indian petition of 1830 signed by nearly 700 which presented a list of Eurasian grievances is worth quoting, not least for the forthright play between paternalism and paternity: "The fourth grievance of your petitioners is that they are not only expressly excluded from all those offices of trust and emolument in the Civil, Military and Marine service of the East India Company's Government, which are open to 'British subjects', but that they are also treated as ineligible to most of those subordinate employments in the Judicial, Revenue and Police Departments, and even in the Military service, which are open without reserve to the Hindu and Muhammadan natives of the country . . . in the Army they are not permitted to fill the posts of native commissioned and non-commissioned officers, nor even that of a naick or corporal in a native regiment, although leave is given to them to shed their blood in ranks as privates, and to officiate in the regiment band as drummers and musicians. Thus, of the many thousand subordinate employments under the local Government, there are few from which they are not excluded except on condition of abjuring the Christian faith, in which case, their eligibility as natives of India would at once be restored . . .". The petition goes on to condemn the "disapproval" or "cold neglect" of every plan for the "improvement" of their "class" by an otherwise "paternal Government". This includes proposed schemes for educating "the sons of European officers by native mothers" in England, reserving cadetships in the army, financial support from the government for their private educational institutions in Calcutta. The petitioners stress their "keen and long cherished conviction of the wrongs they have suffered from *the race of their fathers*" (my emphasis). In the ensuing debate in the House of Commons, some members took the petition in the spirit in which it was intended—a challenge to British paternalism. For instance, Sir James Macintosh said, "these exclusions of the half castes do assume the odious appearance of exclusions made by fathers against their own children" (Thomas Edwards, *Henry Derozio, the Eurasian Poet, Teacher, Journalist* (Calcutta: W. Newman, 1884), pp. 226–28, 242).

110 Tulsi Ram, *Trading in Language: The Story of English in India* (Delhi: GDK, 1983), pp. 42–43.

111 *Report, General Committee of Public Instruction,* 1831, p. 12, quoted in Ahmed, *Social Ideas*, 168.

112 While assessing public reaction to the abolition of widow immolation, James Calder, a Calcutta merchant, wrote to Captain Benson, military secretary to Bentinck, that Prasannakumar Tagore, who was "remarkably intelligent and better informed in English literature" than his cousin Dwarkanath Tagore, was "another useful opponent of the suttee" (James Calder to Benson, undated, Bentinck Papers, quoted in Ahmed, *Social Ideas*, p. 142).

113 Letter to J.C. Villiers on the Education and Improvement of the Natives of India, London, 5 Jan. 1820, Calcutta Journal, 31 Aug. 1820.

114 *Calcutta Christian Observer*, i, 5 (Oct. 1832), p. 213.

115 Letter to his father, 12 Oct. 1836, in George Otto Trevelyan, *Life and Letters of Lord Macaulay* (Oxford: Oxford Univ. Press, 1978), vol. I, p. 421.

116 Macaulay, *Works* (Albany: Longman, 1898), vol. XI, p. 556, quoted in Ram, *Trading*, p. 91.

117 Speech in Charter debate, 10 July 1833, in Macaulay, *Complete Works,* vol. II, p. 583, quoted in Stokes, *English Utilitarians*, pp. 413–14.

118 Trevelyan, *Life*, p. 378.

119 Reformer (1833), in Pradip Sinha, *Nineteenth Century Bengal: Aspects of Social History* (Calcutta: K.L. Mukherjee, 1965), p. 96.

120 *Samachar Darpan,* 6 Nov. 1830, and *Samachar Chandrika,* 5 and 9 May 1831, in *Sambadpatre Sekaler Katha*, ed. Brajendranath Bandhyopadhyay (Calcutta, 1941), vol. II, pp. 231–32, 235–37, quoted in Sarkar, *A Critique,* p. 25.

121 22 Nov. 1831, rpt *India Gazette,* in Ghose, *Selections,* vol. I.

122 Sarkar, *A Critique,* p. 66.

123 Ahmed, *Social Ideas*, pp. 193–95; Kejriwal, *Asiatic Society,* p. 83.

124 The delinking of women's education from colonial utility, on the assumption that they were not participant in the economy like men, was of course ideological. On the relation between women's education in the nineteenth century and domestic labour, see "The 'amenities of domestic life'" in this volume.

125 See, for example, Ward, *A View* (1820), vol. 4, pp. 503–04; Ingham, *Reformers*, p. 86.

126 *Strishikshavidhayak: An Apology for Female Education Evidence in Favour of the Education of Hindoo Females, from the examples of illustrious women, both*

Ancient and Modern (Calcutta: Baptist Mission Press, 1823), pp. 2, 15.

127 *The English Works of Rammohun Roy*, ed. J.C. Ghose (Calcutta: Bhowanipore, Oriental Press, 1885), pp. 300–01, 305, 308, 341, 343.

128 In *Calcutta Journal,* 20 Jan. 1820.

129 Ibid.

130 There is some debate on whether the family were kayasths or subarnavaniks (bankers and bullion dealers) claiming a higher kayasth status through the institution of ostentatious ceremonies, charities, and 'Hinduness'. (See Syamalendu Sengupta, *A Conservative Hindu of Colonial India: Raja Radhakanta Deb and His Milieu 1784–1867* (Delhi: Navrang, 1990), pp. 4, 15–18. See also Kopf, *British Orientalism*, pp. 193–95; De, *Bengali Literature*, pp. 552–53; Ahmed, *Social Ideas*, pp. 16, 31–36.)

Radhakanta publicly declared his support for the government in 1857 and his letter to Queen Victoria rapturously confirmed the self-designating altruism of the colonial state: "Britain has wrenched from the Moslem's hand that iron rod with which they ruled in Hindusthan, and has spread over the country her benignant and fostering sway; she has established here a mighty empire over countless myriads, an empire more glorious than that of Ancient Rome; she has chosen India to be her favourite dependency, and though she is fully capable of maintaining her supremacy over it by the mere exercise of physical power, yet she has preferred to be guided by higher motives, and has sought to found her dominion on the affection and goodwill of her faithful subjects" (Sengupta, *A Conservative Hindu*, pp. 118–19).

131 Priscilla Chapman, *Hindoo Female Education* (London, 1839), pp. 75–76, in Kalikinkar Datta, *A Social History of Modern India* (Delhi: Macmillan, 1975), p. 116. See also Kopf, *British Orientalism*, p. 196.

132 Rev. R. Heber, Record of Conversations of 21 April 1824, in *Narratives of a Journey 1824–25*, vol. 5, pp. 71–73, in Arabind Poddar, *Renaissance in Bengal* (Simla: IIAS, 1976) p. 76; Kopf, *British Orientalism*, p. 195.

133 R.C. Majumdar, *Glimpses of Bengal in the Nineteenth Century* (Calcutta: Firma K.L. Mukhopadhyaya, 1960), p. 60, in Kopf, *British Orientalism*, p. 195. *Stri-sikhar Bidya* was written in collaboration with or commissioned from a pandit, Gourmohun Vidyalankar.

134 Mukherjee, "The Social Implications" in *Indian Society*, ed. Sharma, pp. 365, 367.

135 In Ahmed, *Social Ideas*, p. 217.

136 "Widow Cremation", *Samachar Chandrika*, in *Calcutta Journal*, 18 March 1822, p. 179, quoted in Kopf, *British Orientalism*, pp. 191–92.

137 See "The Counter-petition of some Hindu inhabitants of Calcutta re: Suttee orders of Government", *circa* 18 Aug. 1818, *Asiatic Journal* (July 1819), in *Raja Rammohun*, ed. Majumdar, pp. 115–16.

138 "Native Female Education", *Reformer*, rpt *India Gazette*, 20 Dec. 1831, in Ghose, *Selections*, pp. 89–92.

139 30 June 1833, Letter of H.D. Sircar and editorial comment, *Reformer*, 4 Aug. 1833, in *Bengal*, ed. Chattopadhyay, pp. 145–49.

140 19 Sept. 1833, in *Reformer* of 13 Oct. 1833, in ibid., p. 150.

141 15 Dec. 1833, *Reformer*, in ibid., pp. 159–60.

142 9 Oct. 1833, in *Reformer* of 17 Nov. 1833, in ibid., pp. 151–57.

143 "On Female Education", *Reformer*, 12 May 1833, in Ghose, *Selections*, pp. 174–75.

144 An Instructor, "Native Female Education", *India Gazette*, 24 Nov. 1831, in Ghose, *Selections*, vol. I, pp. 86–87.

145 Mahesh Chunder Deb, "A Sketch of the Condition of Hindoo Women" (1839), Speech to the Society for the Acquisition of General Knowledge, in *Awakening in Bengal in Early Nineteenth Century: Selected Documents*, ed. Gautam Chattopadhyay (Calcutta: Progressive Publishers, 1965), vol. I, p. 89. Subsequent references are cited in the text.

146 See Mukherjee, "The Social Implications" in *Indian Society*, ed. Sharma, p. 372.

147 21 March 1835, *Samachardarpan*, in *British Paramountcy and the Indian Renaissance*, eds. R.C. Majumdar, A.K. Majumdar and D. Ghosh (Bombay: Bharatiya Vidya Bhavan, 1981), pp. 262–63.

148 See Nairn, *The Break-up*, pp. 29, 31–32, 36, 40, 42, 69.

149 See Williams, *The Country*, pp. 140–46; David Aers, "Commitment and Morality: Towards a Reading of Jane Austen" in *Romanticism and Ideology*, eds. David Aers, Jonathan Cook, and David Punter (London: Routledge and Kegan Paul, 1981), p. 122.

150 *The Complete Novels of Jane Austen* (New York: Modern Library, n. d.), p. 753. Subsequent references are cited in the text.

151 Fanny "saw much that was wrong at home, and wanted to set it right. That a girl of fourteen, acting only on her own unassisted reason, should err in the method of reform, was not wonderful" (p. 720).

152 R.S. Neale points out that life in *Mansfield Park*, depending on ancient landed property and commercial wealth, is rooted in slavery and therefore morally degenerate, at least in early-nineteenth century Evangelical terms. His conclusion, however, differs from my own. He says that the "moral dilemma, posed by a system of landed property bolstered by exploitation of slave labour and the slave trade", is comprehended neither by Fanny nor by Sir Bertram, but it may be a comment by Austen on both Fanny and herself as alienated victims of property. See *Writing Marxist History: British Society, Economy and Culture since 1700* (Oxford: Basil Blackwell, 1985), pp. 105–07.

153 *Calcutta Journal*, 11 July 1819.

154 In this context Austen's own disclaimer of the ability to portray a "good", "enthusiastic", and "literary" clergyman is of some interest: "Such a man's conversation must at times be on subjects of science and philosophy, of which I know nothing; or at least be occasionally abundant in quotations and allusions which a woman who, like me, knows only her own mother tongue, and has read little in that would be totally without the power of giving. A classical education, or at any rate a very extensive acquaintance with English literature, ancient and modern, appears to be quite indispensable for the person who would do any justice to your clergyman; and I think I may boast myself to be, with all possible vanity, the most unlearned and uninformed female who ever dared to be an authoress" (11 Dec. 1815, letter to the Prince Regent's Librarian, in *Prose of the Romantic Period 1780–1830*, ed. Raymond Wright (Harmondsworth: Penguin, 1956), pp. 269–70).

155 D.A. Miller, *Narrative and its Discontents: Problems of Closure in the Traditional Novel* (Princeton, N. J.: Princeton Univ. Press, 1981), p. 54.

156 Sir Spenser St John, *Rajah Brooke* (London: Fisher Unwin, 1897), pp. 44, 53, 68, 107, 205.

157 Hannah More, *Strictures on the Modern System of Female Education* (1799; rpt New York: Garland Publishing, 1974), p. 1.

158 'A mother and mistress of a family', comparing England with events in France, writes: "Household authority is the natural source of much national peace: its decline is one of the causes of reckless turbulence in the people" (*Home Discipline or Thoughts on the Origin and Exercise of Domestic Authority* (1841), p. 106, in Leonore Davidoff et al., "Landscape with Figures: Home and Community in English Society" in *The Rights and Wrongs of Women*, eds. Juliet Mitchell and Ann Oakley (Harmondsworth: Penguin, 1976), p. 152).

159 Mrs Sara Ellis, *The Women of England, Their Social Duties, and Domestic Duties*, 2 vols (Philadelphia: E. L. Carey and Art, 1839), vol. I, p. vi. Subsequent references are cited in the text.

160 W.H. Sleeman, *Rambles and Recollections of an Indian Official* (London: J. Hatchard, 1844), pp. iii–iv.

161 John Ruskin, "The Deteriorative Power of Conventional Art over Nations" (1858), in *Sesame and Lilies, The Two Paths* (London: Dent, 1965) p. 89. Subsequent references are cited in the text.

Ruskin's position should be seen in the context of the critiques of British rule in India during the 1857 uprising, many of which were fuelled by fears of territorial empire perverting liberal morality, eroding constitutional liberties, and encouraging conservatism in Britain. For J.M. Ludlow and others the 1857 rebellion proved the long-suspected defects of a non-settler colonialism; they felt that in those territories where settler colonization with its civilizing effects was impracticable, an imperial authority whose power was both *absolute* and *disinterested* was required. Radical critiques sympathetic to Indians were less common. A notable instance is the Chartist Ernest Jones who condemned British rule for being greedy, despotic, marked by atrocities, and for oppressing Indians. See Miles Taylor, "Imperium et Libertas? Rethinking the Radical Critique of Imperialism during the Nineteenth Century", *Journal of Imperial and Commonwealth History*, 19:1 (Jan. 1991), pp. 9–12, 17. The most well known of course are Marx's contemporaneous *New York Daily Tribune* articles which emphasized economic exploitation, stressing British incomes, rapacious land tenure policies, and the physical cruelty practised by tax collectors.

162 "Out of the peat cottage come faith, courage, self-sacrifice, purity and piety, and whatever else is fruitful in the work of Heaven; out of the ivory palace come treachery, cruelty, cowardice, idolatry, bestiality,-whatever else is fruitful in the work of Hell" (p. 90).

163 The specific alignment of the heroic and domestic in Ruskin also encapsulates the intimacy of female altruism and self-sacrifice with a militant masculine will—this was to be displayed in its full vulgarity in several late-nineteenth-century popular British narratives as imperialism entered its most jingoist and virulent phase.

164 Catherine Gallagher, *The Industrial Reformation of English Fiction* (Chicago: Univ. of Chicago Press, 1985), p. 119.

165 Terry Eagleton, *The Rape of Clarissa* (Oxford: Blackwell, 1982), pp. 13, 95; Carol Christ, "Victorian Masculinity and the Angel in the House" in *A Widening Sphere: Changing Roles of Victorian Women*, ed. Martha Vicinus (Bloomington: Indiana Univ. Press, 1977), pp. 158–60.

166 See Terry Eagleton, *Literary Theory* (Oxford: Basil Blackwell, 1983), pp. 26–28; Francis Mulhern, *The Moment of Scrutiny* (London: Verso, 1981); Terry Eagleton, *The Function of Criticism* (London: Verso, 1984), p. 78; Terry Lovell, *Consuming Fiction* (London: Verso, 1987), p. 144; Chris Baldick, *The Social Mission of English Criticism 1848–1932* (Oxford: Clarendon, 1983), p. 9.

This structural and semantic adjacency becomes less surprising if it is integrated with another related set of institutional developments in the nineteenth century. Baldick shows that the three principal factors which ensured English literature a permanent place in British higher education were the administrative needs of British empire as expressed in the regulations and examinations for admission to the Indian Civil Service, the various movements for adult education including Mechanics Institutes, Working Men's Colleges, and extension lecturing, and within this general movement, the specific provisions made for women's education. The emphasis repeatedly fell on English literature as a moralizing, civilizing discipline that was to harmonize class differences, control workers and urban masses, safeguard British administrators from colonial corruption and immorality, contribute to the 'good' of the empire, confirm English women in their established roles and equip them to humanize middle-class men through a combination of altruism, instinct, and literary culture. See *The Social Mission*, pp. 61–63, 105.

167 British military nurses, for instance, argued that their *service* to empire was proof of their reliability as voters. (See Anne Summers, *Angels and Citizens: British Women as Military Nurses 1854–1914* (London: Routledge and Kegan Paul, 1990), pp. 182–83.) Mary Poovey makes an interesting connection between British military assertion, male militancy, maternal tutelage, female nurturance and self-sacrifice, as they coalesced around Florence Nightingale into a single narrative of patriotic service and domestic management. Nightingale's project was squarely based on the management and ideological incorporation of lower classes and the militaristic, civilizing role of middle-class wives. In 1859, presenting India as a lower-class enemy, analogous to the poor helpless patient, Nightingale advocated importing English head nurses to Indian hospitals to ensure discipline and morality in the colony. Later Nightingale was to use familial metaphors and the vocabulary of altruism to argue against the professionalization of nursing which threatened to jeopardize the separate sphere of womanly altruism. For Poovey, Nightingale exemplifies the way mid-nineteenth-century domestic ideolo-gies worked to obliterate class divisions, colonial profit and violence, legitimize England's moral superiority and imperial aspirations, and had the potential to authorize aggressive projects beyond the boundaries of home and England. See *Uneven Developments: The Ideological Work of Gender in Mid-Victorian England* (Chicago: Univ. of Chicago Press, 1988), pp. 169, 187–97.

168 See "Women against women" and "The 'amenities'" in this volume.

169 See "Consent, agency" in this volume.

Women against women

1 James Manor, "The Demise of Princely Order: A Reassessment" in *Peoples, Princes and Paramount Power: Society and Politics in the Indian Princely States*, ed. Robin Jeffrey (Delhi: Oxford Univ. Press, 1978), pp. 307–08; Ian Copland, "The Other Guardians: Ideology and Performance in the Indian Civil Service", ibid., p. 291; D.A. Low, "Laissez-faire and Traditional Rulership in Princely India", ibid., p. 377; S. Natarajan, *A Century of Social Reform in India* (Bombay: Asia Publishing House, 1962), p. 119.

2 See Sumit Sarkar, *Modern India 1885–1947* (Delhi: Macmillan, 1983), pp. 64–65; Peter Reeves, *Landlords and Governments in Uttar Pradesh* (Delhi: Oxford Univ. Press, 1991), pp. 4–5.

3 G.W. Leitner opposed secular education on the ground that "the fear of government will vanish with the fear of God" (*History of Indigenous Education in the Panjab since Annexation and in 1882* (1883; rpt Gurgaon: Deepak Reprints, 1989), pp. 18–19, 27, 42, 75).

4 See Frances Hutchins, *Illusions of Permanence* (Princeton, N.J.: Princeton Univ. Press, 1967), pp. 158, 167–84; Thomas Metcalf, *Land, Landlords and the British Raj: Northern India in the Nineteenth Century* (Berkeley: Univ. of California Press, 1979), p. 180; Ram Gopal, *A Political History of Indian Muslims, 1859–1947* (Lahore: Book Traders, 1976), p. 46.

5 *Stewart's Historical Anecdotes with a Sketch of the History of England and Her Connection with India*, trs. W.T. Adam as *Updesh Katha aur Ingland ki Upakhyanka Chumbak* (Calcutta: Calcutta School Book Society Press, 1825).

6 See James Talboy Wheeler, *A History of India* (London: Trubner and Co, 1867 and 1873), vol. 1, p. 3 and vol. 3, p. 2.

7 Cited in David Lelyveld, *Aligarh's First Generation: Muslim Solidarity in British India* (Delhi: Oxford Univ. Press, 1978), p. 10.

8 See Francis Robinson, *Separatism Among Indian Muslims: The Politics of the United Provinces Muslims 1860–1923* (Delhi: Oxford Univ. Press, 1993), pp. 101, 105, 127, 130.

9 Cited in P. Hardy, *The Muslims of British India* (Cambridge: Cambridge Univ. Press, 1972), p. 88.

10 Duncan B. Forrester, *Caste and Christianity* (London: Curzon Press, 1980), p. 72.

11 See "The 'amenities'" in this volume.

12 See Amalendu De, "Roots of Separatism in Nineteenth Century Bengal" in *Essays in Honour of S.C. Sarkar* (New Delhi: People's Publishing House, 1976), p. 238; A.F. Salahuddin Ahmad, "Muslim Thought and Leadership in Bengal in the Nineteenth Century" in ibid., pp. 633–34.

13 Rajat Sanyal, *Voluntary Associations and the Urban Public Life in Bengal* (Calcutta: Riddhi, 1980), pp. 136–40.

14 See Reeves, *Landlords*, pp. 2, 12; Robinson, *Separatism*, pp. 26, 31–32, 104; Metcalf, *Land*, p. 141; Hardy, *The Muslims*, pp. 47–49, 76, 78, 80; C.A. Bayly, *Rulers, Townsmen and Bazaars: North Indian Society in the Age of British Expansion 1770–1870* (Delhi: Oxford Univ. Press, 1992), p. 363.

15 Metcalf, *Land*, pp. 159–60, 191.

16 See Ahmad, "Muslim Thought" in *Essays*, pp. 635–41; Robinson, *Separatism*, p. 23; Lelyveld, *Aligarh's First*, p. 100; Hardy, *The Muslims*, pp. 36–39, 80–81. In NWP 25 per cent of Muslims were urban (one third of town population) compared to Bengal where not more than 3 or 4 per cent lived in towns (Hardy, ibid., p. 3).

17 Lelyveld, *Aligarh's First*, pp. 58–61, 66–67; Robinson, *Separatism*, p. 40.

18 R.K. Kocchar, "English Education in India", *Economic and Political Weekly* (henceforth *EPW*), 28:48 (Nov. 1992), pp. 2614–15; Robinson, *Separatism*, p. 38; Kenneth Jones, *Socio-Religious Reform Movements in British India* (Cambridge: Cambridge Univ. Press, 1989), pp. 62–63; Lelyveld, *Aligarh's First*, p. 85.

19 Cited in Rahmani Begum, *Sir Syed Ahmad Khan: The Politics of Educational Reforms* (Lahore: Vanguard, 1985), pp. 48–49.

20 Mushir-ul Haq, *Islam in Secular India* (Simla: IIAS, 1972), p. 22; Lelyveld, *Aligarh's First*, pp. 33, 95–96.

21 Lelyveld, *Aligarh's First*, pp. 88–89; Hardy, *The Muslims*, p. 121.

22 See B.D. Misra, *A History of Secondary Education in Uttar Pradesh 1843–1900* (Delhi: Anamika Prakashan, 1989), pp. 25–33; Robinson, *Separatism*, pp. 95–97; Rahmani Begum, *Sir Syed*, pp. 69–71, 101, 122; Christopher King, "Forging a New Linguistic Identity: The Hindi Movement in Benares 1868–1914" in *Culture and Power in Benares: Community, Performance and Environment 1800–1980*, ed. Sandria B. Freitag (Delhi: Oxford Univ. Press, 1989), p. 195.

23 See Robinson, *Separatism*, pp. 35–37, 101; Lelyveld, *Aligarh's First*, p. 82; King, "Forging a New" in *Culture*, ed. Freitag, p. 194.

24 For instance, the Scientific Society (1863) set up by Sayyid Ahmad Khan in Ghazipur with British administrative collaboration to translate European science into Urdu, Persian, Arabic, and Hindi and to search for rare oriental manuscripts had both Hindu and Muslim members. The British Indian Association of the North-Western Provinces (1866) he started to address north Indian demands to parliament had Hindu and Muslim taluqdars and British administrators. The composition of the Allahabad Institute, the Lucknow Jalsa, Sitapur Jalsa, Gonda Jalsa, Rohilkhand Literary Society, and Benares Institute was similarly mixed. Hindus contributed to Aligarh College (1875). The "promotion of friendly feelings" between Hindus and Muslims was the object of Surendranath Banerjee's Indian Association (1877) with which Sayyid Ahmed Khan was also associated. See Gopal, *A Political History*, pp. 48–50; Lelyveld, *Aligarh's First*, pp. 77–80; Robinson, *Separatism*, pp. 17, 85–87, 92–95, 110; Hardy, *The Muslims*, p. 136.

25 There were episodes of communal antagonism in some urban areas of Rohilkhand region in western UP. See Sandria B. Freitag, *Collective Action, Community Public Arenas and the Emergence of Communalism in North India* (Delhi: Oxford Univ. Press, 1990), p. 94.

26 Sayyid Ahmad Khan believed that Hindus and Muslims were one nation or *quam*. On the Deobandis and Ahmad see Gopal, *A Political History*, p. 48; Hardy, *The Muslims*, p. 136; Mushirul Hasan, "Traditional Rites and Contested Meanings: Sectarian Strife in Colonial Lucknow", *EPW*, 31:19 (March 1996), pp. 547–48.

27 A thousand copies of *Mir'at ul'-Arus* (rpt Delhi: Sahitya Akademi, 1982) were purchased by the government for its institutions and recommended for inclusion in school syllabi; the author was given a reward of a thousand rupees. Of the 125 vernacular compositions that were given rewards between 1868 and 1874, one-fifth were on 'Female Education'. *Ritiratnakar* (Allahabad: Govt. Press, 1873) was written on the order of the Lieutenant Governor.

28 In *Mir'at*, tutelage flows from the author to Asghari's father to Asghari and then to Mehmooda who virtually duplicates her mentor. In *Riti* a similar relay is set up between the author, Maina, a learned brahmin woman, a memsahib, and a low-caste servant.

29 As in Khwaja Altaf Husain 'Hali's *Majalis un-Nissa*. See *Voices of Silence: English Translation of Hali's Majalis un-Nissa and Chup ki Dad*, trs. Gail Minault (Delhi: Chanakya, 1986), p. 58.

30 On such educational institutions see Lelyveld, *Aligarh's First*, pp. 50–51, 71, 77, 114; Krishna Kumar, "Hindu Revivalism and Education in North-Central India" in *History, Politics and Culture*, ed. K.N. Panikkar (Delhi: Manohar, 1991), p. 179; Jones, *Socio-Religious*, pp. 60–61; Rahmani Begum, *Sir Syed*, pp. 60, 140; Robinson, *Separatism*, p. 110.

31 A kachahri was a complex of courts and government offices. In the reform of bureaucracy in 1869, the old structure of patronage was replaced by proportionate recruitment in terms of caste and religion and in 1874 examinations became compulsory for tehsildars. See Robinson, *Separatism*, p. 42; Lelyveld, *Aligarh's First*, p. 67.

32 Shiva Prasad, *Memorandum: Court Characters, in the Upper Provinces of India* (Benares, 1868), cited in Christopher King, "Images of Virtue and Vice: The Hindi-Urdu Controversy in Two Nineteenth Century Hindi Plays" in *Religious Controversy in British India*, ed. Kenneth Jones (New York: State Univ. of New York Press, 1992), p. 124. Shiva Prasad, at the time an Inspector in the Department of Public Instruction of the NWP, wrote 18 textbooks. In 1868, Dinanath Gangoly, Secretary of the Etawah Club, also connected Hindi to Hindu religion and nationality. See Robinson, *Separatism*, p. 36; Rahmani Begum, *Sir Syed*, pp. 101–02.

33 In 1868 the centre of government for NWP was moved from Agra, sign of

Mughal glory, to Allahabad, a holy city of Hindus. See Robinson, *Separatism*, p. 101.

34 Propagating Nagri in the 1880s, Shiva Prasad actually did represent the British as having come to India to rescue the Hindu population from Muslim persecution. Cited in Lelyveld, *Aligarh's First*, p. 58.

35 See "Relating histories" in this volume. Whereas the Bengal *bhadralok* sought to displace Persian with English, in UP Urdu and Persian were sought to be replaced by Hindi. In 1867, Hindus demanded that Hindi replace Urdu as the language of administration; this was accepted in 1873 only for use in lower courts in Bihar. (See Jones, *Socio-Religious*, pp. 66–67; Gopal, *A Political History*, p. 40.) Significantly, the alliance between Sanskrit and English was to move from such popular sites to institutional ones. The Arya Samaj split over this issue—the Gurukul party felt only Sanskrit should be taught, while the other faction, to which Lajpat Rai belonged, believed that English should be taught alongside Sanskrit.

36 "The 'amenities'" in this volume also discusses the hinduizing capacities of domestic ideologies in other textbooks and behaviour manuals in this region.

37 Bayly, *Rulers*, pp. 200–01, 214–17, 240–41.

38 Zamindars, no longer permitted armed retainers, needed government assistance to collect rents; tenants hoped for assistance in resisting encroachments from zamindars and moneylenders; commerce and manufacture took place under goverment regulation that specified property rights; courts had ultimate sanction over transference and inheritance; religious leaders relied on government to protect charitable endowments and other forms of patronage or income; personal law covering family and marriage required government enforcement; revenue administrators, policemen, judges presided over personal safety, security, distribution of property, and all kinds of wealth. See Lelyveld, *Aligarh's First*, pp. 63–64.

39 Sen's speech at Victorian Discussion Society in London, 1 Aug. 1870, quoted in Pat Barr, *The Memsahibs: Women of Victorian India* (London: Secker and Warburg, 1871), p. 161; *Nildevi*, cited in Madan Gopal, *Bharatendu Harishchandra* (Delhi: Sahitya Akademi, 1981), p. 31.

40 For Dinananth Gangoly, a supporter of Hindi, the vernacular literally paved the way for its parent Sanskrit, the "national language" of India (cited in Rehmani Begum, *Sir Syed*, p. 101).

41 Pandit Gauri Datta, *Devrani Jethani ki Kahani* (Meerut: Ziyai Chapakhana, 1870), pp. 11–12.

42 Minault, *Voices*, pp. 7, 13; Rehmani Begum, *Sir Syed*, p. 279.

43 These were British roads, communications, transport, commerce, medicine, irrigation, urban hygiene, justice, the possibility of legal redress and reform. *Majalis* won a prize of four hundred rupees and was adopted as a textbook in girls' schools in UP and Punjab and taught for several decades.

44 See "The 'amenities'" in this volume.

45 In *Majalis* 'Hali' laments that though God and the Prophet gave widows permission to remarry, it was considered "an evil worse than adultery" among Muslims, who had surrendered to custom (p. 83). Widow remarriage was uncommon among the higher classes. Three decades later the Deobandi reformer

Thanawi was to argue for widow remarriage among well-born Muslims and condemn its absence as a sign of foolish hinduization. See E.A.H. Blunt, *The Caste System of Northern India with special reference to the United Province* (1931; rpt Delhi: S. Chand, 1969), p. 198; Barbara Daly Metcalfe, *Perfecting Women: Maulana Ashraf Ali Thanawi's Bihishti Zewar* (Delhi: Oxford Univ. Press, 1992), pp. 44–45.

46 *Hadis* are the reported words, deeds, and occasions of tacit approval by the Prophet Muhammad, passed on by a chain of reliable authorities.

47 'Hali's *Majalis* warns housewives to be wary of *new* women vendors and not become too open or informal with them (p. 74).

48 Asghari's father-in-law gets a house, a vehicle, and fifty rupees but sends home twenty claiming that he cannot manage on less since he needs it for maintaining his house, servants, and status in Lahore; his wife protests that she finds the distribution unequal and inadequate. It is the new managerial labour and efficiency of Asghari and the expulsion of Azmat that allow him to continue to keep thirty rupees for his own use.

49 E.P. Thompson's description in *Customs in Common* (New York: New Press, 1991), pp. 69, 85.

50 Cited in Rahmani Begum, *Sir Syed*, p. 92; Statement of 1872 as Secretary of a Select Committee on Education, in Jones, *Socio-Religious*, p. 67.

51 Kahars were classified as sudras and some were also engaged in agriculture. There was an occupational sub-caste among them known as mahar who worked as women's servants. (See Rev. M.A. Sherring, *Hindu Tribes and Castes as represented in Benares* (1872, rpt Delhi: Cosmo, 1974), vol. 1, pp. 339–40; Blunt, *The Caste System*, p. 238.) In *"Lavli aur Malti ka Samvad"* a kaharin named Mahesiya cooks in a bania household where the husband, *lalaji*, works in a *kachahri* (*Balabodhini*, 1874, no. 5).

52 See William R. Pinch, *Peasants and Monks in British India* (Delhi: Oxford Univ. Press. 1996), pp. 75, 95–96, 111, 118, 125.

53 Dasiya's narrative applies to landowners a folklore, already circulating among merchants, which linked degenerate Persian, Muslim, and European ways to the collapse of family credit and bankruptcy. On this folklore see Bayly, *Rulers*, pp. 383–85.

54 Chowbe Raghunath Das, *Bharyahit* (*circa* 1870, rpt Lucknow: Naval Kishore, 1929), p. 2.

55 Farsi-educated groups in both princely and government service had a stake in Persian and Urdu. Of these Kashmiri brahmins and kayasths were close to Muslims, prominent in government jobs, and defended Urdu vigorously. See King, "Forging a New" in *Culture*, ed. Freitag, pp. 196–97; Robinson, *Separatism*, pp. 30–31.

56 Robinson, *Separatism*, pp. 30–31; Gopal, *A Political History*, p. 32; Lelyveld, *Aligarh's First*, pp. 92–93.

57 The self-conception of Awadh taluqdars as a munificent aristocracy took the shape of investing in English education by establishing Canning College in Lucknow in 1862 and in resisting government efforts to terminate the Oriental Department which taught Sanskrit, Arabic, and Persian on the "native method".

The Raja of Bhinga employed a European tutor and a pandit to teach Sanskrit to his sons. The ruler of Balrampur financed both an English school and a Sanskrit *pathshala*. In the 1890s Colvin School which catered to taluqdars put a major emphasis on English but also taught Persian, Arabic, Sanskrit, and employed three religious teachers—a pandit, a Sunni and a Shia maulavi. See Metcalf, *Land*, pp. 319–21, 323, 325, 333, 353.

58 See ibid., p. 359.

59 Bayly, *Rulers*, p. 215; Sherring, *Hindu Tribes*, vol. 1, p. 339; Blunt, *The Caste System*, p. 237.

60 See "Relating histories" in this volume.

61 King, "Forging a New" in *Culture*, ed. Freitag, p. 196.

62 For Sayyid Ahmed Khan's statements on Urdu see Rehmani Begum, *Sir Syed*, pp. 57–58, 63, 90–96, 206; Lelyveld, *Aligarh's First*, pp. 98–99, 125.

63 On 'English' see "Relating histories" in this volume. Sayyid Ahmad Khan's statements on English are cited in Rehmani Begum, *Sir Syed*, pp. 95–96, 201–02; Robinson, *Separatism*, pp. 108–09.

64 In his testimony to the Education Commission in 1882, Sayyid Ahmad Khan said that the aim of Aligarh College was "to form a class of persons, Muhammedan in religion, Indian in blood and colour, but English in tastes, in opinions and in intellect" (cited in Lelyveld, *Aligarh's First*, p. 207).

65 Testimony before Hunter Commission in 1882, cited in King, "Images" in *Religious Controversy*, ed. Jones, p. 139.

66 Cited in ibid., p. 137.

67 In the 1860s Tattva Bodhini, a society for religious and social reform, translated Sanskrit religious works into Hindi and managed to place them in the curricula of government schools. Kempson, the Director of Public Instruction from 1862 to 1878, *did* in fact favour Hindi over Urdu while many of Maina's anti-Urdu arguments can be found in the government's NWP Education Report 1873–74 (cited in Gopal, *A Political History*, p. 41). See also Rahmani Begum, *Sir Syed*, pp. 106–07; Robinson, *Separatism*, p. 73.

68 Dais were usually dhanuk, chamar, or koli (weavers) by caste. See Blunt, *The Caste System*, p. 242; Sherring, *Hindu Tribes*, vol. 1, p. 345.

69 In *Riti* the nain also washes the feet of Maina and her husband and leads them along with the infant to the bedi (raised platform for ritual purposes) where the pandit takes over (p. 51). In Devrani Jethani dais are indispensable while nains visit brides in their marital home and act on their behalf as mediators between the natal and the marital family.

70 In *Devrani Jethani*, nais arrange weddings; a panihaari goes to call a chamar to treat an ailing child, but his medicine makes the child worse and he is eventually cured by a *hakim*, a unani physician (p. 64). *Riti* describes several customs or rituals that involve bhat, mali, tamboli, nai, sonar, darzi (tailor), and lohar (blacksmith).

71 Charles Raikes, *Kshatriyanushasanika* (Agra: Sikander ke Chhapekhane se, 1853), p. 6.

72 See Metcalf, *Land*, pp. 232, 361–62; Sherring, *Hindu Tribes*, vol. 1, p. 22.

73 Pyarelal, *Paddhati Prayagshetra ke Kayastho ki Vivah ki*, trs. from Urdu by

Munshi Bhairavdayal (Allahabad: Govt. Press, 1870), on order of the Lieutenant Governor. Pyarelal makes a point of mentioning the Srivastav kayasths.

74 Pyarelal, *Jagopkarak: Rules for the Reduction of Marriage Expenses among Hindus of the Northwest Provinces on order of Maharajdhiraj Radha Prasad Singh Bahadur Dumrav va Deshadhikari* (Patna: n.p., 1871), p. 39.

75 *Balabodhini*, 1874, no. 1, p. 10.

76 Anjuman-i-Ajmere, *Rasala Kharch Kam Karne ke Vishay Mein* (Lahore: Yantralaya Kohinoor, 1874), pp. 36–38.

77 It seems the performances of bhands were often perceived as "gross and indecent" (S.N.A Jafri, *The History and Status of Landlords and Tenants in the United Provinces* (1931; rpt Delhi: Usha, 1985), p. 290). See also Sherring, *Hindu Tribes*, vol. 1, p. 276.

78 Ramlal, *Banitabuddhi-Prakashini*, on order of Lieutenant Governor for Hamirpur zila school (Allahabad: Govt. Press, 1871), pp. 33–35.

79 Thakur Hanuvant Singh, *Kshatriyakul Timirprabhakar* (Agra: Rajput Press, 1893), pp. 34–35, 66, 69–70, 62–63, 74–76. The book is dedicated to Raja Udai Pratap Singh of Bhinga. This English-educated raja endowed an Anglo-Vernacular school, set up a scheme for a special school for the sons of taluqdars where they would be taught English and get "religious, moral, aesthetic and physical instruction"; he seems to have combined a nonsectarian philanthropy in education with special zeal on behalf of Hindu taluqdars and fellow rajputs. See Metcalf, *Land*, pp. 318, 321–22, 325, 355.

80 *Bihishti Zewar*, pp. 75, 100–01, 113, 118, 125–26, 130–33, 86, 121–23. In his retrospective account of the nawabi elite, Abdul Halim Sharar equated the bad influence of courtesans on men with the influence of "coarse" domnis on women in the *zenana* (*Lucknow: The Last Phase of an Oriental culture*, eds. and trs. E.S. Harcourt and Fakhir Husain (Delhi: Oxford Univ. Press, 1989), p. 192).

81 See Sherring, *Hindu Tribes*, vol. 1, p. 272.

82 See Metcalf, *Land*, pp. 352–55.

83 Reeves points out that in UP villages Muslims in fact operated at most levels as *jati* groups in the late nineteenth century (*Landlords*, p. 3).

84 On landowning patterns see Robinson, *Separatism*, pp. 62–65; Metcalf, *Land*, p. 163.

85 See Burton Stein, "Towards an Indian Petty Bourgeoisie: Outline of an Approach", *EPW*, 26: 4 (June 1991). 'Communities' could be confined as merely local and proximate groups, or solicit, with the aid of print and abstracted ideological appeals, the participation of heterogenous urban and ruro-urban populations. See Freitag, *Collective Action*, p. 88; Kumar, "Hindu Revivalism" in *History*, ed. Panikkar, p. 175.

86 Hardy points out that religious communities in practice meant Hindu and Muslim upper and middle classes, not the mass of Muslims in this region who were in agricultural, artisanal, and service occupations (*The Muslims*, p. 6).

87 In practice caste rather than religious discrimination predominated among the elite, and Hindu and Muslim landowners could join to suppress upstart peasant castes. See Metcalf, *Land*, p. 262; Gyanendra Pandey, *The Construction of*

Communalism in Colonial North India (Delhi: Oxford Univ. Press, 1990), pp. 84, 200.

88 In UP the assertive movements of lower and middle castes took more sanskritized forms because radical tendencies were weak. See Gail Omvedt, *Cultural Revolt in a Colonial Society* (Bombay: SSET, 1976), p. 297.

89 *Banitabuddhi* proscribes abusive songs sung by women at weddings-*maryad ki gaari* and *thattha karna* (p. 35). *Riti* and *Devrani Jethani* also rail against women's bawdiness and abandon at weddings. So does Munshi Jivaram Kapur Khatri in *Stridharma Saar* which was published under the auspices of a khatri caste association. Khatri interdicts going to *melas* and *tamashas*, *sithni* or abuse at weddings, *doha dena* or verbal contests between men and women, the *syaapa* or gathering of women for weeping and lamenting at deaths; the tract has a special section on how women should behave among women entitled *"Striyon mein baithne ki riti"*, which prohibits immoderate laughter, criticism, and gossip (Agra: Gurjar Yantralaya, 1892), p. 8). In *Bihishti*, Thanawi described the gatherings of women for celebrations, marriage, and funeral ceremonies as the "root of excesses" because they involved foolish and sinful customs, showing off, travelling, spending money, singing songs, laughing, gossiping, spending too much time together, and visiting each other's homes (pp. 108, 113, 116, 118, 153, 156).

90 A publication of the Christian Vernacular Education Society, *Ratnamala* or *Reading Book for Women: Advice on Domestic Management*, also condemned the bad marriage songs among Hindus and any gossip or abuse by women (Allahabad: Mission Press, 1869, p. 116).

91 Though islamicization had substantially different ideological, political, and class locations in the Faraizi and Wahabi movements as well as differing locales in the eighteenth and early nineteenth centuries in this region, after 1857 its liberal variants in UP were as tied to class processes as its hinduizing counterparts.

92 Ojhas were supposed to have special jurisdiction over evil spirits of the deceased, *bhoot*, *pret*. Though formerly brahmins, now "shrewd men" from all castes were said to have taken to this increasingly profitable profession (Sherring, *Hindu Tribes*, vol. 1, p. 37).

93 Pasis were dubbed criminal by the British. See W. Crooke, *Natives of Northern India* (1907; rpt Delhi: Royal Reprints, 1980), p. 120.

94 Historians of UP generally acknowledge this though only under the rubric of syncretism between and assimilation from otherwise discrete Hindu and Muslim cultures. See Charles Alfred Elliott, *Laborious Days* (Calcutta: J. Larkins, 1892), p. 28; Metcalf, *Land*, p. 358; Hasan, "Traditional Rites", p. 548; Rahmani Begum, *Sir Syed*, p. 18; Bayly, *Rulers*, pp. 12–13, 192; Gopal, *A Political History*, p. 11.

95 Kayasth families in Karrah, Mirzapur converted to Islam but retained some customs. Some Kapurs among khatris too had converted to Islam in the past; many khatris had Islamic lifestyles and took pride in their close association with Muslim dynasties. The most extreme example of ritual syncretism in this region was an agricultural and trading group known as Vishnuis or Bishnois whose practices were divided evenly between the Koran and Hindu *pothis* or holy books, Hindu ceremonies and Muslim prayer (*namaaz*), the fasts of Ramzaan and Ekadasi.

Muslims could be initiated into this "caste". They buried their dead, were regarded as polluted by Hindus, themselves regarded the Hindus as polluted, and were hated by orthodox Muslims. See Sherring, *Hindu Tribes*, vol. 1, pp. 294–95, 311–12, 281; Bayly, *Rulers*, p. 366, 387.

96 Non-Muslim participation in Shia practices, Muharram processions, recitations, decoration of *tazias* (model of the tomb of Hasan or Imam Husain), and veneration of Husain was widespread in UP and other regions, both with and without state patronage, till the end of the nineteenth century. See Hasan, "Traditional Rites", pp. 544–45.

97 The precise composition of the five saints or Panchpiri varied but the cult centred on Ghazi Miya. The saints ranged from the Shia canon, Hindu deities, mother goddesses, deified men, martyrs, Hindu and Muslim saints, and Amina sati (Amina was the name of the Prophet's mother). They were worshipped by masses of peasantry and the lowest castes. The Panchpiri was also worshipped by some kalwars, sonars, mihtars (sweepers), baheliyas (hunters, fowlers), and luniyas (cultivators). Panchpiriya was recorded as a sub-caste among dhobis in the 1870s and as a sub-caste among telis, barhais, bhangis, halwais (confectioners and sweet vendors), and koris (weavers, an offshoot of chamars) at the turn of the century. In the 1870s Hindu halwais of Benares worshipped Ghazi Miya and undertook journeys to Bahraich. In fact until the early twentieth century Muslims and Hindus of different castes made annual pilgrimages to Ghazi Miya's tomb, and a *Ghazi Miyan ka mela* was enthusiastically celebrated in many places in eastern UP and western Bihar. The 1901 census recorded 53 castes in UP who worshipped Panchpir, among whom Ghazi Miya was the foremost; of these castes 44 were "wholly or partly Hindu" and 16 of "good social standing". The number of Hindu followers was put at 1.75 million, and this took into account only those who declared them the "principal" object of worship. In 1920 it was estimated that the total number of people worshipping was 13.5 million. The annual *mela* at Bahraich at the turn of the century drew over 100,000 people. See Blunt, *The Caste System*, pp. 56, 101, 286, 292–93; William Crooke, *Religion and Folklore in Northern India* (1925; rpt Delhi: S. Chand, n.d.), p. 166; Sherring, *Hindu Tribes*, vol. 1, pp. 300–01, 313, 397; Pandey, *The Construction*, pp. 86–87.

98 Significantly, the 1837 and 1870–71 clashes in Bareilly were related to the coincidence or overlap of Muharram and Ramnavmi. (See Freitag, *Collective Action*, pp. 107–10.) Ghazi Miya is not the only target in *Riti*, it also condemns *shaheeds* like Ahmad Vir and Muhammed Vir, Loona Chamari, devotional bhakti cults practised by Vairagis that centred on ahir and nai devotees (p. 171). Loona Chamari or Nona Chamarin was believed to be a witch who caused calamities and had to be propitiated; Vairagis were followers of Ramanuj and mainly sudras. See Sherring, *Hindu Tribes*, vol. 1, pp. 393, 260.

99 This representation of popular *pirs* or saints as 'Muslim' invaders killed by Hindus in the past and later deified by ignorant Hindus, was incidentally repeated even more virulently by William Crooke. In fact many *pirs*, as Crooke himself acknowledged, had syncretic hagiographies combining motifs from several religions.

See William Crooke, *North-Western Provinces of India* (rpt Delhi: Cosmo, 1987), p. 252; *Religion*, pp. 163–64.

100 See V.R. and L. Bevan Jones, *Women in Islam* (Lucknow, 1941), pp. 309–39, 402–16; Crooke, *Natives*, pp. 249, 257–59.

101 A *chudail* was believed to be the ghost of a pregnant or impure woman. *Mir'at* forbids customary wedding rituals and festivities like *sehra, kangna, manda,* and *aaraish* (p. 107).

102 Sheikh Saddu for instance was revered by women who wished to obtain the upper hand of their husbands and the special saint of barren women; his worship involved magical cults, ecstasy, and possession. See Crooke, *Religion*, p. 167; Blunt, *The Caste System*, p. 291.

103 Deobandis rejected the authority of *pirs*, pilgrimage to saints' tombs, and annual death rites of particular saints as falling outside acceptable Islamic practice along with anything else that appeared to come from Hindu culture. This de-corruption of Sunni and Shia Islam was to accelerate in the twentieth century. See Hardy, *The Muslims*, p. 59; Pandey, *The Construction*, pp. 87–88; Jones, *Socio-Religious*, p. 60; Hasan, "Traditional Rites", p. 548.

104 Thanawi condemned a number of practices as wasteful and un-Islamic: animism, magic, beliefs such as evil eye, jinns (creatures good and bad made from the order of fire), consulting brahmins or astrologers, composite customs, faith in amulets, worship or offering *fatihas*, food or anything else at graves and tombs, worshipping *pirs, melas* including those held at graves (*Bihishti*, pp. 73–76, 120, 136, 150).

105 See Crooke, *North-Western*, pp. 234, 240, 242, 263; *Natives*, pp. 203–04, 213–14, 221, 237–41, 244. Crooke enumerates shared Hindu and Muslim superstitions, popular religious beliefs, common birth, naming, marriage and mourning rites, and practices related to death pollution. Belief in animism and *bhoots* cut across denominations among peasants.

106 Crooke, *North-Western*, pp. 240–42.

107 For instance, the 1872 census for this region stated: "Indeed except for rules of inheritance, in her occupation and mode of life, the Mohammedan female does not differ much from the Hindu, although among Mohammedans marriage takes place at a little more advanced age, but the proportion in the age of the wife and husband is not materially different" (pp. 44–45). See H.G. Keene, "Islam in India", *Calcutta Review*, LXXI (1880), pp. 250–51.

108 Cited in King, "Images" in *Religious Controversy*, pp. 142–43.

109 See "Consent, agency" in this volume.

110 Asghari distributes copies of the Koran, gives alms to the deserving poor, builds a mosque, a *sarai* for travellers, but Maina does not build bathing places, temples, *dharamshalas*, almshouses, resthouses for pilgrims, orphanages.

111 Vamisdhara's *Sutashikshavali* had identified *vidyadaan* (teaching) as the highest form of charity in which women could be active; this could be extended through personal teaching or gifts of money and would multiply since the educated would teach others (Agra: Nurul Ilm Press, 1865, p. 28). *Devrani Jethani* too says that *vidyadaan* is authorized by the Shastras and girls must teach others what they know (pp. 51–52).

112 Munshi Ahmad Husain, *Istri Updesh* (Agra: n.p., 1873), *Mudris Farsi madrasa faiz amne vaste faide aam ke banai.*

113 This device is discussed in "The 'amenities'" in this volume.

114 Bireswar Sen, *Influence of English Education: Bengal and the North West Provinces* (Benares: P.C. Chowdhury and Co., 1876), p. 3.

115 Cited in Lelyveld, *Aligarh's First*, p. 144.

116 Cited in Rahmani Begum, *Sir Syed*, p. 171.

117 Among the some seventy or more caste groups who practised widow remarriage in this region at the time were: the Khagi Chauhans of Bijnor and Etawah, Bishnois, most telis, chamar barhais, gujars, malis, kahars, baaris, kacchis, kurmis, kanjars, bhangis, doms, and tawaifs. Levirate marriage of widows was common among jat, gadariya, gujar, khatik, chamar, dhusia, ahir, bhar, julaha, dhuniya, and mallah (boatmen). See Sherring, *Hindu Tribes*, vol. 1, pp. 161, 166, 301, 316, 328, 337, 340, 350, 404; Blunt, *The Caste System*, pp. 64–65, 219.

118 See Francis W. Pritchett, *Marvelous Encounters: Folk Romances in Urdu and Hindi* (Delhi: Manohar, 1985), pp. 3–4, 7.

119 Ibid., pp. 142, 175, 196.

120 *Chhabili Bhatiyar 'Qissa* (Agra: n.p., 1864); Muhammed Wazir Khan, *Chhabili Bhatiyari* (Agra: n.p., 1868); Ganga Prasad Gupta, *Sangit Chhabili Bhatiyar* (Aligarh: n.p., 1920); Krisna Khattri, *Sangit Chhabili Bhatiyar* (Kanpur: Sri Krisna Khattri, 1926); Chaudhuri Nathu Das, *Sangit Chhabili Bhatiyari* (Meerut: Reformer Press, 1928); Natharam Sarma, *Sangit Bicitra Kumari*, 2nd edn (Hathras: Gaur Book Depot, 1943).

121 *Chhabili Bhatiyari: Sikandar Shah badshah ke shahzade Raman Shah ka qissa* (n.p.: Brahm Press, 1873).

122 One of the four classes of women in classical taxonomy, a *shankhini* is described as tall, handsome with long eyes and hair, marked with three lines on the neck, amorous and irascible, a very demon in look and nature.

123 On Bengal see "Figures for the unconscious" in this volume. For instance, in 1873 *Harishchandra's Magazine* published an effusive review of James Tod's *Annals and Antiquities of Rajasthan* (1829) that praised it for restoring the noble history of raputs.

124 Metcalf, *Land*, p. 113.

125 Robinson, *Separatism*, pp. 30–31.

126 See Metcalf, *Land*, pp. 360–61.

127 Many rajputs worshipped Muslim saints. See James Ludlow, *Mahomedanism in India* (Cambridge: n.p., 1858), vol. 1, p. 177.

128 Branches of several rajput clans in UP had converted to Islam either before or during during Mughal rule. These included sections of the high-ranking Bachgotia Chauhans of Awadh; the Dores and Ujjains of the Pramar clan to which the Raja of Dumraon belonged; the Gaharwar rajputs in Benares district; large branches of the Gautam rajputs some of whom took the apellation of Khan; some of the Pachtoriya branch of *suryavanshi* Dikshit rajputs. In Chail division of

Allahabad district, there were converts called Chauhan Muhammedans. There were some converts among the Tomars of Bulandshahr and Meerut, the Baghels of Rewa, the Bhals of Bulandshahr, and the Naikumbhs of Ghazipur. See Sherring, *Hindu Tribes*, vol. 1, pp. 137, 146–48, 150, 157–58, 162, 166, 170, 176, 203–04, 208–09; Metcalf, *Land*, p. 14; Blunt, *The Caste System*, p. 203.

129 Sherring, *Hindu Tribes*, vol. 1, pp. 118–19, 158, 169, 178, 206, 210, 224, 229, 241–43.

130 The emperor Akbar had introduced customs such as the *barat* at his son's wedding as a sign of tolerance and assimilation. Apart from *nazrana* and *dahej*, the *rasms* described in the qissa are *lagan*, *barauna*, *toran*, *saat phere*, and *gauna*.

131 The Gautam rajputs of Kalyanpur, Fatehpur district, and some of the Pachtoriya rajputs, though professedly Muslim, still practised a number of Hindu rites and ceremonies. The Badjugar rajputs included Muslim clans who maintained rajput titles and marriage customs and celebrated Holi. The Malkana rajputs of Mathura region were regarded as neither Hindu nor Muslim; they combined Hindu and Muslim marriage ceremonies but buried their dead. (See Sherring, *Hindu Tribes*, vol. 1, pp. 203, 209; Lelyveld, *Aligarh's First*, p. 13; Blunt, *The Caste System*, p. 206.) In later decades islamicization banned *pheras*, circumambulating a fire, and other 'Hindu' marriage rituals among converts of all classes.

132 It seems some rajputs at the lower end of the scale had fallen into "low caste habits". The bhats who ranked below rajputs and the Meos of Bharatpur who were regarded as a low group, practised both Hindu and Muslim marriage ceremonies in full form consecutively: *pheras* and *nikaah*. The Meos of Punjab continued Hindu festivals, worship, and dress and were seen as "impure Muslims". See Sherring, *Hindu Tribes*, vol. 1, p. 126; Blunt, *The Caste System*, pp. 201–02; Denzil Ibbetson, *Panjab Castes* (1916; rpt Delhi: Cosmo, 1981), p. 180.

133 The Hindu *rasm* along with the *barat* could signify a sacramental marriage and/or indicate the ritual importance of marriage, and the legal significance of rituals as preconditions for customary rights such as *stridhan* (inherited wealth, gifts, or property a married woman could hold in her own right).

134 Muhammed Husain in *Rasala Kharch*, for instance, argued that status should now be derived from wives rather than wealth or pleasure.

135 See Kumkum Sangari, "Mirabai and the Spiritual Economy of *Bhakti*", *EPW*, 15:28 (July 1990), p. 1540.

136 In *Dastan-e-Amir Hamzah*, Asman Pari's punitive jealousy of Hamzah's many other wives structures the narrative but finds no comparable resolution.

137 In western UP gujars could also be described as degraded rajputs and some as ahirs; in some areas they were clubbed with pasis, slaughtered goats, sold meat, fruit and vegetables, reared poultry and pigs, or were stone cutters. See Sherring, *Hindu Tribes*, vol. 1, pp. 235–37, 337, 400; Crooke, *Natives*, p. 114.

138 These were medieval traditions that had received royal patronage and still continued, especially in Awadh. A favourite device of bahurupiyas was to ask for money, and when refused, to ask that it may be given on condition of the bahurupiya succeeding in deceiving the person who had refused it; some days later the bahurupiya would visit the house again in the disguise of a pedlar, a milkman, etc., sell his goods without being detected, throw off his disguise and claim the stipulated reward. See M. Aslam Qureshi, *Wajid Ali Shah's Theatrical Genius* (Lahore: Vanguard, 1987), pp. 123–25; Sherring, *Hindu Tribes*, vol. 2, p. 201; Ibbetson, *Panjab Castes*, p. 236.

139 Qureshi, *Wajid Ali*, pp. 9–10, 14.

140 The mobile bhamptas and chauras of the Deccan who operated all over the country disguised themselves as well-to-do Mahrattas, prosperous Marwaris, Lingayat traders, mendicants, and wandering minstrels when out thieving or picking pockets. The bowri or bauriah, a so-called criminal tribe of north India, disguised themselves as religious mendicants or *bairagis* (a general term applied to many devotees). See Edmund Cox, *Police and Crime in India* (London: Stanley Paul, *circa* 1910), pp. 234, 248; Sherring *Hindu Tribes*, vol: 2, pp. 326, 336.

141 *Bihishti*, pp. 211, 379.

142 *Letters and Correspondence of Pandita Ramabai*, ed. A.B. Shah (Bombay: Maharashtra State Board for Literature and Culture, 1977), pp. 292–94.

143 Balakrishna Bhatt, *Shikshadana* (Allahabad: Victoria Chhapsthan, 1877), p. 17.

144 The *Manusmriti* recommended conjugal happiness, while conjugal love was celebrated in the *Taittriya Brahmana* and *Satpatha Brahmana*. In Kautilya's *Arthashastra* both husbands and wives were entitled to expect their spouses to fulfil their conjugal duties, the punishment for the husband being double that of the wife (ed. L.M. Rangarajan (Delhi: Penguin, 1992), verse 3.3.2, p. 68).

145 One of the earliest condemnations of polygamy for this reason came in a letter by "Women of Chinsura" in *Samachardarpan*, 21 March 1835, in *British Paramountcy and the Indian Renaissance*, eds. R.C Majumdar, A.K. Majumdar and D.K. Ghosh (Bombay: Bharatiya Vidya Bhavan, 1981), pp. 262–63.

146 Munshi Ramlal, *Putrishikshopkari Granth* (Allahabad: Govt. Press, 1872), p. 31.

147 Pandit Sitaram, *Stri Updesh* (Lalitpur: Lalitpur Press, 1871), p. 17.

148 *Bihishti*, pp. 183, 336, 341.

149 Bayly, *Rulers*, pp. 364–65.

150 Crooke, *Natives*, p. 115; Bayly, *Rulers*, p. 364.

151 Cited in Ibbetson, *Panjab Castes*, p. 308.

152 Bayly, *Rulers*, pp. 129, 219.

153 Blunt, *The Caste System*, p. 205. In Punjab bhatiyars were bakers and sellers of food in *sarais*, and were jhinwar by caste (a classification that seems to have included kahars, Muslim bhishtis and saqqas, and encompassed the occupations of carriers, watermen, fishermen, village menials). As railways had diminished their trade, bhatiyars had also taken to petty carriage, hiring out ponies, ikkas (two-wheeled horse-drawn vehicle), and keeping donkeys. All bhatiyars in the 1881 census in Punjab were Muslims since Hindus did not eat food cooked by jhinwars. See Ibbetson, *Panjab Castes*, pp. 306–08.

154 Lakshmanprasad, *Saas Bahu ka Qissa* (Agra: Madan Mohan Press, 1895), p. 11.

155 See Sherring, *Hindu Tribes*, vol. 1, pp. 119, 249–50.

156 On the latter two practices see "The 'amenities'" in this volume and Blunt, *The Caste System*, p. 154.

157 Cited in Pritchett, *Marvelous*, pp. 80–81, 84, 94. The heartless queen who is willing to risk the king's life to satisfy her curiosity resembles Kaikeyi's mother who is banished for the same reasons in the *Valmiki Ramayana*. See endnote 63 in "Consent, agency" in this volume.

158 See Patricia Parker, *Literary Fat Ladies* (London: Methuen, 1987), p. 13.

159 *Kissa Chavili Bhatiyar* (Delhi: Matba Chivan Prakash, 1884).

160 *Kissa Chhabili Bhatiyari* (Benares: Star of India Press, 1927), pp. 35–36.

161 Slavoj Zizek terms this "surplus" the last "support" of ideological meaning (cited in Terry Eagleton, *Ideology* (London: Verso, 1991), p. 184).

162 Significantly, the 1943 edition is named after Vichitra and this may indicate another alteration in caste configurations.

163 Qureshi, *Wajid Ali*, pp. 9, 31. Bhojpuri oral epic poems often had lower-caste heroes—ahir, teli—and brahmin villains.

164 Bhojpuri folklore mentions the militancy of Dharman bi, Karman bi, and Lakhiya—a lower-caste woman; songs were sung about 1857 by women while some songs satirized the loyalism of the Maharaja of Dumraon. See Badri Narayan, "Popular culture in 1857", *Social Scientist*, 26:1–4 (Jan.-April 1998), pp. 89–92. Pritchett mentions some lower-strata protagonists in *Marvelous*, p. 30.

165 See Frances W. Pritchett, *The Romance Tradition in Urdu* (New York: Columbia Univ. Press, 1991), pp. 14–15.

166 Qureshi, *Wajid Ali*, pp. 24–25. An early twentieth-century account says that the wives of nats were also prostitutes. (See Blunt, *The Caste System*, p. 157.) Significantly, Harischandra was vocal in condemning the spread of troupes of *bhands*, *bhagatiyas* and *ganikas* (courtesans) and characterized most types of popular drama as *bhrasht* or depraved. See Kathryn Hansen, "The Birth of Hindi Drama" in *Culture and Power*, ed. Freitag, pp. 85–86.

167 See Pritchett, *The Romance*, p. 15.

168 *Vidyarthi ki Pratham Pustak*, prepared on goverment order by Doctor Walker Sahib with Pandit Jaishankar and Pandit Madanlal (2nd edn, Agra: n.p., 1854), pp. 11, 13. In Nazir Ahmad's *Fasana-e-Mubtala* (1885), the hero marries a prostitute named Haryali; the story is also structured around the rivalry between her and his first wife and intended to display the defects of polygamy.

169 Later ashrafization and sanskritization involved a growing use of Arabic, Persian, and hinduized names and this along with British classificatory schemas drove many Muslims to shed 'Hindu' names and vice versa. On changes in caste apellations see Pandey, *Construction*, p. 88.

170 The worship of Muslim saints and *pirs* was common among several low-caste, nomadic, tribal, and 'Hindu' peasant groups, as were considerable overlaps in the faiths of the lower classes. The *mazaar* (shrine) of the eighteenth-century sufi, Raja Mubarak Shah, was repaired between 1860 and 1880 by all castes and religious groups in Mubarakpur. See Crooke, *Religion*, p. 165; Crooke, *North-Western*, p. 240; Blunt, *The Caste System*, pp. 149, 157, 286–87; Pandey, *The Construction*, pp. 128–29.

171 Some kurmi families of Chunar and Jaunpur practised parallel-cousin marriage and even adopted the crescent as a symbol, and the Dhaighar gadariyas had taken to Muslim customs. In parts of Allahabad and the western UP Doab there were traditions of intermarriage between chamars and Muslim weavers. See Bayly, *Rulers*, p. 49; Blunt, *The Caste System*, p. 54; Amaresh Misra, "Redefining Tradition", *Times of India*, 8 Nov. 1995.

172 Churihars, dhuniyas, kunjras, and gujars preserved Hindu wedding rites except that a qazi replaced the pandit, and the gods were replaced by Allah, the Prophet, or some saint. Converted gujars, bhats, and Meos employed pandits to fix auspicious days and wedding dates. Blunt lists the maintenance of Hindu festivals, taboos, and deity worship among converts in this region. In Punjab, converted gujars retained many Hindu customs. See *The Caste System*, pp. 201–02, 183–84.

173 Among the lower castes who converted to Islam in this region were one subdivision of telis, some rangers (agricultural workers, sepoys). In two ahir clans, the Kankauria and Nigania, many were Muslim. The ghoṣi subgroup of ahirs was chiefly Muslim but the gaddi subgroup was only partly Msulims; other converted ahirs called themselves shaikhs. The shaikh and bharka subgroups among dhobis were Muslim; there were several Muslim subdivisions among the karouls (hunters and sellers of game); among bhangis and mihtars, the shaikhs were converts as were the chikwas among gadariyas. Qalaigars were Muslim and Hindu and had a separate caste among Hindus. Kalwars could be Hindu and Muslim, had a Muslim branch called rangki, and the Rajasthani counterparts of kalwars, known as kallars, were converted rajputs. Sikligars, who sharpened knoves and swords were Muslim, the same occupational group among Hundus were called barhiyas; however, Hindus could also be called sikligars. There were regional variations not only within UP but in neighbouring states. In Punjab there were both Hindus and Muslims among the gujar, od, khatik, chamar, nai, banjara, nat, julaha, lohar, darzi, ahir, barhai, teli, kalwar; dhobis were mainly Muslims, while gadariyas were entirely Hindu. Duniyas and gujars were both Hindu and Msulim in UP but in Punjab gujars were mostly Muslims. Banjaras could be Muslim and Hindu in NWP though they were Muslim in Rajasthan. See Sheering, *Hindu Tribes,* vol. 1, pp. 236, 270–72, 276, 301, 303, 316–17, 329, 333–35, 338, 341, 343, 345, 347, 353, 388–39, 396; vol. 2, p. 700; vol. 3, p. 90; Robinson, *Separtism*, p. 24; Blunt, *The Caste System*, pp.200–01; Ibbetson, *Panjab Castes*, pp.183–84, 204, 254, 275, 285, 296, 302, 312–13, 321, 324–25.

174 In Awadh, bazigars (conjurous) and mahawats (cattle traders) were Muslim subdivisions of nats. In Punjab too bahurupiyas could be drawn from any caste and no religion is metioned for them. See Sherring, *Hindu Tribes*, vol. 1, pp.271, 276, 388–89; Blunt, *The Caste System,* p. 157; Ibbetson, *Panjab Castes*, p. 236.

175 Though in later decades hinduization dictated the proscription of burial, in this region and period several groups practised it. Only some nats had converted but all practised burial. So did several menial castes such as doms; some subdivisions of mihtars and bhangis burned while others buried their dead. The ods, a wandering tribe, married in Hindu fashion and buried their dead like Muslims. (In Punjab the ods were Hindu and Muslim but all practised burial.) In addition, several sects such as the Bhartharis, Vishnuis, Baitali Bhats, which had cross-caste membership, practised burial. Some of these sects were affiliated to Shaivism (Tridandi, Jangam, Sewara, Gosains—Kanchani), some to Gorakhnath (Kanphatas, Jogis), Nanak (Suthras) or the Jatis (Udasis). See Sherring, *Hindu Tribes*, vol. 1, pp. 255, 257, 259, 261–66, 269, 294, 388–89, 397, 401; Crooke, *Natives*, pp. 141, 215; Ibbetson, *Panjab Castes*, p. 275.

176 H.M. Elliott wrote that bhangis "cannot be said to be of any particular religion, but they are, perhaps, more Muslim than Hindu. . . . They generally, nevertheless, profess to be Hindus" *(Memoirs on the History, Folklore and Distribution of the Races of the North-Western Provinces of India*, 1846, cited in Lelyveld, *Aligarh's First*, p. 13). Sherring points out that chamars were thought to not belong to the "Hindu race" (*Hindu Tribes*, vol. 1, p. 392) and Blunt describes doms as the least hinduized among the untouchables (*The Caste System*, p. 103). See also Ludlow, *Mahomedanism*, p. 77.

177 Duncan B. Forrester, *Caste and Christianity* (London: Curzon Press, 1980), p. 82.

178 According to Blunt, some castes had larger Muslim branches (churihar, darzi, kunjra, dhuniya, manihaar, sikligar, tawaif), and some had larger Hindu branches (ahir, banjara, barhai, bhangi, bhat, chamar, dhobi, dom, gujar, kahar, kumhar, lohar, mali, mallah, nai, nat, sonar, teli) by the early twentieth century, while others lost their mixed character (bhand, bhatiyara, bhishti, julaha) and became entirely Muslim. See *The Caste System*, pp. 200–01.

179 Tawaifs were recruited from all castes and religions. Ramjanis comprised women born into the group as well as those admitted from various other castes; gaunharins, professional singers and dancers, were not a distinct caste but said to be "attached" to all castes. Hindu widows could convert and become dancing girls. See Sherring, *Hindu Tribes*, vol. 1, p. 274; Crooke, *North-Western*, p. 260; Blunt, *The Caste System*, pp. 201–05.

180 Administrative reports of 1872 from Chittagong and Coochbehar stated that Muslim prostitutes assumed Hindu names to enlarge their clientele and maintain the option of marriage, and that prostitutes were converts who had adopted Hindu manners. Cited in Sumanta Banerjee, "The 'Beshya' and the 'Babu': Prostitute and her Clientele in Nineteenth Century Bengal", *EPW*, 28:45 (Nov. 1993), p. 2465.

181 The anonymous *Educational Disabilities of the Children of Dancing Girls in India* represented any and every Muslim woman as able to join the Naikins (a "class" of Hindu and Muslim dancing girls) as well as to give up prostitution at any time to get married (London: n.d.; Bombay: Dnyan Mitra Press, *circa* 1879, pp. 8–9).

182 For such changes see Blunt, *The Caste System*, pp. 52–57, 125, 214–25, 236–38.

183 Christian missionaries too dreaded incomplete or nominal conversions, as is evident in *Ratnamala* (p. 131).

184 Low-caste alignments were only to be posed as a political issue in succeeding decades and fluctuated situationally. An ambiguity about religious identity and being Hindu is evident in Phule's Satyashodhak Samaj in Maharashtra in this period. In 1911 namasudras claimed to be a separate community in Bengal, like Muslims, and to have no connection with Hindus; Ambedkar wanted separate representation and identities for depressed classes, a complete partition from the Hindus who wanted political incorporation but denied social acknowledgement. See Rosalind O'Hanlon, *Caste, Conflict and Ideology: Mahatma Jotirao Phule and Low Caste Protest in Nineteenth Century Western India* (Delhi: Orient Longman, 1985), p. 239; Hasi Bannerjee, "Casteism and the Communal Award, 1932" and Sekhar Bandyopadhyaya, "A Peasant Caste" in *Caste and Communal Politics in South Asia*, eds. Sekhar Bandyopadhyaya and Suranjan Das (Calcutta: K.P. Bagchi, 1993), pp. 155, 124–27.

185 Galvano Della Volpe uses the term to discredit textual autonomy and to designate a form of intertextuality: that is, the way in which earlier texts are imprisoned in later ones, presuppose them "precisely in order to be expressed" and thereby become members of semantic chains (*The Critique of Taste*, trs. Michael Caesar (London: Verso, 1978), p. 115). I am using the phrase more extensively to indicate a principle of cohesion between disparate texts in wider clusters.

The 'amenities of domestic life'

1 Christine Delphy's analysis rests on an untenable dualism between the mode of production and the "domestic mode of production", to which latter household labour belongs. However, she makes a thought-provoking argument for household labour as the tail-end of the production process, where the transformation of raw products for consumption takes place at home instead of taking place in the factory, though it could as well take place outside the home and within the sphere of exchange; she thus locates household labour as one part of the circuit of production and consumption if the labour process is taken in its totality and not broken up, especially since the household is the space for both production and consumption. (See "The Main Enemy", *Feminist Issues*, 1:1 (Summer 1980), pp. 33, 29–30.)

Others have seen domestic labour and the cheaper cost of female labour power as benefiting capitalism, especially in the way the question of family wage has been determined. (See Rachel Harrison and Frank Mort, "Patriarchal Aspects of Nineteenth Century State Formation: Property Relations, Marriage and Divorce, and Sexuality" in *Capitalism, State Formation and Marxist Theory*, ed. Philip Corrigan (London: Quartet Books, 1980), p. 92; and Leger in Christine Delphy and Daniele Leger, "Debate on Capitalism, Patriarchy and the Women's Struggle", *Feminist Issues*, 1:1 (Summer 1980), p. 42.) The sexual division of labour has been seen as allowing capitalism to divide the workforce, thus obtaining lower wages and a reserve army of labour while at the same time gaining cheap physical and ideological maintenance and reproduction of the workforce. (See Anna Davin, "Feminism and Labor History" in *People's History and Socialist Theory*, ed. Raphael Samuel (London: Routledge and Kegan Paul, 1981), p. 178; and U. Kalpagam, "Gender in Economics: The Indian Experience", *Economic and*

Political Weekly (hereafter *EPW*), 21:43 (Oct. 1986), p. ws 63.) Domestic labour has been seen alternately as parallel to capitalism, and as structural to capitalism, determined by the capitalist mode of production or capitalist social relations and the market. (See Kathleen B. Jones, "Socialist-Feminist Theories of the Family", *Praxis*, 8:3 (Oct. 1988), p. 292.)

Maxine Molyneux has critiqued the abstraction, functionalism, and economism of the domestic labour debate and argued for locating it within a wider complex of material relations in determinate historical formations; she stresses that determinate capitals have different labour requirements, and women's subordinate position in the household can have contradictory effects in relation to capitalist states. (See "Beyond the Domestic Labour Debate", *New Left Review*, 116 (July-Aug. 1979), pp. 22, 25–26.) The narrowing of the meaning of productive activity to its definition as wage labour has been discussed as a historical premise of the development of capitalism itself. (See Jones, "Socialist-Feminist", p. 287.) Veronica Beechey draws attention to the interplay of work and family life and suggests that the interrelation between women as wage labourers and as domestic labourers within the family needs to be explored. She points out that the family *appears* to have become separated from the capitalist mode of production, but in reality it is divorced only from the labour process and continues to play a vitally important role in the system of capitalist production as a whole. Domestic labour is itself involved in the reproduction of labour power as a commodity. She also says that the varied and changing relations between the domestic production of commodities and the production of commodities within capitalist manufacture and large-scale industry deserve closer examination since the transformation of the family has been both prolonged and variable. (See *Unequal Work* (London: Verso, 1987), pp. 9, 57–58, 75, 78.)

More recently, Jeanne Boydston has critiqued analytic models of industrialization that examine its *effects* on the household as being "gender less". Since gender was a preeminent organizing principle of labour and authority in preindustrial America, it should be seen as central to shaping the disposition of paid labour in industrial society as well as in defining the very concept of labour on which capitalism was based. The unpaid labour that women performed in households played an integral and constitutive economic role in the larger processes of industrialization as well as in determining its region-specific shapes. (See *Home and Work: Housework, Wages, and the Ideology of Labour in the Early Republic* (New York: Oxford Univ. Press, 1990), pp. 121–22.)

The domestic labour debate has been similarly characterized as subordinating household relations to the dictates of capitalism in a way that is ahistorical, does not address either changes over time or cultural variations in the construction of service or the role of housework in sustaining patriarchal relations in society at large. (See Heidi Tinsman, "The Indispensable Services of Sisters: Considering Domestic Service in United States and Latin American Studies", *Journal of Women's History*, 4:1 (Spring 1992), pp. 41, 43, 51.)

Studies on India have tended to situate women's unpaid labour in the household, that, combined with inferior entitlements, creates and releases a surplus for investment elsewhere; the rural subsistence sector in which women's labour predominates has been seen as providing a wage subsidy for the capitalist sector by assuming the burden of social security and 'freeing' other members of the family for waged work. See Maithreyi Krishnaraj, "Women Craft Workers as Security for Family Subsistence", *EPW*, 27:17 (April 1992), pp. ws 10, 7, 11.

2 See for instance Krishnaraj, "Women Craft Workers", p. ws 8; Gita Sen and Chiranjib Sen, "Women's Domestic Work and Economic Activity: Results from National Sample Survey", *EPW*, 20:17 (April 1985), p. ws 52; Shakti Kak, "Rural Women and Labour Force Participation", *Social Scientist*, 250–51 (March-April 1994), pp. 37–38.

3 Over 92 per cent of women interviewed for the 32nd National Sample Survey reported "pressing need" as the reason for involvement in domestic work; cited in Sen and Sen, "Women's Domestic Work", p. ws 51. For a discussion of consent see "Consent, agency" in this volume.

4 Colette Guillamin, "The Practice of Power and Belief in Nature", *Feminist Issues*, 1:2 (Winter 1981), pp. 12–13, 15. Delphy makes a similar point but relates household labour more narrowly to the conjugal relationship in "The Main Enemy" (p. 25).

5 Cited in David McClellan, *Karl Marx* (New York: Viking, 1975), pp. 31–32.

6 Guillamin, "The Practice of Power", p. 12; and Delphy, "The Main Enemy", pp. 30–31. Delphy points out that in a farm economy, in effect all use values produced in the household are *potentially* exchange values, and it is thus not women's production but women as economic agents who are excluded from the (exchange) market (ibid., pp. 26–28).

7 The home can then be visualized as one stage in a circuit where values are personalized and transformed, and *both* wealth (as patrimonial transmission or inheritance) and services are taken temporarily out of the realm of exchange only to be 'returned' to it at some other stage as capital or to re-enter it as paid public services.

8 See Beechey, *Unequal Work*, pp. 71–72.

9 The historical variations on the subcontinent may in fact be more amenable to analysis in terms of coexisting modes of production, and as what Eric Olin Wright has in a different context termed "complex patterns of decomposition and recombination of elements of modes of production", rather than as entirely discrete and qualitatively discontinuous modes of production. ("Class Analysis, History, Emancipation", *New Left Review*, 202 (Nov.-Dec. 1993), p. 24).

10 "Relating histories" in this volume discusses some of these ideological confluences.

11 The 'non-market' sphere is not of course confined to domestic labour but can include other precapitalist institutions such as caste and kinship as well as subsistence production. The articulation of the latter with the capitalist economy and the state in Maharashtra has been discussed by Krishnaraj in "Women Craft Workers" (pp. ws 7, 10–11).

12 My starting point here is Anna Davin's essay which argues that shifts and variations in the sexual divisions of labour, both in practice and ideology, can be a key to the changing actuality of work, daily life, and struggle, and are central to the analysis of how capitalism maintains itself. The study of work should, however, recognize the contribution and interrelation of all the different kinds of work. (See "Feminism and Labour" in *People's History*, p. 178.) Maithreyi Krishnaraj also emphasizes the relation between the sexual division of labour and the labour process which structures the organization of work within a particular mode of production. See "Research on Women and Career: Issues of Methodology", *EPW*, 21:43 (Oct. 1986), p. ws 69.

13 For a suggestive discussion of the heterogeneity of medieval peasant women's labour in England, see Christopher Middleton, "The Sexual Division of Labour in Feudal England", *New Left Review*, 113–14 (Jan–April 1979), pp. 164–66.

14 Marriage, family, and household become central to relations of production if we follow Maurice Godelier's definition of precapitalist relations of production as those that determine social forms of access to resources and the control of resources, the organization of labour processes including allocation of members, and the forms of circulation and redistribution of the products of individual and collective labour. He says, "for a social activity—and with it the ideas and institutions that correspond to and organize it—to play a dominant role in a society's functioning and evolution . . . it is not enough for it to fulfil *several functions*; in addition to its explicit ends and functions, it must of *necessity directly fulfil the function of a relation of production*" (*The Mental and the Material* (London: Verso, 1988), pp. 19, 147).

15 On the contribution of patrilocal residence to the rational exploitation of female labour in several preindustrial societies and to the origins of gender stratification with women becoming non-owning producers in the marital household while losing control over their natal property, see Nicole Chevillard and Sebastian Leconte, "The Dawn of Lineage Societies", and Stephanie Coontz and Peta Henderson, "Property Forms, Political Power and Female Labour" in *Women's Work Men's Property: The Origins of Gender and Class*, eds. Stephanie Coontz and Peta Henderson (London: Verso, 1986), pp. 84, 111, 122. On north-Indian exogamy see Jack Goody, *The ancient, the oriental and the primitive* (Cambridge: Cambridge Univ. Press, 1990), p. 272.

16 Kumkum Sangari, "Politics of Diversity: Religious Communities and Multiple Patriarchies", *EPW*, 30:51–52 (Dec. 1995), pp. 3381–86.

17 Post-independence failures in agrarian reforms, egalitarian distribution of resources, development of infrastructure, and provision of health and childcare facilities took gender-specific forms. Even as the commodity market expanded and proliferated, livelihood resources for many women dwindled and new ways of curtailing their consumption emerged. At the same time women became the objects of numerous "development" policies. For critiques of development processes as reinforcing and exacerbating divisions of labour, limiting women's access to economic resources and political participation while increasing their labour burden, see U. Kalpagam ("Gender in Economics", pp. ws 64–65). The work of poor rural and urban women functioned as a buffer, increasing their drudgery and shouldering the cost of development: it reduced the impact of depletions and displacements consequent on development, ensured minimal subsistence levels, and helped to retain family land and assets. (See Krishnaraj, "Women Craft Workers", pp. ws 10–15.)

At present the New Economic Policy is reinforcing trends of the informalization of the female workforce, subcontracting and piece-rate production by MNCs, greater utilization in the informal sector, and increasing the numbers of women in the reserve army of labour. On these and other consequences of the Structural Adjustment Programme for women—unemployment, retrenchment, marginaliza-tion in the labour force, increased girl—child labour, prostitution and relegation to the low-wage and unorganized sector, increased drudgery for poor women in acquiring necessities such as fuel and water—see Vibhuti Patel ("Women and Structural Adjustment in India", *Social Scientist*, 22:3–4 (March-April 1994), pp. 16–34).

More recently, it has been pointed out that the policies that are being implemented following a World Bank document of 1995 include an attack on unions, denial of legislative provisions, treating older male and female workers as a "lost generation" with no policy interventions to improve their lot, treating women in organized employment as an "inflexible" and "expensive" workforce, and employing them in informal, insecure work situations. See Sujatha Gothoskar, Nandita Gandhi, Nandita Shah, Amrita Chhacchi, "Towards a Sustainable Future for Working Women: Strategic Perspectives in the Era of Globalization", seminar paper, Jamia Hamdard University, Delhi, Sept. 1997, p. 3.

18 The World Bank and IMF regard the unpaid labour of women (cooking, cleaning, nurture), their augmentation of family resources through fuel, fodder, and water collection, and their subsistence tasks (looking after livestock, poultry, and processing of agricultural goods) as *elastic*, that is, as buffers for inflation. See Patel, "Women and Structural Adjustment", p. 30.

19 Boydston points out that in eighteenth-century America the cash value of housework was embedded in the collectivity of the family, and in large part the wife's labour could not be extracted from the ongoing processes of household life or indeed from the labour of other members such as children. (See *Home Work*, p. 134. See also Meg Luxton, "The UN, Women, and Household Labour: Measuring and Valuing Unpaid Work", *Women's Studies International Forum*, 28:3 (May 1997), pp. 431–40.) However, attempts to measure the unremunerated work of women in quantitative terms continue, the most recent being the UNDP report of 1995 and Fourth World Conference of Women (Beijing, 1995).

20 It has been pointed out that the household is a space of "co-operative conflicts" over distribution; that disparities of consumption in everyday experience are *recognized as constitutive* of family structure and differing family statuses, main-tained by internalizing customary prohibitions and by coercion, and for women, linked to wider ideologies of self-sacrifice. See Amartya Sen, "Gender and Co-operative Conflicts" in *Persistent Inequalities: Women and World Development*, ed. Irene Tinker (New York: Oxford Univ. Press, 1990); Christine Delphy, *Close to Home: A Materialist Analysis of Women's Oppression*, trs. Diana Leonard (Amherst: Univ. of Massachussetts Press, 1984), pp. 42–47, 50–51, 54.

21 Rajni Palriwala, "Economics and Patriliny: Consumption and Authority within the Household", *Social Scientist*, 244–46 (Sept.-Nov. 1993), and "Transitory Residence and Invisible Work: Case Study of a Rajasthan Village", *EPW*, 26:48 (Nov. 1991), pp. 2768, 2770–71.

22 For instance, in nineteenth-century northeast America, it is said to have fostered the cult of domesticity and separate spheres by 'freeing' some women to be exclusively mothers or to pursue public roles in social reform as an extension of the private sphere. See Tinsman, "The Indispensible Services", pp. 44–45, 49, 51–53. See also Henrietta Moore, *Feminism and Anthropology* (Cambridge: Polity Press, 1988), p. 89.

23 See Lakshmi Srinivas, "Master-Servant Relationship in a Cross-Cultural Context", *EPW*, 30:5 (Feb. 1995), p. 272.

24 A sample study in Delhi shows that women in the domestic service sector do all the housework. Men do not help even if unemployed. See Prabha Rani, Poonam Kaul, "For Two Meals a Day: A Report on Tamil Domestic Maids", *Manushi*, 6:5 (July-Aug. 1986), p. 5.

25 The number of women in the domestic service sector has, however, increased substantially. According to the 1971 and 1981 censuses, the percentage has gone up from 37.2 to 50, mainly in urban areas. See Srinivas, "Master-Servant", p. 272.

26 Domestic ideologies are often related to economic behaviour intended to ensure prosperity and can have an economic rationality within specific socio-economic formations. For example, on eighteenth-century England, see Nancy Armstrong ("The rise of the domestic woman" in *The Ideology of Conduct*, eds. Nancy Armstrong and Leonard Tennenhouse (London: Methuen, 1987), p. 120).

Hanna Papanek describes "family status production" work as consisting of the support of paid work of other family members, the future paid work and status aspiration of children, social activities related to status maintenance, and the performance of religious acts and rituals. All of these become prominent at class levels where energy can be spared from survival labour and where mobility is possible. Thus it is here that women's work becomes crucial to class differentiation. However, she distinguishes status production too sharply from "housework". I think that the two overlap quite substantively. See 'Family Status Production: The 'Work' and 'Non-Work' of Women", *Signs*, 4:4 (1979).

27 It has been suggested that male privilege and gender inequality in the home has played a part in undermining the class consciousness and solidarity of wives of British working-class men. See Nicky Hart, "Gender and the Rise and Fall of Class Politics", *New Left Review*, 175 (May–June 1989), pp. 19–47.

28 Christine Delphy has defined property and inheritance systems as forms of capital accumulation through patrimonial transmission and appropriation of the wife's property, as a non-market sphere of the economy where wealth, property, goods change hands without going through the market but through family mechanisms bound up with familial relations, as creating and recreating possessors and nonpossessors within the family, and as producing broad class divisions. See "Patriarchy, domestic mode of production, gender and class" in *Marxism and the Interpretation of Culture*, eds. Cary Nelson and Lawrence Grossberg

(London: Macmillan, 1988), pp. 259, 262; Harrison and Mort, "Patriarchal Aspects", pp. 92–93.

29 Indira Rajaraman, "Economics of Bride-price and Dowry", EPW, 18:8 (Feb. 1983), p. 276.

30 Goody dwells only on the former and fails to understand its double character (*The ancient*, pp. 381–82, 413–15, 453). For a critique of Goody, see Bina Agarwal, "Who Sows? Who Reaps? Women and Land Rights in India", *Journal of Peasant Studies*, 15:4 (July 1988), p. 547.

31 Dowry is not a right and subject to changes and fluctuations in the customary sphere. Since women are seldom in line for future paternal inheritance, especially immoveable property, the dowry and gifts *de facto* define the limits of their claim, overcommitting them to and making them overdependent on the marital family. Women's entitlement to support from the natal family usually comes at the cost of foregoing their rights. Partially as a corollary, women can seldom be responsible for their natal family. Their links with it are attenuated through patrilocal residence and the immobilizing effects of domestic and agricultural labour in marital homes, while their relation with the marital family takes years to consolidate. Women's practical difficulties in claiming and managing land are compounded by the fact that on marriage they usually move from one patriarchal family to another.

32 See Mira Savara, Sujatha Gothoskar, "An Assertion of Womanpower: A Case Study on Organizing Landless Women in Maharashtra", *Manushi*, 3:1 (Nov.–Dec. 1982), p. 28; Govind Kelkar, "Women, Land and Agrarian Reform: Issues of Gender and Class in Improving Women's Effective Access to Land", *National Law School Journal*, 1 (1993), pp. 127–28; Prem Chowdhury, "Persistence of a Custom: Cultural Centrality of Ghunghat", *Social Scientist*, 244–46 (Sept.-Nov. 1993); Jayoti Gupta, "Land, Dowry, Labour: Women in the Changing Economy of Midnapur", ibid.; Kak, "Rural Women", pp. 48–49.

33 Sen and Sen argue that this is in part a feature of partly commoditized rural societies where the dividing line between domestic work and economic activity is ambiguous both in respect of the work itself and its time disposition ("Women's Domestic Work", p. ws 49). Pushpa Sundar points out that there is no clear dividing line between domestic labour and agricultural tasks and production for home and market consumption ("Characteristics of Female Employment: Implications of Research Policy", *EPW*, 16:19 (May 1981), p. 863). Kalpana Bardhan shows the difficulty of a dividing line between economically productive work (generating income for production) and domestic work (processing income or production for consumption) in households that are units for largely noncommercial production and consumption ("Women's Work, Welfare and Status", *EPW*, 20:50 and 51–52 (Dec. 1985), p. 2262). According to Kalpagam, women's work in subsistence agriculture provides a wage subsidy for the capitalist wage sector ("Gender in Economics", p. ws 63).

34 Kelkar, "Women, Land and Agrarian Reform", pp. 127–28.

35 At most, affluence seems to entail a redistribution rather than reduction of women's labour by shifting them from agricultural work in the fields to food and agricultural processsing in the courtyard. See Prem Chowdhury, "High Participation, Low Evaluation: Women and Work in Rural Haryana", *EPW*, 38:52 (Dec. 1993), p. A 137, and *The Veiled Women: Shifting Gender Equations in Rural Haryana 1880–1990* (Delhi: Oxford Univ. Press, 1995).

36 See Kalpagam, "Gender in Economics", pp. ws 60–61. As Maria Mies's *The Lacemakers of Narsapur* (1982) revealed, home-based production can build systemic structures of invisibilization that transform wage work within a subsistence economy into the "leisure" activity of "housewives". See Kumkum Sangari, "The Invisible Worker", *The Book Review*, 7:6 (1983).

37 See ibid.; Kamala Ganesh, "The State of the Art in Women's Studies", *EPW*, 20:16 (April 1985), p. 685; *Moore, Feminism and Anthropology*, pp. 90–91; and Bardhan, "Women's Work", p. 2211. Bardhan argues that capitalist growth seems to harness the superstructures of pre and coexisting relations of production, utilizing patriarchy to hold back the labour movement and preempt the scope of implementation of labour laws; the exploitation of female labour in both home-based out-work and in the dependent family mode is mediated by family patriarchy.

Krishnaraj makes a significant correlation between continuing casteist social and production relations and women's continued and/or increasing presence in the rural household sector. The combination of the two is making low-caste women's labour central to the persistence of upper-caste patronage and customary lower-caste obligations in some regions. Certain income-producing activities defined by caste and the *jajmani* system of hereditary patron-client relationships are mainly or solely done by women: sweeping houses, cleaning latrines, washing clothes and utensils, carrying water, midwifery, and preparing ritual items such as flowers for ceremonies in upper-caste homes. See "Women Craft Workers", p. 15.

38 Esther Boserup, *Women's Role in Economic Development* (New York: St Martin's Press, 1970), p. 75. Between 1971 and 1981 the maximum increase in women's employment took place in the rural household sector. See Krishnaraj, "Women Craft Workers", p. ws 8.

39 Sen and Sen, "Women's Domestic Work", pp. 51–53, 55; Boserup, *Women's Role*, pp 161–63, 166

40 Sen and Sen, "Women's Domestic Work", p. 54.

41 Ibid., p. 55; Boserup, *Women's Role*, p. 187; Bardhan, "Women's Work", p. 2210.

42 Sen and Sen, "Women's Domestic Work", p. ws 51.

43 Krishnaraj, "Women Craft Workers", pp. ws 11–12, 15.

44 The ideology of seclusion is internalized by lower groups as a status symbol because it grants women protection from the harsh conditions of external employment. (See Ganesh,"The State of the Art", p. 687.) Women consent to it not only because it confers status but also because they entered wage work not from choice but for survival. See Kalpagam, "Gender in Economics", p. ws 61.

45 See Krishnaraj, "Women Craft Workers", p. ws 15; Bardhan, "Women's Work", p. 2214; and Chowdhury, "High Participation", pp. A 142, 144. Chowdhury points out that land management remains in men's hands, while women perceive only "male work" as income generating and not their own. The limited access of labouring women in rural households to cash has emerged in a number of field studies. See, for instance, Palriwala, "Transitory Residence", and Chowdhury, "Persistence of a Custom".

46 Krishnaraj, "Women Craft Workers", p. ws 15. Mies's study shows that home-based production can deprive women of access to the market sphere, subsidize the wage work of their husbands, and integrate their labour into global capitalist strategies of decentralized production. See Sangari, "The Invisible Worker".

47 What is more, this type of reformulation of patriarchies will absolve the state for its abdication of welfarist functions.

48 Delia Davin has made a suggestive correlation between a small producer economy, the household as productive unit, and patriarchal power in post-revolutionary China, which, despite favourable legislation, made women more dependent on men and, structurally, made it difficult to implement women's property rights. See "Engels and the Making of Chinese Family Policy" in *Engels Revisited: New Feminist Essays*, eds. Janet Sayers, Mary Evans, and Nannette Redclift (London: Tavistock, 1987), pp. 149–58.

49 On the caste segmentation of the labour market, see Kak, "Rural Women", pp. 44–45. The migration of rural labour from lack of subsistence can also be gender differentiated. At the turn of the century, women could migrate because they were marginalized in the patriarchal family due to barrenness, desertion, or widowhood. Since migration also implied loss of honour, they lost contact with village and family, and consequently, their status in the city fell. They were less able to return to their villages, especially if lured away by middlemen. The hostility to an independent female workforce outside the home created by purdah-related ideology made it difficult for women displaced from artisanal and agricultural occupations or the bazaar economy to relocate, and worked against them in the job market. See Dagmar Engels, *Beyond Purdah? Women in Bengal 1890–1939* (Delhi: Oxford Univ. Press, 1996), pp. 203, 205, 208, 214.

50 Several studies have shown that women do not usually enter the labour market or compete on the same terms as men. The social relations within which they operate—as daughters, wives, mothers, widows—impose both material and ideological restraints upon their identification as 'free labour'. See Hilary Standing with Bela Bandyopadhyay, "Women's Employment and the Household: Some Findings from Calcutta", *EPW*, 20:17 (April 1985), p. ws 23.

51 Single women—unmarried, divorced, or widowed—still tend to enter at and occupy the lowest rung of the workforce—casualized, unprotected, with wages below the minimum standard. (See Amrita Chhacchi, Sujatha Gothoskar, Nandita Shah, Nandita Gandhi, "Mediating the Macro and the Micro: Industrial Restructuring and Women's Lives", seminar paper, Jamia Hamdard University, Delhi, Sept. 1997.) On the restriction of employment opportunities for widows in rural and urban wage work, see Marty Chen and Jean Dreze ("Recent Research on Widows in India", *EPW*, 30:39 (Sept. 1995), p. 2446.

52 Henry Mayhew classified Maidservants as Clandestine Prostitutes and sexualized any female labour outside the home. His list included milliners, dress-makers, hat-binders, slop-women, servants, women who worked in certain kinds of shops. See *London Labour and the London Poor*, vol. 4: *Those that Will Not Work, comprising Prostitutes, Thieves, Swindlers and Beggars* (1861; rpt New York: Dover, 1968), pp. 27, 255, 217.

53 Elizabeth Wilson, "The Invisible Flaneur", *New Left Review*, 191 (Jan.-Feb. 1992), pp. 91–93, 105.

54 Ratnabali Chatterjee, "Prostitution in Nineteenth Century Bengal: Construction of Class and Gender", *Social Scientist*, 244–46 (Sept.-Nov. 1993); Kokila Dang, "Prostitutes, Patrons and the State: Nineteenth Century Awadh", in ibid.

55 The blurred frontiers between domestic service and prostitution were not peculiar to India but existed with specific conjunctural features in urban England and in Latin American towns. The majority of the one million domestics in England were women, and of all single women, 20 per cent were servants. An unusually high proportion of prostitutes were initially domestic servants—estimates range from one-third to half—while a large number of illegitimate pregnancies were those of servants impregnated by masters. See Francoise Barret Ducrocq, *Love in the Time of Victoria*, trs. John Howe (London: Verso, 1991), p. 55; Boserup, *Woman's Role*, p. 103; Theresa Mcbride, *The Domestic Revolution: The Modernization of Household Service in England and France 1820–1920* (London: Croom Helm, 1976), p. 102; George Rosen, "Disease, Debility and Death" in *The Victorian City*, eds. H.J. Dyos and Michael Wolff (London: Routledge, 1973), p. 657; Francoise Basch, *Relative Creatures: Victorian Women in Society and the Novel 1837–67* (London: Allen Lane, 1974), p. 199; Lawrence Stone, *The Family, Sex and Marriage in England 1500–1800* (London: Weidenfeld, 1977), p. 642.

56 Women—rural, nomadic, and tribal—were present in most primary and subsidiary agricultural occupations and animal husbandry, in independent (tattooing, dyeing, other crafts) and supplementary occupations such as the collection and processing of materials for various types of household manufacture (fuel, rope, silk, cotton, pottery), in the provision, processing and preparation of food (foraging, husking, grinding, fetching water, cooking), the gathering of medicinal herbs for sale, and the bearing of loads (sheaves, wood, chaff). (See, for instance, William Crooke, *Natives of Northern India* (London: Archibald Constable, 1907), pp. 161–71.) The list could be longer. The point is that there was an existing 'public' sphere filled with labouring women, unacknowledged by elite historiography. I have critiqued this tendency at length in "Consent, agency" in this volume.

57 This latter is, of course, a continuing process. For instance, there is evidence of the othering of East Bengali refugee women who were forced into eclectic employment patterns. The present practice of *ghunghat* in rural Haryana is also an attempt to control this space by segregating the women who occupy it; it is ideologically reinforced by a regional binary between local Haryanvi and post-partition refugee Punjabi women and a *shehri/dehati* binary between rural and urban culture that is both contradicted and reinforced by actual rural stratification and patterns of consumption. (See Standing and Bandopadhyay, "Women's Employment", p. ws 24; Chowdhury,"Persistence of a Custom".) It disparages *dehati* women's consumption of *shehri* things, makes *shehri* women fair game, and identifies the town with prostitution. Here a cross-class patriarchy is articulated through 'othering' women and gathers power from its simultaneous function as a critique of the privileged economies of urban areas as compared to the rural.

58 See "Women against women" in this volume; Kumkum Sangari and Sudesh Vaid, "Introduction", *Recasting Women: Essays in Colonial History* (Delhi: Kali, 1989), pp. 9–10.

59 See Ann Phillips, *Engendering Democracy* (Cambridge: Polity Press, 1991), p. 32.

60 Calcutta: Baptist Mission Press, pp. 2–4.

61 Tiwari, *Sutaprabodh* (Allahabad: Allahabad Govt. Press, 1871), on order of Lieutenant Governor for girl's schools; Sitaram, *Stri Updesh* (Lalitpur: Lalitpur Press, 1871); citations of *Bihishti Zewar* are from Barbara Daly Metcalfe, *Perfecting Women: Maulana Ashraf 'Ali Thanawi's Bihishti Zewar* (Delhi: Oxford Univ. Press, 1992); Datta, *Devrani Jethani ki Kahani* (Meerut: Ziyai Chapakhana, 1870), on order of Lieutenant Governor; Christian Education Vernacular Society, *Ratnamala* or *Reading Book for Women: Advice on Domestic Management and Training for Children* (Allahabad: Allahabad Mission Press, 1869).

62 This was a series of essays entitled *"Hindustan mein Mashriqi Tamaddun ka Akhiri Namuna"*, published in Sharar's journal *Dilgudaz* between 1913–20, and later collected in his *Mazamin-e-Sharar*. The citations here are from Abdul Halim Sharar, *Lucknow: The Last Phase of an Oriental Culture*, trs. and eds. E.S. Harcourt and Fakhir Husain (Delhi: Oxford Univ. Press, 1989), pp. 192–93.

63 Ramkrishan, *Strishiksha: Striyon ke updesh ke liye* (Allahabad: Govt. Press, 1871), on order of Lieutenant Governor; Gokul Kayasth, *Vamavinod* (Balrampur: Manranjar Bahaduriy Yantralaya, 1875); Munshi Ramlal, *Putrishikshopkari Granth* (Allahabad: Govt. Press, 1872), and *Banitabudhhi-prakashini* (Allahabad: Govt. Press, 1871), on order of the Director of Public Instruction; *Balabodhini*, ed. Harishchandra (Benares, 1874) no. 1, pp. 10–11.

64 Manmatha Nath Dutt, *Heroines of Ind* (Calcutta: The Society for the Resurrection of Indian Literature, 1908). The Bengali Jnanadanandini Debi expressed similar sentiments in her *Strishiksha*, 1882. Cited in Himani Bannerji, "Fashioning a Self: Educational Proposals for and by Women in Popular Magazines in Colonial Bengal", *EPW*, 26:43 (Oct. 1991), p. ws 54.

65 *Majalis-un-Nissa* in *Voices of Silence: English Translation of Hali's Majalis un-Nissa and Chup ki Dad*, trs. Gail Minault (Delhi: Chanakya, 1986), p. 70.

66 Jivaram Kapur Khatri, *Stridharma Saar* (Agra: Gurjar Yantrayalaya, 1892).

67 *Stree Dharma-Neeti*, trs. in Meera Kosambi, *Pandita Ramabai's Feminist and Christian Conversions* (Bombay: SNDT, 1995).

68 Shambhulal Kalurama Sukla, *Hindi Pahila Pustak* (Indore: Holkar Central Book Depot, 1876), on order of Suptd. State Education, Indore.

69 See *Majalis* (pp. 51–52) for the amount of work this required.

70 Vamsidhar, *Sutashikshavali* (1865; 2nd edn, Agra: Nurul Ilm Press, 1867), on order of Lieutenant Governor, p. 36.

71 Lakshmanprasad, *Saas Bahu ka Kissa: Gyan updesh* (Agra: Madanmohan Press, 1895).

72 Tarachand Shastri, *Stridharma Sangreh* (Bareilly: n.p., 1868).

73 See Ishuree Das, *Domestic Manners and Customs of the Hindoos of Northern India, or more strictly speaking, of the North West Provinces of India* (Benares: Medical Hall Press, 1860), pp. 169, 171.

74 In the reformer Ranade's family in nineteenth-century Maharashtra, education for women connoted leisure in a houshold where other women were engaged in manual work. See Uma Chakravarti, "Social Pariahs and Domestic Drudges: Widowhood among Nineteenth Century Poona Brahmins", *Social Scientist*, 244–46 (Sept.-Nov. 1993), p. 152.

75 Perhaps it was such uneven familial configurations that gave rise to sarcastic praise for the perfect wife and daughter-in-law. An early twentieth-century saying in Bengal, which I owe to Anita Roy, went: *Shawbe kamey hira / Maggey baatey jira*, this woman is such a jewel of a worker, she even grinds cumin seeds with her bum.

76 Bhavani Devi, *Agrawal Riti Chandrika arthat Poorvi Agarwal Jatiyon ke Rivaj* (Gaya: Laxmi Press, 1922).

77 Tiwari, *Ritiratnakar* (Allahabad: Govt. Press, 1872), on order of the Lieutenant Governor, William Muir, p. 4.

78 Yashoda Devi, *Grihini Kartavya Shastra* (2nd edn, Allahabad: Hitaishi Press, 1916).

79 See, for instance, the *Manusmriti*, 5.151–66, 8.363, 9.4–12, 9.24–30, in *Manava Dharma Sastra or the Institutes of Manu*, trs. G.C. Haughton (1825; 3rd edn, 1863; rpt Delhi: Asian Educational Services, 1982). The wife, debarred from performing sacrifices or rituals independently of her husband, was not integrated fully into the four *ashramas*, being forbidden voluntary renunciation on her own behalf in order to ensure that she remained under family control. The fourth *ashrama* was also barred to sudras.

80 *Manusmriti*, 5.147–49, 5.154–55, 9.6–7. The nuptial ceremony is stated to be the vedic sacrament for a woman (and equal to initiation), serving the husband (equivalent to) the residence in (the house of) the teacher, and the household duties (the same) as the (daily) worship of the sacred fire (2.67).

81 Thus the student, householder, ascetic, and hermit are all said to be the "offspring" of "married men keeping house" who are superior to all for they support the other three orders (*Manusmriti*, 6.87, 6.89–90).

82 Hariharhiralal, *Strivichar* (Meerut: Chashme Faiz Chhapekhana, 1876). The *Manusmriti* had been translated into Hindi and become popularly accessible in abridged form in this period.

83 *Balabodhini*, 1874, no. 1, pp. 10–11; no. 2, pp. 28–31; no. 10, p. 11.

84 Swami Dayanand Saraswati, *Satyarth Prakash*, trs. Durga Prasad (Lahore: Virjanand Press, 1908), pp. 144, 181.

85 Pandharinath Prabhu, *Hindu Social Organisation* (1940; 4th edn, Bombay: Popular Prakashan, 1963), pp. 232–35.

86 For links between control of women's domestic labour and control of their sexuality, see Jane Humphries, "The Origin of the Family: Born Out of Scarcity not Wealth" in *Engels Revisited*, eds. Sayers et al., pp. 226–67; and Tinsman, "The Indispensible Services", pp. 50–51.

87 Ahmad Husain, *Istri Updesh: Do ladkiyon ki kahani* (Agra: n.p., 1873). See "Women against women" in this volume for a discussion of this textbook.

88 Nazir Ahmad, *Mir'at ul-Arus* (1869; rpt Delhi: Sahitya Akademi, 1982), p. 30.

89 Gangaprasad, *Kumari Tattvaprakashika* (Mirzapur: Orphan School Press, 1871), on order of the Maharaja of Kashi.

90 Significantly, homes for widows such as those opened by Ramabai, followed this same 'vocational' model in which, other than teaching in schools or homes, all the skills involved manual labour and were identical to the accomplishments she also recommended for wives. Widows were trained for nursing, teaching, tailoring, handicrafts, laundry, oil-pressing, dairy work, milling flour, cooking, weaving, sewing, and some work in the fields. (See *The Letters and Correspondence of Pandita Ramabai*, ed. A.B. Shah (Bombay: Maharashtra State Board for Literature and Culture, 1977), p. 360; Kosambi, *Pandita Ramabai's*, pp. 69, 171, 211.) It is interesting to note that scriptural sanctions could be found for home-based work too: according to the *Manusmriti*, the unsupported wife whose husband had departed without providing for her, could "subsist" through "blameless manual work", spinning, and other handicrafts at home (9.75).

91 See Christopher Bayly, *Rulers, Townsmen and Bazaars: North Indian Society in the Age of British Expansion* 1770–1870 (Delhi: Oxford Univ. Press, 1992), p. 436.

92 *Bharyahit* or Hindi translation of *Advice to a Wife* by Henry Chavasse Pye, FRCS, trs. Diwan Bahadur Chowbe Raghunath Das CSI, Diwan, Kotah state (Rajputana: n.p. , 1929), pp. 55, 75, 26. The twelfth edition came out in 1883.

93 Bayly points out that merchant households in nineteenth-century UP were able to expand or restrict consumption in relation to the success of the trading season. There was also a running tension between the lavish sahu (like Khatri Kashmiri Mull) who ran the risk of bankruptcy and whose profligate spending undermined credit, and the self-denying frugal merchant who avoided expense, luxury, too many servants, and was a model of professional probity. Jain, bania, and khatri merchants condemned conspicuous consumption, fusing bad moral and bad economic conduct into one whole. See *Rulers*, pp. 376, 383–85, 388.

94 A related logic can be found in eighteeenth-century England. Laura Brown points out that the misogynist scapegoating of the overconsuming woman could function both as a device which masked the male acquisitiveness that fuelled the energies of imperialism and as a resistance to mercantile capitalism. See *Ends of Empire: Women and Ideology in Early Eighteenth Century Literature* (Ithaca: Cornell Univ. Press, 1993), pp. 101, 155.

95 Boydston points out that at the onset of industrialization in northeast America, households were dependent on paid and unpaid labour. They needed money for cash purchase of goods and services, and unpaid labour for processing these commodities into consumable form as well as to produce other goods and services without recourse to the cash market. The unpaid labour of middle-class wives helped to generate petty capital that could be translated into home ownership, expanded business operations, investment, and savings. See *Home and Work*, pp. 123, 136–37.

96 Crooke, *Natives*, p. 169. A few decades later, as mill cloth and flour became commoner in villages, Malcolm Darling pointed out that home spinning and grinding were directly related to shortages of cash, but at the same time he presented grinding both as a remedy for ill health and a compensation for the outdoor activity denied to secluded women! If no grinding was done then secluded women could only knead, gin, and spin and these were not enough to keep them fit. See *Wisdom and Waste in a Punjab Village* (London: Oxford Univ. Press, 1934), pp. 197, 290–91, 307.

97 It seems that grinding began at 4 am or even earlier, and only the higher classes hired someone to grind for them; the cost was two pice for about ten pounds of grain. See Das, *Domestic Manners*, p. 168.

98 Domestic labour included the management of servants in the Gujarati journal *Streebodh* from the 1850s. See Sonal Shukla, "Cultivating Minds: Nineteenth Century Gujarati Women's Journals", *EPW*, 26: 43 (Oct. 1991), p. ws 63.

99 The tasks a mistress had to oversee daily were: removal of ashes from the stove, filling water, cleaning the *paan daan* (metal box for lime, betel leaf, and nuts), cutting betel nut, the differential serving of meals to each member of the family, returning utensils to the storeroom after they were cleaned. Charcoal had to be set aside from the kitchen fire and stored every day for the *angithis* (moveable stoves) which would be lit in winter. The maidservants had to clean the inner rooms and the sweeper the whole house every morning under her supervision. The spaced out tasks ranged from weekly retinning of utensils, recoating the bottoms of pans every second or third day, replastering the clay *chulhas* (stoves) every fortnight, rechiselling the spice grinding stone every four months, tightening cot strings every ten days, sunning clothes several times a year, sorting winter clothes and restuffing quilts every year. Every summer the house was to be whitewashed, *pankhas* (fans) hung, the garden attended to, water vessels changed, summer clothes sorted. The house had to be repaired, mud plastered on thatched roofs, cracks filled in masonry roofs, gutters and downspouts cleaned and repaired before every monsoon. Broken furniture was to be punctually sent out for repair (*Majalis*, pp. 72–74). Thanawi too insisted that women had to oversee the preparation and storage of all household goods.

100 The mistress had to keep ten kilos of grain husked and ready for the millerwoman every day, weigh it and the flour as well when it came back, and pay her each time. She had to know how much flour, *dal*, *ghee*, rice, etc., were needed on a daily basis, get it weighed and mete it out, increasing the portion on days when there were special needs. Similarly, she had to get the daily rations for the horses and cattle weighed and sent out in her presence. Oil for refilling lamps had to be measured every evening. She had to allocate the daily produce from the garden as well as whatever came from the village land for family use, to relatives, neighbours, and servants. And she always had to be prepared with extra food for unexpected guests and meet all their needs (*Majalis*, pp. 71–74). In *Bihishti* too, women have to keep an account of grain to be mulled, pots given for retinning, and dirty linen for washing, while *Mir'at* also recommends a careful accounting of clothes given to the washerwoman.

101 Jaishankar, *Vyanjana Prakar* (Agra: Nurul Islam Chhapakhana, 1867), by permission of the Director of Public Instruction. In one description the woman who teaches, *bataanewali*, supervises four servant women who knead the dough, roll it, and fry the *puris*—*loi karnewali, belnewali, utarnewali* (p. 34).

102 According to Das, the daily household duties of women were grinding, washing the kitchen floor, drawing water, cooking, and scouring utensils. The only women exempt from most of these were from wealthy families, but even they did the cooking themselves. Cooking a meal for a poor family took an hour, for a wealthy one, two hours. A few Hindu families who were very rich employed brahmin women as cooks. See *Domestic Manners*, pp. 167, 171.

103 *Balabodhini*, 1875, no. 10, p. 74.

104 *Balabodhini* also enjoined women to constantly guard their household goods and valuables to protect them from theft while *Stridharma Saar* recommended paying servants regularly in order to prevent the temptation to steal.

105 For a discussion of this configuration see "Relating histories" in this volume.

106 Mrs Rowe, *Mulsutra* (Calcutta: Baptist Mission Press, 1823), pp. 53–54.

107 Christian Vernacular Education Society, *Lara Lari: Panch jhagralu striyon ki katha* (Allahabad: Allahabad Mission Press, 1875), p. 6.

108 Quoted in Anne Summers, "A Home from Home—Women's Philanthropic Work in the Nineteenth Century" in *Fit Work for Women*, ed. Sandra Burman (London: Croom Helm, 1979), pp. 39–40.

109 Christina Hardymen, *Dream Babies* (London: Oxford Univ. Press, 1984), pp. 79, 152, 63.

110 Her mother was heiress to a Jamaican sugar plantation, an uncle, two brothers and a nephew came to India in colonial service, and she married an officer in the Indian Civil Service.

111 F. Steele and G. Gardener, *The Complete Indian Housekeeper and Cook* (London: William Heinemann, 1898), pp. ix, 3, 6, 229, and p. 243 of the 1909 edition.

112 Parvati Athawale, *Hindu Widow: An Autobiography*, trs. Justin Abbott (1928; rpt Delhi: Reliance, 1986), p. 135.

113 For his conspicuous loyalty during the 1857 uprising, the Maharaja was given most of the business of government, got many marks of distinction from the British, and was, exceptionally, allowed to retain 500 armed retainers and seven cannon. He was the first president of the British Indian Association of Oudh (1861) and opened ten schools of his own on his estate; all these closed by the mid-1870s but the government-aided schools fared better. See Thomas Metcalf, *Land, Landlords and the British Raj* (Berkeley: Univ. of California Press, 1979), pp. 281–82, 319, 333, 345. For a detailed discussion of *Ritiratnakar* see "Women against women" in this volume.

114 In Datta's *Devrani*, a jat *dhai* who breastfeeds a bania child from birth till the age of five in her *own* home for two rupees a month, festival gifts, and a lump sum of twenty-five rupees for the entire period, is not absorbed into the household.

When the child is returned to his parents he believes the jatni to be his real mother and refuses to be parted. She too is overcome with grief. The bania family only invites her to stay for a few days in order to accustom the *child* to his biological mother.

115 For a discussion of other aspects of this shift see "Women against women" in this volume.

116 Cited in Vasudha Dalmia, *The Nationalization of Hindu Traditions* (Delhi: Oxford Univ. Press, 1997), pp. 259–60.

117 Bayly, *Rulers*, pp. 306, 315–16.

118 Reprinted in *Reform and Intellectual Debate in Victorian England*, eds. Barbara Dennis and David Skilton (London: Croom Helm, 1987), pp. 71–73.

119 Dayanand's melioration of brahminical food pollution taboos may also have stemmed from his belief that sudras, as descendents of Aryans, could be absorbed back into the Aryan fold.

120 See Rosalind O'Hanlon, *Caste, Conflict and Ideology: Mahatma Jotirao Phule and Low Caste Protest in Nineteenth-Century Western India* (Delhi: Orient Longman, 1985), pp. 257–58, 262.

121 Cited in S.N.A. Jafri, *The History and Status of Landlords and Tenants in the United Provinces* (1931; rpt Delhi: Usha, 1985), pp. 294–95.

122 In Bengal, a dialogue between women was used as early as Radhakanta Deb's *Strisikhar Bidya* in 1822.

123 *"Lavli aur Malti ka Samvad"* carries a conversation between two women who are childhood friends from the same village; Lavli asks Malti for advice and receives a discourse on *pativratas* and the fasts she should observe. See *Balabodhini*, 1874, no. 5.

124 This is a form that goes at least as far back as the medieval Bengal Puranas in which Parvati appears as a faithful, subservient wife perpetually seeking information or clarification on matters ranging from the most mundane and trivial to those of profound philosophical significance. She even publicly demeans herself saying she is a woman of small intelligence. See Kunal Chakravarti, "Divine Family and World Maintenance: Ganesa in the Bengal Puranas", seminar paper, IIAS, Simla, 1992.

125 *Bombay Chronicle*, 27 March 1925, in *Collected Works of Mahatma Gandhi* (henceforth *CW*), vol. 26, pp. 419–20.

126 *Young India*, 11 Aug. 1921, in *To the Women*, ed. Anand Hingorani (1941; rpt Karachi: Hingorani, 1946), p. 170.

127 *Harijan*, 2 Dec. 1939, in M.K. Gandhi, *The Role of Women*, ed. Anand Hingorani (Bombay: Bharatiya Vidya Bhavan, 1964), p. 25.

128 *Harijan*, 2 Dec. 1939, in *Role of Women*, p. 25. Gandhi was rehearsing an old patriarchal history. Irfan Habib has pointed out that the spinning wheel or *charkha* was associated from the medieval period not only with the gendered division of labour but with minatory discourses about the correct place of women, that is, in the home. See "Pursuing the History of Technology: Premodern Modes of Transmission of Power", *Social Scientist*, 20:3–4 (March-April 1992), pp. 12–13.

129 *Navjivan*, 22 Feb. 1920, and 11 Sept. 1921, in *CW*, vols. 17 and 21, pp. 31

and 94; *Young India*, 17 Sept. 1919, and Speech, 16 Jan. 1925, in *Gandhi on Women*, comp. Pushpa Joshi (Ahmedabad: Navjivan, 1988), pp. 33 and 114; Gujerati, 12 Dec. 1919, in *CW*, vol. 16, p. 193.

130 Speech to women at a meeting in Dakor, *Navjivan*, 3 Nov. 1920, in *CW*, vol. 18, p. 384.

131 *Young India*, 17 Sept. 1919, in *CW*, vol. 16, pp. 129–30.

132 *Daily Herald*, 28 Sept. 1931, in *CW*, vol. 48, p. 181.

133 *Navjivan*, 29 Feb. 1920, in *CW*, vol. 17, p. 49.

134 *Harijan*, 16 March 1940, in *To the Women*, p. 30.

135 *Gujerati*, 16 June 1935, in *Gandhi on Women*, pp. 293–94.

136 *Diary of Mahadev* Desai, p. 189, cited in *Role of Women*, p. 61.

137 *Harijan*, 2 Dec. 1939, in *To the Women*, p. 175.

138 Radha Kumar has connected the retrenchment of women and their declining numbers in the textile industry with the emergence of reformist ideologies centred on the working-class family—glorification of motherhood, the husband as sole provider of a nuclear family, the wife's wages as supplementary—which were designed to legitimate a family wage and to rationalize industry. See "Family and Factory: Women in the Bombay Textile Industry 1919-1939", *Indian Economic and Social History Review*, 20:1 (Jan.–March 1983), pp. 81–110.

139 Boydston points out that pastoralization of housework in America implicitly reinforced both the social right and the power of husbands and capitalists to claim the surplus value of women's paid and unpaid labour. See *Home and Work*, p. 158.

140 Gandhi was not unaware of this process. See *The Hindu*, 26 Sept. 1927, in *Gandhi on Women*, p. 12.

141 20 Oct. 1917, in *CW*, vol. 14, p. 31. See also *Harijan*, 12 Oct. 1934, in *To the Women*, p. 11; *Young India*, 3 Oct. 1929, ibid., p. 2. For a discussion of Ruskin see "Relating histories" in this volume.

142 *Nari Ratna Singar*, ed. Kapurchandji Jain (Shahgunj, Lucknow: n.p., 1931), parts 1 and 3.

143 See *Balabodhini*, 1875, no. 10, pp. 73–75.

144 *Mahila Gitanjali*, ed. Sushiladevi Vaidya Visharda (Moradabad: Saraswati Press, 1930). The booklet was brought out by the Akhil Bharatvarshiya Mahila Sewasangh, a branch of Nikhil Bharatiya Hindi Sanskrit Sahitya Mahamandal Vidyapeeth. This was an organization dedicated to uplifting women, teaching them the Shastras, and Hindi and Sanskrit literature.

145 For details of the debate in Gujarat, Maharashtra, and Bengal, see Alice Clark,"Limitations on Female Life Chances in Rural Central Gujarat" in *Women in Colonial India*, ed. J. Krishnamurty (Delhi: Oxford Univ. Press, 1989), p. 49; Meera Kosambi,"Girl Brides and Socio-Legal Changes: Age of Consent Bill (1891) Controversy", *EPW*, 26:31–32 (Aug. 1991), pp. 1857–61; Tanika Sarkar, "Rhetoric against Age of Consent", *EPW*, 28:36 (Sept. 1993).

146 Kosambi, "Girl Brides", p. 1862.

147 Engels, *Beyond Purdah?*, pp. 200, 203, 205, 213. Before the 1920s, widows formed a sizeable proportion of the women in domestic service in Bengal. After this married women and women from Nepal and Orissa joined this expanding service sector.

148 An Arya Samaji wrote: "Few well-to-do women, even easily circumstanced parents, guardians or husbands will care to allow their girls and wives to engage in service after marriage; but there is a class of females—at present a pest on society, source of untold suffering and crime all around—who can be nicely utilized for the purpose; I mean the Hindu widows" (Letter by Ralla Ram, *Tribune*, 25 April 1894, cited in Madhu Kishwar, "The Daughters of Aryavrata" in *Women in Colonial India*, ed. Krishnamurty, p. 102).

149 For instance, the tussles between women in the reformer Ranade's household were generated between old and new patriarchal arrangements with the widow as a point of tension in the transformations of traditional households into an affective unit consisting of the conjugal couple. See Chakravarti, "Social Pariahs", p. 46.

150 Kosambi, *Pandita Ramabai's*, p. 220.

151 *The Letters and Correspondence of Pandita Ramabai*, pp. 277, 280–81, 287, 290, 292–93.

152 See Chakravarti, 'Social Pariahs', pp. 134–37.

153 When the Hindu Widows' Remarriage Bill was published in 1856, 28 petitions signed by 51,746 persons opposed it, while 23 petitions signed by 5,191 persons favoured it. See Lucy Carroll, "Law, Custom and Statutory Social Reform: Hindu Widows' Remarriage Act of 1856" in *Women in Colonial India*, ed. Krishnamurty; Chowdhury, *The Veiled Women*; Archana Prasher, *Woman and Family Law Reform in India* (Delhi: Sage, 1992), p. 95.

154 Har Bilas Sarda, *Speeches and Writings* (Ajmer: Vedic Yantralaya, 1935), pp. 70–90. In the 1950s the vociferous opposition to the Hindu Code Bill in granting women equal property rights rested in part on the claim that it would break the joint family.

155 See Crooke, *Natives*, p. 166.

156 In Mohammed Hadi 'Ruswa's Umrao Jan 'Ada' (1899), as Umrao grows older, wary, and cynical, she wants to "reform", but who will marry an aging courtesan? 'Ruswa's narrative, or at any rate the subsequent interpolations, seem to indicate that there was no happy ending available except reform, no justification other than a minatory moralism for depicting a fallen women 'realistically'.

157 In Nabakumar Datta's *Swarnabai* (1888), a brahmin widow who chooses prostitution is "converted" by a white missionary woman to the virtues of domesticity, and after a period of domestic service turns into an austere widow. For details of the story see Chatterjee, "Prostitution in Nineteenth Century Bengal", pp. 168–69.

158 See Moore, *Feminism and Anthropology*, pp. 94–95.

159 Harrison and Mort, "Patriarchal Aspects", pp. 79–82.

160 See "Relating histories" and "Women against women" in this volume.

161 *Darling, Wisdom and Waste*, pp. 187, 305, 385.

162 For instance, in Haryana it not only supported bride price, betrothal contracts, legally arranged *karewas* or levirate marriage that reabsorbed the widow's right to property into the family, but also the widow's legal right to control land since she had to pay government revenue. See Prem Chowdhury, "Conjugality, Law and State: Inheritance Rights as Pivot of Control in Northern India", *National Law School Journal*, 1 (1993), pp. 95, 99–100, and *The Veiled Women*.

163 P.L. Chudgar, *Princes under British Protection* (London: Williams and Norgate, 1929), pp. 33–44.

164 See Dang, "Prostitutes, Patrons and the State", pp. 188–89.

165 "These women are not obliged to seek shelter in private haunts, nor are they, on account of their professional conduct, marked with opprobious stigma. They compose a particular class of society, and enjoy the avowed protection of government, for which they are assessed according to their several capacities. . . . They were not driven by financial necessity into a promiscuous intercourse with the world" (George Foster, *A Journey from Bengal to England*, Letter of 1782 (London: R. Fauldner, 1798), pp. 59–60).

Nathaniel Halhed too believed in "the necessity as well as utility of tolerated prostitution" as an effective method for "preserving the peace of families and the health of individuals", and affirmed the virtues of the regulation of prostitutes by the state (*A Code of Gentoo Laws* (London: n.p., 1781), p. lviii).

166 "Those who do not receive any permanent stipend, are little less dissolute and abandoned in their habits of life, than a female of similar description in European countries" (Foster, *A Journey*, p. 60).

167 See Dang, "Prostitutes, Patrons and the State", pp. 185–87.

168 "The prostitute class as we proceed from the pure savage to the highest point of civilization, becomes more and more distinct—being more conspicuous because more isolated." India fell somewhere in the middle of Mayhew's scale because prostitution was diffused across a spectrum that ranged from religion to performance, and because it gave prostitutes a "place in society" and even admitted them into zenanas or women's quarters (*London Labour*, pp. 58, 105–06, 124).

169 The Surgeon-General of Bengal wondered how registering a few prostitutes could help when there were so many. (Cited in Kenneth Ballhatchet, *Race, Sex and Class under the Raj* (London: Weidenfeld, 1980), p. 52.) The unnamed author of *Educational Disabilities of the Children of Dancing Girls in India* represented "Hindu" prostitutes or "Kalawantins" as recognized by the Shastras and Puranas, attached to temples, and the profession as hereditary and caste-bound. All those who fell outside this, especially Muslim women, were dangerous because they could move in and out of prostitution (London, n.d.; Bombay: Dnyan Mitra Press, circa 1879), pp. 8–9.

Consent, agency, and the rhetorics of incitement

1 See Eleanor Leacock, *Myths of Male Dominance* (New York: Monthly Review Press, 1981), p. 218.

2 Mona Etienne and Eleanor Leacock, *Women and Colonization* (New York: Praeger, 1980), p. 4.

3 The division of public and private in liberal democratic discourse located the public as the sphere of universality, nationality, impartiality, equality in the eyes of the law, built on consent, and rested on that cornerstone of capitalism—the possessive proprietorial male operating in the public sphere. (See Anne Philips, *Engendering Democracy* (Cambridge: Polity Press, 1991), p. 32.) The private, incorporating home, family and sexuality, was the sphere of particularism built on the "natural" subjugation of women; it was to be freed from the illegitimate interference of the state and, implicitly, both a non-economic realm and a realm of freedom. Not only did these assumptions invisibilize domestic labour or other work performed in 'private' spaces, efface the fact that women were scarcely proprietors of their own persons, property or labour power, and perpetuate patriarchal arrangements within the family, but the liberal conception of the family as a private sanctuary ideally beyond state intervention assisted the legal reinforcement of women's subordination. The distinction between public and private spheres was challenged by socialist feminists who brought restructuring of the 'private' within the realm of politics and argued for an essential unity of the public and private spheres as integrally related and as reshaping each other. See Alison Jaggar, *Feminist Politics and Human Nature* (Totowa, New Jersey: Rowman and Allenheld, 1983), pp. 144,146–47, 210, 244.

4 See "Relating histories" in this volume.

5 See "Introduction", *Recasting Women: Essays in Colonial History*, eds. Kumkum Sangari and Sudesh Vaid (Delhi: Kali, 1989), pp. 10–11.

6 The division of public and private along the grid of state and civil society has produced a relocation of many coercive functions of the "private sphere". See Ellen Meiksins Wood, "The Uses and Abuses of 'Civil Society'", *Socialist Register* (1990), pp. 73–74.

7 For instance, *peshwai* rule in Maharashtra not only classified and kept a register of all sexual offences but was more intensely involved in family and caste matters than the colonial state. See Meera Kosambi, "Images of Women and the Feminine in Maharashtra", *Economic and Political Weekly* (henceforth *EPW*), 26:25 (June 1991), pp. 1521–23.

8 On the latter point see Michele Barrett, *Women's Oppression Today* (London: Verso, 1980), p. 78.

9 See Henrietta L. Moore, *Feminism and Anthropology* (Cambridge: Polity Press, 1988), pp. 131, 179.

10 Here I refer also to reproduction and to the gender-based division of labour in a caste-class differentiated social formation.

11 Even when women's agency is enhanced through belonging to 'semi-autonomous' forms of female collectivity, for instance matrilineal groups, we still need to ask how these groups connect not only with other structures of dominance (such as caste, religion, law) but also with other operative and adjacent patriarchies.

12 For a related emphasis see Michelle Perrott, Cecile Dauphin et al., "Culture and Power of Women: A Historiographical Essay", *French Studies in History*, vol. 2, *The Departures*, eds. Maurice Aymard and Harbans Mukhia (Delhi: Orient Longman, 1990), pp. 455–86.

13 For subsequent discussion of multiple yet overlapping patriarchies centred on different labour forms and corollary variations as well as caste and religious differences, see "The 'amenities'" in this volume, and Kumkum Sangari, "The Politics of Diversity: Religious Communities and Multiple Patriarchies", *EPW*, 30:51 and 52 (Dec. 1995). In the latter essay I have argued that in the past, caste differentiation, divisions of labour, the coexistence of tribal and agricultural modes of production, of matrilineal and patrilineal systems, and their complex articulation with regional histories including the formation of religious sects, have been significant factors in the crystallization of differing patriarchies. However, many of the overlaps and differences in patriarchal arrangements that functioned around the axes of caste and class were in fact structured, and neither historical accidents nor ideologically neutral. The differences between the patriarchal arrangements of regionally contiguous religious groups were partly a product of discrete religio-legal systems; these systems were, however, subjected to a continuous restructuring by the imperatives of class and the customary domain which produced sets of practices where the areas of commonality were wider than the areas of difference. At present, the political economy that shapes and intersects with all patriarchies is producing new grounds and forms of similarity, and continues, in combination with customary practices, to level many religio-textual differences. The overlaps extend beyond a commonality of patriarchal practices into a denial of customary entitlements and existing legal rights, displaying the operative power of a patriarchal social consensus.

14 This formulation begs two questions which need separate attention—the determination of men by patriarchal structures, and men's consent.

15 For a discussion of domestic labour as one of the bases for the long duration as well as the reformulation of patriarchal ideologies, see "The 'amenities'" in this volume.

16 Since patriarchies are related to so many other systemic oppressions, feminists cannot isolate and challenge patriarchies alone but have to confront all that they are shaped by and embedded in; that is, the very nature of patriarchies requires a wide, thoroughgoing egalitarian project to end all forms of inequality—based in class, caste, distribution of surplus, and division of labour—that women and men are subject to.

17 The fact that patriarchal violence practised against women often also functions on behalf of social consensualities dispersed in 'commonsense' or condensed in symbolic systems, shows how deeply embedded and widely distributed it is across the social formation.

18 The ideological and legal history of 'protection' has, broadly speaking, not only been entangled with essentialist notions of gender difference, relied on a social consensus and naturalized patriarchal arrangements, but has also been implicated in the deferral or denial of women's rights.

19 The class-maintaining/maximizing function of domestic labour is also an arena for varying degrees of women's agency and consent, and these variations are partly determined by different levels and junctures of class mobility. See "The 'amenities'" in this volume.

20 Our own embarrassment about explaining women who oppressed other women in instances of family violence such as dowry murders was in fact one of the starting points for reflecting on the whole issue of consent. For a discussion of a recent display of the collective solidarity of upper-caste women against lower-caste men and women, see Vasantha Kannabhiran and Kalpana Kannabhiran, "Caste and Gender: Understanding Dynamics of Power and Violence", *EPW*, 26:37 (Sept. 1991), p. 2132. For an account by dalit women of their oppression by jat women in a Punjab village, see Interview (Anonymous, rpt from *Jaikara*), "Women Dalit Labourers Speak", *Manushi*, 4 (Dec. 1979-Jan. 1980), p. 21.

21 For instance, female seclusion or male addiction to liquor may be perceived as moral issues by women from the upper strata and experienced as economic ones by women from the lower. Middle-class familial ideologies of male protection, female domestic service, socialization of children, and the sacrosanct nature of family ties may have little correlation with either the economic necessities of poor families or the types of labour performed by poor women.

22 See Stephanie Coontz, *The Social Origins of Private Life: A History of American Families 1600–1800* (London: Verso, 1980), p. 13; Moore, *Feminism and Anthropology*, p. 117; Michele Barrett and Mary McIntosh, *The Anti-Social Family* (London: Verso, 1982), p. 85.

23 Some of these questions on the internal differentiation of families have been pursued in "The 'amenities'" in this volume.

24 On the latter point, see Alex Callinocos, *Making History: Agency, Structure and Change in Social Theory* (Oxford: Polity Press, 1987), p. 156.

25 For instance, a remarkable congruence was created between domestic service as advocated in the Shastras and as enjoined by emergent bourgeois ideologies in the prescriptive literature of the Hindustani belt in the late nineteenth century—virtually turning the *Manusmriti* into a 'modern' primer for embourgeoisement and class management. See "The 'amenities'" in this volume.

26 For instance, women used the doctrine of separate spheres in early nineteenth-century America to gain moral leverage within the family while domestic ideologies in part functioned to give women some control over sexuality and reproduction. See Coontz, *The Social Origins*, p. 218.

27 See "Relating histories" in this volume, and Kumkum Sangari, "Mirabai and the Spiritual Economy of Bhakti", *EPW*, 15:27 and 28 (July 1990). On the use of consenting female voices to contain the disruptive effects of education and curtail the new agential spaces in the economy as well as to refurbish patriarchies in the late nineteenth century see "The 'amenities'" in this volume.

28 See Michael Brown, "History and History's Problems", *Social Text*, 16 (Winter 1986–87), p. 158; Sudipta Kaviraj, "Some Observations on Marxism and Political Causality", Occasional Papers (Delhi: Nehru Memorial Museum and Library, 1989), p. 36.

29 Women's agency is often pejoratively slotted as manipulative. According to Leela Dube, in her field experience, women are not accused so much of manipulation in matrilineal groups whereas manipulation is built into the structure of patriliny. For a discussion of the use of manipulative strategies in the absence of formal power, see Joke Schrijvers ("Make Your Son a King: Political Power through Matronage and Motherhood" in *'Big Man' Political Systems*, ed. M.V. Bebel (Leiden: Brill, 1986), p. 19).

A near-contemporary and virtually archetypal representation in this genre, Shastriji (1945, a Prabhat Studio film on the Peshwas), presents Lalita Pawar in the role of a wife who incites her husband and her advice leads to the loss of his kingdom. She is Bad because she is an explicit surrogate power-sharer in her husband's position as well as an active class agent. The film recognizes and displays the power which exists in structures of surrogacy only to condemn it. Such a woman contradicts bourgeois domestic ideologies which describe women as noncompetitive and as the good conscience of men: her incitement pollutes the domestic space. Those tendencies in elite nationalism which constituted the wife–woman as the conscience of both husband and nation, inversely enlarged the 'criminality' of such 'scheming' women—making them the first antinationals as it were. Their crime lay in wanting to share power overtly while giving no other socially legitimate name to female agency. Since various tendencies in elite nationalism were also engaged in building a consensual patriarchy, the familialist strategies of protonationalist and nationalist reform tended to make the public activity of women a natural extension of domestic activities—only Bad women spoke in their own name.

30 Romila Thapar points out that primogeniture indicated a society where land rights have been established, and would require an extra emphasis where there may have been a variant descent and inheritance system and where an elite group sought to distinguish itself from others. See *Exile and the Kingdom: Some Thoughts on the Ramayana* (Bangalore: Mythic Society, 1978) p. 11.

31 The epic indirectly represents and legitimizes the transition from non-state to state and monarchy; lineage systems did not, however, die out with the emergence of states but continued side by side until the second millennium ad. See Romila Thapar, *From Lineage to State: Social Formation in the Mid-First Millennium bc in the Ganga Valley* (Delhi: Oxford Univ. Press, 1990), pp. 32–34, 171.

32 According to D.D. Kosambi the transition to monarchy carried features from previous tribal customs and was a period not only of providing rationales for monarchy but of a new veneration of force, since the rule of kings not belonging to the tribe depended on a class of armed kshatriyas; in the *Manusmriti* force lies at the foundation of state and social order. See *An Introduction to the Study of Indian History* (Bombay: Popular Prakashan), pp. 153, 252.

33 See Romila Thapar, "Society and Historical Consciousness: The Itihasa–Purana Tradition" in *Situating Indian History*, eds. Sabyasachi Bhattacharya and Romila Thapar (Delhi: Oxford Univ. Press, 1986), pp. 362–64.

34 See Uma Chakravarti, "The Development of the Sita Myth: A Case Study of Women in Myth and Literature", *Samya Shakti*, 1:1 (July 1983), pp. 67–72.

35 See Sarva Daman Singh, *Polyandry in Ancient India* (Delhi: Motilal Banarsidas, 1988), pp. 139–44.

36 Succession agreements at the time of marriage were not uncommon. In the *Mahabharata*, Shakuntala makes a private condition that her son should succeed to the throne, a condition that disappears in Kalidasa's version.

Ramashraya Sharma, whose book I read after this essay was published, reinterprets the marriage agreement significantly. He points out that the idea of *sulka* (price) is present in the marriage of Dashrath with Kaikeyi. She is *rajya-sulka* in the sense that Dashrath has to promise to appoint as his successor a son begotten with Kaikeyi. This securing of the future well-being of a daughter by her father has to be distinguished from securing a bride by purchase. The text uses the word *rajya-sulka* not as a price to be paid to the father but to make Kaikeyi's future secure because she is marrying a much older man. Such promises were elicited by parents in incompatible matches. (See *A Socio-Political Reading of the Valmiki Ramayana* (Delhi: Motilal Banarsidas, 1986), pp. 52–53, 82, 111.) The transactional character of the marriage is further augmented by the likelihood of its representing the type of alliance through which links were forged between political centres, in this case Kekeya and Kosala. (See Thapar, *From Lineage*, p. 95.) Marriage alliances tied to political expansion were a feature of the transition to monarchy. (See Kosambi, *An Introduction*, p. 8.) However, even if it was distinct from bride price, it remains difficult to arrive at any conclusion about the legal ranking and location of such a 'price' in the hierarchy of extant marriage agreements, or about whether such agreements were honoured.

For another suggestive reading of this episode in the *Ramayana* see Sally Sutherland, "Seduction, Counter Seduction and Sexual Role Models: Bedroom Politics and the Indian Epics", seminar paper, Annual Meeting of the Association for Asian Studies, San Francisco, California (1983).

37 I have used the *Valmiki Ramayana*, Part 1 (Gorakhpur: Gita Press, 1988) for this section.

38 How precarious this ideality is (as well as how unsettled primogeniture as a norm and how prevalent the rule of force) can be judged from the fact that Lakshman's response to Ram's exile is to take over the kingdom by force, imprison or kill Dashrath, and destroy all dissenters; as well as from Ram's fear, later in the forest, that Kaikeyi may poison Kaushalya and Sumitra.

39 Significantly, this was the direction in which Kumaradasa's version, based on both Valmiki and Kalidasa, took the episode by making Kaikeyi the protector of *dharma*. In *Janakiharan* (circa ad 400–600) Ram improves on his original injunction to Bharat in the *Ayodhyakhand* to protect his mother Kaikeyi with the statement: "That queen who saved the vow of honesty of her husband is to be worshipped by you." Here Kaikeyi deserves Bharat's protection not only because she is his mother, but because she was responsible for ensuring that Dashrath did not swerve from the path of truth. See C.R. Swaminathan, *Kumaradasa* (Delhi: Sahitya Akademi, 1990), pp. 11, 16.

40 Even Brahma and Indra granted boons for impeccable devotion to demons which later made them helpless, while there are many stories about them and other gods using codicils in their own protection or calling upon some counteracting power. The boons granted by gods are often a means of negotiating, propitiating, containing, or being forced to acknowledge a source of self-accumulated, threatening power—an 'extra-legal' way of settling a 'claim' as it were.

It is interesting to note that Dashrath and Vasishtha also do their best to 'legalistically' circumvent the boons. Dashrath orders that the treasure of the city, attendants, and the army be sent with Ram to the forest since the boon did not specify that he go empty-handed. Vasishtha says that either Sita can rule the kingdom in Ram's absence, or the wealth and population of the kingdom should follow Ram. Kaikeyi has to struggle to maintain her demands.

41 The status of the tribal chief had been hedged by his relationship to various clan gatherings (*gana, vidatha, sabha, samiti, parishad*) which carried a variety of functions—from cattle-raids, rituals, kin gatherings, redistribution of wealth and advice to the king—and declined over time or changed their function. The period of transition to monarchy had features from such previous tribal custom where decision-making was not centralized, citizens had some local autonomy, paid less tribute, and gave formal assent to the coronation; kings began to claim the prerogatives of formal tribal chiefs but did not retain property rights in common. With the rise of the monarchical state, pre-Buddhist, Buddhist, and Mauryan notions about 'contract', at first between gods and kings and later extending to kings, brahmins and the people, underwent a continuously greater elaboration of their mutual obligations and tended more and more to legitimate kingship. The king came to be associated with divine elements, the upholder of order and *dharma*: the concrete contents of *dharma* were property, marriage, family and caste relations. The analogy of king and god underlined the former's role as nourisher and protector and in the avoidance of chaos while election and selection were superseded by hereditary claims. (See Thapar, *From Lineage to State*, pp. 55–62; Kosambi, *An Introduction*, pp. 153, 159; Ram Sharan Sharma, *Aspects of Political Ideas and Institutions in Ancient India* (Delhi: Motilal Banarsidas, 1991), pp. 60–76, 360–61.)

Many of these elements are visible in the *Valmiki Ramayana*. The king is presented as protector of the people, required to uphold the law, and his absence is associated with dystopian *kaliyug* motifs: the breakdown of filial or wifely obedience, proprietory rights, of security for subjects, person and property, and of protection for brahmins. But sovereignty is vested in the people too, they have the right to sanction or stop a king's succession. Dashrath seeks the approval of his subjects to appoint Ram as a *yuvraja*, or his successor, at a *sabha* (a place of meeting for king and ministers, his court of justice, an assembly which discussed important matters concerning the state). The *sabha* here seems to consist more of prominent interests than of ordinary people while its role seems to be somewhat formal since Dashrath has already decided on Ram's coronation before calling a meeting. However, Valmiki recognizes not so much the absolute authority of the king as of *dharma*, that is why Ram has to go to the forest. See Sharma, *A Socio-Political*, pp. 289–91, 300–01, 335–340.

42 This too remains problematic. Why is a context needed at all? Would she have had less leverage if Dashrath, who is about to renounce political power, were also able to renounce the sexual desire which is repeatedly described as enslavement?

43 According to Sharma, ideal conduct was demanded from the king because it was believed that mishaps and evils among the people were caused by the wrongs of the ruler. Kings dreaded public infamy, especially censure of the sages and the good, but there is no indication in the epic of what people can do if the king is bad. (See *A Socio-Political*, p. 301.) I think the references to public perception, approval, stricture, and consent in the Valmiki *Ramayana* could be multilayered. They could evoke earlier tribal systems of elective chieftainship where the chieftain's power was hedged by clan gatherings, that is, signify hovering memories of tribal forms and usages as a memory of limits. They could encapsulate the pressure of the knowledge that people's approval was necessary to institute and consolidate primogeniture which further absolutized kingship. Finally, they could simultaneously constitute an attempt to erase or displace memories of tribal arbitration by making a consensual basis for monarchy in a new type of popular consent. Later, Ram tries to ensure such a consent through his *own* spies who go looking for signs of disaffection among the people. What is also significant is that in the episode of Sita's exile, patriarchy becomes a more explicit basis for popular consent than in this episode.

44 As sources of authority, king, brahmin, and *rishi* were based respectively on land as a source of revenue, the monopoly over knowledge and performance of rituals, and an intangible moral authority that was almost a counterweight to the first two. See Thapar, "Society and Historical Consciousness", p. 362.

45 Viswamitra (who was a *rajarshi* before he ascended to being a *brahmarshi*) and other *rajarshis* were the architects of the plan by which Ram was to defeat Ravana in the epic. (See Sharma, *A Socio-Political Study* pp. 144–45.) *Rajarshis* could dwell in the heaven of Indra such as Viswamitra and Ikshvaku. See John Garrett, *A Classical Dictionary of India* (1871; rpt Delhi: Low Price, 1990).

46 In other words, the epic may have sought to evolve a consensus for a new language of entitlement and obligation that could be embedded in patriarchal arrangements.

47 The new woman practising *naridharma* in the Valmiki *Ramayana* and the brahmin as represented in the *Manusmriti* are curiously similar: both rely on self-punishing structures of legitimation hinging on self-regulation and self-denial.

48 Exactly what Ram has told Kaushalya. That is why Kaushalya becomes Bharat's 'true' mother. Sharma points out that in the epic a wife is expected to support her husband, not her son. (See *A Socio-Political*, p. 95.) This of course raises another question: is Kaikeyi's agency on her own behalf or on her son's, or both?

49 Sita's threatened suicide if she is not allowed to join Ram in exile because she does not want to be left unprotected in the palace, Sita's lament at being abandoned by Ram despite her devotion when she is imprisoned by Ravana, Kaushalya bemoaning her status which has been equal to that of Kaikeyi's servants, Kaushalya's sense of vulnerability and fear of the taunts of junior wives once Ram is exiled as well as her claim that having had no happiness with her husband she had looked forward to *putra-rajya* (son's reign) for an end to her troubles—all testify to this.

50 Ram even claims that he won Sita back not for love of her but in order to restore his own fame, and describes Sita's abduction as her sexual dalliance with Ravana.

51 If they are obscured or resolved at all it is in the latter-day, now hegemonic versions of the epic.

52 Or, to frame this question from another direction, is this because entitlement and obligation are already so deeply implicated in patriarchal arrangements that they cannot but function, simultaneously and inconsistently, to enforce, to mitigate, *and* to seek women's consent for such arrangements? And is it that while women's entitlements are now sought to be embedded more ideologically and more fully in structures of patriarchal enforcement, male obligations remain divided between incompatible pressures?

53 In Dashrath's literal distribution of 'assured' sons in the form of fertilizing *kheer* (milk preparation), the largest portion goes to Kaushalya and the smallest to Kaikeyi. All the sons are parts of Vishnu with Ram being half, or the largest part.

54 Significantly, Ram himself is inclined towards interpreting Kaikeyi's action as preordained. He soothes Lakshman saying that the very suddenness and extremity of Kaikeyi's behaviour shows that it is a part of god's design, otherwise how could a good woman give her husband such pain.

Another question arises here. Would the nature of Kaikeyi's agency and social valuation change if the marriage agreement entered the chain of causality, or would it still go against the social grain? Tentative answers could be sought not only in the other kinds of female agency that Kaikeyi's is counterposed to in the Valmiki *Ramayana* but also in the way Manthara and Kaikeyi are presented in other rescensions or narrative traditions. The Jain traditions for instance did not villainize Kaikeyi; while a later Bhojpuri folk song resolves the inconsistency between preordainment and condemnation by having Ram exonerate Kaikeyi. He declares to Lakshman, "It is no fault of Kaikeyi, what is written on the forehead cannot yield" (cited in Indra Deva, *Folk Culture and Peasant Society in India* (Jaipur: Rawat, 1989), p. 226). Significantly the full structure of Kaikeyi's villainization breaks down in a text that foregrounds the device of preordainment and also makes the marriage agreement central to the narrative—Bhasa's *Pratima Natak* (*circa* second–fourth centuries ad). Ram is being crowned when Manthara comes and whispers in Dashrath's ear, the ceremony is postponed, and later Ram is told that greedy Kaikeyi is the cause. He remains cool and unsurprised, and answers that it should not be forgotten that it was stipulated at the time of her marriage that her son would be king, so it is Ram who can be dubbed greedy but not Kaikeyi. Dashrath is full of grief and anger but Ram does not condemn Kaikeyi. When Bharat arrives and discovers what has happened, he thinks people will hate him—he wants to be an object of respect and affection—and in anger, disowns Kaikeyi. He too knows about the marriage agreement but says that her 'son' could have been interpreted to mean Ram. Kaikeyi answers, "Shall a woman be questioned for claiming what is stipulated at the time of her marriage?" Bharat then wants to know why Ram is to be exiled since that was not in the marriage agreement. Kaikeyi promises to explain at the proper time. Later when Bharat taunts her with the news of Sita's abduction, Kaikeyi explains that Dashrath when out hunting had unwittingly killed the only son of a blind sage and the sage had cursed Dashrath: he too, like the sage, would perish with grief for his son. Kaikeyi claims, "It is not through lust of power that I asked for Ram's exile. I was impelled to ask for it by the sage's curse which was inexorable and could only be fulfilled by the exile of the son." Sumantra and the preceptors Vasishtha and Vamdev know all this too. Bharat then forgives his mother. (See A.S.P. Ayyar, *English One-Act Plays of Bhasa* (n.p.:n.d.), pp. 181, 196.) Here Kaikeyi is not villainized, the marriage agreement is upfront and common knowledge. However, Kaikeyi is not let off simply because she is claiming a 'right' conferred by the agreement but because she is the *instrument* of a curse beyond her control: even her ruse is induced by the curse of the sage.

55 Women had been associated with and participated in a number of clan and tribal assemblies, especially in the early vedic period. In the *vidatha* (a clan or tribal assembly) women had a voice in public affairs including the consecration of a king; significantly the *vidatha* had undifferentiated functions which spanned the economic, military, legal, religious, and social, and indicates an unequal but pre-class society. Women also attended *sabhas* and were a part of *ganas* at this time. The reference to *ganas* of 'mothers' in the *Mahabharata* has been taken to suggest matriarchal formations as well as a time in the vedic past when adult women who took part in battle formed military assemblies; this could have been a pre-Aryan or an Aryan institution. The *parisad*, a tribal military assembly that was partly patriarchal and partly matriarchal, could have included women in vedic times. These limited forms of participation were subsequently undermined with settled agriculture and polygamy, and their demise significantly coincided with kingship becoming hereditary in the later vedic period. In the later vedic period, women may, however, have attended the *samiti*—a folk assembly in which common and rich people gathered; this is said to have been a powerful deliberative body which later became aristocratic and non-tribal. (See Sharma, *Aspects of Political Ideas*, pp. 88–106, 11, 115, 117, 119–27, 136–38, 351, 358, 360.) In this context of increasing 'domestication' with settled agriculture, it is significant that in the rendition of the story of Ram in later Bhojpuri folk songs and folklore, Kaikeyi's assistance on the battlefield is replaced by a mundane service: she removes a thorn/bamboo chip lodged in Dashrath's finger/foot which is causing intense agony. See Deva, *Folk Culture*, p. 229; Vidya Nivas Misra, "The Rama Story in Indian Folk Lore: Some Significant Innovations" in *Asian Variations in Ramayana*, ed. K.R. Srinivasan Iyengar (Delhi: Sahitya Akademi, 1983), p. 104.

56 Bhavabhuti's *Mahavircharitra* (*circa* seventh–eighth centuries ad) displaces the agency of these two women altogether in a chain of incitement. Ravana's minister Malyavat instigates Surpanakha to disguise herself as and/or take possession of Manthara's body, and work through her on Kaikeyi's mind. Kaikeyi's demand, which sends Ram into exile, is shown to result from Malyavat's scheme. Murari's *Anargharaghava* (*circa* ninth century ad) repeats this 'plot'. Later the *Bhusundi Ramayana* (*circa* thirteenth century) displaces Manthara's agency on to the gods. Saraswati, through the connivance of the gods, influences Manthara to incite Kaikeyi. See G. Bhat, *Bhavabhuti* (Delhi: Sahitya Akademi, 1979), pp. 20–21; Arriedale Keith, *The Sanskrit Drama* (Delhi: Motilal Banarsidas, 1982), pp. 109, 227–28; Bhagwati Prasad Singh, "*Bhusundi Ramayana* and its Influence on Medieval Ramayana Literature" in *The Ramayana Tradition in Asia*, ed. V. Raghavan (Delhi: Sahitya Akademi, 1980), pp. 500–01.

57 And provide her with a retinue of dwarf and hunchback women servants!

58 These, as associated with the word *kaatar*, almost a pre-emotion, could range from fear, impatience, excitement, nervousness to cowardice.

59 He not only invokes every possible sin, dishonour, and punishment in the book for her but tells her to walk into a burning fire or hang herself, and says he would kill her himself but for Ram's disapproval of matricide—magnifying her 'sin' beyond endurance and moving Kaikeyi to tears.

60 In one sense personalization also functions to *contain* the action of Manthara and Kaikeyi.

61 See Sangari, "Mirabai", p. 1471.

62 There are repeated images of Kaikeyi *enjoying* power as a widow which haunt Dashrath and even Ram. These carry the implication that there is no ideologically guaranteed certainty that such a woman will suffer upon becoming a widow. Further, the anxiety about royal women who had a potentially separable self-interest because they could form a new unit of joint interest with a son may be related not only to a then extant typology of dangerous queens (found for instance in the *Arthashastra* and *Manusmriti*) but could also have been a potential site of misogyny. At one level, such a relocation of loyalty from husband to son undercuts the instatement of another emerging ideology that was centred on the privations or wretchedness of widowhood. Kaikeyi thus becomes a husband-killer in an epic interested in deifying husbands and universalizing *naridharma* through Kaushalya, Anasuya, Sita, and the choric voices of the faceless women of Ayodhya. However, Kaushalya and Sita make misogynist statements too. (On these statements, see Sharma, *A Socio-Political*, p. 110.) Another type of relation between *naridharma* and misogyny could have been emerging, expressed through making 'good' female voices the bearers of misogyny.

63 Kaikeyi's mother is accused of lacking all competence—*naridharma*, respect for family honour, carefulness regarding her husband's life-and dismissed from any justifiable claim to queenship. However, the real issue, over which she is banished from her husband's home, is her challenge to male control (that of king and priest) of knowledge and her own exclusion from it. Significantly, for Sumantra, who narrates this episode, women inherit their disposition from their mothers. This stands in sharp contrast to dynastic patrilineage and the conferral of male capacity. For instance, in the Upanishads the father bequeaths faculties, fame, and power to the son. It is also significant that Bharat asserts the principle of patrilineage, not only by failing, as Kaikeyi's son, to claim her 'rights' on her behalf but also by refusing to allow her 'rights' to be transmitted to him.

64 Kaushalya eventually translates her husband's 'rejection' into duty and so succeeds in remaining good. Despite latent fraternal and polygamous politics, the onus of disharmony is put on Manthara and Kaikeyi.

Though there is no simple equivalence between law and social practice in the epic, the misogyny in extant legal prescriptions resting on the wife's duties also weighs against Kaikeyi. This has led some commentators to claim that Dashrath deserts her on what were sanctioned legal grounds: she impedes his pursuit of *dharma*, that is, of primogeniture; she is 'unchaste' in the sense of disregarding the will of her husband, excessively wrathful, and also speaks unkindly. Sharma refutes this interpretation: the kingdom was already pledged to her son and there is no evidence of desertion since there is no change in her status in the palace. See *A Socio-Political*, pp. 62–65.

65 We are still left with a set of questions related to the mythic refraction of social practices and norms. What was the precise nature of earlier or extant patriarchal systems of customary entitlements or 'rights' for women, and for guaranteeing licit claims, which were now being eroded or sought to be supplanted? How contingent were these on situations and on women's behaviour, and what were the pressures under which they expanded and contracted? What was the relation between primogeniture, polygamy, and female sexuality as glimpsed in Kaikeyi's transition from wife to mother? What was the wider set of relations between kinship and politics which produced inequality in the palace? Was polygamy one of the breeding grounds for both the ascription of scheming women and of a corollary convolution of women's agency? What was the relation between Dashrath's visibly overpowering love for Kaikeyi and his failure to obey the terms of the marriage agreement? Could hierarchy be altered in the name of love or did polygamy function to split male duty and male desire? Was there an inherent contradiction between *naridharma* and polygamy? Is Kaikeyi's 'banking' of the boons linked to polygamy? Indeed how settled were the 'norms' of polygamy?

66 See "Relating histories" and "Women against women" in this volume.

67 This historiographic model of sexual violence is a subset of the larger nineteenth-century model of hindu patriarchy as a gift of the muslim invader, which I have discussed at some length in "Relating histories" and "Women against women" in this volume: it functions not only to blur the history of earlier patriarchies but also as a form of self-exculpation for hindu men, while the only legitimate voices it confers on hindu women are those of victimage and of hatred for muslim men. It constitutes a grave assault on feminism since it not only pushes women to identify with the right-wing's broader claim to hindu victimage and assertion of a violent 'righting' of 'historical wrongs' but also works to divide women on religious lines: in this schema hindu women, as past and potential victims of sexual violence, can now condone violence against 'other' women. The danger of this discourse is apparent when it is seen in relation to rape as a recurrent feature of communal violence.

This discussion is based on two audio-cassettes circulated during the peak of the Ram Janmabhumi campaign: Sadhvi Rithambara, untitled (*circa* 1991) and Sadhvi Rithambara, *Ram Janam Bhumi-Ayodhya* (*circa* 1991).

68 She claims that now hindus are like the *pehalwan* (bodybuilder) who had maintained his strength through daily *dandbaithak* (exercise), but failing to maintain it after marriage, turned into a weakling. His *samajhdar* (sensible) wife, who he blames for his weakness, demonstrates that he can perform the same feats if accompanied by his five strong young sons.

69 Hindus are asked to give up evil fathers as Prahlad gave up Hiranyakashyap, and renounce evil brothers as Vibhishan did Ravana.

70 She exhorts her listeners to beat up those politicians who object to Ram Janmabhumi.

71 According to Swami Sakshiji Maharaj, a BJP MP from Mathura: "In ancient times kings ruled but holy men held the reins" (*Times of India*, 28 June 1991; see also the statements of Swami Chinmayanand, BJP MP from Badaun (UP) in *Times of India*, 23 July 1991). Rithambara's claim that in Indian history every successful king has had the blessings and advice of a *guru or sant*, is a virtual replay of Annie Besant. Besant, with her notoriously organicist view of India, lectured on the active participation of ancient *rishis* (ascetic saints) in politics: it seems they wandered around the country visiting kings and asking whether they looked after the widows and orphans of those who had died on the battlefield! See *Hindu Ideals* (Benares: Theosophical Publishing Society, 1904), p. 122.

72 Significantly, Rithambara comes from a rural and relatively poor family. The persona of the *sadhvi* also provides a nonconflictual resolution (if not submersion) of her own relatively lower-caste background that must be convenient in a right-wing ensemble where the caste question otherwise remains 'untranscended' and explosive. Hindutva being a complex historical, political, economic, and class–caste differentiated phenomenon, Rithambara's active investment in it, despite the persona of a *sadhvi*, cannot be simplistically seen as an agency which devolves through religious belief.

77 Rithambara also claims that muslims have started all riots and always attacked hindu processions at Dussehra and Diwali, while hindus have been over-tolerant in the past and not attacked Muharram processions, and as a result have always been killed; she concludes that hindus now must retaliate. *Masjids* (mosques), said to be arsenals, are more or less specified as a target. There is both evidence and analysis of the role and deployment of these ideologies during communal riots. (See People's Union for Democratic Rights, *Bhagalpur Riots* (Delhi: PUDR, 1990); and Uma Chakravarti, Prem Chowdhury, Pradip Dutta, Zoya Hasan, Kumkum Sangari, and Tanika Sarkar, "Khurja Riots 1990–91: Understanding the Conjuncture", *EPW*, 27:18 (May 1992.) In such situations instigatory pamphlets have tried to create a paranoid, guilt-free, militant hindu. (See *Bhagalpur Riots*, pp. 8–9.) The call to destroy mosques must be seen in the context of the large number of mosques attacked and damaged in northern India in the course of communal riots during this period.

74 For an account of the active anti-muslim bias of the PAC in recent riots as well as the organized incitement of the PAC by the VHP through letters, video-cassettes, and personalized appeals, see Asghar Ali Engineer, "The Bloody Trail: Ramjanmabhoomi and Communal Violence in UP", *EPW*, 26:4 (Jan. 1991), pp. 155–58.

75 According to her, all of them remember the day when they did not have a *naukari* (job) and prayed to Bajrang Bali for help, promising *prasad* (food offering to idol) in return; further, when they lose their jobs they will have to take Ram's *sharan* (sanctuary). However, the matter does not rest at setting up Bajrang Bali and Ram as an employment agency in order to establish the PAC as true *Rambhakts*. They are asked to desert Mulayam Singh Yadav in the impending showdown on 30 October 1990. When Mulayam asks them to fire they will fire but time will tell whether the bullets will be aimed at *Rambhakts* (devotees of Ram) or *Ramdrohis* (those who have been traitors to Ram). On that day, the PAC will turn into "Bajrang Balis" and undertake a ten to one contest with "Alis", that is, muslims.

76 A man was reported as crying from excitement (*Times of India*, 5 April 1991).

77 *Times of India* (14 June 1991).

78 The Ram Janmabhumi campaign has consolidated a rural base in the past three years, as for instance among labouring classes and the rural elite belonging to intermediary castes in parts of Bihar. (See PUDR, *Bhagalpur Riots*, pp. 29–32.) Along with the BJP base among the petty-bourgeois intelligentsia of Bihar and Uttar Pradesh (UP), it has also acquired a base in western UP among small-town commercial and manufacturing groups, a strata of *mofussil* traders which cannot readily transform into corporate capital, while its base in central UP is more markedly upper-caste. (See Chakravarti et al., "Khurja Riots".) In Maharashtra, the BJP cadre, initially lower-middle class and brahmin, is now shifting to the upper class, professionals and entrepreneur—to 'modernized hindus' as it were—and there has been a conscious effort to enlist non-brahmins. A 'modern' Hinduism is also being expounded by associated organizations attempting to draw in the OBCs, and this is accompanied by relatively liberal positions on women's issues. The spokesperson of the Patit Pavan Sanghatan, which works in tribal regions, has even identified feudalism and religiosity with a reactionary Hinduism and claims to be a hindu without ever having followied a word of Hinduism. In Gujarat it is not the brahmin–bania but the patel–kshatriya, the nouveau riche, non-resident Indians as well as 'westernized' English-speaking youth who support the BJP. In both regions the old-fashioned RSS ideology is being contested by a new managerial group with a different understanding of religion. (I owe this as well as all subsequent information on Maharashtra and Gujarat to Ram Bapat, Vidyut Bhagwat, Vibhuti Patel and Sandeep Pendse.)

79 They draw selectively on existing experiences, frustrations, grievances, inhabited prejudices, presenting them as the only reality in explanatory discourses which make people feel that their 'real' experience is being recognized.

80 For Rithambara, Arya Samajis, Sanatanis, Buddhists, and Sikhs are all hindus who have to be united.

81 As is well known, these organizations place liberal secularism outside the consensus of the 'community' of 'ordinary people' by appealing to 'commonsense' and invoking an exclusivist Indian culture, or brand them as communal through strategic reversals which also help to conceal their own agency.

82 *Times of India* (15 May 1991).

83 In Maharashtra, it is not senior Rashtra Sevikas but a young Rashtra Sevika and ABVP activist in Kolhapur who has publicly criticized Rithambara for using them for their own purposes. Some BJP men have also said that Rithambara's language is not suitable for women while right-wing women resented Bal Thackeray's derogation of women at a recent meeting in Maharashtra.

84 They claim to want neither divine *shakti* nor liberatory feminism. *Stri-mukti* is identified with a caricatured female permissiveness, communism and the Nehruvian legacy, while *stri-shakti* is identified with the mobile mainstream and its platform consists of positions against dowry and violence, demands for *palnaghara* or creches, safety for women commuters, and a uniform civil code. Despite the rhetorical appropriation of feminism, the demand for a uniform civil code is not substantive, it is merely an anti-muslim device.

For a discussion of the Rashtriyasevika Samiti and the particular accommodation of women's militancy and professionalization, see Tanika Sarkar, "The Woman as Communal Subject: Rashtrasevika Samiti and Ram Janmabhumi Movement", *EPW*, 36:35 (Aug. 1991), pp. 2061–62.

85 See "Relating histories" and "Women against women" in this volume.

86 A significant parallel can be drawn with Britain in the 1980s in the use of consent to patriarchies as a vector for consent to right-wing politics. Stuart Hall observes that since "patriarchal positions are absolutely central, as points of condensed articulation, in the discourses of both middle class, petit bourgeois and working class respectabilit—an apparently non-political factor . . . has the effect of stabilizing and securing to the Right a whole range of other discourses" ("The Toad in the Garden: Thatcherism among the Theorists" in *Marxism and the Interpretation of Culture*, eds. Cary Nelson and Lawrence Grossberg (Urbana: Univ. of Illinois Press, 1988), p. 50).

87 Afterword: Though written before the destruction of Babri Masjid on 6 December 1992, some of the tendencies described in this essay later came into sharper focus.

The *sadhus* and *mahants* clustered around the BJP and VHP have moved from surrogate, advisory power to making direct, explicit bids for political power. While women's consent to this right-wing remains caste and class differentiated, Hindutva women have crossed more frequently into direct involvement in communal violence as orchestrators, instigators, looters, and armed rioters. Babri Masjid was broken to the chanting of *karsevikas* (women volunteers) who were active not only as instigators but also in the demolition.

The conjunctural orchestration of voices from this ensemble continues. Sadhvi Rithambara has been astutely stage-managed. For instance, while her voice and presence presided over the demolition she is pulled back from centrestage whenever a moderate image seems judicious. Since militant Hindutva was not a prominent issue for the BJP and Shiv Sena combine in the Maharashtra elections, BJP candidates avoided inviting Rithambara and Uma Bharati, while those who did requested them to refrain from making fiery speeches. (See Gopal Guru, "Assembly Elections in Maharashtra", *EPW*, 30:14 (April 1995), p. 3.) Further, as the BJP sought to prove its eligibility for state power, Rithambara's overt affiliation seems to have been shifted to the Durga Vahini and the VHP. In April 1995 she delivered an instigatory diatribe against muslims and christians, as part of the VHP campaign against conversion and for forcible 're-conversion', on the same site in Udaynagar where a Catholic nun had been murdered two months earlier; her speech was followed by a trail of attacks on churches in Madhya Pradesh allegedly under the aegis of hindu communal organizations. (See *Pioneer*, 5 May 1995; *Hindu*, 7 May 1995; *Times of India*, 25 June 1995; *Statesman*, 30 July 1995.) In the 1996 and 1998 election campaigns as well as after the formation of a BJP-led coalition government, Rithambara seems to have receded further from her earlier prominence even as Sushma Swaraj, the epitome of the puritanical, canny, yet compliant middle-class housewife, has become a major spokesperson.

The intensification of methods of instigation in riots after December 1992— casettes, films, rumours, street events, damaging religious places, creating 'religious' differences among the poor—has located Rithambara and other women as gendering mechanisms within this right-wing formation as a *whole* which instigates communalism and works to maintain a social volatility at both the regional and national level. Male incitement has become prominent within the VHP which recently justified the attacks on Christian priests and nuns in Jhabua, Madhya Pradesh, as a result of the "anger of patriotic youth against anti-national forces" (*Hindu*, 30 Sept. 1998), while Bal Thackeray has outstripped Rithambara in his inflammatory and murderous speeches.

The nature of the violence that she invests in has become even more apparent. Despite the open triumphalism of the ensemble of communal organizations upon demolishing Babri Masjid and over the bloodshed in the subsequent riots or their peculiar combination of anarchism and authoritarianism, violence on communal grounds has received more social consent. In ideological terms, this right-wing ensemble has naturalized violence as a form of social power, as a means for enforcing religious identities and substantiating the symbols of Hindutva, for enlarging consent to communalization through the display of force as well as through a brutalizing combination of guilt and complicity. In material terms riot violence has been used to create systems of 'protection' and profit, as an avenue for the acquisition of street power, to alter demographic patterns, patterns of property ownership as well as the composition of the industrial workforce, to de-class and pauperize muslims, and to break up ordinary civic relations of decency.

The BJP has vociferously appropriated the demand for a uniform civil code and set itself up as a champion of gender justice. However, far from signifying an investment in rights for women, this is part of a continuing anti-muslim campaign. The vengeful opposition to and attack on muslim personal law and its provision for polygamy is usually made on a competitive patriarchal ground of equivalence of 'male' rights while the claim for gender justice is intended as a pragmatic design for a moderate Hindutva that can covertly equalize male privileges. (See Sangari, "The Politics of Diversity".) However, the right-wing appropriation of languages of feminism, citizenship, nationalism, and democracy has been gradually derailing left, democratic and feminist agendas as well as forcing these languages into new ideological locales by changing the very terms of public-political discourse; they now need stringent redefinition and cannot be tamely surrendered to the right.

Index